MARSILIO FICINO: THE *PHILEBUS* COMMENTARY

Published under the auspices of the

CENTER FOR MEDIEVAL AND RENAISSANCE STUDIES

University of California, Los Angeles

Publications of the

CENTER FOR MEDIEVAL AND RENAISSANCE STUDIES, UCLA

1. Jeffrey Burton Russell: Dissent and Reform in the Early Middle Ages

2. C.D. O'Malley: Leonardo's Legacy

3. Richard H. Rouse: Serial Bibliographies for Medieval Studies

4. Speros Vryonis, Jr.: The Decline of Medieval Hellenism in Asia Minor and the Process of Islamization from the Eleventh through the Fifteenth Century

5. Stanley Chodorow: Christian Political Theory and Church Politics in the Mid-Twelfth Century

6. Joseph J. Duggan: The Song of Roland

7. Ernest A. Moody: Studies in Medieval Philosophy, Science, and Logic

8. Marc Bloch: Slavery and Serfdom in the Middle Ages

9. Michael J. B. Allen: Marsilio Ficino: The *Philebus* Commentary

A Critical Edition and Translation

By MICHAEL J. B. ALLEN

Marsilio Ficino:
The *Philebus* Commentary

UNIVERSITY OF CALIFORNIA PRESS

BERKELEY, LOS ANGELES, AND LONDON

1975

University of California Press
Berkeley and Los Angeles, California
University of California Press, Ltd.
London, England

Dedicated
To
E.N.A. & W.

Acknowledgements

Pre-eminently it is a joy to thank Professor Paul O. Kristeller who sat down out of the goodness of his heart two years ago and read through my typescript, correcting errors, providing me with invaluable suggestions and directing my attention to the Pesaro fragments. He is legendary for his kindness, but such spontaneous generosity of time and great learning is surely of the golden age.

For encouragement and help at the dissertation stage I would like to thank my director, Professor Russell A. Fraser, and Professor John D'Arms particularly, and also Professors Gerald F. Else, Frank L. Huntley, William H. Ingram and John R. Knott. My good friend Mr. Ian D. Mackenzie has come to the rescue several times since then, as have several students at UCLA, among them Lynda Boose, Susan Nierengarten and Stephen Sharborough, and my colleagues Professors Herbert B. Hoffleit and Henry A. Kelly.

I am indebted to the Horace H. Rackham School of the University of Michigan, the Ford Foundation and the University of California for the fellowships which made this work possible; and to the British, Vatican, Laurentian, Oliverian and Bodleian libraries and the Bibliothèque Nationale for permission to use their manuscripts and incunabula.

Finally I am deeply grateful to Professor Fredi Chiappelli, Director of the Medieval and Renaissance Center at UCLA, both for his endorsement and for the Center's timely donation towards the costs of publication.

Contents

Sigla

W = Biblioteca Vaticana MS. *lat.* 5953
(the first version)

X = Biblioteca Laurenziana MS. *Plut.* 21, 8
(the second version)

Y = *Commentaria in Platonem,* Florence 1496
(the third version and the *editio princeps*)

P = Biblioteca Oliveriana MS. 620
(fragments of the second version)

¶Collecta curſim eχlectionibus Marſilii Ficini in Philebuȝ q̃ ſit ali
quis finis omniuȝ actionum⁖   Ca i.

QVoniam omnis philoſophiȩ ſũma ad beata uitam refertur⁚atqȝ eã quȩrenteſ homi
nes/ſe ad eius ſtudia contulerunt⁚beata autem vita in ſummo bono cõſiſtit⁚ libȝũ
Platonis Ꝟe ſũmo hominis bono ante alios exponendũ aggredimur· Sũmuȝ quip
pe bonum finis eſt/cuius gratia omnia omnes agimus⁚finis autem vitȩ in pȝimis
noſcendus eſt/ vt ad eum actiones omnes dirigere ualeamus⁚non minus q̃ naui
ganti poȝtus ad quem Ꝟeueniat ante omnia ſtatuendus/ꝛ ſagittario ſignuȝ ⁚ ad quẽ tela dirigat
pȝimuȝ inſpiciendũ.Quod quidem vaticinatus Plato/in Alcibiade/in Euthydemo/ in ſeptimo
Ꝟe re.pu.in legibus/ait ſi boni ipſius nobis cognitio Ꝟeſit⁚arteſ omnes alias ꝛ ſcientias i̅ vtiles
conatus/irritos/noxias actiones foꝛe.Jã ꝟ in arteꝛ cõſilio nihil aliud eſt finis q̃ terminus/ad
quẽ mouetur agentis intentio potiſſimum/ ꝛ inquo quieſcit.Cum ergo in natura motus ſaliqd
pȝopꝛie dirigatur quo habito ceſſet/agit ad finem· Similiter ſe habet diſpoſitio reruȝ inarte ꝛ na
tura ad finem/quo ſublato/non poſſunt cauſe aſſignari.Quãobrẽ ad Phylebi ipſius Ꝟeclaratiõe/
qui Ꝟe ſũmo hominis bono/noſtrarum omniũ actionũ fine diſputae⁚nos pȝimũ parabimus.Oſtẽ
demusqȝ aliquem eſſe finem/ad quem actiones bominum tendant.Deinde quis iſte ſit ꝛ qualis
Ꝟeclarare conabimur⁚ꝛ falſas quideȝ Ꝟehoc opiniones reicere/ueras aſtruere Ꝟemuȝ/quã uia ma
ximȩ ad euȝ perueniatur/monſtrabimus.Jd ergo libȝi buius ꝑpoſitum eſt.Js oꝛdo, ¶Omnis
actio aut a natura coꝛpoꝛum pꝛouenit⁚aut animi ſpetu/aut rationis ꝑſilio/atqȝ habitu/aut men
tis intelligentia.Si a natura coꝛpoꝛum pꝛouenit/ad certum aliquid tendit.Nã coꝛpoꝛ inter ſe
diſtinctȩ ſubſtantiȩ ſunt⁚quare naturȩ erunt vireſqȝ diſcretȩ.Vnde ſingulis coꝛpoꝛibus ſingu
lȩ inſunt/ꝑpꝛieqȝ naturȩ.Exbis proprii motus fiunt.Proprios ſinguloruȝ motus ſecuntur opa
propria ſinguloꝛ⁚inque nature coꝛpoꝛ/motusqȝ nitũe⁚ut efficiẽt/ꝛ effecto ope ꝑqeſcut/Neqȝ
n̅,quelibet aquolibet⁚f a pꝛriis quibuſdã propria quedam ſiũt/ab homine homo/a ficu ficus/ab
igni calor.Quis aũt negabit finẽ eſſe cuiuſqȝ naturȩ effectionisqȝ/id ipſũ ſquod ꝑpꝛie ſepqȝ niti
tur eius ſpetus⁚ꝛ iãdcunqȝ ceſſat.Pꝛeterea diſcoꝛpoꝛ motuſ aut eo tẽdit ut uitet iteritũ/aut
qdẽ ſibi ꝑueniẽs adſciſcat/aut pimat ꝑtrariũ/ſimile gignat.Dum nitat ꝛadſciſcat/ad ſui ipſuſ cõ
ſeruationẽ mouet.Dum pimit atqȝ gignit/ad ſimilis generationẽ.Omniũ ergo corporaliũ motio
nũ/ꝑſeruatio generatioqȝ eſt finis.¶Accedit ad bec/q̃ ſi natura corporis alicuius dũ agit/ad al
iquẽ effectũ Ꝟeterminatũ nõ tenderet/omẽs et effectus i̅differẽtes eſſet⁚quod aũt eque ſe bẽt ad
multa/nõ magis unũ/e/pluribȝ q̃ aliud efficit.Quare unũ qȝqȝ coꝛpus uel oſa faceret/ uel nihil
utrũqȝ ipoſſibile eſt.Naȝ quod facit oſa primũ reχ pꝛicipiũ eſt⁚quod agit nibil/eſt otioſũ.Qua
re adcertum quendã tendit effectum.Certus aũt euentus actionis finis cognominaꝛ.¶Jtem
corporis uis aut caſu in opus ſcidit/aut neceſſaria quedam ſtentione nature.Non caſu/ ga ſque
cũqȝ opa/quodcũqȝ coꝛque iſcurreret/atȝ ita quelibet aqȝbibeꝛ fieret/neqȝ certo res ſemine in
digerent/ꝛ illud Lucretiu eueniret.Nã ſi Ꝟe nibiloſierent/expibȝ rebȝ omnegnũs naſci poſſet/ ni
bilſemine egeret/e/mari primuȝ bomiẽs/e/terra poſſit oriri ſquamigeꝛ genus ꝛ uclucres erum
pere cȩlo ꝛ pfecto quod caſu ſit raro cõtigit nec uno dumtaχat modo f uariis ꝑuenit. ViꝞemuſ
autẽ propria quedam a ſingulis/certo ſemine/inſtituto tempore/ſolito ordine/modoqȝ/ digeſta ſe
rie/iiſdẽ mediis eadẽ rõeꝛvt plurimi fieri.Ergo cuȝ neceſſaria quadã intentiõe corporea uis eſſe
ctum producit/proprie illum intendit.Et quod intendit/naturali inſtinctu appetit / quod ab ali
quo agente appetitur/actionis eſt finis.Omnis ergo actio corporum ẽ ad fineȝ.Quinetiã actio
quȩ animi impetum/vt iram/metum/cupidineȝ/ſequitur/finẽ aliquẽ reſpicit.Nam ſi nihil moue
ret extrinſecus⁚animi ſpetus nulluſ inſurgeret.Ab aliquo ergo exteriori impetus iſte Ꝟependet/
quod vel bonum iudicatum eſt/vel malum/ vel neultrum . Si ueultrum nouus exco impetus

Commentaria in Platonem. Florence, 1496. (see p. 75. In the 1496 corrigenda
in quodcunque cessat of paragraph two, line 9, is corrected to *in quo denique
cessat*)

posuerit dicebas. Illis ego rationibus tuis iam ita
respondi, ut et eas libenter ad miserim et tanquam
uerissimas approbauerim et Platonis nostri defenderim mixtionem. Reliquis tuis circa Platonem
subtilissimis questionibus alias respondebimus.

Explicit liber primus commentarioru Marsilij ficini florentini in Platonis philebum de summo
hominis bono.

Secundus liber commentariorum Marsilij ficini
florentini in Philebum.

OMNIA Que nunc in uniuersa sut
Postqi in prima libri parte quod
tractandum erat proposuit Plato
et in secunda tractandi mundua
quoniam et ingressum tradidit in 3ª. qua cautione differendum sit docuit. in quarta tractare cepit de bono. Et quoniam collaturus ad ipsum erat uoluptatem et sapiam ut inspiceretur, nunquid istorum alterum ipsum sit bonum, et quid bonum sit explicuit. et ad ipsum
utraque conferens, neutrum ee ipsum bonum
ostendit. hec hactenus. Deinceps inuestigandu
restat. utrum istorum magis ad bonum conf-
rat. quod inueniri non pot, nisi et definiatur
et diuidatur in pes utrumq. Definitio aut genus requirit primo. post modum differentia
Ideo quinta hac inpte genera utriusq; equirit
et infiniti quoddam genus: nec non termini genus inducit. ad infinitum uoluptate ad terminu

Vat. lat. 5953. f. 402v (see pp. 381, 383, 385)

nij celeritatem, breuitate admodum delectari.

Finis De Quatuor sectis phoix Marsilij ficini floretur

PROHEMIVM MARSILII FICINI IN PHILE
BUM PLATONIS AD MAGNANIMUM LAVRE
TIVM MEDICEM PATRIE SERVATOREM

RES ESSE VITAS
NEMO RATIONE UIUENS
DUBITAT Contemplatiuam.
Actiuam. Voluptuosam Quoni
am .v3. tres ad felicitatem uia'
homines elegerunt. Sapien
tiam. Potentiam. Voluptatem. Nos autem sub Sapien
tie nomine quodlibet liberalium artium studium re
ligiosumq; ocium intelligimus. Sub apellatione poten
tie auctoritatem in gubernatione ciuili pariter atq; mi
litari. Diuitiarumq; affluentiam. & splendorem glorie
negociosamq; uirtutem comprehendi putamus. Sub
voluptatis deniq; cognomento Quinq; sensuum oblecta
menta & laborum curarumq; declinationem contine
ri non dubitamus Primam igitur Poete Mineruam. Se
cundam uo Iunonem. Tertiam deniq; Venerem nomi
nauerunt. // Tres olim apud Paridem de pomo aureo

Laur. Plu. 21, 8. f. 146r (see pp. 481, 483)

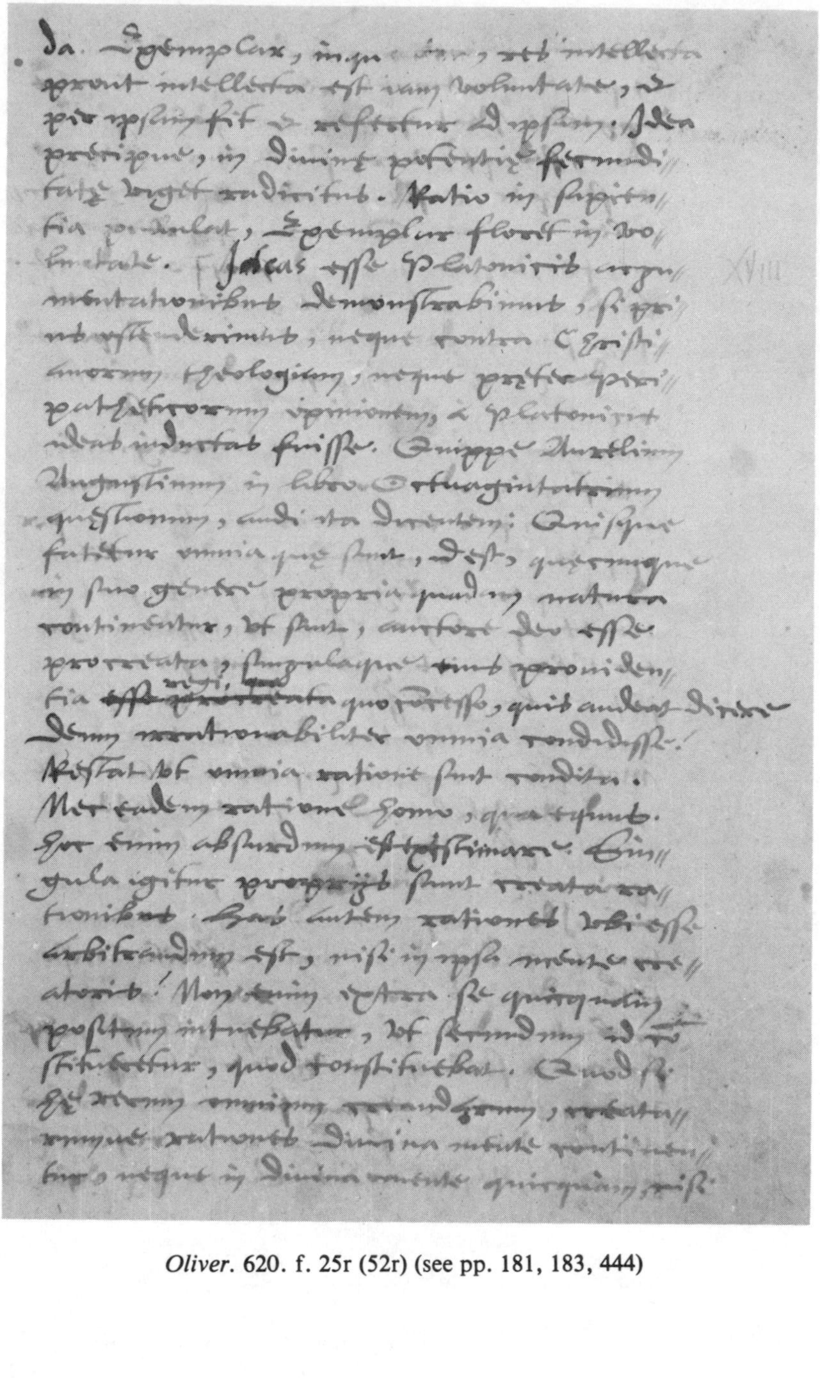

Oliver. 620. f. 25r (52r) (see pp. 181, 183, 444)

Introduction

In 1462 Cosimo de' Medici granted Marsilio Ficino a villa at Careggi and put at his disposal a number of precious Greek manuscripts, including a complete manuscript of Plato. Afterwards two or three dialogues became especially dear to Ficino, among them the *Philebus*. Like the majority of the Platonic dialogues, the *Philebus* had been unavailable to the Latin west since antiquity, and it was Ficino who translated it from the Greek for the first time.[1] More than this, he deliberately placed it in the climactic final position of the initial decade of dialogues he prepared for Cosimo's study. Cosimo and his friends discussed the decade culminating in the *Philebus* and these discussions informally constituted the inaugural meetings of the Florentine Academy. In 1464, as Cosimo lay dying in the last two weeks of July, it was the *Philebus* that was read to him; and during the reign of his successor, Piero, it was on the *Philebus* that Ficino first chose to lecture to the city's patricians, including the young Lorenzo. Since the lectures were composed on the broad problems posed by the dialogue, they were of seminal importance: they contributed an introduction not just to the *Philebus* but to Platonism itself.

Platonism had never died during the Middle Ages. In the west it flourished under the guise of Augustinianism and mysticism, and even such staunch Aristotelians as St. Albert and St. Thomas Aquinas were imbued with certain Platonic concepts. In the Byzantine east Plato always occupied a premier position and in the last decades of the empire's existence it was Pletho's outspoken championship of Plato which initiated a prolonged academic controversy among the Greek exiles in Italy.[2] But the actual face-to-face encounter with Platonic and Neoplatonic texts which took place in the Florentine Academy under the leadership of Ficino was responsible for the European diffusion of Platonism in its distinctively Renaissance form. As Paul O. Kristeller observes, the "direct access to the work of Plato, of Plotinus, and of the other Platonist philosophers of Greek

antiquity ... was in itself a major event in the intellectual history of Europe, and its importance was not diminished by the
fact that the understanding of these Platonist sources continued
to be affected by Neoplatonic and medieval ideas."[3] The first
public articulation of Ficino's "direct access" to the Plato text
was the series of lectures he delivered on the *Philebus,* a series
which later formed the basis of the written commentary. Consequently, the *Philebus* was in the vanguard of what was both a
revival of an ancient academic philosophy, and also a wide-
ranging religious, cultural and intellectual movement peculiar
to the Renaissance and constituting one of its chief glories,
Florentine Platonism.

Apart from its historical importance, the commentary had a
crucial role to play in the development of Ficino's own philosophical system; for along with the *Symposium* commentary
(1468-69), the huge *Platonic Theology* (1469-74) and the treatise
On The Christian Religion (1474) it bears witness to the
generation of his most profound and luminous ideas. It is
remarkable for its broad orientation, the profusion and scope
of its major theses, and the suggestiveness of its detail. Even in
the longueurs, one can detect Ficino's enthusiasm for the
dialogue's intricacies and his sense of continual intellectual
excitement. After lavishing much energy and concentration
upon the commentary initially, he returned to it at least twice
and he made it the longest of his Plato commentaries with the
exception of the commentary on the *Parmenides.*

Despite its signal interest, however, scholarship has hardly
begun to give it its due. Its various arguments, and
particularly those concerning the universal act, the primacy of
the intellect and the psychology of perception, have been referred to individually, but the whole commentary has not been
studied carefully for its own sake. Hidden away in three manuscripts, in the first edition of Ficino's *Commentaria in
Platonem,* and in the corrupt, mispunctuated texts of the Basle
and Paris editions of his *Opera Omnia,* it has neither been
edited in modern times nor ever translated. Now, by chance, it
follows the *Symposium* commentary as the second principal

work of Ficino's to appear in English. Such a place is not undeserved though, as the two commentaries are in many ways companion pieces.[4]

My introduction has seven sections dealing with: the historical genesis, provenance and composition of the commentary; the reasons for Ficino's choice of the *Philebus;* the external aspects of the commentary; its main ideas; the intellect/will controversy; the problem of the dating; and editorial and translation practice. Much of what follows is necessarily provisional in the light of the many gaps in our understanding of Ficino's life and work.

I

In 1463, having asked Ficino to translate the *Pimander (Poimandres)* of the legendary Hermes Trismegistus, Cosimo also asked him to translate "ten of Plato's dialogues containing every precept for living, all the principles of nature and all the sacred mysteries of divine things."[5] In the last years of his life Cosimo was anxious to read the newly discovered texts and to begin the revival of Platonism in his own city. There is even the possibility, as Raymond Marcel suggests, that he and Ficino consulted each other beforehand on the particular dialogues which should make up the initial group.[6]

In the early days of 1464 Cosimo sent an impatient note to Ficino: "I arrived here at Careggi yesterday, not in order to till my fields, but to cultivate my soul. Come as soon as possible, Marsilio. Bring with you Plato's book on the highest good— which by now I assume you have translated as you promised from the Greek into Latin—for there is nothing I desire more ardently than to know the way that leads most surely to felicity. Farewell, and do not forget your Orphic lyre when you come."[7] This note testifies to the esteem which Cosimo accorded the unknown *Philebus,* and specifically designates the dialogue as the one most likely to lead him to felicity. Two manuscripts are of importance here. In a fifteenth century manuscript in the Bodleian library (*Canonicianus latinus* 163) is the anxiously awaited translation, and we discover what the ten dialogues

were; but the prefatory letter to Cosimo and the introductions
to each of the dialogues are in an even earlier manuscript too.[8]
While the introduction to the *Philebus* translation continued to
accompany the *Philebus* translation in the various editions of
the complete Plato translation, it also reappeared as the proem
to the Basle editions of the *Philebus* commentary (see Appendix
III). The ten dialogues (4-6 of which are now usually accounted
spurious) consisted of: the *Hipparchus, On Philosophy,
Theages, Meno, Alcibiades I, Alcibiades II, Minos, Euthyphro,
Parmenides, Philebus.* In the letter Ficino explained his choice
and justified the sequence he had adopted, concluding, "as our
happiness consists in the vision of God, it seems just that the
Philebus which treats of man's highest good should follow the
Parmenides which treats of the highest good of all nature."[9]

Kristeller says "this explanation is not too plausible" and the
arrangement simply represents the chronological sequence in
which Ficino translated the dialogues, Ficino's "unexpressed
principles of selection" being: one, that the first eight dialogues
in the decade were all "comparatively short or easy"; and two,
seven of them had never been translated before and the three
which had been Ficino may not have known about. He concludes therefore, "Ficino began his translation [of Plato] with
ten dialogues which he considered to be 'new' to his Latin
readers...."[10] This is too dismissive. The *Philebus* and the
Parmenides are two of Plato's longest and most difficult works
even if the other eight are short and easy. Furthermore, there
are several things of note in the prefatory letter. The *Philebus* is
the culmination of the decade, Ficino says, because it treats of
the goal of human endeavour, namely "the divine vision," or in
Cosimo's words, "felicity"; even the *Parmenides* is made to
precede it. Ficino may have been personally indebted for his
conception of the *Philebus'* importance to Greeks like
Bessarion who were then living in Italy. Or he may have been
influenced directly by Olympiodorus' commentary on the
Philebus, which he certainly knew since at one time he owned
and wrote marginal notes on a manuscript containing
it—though he made little use of Olympiodorus, surprisingly, in

his own commentary.[11] Most likely, however, he derived the conception from Neoplatonism itself. First, the Neoplatonists also put the *Philebus* at the end of a decade of dialogues in a teaching cycle, though the other members of the ancient decade do not correspond to those in Ficino's group, nor did they always remain constant among the ancient Neoplatonists themselves.[12] Second, starting with Iamblichus, it had become ancient Neoplatonic practice to define the *skopos* or purpose of each of Plato's dialogues as a preliminary step to the study of it.[13] In two places in the dialogue (11B and 60A) Socrates had said Philebus' view was that pleasure was the goal for all living creatures and not just for man alone. This suggested to the Neoplatonists Plato was concerned with something more than a specifically human pleasure, therefore with something more than a specifically human wisdom. Since Iamblichus, the accepted view had been that the *Philebus* was concerned with man's very highest good which was at the same time the very highest good for all things. As Henry Sidgwick noted years ago, the traditional distinction between the good for man and the absolute or universal good loses its force for someone who subsumes ethics into metaphysics. In Platonism the two goods have always been indissolubly blended.[14] A.E. Taylor, for instance, suggested that in the *Philebus* Plato himself was actually "moderating" a *quaestio disputata* on the Idea of the good which was then narrowed down to a discussion of the good for man.[15] Although Plato may have lost interest in the theory of the Ideas as he got older, his successors elaborated on the passages in the sixth and seventh books of the *Republic* (and elsewhere) where the Idea of the good is made to subsume the other Ideas and even in some sense to transcend both them and its own nature as an Idea. Eventually the Idea of the good became identified with Plotinus' first principle, the one beyond being, and the last section of the *Enneads* is in fact entitled: "On the good, or the one."[16] For Ficino, then, the *Philebus*—traditionally defined as a dialogue dealing with man's highest good rather than with pleasure or wisdom—was obviously not only concerned with the ethical good, but with

the metaphysical good too, that is, the one, the absolute principle, the unitary source of all being and all felicity. The commentary's opening sentence testifies to the easy movement from the ethical to the metaphysical; and the entire conception, it seems to me, accounts for the *Philebus'* close association from the beginning with the *Parmenides* (the dialogue most favoured by the Neoplatonists), for the otherwise inexplicable esteem it was accorded in the 1460's, and for the overridingly metaphysical content of the commentary Ficino wrote upon it.

Marcel, in commenting on Ficino's introductory letter, says: "With what ingenuity Ficino applied himself to making a unity out of these somewhat disparate elements! He has linked them together in a continuous progression, which, commencing from the desire for terrestrial goods [the *Hipparchus*], has blossomed into the plenitude of the sovereign good."[17] He goes on to suggest the decade represents a sort of *summa platonica.*[18] Certainly, the enunciation in sequence of the fundamental Platonic definitions of philosophy, of wisdom, of virtue, etc., leading to the ascent to the good adds force to his suggestion and ties it in with what has been said above.

Vespasiano da Bisticci tells us that while Cosimo waited for the *Philebus* translation in the year before his death in the August of 1464, he had the Florentine chancellor, Bartolomeo Scala, read him Aristotle's *Nicomachean Ethics.* Bartolomeo also read him the lecture notes which Donato Acciaiuoli had taken on Argyropoulos' influential lectures on the *Ethics.*[19] It is interesting Aristotle's *Ethics* should be linked from the beginning with the rebirth of the *Philebus,* not only because of the characteristics they share in common and the obvious indebtedness of Aristotle's work to its predecessor, but also because of the prevailing controversy among the Aristotelians and Platonists over the *Ethics,* a controversy in which the Florentine Academy was necessarily involved.

As Cosimo lay on his deathbed in the late July we learn from Ficino himself in a letter to Lorenzo that at last Cosimo heard the *Philebus:* "So, as you yourself know since you were there,

he died not long after we had read him Plato's dialogues on the one principle of things [the *Parmenides*] and on the highest good [the *Philebus*]. It was as if he did not want to wait to enjoy fully the good which had been the theme of the discussion."[20] The "not long after" was, in Ficino's own recollection, twelve days.[21] Once again, this is evidence for the felt connection between the two dialogues, though, parenthetically, Ficino was to postpone commenting on the *Parmenides* until much later. From the ensuing discussions on the *Philebus* and the other nine dialogues which Ficino managed to complete before Cosimo died, Marcel suggests the meetings of the Academy as a religio-philosophical society were informally inaugurated among Cosimo's friends. Till then the Academy had been simply an unrealized ideal.[22]

Under the reign of Cosimo's successor the Medici patronage seems to have been less certain.[23] Piero had been a pupil of the Aristotelian Marsuppini. Nicolò Tignosi, Ficino's Aristotelian teacher, had dedicated his anti-Platonic commentary on the *Ethics* to Piero[24] and there is other odd evidence to suggest Piero was predisposed to the Aristotelians rather than the Platonists. Nevertheless, Corsi, Ficino's first biographer, says Ficino and Piero were in frequent contact and Ficino used to visit him to expatiate on the merits of Plato. Piero in turn encouraged Ficino to continue with his Plato translations: he gave him Greek and Latin books and also urged him to comment on Plato in public. Corsi goes on to say it was at that time (*eo tempore*), meaning in the reign of Piero, that Ficino did formally lecture on the *Philebus* before a large audience.[25] Marcel supposes that after Cosimo's death, Ficino had discussed the *Philebus* with his associates (this being his customary method) and "it was the enthusiasm aroused by his exposition of Platonic thinking on the sovereign good which led his friends and patrons to wish a bigger audience could take advantage of his teaching."[26] Having moved from Ficino's desk to Cosimo's bedchamber to the immediate Medici circle, the *Philebus* was now reaching the Florentine intellectuals. But it is doubtful if Piero himself played any part in this

dissemination; he left it to his sons, Lorenzo and Giuliano, and to other Platonic enthusiasts like Landino and Valori.

Corsi claims there once existed a manuscript containing Ficino's lecture notes *(collectanea)* plus the four books of Ficino's youthful *Institutiones Platonicae;* neither are extant.[27] But we have another fifteenth century manuscript, *Vaticanus lat.* 5953, containing the putative first version of the *Philebus* commentary. What precise relation this version bears either to the actual lectures Ficino was delivering or to the *collectanea* mentioned by Corsi has to be a matter for speculation. The preface to the commentary in MS. 5953 begins: "Since we are going to interpret the sacred philosophy of the divine Plato in this celebrated place at the request of our best citizens, I have thought it important we first briefly consider what philosophy is."[28] And Ficino goes on to deal with the nature of philosophy and the life of Plato. This material he later transformed into two letters: one to Giovanni Francesco Ippoliti, Count of Gazzoldo *(Op. Om.,* 761-763), and the other to Francesco Bandini *(Op. Om.,* 763-770). The commentary's preface concludes: "I am deeply grateful to you illustrious gentlemen for having honoured my lecture with your presence. May the immortal God give you immortal thanks,"[29] and the manuscript itself ends with a note saying Ficino has not yet completed or revised the commentary (see my p. 425). The preface points to a close connection between the public lectures and the written commentary as we have it and we must accede to Kristeller's observation that "Ficino's own public teaching in Florence left a permanent trace in his commentaries on St. Paul's Epistle to the Romans, on Plato's *Philebus* and on Plotinus' *Enneads....*"[30] Kristeller suggests the public teaching took place "mostly in the church of S. Maria degli Angeli and presumably before an audience that was not limited to the members of his own circle."[31] Marcel too suggests "this celebrated place" of the preface was the convent church of S. Maria degli Angeli. He alludes to the speech entitled *Oratio in principio lectionis (Op. Om.,* 886, 2), while acknowledging it may in fact be concerned with Ficino's later lectures on the

Enneads (which we know for certain took place in S. Maria degli Angeli).³² In the *Oratio* Ficino refers to the use of temples by the ancient sages who wished to study or teach the "sacred mysteries of philosophy" and he continues: "Following in the footsteps of the ancient sages therefore we will study to the best of our powers the religious philosophy of Plato in the midst of this church. In this dwelling place of the angels we will contemplate the divine truth."³³ The allocation seems reasonable. S. Maria degli Angeli was near the Medici palace and it had been made into one of the first centres of humanism by Ambrogio Traversari, the Minister General of the Camaldolese, the architect of the decree of union at the Council of Ferrara-Florence, and the renowned translator of Diogenes Laertius, the pseudo-Dionysius, and other Greek patristic texts.

One can picture the scene as Marcel describes it: "For the first time a Latin, text in hand, explicates one of Plato's dialogues at the request of the noble citizens and before an audience as attentive as it was numerous. In fact, the choice of the *Philebus* was an extremely judicious one, for the thesis concerning the sovereign good which one finds expounded there could only seduce this élite which had grown up searching for the solution to the problem as they listened to their teachers commenting upon Aristotle's *Ethics*."³⁴ Although Ficino had approached the same question in his early tract *On Pleasure* (1457), the lectures were the direct outcome of his newly acquired mastery of the actual Plato texts and of the philosophical stimulus they supplied. The long complicated section on the final cause, serving as it does as the prolegomenon to the commentary itself, bears witness to Ficino's sense of his audience (for it takes up the opening propositions of the *Ethics*), and to his missionary purpose (for it proceeds to incorporate these universally familiar propositions into a Platonic analysis of the general good and in so doing makes extensive but absolutely unacknowledged use of the *Summa Contra Gentiles*).³⁵

The lectures in their turn drew considerable attention. One clue to the contemporary reaction is provided by Landino's *Camaldulensian Disputations*. In the second book one of the

interlocutors, Alberti, observes: "The Christians say then that God is the highest good. But Plato agreed before Christ was born and made man. You can easily see this, if you want to, from the commentaries Marsilio has composed on Plato's *Philebus*. They are not only profound but also particularly clear and simple."[36] Ficino eventually succumbs to Alberti's entreaties and to those of Lorenzo, another of Landino's *dramatis personae*, and undertakes to elucidate the theories he had developed in the *Philebus* commentary. The reference is sufficiently distinct for us to be able to recognize the sort of impact the commentary was having.[37] Ficino never managed to complete the task he had undertaken.[38] Marcel comments: "After Ficino had announced to his listeners that the *Philebus* is divided into twelve sections, without any warning he interrupts his exposition after the fifth section; and although subsequently—twice in fact—he showed his regret at not having been able to complete his exposition, we see him contenting himself with illustrating it with apologues, an odd conclusion for the treatise."[39] (See Appendix II for the ten excerpts—not all of which are apologues, however—which make up the "odd conclusion.")

Marcel's suggestion that the interruption was caused by the political situation, precipitated by the death of Francesco Sforza in the March of 1466 and the collapse of the alliances dependent on him, is completely untenable (see the penultimate section of my introduction), as is Arnaldo della Torre's thesis that Ficino was saddened by the charge that what he was doing was unchristian. Della Torre thought that Ficino passed through a period from 1459 to 1469 of "moral depression resulting from an internal struggle between his philosophical convictions and his religious feelings,"[40] because Corsi, having talked of Ficino's *animi dolor,* specifically referred it to the period of the *Philebus* lectures. Corsi said Ficino intended at that time to compose a book of Platonic theology and "to publish the *Hymns* of Orpheus and the *Sacrifices* [alluding possibly to Proclus' *De Sacrificio et Magia*], but from day to day a truly divine miracle prevented him from doing what he

wanted. His spirit, he said, was distracted by a certain sadness. This is said to have happened in the same way to St. Jerome with regard to Cicero."[41] Della Torre took this to mean, in conjunction with other material he worked up into proofs, that Ficino was undergoing a long crisis of conscience. But in actuality Corsi is not talking about a ten-year period at all and the "certain sadness" is mentioned in a theological context, i.e., whether to write a Platonic *theology*. In dismissing Della Torre's theory, Marcel attributes Corsi's remarks to Ficino's distress at his own inability to reconcile Platonism and Aristotelianism over the problem of the soul's immortality.[42] Kristeller too rejects the crisis theory, refuting one by one Della Torre's proofs and arguing "it is not the transition from paganism to Christianity that determines the development of Ficino's thought . . . he was a Christian throughout his entire life."[43] We must acknowledge the force of their refutations of Della Torre.

However, though there is no evidence in the commentary itself that Ficino was depressed, there is also no reason to deny Corsi his point. Assuming Ficino had started to write the commentary while he was still lecturing on it, and that Corsi is specifically referring to Ficino's state of mind vis-à-vis the *Philebus*, we can easily suppose Ficino became somewhat dispirited when he eventually realized he was being led into an endless series of abstractions and that the commentary, while being multifariously suggestive, was nevertheless lacking in direction and plan.[44] Hence his decision to start on the much more clearly organized *Platonic Theology*. The *Philebus* commentary, concerned as it is with basic metaphysical principles and the Neoplatonic one in particular, obviously contributed in its own discursive way towards the establishment of the ontological and ethical framework which Ficino was going to elucidate systematically and at length in the early books of the *Platonic Theology*. Indeed, the *Philebus* commentary and the *Platonic Theology* have more in common from the metaphysical viewpoint than either has with the *Symposium* commentary and in neither, significantly, does the theory of love

play a preponderant role.⁴⁵ In a sense, therefore, the *Philebus* commentary was a rough draft for the major work, though Ficino himself would not have conceived it as such.

There is still one recurrent misconception which must be dispelled. Although the *Philebus* commentary may have been the first of Ficino's major extant writings to be conceived (and the public lectures suggest it was) and although its composition may antedate the composition of the *Symposium* commentary,⁴⁶ it cannot be dismissed as juvenilia. Michele Schiavone, for example, discounts Ficino's exaltation of the intellect over the will in the *Philebus* commentary as merely the result of a "neophytic" zeal to stand by Plato or a temporary inability to move beyond the "static" conceptions inherited from classical philosophy.⁴⁷ But the *Symposium* commentary and the *Platonic Theology*—works which he admires unequivocally for containing Ficino's most daring contributions to modern thought—are products of the same period of thinking and the three works followed close upon each other, as we shall see.

In the August of 1490, having just finished his commentaries on the *Enneads,* Ficino again turned his mind towards the *Philebus,* that is, seven years after the complete Plato translation had gone to the press. Since Ficino had revised his translation at least twice (in the period from 1477 to 1482 and then apparently again in 1483 just before sending it off to the press), the *Philebus* commentary was written presumably on the basis of Ficino's first draft of the *Philebus* translation. Some of the changes in the second version of the commentary (and possibly some of the changes in the first edition of the commentary, though this is logically far less likely) may therefore be the direct outcome of his revision of the translation. However, the textual history of Ficino's Plato translation has yet to be explored before we can proceed further in this direction.

In a letter to Francesco Soderini Ficino wrote: "It has just occurred to me again to finish the commentary on Plato's *Philebus* on the highest good which at one time I had almost half completed."⁴⁸ This is the second version of the commentary as preserved in the fifteenth century manuscript

Laurenziana Pluteo 21,8. The original introduction has disappeared, transformed as we saw into two letters, and in its place is a proem addressed to Lorenzo, dated the fifteenth of February, 1490 (see Appendix III). But February the eleventh is the date found in the subscription (p. 425) where we are also told that the manuscript was transcribed by Sebastiano Salvini, Ficino's relative on the side of a paternal aunt, probably a first or second cousin.[49] Since the Florentine year began officially on March 25, the February dating must refer to the year 1491. The second version not only contains nearly all the passages omitted in the first version but found in the first and subsequent editions, it also contains two extracts not found elsewhere (see Appendix I). Also, Ficino has made chapter numbers and divisions—though they do not always correspond exactly with those found in the editions (in the first version he had only a few headings and intermittent breaks where the later chapter divisions were going to occur). The manuscript still concludes with the ten excerpts, but now he has divided them into two series. Those numbered fourth, seventh, ninth and tenth in the MS. *Vat.* 5953, have been relegated to the end of the group and entitled "apologues on pleasure."[50] A month or so later, sometime between March and April, Ficino took the four pleasure apologues and put them at the end of the tenth book of his letters, dedicating them to Martinus Uranius (*Op. Om.,* 921, 2). During that same year he then had the whole commentary transcribed for Uranius, for on the 24th of November he was sending the last four quinternions to him (*Op. Om.,* 928, 2; 929, 3). The second version is also partially preserved in a fragmentary sixteenth century manuscript now in the Biblioteca Oliveriana in Pesaro (see Appendix IV).

The third and final version, that of the first edition printed in Florence in 1496 and of all subsequent editions either of the *Commentaria* or the *Opera Omnia,* seems to have been completed in 1492 when Ficino was putting together his Plato commentaries.[51] The apologues on pleasure and the other six excerpts have been removed. In their place are four unattached chapters and a breakdown of all the "chapters" in the *Philebus*

and summaries of their contents. These summaries, incidentally, have not been translated as they are of diminutive interest. Since neither first, second nor third version represents the completed commentary, it is still referred to in the catalogue of Ficino's works compiled in 1493 as a commentary on part of the *Phile-bus*. The third version is the definitive version both from the point of view of content and text and it is the one translated here.

Later, to the 1496 edition of his Plato commentaries, Ficino appended a letter to his friend Orlandini for which the *Philebus* supplies the subject matter (see Appendix III and below); and up to the very last Ficino attempted to complete commentaries on the dialogues which seemed to him, as to the Neoplatonists before him, to represent the foundations of the Platonic system: the *Parmenides, Timaeus, Theaetetus, Phaedrus, Sophist* and the *Philebus*. As Corsi laconically notes, however, death came and prevented him.[52]

In the postscript to book one of the commentary in all three versions Ficino says his work is a response to the insistent queries of a great friend, the monk from S. Miniato, Michele Mercati, who was also a friend of Ficino's medical tutor, Nicolò Tignosi. At various points in his life Ficino addressed letters to Mercati; he dedicated a theological dialogue between the soul and God to him and also a *summa* of philosophy; and he was one of the few people to whom Ficino confided he had written a commentary on Lucretius, a work which he felt compelled to burn soon after it was written.[53] By way of digression, Baronius has a marvellous story about the two friends.[54] Ficino and Mercati were supposed to have agreed one day, while they were discussing philosophy and in particular the problem of the soul's immortality, that whoever died first should return to contact the other and tell him about the mysteries of the afterlife. On the night of Ficino's death, Mercati, who was sitting inside his room pondering abstractions, was suddenly visited by the ghostly spirit of his friend on a white horse. Ficino galloped up to the door and shouted, "O Michael, Michael, vera, vera sunt illa" (O Michael, Michael, everything we said is utterly true). Mercati rushed out in time to see the back of his friend

disappearing into the darkness. After a vain attempt to catch up with the white horse, Mercati sped to Florence where Ficino was staying, only to find he had died at the same hour as the equestrian visitation. Mercati, needless to say, was suitably moved.

The *Philebus* commentary has received some notice from modern scholars. Giuseppe Saitta talks of "the extremely beautiful commentary on the *Philebus* in which the superiority of the good over the beautiful is vigorously affirmed. All beauty is good, but not all good is beautiful: this is the Platonic concept that Ficino is continually attempting to illustrate in his own way. However, a common bond exists between the good and the beautiful, and this is supplied by the appetite . . . etc." Later he talks of the "magnificent commentary on the *Philebus*" in which Ficino "had explicitly identified the universal act with the good."[55] Paul Kristeller has frequently referred to it and Michele Schiavone has used it as a whipping boy while devoting careful attention to certain theses. It would be interesting to speculate on the influence the commentary has had in subsequent centuries; but, as Saitta says, Ficino was often robbed but rarely acknowledged.[56] Much more work has to be done on specific ideas and theories in Ficino and Renaissance philosophy in general before anything can be said with accuracy about the influence of a particular commentary and this is true even of the *Symposium* commentary.[57]

What we do know, however, is that the *Philebus,* more perhaps than any other Platonic dialogue, including the *Symposium,* seems to have dominated the early days of the Platonic revival, and it is important we take note of its popularity if we want to understand the genesis of Florentine Platonism. It was through the *Philebus* that the newly revived interest in Plato began to broaden into what was later to become a European movement. The commentary translated here is our chief witness to the crucial point of transition.

II

I turn now to consider some further aspects of Ficino's choice of the *Philebus.* Given the humanists' particular concern with

ethical problems and that the standard topic of classical ethics
was happiness or the supreme good for man,[58] the designated
theme of the *Philebus,* it was inevitable a humanist would write
directly on the *Philebus* once it was made available. This
humanist was to be Ficino himself. However, Saitta is not
strictly correct when he says "the ethical interest in Ficino
dominates over the speculative one."[59] Although man occupies
a central position in Ficino's thinking, Ficino has, as Kristeller
observes, no real system of ethics; for in the Renaissance
". . . we do not find any system of ethics based primarily on
Plato, as so many were on Aristotle. . . . The leading Platonists
of the Renaissance . . . were interested in questions of metaphysics and cosmology rather than of ethics."[60] This is mainly
because the perfection of the soul ". . . is entirely bound up with
its spiritual ascent and with the contemplative attitude."[61] As in
the case of the ancient Neoplatonists, Ficino's ethical ideas are
part and parcel of a metaphysical framework: as a humanist
Ficino would be drawn towards an ethical dialogue, but as a
Platonist he would be drawn towards it for metaphysical
reasons.

   Aristotle's *Ethics* had long been the classical source for
ethical studies. In the thirteenth and fourteenth centuries we
find not only the great editions and translations of Grosseteste,
William of Moerbeke and Gerard of Cremona but also the
extended commentaries of such eminent scholastics as St.
Albertus Magnus, Giles of Rome, St. Thomas Aquinas and
many others. But in the fifteenth century, after Bruni's new,
controversial translation and Argyropoulos' lectures too had
again stimulated interest in the *Ethics,* the commentaries began
to shift their emphasis. In Eugenio Garin's words: "They . . .
ceased to interpret this work in the narrow terms of social and
political problems and of man seen as a political animal. They
interpreted the *Nicomachean Ethics* as a final exaltation of the
contemplative and separated intellect."[62] There is much resulting controversy over the nature of the separation and the relationship between the soul's natural and supernatural powers,
and the book becomes a touchstone in the battle with Latin

Averroism. Many eminent thinkers were, therefore, involved in restating and reassessing the *Ethics'* arguments throughout the period, including Bruni, Donato Acciaiuoli, Ermolao Barbaro, Filelfo, Lefèvre D'Étaples, and Philip Melanchthon. But, since the principal Aristotelians were primarily interested in their master's ethical writings,[63] their opponents were forced to become familiar with them too. Ficino himself had studied under a dedicated Aristotelian (Nicolò Tignosi, who had taught theoretical medicine and natural philosophy at the Studio in Florence) and he knew his Aristotle well, valuing him in particular for his work in logic and physics.[64] In the May of 1455 he had copied out Bruni's translation of the *Ethics* and written his own notes in the margin; and, according to Eugenio Garin, his notes are even to be found in a copy of the first edition of Acciaiuoli's commentary on the *Ethics* (which was based on Argyropoulos' earlier lectures).[65]

When Ficino started to write on the *Philebus,* he aimed to do three things: first, to counter the naturalist and activist ethics that had stemmed from the *Ethics'* commentators with new arguments drawn from Plato's counterpart to the *Ethics;* second, to reconcile and synthesize the two masters like the Neoplatonists before him. The first meant proving Aristotle had been betrayed by his commentators, the Alexandrists and Averroists; the second that he and Plato were not in real conflict, but concerned, rather, with different levels of moral experience (hence the *Philebus* was to subsume not supersede the *Ethics*—the appearance of the theory of the mean in both works was merely the most obvious instance of what Ficino saw as the absence of any "real conflict"). Third, apart from the two ethical aims there was a metaphysical aim. Ficino's own city had seen a prolonged controversy, in which the *Ethics* had played a central role, between the Aristotelians and the Platonists on the subject of Plato's Ideas. The *Philebus* lectures were Ficino's own initial contribution to the controversy, so he obviously felt the dialogue was specially suited to combat Aristotle's attack on Plato's metaphysics. The course of this local dispute seems to have been as follows.

On the death of Carlo Marsuppini, Bruni's illustrious successor as chancellor of Florence and an Aristotelian, there was a
struggle for his chair. The Platonists and their Medicean allies
backed Cristoforo Landino, while Marsuppini's own disciples
backed Antonio Rossi. The Aristotelian candidate was eventually defeated and the chair divided: Argyropoulos was
appointed to the chair of Greek in 1456 and two years later
Landino was appointed to the chair of Latin. The Platonists
were triumphant.⁶⁶ In the year 1457-58, before Landino's
installation, Argyropoulos took the opportunity to lecture on
the *Ethics* in the Studio, but used the occasion to champion
Plato too.⁶⁷ In the course of his lectures, Argyropoulos wanted
to prove Plato and Aristotle were in accord, but, in commenting
on the key fourth chapter of book one of the *Ethics,* he
maintained Aristotle did not understand the Ideas. (It was on
these lectures that Donato Acciaiuoli had taken the notes which
Cosimo wanted to peruse.⁶⁸) In 1460 Nicolò, Ficino's former
teacher, took issue with Argyropoulos and published a
polemical commentary on the *Ethics* which he dedicated to
Piero, and also a tract actually on the Ideas. Finally, in 1469,
the probable date of Ficino's *Philebus* commentary, Bessarion
published his eirenic *In Calumniatorem Platonis.* Material from
the *Ethics* appeared here, and Bessarion used St. Augustine and
St. Thomas in an attempt to bring Aristotle and Plato together
in a Neoplatonic synthesis.

It is significant Ficino initially chose the *Philebus* in his own
attempt to defeat the more militant Aristotelians and to make
Florence into a Platonic city. He obviously felt it ideally
adapted to the general defense of the Ideas and their ultimate
reality. To us this is ironic, since the only reference to the Ideas
in the *Philebus* is at 15B-C where Plato seems to be referring
directly to problems enumerated in the *Parmenides,* a dialogue
which A.E. Taylor says is "clearly presupposed" by the
*Philebus.*⁶⁹ Instead of the Ideas Plato is concerned with the four
classes and with conceptual forms and unities alone. Consequently, scholars dealing with the unity of Plato's thought
have found it difficult to reconcile the Ideas with the classes,⁷⁰

and it is interesting Ficino simply avoids the problem of reconciling the two.

Apart from such external considerations, the *Ethics'* Platonic predecessor clearly had an intrinsic fascination for Ficino just as it did for the ancient Neoplatonists, Proclus and Damascius, who commented on it.[71] Modern scholars have been somewhat more hesitant or tentative in assessing the *Philebus*. Benjamin Jowett adverted to its "degree of confusion and incompleteness in the general design . . . [in which] the multiplication of ideas seems to interfere with the power of expression," while at the same time he admitted it "contains, perhaps, more metaphysical truth more obscurely expressed than any other Platonic dialogue."[72] R.G. Bury thought it indisputable it was "jagged and distorted in composition," though "beneath the difficulties of expression and the peculiarity of form" he found "a sound core of true Platonic thought."[73] J. Gould talks of its "fundamental tension between two opposed concepts, those of purity and mixture" in which Plato was fighting against his "sense of reality," in turn accepting and fleeing from the "inextricable and everpresent mixture of opposites" in human life. The result in Gould's view is eccentricity of form and structure, a concern with the concrete rather than the abstract and an "aggressive allegiance" to a contemplative ideal which Plato knows is impractical.[74] However, others have recently demurred. R. Hackforth says "the formlessness of the work has been often exaggerated," and the more he has studied it "the clearer has its structure become, and the more understandable its transitions, digressions, and postponements."[75] Auguste Dies talks at first simply of "a singularity of construction" and the "scholastic character of the discussion,"[76] and he divides the *Philebus* into three parts: 11A-23B where it is proposed that the good life consists neither in pleasure or wisdom alone but in a mixture of the two (this part is Ficino's first book); 23C-59C where it is proposed that intelligence predominates in the mixture; 59D-end where Plato establishes the hierarchy of goods. Part two, however, contains long sections on the types of pleasure and wisdom, the section on the types of pleasure (31A-55C)

constituting more than half the dialogue. Dies calls these two sections a "mass in the interior of the dialogue" and the analysis of pleasure "a block" inside the mass.[77] Close consideration leads Dies eventually to talk of the "perfect logical continuity of development" in the *Philebus,* of its "abundance," of its "freedom" and "variety."[78]

Ficino was obviously drawn to the dialogue in part because of the extensive pleasure "block"; although, ironically, his commentary stops just before the block begins. He was well into the digression on the divisions of reality (23C-27C) and the chapter summaries he affixed to the first edition indicate he was intending to deal at length with true and false pleasures, with pleasure and pain, with the pleasures in rest and in motion, etc. However, as we have seen, Ficino believed the true theme of the discussion was not pleasure but "man's highest good" and he says all the arguments in the dialogue are introduced for the good's sake (p. 127). Accordingly, the dialogue has a twelve part structure, designed with the express intention of making it particularly clear what man's highest good is. We only need examine chapter nine to discover how Ficino thought of the structure: a simple ascent to the highest good effected by contrast and comparison. Patently, Ficino had a coherent theory about the transitions and digressions in the *Philebus* and was convinced of the dialogue's essential unity of purpose. The fact he felt it needed such extensive commentary suggests, however, he was well aware of its difficulties for the ordinary reader.

What would have presented itself to Ficino as a thematic question tends to be complicated for us by other considerations. Although he was not completely oblivious to chronological problems (he was convinced for instance that the *Phaedrus* was Plato's first dialogue), he did not concern himself with the modern concept of an evolving or changing Plato.[79] Consequently, he was not cognizant of the fact the *Philebus* is a middle or late dialogue in which Plato, if not actually abandoning, is moving away from his earlier concern with the Ideas and ethical intellectualism towards a new interest in logical, taxonomical and even psychological problems.[80] Rather, Ficino, like

the ancient Neoplatonists, assumed the unity not only of Plato's thought, but of the whole Platonic tradition; and his life's work was to make the whole unified tradition available in translation and in commentary—hence his work on the Areopagite, on Plotinus, on Iamblichus, on the *Pimander,* on the Orphic *Hymns,* on the *Symbola* of Pythagoras, etc. The Platonic tradition, and again this is a Neoplatonic assumption, not only embraced Plato and his successors but also those enigmatic figures who were thought to precede Plato: Philolaus, Pythagoras, Aglaophemus, Orpheus, Hermes Trismegistus and Zoroaster. These collectively Ficino referred to as the *prisci theologi,* the ancient theologians,[81] the interpreters of a perennial wisdom stretching back long before Plato.

Such an approach does away with the need to decide on the authorship of particular concepts or to differentiate the peculiarities of individual dialogues (hence the ease with which apocryphal works were accepted as part of the canon). So, wherever possible, Ficino attempted to syncretize and reconcile the positions adopted in Plato's various works. In examining the *Philebus* commentary, one is gradually made aware of the other dialogues which were constantly in the forefront of Ficino's mind, dictating the structure of his proofs and providing further authentication for his conclusions. They were drawn in the main from Plato's middle and late periods—they are notably the *Sophist,* the *Timaeus,* the *Parmenides,* the *Republic,* the *Laws* and the *Phaedrus*[82]—and they constituted for Ficino a unified body of metaphysical "doctrine," a word he himself used.[83] Hence the wholly philosophical nature of the *Philebus* commentary. As Roberto Weiss observes, Ficino was not a philologist or a grammarian; he was untouched by the philological zeal of humanists like Valla and Politian, and was concerned solely with exposition, not with textual problems[84] — which was as well perhaps considering the notorious difficulties the *Philebus* presents to the textual scholar.

In elucidating the "secret" Platonism he assumed Socrates was imparting to the assembled adolescents, Ficino was quick to perceive the local dramatic ironies, and he took an obvious

delight in imagining the personal aspects of the crossfire between Socrates, Protarchus and Philebus. But he was not
oriented towards the modern concern with the ambiguities
created by the dialogues' dramatic structure. Because he believed in their collective wisdom and the power of allegoresis to
"explain" intractable or figurative passages, he refused to
acknowledge the exploratory or interrogatory nature of many
of the propositions. Hence his anticipation of Plato's conclusions in the *Philebus:* the idea, for example, that there is a
tertium quid is indeed mentioned briefly at the beginning
(11D-12A); but it is essentially something Plato arrives at in the
course of the argument. Ficino, however, used it throughout his
commentary as an established principle. For him the *Philebus*
was obviously a normative work, concerned with Plato's unchanging conception of the unitary good; and he must have felt,
therefore, it was an ideal text for educating his peers into the
true secrets of philosophy, as well as for combating the
Aristotelians.

In short, Ficino chose the *Philebus* for a variety of intrinsic
and extrinsic reasons—historical, philosophical, polemical and
pedagogical—all stemming ultimately from the particular interpretation he accorded to it.

III

Initially the commentary confronts us as a medieval work.
Kristeller says of Ficino, "the strongly medieval, scholastic
character which we notice in his works . . . consists not so much
in specific philosophical ideas, but rather in the terminology
and in the general method of arguing." But he goes on to say
this scholastic element "was not due to an extensive reading of
the scholastic authors of the twelfth and thirteenth centuries,
but rather to the training which Ficino must have had in the cur-
rent Aristotelianism of the schools as a student in the University
of Florence."[85] Kristeller maintains Ficino did not have any
extensive firsthand knowledge of the medieval philosophers
with the notable exception of Aquinas, but was able "to build
his Platonism on the method and terminology of late medieval

Aristotelianism.''[86] The result is daunting: the reader is confronted with chains of syllogistic reasoning which have the appearance of being tightly organized and utterly logical. But the logic frequently begs the very questions it is attempting to answer; in this it is reminiscent of much medieval philosophy, the texture of which more nearly resembles a row of mental walnuts than it does a series of Euclidean proofs.

The commentary is eclectic in its approach. This is typical not only of the Renaissance but of most medieval philosophy and, indeed, of patristic and Neoplatonic thinking.[87] Ficino was not trying to be original; he was trying to synthesize, as Charles Trinkaus has recently reemphasized.[88] Besides the many quotations and references to other Platonic dialogues in the commentary, there are references to other ancient authors, real and fictive, and to a few medieval ones; but Ficino rarely cites the specific works he is referring to. In addition to the acknowledged references, there are some which are unacknowledged. Most notable are the extensive borrowings from Aquinas in several of the chapters, which are in paraphrase rather than direct quotation. Marcel suggests in his new edition of the *Platonic Theology* that Ficino habitually reduced his quotations to the essential meaning and adapted them to his own context. Perhaps Ficino assumed some of his allusions were too familiar to need acknowledgment, but at times it seems as if he were deliberately concealing his authorities. Marcel observes: "It is almost as if he wanted to appropriate their thinking or [wanted] to constrain his readers to admit principles or arguments which they would have refused to examine on principle [a priori] if they had known the source."[89] Ficino often groups his references by school and these group references are frequently taken *en masse* from later authorities: the list of ancient physicists and moralists, for example, he could have derived from Diogenes Laertius or Aristotle or Cicero or Augustine or Lactantius or Aquinas or from half a dozen medieval or contemporary sources. Marcel freely admits to resorting to "resonances" in order to suggest a source and the task is fraught with indecisions. I have tried to supply Ficino's particular references (and

some of his vaguer ones) but rather, in Marcel's words, "to call
attention to the problem" than to pretend to offer "a definitive
list."[90] More work has to be done on Ficino's indebtedness to
scholastic philosophy as well as on his own development before
we can move with any certainty here.[91]

Structurally the commentary is confusing because it is cumulative rather than systematic in its approach. While it purports
to follow the order of the *Philebus* itself (though in actuality it
gets no further than 24A, hardly more than the opening fifth of
the dialogue), the *Philebus,* which it must be remembered is
itself a multifaceted work, simply serves as the starting point for
trains of thought which bear no organized relationship to it.
While individual sections or paragraphs are systematic in their
construction, the commentary itself follows a much more
leisurely plan, gradually unfolding the central propositions of
Ficino's metaphysics and epistemology with many repetitions
and digressions (and in one instance a whole proof is repeated
word for word).[92] But the absence of structural rigour does not
prescind from the philosophical unity of Ficino's system as a
whole, nor does it detract from the ferocious rigour Ficino
often applies to the individual parts. Readers of Ficino's other
works will half recognize many of the passages and proofs.
Given the relative priority of the *Philebus* commentary among
Ficino's mature works, it must be the source for many of these
recurring formulations, though earlier works like the lost
Institutiones Platonicae (1456) must account for others. The
cumulative approach can make for difficulties. Before any one
section can be understood, it is often necessary to understand
the metaphysical principle involved. Since, in Trinkaus' words,
Ficino's philosophy is "to a very great extent a seamless
garment,"[93] single propositions tend to stand or fall on the
truth or adequacy of a few a priori assumptions. But this has
one overwhelming advantage: the commentary is more than a
series of scholarly notes for it explores propositions with endless
ramifications—something it shares with other Neoplatonic and
scholastic commentaries derivative in appearance but often
containing truly original insights.

However, despite its medieval tone and texture, the *Philebus* commentary is a Renaissance document and in it we can hear echoes of numerous Renaissance themes and preoccupations. There are passages of interest to historians concerned with: the "dignity of man" theme; educational theory; aesthetics; psychology; the debate over the merits of the active or contemplative lives; the concepts of the intellect, the will and freedom; Pelagianism; Epicureanism; Averroism; Thomism; the inception of the idea of natural religion; iconography and myth, etc. Although the commentary is a piece of formal philosophical writing, it does spring directly from the imaginative and intellectual worlds of the humanists and reflects many of their obsessions. There are several suggestions, even, that it is more closely interwoven with Renaissance Hermetism and occultism than might appear feasible from its uncompromising facade. First, Ficino spent the year or so before Cosimo died not only translating the ten dialogues, including the *Philebus,* but also Hermes Trismegistus' *Pimander.* Second, Johannes Pannonius charged that at the time Ficino was writing the commentary he was overindulging himself in *pagan* lore. Third, some of the sections dealing with dialectic and the dangers attending its use can be linked to the belief that a word has power over its referent and the proper manipulation of words can result in the manipulation of things. Fourth, it is more than curious Ficino should spend so much time warning us about the *dangers* of admitting apprentice adolescents to the secrets of dialectic's sorcery. Finally, the whole idea of the mediating principle and the mixture, and the idea that the species exist in the seed-plot of the mind have implications extending far into the realms of magic theory. I do not believe for one moment that the commentary is an introduction to magic; I merely suggest there may well be some profitable connections to be made between it and the Hermetism which Ficino, Frances Yates says, rejuvenated for all of Europe.[94]

The *Philebus* commentary is also the work of the greatest Christian rationalist of the Renaissance. In his preface to the *Concerning the Christian Religion* Ficino talks of the

intelligence and the will as the soul's two wings enabling it to fly back towards its home: "the intelligence illuminates the will" and "the will embraces the intelligence" and so philosophy, the activity of the intelligence, being a gift from God must be used to defend religion.[95] In a letter to Pico della Mirandola, his "brother philosopher," he refers to Platonism (which for him is synonymous with philosophy) as the way which leads men to Christianity; it is the necessary first step which takes the unbeliever towards the concept of a natural religion and thence towards Christianity itself.[96]

For a Christian the intelligence can be seen from two angles: either it is moved naturally by God towards the apprehension of a truth which the will does not yet believe in; or it is moved supernaturally towards the defense of a truth which the will already believes in.[97] Ficino is writing in order to lead men towards faith: hence his insistence that "the intelligence illuminates the will" and his subordination here of the will to the intelligence, an aspect we shall return to. Consequently, certain fundamental Christian ideas associated with the will are absent: the fall of man and his consequent need for atonement and grace are never mentioned and the concept of sin is subsumed into that of error. Nevertheless, the Christian context is there. As Kristeller says, "the Platonic Academy of Florence was Christian in its tendency and a center of religious as well as of philosophical and of literary importance."[98] More particularly, the *Philebus* lectures took place in a church and were part of a conscious programme to harness the "divine Plato" to Christianity. So the emphasis on the withdrawn, contemplative life in the lectures must have had religious—perhaps even specifically Augustinian—implications for Ficino's contemporaries.[99] At all events, it can be placed, as we shall see, in the context of at least one major theological controversy.

IV

I turn now to the commentary's ideas. First to its ethics. Ficino, like Plato before him, works in a very restricted area here: he has little to say about the problems of intention and

motivation and there is no anticipation at all of the concepts of duty and utility as we find them in post-Kantian ethics. Equally unmodern is his refusal to use a technically self-defining vocabulary for ethical discussion, which he consistently sees against the backdrop of a comprehensive metaphysical system.

Man is a being in internal discord, subject to the conflicting demands of wisdom and pleasure. Ficino had long been intrigued by the concept of pleasure and by Epicureanism in general.[100] In 1457 he actually laid aside Plato to read and comment on Lucretius and he was familiar with the debate about the nature of pleasure involving such renowned humanists as Raimondi, Valla and Poggio. The debate was the result of the rediscovery of Lucretius and Diogenes.[101] Their enthusiasm for Epicurus' doctrines, which offset Cicero's hitherto unquestioned censure, did away with the feckless libertine. Epicurus became a true philosopher, wholly engaged in the intellectual life and in promulgating a doctrine of strictly noetic pleasure. It is important to remember this, because Ficino envisaged Socrates fighting against the sensualism, materialism and scepticism of Philebus and the atheism it implied, but not against hedonism as such. Moreover, it is obvious Plato himself used Philebus and Protarchus to indicate he was differentiating between sensual hedonism and hedonism of a more subtle or refined kind. A.E. Taylor has argued that "the Hedonists of the *Philebus* are more or less serious thinkers, with a reasoned-out view of 'values' " and that the difference between the *Philebus* and the *Republic* over this point is the consequence of the rise of "a *reasoned* doctrine of *philosophical* Hedonism" (which he ascribes to Eudoxus).[102] It is reasonable to suppose Ficino not only perceived this but wanted to exploit it. Both the dialogue and the commentary plainly defend pleasure, though a pleasure that has been carefully circumscribed. Hackforth says the *Philebus* is constructive rather than destructive, and "seeks to do justice to the rightful claim of pleasure to be a factor in human happiness"; and Taylor has argued it is "part of his [Plato's] view that for a sentient being like man pleasure *must* [his italics] be an ingredient in the 'best

life.' "[103] Ficino, while recognizing pleasure's claims, usually insists on its subordination to wisdom. Periodically, however, he suggests happiness and intellectual pleasure are the same and there are ecstatically happy states in which wisdom and pleasure are fused and the soul becomes identified with its intelligence *(mens)*. Since the will is associated with pleasure rather than the intelligence, and since true pleasure is accordingly "the expansion of the will into the good and the rest of the will in the good,"[104] it means the ecstatically happy state is one in which the intelligence, the will and pleasure are one. As Kristeller observes: "In this highest act . . . the knowledge of divine truth coincides with the enjoyment of divine goodness."[105] Once a man has attained this state he can then become mystically identified with the heavenly intelligence itself.[106] Protarchus, in contradistinction to Philebus, never entrenches himself behind any dogmatic view of pleasure, and proffers sundry sophisticated arguments which Socrates does not so much reject as modify. On the other hand, it is clear Ficino wanted to use Protarchus primarily as a springboard for the various problems raised; there is no such thing, that is, as a Protarchan position to offset the Socratic one at any fundamental level. It is unlikely, besides, that Ficino was attacking any particular philosopher or philosophical sect in Florence and there is no reason to believe the "partisans" of pleasure refer to any persons in particular, as they may well do in the case of the *Philebus* itself.[107]

Granted the ultimate goal is the mixed life of wisdom and pleasure, which are individually the goals of the intelligence and the will, the main problem then becomes: Does the intelligence or the will contribute more to the mixture? Since we must go into Ficino's presentation here in some detail, as it is one of the commentary's distinguishing features and has important consequences, the next section is specifically reserved for a consideration of the internal reasons Ficino educes for the subordination of the will to the intelligence.

Apart from the internal reasons, there is an overwhelmingly important external one which I shall mention now. Ficino is

ultimately trying, as Saitta suggests,[108] not only to reconcile Platonism and Christianity, but also to explore the possibility of a natural religion, a religion inherent in man's nature from the beginning as opposed to one supernaturally revealed to him subsequently. The genealogy of Platonists stretching back prior to Plato to Hermes and Zoroaster is the genealogy of those professing this natural religion,[109] which takes the form, inevitably, of a variety of rationalism, that is, belief in the natural powers of man's own intelligence to apprehend the supreme good. Since any introduction of an all powerful "perverted will" would undermine such a belief, another concept has to be employed in order to account for man's fundamental instincts and energies; and it will be subordinate to, rather than opposed to, the intelligence. Hence Ficino more often talks about the "natural appetite" than he does about the will. Arguments from its existence can be used extensively to support the thesis there is a final cause towards which all things are drawn, and anyway it is the concept Plato himself is dealing with in the *Philebus*.[110] Although the appetite is beneath the will, functions at a lower level, and is distinct in its own right, it is universally understood as the source of instinctual energy; it is uninvolved in the sort of moral choices that weaken and trap the will, and it can be harnessed by the intelligence without any sense of real conflict. Since the intelligence is indisputably superior to the natural appetite, Ficino tends to argue therefore that the intelligence is superior to all non-intellectual activity. The distinction between the intelligence and the appetite seems to rub off onto the distinction between the intelligence and the will (this is prescinding of course from the broader problem of Ficino's drive to subsume all three "faculties"). The result is a special emphasis on the intelligence and its unique ability to perceive the universal good.

Ficino's search for the natural rational religion not only involved dealing with the intelligence but with the *ideal* intelligence, "the erected wit," which we find in the philosopher, but not in the active man immersed in business, society and politics. As a result of the natural appetite all men have a natural desire

for the good; but the philosopher is the only one who can perceive what the good truly is. He is therefore the rational animal *par excellence,* the wholly religious man. Over and against the fideism and scepticism of the Ockhamists, which sprang from an emphasis upon man in all his weakness and dependency, Ficino reaffirmed the power and validity of man's intelligence when it is used to contemplate eternal truth. This reaffirmation (which some would call Pelagian) understandably adopted many Thomist positions, since Thomas Aquinas was the great Christian apologist for the mind, but preeminently it was invoking the authority of Plato. It was reaching out towards a revitalised concept of the intelligence in order to affirm the reasonableness, and indeed the logical necessity, of a natural ethic.

There are two further points with regard to the intelligence. One, its nature was the subject of controversy between Averroists, Alexandrists, and other integral Aristotelians and the orthodox theologians. Inevitably Ficino had to concentrate on it when he brought Plato's authority to bear on his opponents' belief in the existence of a unitary and separated intelligence, a belief which made the possibility of personal immortality undemonstrable. Two, there are times when Ficino uses the terms "man," "soul," and "intelligence" almost interchangeably,[111] because man's highest part is his soul, and the highest part of the soul is the intelligence. Everything Ficino says in the *Philebus* commentary about the intelligence and its knowledge of the species is therefore being said about the soul. As such it prepares us for the *Platonic Theology,* where Ficino not only defends immortality but offers us an extensive examination of the soul's metaphysical role as the universal bond and copula, that is, of its intelligential and dialectical powers and its ability to mediate between the corporeal world and the world of Plato's Ideas.

Neoplatonism had fully elaborated the major development of Plato's successors, namely, the theory that the Ideas exist in the divine intellect: in Ficino's terminology *species, ratio, idea, regula, forma* all signify, in Heitzman's words, "a universal

existing in the divine intellect.''[112] This is in contradistinction to *natura* which refers to the universal's embodiment in matter. Ficino occasionally gives other names to the universal in its disembodied form, e.g., *unitas,* when he is making a particular distinction;[113] but the term abounding in this commentary is *species*. Although it is true, as Huit, Saitta, and Kristeller have pointed out, that the Platonic theory of the Ideas as such has little impact on Ficino[114] (as such it had, of course, little impact on Plotinus,[115] or even, arguably, on the later Plato), Ficino does, in Kristeller's words, ''[discuss] the theory of Ideas more explicitly and more clearly . . . [under] the direct influence of the ancient sources.''[116] This not only has a direct bearing on his monism, but because of the ubiquitous influence of the concept of ''participation''—the concept that ''what is more or less such and such is so called because of its smaller or greater distance or propinquity to that which is primarily and totally such and such,''[117]—the theory of the sovereignty of the intelligible world (signified by the prior existence of the universal species) does have an impact of overwhelming proportions on Ficino's whole metaphysical system. Chapters 16 to 22 of Book I of the *Philebus* commentary are specifically concerned with establishing the higher reality of the species as contained in and perceived by the illuminated intelligence, which is the receptacle of the Ideas, as opposed to the reality at a lower level of their embodiment in matter. Because the lower ''participates'' in the higher, the intelligible world of the Ideas can be reached both by deduction and analysis, that is, by logic, and by the greater discipline of dialectic. Consequently, chapters 23-28 and the unattached chapter IV of the *Philebus* commentary are specifically concerned with dialectic—in Plato's phrase—the ''coping stone'' of the sciences.[118]

Dialectic was the major instrument of a rationalist. Since the time of Berengarius, Lanfranc and Damian there had been a continuous and sometimes rancorous debate on the nature of dialectic, on its relationship to faith and on its validity as a weapon in the fight against epistemological scepticism. As a rationalist Ficino was bound to champion dialectic and to

justify it and its function, just as Lull and other apologists had done before him. In distinguishing it from logic, Ficino writes: "Dialectic is a divine craft no longer concerned with words, but with things. By the pure probing of the intelligence above the senses it inquires into each thing's substance, and from all things it ascends to their one principle without the need for any other principle."[119] So logic is the art of the reason, dialectic is the art of the intelligence. The distinction was first introduced by Boethius who distinguished between the concepts of the intelligence and the reason. The *ratio* abstracts universals from matter; the *mens* or *intelligentia* contemplates the reality of the universals within itself primarily, only then does it compare them to the universals as perceived through abstraction.[120] One must remember the intelligence is not the specifically human aspect of the soul, but its highest part, its angelic face,[121] and being the receptacle of the innate Ideas, it is therefore essentially passive,[122] awaiting illumination or activation by God.[123] Once activated by God it operates dialectically and logic is arrogated rather than rejected. Both logical and dialectical processes result in "true" knowledge, knowledge of the world of the species as abstracted from matter and as illuminated in the intelligence. Moreover, both logic and dialectic share in an ascent within the intelligible world up through the hierarchy of the Ideas in their search for greater truth. This epistemological ascent takes on ethical and ultimately spiritual meaning. Since, in Kristeller's words, "all knowledge is implicitly directed to God [as the source of the Ideas], it is easy to consider thought in general as a way of the Soul toward God."[124] Dialectic becomes a spiritual ascent into the divine reality.

There are several stages in the ascent to pure knowledge.[125] One reason why Ficino subordinates pleasure is because it is content with opinion; and since the will and pleasure are associated, the will is associated with opinion too.[126] Ficino, like Plato, does not dismiss opinion, but he does place it lower down on the scale of authenticity. The intelligence does not rest content with opinion, but contains within itself the species which are the touchstone of truth. Ficino introduces the Saturn

and Prometheus myths in order to personify his ideas on the way in which the species in the intelligence are illuminated.[127] The species in the intelligence and the species as they are embodied in things are not the eternal species themselves as they exist in the divine intellect, but rather reflections or images of them, *formulae idearum.*[128] So the crucial problem devolves upon the three-way relationship between the three "existences" of the species and their need for each other. The images in things, the *simulacra,* are occasions for the activation of the reflections in the intelligence, the *formulae idearum,* which have been there potentially from the beginning.[129] The occasion has, however, to be accompanied by activation by God; for, as Heitzman observes, "the existence of the innate ideas in our soul is not yet equivalent to their being known and comprehended."[130] That is, the method of ascent corresponds to the ascending structure of reality from things' essences to the innate ideas, to the eternal Ideas, to the Idea of the good.

Since Plato said essences were known through dialectic,[131] and since the name is what denotes the essence,[132] dialectic is concerned with names and with naming: "the power of a natural object reaches through the senses to the imagination, through the imagination to the intelligence itself by which it is apprehended and enclosed in a name."[133] Chapters 11-12 have a number of things to say about the power this in turn bestows on the dialectician. The naming of an essence becomes the same as its activation in the intelligence: the external and internal "existences" of the essence are brought together by the articulation of the name and gradually as the whole macrocosm is named it becomes activated within as the intelligible reality. The elaboration of such perceptual and conceptual problems in turn requires a metaphysical explanation of the sort of correspondence existing between the mental and physical worlds. Since this would take us into the theories of innatism, nativism, occasionalism, as well as into the more familiar debate over nominalism and realism, I refer further discussion to the specialized studies of Heitzman, Kristeller and Schiavone.[134]

However, dialectic is not only the instrument of ascending knowledge, but of descending knowledge too. Miss Yates' remarks on Ramus pertain equally to Ficino here: "...natural dialectic is the image in the *mens* of the eternal divine light.... It is a way of ascent and descent from specials to generals, from generals to specials...."[135] The conception goes back to Plato: dialectic is less a method than a spiritual movement, mounting by provisional hypotheses, i.e., by supposition, to the universal principle and thence returning to readjust the hypotheses in the light of pure intellection, that is, "demonstrating" them in the light of its understanding of the one alone.[136] It is an intuitive contemplation rather than a discursive process of reasoning: initially it makes use of logical induction and deduction, but then it becomes mysteriously creative.[137] Ficino's view of method resolves the traditional dichotomy between a priori and a posteriori knowledge into an organic unity and is part of his reappraisal of the problems of consciousness. Through the dialectical method the intelligence and will are united in the contemplative descent: the intelligence having seen the one then wills it as it turns to contemplate the many in the one. In so doing it is demonstrating man's godlike knowledge and godlike powers.[138]

The nature of dialectic with its dual concern for the one and the many, identity and change, rest and motion, is in many tantalizing ways suggestive of the nature and function of love as it is explicitly dealt with in the *Symposium* commentary and briefly but lyrically in this commentary.[139] They both fulfill similar unitive functions, for the magical power dialectic has over essences and therefore over things, its ability to divide and unite reality itself, is something it shares with love. In the Platonic tradition they have always been related: the dialectician is a lover; love is an instrument of knowledge.[140] What Ficino was bringing to both concepts in the period in which he wrote the two commentaries was a heightened awareness of the kinship.

Other Platonic ideas are introduced too: the nature and existence of the world-soul, the hierarchical series of the Ideas

and the hierarchy of the goods, the relationship of these two hierarchies to the Idea of the good, the various categories of reality headed by the limit and the infinite,[141] attacks on the eristics and sophists, etc. However, I wish to close this particular section with three consequences of the theory which has been with us since the beginning, namely the theory of the one. First, unlike St. Thomas who talks about unity as one of God's attributes but not as His essence, Ficino is a radical monist: the one is beyond being but is the principle of all being, it is God's essence.[142] Hence the one supplies the cardinal premise in any argument and there is no philosophical question in the commentary for which this is not true: it is what makes the commentary central to the development of Ficino's views as a metaphysician, not his *ad hoc* positions, important though they may have been at the time. Second, the digressive, convoluted appearance of the commentary takes on new significance in the light of Ficino's unmitigating search for the universal principle. The commentary is unified by its preoccupation with the participation of all things in the one, and with the unitary consciousness which enables us both to perceive and to create the mysterious participation of our being and actions in the being and the actions of all other things. The reader cannot fail to detect Ficino's sense of awe and exhilaration whenever he approaches this body of ideas. Third, Ficino's constant concern with the one has a bearing on the unfinished state of the commentary. Ultimately, it seems to me, it could never have been finished. Ficino's subsequent writings are essentially a profound and continuous commentary on the *Philebus* and the metaphysics Ficino saw embodied in it. Which is to say, the sermons he delivered to the cultural élite of Piero de' Medici's Florence were early reactions to ideas which he continued to explore to the grave.

V

I turn now to the intellect/will controversy. The *Philebus* commentary is among other things an apology for ethical intellectualism; it is concerned with contemplation rather than the

moral virtues and is philosophical rather than psychological in
its approach. As both Kristeller and Sears Jayne have explained,
the Platonic way of describing the pursuit of the highest good
"is to relate the various parts of the soul to the characteristics of
its goal" and this means equipping the soul with three principal
faculties: the intellect, will and love.[143] But the issue is complicated by the fact that "Ficino regards love and will as essentially
identical ... he sets them off together as differentiated from
intellect."[144] Consequently, whenever Ficino asserts the will is
higher than the intellect, it is because he is identifying will with
love. Yet Ficinian love, in Jayne's words, is "essentially an
epistemological term meaning desire for truth ... [it] remains
...essentially an intellectual rather than an emotional process.
...Although he [Ficino] talks about love as the unifying force
in the universe, he preserves the primacy of the intellectual life
by the way in which he defines that love.... His whole life
testifies to the fact that the supreme value is for him intellectual
...he regarded the principal objective of the soul as an
intellectual objective."[145]

The relationship between the intellect and the will was a
traditional subject of debate between Scotists and Thomists.
Initially, Ficino was drawn towards the Thomist position, the
position upholding the primacy of the intellect. As we have
seen, it is to the *Summa Contra Gentiles,* Book III, that we
must turn for his model. Here the argument proceeds from the
proposition that "all things are directed to one end, which is
God";[146] and therefore "the knowledge of God is man's last
end. Now the last end of man and of any intelligent substance is
called *happiness* or *beatitude* ... therefore the last beatitude or
happiness of any intelligent substance is to know God."[147]
Aquinas goes on to make the crucial point that "that operation
of man whereby he first obtains God is essentially his happiness
or beatitude. And this is understanding: since we cannot will
what we do not understand. Therefore man's ultimate
happiness is essentially to know God by the intellect, and not an
act of the will."[148] Later Aquinas concludes, "man's ultimate
happiness consists in the contemplation of the truth [and] ...

all other human operations seem to be directed to this as their end."[149] Therefore the truly ethical life is intellectual and the civic and moral virtues are subsumed into the intellectual ones.

This is not only the position which is broadly adopted in chapter 37 of the commentary on the *Philebus*, it is also the position attributed to "Marsilio" in Landino's *Camaldulensian Disputations*. "Alberti" has pointed out that although there is complete agreement among the Christian theologians that God is the highest good, there is marked disagreement over whether speculation or love is the true means of attaining it (it is interesting, incidentally, that "Alberti" should contrast speculation to love rather than to the will, for it means that for him also the two have become identified). Landino brings in Ficino to champion the Platonic viewpoint and to argue that the highest good is to be reached via the intelligence rather than the will. James Wadsworth maintains Landino misrepresented Ficino's views here and that Ficino's *On Happiness* is a "fully reasoned refutation of the thesis on the supremacy of the Intellect" which Landino had erroneously attributed to him.[150] Still, it is interesting to note Landino was obviously convinced at the time of writing his second book of the *Camaldulensian Disputations* that Ficino did put the intellect above the will, and that his conviction was the result of Ficino's discussion of the *Philebus*.

However, in the light of other works of Ficino's "middle period" particularly the *On Happiness,* parts of the *Platonic Theology* and some of the letters, the Thomistic approach is surprising, and commentators have drawn attention to what seems to be genuine inconsistency. Let us examine the charges with specific regard to the *Philebus* commentary.

Giuseppe Saitta took an extreme view. He not only maintained the mature Ficino was always a voluntarist (a view that, as we shall see, certainly cannot be substantiated for Ficino's last years), but that he was already a voluntarist when he composed the *Philebus* commentary. He argued the commentary is fundamentally at odds with Plato's position: "in the commentary on the *Philebus,* which, as you know, is one of the most significant of Plato's dialogues, what refers to the voluntaristic

nature of the good is treated with breadth and profundity, but the reason for this is obvious: Ficino, in dealing with the various problems touched on in this Platonic dialogue, is unable to disobey the demon spurring him on. It takes the form of positing an ethical idealism that is strictly voluntaristic, at the expense, as you can see, of rationalism.''[151] The comment has to be taken in the context of Saitta's particularly "idealistic" approach to Ficino, but it does point up a central issue: the *Philebus* commentary, in using such detailed and powerful proofs to set up the intellect over the will, seems to belie Ficino's real intentions as one can deduce them from some of his other works.

In his extended study of Ficino's philosophy Kristeller, when speaking to this precise issue, also saw Ficino as a committed voluntarist, though unlike Saitta he recognized that the position expounded in the commentary was intellectualistic. He argued it was an early work and that Ficino upheld the superiority of the intellect because he still saw it as an independent and static faculty—"the old ontological contempt for movement apparently still has some influence."[152] He juxtaposes the key proofs from Book I, chapter 37 of the commentary with quotations from the *Platonic Theology* and the *On Happiness,* arguing for the "close connection" if not the "identity" of the two systems of will and love in Ficino,[153] and for the primacy of the *will* as Ficino's mature, sustained conception. Significantly though, Kristeller's most convincing illustrations are all drawn from the *On Happiness* alone.[154] It is undisputable that in the *On Happiness* Ficino is indeed a committed voluntarist, since the arguments are there, and Ficino himself later singled it out as pro-voluntaristic; but it was the one piece he did so single out, and he must have felt that it was alone among his many works in maintaining an unequivocal voluntarism.

One reason for this apparent indecisiveness or inconsistency is obvious. Ficino's analysis of the soul into parts, influenced as it is by classical tradition, does not include the will. The *idolum* does contain an aspect referred to as the "vital force" and the body contains an image of this, the *natura* or "vital complexion" which Ficino usually calls the irrational soul. However,

apart from these two aspects which are concerned with the biological functions such as growth, reproduction, nutrition, etc., which were then attributed to the soul, the parts of the soul are the direct outcome of classical and medieval attempts to arrive at a theory of knowledge and perception; that is, their *raisons d'être* are epistemological.

It is only fair to point out Kristeller not only acknowledges this, but assumes Ficino's intellectualism throughout his study, except when he is arguing with particular reference to the conflict between the *Philebus* commentary and the *On Happiness*. He writes, "from the beginning it [the will] is related to the intellect and, so to speak, leans on it";[155] and he quotes Ficino on the will's derivation from the appetite, "as the irrational appetite follows sensation, so the will, which is rational appetite, follows the intellect."[156] The will is distinguished from other forms of appetite because it is allowed to choose. The process of choosing is, however, an intellectual process; it depends on the reason and its deliberation: "the will desires the good to the extent to which the intellect offers it."[157] In the section in which Kristeller identifies will and love he admits that together they occupy a "double position in relation to the theory of knowledge, being conceptually dependent on it in many points."[158] Ficino had defined will as "an effort of the thought" *(nixus intelligentiae);*[159] he repeatedly talks of the will *following* the intellect;[160] and although the intellect is properly directed towards truth, the will towards goodness, he frequently failed to make this distinction and assigned both goals to the intellect, "[the *intellect*] knows all things under the concept of truth and desires all things under the concept of goodness."[161] Kristeller admits "the knowledge of God through the intellect and the love for God through the will are after all only two conceptual formulae [elsewhere he calls them "indifferently parallel"] indicating the same concrete fact—in other words, the inner or spiritual ascent of consciousness to the highest grade of contemplation."[162] At the same time, he maintains, "the real essence of inner or spiritual consciousness is revealed more deeply and more directly by the theory of the will than by

that of knowledge."[163] Yet the goal of the inner ascent is the *knowledge* of God. Kristeller says that happiness for Ficino "can consist only in the speculative virtue—that is, in contemplation. Above all, it consists in that knowledge of God which the soul attains after separation from the body and in the joy connected with it."[164] Hence, he continues, "the contemplative attitude is considered the real content and measure of human life"[165] and the contemplative experience is "identified" with philosophical knowledge.[166] As we have seen, Ficino insisted that philosophy and religion were one and the same, and the soul had two wings, the intellect and the will, the philosopher depending mainly on the former, the priest on the latter. But from early on he upbraided those "who too impiously separate the study of philosophy from sacred religion" since wisdom and love, "true intelligence" *(intelligentia vera)* and "right will" *(voluntas recta)* are one.[167] In the light of Kristeller's repeated recognition of these various points, it is surprising he adopted a negative approach to the intellectualism of the *Philebus* commentary.

Yet such an approach does receive some support from Ficino's own postscript to the commentary addressed to Michele Mercati, and from a short letter Ficino wrote in 1496 to another Camaldolese friend, Paolo Orlandini, which is devoted entirely to the problem under debate. Ficino acknowledged that Orlandini and apparently others had asked him why he had preferred in the *Philebus* commentary the intelligence over the will, in accordance with Plato's own view, and then in the letter *On Happiness* the reverse. To Orlandini Ficino wrote: "I could reply that in the *Philebus* [commentary] I am giving you Plato's view, in the letter my own view. But I do not want Marsilio's view to differ from Plato's. So, briefly, I will say in reply that our intelligence operates in two ways, one natural, but the other supernatural, which might properly be referred to as the way of ecstasy. In the first case, the intellect guides the will, just like a friend, as a result of some naturally innate light; eventually, when it has guided the will correctly, it satisfies it, and is therefore superior to it. In the second case, the case of ecstasy,

however, a new light and power poured in by God does not fill the intellect with the divine splendour, until it has kindled the will with a wonderful love." Ficino went on to say, "We have discussed the intelligence's natural process in accordance with Plato in the *Philebus;* but we touch on the ecstasy which is higher than the natural motion in the letter, and we have treated it in accordance with Plato in the *Phaedrus* and *Symposium.*"[168] Ficino obviously thought he was reconciling the two viewpoints satisfactorily. Despite the traditional nature of his distinction, his critics think otherwise. Saitta, in commenting on the Orlandini letter, says, "These latest words are a protest we can make nothing of."[161] And Kristeller, in commenting on the postscript and the letter, says, "...it is not necessary to take these explanations ... literally, for they were obviously added subsequently. It is sufficient for us to recognize in them an admission of the difficulty and of the change of doctrine. Therefore we must accept the superiority of will and love over the intellect as Ficino's more mature and conclusive theory." He goes on to observe, however, that "the inner or spiritual ascent of the soul toward God ... received its first systematical interpretation in the theory of knowledge" and was then "caught, in its dynamic element, in the theory of will and love.[170] His viewpoint here was adopted, necessarily, before the discovery of the letter written to Colet by Ficino in 1499.

Three decades later, however, Kristeller came to a less sweeping conclusion. In his review of Renaissance Thomism he traces the history of the will-versus-intellect debate. In general, Aquinas had affirmed the intellect was ultimately superior, though he conceded the will may be superior in this present life.[171] It is important to note that from the standpoint of the present and future lives this is the exact reverse of the view adopted in the Orlandini letter. Scotus, incidentally, took the extreme anti-intellect view, maintaining the will was always superior in the present life and in the future one.[172] Kristeller reviews the problem in Ficino succinctly: "The problem preoccupied Marsilio Ficino on several occasions at different points in his life. Indeed, it is one of the points on the subject of

which one can observe oscillations and changes in his thinking.''[173] Again Kristeller contrasts the position adopted in the commentary with that in the *On Happiness* and various letters. He continues: "Towards the end of his career, however, he showed that he was again undecided. In preparing his commentary on the *Philebus* for publication, he admits, at an appropriate moment, to having resolved the question elsewhere in an opposite sense, and he tries to propose a compromise distinguishing between the will as a distinct faculty and the will as part of the intellect.''[174] Kristeller refers to the Orlandini letter with its crucial distinction between the soul's natural and supernatural powers in which the intellect and the will are superior respectively, and concludes: "The solution is not very clear or convincing, but it does make us see that the problem continued to preoccupy him and that he had not succeeded at all in reaching a firm or categorical opinion on this particular point.''[175] A contemporary of Ficino, Vincenzo Bandello, was provoked by the *On Happiness,* which Ficino had sent to Lorenzo in 1474, and proceeded to attack Ficino on Thomist grounds, choosing to ignore the modified Thomist position Ficino had himself adopted in the *Philebus* commentary. The issue centred around Ficino's theory of knowledge and its relationship to the will in the future life.[176] Bandello made a radical break between this life and the next and followed Aquinas exactly in making the will dominate the one, the intellect the other. Ficino cannot consistently make such a radical break. Even though it undermines his previous insistence on the incongruity of Ficino's two views, Kristeller emphasizes this: "Ficino, for his part, as heir to the Neoplatonic tradition, does not admit that the difference can be that radical between the present and future lives. He is convinced that the supreme experience of contemplation to which philosophy can attain in this life is an authentic anticipation of the future life. . . . He insists on the fact that the experiences of the present and future lives are profoundly similar.''[177] He comments: "It is interesting to find echoes of the debate in the writings of the humanists, who otherwise show such little

interest in theological questions and in the questions raised by scholastic philosophy."[178] It was an especially live issue among Ficino's pupils: Alamanno Donati wrote a little treatise on the theme and Lorenzo in his *L 'Altercazione* introduced "Marsilio" into his shepherd world to defend voluntarism.

I have dealt with Kristeller's remarks at length because they offer us by far the best account of the differences over this fascinating issue between the *Philebus* commentary and the *On Happiness.* Even if we grant for the moment Kristeller's particular approach to the commentary, certain points are already established. First, Ficino showed continuing hesitation over assigning the primacy either to the intellect or the will. Second, Ficino's position in the *Philebus* commentary though certainly not Scotist, was not strictly Thomist either. Third, it was Ficino's "first systematical interpretation . . . [of the] inner or spiritual ascent of the soul to God," and as such provides us with the basis for exploring the origin and nature of his subsequent views. Fourth, the *Philebus* commentary brought the authority of Plato to bear on the issue for the first time, independently of Aquinas; and the impact of this integral Platonism should not be overlooked. Fifth, the debate was a long-standing one, where both extreme positions, their modifications and possible combinations had already been explored by the Dominican and Franciscan schoolmen; there was obviously no incontrovertible solution and so Ficino could espouse a number of views with equal respectability. Finally, if it is true that Ficino refused to envisage a radical break between the present and future lives, then anything said about either life will impinge on the other too. Ficino's indecision becomes not a matter of being unable to make up his own mind, but the inevitable consequence of a fundamental circularity in his thinking which is monistic and ultimately perhaps mystical.

However, it is odd Kristeller's study of Thomism should make no mention of Jayne's work on Ficino and Colet, not only because of Jayne's carefully argued claim that Ficino was never an authentic voluntarist, but also because of the important evidence of the letter Ficino wrote to Colet in the July of 1499

which is printed and translated by Jayne as Letter D. Here Ficino takes an extreme intellectualist position: "intellect is primary and love is secondary. Intellect produces love; love is brought forth in intellect. Intellect faces inward; love faces outward. Intellect finally is purer, clearer and truer; love is more mixed, denser and thicker.... Will is crude intellect and intellect on the other hand is pure and refined will."[179] The letter is important on several counts. One, Ficino in his old age has taken up the cudgels again having been conciliatory for so long. Two, both love and will are now subordinated to intellect. Three, written in the last year of his life, it represents his final and unequivocal stand. Four, and most importantly, when taken in conjunction with the postscript to Mercati and with the fact that revising the *Philebus* commentary was one of the last of Ficino's projects, it suggests perhaps that it was the rereading of the commentary which brought Ficino back to the unequivocal intellectualism he had espoused at the beginning of his career.

There is one other recent commentator whose views, though expressed prior to Jayne's book and to Kristeller's later book, are particularly significant, since his overall approach to Ficino opens up a number of provocative and fundamental questions about Ficino's modernity. Michele Schiavone's dynamic interpretation of Ficino's metaphysics is very persuasive. But I do feel his account of the *Philebus* commentary, attractive as it is from the viewpoint of his immediate thesis, has to be severely modified in the light of his own total reading of Ficino. While recognizing Ficino hesitated over the problem of the primacy of the intellect, Schiavone explains it in terms of Ficino's historical position rather than admitting the possibility of genuine oscillation and doubt on Ficino's part. He posits a Ficino who was gradually breaking away from a received metaphysics towards one that was "intimately phenomenalistic and modern."[180] It involved breaking away too from a received vocabulary: "beneath a classification and a terminology which are classical new significances and new possibilities are hidden."[181] In the process of liberation from the structures of classical thought which

Schiavone sees as typical of Ficino's early thinking, the *Philebus* commentary occupies a temporary position. It is "a youthful piece of writing" in which Ficino momentarily accepts Plato's intellectualism. Accordingly, Ficino's attempt to bring it and the *On Happiness* into accord by distinguishing between the natural and supernatural understandings (which are controlled respectively by the intellect and the will) is unconvincing, "because it shows too many traces of a compelling desire to agree completely with Plato."[182] Schiavone goes on to give an explanation with a sirenic attractiveness: "In the commentary on the *Philebus* the reason for his assigning the primacy to the intellect is indicated by the superiority of activity without becoming, that is, dynamic concreteness ... in this youthful phase dynamism is understood as static action on another and not as self-determination by means of the determination of otherness; the result is an absence of that circularity and dialecticity which we can point to in Ficino's maturity."[183] Even if the theory is correct (and I believe it is), this is to dismiss the *Philebus* commentary too precipitately.

As Saitta alone acknowledged in talking of "the breadth and profundity" of Ficino's treatment of "the voluntaristic nature of the good," some of Ficino's best thinking here is very much concerned with the dynamic interrelationship, the "dialecticity," existing between any one entity and all other things as a result of their mutual participation in the one good. The major portion of Book I, chapter 31, for instance, is devoted to a consideration of the one as act: "all things gather themselves together into their one act [previously defined as the centre of each object 'to which and from which all the rest of the things in it come and go'], so that through this, their one centre, they may adhere to the centre of all things."[184] Ficino proceeds to elaborate on the circularity of the ontological process and on the intelligence's role in mediating the creative flow from the one to the soul and to matter and the reverse. Here we have one of several instances (the iconology of the Saturn, Jupiter, Prometheus group is another in chapter 26), in which Ficino deals with the triadic nature of the many's emanation from, turning

back towards, and return to the one in a continuing dialectic which passes through the intelligence: "The highest good of the intelligence is the perfected act of its nature: that is, when it has been turned back through one act towards the one act for it to become all acts and all things in act.[185] ... The highest good of the intelligence [is] ... the one comprehension of the highest one in all the species."[186] Beneath the intelligence the dialectical process is repeated in the soul's relationship to the intelligence and in matter's relationship to the soul. Consequently, the totality of existing things is involved in an ascent to and a descent from the one which both devolve upon the participation of each thing in the one and so in each other. Throughout the commentary, Ficino recurs to the ceaseless movement between the different levels of being and its consequence, the continual metamorphoses of matter into soul, of soul into intelligence, of intelligence into the one and back again.[187] Ficino is using, admittedly, the traditional distinction between the one's trans-cendence, which he calls its "sublimity," and its immanence, which he calls "the beneficent glance of the divine countenance."[188] But in elaborating on the two unities proceed-ing from the dual aspects of the one, he concentrates on the "beneficent glance" of the divine immanence. While God's sublimity is "the cause of the unity which preserves the proper simplicity of each thing," God's countenance is "the cause of the unity which results in things joining together."[189] It is not only the ground of each thing's own individual unity but the cause of each thing's perpetual desire to be at one with all other things; that is, the one's immanence is not only reflected in the plenitude of the cosmos, the procession from the one, but in each thing's relationship to that plenitude, the return to the one. Moreover, the return is in an enigmatic sense "better" than the procession: "So God bestows the good on things in putting them forth; but in turning them back He gives them the highest good."[190] Through its creative relationship with the one each thing is involved in a creative relationship with all other things, the one's creativeness insuring there is a like creativeness in the many. The whole of existence outside the one is therefore the

result of a ceaseless flow of energy not merely downwards from the one but upwards from the many as well. Ficino writes of the soul, for instance: "The highest good of the soul is the completion of the soul's one act: that is, when it has been turned back through its one act towards the one act of the intelligence and the one act of all things, for it to become all acts, that is, the plenitude of all the species."[191] We have here an ontological system with an emphasis on the organic union of all being and activity, an emphasis leading in turn to a new conception of consciousness, and more particularly of the intelligence.

In the Neoplatonic system the intelligence constitutes the second hypostasis and alone mediates between the absolute and all subsequent hypostases. Therefore, since the one is regarded here in terms of its creative immanence, the intelligence has to possess creative attributes too. They would normally be ascribed to the will, if the will as we know it in its Christian form existed in the Neoplatonic system. In transforming the Neoplatonic system which he saw articulated in the *Philebus,* Ficino was faced with the task of transforming the intelligence into a faculty which also functioned as the will. Or rather, the intellect/will dichotomy was caught up by Ficino's drive towards a unitary psychology, in which he was not going to subordinate or even combine mental faculties but do away with them as separate entities altogether. In their stead he was introducing a new awareness of subjective reality and the indissoluble unity of the inner world.

I must refer further discussion to Schiavone's own extended work on Ficino's monism, but one thing is clear: if he is correct in his view that Ficino was moving away from a static Neoplatonism towards a modern dialecticity, then it is ideas such as these (which Ficino had derived from Plotinus, Proclus, the Areopagite and Augustine but was working up into his own system) which testify to the movement. Ficino was already formulating those very conceptions which Schiavone finds proleptically modern and though they are clustered here around the concept of the intellect it does not mean they are any the less significant. We must recall Schiavone talks as if there were a

lengthy period of development between the approach adopted in the *Philebus* commentary and the one adopted in the *Symposium* commentary and the *Platonic Theology,* key texts in his argument that Ficino was moving towards proto-Hegelian positions. However, since the three works were generated close upon each other, it indicates rather the simultaneity of the conflicting theses in Ficino's mind. Ficino was not unaware of the conflict, he was simply exploring the various possibilities in his search for a new, organic synthesis. My disagreement with Schiavone lies in the fact that I see such a search already well underway in the *Philebus* commentary.

VI

I turn now to the problem of the dating. Since Corsi's remark that Ficino was lecturing on the *Philebus* during the reign of Piero there have been three attempts to date the written commentary. The first was by the great historian of the Florentine Academy, Arnaldo della Torre, who says: "A little after he had finished the *Symposium* commentary, Ficino started on the *Philebus* commentary, but at this point Piero invited him to expound his interpretation in public."[192] This is notable on two counts: it puts the *Philebus* commentary after the *Symposium* commentary; it suggests the written commentary preceded the public lectures. A few pages later, he notes that the second version of the *Philebus* commentary is grouped in the MS. *Laur.* 21, 8 with Ficino's youthful writings; and later still, while arguing Ficino chose the *Symposium* commentary and the *Philebus* commentary to divert himself from a personal "crisis," he says the public lectures took place in 1468, i.e., the year in which the first draft of all the Plato translations reached completion.[193] This series of arguments is based entirely on Corsi's ambiguous words *eo/hoc tempore,* and on the contents of MS. *Laur.* 21, 8; it implies amongst other things that the *terminus ante quem* for both the *Symposium* and *Philebus* commentaries is 1468.

Raymond Marcel offers us the most recent and elaborate attempt to date the commentary. First he argues from the

specific references in Landino's *Camaldulensian Disputations* Book II that the *terminus ante quem* for the commentary must be the summer of 1468 since, he says, Landino's first two books were completed by that date.[194] But there is no proof that they were completed then. The references in Landino to the *Philebus* commentary are clear enough—there are in fact verbal echoes—but the date of actual composition must not be confused with the date at which Landino imagines the conversation between Alberti, Lorenzo and Ficino to be taking place. Marcel argues that since the second book must have been written before the death of Piero on December 2, 1469 (because "Alberti" refers to Piero as being ill not dead), it was written during the summer of 1468—he gives no explanation why it should be 1468, however, when Piero did not die until the December of 1469.[195] But "Alberti's" remark only proves Landino is projecting the conversation back to the time preceding Piero's death. The references in the second book indicate the sort of impact Landino recalls the *Philebus* commentary having at the time of Piero's fatal illness; they do not prove Landino was writing it then, only that the commentary must have been written before 1474 when the *Camaldulensian Disputations* were dedicated to Count Federico of Urbino.[196] The uncovering of new evidence to date the actual composition of Landino's second book more precisely would alone enable us to proceed further.

Marcel's arguments to advance the *terminus ante quem* to 1466 are even more unsatisfactory. In April 1466, we know Ficino had the *Cratylus* translation in hand.[197] Marcel argues the *Philebus* commentary must have been composed before this because "the references to the *Cratylus* for example are not in the first version"; and in a footnote he writes: "For example the citation from the *Cratylus* at the beginning of chapter 23 and those in chapters 24 and 31 are wanting in the MS. *Vat. lat.* 5953."[198]

It is perfectly true the references at the beginning of chapter 23 and in chapter 31 (my pp. 215, 299) are missing in MS. 5953 (one to the *Cratylus* and one to Ficinos *argumentum* are also missing

in chapter 26 [p. 247] but Marcel does not mention these[199]). But the reference in chapter 24 (p. 229) is certainly there (though the paragraph following it has been transposed); and there are three further references to the *Cratylus* in the MS., two in chapter 11 (pp. 139, 141) and one in chapter 14 (p. 165), which Marcel completely ignores. Since his 1466 argument depends solely on this initial absence of *Cratylus* references, it is invalidated by the presence in MS. 5953 of four of the seven references in the 1496 *editio princeps*. Indeed, since three of the four references occur as early as chapters 11 and 14—and the specific reference in chapter 14 is to the latter portion of the *Cratylus* (428D), which may suggest Ficino was almost through if not completely finished with the translation—it would seem that even the early parts of the commentary were written after April 1466. I have compiled my own statistics on the incidence and frequency of the references to the various Plato dialogues but can come to no watertight conclusions: there are just too many variables.

Marcel is inconsistent on another issue affecting his attempt to date the *Philebus* commentary before the *Symposium* commentary. The genealogy of the six links in the gold chain of ancient Platonic philosophers ending with Plato himself—the *prisci theologi*—appears for the first time in the preface to Ficino's translation of the *Pimander* (1463) and it runs: Hermes, Orpheus, Aglaophemus, Pythagoras, Philolaus, Plato. In the *Platonic Theology* Book VI, chapter 1, as Marcel observes, the chain has become: Zoroaster, Hermes, Orpheus, Aglaophemus, Pythagoras, Plato. In order to preserve the symbolic hexad and include Zoroaster, Ficino dropped Philolaus and relegated Hermes to second position. Eventually, in the preface to his commentary on the *Enneads* Ficino no longer subordinated Hermes but bracketed him in first place with Zoroaster. I am not concerned here with the last development, or with the origins of the idea of the chain, or with the controversy over whether it was Pletho who first suggested the particular philosophers who should make up the links (though what I am going to say weakens Marcel's whole thesis). Rather, I am concerned with Marcel's claim that Ficino uses Zoroaster

for the *first* time as a theologian (as opposed to a mere magician) in his *Symposium* commentary (completed according to Marcel's own authoritatively argued dating in 1469). Now in actuality the second version of the chain, the one commencing with Zoroaster, is cited in its entirety in Book I, chapters 17 (p. 181) and 26 (p. 247) of the *Philebus* commentary (and Zoroaster is cited in Book I, chapter 29 and Book II, chapter 1 [pp. 271 and 403] in theological/philosophical contexts too). So, either Marcel is wrong in saying the "theological" Zoroaster appears for the first time in the *Symposium* commentary; or, if he is right, then the *Philebus* commentary must come after the *Symposium* commentary. In either case, Marcel fails to mention the appearance of the "mature" second version of the chain in the *Philebus* commentary, citing the one in the *Platonic Theology* Book VI as the first instance.[200] However, nothing can be proven incontrovertibly from the mention of Zoroaster in the *Symposium* commentary: Marcel's statement that Zoroaster occurs in a theological context for the first time in the *Symposium* commentary and yet remains subordinate to Hermes, the commentary's "uncontested master,"[201] is based entirely on the unsubstantial evidence of the reference in Book I, chapter 3, where Ficino is explicating the enigmatic passage from Plato's *Epistle* II, 312E-313A. There is no evidence in the *Symposium* commentary that Ficino had actually decided on the relationship between Zoroaster and Hermes. The enunciation of a Platonic hexadic chain does not occur in it at all; nor are Hermes and Zoroaster juxtaposed, for Zoroaster is mentioned only twice and Hermes once and then in quite separate contexts.[202] All this suggests the *Philebus* commentary postdates the *Symposium* commentary, as Della Torre originally supposed.

I have dealt with Marcel's arguments at length, not only because they are the most detailed ones adduced so far, but also because they indicate the sort of approach that dating the commentary entails. Their refutation merely underscores the difficulties facing the investigator and does not, I hasten to add, detract from the importance of what

Marcel attempted to do, and succeeded so brilliantly in doing in other related areas.

Paul Kristeller's proofs in his *Supplementum Ficinianum* I, p. cxxii, though prior to Marcel's, are the only ones which can stand scrutiny. He cautiously concludes the *Philebus* commentary must have been written before 1474, since it is mentioned in the brief *Five Questions on the Intelligence* and in the *argumenta* to the *Cratylus* and the seventh and tenth books of the *Laws* (*Op. Om.*, 677, 1309, 1507, 1520) and also in the first catalogue (*Op. Om.* 619.3). We have already seen the evidence from Landino and Corsi also points to a date before 1474 and the words addressed to Michele Mercati at the end of the first book do the same. Kristeller agrees with Della Torre that the *Philebus* commentary succeeds the *Symposium* commentary but he departs from Della Torre in insisting that the lectures preceded the written commentary. In his later book, *The Philosophy of Marsilio Ficino,* Kristeller is more specific; he says Ficino "wrote his commentaries on Plato's *Symposium* and *Philebus* in 1469,"[203] but he gives no reason for being so specific. I believe, though, that 1469 is the correct date.

So far the available evidence has pointed to a date prior to 1474 and that is all. However, we do know Ficino completed his *Symposium* commentary in the July of 1469,[204] and it would be important if we could establish whether the *Philebus* commentary was *written* before or after this. (Corsi of course tells us Ficino was *lecturing* on the *Philebus* before this, but that is not the issue at stake.) There is a little evidence, hitherto unnoticed, which has a bearing on the relationship between the two written commentaries. In order to discuss this evidence I propose to use the following sigla:

S   =   *Symposium* commentary

W   =   *Philebus* commentary: first version

XP =   *Philebus* commentary: second version

Y   =   *Philebus* commentary: third version

In Y there is a passage which extends from "Omne enim corpus ab alio quodam movetur" (p. 99, para. 2) to "ergo ipsa principium motus existit" (p. 103, top 2 lls.). This I shall divide

into five sections: "Omne enim corpus ab alio quodam movetur
...secundum participationem talia fiunt," I shall call *a*;
"Rursus anima quoniam a se ipsa movetur ... ante ipsam esse
quod primo est intelligens," I shall call *b*; "Id totum sic ab
initio ... Hoc ad materiam declinat magis, anima magis ad
mentem," I shall call *c*; "Cum dicimus animam se ipsa moveri
... rationis cogitationis discursiones," I shall call *d*; and "Agit
mens sed cum aeternitate ... ipsa principium motus existit," I
shall call *e*. A glance at the *apparatus criticus* will show that W
has the sequence *a-b*, XP has *a-b-c-d*, and Y has *a-b-c-d-e*.
Moreover, with regard to the sections shared, the *variae lectiones* are virtually confined to XP; that is, W and Y are
virtually identical.

In the *Symposium* commentary Book VI, chapter 15 (Marcel's ed. pp. 230-31) we find the following passage:

> Omne corpus ab alio quodam movetur; movere autem se ipsum
> natura sua non potest, cum nec agere per se quicquam valeat. Sed
> propter anime presentiam se ipso moveri videtur et propter ani-
> mam vivere et, presente quidem anima, se ipsum movet quodam-
> modo, absente vero, ab alio duntaxat movetur, utpote quod hanc
> ex se ipso naturam non habeat sed anima proprie vim ad se ipsam
> movendi possideat. Nam cuicumque adest, vim ad se ipsum
> movendum impertit. Quod autem ipsa sui presentia impertit aliis,
> hoc ipsa multo prius magisque debet habere. Est igitur anima
> supra corpora, utpote que se ipsam secundum essentiam suam
> movere queat atque iccirco supra illa debeat esse, que non ex se
> ipsis sed aliorum presentia ut se moveant assecuntur. Cum dici-
> mus se ipsa moveri animam, non transitive, ut ita dixerim, que-
> madmodum a Platone accipi voluit Aristoteles, sed absolute ver-
> bum illud proferimus, ut cum stare per se deum, lucere solem per
> se, calere ignem asseveramus. Non enim pars anime movet, pars
> agitatur, sed tota ex se ipsa, id est, sua natura, movetur; hoc est,
> ab alio in aliud ratione discurrit ac nutritionis, augmenti, gener-
> ationis opera per intervalla temporum transigit.

This I shall divide into two sections. "Omne corpus ab alio
quodam movetur ... presentia ut se moveant assecuntur," I
shall call *a**; "Cum dicimus se ipsa moveri animam ... intervalla temporum transigit," I shall call *d**. A cross-comparison
between the passage in Y and this one in S will show *a* and *a**

are parallel as are *d* and *d**; there are significant local variations however.

Prescinding from the remote possibility there may be an
earlier archetype which we do not know about and to which
both refer, can we determine which of the texts is the archetype?

Let me turn momentarily to the omissions in W and in S. If *d*
were in W, we would have the convenient progression (S) *a*-d**
(W) *a-b-d* (XP) *a-b-c-d* (Y) *a-b-c-d-e*. The constant accretion
would indicate that S were the archetype and so predated W.
But *d* is not in W. Conversely, if *b* were in S (as *b**), we would
have the progression (W) *a-b* (S) *a*-b*-d** (XP) *a-b-c-d* (Y)
a-b-c-d-e. Again, the constant accretion would indicate that W
were the archetype and predated S. But *b** is not in S. This is to
say that from a strictly logical viewpoint arguing from the omissions gets us nowhere.

Nevertheless, I do feel there are two arguments which cast
some light on the problem. First, the fact that *a* is virtually the
same in the three versions W, XP and Y, but *a** presents us with
a number of variations, suggests XP and Y depend directly on
W without referring to S at all. But when he was at stage XP,
Ficino must have resorted to S for *d*, since *d* is not in W and we
know XP postdates S. But if W were the archetype, then we
would have this situation: S would be looking to W for *a** and
XP would be looking to W for *a* but looking to S for *d*. But why
at stage XP would the rereading of *a* in W remind Ficino of S, if
S were not the archetype for *a* as well as *d*? I am arguing here,
obviously, on psychological grounds. The following completely
plausible situation would result if S were the archetype. At stage
W Ficino looked to S for *a*, then added *b* independently. At
stage XP, having read *a* in W, he was reminded of *a** in S;
whereupon he saw the significance of *d** and decided to borrow
it too. But before doing so he introduced *c* to serve as a bridge
between *b* (which he still wanted to keep) and *d*. That is, in
working on expanding the whole passage at stage XP, it was
completely natural for Ficino to return to S (since it was the
archetype) and to borrow again from it.

This argument is necessarily speculative, but my second argument is, I believe, less so. The sections *a* and *d* in W, XP and Y are not just somewhat varied versions of *a** and *d**; they are abbreviated versions. If we turn to consider Ficino's extensive borrowings from Aquinas (my pp. 81-83, 87-89, 295-297, 375-379) we find invariably that the fuller version is the original one. In the process of incorporating Aquinas' argumentation into his own text Ficino habitually abbreviated by omitting the odd word, phrase, sentence or group of sentences, in the same way as we all do when we are taking notes. From this perfectly legitimate analogy, we may conclude, therefore, that *a** and *d** (being the fuller versions) are the archetypes. S therefore predates W.

There is another parallel passage. The passage in the *Philebus* commentary (my pp. 109-11), "Sol profecto corpora visibilia.... Ut pulchrum illuminat gratiamque infundit" (the first part of which is repeated verbatim on my pp. 303-05), parallels the second half of chapter two in the second book of the *Symposium* commentary (Marcel's ed. pp. 146-67). Except for one sentence, the three texts of W, X and Y are virtually identical (apart from the opening few words, P is not involved this time), whereas the text of S has a fuller version. Both the arguments elaborated above apply to this passage as well and would again suggest that S is the archetype. Oddly, though, W has one sentence missing which is present in the others: "Ut in obiectis quae noscenda sunt tres illas cognoscentes animae vires allicit, gratia, pulchritudo." At first glance this would seem to be counterevidence. However, we are almost certainly dealing here with a mechanical error. The scribe's eye as he looked at the manuscript he was working from must have skipped over this sentence to the next sentence which also begins "Ut in...." In the formal hand of the W scribe the missing sentence would have occupied almost exactly two lines; something of the same was probably true also for the manuscript he was working from, in which case there would have been five *Uts* in near vertical succession and it would have been only too easy to slip over one of them.

The two arguments, applying as they do to both the parallel pairs I have been able to find, reinforce each other: they suggest the *Symposium* commentary preceded the *Philebus* commentary. This means the *terminus post quem* for the latter is July 1469.

The only *terminus ante quem* we have is still 1474, but it is psychologically unlikely (though logically possible) that Ficino would have done much work on the *Philebus* commentary when most of his energies were being absorbed by the composition of the *Platonic Theology,* a work he began in 1469.

In conclusion, then, I would argue for the latter half of 1469 as the period in which Ficino wrote the *Philebus* commentary. The sequence of his compositions from 1468 to 1474 would therefore run as follows: completion of the Plato translation (1468); composition of the *Symposium* commentary (Nov. 1468—July 1469); composition of the *Philebus* commentary (July 1469 to winter 1469); composition of the *Platonic Theology* (winter 1469-1474); composition of the *On The Christian Religion* (1474).

If we accept this series of arguments and counterarguments, we must acknowledge that the *Philebus* commentary, far from being a youthful piece, is an integral part of Ficino's most productive years. Necessarily, this is to question the validity of much of the interpretation of the commentary which has so far been put forward by other scholars.

VII

The present text is based on the third version of the *Philebus* commentary found in the 1496 edition of the *Commentaria in Platonem* printed in Florence (this incidentally has a corrigenda list which is easily overlooked). However, the edition has been collated with the three extant MSS., *Vat. lat.* 5953, *Laur. Plut.* 21, 8 and *Oliver.* 620, and all four readings have been recorded. None of the manuscripts is an autograph;[205] they represent the commentary's two earlier stages as we have seen, and Ficino himself saw the 1496 edition, i.e., the third and final version, through the press. The first edition is therefore authoritative.

An examination of the variant readings will show that Ficino made a number of minor stylistic changes. Usually the manuscripts agree with each other on a reading but differ from the edition. In a few instances the changes are substantive, but, again, attributable to Ficino's final revision. In most instances, therefore, the first edition's readings have been adopted. Occasionally the first version provides the obviously correct reading, but the second version rarely provides a good reading on its own. On a handful of occasions grammar or sense have necessitated emendation, but this has always been noted. The corrigenda list in the first edition has been incorporated without comment and non-substantive typographical errors ignored. The word-order is the first edition's, though it is virtually the same in all three versions.

The text of the *Philebus* commentary in the 1496 edition of Ficino's *Commentaria in Platonem* was reprinted in the first edition of his *Opera Omnia,* printed in Basle in 1561 and again in Paris in 1641. By now the text was peppered with variants and mistakes. The text in the second Basle edition of the *Opera Omnia* of 1576 (which is based on the first Basle edition) introduced further corruptions. My text has been compared word for word with these two editions of the *Opera Omnia* and in no single instance do they provide a better reading. With regard to the *Philebus* commentary anyway, the conclusion must be that the variants and mistakes were introduced by a printer's assistant or a compositor; there is no point in collating them. However, all my references are to the 1576 edition since it is the one generally available in the Turin reprint of 1959.

My paragraphing is the 1496 edition's since the manuscripts are largely unparagraphed (as are the Basle and Paris editions). All abbreviations have been expanded and the spelling regularized, the most important feature being the *ae/e* differentiation which is not consistently preserved in either the manuscript or printed versions and is merely the result of scribal and editorial preference. The punctuation has been modernized; in the manuscripts, predictably, it does not conform to modern usage, but in the various editions it is also repeatedly misleading.

Ficino enthusiasts of the sixteenth and subsequent centuries must have spent hours of irritation following the logic through the maze of colons and commas.

Translating Ficino demands, Marcel says, clarity, elegance and concision.[206] I have only tried to be clear; but by using such contractions as "can't" and "we've" to remind the reader the commentary was first delivered orally as a lecture I hope I have achieved a certain concision as well. The main problem is the scholastic terminology. With two recent translations of the *Summa Contra Gentiles* in mind,[207] I have normally chosen to translate *actus* and *principium,* for instance, as "act" and "principle," even though they derive ultimately from *energeia* and *arche,* terms which require two or more equivalents in modern English. Although Aquinas' terminology derives from Aristotle, it is self-defining. In order to keep my notes to the minimum, therefore, I have made no attempt to gloss the commonplaces of medieval philosophy; rather, I would refer the interested reader to such recent works as the Aquinas lexicon.[208]

Two further items need a word of explanation. The terms *anima* and *animus* do not seem to be differentiated by Ficino and I have translated both as "soul," even though *animus* usually refers specifically to the rational part of the human soul (or sometimes it means "courage" or "intention"). Second, *mens* has been translated throughout as "intelligence" rather than as "mind" (I have been swayed here by Marcel's example) and it means the same as *intellectus*; Ficino moves indifferently from one term to the other.[209]

The foliation of MS. 5953 is shown in the body of the Latin text; and in the left-hand margin of the English translation is the pagination of the Stephanus edition of the *Philebus*. There are only a few, true lemmata, as distinct from Ficino's para-phrasis and commentary, and these are in bold face. Italicized Latin and English texts indicate Ficino's unacknowledged citations from Aquinas.

Synopsis of the Commentary

(The numbers in parentheses refer to the pagination of the Basle 1576 edition of the *Opera Omnia*.)

BOOK I.

Chapter 1, p. 73 (1207): The need to establish an end for life. Everything acts for some end including the body, the reason, the intelligence; this proves there is a universal end cause.

Chapter 2, p. 81 (1208): Various proofs arguing for the necessity of an ultimate end and the impossibility of an infinite series. The end for the natural appetite, and the ends of execution and intention.

Chapter 3, p. 87 (1209): Various proofs establishing that the ultimate end has to be the good.

Chapter 4, p. 89 (1209): What the good is. The necessity for cosmic unity. The primacy of the one over multiplicity and over being. Above bodies is the soul; above souls is the intelligence; above intelligences is the one itself. Various proofs for this drawn from motion. The identity of the one and the good.

Chapter 5, p. 103 (1211): The reasons why everything seeks for the one and the good. The primacy of the good over being. The relationship of the good and the beautiful and the analogy with light.

Chapter 6, p. 111 (1213): The need to refer man's good to the absolute good. The other unsatisfactory ethical systems. The good is best apprehended and enjoyed by the intelligence.

Chapter 7, p. 115 (1213): Ficino returns to the text of the *Philebus* and, in the process of defining different sorts of wisdom and pleasure, he explains why Plato had chosen to compare these two terms.

Chapter 8, p. 121 (1214): The different sorts of good things. The contribution of wisdom to felicity. The two sorts of knowledge: the morning and evening knowledge. The distinctions that must be made between what leads to happiness, happiness itself and God. The relationship of all three to wisdom.

Chapter 9, p. 127 (1215): The real subject of the dialogue is man's highest good; other suggestions are dismissed. The dialogue's twelve part structure.

Chapter 10, p. 131 (1216): Socrates proposes initially that he and Protarchus should each champion wisdom and pleasure respectively, but be prepared to abandon their positions should some third alternative appear. Socrates refuses to accept that Venus can be identified with pleasure.

Chapter 11, p. 135 (1216): The divine names. The iconology of Uranus, Saturn, Jupiter and the two Venuses. The reason why divine names ought to be venerated. The power and origin of divine names.

Chapter 12, p. 143 (1217): The power inherent in the divine name and its various forms.

Chapter 13, p. 145 (1218): The importance of the species as opposed to the genus or the individual. The method for establishing a definition. The genus of pleasure. Socrates refutes Protarchus' argument that all pleasures must be alike because they are pleasurable, and maintains that some of Protarchus' pleasures are actually opposed to each other. Socrates differentiates between being good and being pleasurable. The good does not embrace opposites.

Chapter 14, p. 157 (1220): Socrates again emphasizes the difference between the genus and the species and warns us against verbal sophistry. The two protagonists agree there are dissimilar pleasures and dissimilar types of knowledge. Ficino warns us against self-deception.

Chapter 15, p. 165 (1221): The nature of the intelligence. The nature of truth and the theory that knowledge consists of the correspondence between the thing and the intelligence. The correspondence takes place in the human intelligence and in the divine intelligence. The light of truth that comes from the good. The one and the many and the psychology of perception.

Chapter 16, p. 171 (1222): The nature of the relationship between the one and the many and the paradoxes it originates. Three ways the one can be many. The Platonic Idea really exists and exists prior to and more absolutely than the sensible object.

Chapter 17, p. 177 (1223): Three problems raised by the Ideas: one, whether they are merely mental concepts; two, if they actually exist, whether they are unitary and immutable; three, if they are unitary and immutable, how do they impart themselves to things which are many and mutable. Why the species are called unities or Ideas. The pagan and Christian writers who have testified to their existence.

Chapter 18, p. 181 (1223): The existence of the Ideas in God's intelligence. The testimony of Augustine, Averroes and others. The contingent nature of the world and its dependence on the incorporeal species. Arguments from change, operation, movement, etc., to prove the existence of a higher cause which is self-sufficient, self-activating and contains all the Ideas.

Chapter 19, p. 191 (1225): More arguments to prove the reality of the Ideas and the unreality of bodily objects. To some extent the soul possesses the true species; but above the soul is the first intelligence which contains the first and truest species. These species are identified with the intelligence itself.

Chapter 20, p. 199 (1226): More arguments drawn from repro-duction, etc., to prove the reality of the Ideas. The world is con-tained in the first intelligence.

Chapter 21, p. 205 (1227): The argument from the world's design is taken to prove the existence of the prime intelligence and to prove that it contains the Ideas. The coincidence of the intelligence and its Ideas. The eternal contemplation of the Ideas is independent of the intelligence's need actually to create them.

Chapter 22, p. 209 (1227): More proofs for the existence of the Ideas drawn from the fact of corruption, etc. The shadowy existence of everyday things. The need to believe in the Ideas, even if we do not understand exactly how things participate in them.

Chapter 23, p. 215 (1228): To establish truth, dialectic is neces-sary because of its concern with the species. Ficino returns to the *Philebus* and inveighs against obstinacy in debating. The three cautions that must be observed with regard to dialectic: one, adolescents should not be allowed to use it; two, those who do use it must guard against the illusions which derive from the senses and the phantasy, and proceed via the intelligence; three, you must not go from one extreme to another without going through the intermediary points. The distinction between logic and dialectic. Dialectic is the instrument of philosophy *par excellence*. In the processes of uniting and dividing upwards and downwards, dialectic is constantly concerned with the one and the many. By using the one and the many, dialectic resolves, de-fines and demonstrates.

Chapter 24, p. 225 (1230): The relationship between definition and demonstration and the process of reasoning syllogistically. On resolving, dividing and compounding.

Chapter 25, p. 231 (1230): Socrates again inveighs against adolescents, sophists and Cyrenaics, and their ethical relativism

and scepticism (i.e., the first caution). Ficino returns to the *Philebus*. Altercation between Protarchus and Socrates. Socrates insists on the crucial importance of dialectic.

Chapter 26, p. 239 (1231): The illumination theory. The three angelic motions. The triple intelligence as personified in Saturn, Jupiter and Prometheus. The triple powers of the soul. The Epimetheus/Prometheus parable. The iconology of Minerva, Vulcan and Mercury and their various gifts. The Uranus, Saturn, Jupiter triad and what they symbolize. Prometheus' gift of fire symbolizes the illumination that comes from God; so dialectic must be practised by the intelligence (i.e., the second caution).

Chapter 27, p. 249 (1233): The three arguments transmitted by the ancient theologians: one, everything subsequent to the one is compounded from the one and the many; two, the species are finite, but individuals are infinite; three, mediation is necessary to pass from one extreme to another. Various supporting proofs. On emanation from the one to the finite many to the infinite many. On the types of division (i.e., the third caution).

Chapter 28, p. 261 (1234): Dialectic and the enemy discipline (which proceeds too quickly or too slowly from the one to the many). Various instances of the enemy discipline furnished from the ancients who ignored the importance of the intermediary stage between the one and the many — a stage involving the species. Ficino introduces the examples of music and dancing to illustrate the importance of the species in effecting the transition from the one to the many.

Chapter 29, p. 271 (1236): Grammar is used as an example of going from the many to the one. The history of letters and their introduction by Hermes Trismegistus. The need to draw things out of the one into the infinite many via the finite many which exist between them; and the reverse. Protarchus urges Socrates to proceed at once to instruct them all in dialectic.

Chapter 30, p. 283 (1238): The need to define the good and the positive and negative ways to do this. The negative way is to say that neither pleasure nor wisdom is the good itself. The good is above being and above the intelligence. It is the absolute act. The god of love is the divinity inspiring Socrates when he talks about the good. The relationship between love, beauty and the good, where the good is prime. Various proofs establishing that the good is sufficient, perfect and desirable.

Chapter 31, p. 299 (1240): The two acts: form and operation. The identity of the good and act. Act consists in unity. The good is compared to the sun. God as the good is all acts and all potentialities. The reflection of the one in everything is what unites everything. The emanation from the one and conversion to the one. The participation of the intelligence, the soul and matter in unity and goodness. The one is present in everything. The creativeness of the one and the resulting beauty. The good is prior to the beautiful and desired by the natural appetite. The difference between rational and irrational pursuit of the good.

Chapter 32, p. 315 (1242): In order to prove that neither is the good Socrates divides wisdom from pleasure, by dividing all mental activity whatsoever from it. The jelly-fish is a model for the life of pure sensation devoid of mental activity. The reason why such "deprived" organisms exist in nature. The great chain-of-being. Pleasure is insufficient in itself; likewise wisdom. The psychology of perception involves both wisdom and pleasure. In the case of both physical and mental events total act is pleasure. There are two sorts of pleasure: that in knowing and that which is the assent of the appetite. The mixture of the two makes for sufficiency in human and indeed all animate life. The life that does not have this mixture is chosen through ignorance or coercion.

Chapter 33, p. 333 (1245): Socrates differentiates between the prime intelligence (which is unitary and unites pleasure and wisdom in itself) and the human intelligence. The prime intelligence

is not the good itself, but next to and inferior to it. After the prime intelligence are the derivative intelligences; and next to them is the soul which becomes its intelligence when purified from all other associations. The soul's happiness consists of wisdom and pleasure. The morning and evening visions of the good. Socrates prepares to define the good positively having already defined it negatively: this consists in finding out whether wisdom or pleasure is nearer to the good (since it has already been established that neither is the good itself). He intends to maintain that wisdom is nearer to the good. The hierarchy of goods with pleasure at the bottom. The company agrees that neither wisdom nor pleasure is the good. Socrates procrastinates in order to make the group docile. He must now define wisdom and pleasure and proceed very cautiously.

Chapter 34, p. 347 (1247): The need for there to be one end. Man's end must be one and compounded from wisdom and pleasure. Wisdom and pleasure are made one by the one which is above. We apprehend the highest good by the unity in ourselves, which is like the charioteer in the *Phaedrus* who has two horses: the intellect and the will. The unity in ourselves converts these two into the one. So there are three happinesses: the human happiness when the charioteer controls the horses and directs them towards the heavens; the divine happiness when the soul becomes its intelligence; the happiness when we are made one by the one and so become one with God, that is, become gods.

Chapter 35, p. 355 (1248): To obtain the right mixture of wisdom and pleasure you must have truth, proportion and beauty.

Chapter 36, p. 359 (1249): The highest good is the measure that gives truth, the moderator that gives proportion, the suitable that gives beauty. Various ways in which God is the measure, the moderator and the suitable. As the one He is all three. Things which share in Him share in all three. The one and the unity the one bestows are both acts. Therefore the highest good

is the one act of the mixed life. This act occurs when the intelligence and the will have been directed to the one through wisdom and pleasure (when these in turn have been joined in accordance with three attributes deriving from the power of the one, namely, truth, proportion and beauty). The one act of the one soul, which is from the one, for the one and in the one, is man's highest good.

Chapter 37, p. 369 (1250): The subordination of the will to the intellect and their respective relationships to things. Various proofs to establish the primacy of the intellect. The ultimate end concerns the intellect more than the will. The need for something to be the first intelligible object. Pleasure's nature and use. God is our end: our understanding reaches Him first and our will follows the understanding. Ficino admits he has argued that the opposite is true in an epistle on happiness. Perhaps the best solution is to consider the will as part of the intellect rather than a separate faculty, and pleasure as something in the intellect. Ficino concludes man's end is one. Thus he claims to have resolved the doubts raised by his great friend, Michael from S. Miniato, who had wondered why Plato posited a mixed end for man.

BOOK II.

Chapter 1, p. 385 (1253): Socrates introduces two concepts, the limit and the infinite, and attributes wisdom and pleasure to them respectively. There are two sorts of infinity: the first excludes the limit, the second is in need of the limit. The first is the infinite limit of everything and is God, the second needs to be limited by something else. The *Philebus* is concerned with God as things' limit, not as the infinite. In the *Philebus,* therefore, the infinite means matter. As the infinite, God transcends creation; but as the limit, He embraces it. The hierarchy which proceeds from nothingness to matter to form and is the result of varying degrees of participation in the limit and the infinite. On the nature of potentiality. The passive potentiality characteristic

of matter precedes all else. On the nature of matter. All things subsequent to God are compounded from act and potentiality, being and essence. The existence of the being whose essence is being itself. Arguments derived from the fact that nature is subject to possibility and limitation and made from the mixture of essence and being prove that all contingent things are compounded from potentiality and act. On matter as the receptacle of all the forms.

Chapter 2, p. 403 (1255): The hierarchy among the principles of being is headed by the one. The general character of an entity incorporates the idea of being; so, apart from being, there are five other elements: essence, rest, motion, identity and difference. There are also the two principles of the limit and the infinite. Depending on our approach, the full hierarchy can therefore consist of six, seven or nine members.

Chapter 3, p. 409 (1256): Six elements derive from the limit and the infinite. These six are equally divided between the limit and the infinite, since each is universally present in the intelligence, the soul, bodies, quantity and quality. Their presence creates a hierarchy that descends towards the infinite.

Chapter 4, p. 415 (1257): How the limit and the infinite are disposed under God. The distinctions between creating, forming and generating. What is mixed from the limit and the infinite. The fourth principle, namely the cause of the mixture, is above the universe. The possibility that a fifth principle exists, namely the cause that subsumes all mixture, is not denied but put aside by Socrates. On the sublimity of God, i.e., His transcendence, and on His countenance, i.e., His immanent presence. The hierarchy existing among the principles and the right way to deal with it. The need to examine the limit and the infinite first.

UNATTACHED CHAPTERS

I, p. 425 (1259): In the height of the understanding pleasure and understanding are identical. The usual differences between them.

II, p. 427 (1259): The good is the end. The reasons why pleasure and wisdom are not the end. The uses of pleasure.

III, p. 431 (1259): The relationship between the one, the many, the limit, the infinite, and their compounds, that is, rest, motion, identity and difference.

IV, p. 433 (1260): The art of dialectic, which is concerned with uniting and dividing. The nature of dialectic and its transmission. Its preoccupation with the species. The various steps in the dialectical method.

A note explaining that this is all there is so far, and what follows are merely chapter divisions and summaries. (See Appendix V).

[*See p. 447 for a synopsis of the ten excerpts.*]

THE COMMENTARY OF MARSILIO FICINO, THE FLORENTINE, ON PLATO'S PHILEBUS ON THE HIGHEST GOOD

MATERIAL THAT HAS BEEN HASTILY COLLECTED FROM MARSILIO FICINO'S LECTURES ON THE PHILEBUS

COMMENTARIA MARSILII FICINI
FLORENTINI IN PHILEBUM PLATONIS
DE SUMMO BONO*

COLLECTA CURSIM EX LECTIONIBUS
MARSILII FICINI IN PHILEBUM**

*the title in W; apparently it reflects Ficino's initial optimism, for it anticipates the completion of the whole commentary

**the title in X and Y (in X it is boldly printed above the first chapter heading, in Y it is incorporated into the first chapter heading); it recognizes the commentary is still incomplete and is probably by an editor. See the subscriptions in texts W and Y (p. 425), and more particularly the postscript in Y after the four unattached chapters (p. 439)

Chapter 1. *That there is some end to all actions.*

   As the chief aim of all philosophy is concerned with the
happy life and men seeking it have given themselves to its study,
and as the happy life consists in the highest good, we will start
to expound Plato's book on man's highest good before the rest.
The highest good is the end for the sake of which all men do
everything. But life's end must be known in particular, so that
we can direct all actions towards it. In the same way a pilot has
to decide above all on the port he's making for, or the archer
has to first inspect the target at which he's aiming his arrows.
Plato foresaw this in the *Alcibiades*, in the *Euthydemus*, in the
Republic Book 7 and in the *Laws*.[1] He says, if we don't know
the good itself, all the other arts and sciences will be useless,
endeavours pointless, actions harmful. Now in art or deliberation an end is nothing other than the terminal point towards
which the agent's intention is mainly directed and in which it
comes to rest. As in nature motion is properly directed towards
something, and as it stops once it has that something, it is therefore moving towards an end. Things in art and nature are both
disposed towards an end in the same way, and once the end has
been removed, causes for them cannot be assigned. So we'll
first discuss Philebus' view—he is arguing about man's highest
good, the end of all our actions—and we'll demonstrate there is
some end towards which men's actions can tend. Then we'll try
to show what this is and of what kind it is, and reject false opinions about it, and arrive at true ones. Finally, we'll point out the
best way to get there. This then is the proposed order of dealing
with the book.
   Every action arises either from the nature of bodily things, or
from the impulse of the soul, or from the deliberation and disposition of the reason, or from the understanding of the intelligence. If it arises from the nature of bodies, it tends towards
something definite. For the substances of bodies are mutually

[*326r*] *Quod sit aliquis*[1] *finis omnium actionum. Cap. I.*[2]

Quoniam omnis philosophiae summa ad beatam[3] vitam
refertur, atque eam quaerentes homines se ad eius studia con-
tulerunt, beata autem vita in summo bono consistit, librum
Platonis de summo hominis bono[4] ante alios exponendum
aggrediemur.[5] Summum quippe bonum finis est cuius gratia
omnia omnes agimus. Finis autem vitae imprimis noscendus est,
ut ad eum actiones omnes dirigere valeamus, non minus quam
naviganti portus ad quem deveniat ante omnia statuendus, et
sagittario signum ad quod[6] tela dirigat primum[7] inspiciendum.
Quod quidem vaticinatus Plato in Alcibiade, in Euthydemo, in
septimo de Republica, in Legibus: ait, si boni ipsius nobis
cognitio desit, artes omnes alias et scientias inutiles, conatus
irritos, noxias actiones fore. *Iam vero in arte et consilio nihil
aliud est finis quam terminus ad quem movetur agentis intentio
potissimum et in quo quiescit. Cum ergo in natura motus in
aliquid proprie dirigatur quo habito cesset, agit ad finem.
Similiter se habet dispositio rerum in arte et natura ad finem
quo sublato non possunt causae assignari.** Quamobrem ad
Philebi ipsius declarationem,[8] qui de summo hominis bono nostrarum omnium actionum fine disputat, nos primum parabi-
mus, ostendemusque aliquem esse finem ad quem actiones
hominum tendant. Deinde quis iste sit et qualis declarare cona-
bimur, et falsas quidem de hoc opiniones reicere, veras astruere.
Demum qua via maxime ad eum perveniatur monstrabimus.
[*326v*] Id ergo libri huius propositum est, is ordo.

Omnis actio aut a natura corporum provenit, aut animi
impetu, aut rationis consilio atque habitu, aut mentis
intelligentia. Si a natura corporum provenit, ad certum aliquid
tendit. Nam corporum inter se distinctae substantiae sunt,

---

[1]ultimus *add. W*   [2]*Y reads* Collecta cursim ex lectionibus Marsilii Ficini in Philebum quod sit
aliquis finis omnium actionum *(cf. p. 71)*   [3]beata *Y*   [4]qui Philebus inscribitur *add. WX*
[5]aggredimur *Y*   [6]*em.,* quem *WXY*   [7]inprimis *WX*   [8]declaratione *Y*
*-**om. WX*

distinct, so their natures and powers are distinguished. So individual and appropriate natures are present in individual bodies. From them proceed appropriate movements. Succeeding the individually appropriate movements are the individually appropriate effects. The natures and movements of bodies strive towards the effects in order to achieve a result, and to rest once the result has been achieved. For anything doesn't come from anything, but proper effects proceed from their proper causes: a man from a man, a fig from a fig tree, heat from fire. But who'll deny the end of every nature and every activity is that towards which its force is always impelled in its own way and in which it can finally rest? Besides, every bodily movement either tends to avoid destruction or acquire something convenient for itself, or destroy an opposite or create something like itself. In avoiding and acquiring it is moved to its own preservation; in destroying and creating, to the generation of something similar to itself. So self-preservation and generation are the end of all bodily movements.

Furthermore, if the nature of any body when it acts did not tend towards some determined effect, all effects would be indifferent to it. But what is disposed equally to many things doesn't effect one thing more than another out of the many possibilities. So every single body would either do everything or nothing. Each is impossible. For what does everything is the first principle of all, what does nothing is inactive. So the body tends towards a definite effect. But a definite outcome is called the end of an action.

Again, the body's power either produces something by chance or by a necessary intention of the nature. It isn't by chance, because any one body would produce all possible effects and so anything would result from anything. Things wouldn't need a definite seed and the argument [discussed] by Lucretius would come to pass: "If things were made from nothing, every genus could be born from every thing; nothing would need a seed. First, men could arise from the sea and the genus of fishes from the land and birds could burst from the sky."[2] And surely what happens by chance rarely happens, and

quare naturae eorum[1] viresque discretae. Unde singulis corporibus singulae insunt propriaeque naturae. Ex his proprii motus fiunt. Proprios singulorum motus sequuntur opera propria singulorum in quae naturae corporum motusque nituntur ut efficiant et effecto opere conquiescant.[2] Neque enim quaelibet a quolibet sed a propriis quibusdam propria quaedam fiunt, ab homine homo, a ficu ficus,[3] ab igni calor. Quis autem negabit finem esse cuiusque naturae effectionisque id ipsum in quod proprie semperque nititur eius impetus et in quo denique cessat. Praeterea omnis corporum motus aut eo tendit ut vitet interitum aut quod[4] sibi conveniens est[5] adsciscat aut perimat contrarium simile gignat: dum vitat et adsciscit ad sui ipsius conservationem movetur; dum perimit atque gignit ad similis generationem. Omnium ergo corporalium motionum conservatio generatioque est finis.

Accedit ad haec quod si natura corporis alicuius dum agit ad aliquem effectum determinatum non tenderet, omnes ei effectus indifferentes essent. Quod autem aeque se habet ad multa non magis unum e pluribus quam aliud efficit. Quare unumquodque corpus vel omnia faceret vel nihil. Utrumque impossibile est. Nam quod facit omnia primum rerum principium est. Quod agit nihil est otiosum. Quare ad certum quendam tendit effectum; certus autem eventus actionis finis cognominatur. [*327r*]

Item corporis vis aut casu in opus incidit aut necessaria quadam intentione naturae. Non casu, quia in quaecumque opera quodcumque corpus incurreret, atque ita quaelibet a quibuslibet fierent, neque certo res semine indigerent et[6] illud Lucretii eveniret. Nam si de nihilo fierent ex omnibus rebus omne genus nasci posset[7]; nihil semine egeret, e mari primum homines, e terra possit oriri squamigerum genus et volucres erumpere coelo. Et profecto[8] quod casu fit raro contingit, nec[9]

---

[1]erunt *Y* [2]conquiescunt *XY* [3]et *add. W* [4]quidem *Y* [5]est *om. Y*
[6]et *om. W* [7]posse *W* [8]profecto *om. WX* [9]non *X*

it happens not just in one way but in various ways. But we see certain appropriate effects coming from individual things — from a particular seed, at the established time, in the usual order and way, in a set sequence, with the same middle terms and the same rational principle and most of the time. So, as the corporeal power produces the effect from a necessary intention of the nature, it intends the effect in the proper way and what it intends it desires by natural instinct. What is desired by some agent is the end of [its] action, so each corporeal action is for an end. Moreover, the action which follows the soul's impulse, like anger, fear, greed, has some end in view. For if nothing were moving [the soul] from the outside, an impulse would not arise in the soul. So the impulse depends on something outside, which can be thought of as good, bad or neutral. If it were neutral, no new impulse would be occasioned by it. If it were good, it proceeds to attain it, if bad, to avoid it. Therefore the end of every action following the impulse of the soul is either the acquisition of good or the avoidance of bad.

Also, the operation following the reason's deliberation seeks some end. For to deliberate is to inquire. The person who inquires wants to find something out; for he doesn't seek what he has, he wants to discover something so he may rest in what he's discovered. But rest in what is discovered (which is what he was seeking) is the action's end.

Also, the action coming from the rational disposition, that is, the one depending on moral virtue and the arts, is directed towards a definite end. If the action comes from virtue and art, it isn't fortuitous, but follows the rational principle of the disposition itself. The disposition draws itself towards a suitable operation or a suitable effect. But eventually it stops in the thing it was drawn towards. Therefore the operation or the effect suitable to the disposition exist as the end of the movement which is born from the reason's disposition.

There remains the operation which comes from the understanding of the intelligence; this must be referred to a definite end. For the intelligence, before it can act, forms an inner conception of what it is going to perform through the action, and

uno dumtaxat modo sed variis provenit. Videmus autem propria quaedam a singulis, certo semine, instituto tempore, solito ordine modoque,[1] digesta serie, iisdem mediis, eadem ratione et ut plurimum fieri. Ergo cum necessaria quadam intentione naturae[2] corporea vis effectum producat,[3] proprie illum[4] intendit et[5] quod intendit naturali instinctu appetit. Quod ab aliquo agente appetitur actionis est finis. Omnis ergo actio corporum est ad finem. Quin etiam actio[6] quae animi impetum, ut iram, metum, cupidinem, sequitur finem aliquem respicit. Nam si nihil moveret[7] extrinsecus, animi impetus nullus insurgeret. Ab aliquo ergo exteriori impetus iste dependet, quod vel bonum iudicatum est vel malum vel neutrum. Si neutrum novus ex eo impetus nullus concitaretur. Si bonum ad consequendum[8] pergit, sin malum ad devitandum. Quapropter omnis actionis,[9] quae impetum animi sequitur, vel boni consecutio finis est vel vitatio mali.

Operatio quoque rationis consilium sequens aliquem expetit finem. Consultare enim inquirere est; quisquis inquirit ut inveniat quaerit. Neque enim quaerit quod habet,[10] invenire autem vult ut in[11] re inventa quiescat. [*327v*] Quies autem in eo quod inventum actionis ipsius quod quaerebat est finis.

Necnon et actio ex habitu rationis, id est, morali virtute et artibus pendens, ad finem certum dirigitur; si ex virtute et arte procedit,[12] non temere fit, sed rationem habitus ipsius sequitur. Habitus ipse vel ad operationem trahit sibi convenientem, vel ad opus conveniens. In eodem vero sistit demum quo traxit. Operatio itaque vel opus habitui congruens motus ipsius, qui ex rationis habitu nascitur, finis existit.

Restat operatio illa quae ex intelligentia mentis exoritur, quam ad finem certum referri necesse est. Mens enim prius quam agat, quod est per actionem paritura, concipit in se

---

[1]modo *WX*   [2]naturae *om. Y*   [3]producit *Y*   [4]illud *X*   [5]et *om. WX*
[6]operatio *W*   [7]movere *WX*   [8]consequentem *Y*   [9]operationis *W*   [10]habeat *Y*
[11]in *om. WX*   [12]procedit *om. Y*

from this notion it acts—for the action is led towards the conception. So the conception is the action's end. The intelligence acts either by knowing or by not knowing. If by not knowing, it isn't acting as the intelligence, but as some life or substance, for knowing is proper to the intelligence. So the intelligence knows what it does, for what it does is to know. Can it will too? Certainly it wills, for the intelligence isn't forced to act. For things are compelled when they are passive. Bodies are passive and those things connected to bodies. But the intelligence is free of the body. Therefore the intelligence wills what it knows and does. But whoever desires something comes to rest in it as an end when he possesses it. So the action of the intelligence is directed to some end. For in so far as it understands, its end is the truth; in so far as it wills, its end is the good; in so far as it acts, its end is the beautiful. For the intelligence arranges all things according to number, weight and measure, mode, species and order.

From this one infers that the operations of the nature, of the soul, of the reason and of the intelligence are directed by some ingenious and rational order to some proper end. They are not merely produced by matter's necessity, as Anaxagoras and Empedocles wanted; nor do they wander about without a definite end as the followers of Democritus and Epicurus argued. Not only reason, but also the senses themselves refute these views. For we don't see the elements borne just anywhere, but always to their proper places. Nor, in the case of animals and trees, do we see the parts of any of them joined at random; but single things are always distinct in their own little parts and the little parts are in turn so arranged that each seems created for the others' sake. And we always see in the earth's movements the same steady course is maintained, which also shows there is a definite end for everything and an ingenious rational principle is present. It shows there is one wise intelligence in command, the leader of all things, which can give a beginning to everything and establish an end, and can lead all movements to the end through the requisite intermediary stages, and bring them back to the beginning.

ipsa, atque ex ea notione agit. Actio enim[1] haec ad illud quod conceptum est inducitur. Quare quod conceptum fuit actionis est finis. Aut enim intelligendo mens agit aut non intelligendo. Si non intelligendo non ut mens agit sed ut vita aliqua vel substantia. Nam proprium mentis intelligere est. Cognoscit ergo mens quod agit, agere enim ipsius cognoscere est. Utrum etiam velit? Vult certe. Non enim coacta mens agit; coguntur enim quae patiuntur. Patiuntur corpora et quae corporibus sunt coniuncta. Mens autem a corpore libera. Vult igitur mens quod intelligit atque agit. In eo vero quod quis appetit ut in fine quiescit cum possidet. Ad finem igitur aliquem actio mentis dirigitur. Nam quod intelligit finis eius est[2] veritas, quod vult finis est bonum, quod peragit finis pulchrum. Omnia enim mens in numero, pondere, et mensura, modo, specie et ordine transigit.

Ex his colligitur et naturae [*328r*] et animae et rationis et mentis operationes artificioso et rationali quodam ordine ad finem proprium dirigi, neque a materiae necessitate dumtaxat produci, ut Anaxagoras et Empedocles voluerunt, neque sine certo fine vagari, quod Democriti et Epicuri sectatores disputavere. Quos non ratio solum, sed et sensus ipsi redarguunt. Neque enim quocumque ferri elementa videmus, sed ad loca propria semper; neque in animalibus et arboribus cuiuscumque partes quibuscumque coniungi, sed singula suis[3] semper distincta particulis, easque invicem ita digestas ut una alterius gratia genita videatur. Semperque eundem in mundi motibus cernimus servari tenorem quod et finem rebus adesse certum testatur rationemque[4] inesse artificiosam, mentem unam praeesse sapientem, rerum omnium ducem, quae et principium det cunctis, finem statuat, motus omnes debita per media ad finem ferat, ad principium referat.

---

[1]autem *WX*   [2]est *om. Y*   [3]fieri *Y*   [4]-que *om. WX*

Chapter 2. That there is an ultimate end to all actions.

Notwithstanding, perhaps someone will say all things always direct their movements to an end, but are ceaselessly going from one end to another. So what remains to be shown next is that an ultimate end is given to agents.[3] *Surely, in the case of all things which act for an end, we call the ultimate end the one beyond which the agent seeks nothing more, just as a doctor's activity extends no further than getting you well again. But something is discovered in the activity of any agent beyond which the agent demands nothing more, otherwise actions would go on to infinity. This is impossible, because, since nothing can pass through an infinite series,[4] nothing would ever start to act. For nothing is moved towards something it is impossible to reach. Besides, if the actions of any agent proceed to infinity, either some result will follow the actions, or no result. If some result, the substance of the result emerges after infinite actions. But what demands an infinite series before it can never exist, since one can't pass through an infinite series. It can't be and can't become either. But the agent cannot make such a thing. So it is impossible for any agent to start to do something which demands infinite actions beforehand for its completion. However, if there is no result consequent on the actions, the disposition of the actions must be such that they either follow the order of the powers involved in acting, as when some man feels in order to think, thinks in order to understand, understands in order to will. Or they follow the series of the things constituting objects for us; for instance, if I look at the body in order to contemplate the soul itself, but at the soul in order to contemplate the celestial beings, but at these in order to contemplate God Himself. But you can't proceed to infinity with the powers involved in acting, just as you can't with the forms of things, for the form is the principle of acting; nor can you with the things constituting objects for us. For things are not infinite, but (as we've shown elsewhere) the one is the principle of all. Consequently, actions cannot be extended to infinity. So there must be something [ultimate], and once it is obtained, each agent's drive ceases.*

Quod sit finis omnium[1] *actionum ultimus. Cap. II:*[2]

Ceterum[3] dixerit forte quispiam res omnes ad finem semper suos motus dirigere, sed de alio fine in alium perpetuo pertransire. Quare deinceps ostendendum restat finem dari agentibus ultimum. *Profecto in omnibus quae propter finem agunt, hunc esse finem ultimum dicimus ultra quem quod agit aliud nihil quaerit, quemadmodum actio medici usque ad sanitatem protenditur. Verum in actione agentis cuiuslibet aliquid reperitur ultra quod agens nihil exigit, alioquin actiones in infinitum progrederentur, quod quidem impossibile est, quia cum infinita transire nihil possit nihil agere umquam inciperet.*[4] *Nihil enim ad id movetur ad quod pervenire impossibile est. Praeterea si agentis alicuius actiones in infinitum procedant, aut has actiones aliquod [328v] opus sequetur aut nullum. Si aliquod, substantia operis post infinitas actiones emergit; quod autem ante se exigit infinita, esse numquam*[5] *potest cum infinita transiri non possint.*[6] *Quod esse non potest nec potest fieri; id vero quod tale est agens ipsum efficere nequit. Quapropter impossibile est ut agens aliquod facere incipiat aliquid ad cuius expletionem actiones infinitae antea exiguntur. Sin autem opus nullum actiones eas sequatur, oportet actionum huiusmodi dispositionem esse, vel secundum ordinem earum virium quae in agendo versantur, sicuti cum homo aliquis sentit ut cogitet, cogitat ut intelligat, intelligit ut velit; vel secundum obiectarum nobis rerum seriem, velut si corpus intueor ut animum ipsum considerem, animum vero ut coelestia numina, haec autem ut Deum ipsum contempler. Procedi vero in infinitum non potest, neque in agendi virtutibus, sicut neque in formis rerum, forma enim est agendi principium; neque in rebus quae nobis obiciuntur, neque enim res infinitae sunt, sed unum omnium est principium ut alias ostendimus.*[7] *Quo fit ut actiones in infinitum porrigi nequeant. Oportet igitur esse aliquid quo habito conatus agentis cuiusque desistat.*

---

[1]omnium *om.* X   [2]*no ch. break or heading* W   [3]certum W   [4]incipiet Y
[5]unquam W   [6]possunt W   [7]ostendemus WX

Again, in the case of the things which act for an end, all those things between the first agent and the last end are the ends of the things preceding them and the principles of the things following them. So, if the agent's drive doesn't refer to something certain, but actions go on to infinity, the principles of acting will have to proceed to infinity. This is impossible, for whether you regard preceding or succeeding things, in no respect are they infinite. For if they were infinite according to a subsequent series, then every single thing you have possesses infinities under it. Therefore it is the cause of infinities. Therefore it has infinite power. Therefore all things are equal, for infinities are equal to each other. But if things are infinite according to a preceding arrangement, whatever you have will be the result of infinite causes. Therefore it will preserve in itself the countless powers of countless causes and every possible thing will be infinite and any effect will be equal to the cause, or rather to infinite causes. And so, since we see effects are exceeded by their causes, we can't discover infinities either by going upwards or downwards. For this reason, Aristotle says, we don't choose everything for the sake of another;[5] for in such a case we would go on to infinity and the result would be a vain and senseless greed. Therefore there's something we want for its own sake, and all the rest because of it. This is the ultimate end.

Natural appetite is the necessary inclination of [a] nature trying to go from a want to fullness. Fullness and the ultimate end are the same. If the appetite has nowhere been given an ultimate end, but goes on from end to end endlessly, it can never be satisfied. So it tries to be satisfied in vain. Or rather, it will not even try at all; for no species of things will be moved towards that which is utterly impossible, since to be moved is to progress gradually from potentiality into act.

Moreover, there are two sorts of ends: one is the end of intention, the other of execution. But in either case something must come first. For what comes first from the point of view of intention is the principle which moves the appetite. When this has been taken away, the appetite won't be moved by anything. But that which is the execution's principle is what an operation

Item in his quae propter finem agunt, omnia quae inter agens primum et finem postremum sunt fines quidem sunt praecedentium, principia vero sequentium.[1] *Quare si conatus agentis ad certum aliquid non refertur, sed in infinitum abeunt*[2] *actiones, oportet agendi principia in infinitum procedere quod impossibile est.* Nullo enim pacto res infinitae sunt, neque si ad praecedentia respexeris, neque si [*329r*] ad sequentia. Nam si secundum seriem subsequentem infinitae sint,[3] tunc omne quodcumque ceperis infinita sub se habet; est igitur[4] infinitorum causa; vim itaque infinitam habet; idcirco paria omnia, infinita enim inter se paria. Sin autem secundum praecedentem ordinem infinitae res sint,[5] quicquid ceperis ab infinitis causis erit effectum; innumerabilium igitur causarum vires in se ipso servabit innumeras et[6] infinitum erit quodcumque et quilibet effectus causae par, immo infinitis par causis. Ideoque cum opera excedi a causis videamus, neque ascendendo neque descendendo infinita possumus reperire. Hinc[7] Aristoteles: non omnia propter aliud exoptamus; sic enim in infinitum foret progressus vanaque et stulta resultaret cupiditas. Ideo est aliquid quod propter se volumus et cetera propter ipsum. Is est finis ultimus.

Appetitus enim[8] naturalis est necessaria naturae inclinatio ab indigentia quadam adnitens ad plenitudinem. Plenitudo ac finis ultimus idem. Si nusquam ultimus huic praescriptus est finis sed de fine in finem absque fine progreditur, numquam impleri potest. Frustra igitur conatur impleri; immo neque conabitur quidem ullo modo, nulla enim rerum species ad id quod penitus impossibile est movebitur,[9] siquidem moveri est a potentia in actum progredi paulatim.

Accedit ad haec quod duplex est in finibus ordo: intentionis unus, executionis alter. In utroque autem ordine primum aliquid esse oportet; quod enim primum est in ipso intentionis ordine principium est quod appetitum movet.[10] Subtracto autem principio appetitus a nullo movebitur. Quod vero in exequendo principium est id est unde operatio incipit, quo

---

[1]effectiva *add. W*   [2]abebunt *Y*   [3]sunt *WX*   [4]ergo *WX*   [5]sunt *Y*
[6]in *add. X*   [7]Hinc *om. WX*   [8]enim *om. WX*   [9]movetur *WX*
[10]monet (*or possibly* manet) *W*

begins from. If you remove it, nobody can begin to do anything. But the intention's principle is the ultimate end. The execution's principle is the principle of those things contributing to the end. So in neither case can we proceed to infinity. For if there were no ultimate end, absolutely nothing would be desired: there would be no limit to an operation, and no agent's intention would come to rest. But if there were no first thing in the case of the things contributing towards the end, nobody would begin to do anything; nor would there be any limit to deliberation, but you would go on deliberating for ever.

Next, the desire in things for some end is either there as a result of chance, usage or nature. It isn't there by chance, as it would rarely happen, nor only as a result of usage, since present in men before all usage is at least the desire for the things which we become used to afterwards. Therefore it is naturally there. In fact, what is always present to all things comes from the species and from nature, so from that which is the principle of nature and the species, that is, God. For nature, as Plato says in the *Statesman*, is either God's art or God's instrument of art.[6] Therefore the appetite has not been given in vain; so sometime it will come to rest; so it attains the ultimate end. For the king who is wise and good doesn't give orders or move in vain, but God impels all things through the appetite.

If we don't go on to infinity with the grades of forms, of materials, of agents but arrive at the highest grade, we shall certainly not proceed endlessly with ends but arrive at the highest end. But the highest end is the ultimate end in which the entire rational principle of the end can exist. So whoever takes away the ultimate end from ends, takes away the nature of the end from ends. But if there is a first factor with agents, there is a last factor with ends. For the agents act for its sake. Therefore the first agent does everything for its sake. Therefore it's the ultimate end of all.

Aristotle says in the *Metaphysics* Book III that those who take away the end from things and create infinity are taking away the nature of the good, for the good contains the rational principle of the end and the end contains the rational principle

subtracto operari aliquid nullus [*329v*] inciperet. Principium autem intentionis est finis ultimus; executionis principium est eorum quae ad finem sunt principium. Atque ita neutra ex parte in infinitum progredi possumus; nam si ultimus non esset finis, nihil prorsus appeteretur, nec operationi ullus esset terminus, nec agentis alicuius intentio conquiesceret. Si autem non esset aliquid in his quae sunt ad finem primum, operari aliquid nullus inciperet; neque terminus esset ullus consilii, sed ulterius semper consultaretur.[1]

Adde quod appetitio finis cuiusdam in rebus aut casu est aut usu aut natura. Non casu, quia raro contingeret; non usu tantum quoniam[2] ante omnem[3] usum inest hominibus appetitus saltem ad ea in quibus post adsuescimus. Ergo natura; etenim quod inest omnibus et semper a specie est atque natura, ergo ab eo quod est naturae et speciei principium, id[4] est Deus. Natura enim ut dicit Plato in Politico vel Dei ars est[5] vel artificiosum Dei organum. Ergo non frustra datus est appetitus;[6] ergo quiescet quandoque; ergo ultimum consequitur finem. Non enim frustra praecipit et movet rex sapiens atque bonus,[7] Deus autem per appetitum concitat omnia.

[8]Si in gradibus formarum materiarum agentium non progredimur in infinitum, sed pervenimus ad summum, quanto magis in finibus non procedimus absque fine, sed ad summum pervenimus. Summus finis est finis ultimus, in quo sit tota ratio finis. Sic qui aufert in finibus finem ultimum hic finibus aufert naturam finis. Quod si est in agentibus primum, est in finibus ultimum. Agentia enim sui gratia agunt. Ergo agens primum sui gratia agit omnia; ergo illud est ultimus omnium finis.

*Aristoteles tertio metaphysicorum[9] dicit,[10] qui auferunt finem[11] rebus et faciunt infinitatem, hi auferunt naturam boni. Nam et bonum habet rationem finis et finis rationem boni. Ergo contra rationem boni et finis est quod procedatur in infinitum.

Praeterea** quemadmodum se habet quaeque ars ad

---

[1]consuleretur *X*   [2]quia *WX*   [3]communem *Y*   [4]illud *WX*   [5]est *om. WX*
[6]est appetitus *om. WX*   [7]atque bonus *om. WX*   [8]Praeterea *add. W*
[9]Metaphysicae *X*   [10]quod *add. X*   [11]in *add. X*   *-**om. W*

of the good.[7] Therefore to proceed to infinity is contrary to the rational principle of the good and the end.

Besides, just as each art is related to its appropriate end, so the universal art of living, whose parts are in a way the arts, is related to a universal end. But individual arts reach an ultimate point, at which point they are perfected and beyond which their functioning and effort do not extend; for instance, medicine has health, the art of war has victory. So each life looks to some universal ultimate good by which it can be perfected. The ultimate end is the good which is the principle of movement in desire. So whatever moves the appetite moves it through the power and grace of the ultimate end, even if we aren't aware of it. If there weren't somewhere an ultimate end to intention, what moves the appetite wouldn't be anywhere, since one can't transcend an infinite series. So the influence of the good will not reach as far as the appetite if it goes from one good to another without end.

Again, what desires, desires as an end either some result or operation, and the steps of each are infinite and terminate in the highest step. The highest step will be the ultimate end of the appetite.

Chapter 3. *The end of all actions is the good.*

Now we have shown there is an end to all actions and there is some ultimate end, we will show what this end is.[8] *But the end for whose sake all things operate is the good. For what is moved (as we said above) is not moved indifferently towards anything, but to something appropriate and suitable to it; for it isn't moved towards it, unless it has some agreement with it. But what is appropriate and suitable to each thing is the good for it.*

Again, the end is in what the mover's appetite and the appetite of what's moved come to rest. But the rational principle of the good is that it can satisfy the appetite. For the good is what all desire. So every movement leads towards the good.

Moreover, in a way every action and movement seem to be moved towards being itself: either in order to preserve the being

proprium [*330r*] sibi finem, ita et communis ars vivendi, cuius partes quodammodo artes sunt, ad communem se finem habet. Singulae vero artes extremum quiddam habent quo perficiuntur et ultra quod earum officium laborque non extenditur, ceu medicina sanitatem, res militaris victoriam. Omnis igitur vita ad ultimum quiddam respicit commune bonum quo perficiatur. *Finis ultimus est illud bonum[1] quod est principium motus in appetendo, ita ut quicquid movet appetitum eius vi et gratia moveat, etiamsi nequaquam animadvertamus. Si nusquam sit finis intentionis ultimus, nusquam erit quod moveat appetitum, quia infinita non transeuntur. Ideo influxus boni non pertinget usque ad appetitum, si de bono in bonum abeatur sine fine.

Item quod appetit vel appetit tamquam finem opus aliquod vel operationem,[2] utriusque gradus sunt finiti et terminantur ad summum gradum. Summus gradus erit finis ultimus appetitus.**

Finis omnium actionum est bonum. Cap. III.[3]

Postquam finem esse omnium actionum et ultimum aliquem esse finem ostendimus, quis iste finis sit monstrabimus. Est autem finis cuius gratia omnia operantur bonum; quod enim movetur (ut supra diximus) non ad quodlibet[4] aeque, sed ad proprium aliquid fertur sibique conveniens; neque enim ad illud, nisi propter aliquam cum eo convenientiam moveretur. Quod autem[5] proprium cuique est atque conveniens id cuique bonum.

Item finis est in quo appetitio eius quod movet eiusque quod movetur quiescit. Ratio autem boni est ut appetitum# impleat. Nam bonum est quod omnia appetunt. Omnis itaque motus ad bonum ducit.

Quin etiam omnis actio atque motus ad ipsum esse quodammodo ferri videntur, vel ut esse singulorum vel speciei

[1]bonum *om. Y*   [2]vel operationem *om. X*   [3]*no ch. heading or break W*   [4]quolibet *W*
[5]autem *om. WX*   *-**om. W*   #*P frag. I (17r) begins*

of individual things or of the species, or in order to reacquire it. But this, which is being itself, is the good.

In addition, every action and movement turn towards some perfection. For, if the action itself is the end, obviously it is a second perfection of the agent. But if the action is the transmutation of external matter, obviously the mover is trying to introduce some perfection into what is being moved. But we say to be perfect is to be good.

Again, every agent acts according as it is itself in act. But in acting it aims at something like itself. So it aims at some act. But every act contains the rational principle of the good; for the bad isn't found anywhere except in that potentiality where act is missing.

Again, what avoids one opposite, necessarily follows the other. But everything always avoids the bad as far as it can. So everything follows the good. Next, just as we move away from a lower place with the same motion as we seek out a higher, so it is the same thing too that makes us avoid the bad and follow the good. But everything avoids the bad. For things that can think move away from something because they think it is harmful or bad, and things that can't think and are just naturally impelled move away from unpleasant places and seek out pleasant ones, avoiding things which are opposite to them and looking for things like them. So it is with the same impulse that everything abhors the bad and seeks the good.

Chapter 4. What the good is; or that above the body is the soul, above the soul the intellect, above this the one itself and the good.

Having said the end towards which everything is moved is the good, obviously we ought now to show what the good is. The entire structure of the world consists of multiplicity and unity, because it consists of many things which have been bound together by continuity, contiguity, similarity, equality, suitability. If there were no union in the world's many parts, they wouldn't

*servetur, vel denuo acquiratur. Hoc autem ipsum quod est esse
bonum est.*

*Adde quod omnis actio motusque ad aliquam vergit perfec-
tionem. Si enim ipsa actio sit finis, patet quod secunda agentis
ipsius perfectio est. Sin autem actio exterioris materiae transmutatio est, patet quod perfectionem aliquam in eo quod movetur ipsum quod movet inducere nititur; hoc autem dicimus esse
bonum quod est esse perfectum.*

*Item omne agens ut¹ actu est agit. Agendo autem in aliquid²
sibi simile tendit; [330v] igitur aliquem in actum tendit. Actus
autem omnis boni rationem habet. Nam malum nusquam reperitur, nisi in ea cui deest actus potentia.*

*Item quod contrarium unum fugit³ necessario sequitur
alterum. Omnia vero semper quoad possunt malum fugiunt.
Omnia itaque bonum sequuntur. Porro sicut idem motus est
quo locum inferiorem fugimus et quo superiorem petimus, ita et
idem quo a malo declinamus, bonum sequimur.⁴ Malum vero
fugiunt omnia. Nam quae cognitione moventur, quia pernicio-
sum malumque aliquid putant, ideo fugiunt; quaeve natura sine
cognitione feruntur loca sibi noxia fugiunt, convenientia petunt,
contraria vitant, similia quaerunt. Eodem itaque nixu et malum
horrent omnia et bonum expetunt.*

**Quid bonum, quodve supra corpus anima, super animam
intellectus, super hunc est ipsum unum atque bonum.
Cap. IV.⁵**

Postquam finem ad quem moventur omnia bonum esse
diximus, quid ipsum bonum sit declarandum iam esse videtur.
Universa mundi machina ex multitudine constat et unitate, quia
ex multis rebus quae unitae⁶ sunt continuitate, contiguitate,
similitudine, aequalitate, convenientia. Si nulla esset unio in

---

¹aut *W*   ²aliquid *om. WXP*   ³facit *W*   ⁴sequitur *W*   ⁵*ch. heading in W reads*
Quid bonum, c. III; *in X and P it reads* Quid sit bonum, c. IV   ⁶multae *XP*

remain together, but be scattered in all directions; nor would there be any conformity in shape or quality or in anything else. So there is unity in the plurality of things. Because the unity is in another, it is also from another. It doesn't come from a compound thing, because it is the function of the simple and the one to give unity. Nor again is that unity in its turn in another, otherwise we shall go on to infinity.

Again, all the multiplicity of things which we see participates in some unity. For, if it didn't, this, the universal genus of things, wouldn't be one, nor any part of it one. It would be made from various things and these in turn from other things and so on to infinity; and any of the things would be an utterly infinite multiplicity, for, since each would not participate in the one itself in any way (neither the whole of each nor any part of each), each would be utterly and entirely infinite. Next, any individual thing you take will either be one or not one. If it isn't one, it will either be many or nothing. But if individual things are nothing, the totality is also nothing. But if it's many, anything will consist infinitely of infinities. However, these are impossibilities; for nothing consists infinitely of infinities for nothing is bigger than the infinite. But what is made from all things is bigger than individual things. Nor is something made from nothing. Consequently, the entire plurality of things participates in unity.

Therefore the one exists above all multiplicity. For, if the many came before the one, the one would participate in multiplicity and wouldn't be one; on the other hand the many above the one wouldn't participate in the one at all, since the many would be existing prior to the one itself. However, it is impossible for any multiplicity to be without the one. So there isn't a many before the one. But if the many coexists with the one and is naturally arranged with it, the one will not be the many because of what it is; nor will the many be the one because of what it is, (since they are mutually different and contrary as neither is prior or posterior to the other). Accordingly, the many won't participate in the one in any way; which is impossible, for it would be infinitely infinite. So the many must be one and

multis mundi partibus, neque simul starent, sed spargerentur;[1] neque in figura vel qualitate vel in aliqua cum aliquibus congruerent. Ideo est in rerum numero unitas, quae quia in alio est, est[2] et ab alio. Non a composito quodam, quia unitatem dare unius est simplicisque officium; neque in alio est iterum, hoc est ne in infinitum eatur.

Item omnis haec quam cernimus multitudo [*331r*] rerum unitatis alicuius est particeps. Nam si nullius, neque universum hoc rerum genus unum esset, neque aliqua eius pars unum, sed ipsum ex aliquibus erit, illaque rursus ex aliis in infinitum, horumque quodlibet multitudo erit penitus infinita. Nam cum nullo modo ipsius unius sit particeps, neque totum ipsum neque pars aliqua, omnino et secundum omne infinitum erit. Porro quicquid singulorum acceperis vel unum erit vel non unum. Si non unum, vel multa vel nihil. Verum si singula nihil, totum quoque nihil. Sin multa, quodlibet ex infinitis infinite constabit. Haec autem impossibilia sunt, neque enim ex infinite infinitis quicquam constat. Nam nihil infinito maius. Quod vero ex omnibus constituitur singulis maius est. Neque ex nihilo quicquam conficitur. Quo concluditur omnem hunc rerum numerum unitatis esse participem.

Igitur super omnem multitudinem unum existit. Nam si multitudo ante unum esset, unum quidem multitudine participaret, neque esset unum. Multitudo vero quae supra unum est nullo modo esset unius particeps, siquidem, antequam unum ipsum sit, multitudo haec existeret. Impossibile autem est multitudinem esse aliquam unius expertem. Non est igitur multitudo ante unum. Sin autem simul cum uno sit cumque illo secundum naturam coordinata, neque unum secundum se ipsum multa erit, neque multitudo secundum se unum, quippe cum contra se invicem discreta sint, siquidem neutrum altero prius est aut posterius. Quare multitudo nullo modo unius erit particeps, quod impossibile est, esset enim infinite infinita. Quare necesse est ut [*331v*] multitudo unum sit et quicquid in ea est sit unum. Sin

---

[1]dispergerentur *WXP*   [2]est *om. XP*

whatever is in the many must be one. But if the one doesn't naturally participate in the many, at least the many will be subsequent to the one, participating in the one, but in no way participated in by the one. But if the one participates in the many, it will be one from the point of view of its own substance, but not be one from the point of view of its participation; it will be a united many. In which case the one will communicate with the many and the many with the one. But if things which agree and communicate with each other are joined together by another, they exist subsequent to that other. If, however, they join themselves, they aren't mutually opposed; for things which are mutually opposed do not seek each other. However, if there is something prior to them, which can join them together, it is either the one, or not the one. If it is not the one, it is either the many or nothing. Yet it is not the many, otherwise the many will be prior to the one. And it isn't nothing; for how would it join other things together? So it is the one alone; for the one cannot be at the same time the many as well, otherwise we would go on to infinity. So there is something which is one because of itself and outside the multiplicity of all things; from it all multiplicity proceeds. In fact, this is the principle of all things.

Nobody should maintain, as the Manicheans and Gnostics maintain, that there are two principles both of which are one, for from two ones is the number two.[9] Unity comes before all number. Again, either the entire power which is in the one is in the other too; or more of it is in the one than in the other. If the entire power is in them both, they are identical and one of them is enough. If more is in one of them, that one is the principle, the other is subordinate to it. Again, either the total perfection is in each principle, or a part of it is in each. If the total, one is enough; if a part, each is imperfect. So above them both will be what is perfect. Again, either they agree entirely or not at all or partially. If entirely, they are one thing. If not at all, they won't agree in the fact that each is a principle. If they agree and differ, there is one nature in common in each of them beyond their individual differences. So each one is a compound and the unity which is in each one, being in another, is from another,

autem ipsum secundum se unum multitudine non participat, erit utique multitudo uno posterior, participans quidem uno, nullo modo ab uno participata. Quod si unum est multitudinis particeps secundum substantiam suam unum erit, secundum participationem vero non unum, eritque multitudo quaedam unita. Quare et unum cum multitudine et multitudo cum uno communicabit. Quae vero congrediuntur communicantque vicissim, si ab alio copulantur, post illud existunt. Sin autem ipsa se iungunt, nequaquam sibi invicem *opponuntur. Nam quae opposita inter se sunt haud se invicem** expetunt. At vero siquid est ante ipsa quod ea invicem copulet aut unum est[1] aut non unum. Si non unum, vel multa est vel nihil. Non tamen multa est, ne ante unum multitudo sit; nec etiam nihil. Nam quo pacto alia iungeret[2]? Unum itaque solum. Neque enim et hoc unum simul erit et multa, ne in infinitum progrediamur. Est itaque aliquid per se unum extra rerum multitudinem omnium, a quo omnis multitudo procedit. Quod quidem principium omnium est.

Neque dixerit quispiam quod Manichaei et Gnostici dicunt duo esse principia, quorum quodlibet unum est. Nam[3] ex duobus unis est duitas numerus. Ante omnem numerum est unitas. Item vel tota vis quae in uno est, est et in alio, vel maior in uno quam in[4] alio. Si tota, idem sunt et unum sufficit. Si maior, in quo maior illud principium est, aliud vero sub eo. Item vel tota perfectio in utroque vel pars in utroque. Si tota, unum sufficit. Si pars, utrumque imperfectum. Supra utrumque igitur erit[5] quod perfectum. Item vel omnino conveniunt [*332r*] vel nullo modo vel partim. Si omnino, unum sunt. Si nullo modo, neque convenient in hoc,[6] quod utrumque principium sit. Si conveniunt et differunt,[7] una communis natura est in utroque praeter proprias utriusque differentias. Compositum igitur est[8] utrumque et unitas quae est[9] in utrisque, quia in alio est, est ab

[1] est *om.* W   [2] iungit Y   [3] Nam *om.* W   [4] in *om.* Y   [5] erit *repeated* W
[6] haec Y   [7] dicunt W   [8] est *om.* W   [9] est *om.* P   *-**om.* W

[namely] the one which is above them both. Or rather, as they agree in having the common reason of a principle, one reason is what makes each one a principle. But because of their individual differences neither is the universal principle, since through the difference each differs from the other principle. So in so far as they are a principle they are one; therefore they ought to be reduced to one principle. We call it one with respect to itself and to others: with respect to itself, because it is completely simple; for were it to have plurality of parts, its power would be diffused through the many. (But the most unitary power is the most perfect.) So it wouldn't be stronger than every other power. Rather it would be deficient, for it would need parts to depend on. So it wouldn't be totally sufficient, nor totally happy, for it wouldn't be enjoying itself completely as it wouldn't be wholly converted to the whole. The one is called one with respect to others, because it doesn't share the reason for its being a principle with anyone.

Besides, just as individual orders of things are related to their own principles, so the universal order is related to the universal principle. But all individual orders are led back to some one species. So the whole order of nature is led back to the one principle.

One soul suffices for a body, one master for a household, one king for one state—won't one God suffice for one world? From the fire's one heat comes all heat, from the sun's one light all light, from the one good all good things. All bodies fall under the world's one body, all natures under one nature, all souls under one soul, all intelligences under one intelligence. But the good and the one is every single one of these. So all good things and all things that are one fall under the one good, just as all numbers can be reduced to unity. So the one is the principle of all. For each order, because it is unified in itself in so far as the single members are of the same order, comes from the one above the order. For the unity of an order doesn't proceed from some one member of the order; for it would be peculiar to that member, and wouldn't be appropriate to all the members. So it comes from the one above the order, which is the first of its

alio, uno quod super utrumque. Immo vero cum in communi ratione principii conveniant,[1] una ratio est qua utrumque est principium. Secundum vero proprias differentias neutrum omnium est principium cum per illam ab alio principio differat. Qua[2] ergo principium sunt unum sunt, ad unum ergo principium reducendum. Quod unum vocamus respectu sui et aliorum; sui quia simplicissimum, si enim habet numerum partium, vim habet diffusam per multa. Vis autem unitissima perfectissima. Non ergo esset omni[3] alia vi potentius, immo esset indigum. Nam partibus egeret quibus dependeat.[4] Non ergo sufficientissimum, neque esset beatissimum;[5] non enim[6] se omnino frueretur, quia non totum in totum conversum. Respectu alterius[7] dicitur unum, quia in ratione principii non habet comitem.

Praeterea sicut se habent singuli rerum ordines ad propria sui principia, sic universus ordo ad universale principium. Sed omnes illi ad unam quandam speciem reducuntur. Quare et omnis ordo naturae ad principium unum.

Uni corpori una sufficit anima, uni domui unus dominus, civitati uni rex unus, uni vero mundo Deus non sufficiet unus? Ab uno ignis calore omnes calores, ab una solis[8] luce omnia lumina, ab uno bono omnia bona. Omnia corpora ad unum mundi corpus; omnes naturae ad naturam unam; [*332v*] omnes animae ad unam animam; omnes mentes ad unam mentem. Bonum vero et unum unumquodque istorum est, ergo omnia bona et una ad unum bonum, sicut numeri omnes ad unitatem. Unum ergo omnium est principium. Omnis enim ordo quia in se habet unionem in quantum singula eiusdem sunt ordinis ab uno est supra ordinem. Nam unio ordinis non ab uno quodam ordinis est,[9] esset enim[10] illius proprium neque omnibus conveniret. Ergo ab uno supra ordinem quod est primo tale, ideo

kind, therefore nothing but its kind. So the principle of good things is the good alone; because, if some good entity or good soul were the good, it wouldn't be the absolute good or the integral good, but good only according to the capacity of its companion. So it wouldn't be the first; for the first of a kind is absolute and integral. Therefore the first good, the first one, is nothing else but good and one.

In fact, the principle is that above which there is nothing. But the one itself has nothing above it; for it would be participating in something higher and wouldn't be one but many. So the principle of all things is the same as the one in itself.

This isn't the body, as the Democritians maintain, for a body has many parts. Nor is it the corporeal quality, as Strato maintains, which is coextensive with the body's parts.[10] Nor is it the soul, as Varro maintains,[11] since the soul participates through its powers and operations in multiplicity. For through one power it understands, through another it acts; for it does many things unconsciously and understands many things without doing anything. Nor is it the intelligence, as Anaxagoras maintains,[12] for the intelligence acts in order to understand itself. So in the intelligence there is what understands, understanding, and the thing understood. Nor is it life, as Zeno maintains,[13] for life is the movement of essence. So in life there are at least two things—to be and to be moved. Nor is it essence itself, as David of Dinant says,[14] for all things participate in the one, but not all in essence. For fluxes and privations don't have essence, but nobody denies they are one. Nor is it being itself, as Alfarabi and Avicebron maintain,[15] for being is the act of essence and the participation of essence in the present moment, as Plato says in the *Parmenides*.[16] But if the one and being were the same, perhaps multiplicity and nothing would be the same. So you wouldn't find any multiplicity in things. Again, being is just as appropriate to an army as to a house, but it has less of the one in it. So being is one thing, the one another.

So either these are equal, or being is above the one, or the one is above being. If they are equal, being is without the one, so the class of things existing under being will also be without the one.

nihil aliud est quam tale, ut bonorum principium sit[1] solum bonum; quia si bonum ens vel bona anima esset bonum, hoc[2] non absolutum bonum, et esset bonum non integrum sed pro socii captu; ergo non primum.[3] Primum enim absolutum est et integrum; primum ergo bonum, primum unum, nihil aliud est quam bonum et[4] quam unum.

Principium sane id est supra quod est nihil. Ipsum vero unum supra se nihil habet. Nam superiori participaret, essetque plura non unum. Idem ergo est principium omnium et ipsum per se unum.

Quod quidem corpus non est, ut Democritii dicunt, multas enim corpus habet partes. Neque corporis qualitas, ut Straton, quae cum corporis partibus est extensa. Neque anima, ut Varro, quippe cum et in viribus et in operationibus anima sit multitudinis particeps, alia enim potentia cognoscit alia facit, facit enim multa non cognoscendo et[5] cognoscit multa non agendo. Neque mens, ut Anaxagoras, mentis enim actio est ut se ipsam intelligat; est igitur in mente quod intelligit intellectioque et quod intelligitur. Neque vita, ut Zenon, est enim vita motus essentiae, in ea igitur [*333r*] duo sunt saltem et esse scilicet et moveri. Neque essentia ipsa, ut Dinantes, nam uno quidem participant omnia, essentia vero non omnia; fluxus enim privationesque essentiam nullam habent, unum tamen esse non negantur. Neque ipsum esse, ut Alpharabius et Avicebron, est enim actus essentiae et essentiae cum praesenti momento participatio, ut in Parmenide dicit Plato. Quin Immo si idem esset unum atque esse, Idem forsan[6] esset multitudo atque nihil, itaque[7] nulla forsan[8] multitudo in rebus inveniretur. Item non minus esse competit exercitui quam domui, minus tamen illi unum convenit. Aliud itaque esse, aliud unum.

Aut ergo paria haec sunt, aut esse super unum, aut unum super esse. Si paria sunt, esse unius est expers, ergo et rerum

---

[1]sit *om. WXP*   [2]huius *XP*   [3]principium *Y*   [4]et *om. W*   [5]et *om. Y*
[6]forsan *om. WXP*   [7]Atque ita *WXP*   [8]forsan *om. WXP*

But if being is above the one, the one will participate in being itself and won't be one but many. But being will be without the one, so it will either be nothing or an infinite plurality. But unity exists above all plurality. There is nothing above unity, for it wouldn't be unity. So the first principle of all things is the same as the one itself. What exists above the body, soul, intelligence, life, and essence is nothing other than the one, which Plato's *Parmenides* indeed tells us.[17]

Moreover, you can learn from the *Laws* Book 10 that above all bodies is the essence of the soul itself, above all souls is the intelligence, above all intelligences is the one itself.[18] For each body is moved by something else: it can't naturally move itself. But because of the soul's participation it is virtually moved by itself, and it lives through the soul. When the soul is present, in a way the body moves itself; but when the soul is absent, it is only moved by another (since it doesn't have this nature in itself and the soul possesses the substance which moves itself). For to whatever body the soul is present it imparts the power to move itself. But what imparts [this power] to others by its mere presence, exists prior to them and more totally than they. So the soul is above bodies, that is, the soul which can move itself because of its essence is above those things which become self-moving because of participation.

Again, the soul, seeing it is self-moving, belongs to the class which is second to the nature whose essence and operation are motionless. Indeed, what moves itself comes before everything which is moved by another, but what is motionless before all moving things. So, if the soul, being moved by itself, moves others, there must be something before the soul which moves others and is motionless. But the intelligence moves and is motionless; it is steadfast and always operates in the same ways. In fact, through the intelligence the soul always possesses the ability to understand, just as through the soul the body can move itself. For if the understanding were always first present in the soul, it would be appropriate to all souls, like self-moving. So the understanding is not first present in the soul. So that which is primarily understanding must be above the soul. This is

ordo sub eo existentium expers erit unius. Sin esse[1] super unum, unum quidem ipso esse participabit eritque non unum sed plura, esse autem unius expers erit, quare aut nihil erit aut numerus infinitus. Supra vero omnem numerum unitas extat, supra unitatem nihil, non enim unitas esset. Idem igitur primum rerum principium est et ipsum unum. Quod supra corpus, animam, mentem, vitam, essentiamque existit neque aliud quicquam est quam unum, quod quidem ex Parmenide Platonis libro colligi potest.

Praeterea sic ex decimo Legum colligi potest: supra[2] corpora omnia est animae ipsius essentia; supra[3] omnes animas mens; supra mentes omnes ipsum unum. Omne enim corpus ab alio quodam movetur. Movere autem se ipsum natura sua non potest, sed propter animae[4] participationem ferme[5] se ipso movetur vivitque per animam. Et praesente quidem anima se ipsum movet quodammodo, [*333v*] absente vero ab alio dumtaxat movetur, utpote quod hanc ex se ipso naturam non[6] habeat et anima substantiam sese moventem possideat. Nam cuicumque adest vim ad se ipsum movendum impertit; quod autem ipso esse impertit aliis, hoc ipsa multo prius magisque existit. Est igitur supra corpora, tamquam quae se ipsam movere potest secundum essentiam supra illa quae secundum participationem talia fiunt.[7]

Rursus anima quoniam a[8] se ipsa movetur secundum obtinet ordinem ad eam naturam cuius et essentia et operatio est immobilis. Nempe omnibus agitatis praecedit quod se ipsum movet, omnibus autem moventibus quod immobile. Si igitur anima a se ipsa mota, movet alia, oportet ante ipsam esse quod immobile movet. Mens autem movet immobilis perseverans et semper secundum eadem operans. Etenim anima per mentem habet quod semper intelligat, sicuti corpus propter animam quod sese moveat. Si enim inesset animae semper intelligere primum, omnibus competeret animis, quemadmodum sese movere. Non igitur animae hoc primum inest. Oportet itaque ante ipsam esse

---

[1]esset *W*   [2]super *W*   [3]super *WXP*   [4]animi *P*   [5]ferme *om. WXP*
[6]non *om. WXP*   [7]*cf.* De amore *VI, xv*   [8]a *om. WXP*

all confirmed from the beginning as follows. Since the body is
made from matter and has quantity only because of matter and
is divided only because of quantity, it follows it can be passive
not active. So since bodies are seen to act, they act because of
another. Is it perhaps because of quality which in itself is incorporeal (since many qualities can exist in the same body)? But
quality is not through itself the principle of action. For what
doesn't exist through itself, doesn't act through itself. Therefore one must turn towards an incorporeal something which can
subsist through itself and can't be divided with the body. The
soul will be like this. Because it is turned back towards itself, it
subsists through itself. The power to act and so to move will be
present in bodies from the soul. So every act and movement of
bodily objects is from the soul, which is an incorporeal essence
joined to but not mixed with the body, connected to but not
dispersed through it. Above the soul is the intelligence. It is
both an incorporeal essence and is entirely cut off from the
body, so it has nothing in common with the body. The intelligence stays the same in essence and operation; the body changes
in both; the soul stays the same in essence but changes in operation. The intelligence is completely in eternity; the body is in
time; the soul is in both. The intelligence moves, is not moved;
matter is moved, does not move; the body moves, moved by
another; the soul moves, moved by itself. So the intelligence
and matter are extremes, but the body and soul intermediaries.
The body inclines more to matter, the soul more to the intelligence. When we say the soul by itself is moved, we mean the
verb intransitively not transitively (as when we say the intelligence remains still, the sun shines, the fire is hot).[19] For one part
of the soul doesn't move while another part is moved, but the
whole soul is moved by itself: that is, it runs to and fro and
brings to completion by means of time's intervals the works of
nutrition, growth and reproduction, the products of reasoning
and cogitation. The intelligence acts, but in eternity; the soul
acts, but in time. What is the soul's movement? Action in time.
And as the first action in time is in the soul, consequently the
first movement is in the soul, and in the soul's rational principle

quod primo est intelligens. *Id totum[1] sic ab[2] initio confirmatur. Cum corpus ex materia constet et quantitatem[3,4] ratione materiae solum capiat, et[5] ratione quantitatis solum dividatur, sequitur ut per haec pati possit non agere. Siquidem[6] ergo agere videntur corpora, per aliud agunt, forte per qualitatem quae ex se[7] est incorporea, cum plurimae sint eodem in corpore qualitates. Sed neque qualitas est per se principium actionis; quod enim non est per se, per se non agit. Eundum igitur est ad incorporale aliquid quod per se subsistat neque cum corpore sit divisum, talisque erit anima, quae quia ad se convertitur per se subsistit. Ab ea inerit vis agendi corporibus, ergo et vis movendi. Omnis ergo actus et motus corporum est ab anima, quae essentia incorporalis est, unita corpori non commixta, coniuncta non dispersa. Supra quam est et mens, et essentia incorporalis et a corpore penitus separata. Ideo nihil habet commune cum corpore. Illa stat essentia et operatione; corpus utroque fluit; anima essentia stat, operatione fluit. Illa omnino in[8] aeternitate; corpus in tempore; anima in utroque. Illa movet non movetur; materia movetur non movet; corpus movet ab alio motum; anima movet a se mota. Ergo et mens et materia sunt extrema; media vero corpus et anima. Hoc ad materiam declinat magis; anima magis ad mentem. Cum dicimus animam se ipsa moveri, absolute non transitive verbum illud proferimus, ut cum stare mentem, lucere solem, calere ignem. Non enim pars animae movet pars movetur, sed tota ex se ipsa movetur, id est, discurrit, transigit per temporum intervalla nutritionis augmenti generationis opera, rationis et[9] cogitationis discursiones. **Agit mens sed cum aeternitate; agit anima sed cum tempore. Quid motus animae? Actio cum tempore, et quia prima actio cum tempore est in anima, ideo primus motus in anima et est in ea ratione sui in quantum iam a statu mentis degenerat.***

---

[1]iterum *XP* [2]alio *add. XP* [3]quantitate *XP* [4]et *add. XP* [5]et *om. XP*
[6]siquid *XP* [7]sese *P* [8]in *om. Y* [9]et *om. Y* *-***om. W (cont.)*
-*om. XP (cont.)*

to the extent it has already degenerated from the unchanging condition of the intelligence. Therefore movement is naturally present to the soul. So the soul exists as the principle of movement. Therefore the intelligence precedes the soul.

But the one itself exists above the intelligence, for, although the intelligence doesn't move, still it isn't the one; for the intelligence understands itself and operates with regard to itself. Now all participate in the one, whatever their condition, but not all participate in the intelligence; for the intelligence's participation is proper to whatever has to participate in knowing, since the intelligence itself is the principle and the prime cause of knowing. Again, the power of the one reaches as far as privations and matter, for they are one, but not the power of the intelligence, because the intelligence is the species and acts with the species (so it only acts upon the species). So the one itself is above the intelligence. And there isn't anything beyond the one which is higher than it; for the one and the good itself are the same, but the good itself is the principle of all.

Chapter 5. The one and the good are the same thing; and it is the principle of all.

Now I will show the one and the good are the same, and the good is the principle of all. All things seek the good, because it preserves single things in their state. But what preserves is what unites the parts of things to each other and to the whole, and the whole to the cause. But to unite is peculiar to the one itself, just as to heat is peculiar to heat itself. So the one and the good are the same. Now all things are preserved by unity, but perish from disunity. The good is present to everything; it preserves things because it unites them and makes them one and contains them in the one. But to make one is the office of the one itself. So, if for each thing being united is well-being, union is goodness for each thing; and the simply one and the simply good are the same thing, and this gives unity and goodness to everything at the same time. So whatever departs from the good falls away from

*Ideo ex sua natura inest ei motus; ergo ipsa principium motus existit.** Quare animae mens praecedit.

Sed enim supra mentem unum ipsum existit, licet enim mens immobilis sit, non tamen unum est. Intelligit enim se ipsam et circa se ipsam operatur. Quin et uno cuncta participant, quomodocumque sint, mente vero non omnia. Quibus enim participatio mentis convenit ea cognitione participent necesse est, quia[1] intelligentia ipsa principium est[2] et causa prima noscendi. Item vis unius usque ad privationes et materiam currit, unum enim haec sunt, [*334r*] mentis[3] vero[4] non, quia mens est species[5] et speciebus agit, species igitur[6] tantum agit. Igitur supra mentem ipsum unum est. Nec ultra aliquid est uno superius. Idem enim unum et ipsum bonum, ipsum vero bonum principium omnium.

Unum idem est atque bonum, atque omnium est principium. Cap. V.[7]

Quod vero unum et bonum idem sit[8] bonumque omnium sit principium iam ostendam. Bonum quidem omnia expetunt, quia singula suo in statu servat. Servat autem quod partes rerum unit invicem et ad totum et totum ad causam. Unire vero ipsius unius est proprium, sicut caloris ipsius est calefacere. Unum ergo et bonum idem. Unitate porro servantur omnia, dissolutione autem[9] intereunt. Bonum quibuscumque adest; ea servat, ex eo quod unit unumque ea reddit et in uno continet. Unum vero efficere est ipsius unius officium. Quare si cuique unitum esse bene esse est, cuique unio bonitas est et simpliciter bonum simpliciterque unum idem est, quod quidem unitatem omnibus simul praestat et bonitatem. Ideo quaecumque a bono

---

[1]quare *XP*   [2]est *om. P*   [3]mens *XP*   [4]vero *om. WXP*   [5]*WXP read* quia species
est mens   [6]ergo *WXP*   [7]*no ch. break or heading WX; a chapter sign P*   [8]sit *om.*
WXP   [9]autem *om. XP*   *(cont.)* *-**om. WXP*

the one too; and the things which depart from the one because of discord, depart from the good also. So unity is goodness and goodness is unity; and the good is the one, and the one in the first place is the good.

This is also obvious because something is perfect and desirable because it comes from the good. But the one itself bestows this. For in ascending from bodies to the intelligence you can see that the greater the increase in unity the greater the increase in perfection. Therefore the good and the one are the same.

But being itself is not enough for things, otherwise they wouldn't need anything over and beyond the fact that they are. So they try to find being-with-the-good and well-being. But they are well if they preserve or recover their complete nature. This comes from the mutual union of parts and of parts to the whole and of the whole to the cause. So all try to find the one above being. The more something is one, the more sufficient and perfect it is, since it is less in want and more powerful because its power is united. So the one is the good itself, since it gives sufficiency and perfection.

Again, the best evidence for good being present is pleasure. But all pleasure results from the unity of each thing with itself, pain from disunity. So union is good, disunion is bad.

The one is not the same in things as being. For being derives from the one that it is integral, sufficient, capable, perfect, pleasing, desirable, and therefore good. So the one and the good are the same.

Now the good itself is the first cause of all things; for, since all things come from one principle, the principle is either the good itself, or something better than the good. If it is better than the good, something passes into the universe from it, or nothing does. It's absurd if nothing does, for it wouldn't be the principle of things, unless something were given by it to things. However, if something is given to things by the principle (just as something is given to things by the good, namely, of course, goodness), it will be something given to things by the first cause better than goodness. For if it is above the good and better than it, surely it gives better gifts to things than the good itself. But

discedunt ab uno quoque decidunt. Et quae ab uno abeunt propter discordiam abeunt et a bono. Est igitur unitas bonitas, et bonitas unitas, et bonum unum, unumque primo bonum.

Quod ex eo insuper patet, quia ex bono est, quod perfectum sit aliquid atque expetendum. Hoc autem unum ipsum praestat. Nam a corporibus ad mentem ascendendo patet quo crescit unio magis eo perfectionem[1] magis excrescere. Bonum igitur et unum idem.

Esse quidem ipsum rebus non sufficit, alioquin[2] eo ipso quod sunt nihil ultra requirerent. Quaerunt ergo esse cum bono et bene esse. [*334v*] Bene autem sunt si vel integram naturam suam servant vel restituunt. Hoc fit unione partium inter se et ad totum et ad causam. Unum igitur super esse expetunt omnia. Quo magis unum est aliquid eo sufficiens magis perfectumque, cum minus indigum[3] sit, sitque potentius ex unita virtute. Unum ergo bonum ipsum est, cum sufficientiam et perfectionem praestet.

Item signa praesentis boni maxime voluptas est. Ex unione vero cuiusque secum ipso omnis resultat voluptas, ex dissolutione dolor. Unum itaque bonum, dissolutio malum.

Neque unum idem est in rebus quod esse. Ex uno enim esse habet quod integrum sit, quod sufficiens quod potens quod perfectum quod gratum quod expetendum, ergo quod bonum. Unum igitur et bonum idem.

Atqui et ipsum bonum prima est rerum omnium causa. Nam cum omnia ab uno principio sint, principium illud vel ipsum bonum est vel ipso bono melius. Si bono melius, aut aliquid ex ipso in naturam rerum procedit aut nihil. Si nihil, absurdum id quidem; non enim esset rerum principium, nisi aliquid ab ipso rebus tribueretur. Sin autem aliquid a principio isto rebus datur,[4] quemadmodum et a bono rebus ipsis datum est aliquid, quod quidem bonitas est,[5] erit aliquid in rebus melius bonitate a causa prima tributum. Nam si super bonum sit ipsoque[6] melius,

[1]perfectiorem *W*   [2]nam *WXP*   [3]indignum *WX*   [4]daretur *X*   [5]est *om. W*
[6]bono *add. X*

what is better than goodness—as something is said to be better because it has a bigger share of goodness? Moreover, since all things want the good only, if there is something above the good, will they want it or not? If they don't want it, it's absurd not to desire the first cause by which all are preserved and created and converted. If they do want it, they won't be wanting the good most nor seeking everything for the sake of the good. However, since it is the good towards which all things are turned by desire, the good will be that by which all are created. Because it produces all, it is the principle; because it draws the appetites of all to itself, it is the end; because it preserves all, it is the intermediary. So the one and the good itself is the principle, middle and end of all things.

It is called the one, because it surpasses all; it is called the good, because it is extended through all. So, as the one it is investigated by Plato in the *Parmenides* through negatives; as the good in the *Republic* Book 6 through analogies.[20] Although it extends itself through all things as the good, still it precedes being itself and all things. Plato says this in the *Republic* and Dionysius the Areopagite agrees in his book *On the Divine Names*.[21] The power of the good itself spreads further than the power of being; for formless matter and privation and flux aren't said "to be," for being comes through form and they are devoid of form. Yet they are in a way said "to be good," in so far as they tend towards act and towards the good because of some power instilled in them by the good. Therefore, when you say "the good itself," you must mean the good alone, not a good body, or good soul, or intelligence, life, essence, or good being. For you stain the good's purity by mixing it; you reduce its integrity by a subject; you refuse it fullness by adding to it. So do away with this good or that good, as Augustine tells you in the *On the Trinity,* and accept the good which is the good of all good, and you will know what God is.[22] As Dionysius says in the *On Mystical Theology,* we can't reach Him by affirmation.[23] For whatever we affirm about Him has been conceived in the intelligence, therefore it is something peculiar to us and limited. Therefore God is exalted above every concept. So what

meliora certe rebus munera elargitur quam ipsum bonum. At vero quid bonitate melius, quippe cum melius aliquid ex eo dicatur quod bonitatis magis est particeps. Quin etiam cum omnia bonum dumtaxat cupiant, si supra bonum est aliquid, utrum et illud appetant necne. [*335r*] Si non appetunt[1], absurdum est causam primam a qua quaeque servantur fiunt et convertuntur non appetere. Si appetunt, non bonum maxime appetent neque sub ratione boni cuncta perquirent. Cum vero bonum sit ad quod omnia appetendo convertuntur, bonum erit a quo omnia procreantur. Quia producit omnia, principium est; quia appetitus omnium ad se rapit, finis; quia conservat omnia, medium. Ipsum igitur unum ipsumque bonum principium est mediumque et finis omnium.

Quod quidem unum dicitur ut supereminet omnia; bonum ut se per omnia porrigit. Ut ergo unum est, per negationes a Platone in Parmenide investigatur; ut bonum est, per comparationes ab eodem in libro de Republica sexto. Etsi ut bonum est se per omnia porrigit, ipsum tamen esse omniaque praecedit, ut et Plato ibi testatur et Dionysius Areopagita in libro de Divinis Nominibus assentitur. Nam boni ipsius vis ulterius se diffundit[2] quam ipsius esse potentia. Informis enim materia privatioque et fluxus esse non dicuntur[3], esse enim est per formam, ista forma carent. Bona tamen quoquomodo dicuntur quantum[4] ad actum bonumque propter aliquam vim ipsis a bono insitam tendunt. Cum ergo ipsum bonum dicis, solum bonum intelligas, non bonum corpus vel bonum animum aut mentem vitam essentiam vel[5] bonum esse. Inquinas enim boni puritatem commixtione; minuis integritatem subiecto; excludis plenitudinem additamento. Tolle igitur bonum hoc et tolle bonum illud ut Augustinus de Trinitate iubet, et accipe illud bonum quod est omnis boni bonum, et scies quid est Deus, ad quem, ut Dionysius de Mystica [*335v*] Theologia dicit, affirmando ire nequimus. Quicquid enim de eo affirmamus mente conceptum est. Ergo proprium nobis aliquod[6] et terminatum. Ergo super omnem

---

God is not we can find out by negation; and how He acts and how others exist with regard to Him we can find out by analogy. But what God is is a secret.

Now it can be shown from the foregoing how Plato ascends by negation to the good itself, but how he does it by analogy will emerge from the following. Whatever is beautiful in the natural order is also good. Whatever is good is in a way beautiful; for to attract the appetite is just as appropriate to the beautiful as it is to the good. Beauty is nothing but the splendour of the highest good, which blazes out principally in the things perceived by the eyes, the ears, the intelligence. The splendour converts the sight, the hearing and the intelligence through these things towards the good itself. Consequently, beauty exists as a circle of divine light, emanating from the good, remaining in the good, eternally turned back through the good and towards the good. Plato revealed this mystery, which he received from the Sibyl, Diotima, to few people. What is the good itself? It is the one itself, the principle of all things, pure act, the act giving life to all succeeding things. What is beauty itself? It is act giving life, issuing from the first fountain of good things. First of all it adorns the divine intelligence with the order of Ideas; then it fills the subsequent spirits and intelligences with the series of the reasons; thirdly it adorns souls with numerous arguments; fourthly it adorns natures with seeds; fifthly it adorns matter with forms. As Plato says in the *Republic,* certainly the sun produces both visible bodies and eyes that see.[24] It pours lucid spirit into the eyes so that they may see. It paints bodies with colours so that they may be seen. Still, a light-ray belonging to the eyes, or colours belonging to bodies, are not enough to perfect vision, unless the one light itself above the many (from which the many and appropriate lights are distributed to eyes and bodies) comes down, illuminates, stimulates and strengthens. In the same way the first act itself, in the process of creating, has bestowed a species and an act on single things. This act is weak and powerless to do anything when it has been received in the passive subject. But the one invisible and everlasting light of the divine sun is always

conceptum supereminet Deus. Quid ergo non sit invenire possumus negando; et quo ordine agat et alia ad illum se habeant
comparando perquirimus. Quid vero[1] sit latet.

Atqui quo pacto ad ipsum bonum Plato per negationes
ascendat ex superioribus patere potest, quomodo vero per comparationes ita patebit. Quicquid ex ordine rerum pulchrum est,
idem et bonum. Quicquid bonum, idem quodammodo[2] pulchrum. Nam tam pulchri quam boni proprium est appetitum
allicere. Pulchritudo quidem nihil aliud est quam summi boni
splendor, fulgens praecipue[3] in his rebus quae oculis auribus
mente percipiuntur, perque illas[4] ad ipsum bonum visum
auditum mentemque convertens. Quo fit ut pulchritudo circulus
quidam divinae lucis existat, a bono manans, in bono residens,
per bonum et ad bonum sempiterne reflexus. Hoc Plato mys-
terium quod a Diotima Sibylla accepit[5] paucis revelavit. Quid
ipsum bonum? Ipsum unum omnium rerum principium, actus
purus, actus sequentia cuncta vivificans. Quid ipsum pulchrum? Vivificus actus e primo fonte bonorum effluens: mentem primo divinam idearum ordine[6] decorans; numina deinde
sequentia mentesque rationum serie complens; animas tertio
numerosis discursibus ornans; naturas quarto seminibus;
formis quinto materiam. Sol profecto, ut in Republica tradit
Plato, corpora visibilia et oculos videntes procreat: oculis ut
videant lucidum infundit spiritum; corpora ut videantur [*336r*]
coloribus pingit.# Neque tamen proprius oculis radius propriive
corporibus colores ad visionem perficiendam sufficiunt, nisi
lumen ipsum unum supra multa, a quo multa et propria lumina
oculis et corporibus distributa sunt, adveniat, illustret, excitet
atque roboret. Eodem modo primus ipse actus speciem actumque rebus singulis producendo largitus est. Qui sane actus cum
in subiecto patiente susceptus fuerit debilis est et ad operis executionem impotens. Sed divini solis perpetua et invisibilis lux

---

[1]vero *om. WXP*   [2]quodammodo *om. WXP*   [3]praecipue *om. WXP*   [4]illas *X,* illam *P*
[5]accipit *Y*   [6]ut in re. pu. tradit Plato *add. W*   #*P frag. I (24v) ends*

present to everything, cherishing, giving life, stimulating, fulfilling, and strengthening. Orpheus says divinely about it: "He is the one that cherishes all and bears himself above all things."[25] As the act of all and as it strengthens, it is called the good. As it gives life, assuages, smoothes, and stimulates, it is called the beautiful. As it draws the three cognitive powers of the soul[26] towards the objects they ought to know, it is called grace and beauty. As it is in the cognitive power and joins it to the known object it is called truth. As the good it creates and rules and fulfils. As the beautiful it illuminates and pours in grace.

However, in order to receive the grace of the divine light everything has to be prepared: bodies by the proportion that consists in order, mode and species; voices by the harmony that comes from numbers and intervals; moral duties by being directed by righteousness towards the good end; the various sorts of learning by being directed in order towards the true object; the soul by the purity which turns away from lower things and turns back towards higher ones; the intelligence by eternally gazing at the good itself. The ray of the divine goodness and beauty penetrates gradually through all these things. It surrounds body, shining out in the measured proportion which is subjected to place and movement. It surrounds voices in the harmony which is independent of a definite place but which is spread through movement. It surrounds the duties and the various sorts of learning and the soul, where it is indeed in motion but where it endures because of some vital reason. It surrounds the intelligence, where it sparkles above movement in the eternal series of the Ideas. It surrounds the good itself as the pure act inserting life and grace into all things.

Chapter 6. In what the human good consists; and on the comparison of pleasure and wisdom to each other and to the good itself.

It has been sufficiently shown, I think, that all things seek some end and are brought back to the ultimate end, and that

una semper omnibus adstat, fovet, vivificat, excitat, complet et roborat. De quo[1] divine Orpheus: Cuncta fovens atque ipse ferens super omnia sese. Ut est actus omnium roboratque, bonum dicitur. Ut vivificat, lenit, mulcet et excitat, pulchrum. *Ut in obiectis quae noscenda sunt tres illas cognoscentes animae vires allicit, gratia, et[2] pulchritudo.** Ut in cognoscente potentia eam applicat cognito,[3] veritas. Ut bonum procreat, regit et complet. Ut pulchrum illuminat gratiamque infundit.

Praeparata autem esse oportet omnia ad gratiam divini fulgoris excipiendam: corpora quidem proportione quae ordine modo et[4] specie constat; voces harmonia quae numeris intervallisque conficitur; officia morum rectitudine ad finem bonum; disciplinas ordine ad obiectum verum; animam puritate per aversionem ab inferis et conversionem ad supera; mentem per aeternum in ipsum bonum intuitum. Per haec omnia gradatim divinae bonitatis et pulchritudinis radius penetrat: circa corpus in aequalitate numerosa refulgens loco motuique subiecta; circa voces in harmonia extra certum locum sed motu dispersa; circa officia disciplinasque et animam in motu quidem sed ratione vitali consistens; circa mentem super[5] motum in aeterna idearum serie micans; circa [*336v*] ipsum bonum actus purus vitam et[6] gratiam omnibus inserens.

In quo[7] consistat humanum bonum et de comparatione voluptatis cum sapientia inter se et ad ipsum bonum. Cap. VI.[8]

Quod omnia finem aliquem expetant et ad ultimum reducantur finem, idque sit ipsum bonum et ipsum unum sitque

---

[1]quo *om. W*   [2]et *om. Y*   [3]cognitio *Y*   [4]et *om. Y*   [5]supra *WX*   [6]et *om. W*
[7]quae *Y*   [8]*no ch. heading but break W; same heading but numbered five X*   *-**om. W*

this is the good itself, the one itself, and the principle of all things. As a result the objections of the Aristotelians to divine Plato have now been exploded. But this good is the absolute good common to all. However, we are seeking the highest good for man. To find it we'll turn to Plato's text. He thinks man's highest good, that is, man's felicity and the happy life, consists in the enjoyment of the absolute good itself, since all that is conditional depends on the absolute. He will show what the possession of the good itself, which we call felicity, principally consists in. Next, the opinions of the people who don't refer our good to the first good have to be rejected as useless. Such was the opinion of Democritus, who was happy with quietness alone, which is the felicity of the stone; or of Aristippus, who pursued bodily pleasure, which is always contaminated by many opposites and shared with the individual beasts. Epicurus' tranquillity must also be rejected, for it isn't sought for its own sake, but in order to free us from worries and make us more prepared to attain the supreme good (on which our good also depends). Nor is the felicity of the Stoics and the Cynics enough for us; for above moral virtue, inasmuch as it's busily occupied and merely human, exists contemplation which is utterly at peace and is divine. Since our good can be nothing else but the complete possession of the first good itself according to our natural capacity, and since we can grasp what is highest in nature principally with our highest part, and since the highest part is the intelligence (as it is the leader of the rest of the parts), we are able to enjoy the good itself principally with the intelligence. But the intelligence enjoys by understanding and by loving. And so Plato will attribute the ability to attain felicity to the intelligence. But before he can take up this problem, he will reduce all the opinions about felicity to three main types. For either felicity is said to be pleasure or knowledge or some third thing. Under the general term "pleasure" are comprehended all the views of the people who reduced happiness either to the delights of the bodily senses, like Aristippus and Dionysius [of Heraclea], or to the gaiety of the soul as well, like Eudoxus. But under the term "knowledge" are comprehended the views of the

rerum omnium principium, satis est, ut arbitror, demonstratum. Ex quo Peripateticorum contra divum[1] Platonem
cavillationes explosae iam sunt. Verum absolutum id bonum est
omnibusque commune. Nos autem summum hominis bonum
expetimus. Quod ut nobis pateat textum Platonis aggrediemur,
qui summum hominis bonum, id est, hominis felicitatem bea-
tamque vitam in ipsius absoluti boni[2] fruitione consistere arbi-
tratur, quippe cum omne quod cum conditione est ab absoluto
dependeat. Declarabitque qua in re potissimum consistat ipsius
boni possessio quam felicitatem vocamus. Porro sententiae
illorum qui bonum nostrum ad bonum primum non referunt
utpote vanae reiciendae sunt. Qualis fuit Democriti, qui sola
quiete contentus fuit, quae lapidis felicitas est. Item Aristippi,
qui voluptatem corporis sectatus est, quae semper plurimis est
inquinata contrariis bestiisque singulis est communis. Mittenda
est et Epicuri tranquillitas, neque enim propter se ista quaeritur,
sed ut a perturbationibus liberi expeditiores[3] simus[4] ad supremi
boni, unde et nostrum pendet bonum, adeptionem. Neque Stoi-
corum et Cynicorum felicitas nobis sufficit. Nam supra mora-
lem virtutem utpote negotiosam et humanam contemplatio est
pacata prorsus atque divina. Etenim cum bonum nostrum nihil
esse aliud possit quam integra pro capacitate naturae boni ipsius
primi possessio, quod vero supremum est in natura, suprema
praecipue nostri parte capere valeamus et pars suprema sit
mens, quia dux partium reliquarum, mente frui praecipue ipso
bono possumus. Mens autem intelligendo fruitur et amando.
Atque idcirco menti felicitatis assequendae Plato tribuet facultatem. Et antequam hoc exsequatur ad tria potissimum capita
sententias omnes de felicitate reducet.[5] Aut enim voluptas esse
dicitur, aut scientia, aut[6] tertium aliquid. Sub communi voluptatis nomine omnes eorum sententiae comprehenduntur, qui vel
ad sensuum[7] corporis oblectamenta ut Aristippus Dionysiusque,
*vel insuper ad animi hilaritatem ut Eudoxus** beatitudinem
retulerunt. Sub nomine vero scientiae eorum opiniones,[8] qui vel

---

[1]divinum *W*   [2]posse *add. W*   [3]expediores *W*   [4]sumus *W*   [5]reducit *WX*
[6]ut *Y*   [7]sensum *W*   [8]opiniones *om. WX*   *-**insuper hilaritatem ut Eudoxus et
animi *W*; vel et animi hilaritatem insuper ut Eudoxus *X*

people who assessed happiness either in terms of the moral virtues, like Zeno and Antisthenes, or like Epicurus in terms of tranquillity, or in terms of the contemplative virtues, like Solon and Anaxagoras. But the people who want them both combined for the sake of felicity in a way follow the third alternative, which Aristotle followed and before him Heraclitus and Empedocles.

Chapter 7. The book's introduction in which the subject is proposed. About wisdom, pleasure and good things.

11A-C   As Philebus and Socrates had argued together at length about the highest good one way and another and Philebus was tired of arguing, he greeted Protarchus, who had just arrived, and allowed him to take over his side in the dispute. Protarchus, being a young man, immediately agreed. Socrates, having turned to him, said, "Think about the job you're taking on, and don't rush into the argument rashly. Rather, listen first to each point of view, and when you've thought about it correctly and rationally take up the defence of the view that seems to you to be the more probable. Philebus says the highest good for all animate beings is gladness and pleasure and delight and the rest of the same class like joy, etc. But I say it isn't these, but to know, to understand, to remember, to judge correctly, to reason truly and suchlike. I say they are better and more excellent, that is, more desirable and more outstanding than pleasure —not for all animals, as pleasure is, but for those capable of them, that is, for men and spirits. And I don't say the possession of them is only good and desirable in itself, but it is the most useful of all things to other people (and for other purposes), both to those who are alive now and to posterity." Socrates is showing his terms surpass pleasure, which is useful neither to the person who has it, nor to others, nor to posterity. Socrates doesn't say knowledge is the highest good, but that it is more outstanding and better and more useful than pleasure, since it is more suitable to the person living the better life and to

morales virtutes ut Zenon et Antisthenes, vel¹ tranquillitatem ut Epicurus, vel contemplativas ut Solon et² Anaxagoras beatitudinem censuerunt. Tertium vero quodammodo hi sequuntur, qui utraque volunt ad felicitatem esse coniuncta, quod secutus est Aristoteles et ante ipsum Heraclitus atque Empedocles.

*Prooemium libri in quo subiectum proponitur. Item de sapientia, voluptate, bonis. Cap. VII.*³

Cum multa de summo bono ultro citroque Socrates et Philebus invicem contulissent essetque Philebus dicendo defessus, Protarcho nuper advenienti gratulatus est Philebus, annuitque ut provinciam in disputando suam susciperet. Protarchus utpote adolescens statim assensus est. Ad quem conversus Socrates: Considera, inquit, qualem tutelam suscipias, neque temere in⁴ disputationem properes. Immo audi utriusque sententiam prius, et eam quae tibi recta ratione examinanti probabilior [*337v*] apparet accipe defendendam. Philebus quidem summum bonum animantibus omnibus laetitiam esse dicit voluptatemque et delectationem et cetera generis eiusdem ut gaudium, etc. Ego autem non haec, sed sapere, intelligere, meminisse, recte opinari, vere ratiocinari et similia, meliora et potiora id est optabiliora et praestantiora voluptate esse dico, non omnibus animalibus, ut voluptatem esse,⁵ sed his quae horum capacia sunt, hominibus scilicet et daemonibus; nec esse horum possessionem dumtaxat per se bonam expetendamque, sed et aliis et ad aliud aliorum omnium utilissimam, tam praesentibus quam posteris omnibus. Quod ostendit ista voluptati praestare quae nec utilis est habenti nec aliis nec in posterum. Neque dicit Socrates scientiam esse summum bonum sed praestantiorem meliorem utiliorem esse quam voluptatem, quia et praestantiori viventi et potentiae magis propria est et meliorem virtute reddit habentem et aliis prodest magis. Quia vero

---

¹et *WX*   ²et *om. W*   ³*no ch. heading or break W; a break but no heading X*   ⁴ad *WX*
⁵*em.,* iste *WXY*

his abilities, and it makes the person who has it more virtuous, and it benefits others more. But since he said "the good and useful," you ought to recall the distinction Plato made in the *Laws*, where he calls "the good" what is sought for its own sake, "the useful" what is sought for the sake of attaining the good, "the necessary" what is sought in order to avoid the bad. The first is quietness, the second is victory, the third is war.[27] He said this too in the *Republic* Book 2.[28] He maintains the good and the desirable are the same, and what is sought for its own sake exclusively, like honest and moderate pleasures, is exclusively good. What is sought for itself and for some other purpose, like feeling and knowing, is both good and useful. What is sought merely for something else, like curing a sick person, exercising, working, etc., is merely useful. He maintains the same in the *Gorgias*.[29] The four terms, "joy," "gladness," "delight," "pleasure," mean the following. The first means the joy of the intelligence in the contemplation of the truth; the second, the gaiety and gladness of the reason or opinion; the third, the amusements and the delight of the eyes and ears; the fourth, the sweetness of the remaining senses, that is, pleasure. But the Latins along with the Greeks use the term "pleasure" in an argument to mean any enjoyment. This is Plato's assertion in this book, Aristotle's in the *Nicomachean Ethics* and Cicero's in the *De Finibus*.[30]

When Plato says "to understand," he means the contemplation of divine things; when "to know," prudence in dealing with human things. But "to remember" is to preserve one's thoughts. "Right opinion" is to have a true estimate through probable conjecture. "Truly discursive reason" is the induction of reason resulting in knowledge. But the power of all these he includes under the heading "wisdom" or "knowledge." Granted such, he says that the truth about them must be completely determined. For nothing is more important when it comes to living well or badly than to think correctly or incorrectly about life's end.

Perhaps somebody is wondering why in the dispute over the good itself Plato mainly proposed these two from among the

bonum et utile dixit, meminisse oportet distinctionis illius quam
in Legibus Plato tradidit, ubi bonum vocat quod per se petitur,
utile quod propter bonum consequendum, necessarium quod
propter malum vitandum. Primum quies, victoria secundum,
bellum tertium. Quod secutus in secundo de Republica: bonum
et expetibile[1] idem esse dicit, et quod per se expetitur tantum
bonum tantum, ut honestae et moderatae voluptates; quod
propter se et propter aliud bonum et utile, ut sentire et sapere;
quod propter aliud tantum utile, ut aegrotantem curari,
exercitari, laborare, etc. Idem in Gorgia docet. Quattuor ista
nomina: gaudium, laetitia, delectatio, voluptas[2] ita se habent
quod [*338r*] primum significat mentis in veritatis contemplatione gaudium; secundum vel rationis vel opinionis hilaritatem
atque laetitiam; tertium oculorum et aurium oblectamenta
delectationemque; quartum reliquorum sensuum suavitatem id[3]
est[4] voluptatem. Sed tam Latini quam Graeci cum disputandum
est voluptatis nomine pro qualibet iucunditate utuntur. Quod
Plato hoc in libro, Aristoteles in libris de moribus et in libris de
finibus Cicero perhibet.

Cum intelligere dicit Plato contemplationem divinorum intelligit; cum sapere humanorum prudentiam. Meminisse vero cogitationes suas conservare est. Recta opinio vera per probabilem
coniecturam existimatio est. Veri rationis discursus inductio
rationis ad scientiam conferens. Sed sub sapientiae vel scientiae
nomine omnium istorum vim comprehendit. His positis infert
omnino quid verum sit de his esse determinandum. Nihil enim
magis ad bene vel male vivendum refert quam de fine vitae recte
vel non recte sentire.

Ambigat forte quispiam cur e multis, quae bona dicuntur,
duo haec potissimum, communem scilicet voluptatem

---

[1]exoptabile *W*   [2]*X supplies the Greek terms as well* εὐφροσύνη, χαρά, τέρψις, ἡδονή
[3]id *om. X*   [4]et *X*

many things which are referred to as good, that is, general pleasure and general wisdom. It's because all the soul's powers are
referred to the two main ones, the power which knows, and the
power which desires. The former seeks the true, the latter the
enjoyable. Therefore men either decide to live for the former,
or for the latter. If for the former, they refer everything to the
truth as the end. If for the latter, they refer everything to what
pleases. For wisdom is concerned with the truth, pleasure with
what delights. Now just as some truth is obtained from each
single object or art, so in all of them there is a certain wisdom,
although in pre-eminent things there is pre-eminent truth and
pre-eminent wisdom. And so in this book the term "wisdom"
or "knowledge" embraces all inner thinking. In the same way,
"pleasure," although it is properly corporeal, in this debate includes all enjoyment, since the term is better known, being used
more often and more generally understood.

But why isn't the object of the irascible power introduced
here into the debate?[31] It's because it helps the reason or the
desire vis-à-vis what they choose as worth pursuing out of
bravery, or abhor as what ought to be shunned out of rage.
Similarly, there is no mention of the cause of the active life. For
those who strive to do things make sure that things are arranged
so as to satisfy either the affections of the senses or the longing
of the intelligence; for nobody works for the sake of work, or is
moved for the sake of moving.

But if someone says "active control" refers to what can
accommodate itself alike to bodily lust and mental contemplation, he will be trying in vain to mix things which are mutually
repugnant. But if he is going to mix them, he will put a mean
between them which will be more useless than both for attaining
the good of the one or the other. In the *Euthydemus* this mean
is proved to be worse than the extremes.[32] Finally, in the
Euthydemus it is shown that felicity consists not in the possession of good things, but in their use.[33] But the soul uses them
either in knowing or in enjoying; and since felicity is an inner
good, it doesn't refer to external or corporeal things but to
inner acts, that is, thinking and feeling.

communemque sapientiam, in boni ipsius disceptatione Plato proposuit. Quia omnes animi vires ad duas praecipuas referuntur: unam quae cognoscit, alteram vero quae appetit. Illa verum quaerit, ista iucundum. Aut[1] ergo homines ad illam vitam instituunt aut ad istam. Si ad illam, omnia ad veritatem velut ad finem referunt; si ad alteram, ad id quod placet omnia. Circa veritatem vero sapientia, circa id quod delectat voluptas. Atqui, quemadmodum ex unaquaque re et arte veritas quaedam excutitur, ita in omnibus [*338v*] illis quaedam sapientia est, quamquam in rebus praecipuis praecipua veritas, sapientia praecipua est. Unde et sapientiae nomen vel scientiae hoc in libro intrinsecam omnem cognitionem complectitur. Quemadmodum voluptas, etsi proprie in corpore est, quia nomen ex usu rerum frequentiore et communiori perceptione notius est, omnem continet hac in disputatione iucunditatem.

At cur non adducitur hic in disputationem[2] irascibilis virtutis obiectum? Quia vel rationis vel concupiscentiae ministra est ad illa, quae vel eligunt audacter exsequenda[3] vel abhorrent per iracundiam devitanda. Simili de causa activae vitae nulla fit mentio, qui enim laborant agendo, id contendunt quo[4] res suas ita disponant, ut vel sensuum affectibus vel intelligentiae desiderio satisfaciant. Nemo enim gratia laborandi laborat et movendi movetur.

Siquis autem dixerit gubernationem activam ad id referri[5] ut tam corporeae libidini obsequatur[6] quam mentis contemplationi, repugnantia miscere invicem frustra conabitur. Quod si miscebit, medium constituet inter haec utrisque ineptius ad bonum vel huius vel alterius consequendum. Quod medium in Euthydemo deterius extremis esse convincitur. Denique in Euthydemo probatur non in possessione sed usu bonorum felicitatem consistere. Utitur autem his anima vel cognoscendo vel gaudendo, et cum felicitas intimum bonum sit, non ad externa vel corporea, sed ad intimos refertur actus, cognitionem scilicet[7] et affectum.

---

[1]At *W*   [2]disceptationem *WX*   [3]et sequenda *WX*   [4]quo *om. W*   [5]referri *om. W*
[6]consequatur *W*   [7]scilicet *om. W*

Moreover, since Plato in other places often compared wisdom to the rest of the things called good, but nowhere compared it to pleasure, it's fitting that in this book he should compare wisdom and pleasure properly together—to complete the comparison among good things and to find out about the good itself.

Chapter 8. The distinction between good things. How wisdom contributes to felicity. Concerning knowledge of the good; that it is every virtue and makes people happy.

But if someone wants to understand the comparison above, he may first read about it in the *Clitophon,* the *Meno*, the *Alcibiades* and above all in the *Laws*, where Plato makes some of the goods human, others divine.[34] The human are those pertaining to the body, the divine those pertaining to the soul. Among the human bodily health holds first place, then beauty, third comes strength, fourth riches. Among the divine firstly comes prudence, that is, wisdom, then the ordered disposition of the soul, thirdly justice, fourthly fortitude. He wants all the human ones referred to the divine: external riches to bodily health, bodily endowments to morality, morality to prudence finally and to the intelligence as the leader. In the intelligence is the knowledge of the true and the good. Plato argues men are made happy by this knowledge in the *Euthydemus,* when he compares wisdom to other things.[35]

Everybody defines felicity as getting what you want. But in any art or study knowledge is the means by which we get hold of the things we want. Military knowledge gets us victory; knowledge of navigation gets us to the port; medical knowledge gets us well.

Again, we say those people are happy who have lots of good things, that is, external things, the advantages of the body and the gifts of the soul. We don't say they are happy simply because they have the gifts, unless they use them; and not just use them, but use them properly. For the gifts aren't any good to us, unless they benefit us; and they do not benefit us, unless we use

Quin etiam cum Plato saepe alias sapientiam ad cetera quae bona dicuntur comparaverit, ad voluptatem vero non alias, merito ut bonorum comparatio ad ipsum bonum comperiendum [*339r*] absolveretur hoc in libro proprie ad voluptatem sapientiam comparavit.

Distinctio bonorum. Quomodo sapientia conferat ad felicitatem, de scientia boni, quod sit omnis virtus efficiatque beatos. Cap. VIII.[1]

Superiorem vero comparationem intelligere siquis cupit, Clitophontem, Menonem, Alcibiadem[2] et[3] imprimis librum de Legibus primum legat, ubi bonorum[4] alia humana, divina alia ponit. Humana quae ad corpus, divina quae ad animum pertinent. Ex humanis primum locum tenet sanitas corporis; secundum forma; tertium vires; quartum divitiae. Ex divinis primum prudentia, id est, sapientia; secundum moderatus animi habitus; tertium iustitia; fortitudo quartum. Omnia illa humana ad divina referri vult: externas divitias ad corporis cultum, corporis dotes ad mores, mores denique ad prudentiam mentemque tamquam ad ducem, in qua veri ac boni scientia est, qua scientia felices fieri homines in Euthydemo sic disputat, dum sapientiam ad alia comparat.

Felicitatem definiunt omnes rerum consecutionem ad votum. In quacumque vero arte et studio ut rerum pro desiderio potiamur scientia praestat: scientia militaris victoriae, gubernatoria portus, medicina sanitatis consecutionem.

Item beatos dicimus eos qui bona habent plurima scilicet[5] externa et[6] commoda corporis animique[7] dotes. Neque possessione horum sola beatos nisi utantur dicimus; nec usu, nisi recte

---

[1] *no ch. heading or break* WX   [2]et Phaedonem *add.* WX   [3]et *om.* W   [4]horum Y
[5]scilicet *om.* WX   [6]et *om.* WX   [7]-que *om.* WX

them and use them properly, for the misuse of them is harmful (so it is better to do without than to misuse). But knowledge of things makes us use everything skillfully, for, in the case of particular skills, the person who has knowledge of that skill uses the instruments and material properly. Therefore, since felicity comes from the acquisition and correct use of good things, and since knowledge of the good bestows this, knowledge of the good contributes mainly, or rather totally, to felicity.

Again, when wisdom is in charge everything else is good for us. But when stupidity is the leader everything becomes pernicious—riches, power, health, comeliness, vigour, quickness of mind, memory, magnanimity, a steadfast and invincible disposition, the subtlety of all the other arts and sciences. So knowledge of the good makes everything good. Plato calls this knowledge by three names: "eudaemonia," "eutychia," "eupragia." In Plato the three mean: "happiness," "felicity," "right action." They all coincide with knowledge of the good. Because it perceives good things and bad things, it is called "eudaemonia," that is, "happiness"; because it shuns bad things and attains good things, "eutychia," that is, "felicity"; because it uses advantages properly, "eupragia," that is, "right action." From this it is obvious that knowledge of the good is most able to attain the highest good.

Indeed, as you can gather from Plato's *Protagoras,* knowledge of the good contributes most towards the highest good because it is itself all virtue.[36] For wisdom is the knowledge of the absolute good. But prudence is the knowledge of bad things and secondary good things. Justice is the knowledge that distributes good and bad things. Fortitude is the knowledge that properly dares to confront or is afraid of good or bad things. Temperance is the knowledge of how to pursue or avoid what is good or bad. So there is one virtue in which the entire rational principle of virtue is included, knowledge of the good; every faculty is present in it for the sake of the good itself. For knowledge considers the good and directs all things towards the good and attains the good, the attaining of which is man's felicity.

utantur. Nam non sunt nobis bona,[1] nisi prosint; non prosunt, nisi utamur et recte utamur. Abusus enim nocet, quare melius est carere quam abuti. Uti autem scite rebus omnibus scientia rerum efficit. Nam in singulis artibus is instrumentis et materia ut decet utitur qui scientiam artis habet. Quapropter, cum felicitas ex bonorum consecutione rectoque usu proveniat, idque scientia boni praestet, haec utique ad felicitatem [*339v*] plurimum immo totum valet.

Item hac ducente bona sunt nobis reliqua omnia. Insipientia vero duce cuncta perniciosa, divitiae, potentiae, sanitas, forma, robur, acumen ingenii, memoria, animi magnitudo, constans et invictus habitus, artium omnium reliquarum et scientiarum subtilitas. Quare scientia boni bona efficit omnia, quam tribus nominibus Plato significat: eudaemonia, eutychia, eupragia.[2] Haec apud Platonem tria nomina sunt: beatitudo, felicitas, bene agere. Haec omnia boni scientiae competunt. Nam, quia bona malaque cognoscit, eudaemonia,[3] id est, beatitudo vocatur; quia vitat mala consequitur commoda, eutychia,[4] id est, felicitas; quia commodis recte utitur, eupragia,[5] id est, bona actio. Ubi patet quod *scientia boni ad summum bonum potest plurimum.

Atque, ut ex Protagora Platonis colligitur,** scientia boni ex eo maxime ad ipsum bonum confert, quoniam ipsa omnis est virtus. Sapientia namque absoluti boni scientia est; prudentia vero †scientia malorum bonorumque secundorum; iustitia†† scientia bonorum malorumque distribuendorum;[6] fortitudo scientia circa bona et mala ‡ut decet audendi atque metuendi; temperantia scientia circa bona et mala‡‡ adsciscendi et fugiendi. Una ergo est virtus, in qua tota ratio virtutis includitur, scientia boni, in qua omnis ad ipsum bonum facultas inest. Ista enim et bonum inspicit et ad bonum omnia dirigit et bonum consequitur, quae consecutio hominis est felicitas.

---

[1]bona *om. W*   [2,3,4,5]*the terms are missing in W; in X they are in Greek script*
[6]-que *add. W*   *-***om. W*   †-††*om. W*   ‡-‡‡*om. Y*

Although moral virtue and wisdom contribute most to the good itself, still, neither moral virtue nor wisdom is the good itself, as you can see from the *Republic* Book 6.[37] Moral virtue isn't, for it is usually enough for many people just to appear to possess it. But the good is what everybody wants to possess in reality. Wisdom isn't, because it is understanding. But understanding is drawn towards understanding something, and when it has understood it, it comes to rest. So its perfection derives from something else. So its good is from something else.

However, so we may know Plato's mind more clearly in different places, we must posit two steps in the knowledge of the good. The first is whereby we can conjecture from all the things which come from the good itself that there is some principle for everything, which is the one and the good. When through negation we have freed it from all other things, we can know what it isn't; and then when we've compared it to everything else by means of analogies, we can know what it is like. This knowledge is called by the theologians the "evening" knowledge. It is in the splendour of the good. The second step is the one whereby we comprehend without any hindrance what the principle is in itself, and this knowledge is called the "morning" knowledge. It is in the light of the good.[38] The first degree of knowledge and wisdom is the way closest to felicity. The second is felicity itself. And whenever Plato says wisdom is "felicity," he means the second sort; whenever he denies it, he means the first sort. Yet, it must be understood the absolute good is one thing, our good another. The former is called God and the good itself; the latter is called felicity. Certainly, felicity is not the first sort of wisdom, but the second. The good is neither the first nor the second sort, as is evident from the *Republic* Book 6.[39] But when Plato calls knowledge of the good and wisdom "happiness," "felicity," "right action," he means the second sort. For if he were talking about the first sort, he'd be misusing words and confusing happiness and felicity with the way that is closest to them.

Certainly, to judge from the reasons we've brought to bear from the remaining dialogues, Plato puts knowledge itself and

Etsi virtus moralis et sapientia plurimum ad bonum ipsum conferunt,[1] neque tamen virtus moralis aut sapientia ipsum bonum est, quod in sexto de Republica patet. Non virtus moralis, plerumque enim[2] sufficit multis ut habere eam appareant; bonum vero habere revera omnes volunt. Non sapientia, quia haec intelligentia est. Intelligentia vero ad aliquid intelligendum fertur, in quo percepto quiescit. *Aliunde igitur eius perfectio pendet.** Aliunde igitur [*340r*] ipsius bonum.

Ut autem mens Platonis nobis passim clarius innotescat, duo gradus in boni scientia ponendi sunt. Unus quo ex omnibus rebus quae a bono ipso sunt esse coniectamus[3] aliquid omnium principium quod unum sit et bonum; ipsumque per negationem ab omnibus aliis eximentes, quid non sit cognoscimus,[4] et deinde per comparationes referentes ad omnia, quale sit agnoscimus,[5] quae cognitio vespertina dicitur a theologis, quae est in boni[6] splendore. Alter gradus, quo quid sit in se ipso expedite comprehendimus, quae cognitio matutina dicitur in boni luce. Ille gradus scientiae et sapientiae proxima est ad felicitatem via. Iste est ipsa felicitas. Et siquando dicit Plato sapientiam esse felicitatem, de gradu secundo intelligitur. Siquando negat, de[7] primo. Intelligendum tamen aliud esse bonum absolutum, aliud nostrum; illud dicitur Deus et ipsum bonum, hoc vero[8] felicitas. Felicitas profecto[9] non est primus sapientiae gradus, sed secundus. Ipsum bonum neque primus gradus est, neque secundus, ut sexto de Republica patet. Cum vero scientiam boni et sapientiam vocat beatitudinem, felicitatem,[10] bene agere,[11] de secundo eius gradu intelligit. Nam si de primo dixerit, abutitur vocabulis et beatitudinem felicitatemque capit pro via ad eam quam proxima.

Profecto per eas quas attulimus rationes in ceteris dialogis Plato scientiam ipsam sapientiamque reliquis omnibus

---

[1]conferant *WX*   [2]ut *W*   [3]coniectamur *WX*   [4]agnoscimus *WX*   [5]noscimus *WX*
[6]bono *W*   [7]re *add. W*   [8]vero *om. WX*   [9]profecto *om. WX*   [10]felicitatis *X*
[11]et *add. W*   *-**om. W*

wisdom before all else. But in this dialogue he prosecutes the comparison with pleasure, so that, having looked at the comparison, we can understand what each contributes to the highest good and what the highest good is. In the beginning of the discussion in this dialogue he will not accept that "wisdom" stands only for knowledge of the good; rather it stands generally for knowledge of every possible truth. In the same way he will use "pleasure" to stand not just for some particular enjoyment, but generally for all delight.

Chapter 9. What human felicity consists in, namely the enjoyment of God. Also concerning the subject of the book.

In the foregoing Plato has declared the theme of the discussion, namely to find out what man's highest good is (for that's the theme and subject of each argument: they are all introduced for its sake). But in order to make especially clear what the good is, he introduces pleasure and wisdom into the controversy—it is apparent here and will often appear subsequently, particularly when he adds a third thing over and above them, and it shows you the error of the people who entitled this dialogue "On pleasure."[40] Why not "On wisdom"—since Plato doesn't talk any less about that than about pleasure? Why not "On the life compounded from wisdom and pleasure"—he refers both to that life? Why not "On felicity"—since he investigates all these things for the sake of discovering felicity (as he himself repeats a thousand times)? Accordingly, since the book's theme has been described, now the structure of the whole argument must be outlined.

It is divided into twelve parts.[41] In the first part he proposes the subject of the debate, which we've already discussed above: that is, what is man's good and whether wisdom or pleasure contribute more towards it? In the second part Plato tells us about the proper circumstances of the life of pleasure and also of wisdom, so that we can see which is more conducive to felicity. He must also see whether some third sort of life

anteponit. Voluptatis vero comparationem in hoc dialogo peragit, ut hac comparatione inspecta quid utrumque ad summum bonum conferat, quidve summum sit bonum intelligamus. Neque accipiet hoc in dialogo in principio disputandi sapientiam pro cognitione boni dumtaxat, sed [*340v*] communiter pro cuiuscumque veritatis scientia, sicut et voluptatem non pro certa suavitate, sed pro omni communiter iucunditate utetur.

In quo consistat humana felicitas, scilicet in fruitione Dei; et de subiecto libri. Cap. IX.[1]

In superioribus declaravit Plato quid disputationis huius propositum sit,[2] invenire scilicet quid summum hominis bonum sit, illud enim disputationis cuiusque propositum et subiectum est, cuius gratia cetera omnia inferuntur. Sed, ut quid bonum sit potissimum pateat, voluptatem et sapientiam in controversiam trahit, quod et hic patet et saepe in sequentibus apparebit, praesertim cum praeter ista tertium insuper addet. Qua in re eorum patefactus est error, qui huic dialogo de voluptate inscripserunt. Cur non de sapientia, cum non minus de illa quam de voluptate loquatur? Cur non de vita ex sapientia voluptateque composita? Ad quam utraque refert. Cur non de felicitate, cum felicitatis inveniendae gratia (ut ipse millies[3] repetit) haec omnia investiget? Quare cum propositum libri huius praescriptum sit, iam disputationis totius ordo est tradendus.[4]

Haec duodecim in partes distribuitur. In prima parte quod tractandum est proponit, quam iam supra exposuimus, quid scilicet bonum hominis sit et[5] utrum ad id conferat magis, sapientia an voluptas. In secunda ponendam Plato monet vitae voluptuosae necnon sapientis conditionem, ut videatur utra magis ad felicitatem conducat. Videndumque utrum tertius

---

[1] *no ch. heading but break W; in X the ch. is numbered six and* et de subiecto libri *is omitted*
[2] sit *om. W*   [3] miles *Y*   [4] *see appendix I for passage added by X*   [5] et *om. W*

appears, which is better than the other two and leads to felicity more. If it does appear, we must consider which of the two is more nearly related to the perfection of this third thing, pleasure or wisdom. In this way we can not only know what felicity is, but also what the best way is to it. Here [Plato] will try to divide pleasure and wisdom in order to effect the comparison. In the third part he'll point out why caution is necessary in the dispute. For he'll show that things have to be defined and divided before they can be mutually compared, and he'll demonstrate how it ought to be done. In the fourth part he'll describe what the conditions of the good itself are. For the person who's going to compare wisdom and pleasure to some third thing has to know about the third thing. Here Plato shows that neither is the highest good. This is a negative comparison for which the knowledge of the third thing together with a general perception of the extremes is quite enough. But for an affirmative comparison it is necessary to have in addition a distinct knowledge of the extremes. So, before he can complete the affirmative comparison (in which it has to be decided, since neither is the good itself, at least which is closer to it), he thoroughly examines what each is. And he comes to the fifth part in which he looks into each one's genus. To define something, the genus must be known first of all, likewise the difference has to be added. In this part Plato explains there are two universal genera which penetrate through all things after God, the finite and the infinite. He shows that something is mixed from them and he has a presentiment of the cause of the mixture. In the sixth part, as some spark of knowledge has been kindled through the genera, he starts on the comparison. In the seventh part he describes the mixture's cause more fully, and talks about the world soul and providence. Here he is exploring the comparison more explicitly. In the eighth part, now the principles and genera have been clarified, he looks into the differences. Here he is exploring the consistency of pleasure and pain, the manner in which they are appropriately born from passivity, and also how many parts they have. In the ninth part he examines what knowledge really consists in and divides it up.

aliquis vitae status appareat utrisque melior et ad felicitatem potior. Qui si apparuerit, considerandum utra illarum sit istius perfectioni cognatior, voluptasne an sapientia, ut non solum quid sit [*341r*] felicitas, sed quae via ad illam commodior cognoscamus, ubi tentabit voluptatem sapientiamque ad comparationem faciendam dividere. In tertia parte docebit qua cautione sit disputandum. Nam ante definienda esse et dividenda quaeque monstrabit quam inter se comparentur, et qua ratione id fieri debeat demonstrabit. In quarta quae sint boni ipsius conditiones describet. Nam tertium cognoscat oportet, qui ad illud duo quaedam sit comparaturus. Ubi Plato neutram summum esse bonum ostendit. Quae comparatio negativa est, ad quam cum communi quadam extremorum perceptione sufficit cognitio[1] tertii. Ad affirmativam enim extremorum quoque distincta cognitio necessaria. Ideo antequam comparationem affirmativam absolvat, in qua iudicandum est postquam neutra[2] ipsum est bonum utra saltem illi sit propinquior, quid utraque sit perscrutatur. Et quintam aggreditur partem, in qua investigat utriusque genus. Nam primo genus ad definitionem accipiendum[3] est, addenda propemodum[4] differentia. Qua in parte duo quaedam[5] genera rerum, quae post Deum per omnia penetrant, aperit, finitum et infinitum, ex quibus mixtum ostendit et mixtionis causam[6] praesagit. In sexta, quia per illa genera scintilla quaedam cognitionis accensa est, comparationem inchoat. In septima causam mixtionis illius explicat latius, deque mundi anima et providentia disserit, ubi planius comparationem exsequitur. In octava principiis iam patefactis generibusque differentias investigat, ubi in quo voluptas dolorque consistunt indagat, qua proprie ex passione nascuntur, quotque partes habent. In nona in quo proprie consistit scientia

---

[1]agnitio *WX*   [2]neutrum *W*   [3]decipiendum *W*   [4]postmodum *WX*
[5]quaedam *om. X*   [6]causa *W*

Here he is now setting up the comparison: that is, there is some third life that takes the lead over wisdom, as wisdom over pleasure. In the tenth part he tells us how these two are mixed together and that our good consists in such a compound. In the eleventh part he investigates what is in the compound, and what the chief element is by reason of which it is felicity. Here our good and the absolute good shine forth. At last in part twelve, having carefully and gradually ascended to the highest good, suddenly Plato enumerates all the degrees of good things from the highest to the lowest and draws a picture of the happy man. And that's the end of the dialogue.

Chapter 10. The arrangement of the arguments in the text; on the happy life and Venus and reverence for the gods.

11D-
12A

Notwithstanding, let's come to the second part. Socrates, having turned to Protarchus, says, "This is the best approach if you want to extol pleasure and I want to extol wisdom. In order to make each man completely happy, you introduce an affection of the soul, and I'll introduce a mental attitude. You can call the affection one of pleasure and I'll attribute the mental attitude to wisdom. Still, we oughtn't to argue so stubbornly that we reject a third alternative should it appear to be better than them. But we each ought to look on it favourably, and when it has been ascertained that it is better, we ought to find out whether wisdom or pleasure is closer to it. For since things are good to the extent they contribute towards the end, we ought to consider what disposition of the soul leads entirely to the end, then see whether wisdom or pleasure belongs to it. And if neither disposition seems to be sufficient to reach the end, we'll have to seek a third disposition to which you can compare each, and better conclude what is closer to it. Before, you concluded in the same way that the totally good was what led totally to the end.

"To be sure, should a more perfect life be discovered, it will contain in itself and in a more enduring way whatever is good in

eamque partitur, [*341v*] ubi comparationem iam expedit, quod scilicet tertia quaedam vita sapientiae praeest, sapientia voluptati. Decima in parte docet quo pacto haec duo invicem misceantur quodve in composito huiuscemodi[1] nostrum est bonum. In undecima vero inquirit quid insit in eo composito quidve praesit cuius ratione felicitas sit. Ubi et bonum nostrum et bonum absolutum emicat. In duodecima tandem postquam ad supremum bonum sensim gradatimque conscenderat, subito gradus omnes bonorum a supremo ad infimum numerat, felicemque figurat hominem atque ibi libri huius[2] est finis.

Dispositio verborum textus et de vita felici et Venere et reverentia deorum. Cap. X.[3]

Ceterum ut ad secundam veniamus partem; conversus ad Protarchum Socrates ait: si voluptatem extollere tu et ego sapientiam volumus, optima[4] haec est ratio, ut et tu affectionem quandam animi et ego habitum inducamus, quo maxime felix quisque reddatur, et tu quidem affectionem eam voluptatis esse dicas, ego sapientiae habitum illum tribuam. Neque tamen usque adeo pertinaces esse in disputando debemus, ut siquis tertius status utrisque praestantior apparuerit eum reiciamus; sed utrosque illi favere decet et illo tamquam potiori posito utra cognatior illi sit investigare sapientiane an voluptas. *Cum enim[5] quaelibet eatenus bona sint quatenus conducunt ad finem, considerandum est quae animi dispositio omnino ad hunc[6] conducat, deinde videre utrum ad illam attineat sapientiane an voluptas. Et si appareat neutram[7] dispositionem sufficere ad finem, quaerenda est tertia ad quam conferas utrumque et concludas melius quod similius; sicut antea[8] concludebas omnino bonum quod omnino conducat.**

Certe siqua vita perfectior reperitur, quicquid est in voluptate vel[9] sapientia boni ipsa in se et stabilius insuper continet;

---

[1]eiuscemodi *X*   [2]istius *WX*   [3]*no ch. heading or break* WX   [4]et *add. W*
[5]enim *om. X*   [6]id *X*   [7]neutrum *W*   [8]ante *X*   [9]in *add. X*   [*-**]*om. W*

pleasure or wisdom; for every single thing endures longer in something better than it does in something worse. So your pleasure and my wisdom will be completely overthrown by this life. But we'll have to see which of them is closer to this life's perfection. If pleasure is, it will defeat wisdom; if wisdom is, it will defeat pleasure, for all the less good things are in turn compared by the standard of the greater good." But Socrates will maintain subsequently that the third more perfect life is the one which joins pleasure to wisdom in a marvellous way. Because of the joining together the whole of life is more complete; furthermore, the pleasure is more lasting, since it comes from something that lasts and it comes with supreme moderation; and the contemplation of wisdom is more constant too, since what is done with delight is done for a longer time.

12B

But, since in this dialogue Socrates is about to derogate pleasure and Philebus had called pleasure, "Venus," he hastens to make atonement, fearing a goddess' name especially as a pious man should. Atonement is the restoration of holiness that has been destroyed. Holiness is devotion to holy things, as in the *Euthydemus*.[42] But Socrates had sinned against a god's name. Therefore he purges himself in the presence of Protarchus, so that Protarchus may excuse him before other men. He tells them he venerates both the goddess and the goddess' name: for fear he should offend somehow in using divine names, he trembles so much, he says, that for men no other horrendous source whatsoever can cause anything like this horror. Rather, it's the extreme limit of the greatest consternation possible, that is, beyond it nothing can be feared more strongly. Socrates says he is

12C

prepared to call Venus by any name most pleasing to her, if he could hear her true names alone; for instance "Ciprogenea," or "Citharea," or "Philomidia."[43] But for the present he doubts "pleasure" is her name, since Venus, being a goddess, is one simple something, but pleasure signifies something varied and multiple and doesn't signify the goddess Venus, as Philebus wanted (he was young still and a follower of Eudoxus and Aristippus, whom the Epicurean philosopher, Lucretius, also copied. Lucretius writes:

unumquodque enim in re meliore stabilius quam in deteriori permanet. Unde ab ea vita longe et voluptas tua et mea sapientia superatur. Sed videndum erit utra istarum sit illius perfectioni cognatior: si voluptas, superabit sapientiam; si sapientia, voluptatem superabit. Omnia namque minora bona secundum maioris normam [*342r*] invicem comparantur. Tertiam vero hanc vitam et perfectiorem eam in sequentibus esse dicet, quae iungit mirabili quodam modo cum sapientia voluptatem, qua copulatione tota vita integrior est. Quin etiam[1] voluptas firmior, cum ex re firma et optima moderatione sumatur, et sapientiae quoque contemplatio assidua magis, quod enim cum delectatione fit diutius agitur.

Verum cum hoc in dialogo Socrates sit voluptati derogaturus, Philebus autem voluptatem Venerem appellaverit, Socrates in primis nomen deae veritus ut hominem pium decet expiare se properat. Expiatio est sanctitatis abolitae restitutio. Sanctitas divinorum cultus est, ut in Euthydemo. Peccaverat autem in dei nomen. Purgat ergo se coram Protarcho ut coram hominibus aliis eum excuset. Praedicitque illis venerari se et deam et deae nomen atque ita se contremiscere in divinorum nominum usu ne quid peccet, ut nullus sit hominum pavor ex aliis quibuscumque rebus horrendis concitus huic horrori similis, sed maximae cuiuscumque trepidationis hunc esse[2] extremum, id est, ultra quem metui vehementius nihil possit; et eo nomine vocare illam paratum se esse, quod magis illi placeat, si modo vera illius audierit nomina ut vel Ciprogeneam,[3] vel Cithaream,[4] vel Philomidiam.[5] In praesentia vero diffidere se voluptatem nomen illius esse, quia Venus utpote dea unum quiddam[6] est simplex, voluptas autem variam rem multiplicemque significat non deam Venerem, ut Philebus iunior adhuc et Eudoxi et Aristippi sectator volebat. Quos Lucretius Philosophus Epicureus imitatus, inquit:

---

[1] *for* Quin etiam *WX read* et   [2] esse *om. Y*   [3] Ciprogenea *Y*   [4] vel Cithaream *om. X*
[5] intuetur eam veneratumque et in ipsa admodum delectatur *add. X*   [6] unum quiddam *om. Y*

"Mother of Aeneas and his race, delight of men and gods,
Life-giving Venus, under the wheeling constellations of the
sky,
You, who over the ship-bearing sea, the fruit-laden land
Frequently wander, each race of living things is conceived
Through you, and having risen it gazes on the rays of the
sun"[44]).

Chapter 11. On Venus and the gods; and on the gods' names and reverence for them.

Three things must be asked here. In Plato what sort of divinity is Venus? How did the error arise of those who've called Venus "pleasure"? Why must the gods' names be held in reverence? To be sure, Orpheus (whose theology Plato followed) in his *Book of Hymns* calls the heavens, which most people refer to as the Sky, "the progenitor of all things" and "the beginning and end of all."[45] Perhaps Plato too wants the sky to be the first divinity—not the sky which one sees with the eyes (for in the *Timaeus* he argues that this was created[46]), but the first principle of the sky and of all things. He says in the *Epistles* that all things surround this king and all things exist for his sake, and he is the cause of all good things.[47] In the *Republic* he called him "the sun of the upper world."[48] He maintains that his son is Saturn, a divine intelligence begotten immediately by God. This intelligence Porphyry calls "the reason or word of God the father."[49] In the *Timaeus* Plato calls the intelligence "the maker of the world and the father of the gods."[50] In the *Statesman* he calls him "Cronos," that is, Saturn, the king of the eternal city, the converter of souls, the author of the resurrection of all things.[51] In the *Laws* Book 4 Plato said he contains the beginning and end and all the middle points of things, and orders individual things with uprightness according to [his] encircling nature.[52] Also in the *Protagoras* Plato calls him "the merciful giver of divine and human laws."[53] In the *Epistles* he calls him "father and master."[54] Out of this divine intelligence a certain living spirit is granted to the universal mechanism of the world;

Eneadum genetrix hominum divumque voluptas,
Alma Venus coeli [*342v*] subter labentia signa
Quae mare navigerum, quae terras frugiferentes
Concelebras; per te quoniam genus omne animantum
Concipitur, visitque exortum lumina solis.

De Venere atque diis; de nominibus deorum et reverentia circa illa. Cap. XI.[1]

Hic tria quaerenda sunt: quod numen apud Platonem sit Venus? Unde ortus sit[2] eorum error qui Venerem voluptatem cognominarunt? Cur deorum nominibus reverentia sit[3] habenda? Orpheus profecto cuius theologiam secutus est Plato coelum quem plerique coelium[4] vocant in libro hymnorum genitorem omnium vocat[5] principiumque et finem omnium. Hunc forsan[6] et Plato primum Deum esse vult, non coelum, hoc quod cernitur oculis, nam[7] genitum esse disputat in Timaeo, sed primum coeli omniumque principium. Circa quem regem in Epistolis ait esse omnia eiusque gratia omnia[8] et ipsum bonorum omnium causam esse; et[9] in Republica hunc mundi superioris solem vocavit. Huius filium Saturnum asserit mentem quamdam divinam statim a Deo genitam, quam Porphyrius[10] Dei patris rationem seu verbum vocat.[11] Hanc mentem in Timaeo mundi opificem patremque deorum nominat Plato, et in libro de Regno, Cronon, id est, Saturnum, regem civitatis aeternae, conversorem animorum, resurrectionis omnium auctorem. In quarto Legum hunc[12] continere dixit principium et finem et media omnia[13] rerum, rectitudine disponere singula secundum naturam circumeuntem. In Protagora quoque clementem divinarum humanarumque legum datorem hunc esse dicit; in Epistolis patrem ac dominum. Ex hac divina mente universae mundi machinae vivens quidam spiritus est tributus,

---

[1]*no ch. heading or break WX*   [2]sit *om. Y*   [3]sit *om. X*   [4]*Late Latin form used consistently by Ficino in this context*   [5]vocat *om. W*   [6]ergo *WX*   [7]natura *Y*
[8]eiusque gratia omnia *om. X*   [9]et *om. W*   [10]Porphyrius *om. Y*   [11]vocant *Y*
[12]In quarto Legum hunc *om. W*   [13]media omnium *W;* medium omnium *X*

a spirit, indeed, which is borne above the waters, that is, above the flowing matter of the world. In the *Timaeus* Plato calls the spirit "the world's soul"; in the *Republic* Book 10 "necessity"; in the *Statesman* "fate"; in the *Laws* "the law of the stars and the rational life of the world"; in the *Epistles* "the ruler of past, present and future things"; in the *Phaedrus* "Jove, the lord who sets the winged chariot into motion in the sky."[55] In this dialogue the world's soul will be called by Plato "the intelligence," "the all-governing wisdom," "the queen of earth and sky," "Jove" (in whom dwells royal intellect and royal soul).

At least three powers are considered to be in this soul: one whereby it always adheres to the good itself, the first principle of things; another whereby it gazes on the beauty of the divine intelligence; a third whereby it extends the forms of things into matter. The first power is called "Jupiter," the second "celestial Venus," the third "inferior Venus." And so in the *Symposium* Plato introduces two Venuses, the mothers of twin loves:[56] one was born the daughter of the sky without a mother; the other was conceived by Jove and Dione. From the former, generous loves are born, from the latter, base loves. Since the rational principle of the soul itself has been turned back towards the glory of the divine intelligence, it sees her and worships her and delights completely in her. Conversion and recognition are called "the celestial Venus." But worship is divine love, delight, supernal joy and true pleasure. Hence love and the pleasure similar to her accompany the celestial Venus. Moreover, the power of that part of the soul, which is concerned with moving corporeal objects, longs to model the beautiful forms of things in the matter of the world. In this way, just as the former part strives to contemplate the beauty of the divine species, so the latter part turns to the exemplar of higher things in order to bring forth the beauty of corporeal forms. So the latter part of the soul is also called "Venus": its drive to procreate is "love," its peace in the fulfilment of procreation is "pleasure." So you have twin Venuses, twin loves and twin pleasures.

Because she's the one who does not look towards matter, the superior Venus is said by Plato to be without a mother. The

qui vere super aquas fertur, id est, super fluxam mundi materiam. [*343r*] Hunc[1] mundi animam nominat in Timaeo; in decimo[2] de Republica necessitatem; in libro de Regno fatum; in Legibus legem[3] siderum ac vitam mundi rationalem; in Epistolis rerum praeteritarum praesentium[4] et futurarum ducem; in Phaedro Jovem ducem, qui alatum in coelo citet currum; in hoc libro dicet hanc mundi animam mentem esse et sapientiam omnium gubernatricem, coeli terraeque reginam, esseque Jovem in quo regius intellectus et regia insit anima.

In hoc utique tres vires considerantur: una qua ipsi bono primo rerum principio semper inhaeret; altera qua divinae mentis pulchritudinem[5] intuetur; tertia qua rerum formas explicat in materia. Prima Jupiter dicitur; secunda coelestis Venus; tertia Venus inferior. Ideoque in Symposio Plato duas inducit Veneres geminorum matres amorum: unam coeli filiam[6] sine matre natam; alteram ex Jove genitam atque Dione. Ex illa generosos amores nasci, ex ista vulgares. Ratio siquidem[7] ipsius animae ad mentis divinae decorem conversa, intuetur eam veneraturque et in ipsa admodum delectatur. Conversio quidem[8] agnitioque coelestis Venus dicitur. Veneratio vero[9] amor divinus, delectatio, supernum gaudium veraque voluptas. Unde coelestem Venerem et amor et voluptas similis comitatur. Quin etiam vis animae istius quae ad corpora movenda porrigitur speciosas rerum formas in mundi materia exprimere concupiscit. Quare sicut pars illa ad pulchritudinem divinarum specierum contemplandam nititur, ita haec ad pulchritudinem corporalium formarum gignendam ad superiorum exemplar se confert. Quapropter et haec pars animae Venus est [*343v*] dicta; eius nixus ad gignendum amor; quies in generationis expletione voluptas. Geminam itaque habes Venerem, amorem geminum, geminam voluptatem.

Superior Venus, quia ad materiam[10] minime respicit, ideo sine matre esse dicitur a Platone. Venus inferior ex Jove,[11] id est,

---

[1]*em.,* hanc *WXY*   [2]sexto *Y*   [3]lege *W*   [4]praesertim *W*   [5]pulchritudine *W*
[6]filam *Y*   [7]quidem *W*   [8]ipsa *WX*   [9]vero *om. WX*   [10]materia *W*
[11]est *add. WX*

inferior Venus depends upon Jove, that is, the higher part of the soul which we've called Jove, and upon a mother as well, Dione, because she does look towards matter. So there are two loves, two pleasures, also two procreations in men: on one part as regards the divine species, on the other as regards the corporeal form. But what Hesiod says of Venus in his *Theogony* (when he says Saturn castrated the Sky and threw the testicles into the sea, and from these and the swirling foam Venus was born[57]) must be understood perhaps as referring to the fertility for creating all things. The fertility lies hidden in the first principle of things; and the divine intelligence at first drinks it down and unfolds it inside itself, then pours it out into the soul and into matter. It is called "the sea" because of movement and time and the wetness of procreation.

When the soul is first abundant with that fertility, it produces intelligible beauty in itself by turning towards higher things. It begets the glory of sensible forms in matter by turning towards lower things. But from turning like this towards beauty and from the generation of beauty the soul is called Venus.

And since pleasure has been mingled into every glance at beauty and into beauty's every generation, and since all generation is from the soul (which is called Venus), the majority have thought Venus is pleasure itself. Again, the pleasure in thinking imparts an almost ceaseless action; and the pleasure in nourishment preserves the individual for a long time, and in generation makes the species everlasting and transforms the lover into the beloved and creates all things in art and nature. These operations are divine, so people call pleasure a goddess. In addition, since all desire pleasure as the end, therefore as the principle, and since they take pains to direct themselves to her, accordingly, people call her a goddess. But they call her Venus, because she is the companion of venery.

But since he was going to impugn pleasure, Socrates feared the name of Venus and didn't want pleasure to be the name of the goddess herself. As Plato says in the *Cratylus,* a name is some of the power of the thing itself.[58] Initially it is conceived in the intelligence, then articulated by the voice, finally expressed in

superiori ipsius animae parte, quam Jovem diximus, pendet, ex matre quoque Dione quia respicit in materiam. Ideo in hominibus amores duo sunt, voluptates duae, duae quoque generationes partim ad divinam speciem partim ad corpoream formam. Quod autem de Venere in Theologia[1] tractat Hesiodus, cum dicit Saturnum castrasse coelium testiculosque in mare iecisse ex quibus et spuma agitata nata sit Venus, intelligendum est forte[2] de foecunditate rerum omnium procreandarum, quae in primo rerum latet principio, quam divina mens haurit explicatque in se ipsa primum, deinde in animam[3] materiamque effundit, quod mare dicitur propter motum ac tempus et generationis humorem.

Anima cum primum ea foecunditate referta est per conversionem ad supera intelligibilem in se ipsa procreat pulchritudinem; et per conversionem ad infera sensibilium formarum in materia gignit decorem. Ex eiusmodi[4] vero conversione ad pulchritudinem eiusque generatione anima ipsa Venus est nuncupata.

Et quia in omni tam aspectu quam generatione pulchritudinis voluptas inserta est, et omnis generatio ab anima est quae Venus dicitur, plerique Venerem voluptatem ipsam esse existimaverunt. *Item voluptas et in considerando actionem reddit quasi perpetuam, et in nutritione conservat diu individuum, et in generatione speciem facit sempiternam et transformat amantem in amatum et omnia procreat in arte et natura. Haec divina opera sunt ideo appellatur dea. Adde quia omnia appetunt illam quasi finem ergo ut principium et in eam[5] se convertere student, ob haec nominant eam deam, Venerem vero quia comes est veneris.**

Socrates vero cum esset voluptatem [*344r*] impugnaturus Veneris nomen veritus est, neque voluit deae ipsius voluptatem nomen esse. Nomen sane, ut a Platone describitur[6] in Cratylo, rei ipsius vis quaedam est mente concepta primum, voce deinde

---

[1]*X also has* Theogonia   [2]forte *om. WX*   [3]anima *W*   [4]huiusmodi *WX*   [5]ea *Y*
[6]scribitur *X*   *-**om. W; shifted back (see p. 141) X*

writing. But the power of a divine thing is also divine. So we ought to venerate the names of God (since the divine power is present in them) much more than we venerate the shrines and statues of the gods. A clearer image of God is preserved in something made by the intelligence than it is in the works of the hands. In fact, in the *Cratylus* Plato wants the first and purest names of God to be in the intelligences of the heavenly spirits (by whom God is conceived with greater clarity), the second-order names to be in the demons, the third in men's souls.[59] He also says the names were revealed by the ancient holy men when they were either enraptured by God, or instructed by the intelligence's light. So God's names are like images or sunbeams of God Himself, penetrating through the heavenly beings, the heroes, the souls of men. However, whoever admires the sun venerates the sun's light too. So you must worship both God and God's sunbeams, the powers, the images lying concealed in the significance of names. Therefore, in the *Phaedrus* Plato introduces Socrates as having been seized by a demon, since he had sinned against Love, the name of a god.[60] In the *Laws* Book 11 Plato wants those people accounted sacrilegious who defile the names of gods with lying and perjuries, and to be scourged to death by anybody with impunity; moreover, if some able person doesn't punish them, he is to be accounted a traitor to the laws (Plato himself decrees this).[61] Also in the *Parmenides,* since he's compared everything to the one God, he didn't think God's names ought to be despised.[62] Dionysius the Areopagite, having copied Plato here, searches in the divine names for all the mysteries of theology.[63] Origen in his book *Against Celsus* says a miraculous power exists in certain holy names, which would not be there if the names were altered; so they mustn't be altered.[64] For this reason the Hebrews placed a miraculous power in the name "tetragrammaton." Paul gave to Him a name which is above all names.[65] Virgil wrote, "Virgin, what shall I name you?"[66] Homer says many things are named one thing among the gods, another among us.[67] Paul writes that God's word is alive.[68] Plotinus and Proclus also have things to say about names. Paul inherited a name how very different compared to those.

expressa, litteris demum significata. Rei autem divinae divina quoque vis est; quare Dei nomina cum illis divina vis insit venerari debemus, multo etiam magis quam delubra statuasque deorum. Expressior enim imago Dei in mentis artificio quam manuum operibus reservatur. Nomina vero Dei prima et sincerissima in Cratylo apud mentes numinum coelestium esse vult, a quibus expressius Deus concipitur; secunda in daemonibus; in animis hominum tertia. Et a priscis viris sanctissimis fuisse prolata, sive Deo raptis seu lumine mentis instructis. Dei itaque nomina tamquam imagines et[1] radii ipsius Dei sunt per coelicolas heroas animos hominum penetrantes. Quisquis autem solem admiratur veneratur et solis lumen, ita et Deum colere oportet et Dei radios, vires, imagines in nominum significatione latentes. Ideo in Phaedro Socratem inducit Plato cum in amorem dei nomen peccasset correptum a daemone. Et in XI Legum eos qui mendacio et periuriis nomina deorum inquinant sacrilegos haberi vult, et a quolibet impune verberibus caedi; et siquis potens[2] non punierit, legum ut ipse iubet proditor habeature. In Parmenide quoque cum omnia ad unum Deum compararet nomina illius spernenda non censuit. Quod imitatus Dionysius Areopagita omnia theologiae mysteria in divinis nominibus exquisivit.[3] *Origenes in libro contra Celsum dicit quibusdam nominibus sacris inesse mirificam virtutem quae mutatis nominibus non inesset. Ideo illa non esse mutanda. Hinc Hebraei in nomine tetragrammaton[4] miraculosam ponebant virtutem. Paulus dedit illi nomen quod est super omne nomen. Virgilius, Quam te memorem virgo? Homerus aliter apud superos aliter apud nos multa dicit nominata. Paulus, Vivus est sermo Dei. De his etiam Plotinus et Proclus. Paulus quanto differentius prae illis nomen hacreditavit.**

---

[1]et *om. W* *inserted here X* [2]praesens *WX* [3]*passage* "Item voluptas et ... est veneris" *(see p. 139)* [4]tetragammaton *Y* *-**om. W (cont.)*

Chapter 12. That there is a living force in names, especially in divine names.

It is not without great mystery that Paul attributes all the acts of a living being to the divine word, making it penetrate the spirit and the soul and the body, making it distinguish between affections and thoughts and see and hear all. It's as if God Himself were there in His words even when they're presented through the prophets, just as the power of the intelligence is there in the conception of a name even when it's presented beyond the intelligence in the imagination.

Notice that the power of a natural object reaches through the senses to the imagination, through the imagination to the intelligence by which it is apprehended and enclosed in a name, just as life and understanding are enclosed in the body. But notice that the divine power reaches through the heavenly intelligences to our intelligence by which it is apprehended and similarly named with a living name. And this name is more alive than the names of bodily objects to the extent that the movement coming down to us from those above is more powerful—coming down to us, I say, when we become more like God, that is, when we recall our intelligence from lower things.

But so great is the divine force preserved in these names that even men far removed from God and wrong-doers can work miracles by them. Finally, if permitted, I would remind you how great a power is present in the five words of the sacrament (I pass over the heretical concept that John was transformed into Christ, that is, with the words, "Woman, behold your son,"[69] and, "You, behold your mother.") These things confirm the view that many names have been found from the individual peculiarity of things.

Why does everybody call God by four letters? The Hebrews by the four vowels "he ho ha hi"; the Egyptians by "Theuth"; the Persians by "Syre"; the Magi by "Orsi" whence "Oromasis"; the Greeks by "Theos"; ourselves by "Deus"; the Arabs by "Alla"; Mahomet by "Abgdi." Again, we accepted "Jesu" from Gabriel, in which name etc.[70] Surely,

Esse vivam in nominibus virtutem praesertim divinis.
Cap. XII.[1]

*Non absque magno mysterio Paulus divino sermoni omnes viventis actus tribuit: penetrare spiritum et animam et corpus, discernere cogitationes et affectus, videre omnia et audire. Quasi Deus ipse ita sit in verbis suis etiam per prophetas prolatis, sicut mentis acies in conceptione nominis etiam praeter mentem in ipsa imaginatione prolati.

Attende vim rei naturalis per sensus ad imaginationem per hanc ad mentem pervenire, qua concipitur nominique includitur quasi vita et intelligentia corpori. Vim vero divinam per mentes superiores ad nostram, qua concipitur similiterque nominatur nomine vivo; et tanto magis vivo quam[2] nomina corporum quanto potentior a superioribus in nos provenit motus. In nos inquam cum Deo similiores evadimus, id est, quando mentem ab inferioribus sevocamus.

Tanta vero divinitatis virtus his servatur nominibus ut etiam viri a Deo remotiores atque malefici his nominibus mirabilia operentur. Denique, si fas esset, commemorarem quanta vis insit quinque sacramenti verbis (mitto haeresim, fingentem Joannem in Christum fuisse conversum, illis videlicet verbis, Mulier ecce filius tuus, et, Tu ecce mater tua). Per haec confirmatur opinio multa nomina ab ipsa rerum proprietate inventa fuisse.

Cur omnes Deum quattuor vocant litteris? Hebraei quattuor vocalibus, he ho ha hi;[3] Aegyptii, Theuth; Persae, Syre; Magi, Orsi unde Oromasis; Graeci, Theos; Nos, Deus; Arabes, Alla; Macometh,[4] Abgdi. Nos item Jesu a Gabriele accepimus, in**

---

[1] *no ch. heading or break in W; X reads* Caput Septimum. Utrum felicitas sit in voluptate an scientia aut potius in quodam mixto. Item de genere speciebusque tum voluptatis tum scientiae *(cf. ch. 13 heading on my p. 145)*   [2] quanto Y   [3] hae ho hai Y   [4] Maumethes X *(cont.)* *-**om. W (cont.)*

such diverse races would not otherwise have agreed on the one name of the unknown God, unless they were divinely inspired? And if they received it from Adam, it was by divine inspiration they received that name rather than others.

The Hebrews say that, if pronounced correctly, all miracles can be wrought in that name—which is the most difficult thing of all to do; it takes a miracle alone to pronounce it. I think God made it so difficult so nobody should say it and work miracles through it, unless like a trumpet God should proclaim through him (which shows the most acceptable of all to God was Jesus, whom the Jews acknowledge worked miracles by pronouncing that name correctly). The Jews themselves pronounce it by "Elohim"; the Greeks by a four letter word. God puts all things in order by means of four: essence, being, power, action. Celestial things He orders by means of four sets of three,[71] sub-celestial things by means of the four elements. Accordingly, He wanted to be represented by four letters.

Chapter 13. Whether felicity is in pleasure, or knowledge, or rather in some third thing. Again, concerning the genus and the several species both of pleasure and of knowledge.

Since Socrates wanted to know the good itself, he brought pleasure and knowledge into the argument (which are thought to be the greatest goods among men), so it might be apparent from a comparison between them which is the better one and whether either of them is the good itself, or both are, or some third thing is. But in order to make the comparison and decide, it is necessary to know about them both beforehand. But each one is a certain genus containing many species under it and under the species an infinite number of individual things, so it is necessary to divide each one into its species for it to be understood by knowledge. For, as Plato says in the *Sophist* and the *Statesman*, whoever is going to understand any genus of things perfectly mustn't rest content with the general notion itself of the genus, nor wander about through an infinite number of

*quo nomine etc. Certe non aliter tam diversae gentes in uno ignoti Dei nomine convenissent, nisi divinitus. Ac si acceperunt ab Adam divinitus hoc potius quam alia acceperunt.

Tradunt Hebraei in nomine illo omnia fieri posse miracula, si vere pronuntietur quod est[1] omnium difficillimum et miraculo solo[2] pronuntiatur. Deum puto adeo difficile instituisse, ut nemo pronuntiaret miraculaque per ipsum faceret, nisi Deus per ipsum quasi per tubam clamaret. Quod ostendit Jesum Deo fuisse omnium acceptissimum, quem fatentur Judaei per id nomen recte pronuntiatum fecisse miracula. Ipsi vero id per Heloin pronuntiant;[3] Graeci per tetragrammaton.[4] Deus omnia disponit per quattuor:[5] essentiam, esse, vim, actionem. Coelestia per quattuor triplicitates; sub coelum per quattuor elementa. Sic quattuor voluit litteris exprimi.**

Utrum felicitas sit in voluptate an scientia aut potius in quodam tertio. Item de genere speciebusque, tum voluptatis tum scientiae. Cap. XIII.[6]

[*344v*] Quoniam cupit Socrates bonum ipsum cognoscere, voluptatem et scientiam, quae maxima inter homines bona existimantur, in disceptationem traxit, ut his inter se comparatis utrum[7] horum melius sit eluceret, et numquid istorum alterum ipsum bonum sit, vel utrumque vel tertium. Ad hanc vero comparationem iudiciumque necesse est ante utriusque illorum habere scientiam. Sed utrumque genus aliquod est multas sub se species et singula sub speciebus continens infinita, quare necesse est utrumque in species suas dividere ut utrumque scientia comprehendatur. Nam, ut in Sophiste et in libro de Regno docet Plato, quisquis aliquod genus rerum perfecte est cogniturus, neque in ipsa communi generis notione quiescere debet, neque per singula infinita vagari. Scientia siquidem[8] perfecta est et

---

[1]est *om. Y*   [2]solo *om. X*   [3]pronuntiat *Y*   [4]tetragammaton *Y*   [5]*for* per quattuor *Y reads* scilicet per   [6]*no ch. heading or break W; a break only X*   [7]quid *WX*
[8]quidem *W*   *(cont.)* *-**om. W*

single things, since knowledge is the perfect and certain comprehension of each thing.[72] But a universal power and potentiality
for the many species lies concealed in any genus; and the person
who doesn't know about a thing's power doesn't perfectly comprehend the thing itself. So you have to understand the power
of the genus, if you're going to profess knowledge of the genus.
However, power either aims at giving something through
action, or receiving something through passivity. In the end it
arrives at some result. But the genus' power and potentiality for
the species is terminated through the differences. So the person
who's going to understand the creative power of a genus and the
result of its creativeness has to know about the differences and
the species. When you know about the species, there's no point
wandering around through single things. For they can't be
enumerated, because they're infinite, and there's no firm and
definite comprehension of them in the soul, because they are
changed every single moment. So whoever wants to know about
any genus of things can neither remain in the genus nor roam
about to infinity through individuals. But rather, having a
notion of the common genus, he must seek out a distinct and
unconditional understanding of it in its species where the whole
power of the genus is perfected. For individuals add nothing to
the species that can increase the power of the genus. Rather,
those things peculiar to individuals are certain extraneous passivities; they are completely foreign to the substance of the
species. For this reason the species of both pleasure and
knowledge must be investigated since both are genera.

But if someone's wondering that Plato should attempt to
divide these things before defining them, he must understand
that some ordinary natural description of a thing has to precede
all division of it. Given this, you have to try to divide the general
concept into its properties so the definition can be more clearly
and precisely understood. Accordingly, since everybody understands what is meant by the term, pleasure or knowledge, that is
to say, recognition of the truth and enjoyment of life, they can
work out from the general description how many ways pleasure
can be obtained and knowledge can be perceived—in which case

certa cuiusque comprehensio. Sed in genere quolibet vis quaedam communis et potentia ad species multas latet; et qui rei vim
ignorat rem ipsam haud perfecte comprehendit. Vim ergo
generis teneat oportet, qui generis scientiam sit professurus. Vis
autem seu per actionem ad aliquid dandum, sive per passionem
ad accipiendum tendat; ad effectum denique nonnullum pervenit. Vis autem generis et potentia[1] per differentias ad species
terminatur. Differentias ergo et species teneat opus est, qui
generis vim foecundam et effectum foecunditatis ipsius sit
cogniturus. Cognitis autem speciebus vagari per singula irritum
opus est. Nam cum infinita sint dinumerari non possunt, et quia
singulis momentis mutantur nulla de his [*345r*] firma est in
animo certaque comprehensio. Quisquis ergo genus aliquod
rerum cognoscere cupit, neque resistat in genere, neque per singula in infinitum pererret,[2] sed communis[3] generis habita
notione distinctam eius et absolutam in speciebus ipsius quaerat
intelligentiam, in quibus tota vis generis adimpletur. Nihil enim
singula speciebus addunt quod vim generis augeat. Sed
quaecumque singulis propria sunt extraneae quaedam passiones
sunt, et a speciei[4] substantia penitus alienae. Quare et species
voluptatis scientiaeque investigandae sunt, cum genera quaedam sint utraque.

Siquis vero admiretur quod Plato divisionem istorum tentet
prius quam definitionem, intelligat ante omnem rei partitionem
naturalem quandam et vulgarem ipsius rei haberi descriptionem. Qua posita, ut definitio distinctior et certior comprehendatur, divisio communis conceptionis in proprias quaeritur.
Ideo cum quid nomine voluptatis et scientiae significatur omnes
intelligant scilicet veritatis cognitio et iucunditas vitae, ex hac
communi descriptione investigant quot modis comparari illa et
haec percipi possit, ubi dividunt. Quo invento, et communis[5]

---

[1]potentiae *X*   [2]pergeret *X*   [3]communi *XY*   [4]rei *WX*   [5]communius *X*

they are dividing. When they have discovered this, they comprehend perfectly all the power of the common genus and its individual parts, that is, they grasp the rational principle of the species. So Plato tells us to use a common description everyone knows when we divide, to define from this division, finally from the definition to reassess the division more carefully and to demonstrate in a more precise way the power and the quality of a thing.

However, Socrates begins with the genus of pleasure, as it is better known than the genus of knowledge. And he shows plea-
12C   sure is usually a genus thus: "Everybody thinks the genus is what is predicated about many species with reference to what it is. But pleasure is predicated of many species, for pleasure seems to have one particular nature: namely, a person is delighted when it is present; and because of this one nature, pleasure is said to be some one thing. But it ought to be called many things as well, because it contains various and dissimilar forms, that is, species under it. For to be delighted, which properly comes from pleasure, occurs in many ways and from different things. We say an intemperate man is delighted by some lewdness, a temperate man by sobriety; an insane man is delighted by some foolish hope and wild opinions, the prudent man by reasonable hope and mature reflection.

"But the person who denies these four species of pleasure are different and dissimilar is indubitably deranged. For what else are these delights if they're not particular movements or dispositions of souls or bodies? But the movements and dispositions, which have been brought about in men in dissimilar ways from dissimilar occasions for dissimilar effects and ends, are certainly dissimilar also among themselves."

Protarchus did not assent immediately to Socrates' argument
12D   but interrupted, "Socrates, although these pleasures proceed from opposites, they aren't, nevertheless, opposite among themselves. For in so far as they are pleasures, among themselves they are of all things most alike."

12E   Socrates counters him thus, "If you deny on this account that the species of pleasure are dissimilar, because each one is a

generis vim omnem perfecte comprehendunt et singularum partium, id est, specierum rationem tenent. Ideo Plato ex communi descriptione omnibus nota dividendum monet, ex hac divisione definiendum, denique ex definitione divisionem distinctius iudicandam et rei vim et qualitatem certius demonstrandam.

A voluptatis autem genere incipit Socrates, quia notius est quam scientiae genus. Atque ita ferme voluptatem esse genus ostendit: genus esse id omnes [*345v*] putant quod de speciebus pluribus in eo quod quid est praedicatur. Voluptas autem de pluribus dicitur speciebus, una enim quaedam videtur esse voluptatis natura, ut scilicet ea praesente quis delectetur; et propter hanc naturam unam unum quoddam voluptas dicitur. Dici quoque debet et multa, quia formas, id est, species sub se varias et dissimiles continet. Nam delectari quod proprie ex voluptate est multis contingit modis diversisque ex rebus. Delectari dicimus intemperantem hominem lascivia quadam, temperantem[1] sobrietate; delectari insanum levi quadam spe temerariisque opinionibus, prudentem consulta spe et matura sententia.

Atque has quattuor species voluptatum siquis differentes et dissimiles esse negaverit, procul dubio delirabit. Quid enim aliud delectationes istae, nisi vel motus quidam vel affectiones aliquae animorum vel corporum. Motus autem affectionesque in hominibus dissimiliter affectis ex dissimilibus occasionibus ad effectus terminosque dissimiles dissimiles certe inter se et ipsi sunt.

Huic autem Socratis rationi haud statim consensit Protarchus, sed intulit: Voluptates istae, O Socrates, quamquam contrariis a rebus proficiscuntur, non tamen invicem ipsae contrariae. Nam qua voluptates sunt inter se omnium simillimae sunt.

Contra eum ita Socrates: Si ex hoc voluptatis species dissimiles esse negaveris, quia unaquaeque voluptas sit, in quolibet

---

[1]temperantem *repeated Y*

pleasure, you'll deny in the same way that there are dissimilar species in any other genus whatsoever, because the nature of each genus is found in its species. Therefore you'll say white and black are like each other, because each is a colour, when nevertheless, they are not only unlike but opposite, because within the genus of colour they are as far from each other as possible. Certainly, the colour white and the colour grey are alike; but white and red are unlike; and white and black are opposite. For each quality is like the one next to it, unlike the one further off, but opposite to the one furthest off. You're at liberty to see this in the case of tastes, and in a way with sounds and smells and things affecting the touch. Moreover, within the genus of shape itself mutually dissimilar and (in some respects) opposite species are present. For the triangle is sufficiently like a quadrangle, very unlike a pentagon, completely opposite to the circle. Although the one genus, shape, is included in all these species, still, nothing prevents the shapes from being very dissimilar. For any genus whatsoever (in that the species are under it) has to be divided into the species by means of opposite differences; a species is constituted from the genus and a difference. In the same way as we say a higher place and a lower place are opposites not because of their dimensions, but because of the opposite powers inherent in them, so we say the cube, i.e., a figure with six faces, is opposite to a pyramid. We are following the Pythagoreans here, because it is they who think the cube is appropriate to the earth, the pyramid to fire. Colour in fact exists in whiteness, but it is a transparent colour; it also exists in blackness, but it is opaque. Animality is present in man, but it is rational; it is present in a beast, but it is irrational. As long as a genus remains one in itself and simple and everywhere similar to itself, no species is produced; hence it's not a genus either. As soon as a number of species is produced, what was one genus in itself is now shown to be distinguished by various differences. And since the species are made from the division of the genus through the differences, the genus' division (and limitation) through the differences precedes every possible species. The differences were lying hidden

itidem alio genere species sub eo dissimiles negabis esse, cum
generis cuiusque natura in speciebus suis reperiatur. Dices
itaque album et nigrum similia invicem, quia color utrumque
sit, cum tamen non dissimilia [*346r*] tantum ista sint, sed contraria, quia maxime inter se sub coloris genere distant. Profecto
albus color et glaucus similes, albus autem et rubeus dissimiles,
albus et niger contrarii. Nam qualitas quaeque ad propinquam
similis, ad remotiorem dissimilis, ad remotissimam vero contraria. Quod in saporibus vocibus quodammodo et odoribus et
his quae ad tactum pertinent intueri licet. Quin etiam in figurae
ipsius genere species inter se dissimiles et quodammodo
contrariae insunt. Nam triangulus quadrangulo satis similis,
pentagono dissimilior, circulo ferme contrarius. Quamvis in
omnibus his speciebus unum figurae genus sit inclusum, nihil
tamen prohibet quominus dissimiles figurae sint. Nam in quolibet genere eo ipso quod species sub eo[1] sunt per oppositas differentias divisum in eas genus sit oportet, ex quo et differentia
fuerit species constituta. *Sicut locum superiorem et inferiorem
contraria dicimus non propter dimensiones sed virtutes
contrarias in illis constitutas, ita figuram cubicam, id est, sex
facierum contrariam dicimus pyramidi secundum Pythagoricos.
Propterea quod cubicam terrae, pyramidem igni propriam esse
putant.** Color quidem inest albo sed lucidus color; inest et
nigro sed opacus. Inest animal homini sed rationale, inest bruto
sed rationis expers. Quoad[2] genus in se ipso unum et simplex
manet et sibi undique simile, nulla nascitur species; unde neque
est genus. Cum primum multae nascuntur species, quod unum
in se erat genus differentiis variis significatur iam esse distinctum. Cumque ex partitione generis per differentias species
constituantur, quamcumque[3] speciem generis praecedit partitio
limitatioque per differentias quae sicut in materia potentia

---

[1]ipso *X*   [2]Quod ad *Y*   [3]quacumque *W*   *-**om. W*

in the genus like potentiality in matter, but they are led into act to make the species. Therefore the genus has already been made different and particular when the species arises. So the species differ inside the genus, because the genus accords with one or other of the species under one or other of its properties now issuing into act. Species are distinguished among themselves by these substantial differences.

"So Protarchus' objection is futile; and it isn't convincing either, since the same reasoning applies to all the other genera. He will argue that all that's in the genus is entirely one. There won't be any opposites in any genus or opposing differences. So there won't be species either. So you won't find any genus in things. Protarchus' reasoning was: the species are under the same genus, so they aren't dissimilar. To this we'll add: so they aren't different. So the species won't be mutually distinguishable through the differences. So with every difference excluded we'll find only the genus in the species. But the genus without the differences is one. So everything in the genus will be one. So the opposite qualities which are in the same genus will also be utterly the same."

To this argument in which he confirms that the genus of pleasure contains dissimilar species in it, Socrates adds another. He says he's afraid some pleasures can be found to be not only perhaps unlike but mutually opposite too: for instance, the pleasure sensed in repletion compared to that from evacuation, the pleasure from heat compared to that from cold, the pleasure from movement compared to that from rest, the one from contemplation compared to that from intercourse. For movements are like the ends for which they exist, the subjects in which they are, the affections from which they come. The pleasures we've described dwell in these opposites and come from opposing desires and mutually impede and avoid each other; nor can the results of opposites come together. Being young, Protarchus replied to the points with too little caution. Since Socrates had said he was afraid some pleasures would be found even mutually opposed, Protarchus casually replied, too confident as it were, "But how will this run counter to my view?" Then Socrates

13A

latebant in #genere, in actum vero reducuntur ad speciem fabricandam. Iam igitur differens et proprium factum est genus cum species oritur. Unde differunt [*346v*] in genere species, quia sub alia et alia sui proprietate iam in actum exeunte aliis et aliis competit speciebus, quibus substantialibus differentiis inter se species distinguuntur.

Quapropter obiectio illa Protarchi futilis est neque illi est credendum, quia per omnia alia genera eadem ratio repetita. Unum omnino quodcumque sub genere est esse concludet. Neque in aliquo genere ulla erunt contraria, neque oppositae differentiae; ergo neque species. Quare nec in rebus genus ullum reperietur. Ratio Protarchi erat haec: species sub eodem genere sunt, ergo dissimiles non sunt. Huic nos addemus: ergo neque differentes, ergo species invicem per differentias non distinguentur. Solum ergo genus omni exclusa[1] differentia in speciebus reperietur. Genus autem sine differentiis unum est. Unum igitur erunt omnia quac in genere. Ergo et contrariae qualitates quae in eodem sunt genere idem erunt omnino.

Huic argumentationi qua[2] confirmat Socrates voluptatis genus dissimiles sub se species continere, addit ipse idem ulterius, metuere se ne forte voluptates quaedam non modo dissimiles sed et contrariae sibi invicem reperiantur: puta voluptas quac in repletione percipitur ad eam quae in evacuatione provenit; voluptas quae ex calore ad eam quae ex frigore; quae ex motu ad eam quae ex quiete; quae ex contemplatione ad eam quae ex coitu. Tales enim sunt[3] motus quales termini ad quos, qualia subiecta in quibus, quales affectiones ex quibus exeunt. Atqui voluptates quas narravimus circa contraria ista versantur et ex oppositis appetitibus[4] et sese impediunt fugantque [*347r*] neque invicem congredi possunt quae contrariorum[5] opera sunt. Protarchus ad haec utpote adolescentulus parum respondit caute. Quippe cum dixisset Socrates metuere se ne etiam contrariae quaedam inter se voluptates reperiréntur,[6] forte respondit: At hoc opinioni meae quomodo adversabitur; quasi nimis

¹conclusa *W*   ²quia *WXP*   ³ut *add. W*   ⁴et ex oppositis appetitibus *om. WXP*
⁵contrariora *W*   ⁶reperientur *W*   #*P frag. II (41r) begins*

suddenly blasts pleasure by an unexpected attack. He immediately goes back to the proposed division, for he says, "The concession that some pleasures are mutually opposed doesn't invali-
date your view that all the species of pleasures exist as pleasures
although in dissimilar things; for no reason prevents all the
species of pleasure from being pleasures. But it does affect your
desire for pleasures to be good. We maintain most are bad, because many are mutually dissimilar. However, you're forced to
acknowledge some are both dissimilar and opposite, and yet,
you don't hesitate to call them all good. So you find out what is
common and identical in all pleasures, the good as well as those
which it is agreed are bad, and by the participation of this common factor you call all pleasures good. It's as if you were
saying: 'We find a common factor in all pleasures, the nature of
pleasure.' But we see some pleasures are bad, namely, those
opposite to the good ones. But this is contrary to the view you
were maintaining that the nature of pleasure and of the good is
the same. For if it were, just as the nature of pleasure is common to all pleasures and makes them all pleasures, so the nature
of the good would be common to them all as well. So all pleasures would be good. But they aren't all good. So the nature of
the good is not common to them all, and yet the nature of pleasure is common to them all. So the nature of the good is not the
same as the nature of pleasure. So pleasure isn't the good itself,
for the entire rational principle of the good would be in it."

Health is predicated through analogy: firstly, of a stable con-
stitution; secondly, of the things which contribute towards it;
thirdly, of the symptoms attesting to it. It can also be predicated
of the sharpness of the senses which both contribute and refer
to it. Similarly the human good is predicated through analogy:
firstly, of felicity; secondly, of the moral attitudes contributing
towards it; thirdly, of the pleasure which attests to it; fourthly,
not of the degree but of the kind of knowledge referring and
contributing to it. Certainly, all that's correctly denominated by
one particular name agrees in one particular nature, just as you
denominate all delights by the general name of pleasure because
they all share in the one disposition of pleasure. But if pleasure

confideret. Unde Socrates subito quodam et inopinato impetu voluptatem effulminat, at statim ad propositam divisionem revertitur. Inquit enim: Concessio ista quod voluptates quaedam inter se contrariae sunt nihil ad id nocet quod ais omnes species voluptatum licet dissimilibus in rebus voluptates existere; nulla enim ratio prohibet quin omnes species voluptatis voluptates sint, sed ad illud officit quod volebas[1] omnes voluptates bonas esse. Nos enim plerasque malas asserimus, cum multae invicem dissimiles sint. Tu autem fateri cogeris nonnullas et dissimiles et contrarias esse, et tamen bonas omnes appellare non dubitas. Quid ergo commune et idem in omnibus reperis voluptatibus tam bonis quam[2] illis, quas esse malas constat, cuius participatione bonas omnes praedicas. Quasi dicat: commune aliquid reperimus in omnibus voluptatibus voluptatis naturam. Videmus autem aliquas esse malas eas scilicet quae bonis contrariae sunt. Id autem[3] contra illam positionem est, qua[4] ponebas eandem esse voluptatis bonique naturam; si enim ita esset, ut communis[5] est[6] voluptatis natura omnibus voluptatibus unde omnes sunt voluptates, ita et boni natura omnibus esset communis;[7] unde omnes essent bonae. Non sunt autem omnes bonae; ergo non omnibus natura boni communis. Et tamen voluptatis natura omnibus [*347v*] est communis; ergo non eadem boni voluptatisque natura. Non ergo voluptas ipsum est bonum, esset enim in ea tota ratio boni.

Sanum per analogiam praedicatur: primo de firma habitudine; secundo de his quae ad eam conferunt; tertio de signis quae referunt. Potest etiam[8] praedicari de perspicacia sensuum quae et confert et refert. Similiter humanum bonum per analogiam: primo de felicitate; secundo de moribus ad eam conducentibus; tertio de voluptate eam repraesentante; quarto non quidem gradu sed modo de scientia et referente et conferente. Certe quaecumque uno quodam nomine vere denominantur una quadam in natura conveniunt, ut omnes delectationes communi

[1] nolebas *W*   [2] quam *om. Y*   [3] quod *add. W*   [4] quia *XP*   [5,7] communius *Y*
[6] esset *P*   [8] etiam *om. W*

were the good itself, the rational principle of pleasure and the good would be the same. So wherever one came upon the rational principle of pleasure, there would be the rational principle of the good as well. But the rational principle of pleasure is peculiar to all the species of pleasure, so the rational principle of the good would be peculiar to them as well; so all the pleasures would be good. Yet all the pleasures can't be good, since most of them are unlike and opposite. But the good is neither opposite to nor unlike the good. In fact, the nature of the good is to preserve and to be desired, but the nature of the opposite is to destroy and put to flight. No one good destroys or puts to flight another good. On the contrary, a higher good preserves and perfects a lower, but the lower desires the higher. However, to the extent that something called good were to destroy something else that was good, it would be bad, since badness is the deprivation of good. But the deprivation of good is bad. The bad is also what destroys good. Good things are not unlike each other; rather, they are alike, since it's proper for similar things to preserve themselves and mutually and freely to admit each other. But all preservation is good from the good, and it is for the good. Each desire too, which is excited by the good, turns towards the good. Therefore, since good things are not mutually unlike or opposite, but lots of pleasures are mutually unlike or opposite, not all pleasures are good. On the contrary, lots of them are bad, namely those unlike or opposite to the good ones. So pleasure is not the good itself.

Chapter 14. Pleasures are mutually dissimilar, otherwise impossibilities would result. Again, concerning the differences of the [several] species within the genus.

Protarchus does not admit Socrates' reason whereby pleasure is overthrown. But he says he rejects the division in which it is maintained some pleasures are good and some bad, so that he won't be forced to acknowledge pleasure is not the good itself. Socrates says to him, "But you can't reject this division, if you

13B-D

nomine voluptatis appellas, quia omnibus convenit voluptatis unus affectus. Sin autem voluptas ipsum bonum esset, eadem esset et boni voluptatisque[1] ratio. Ubicumque igitur ratio voluptatis ibi et ratio boni inveniretur.[2] Voluptatis autem ratio omnibus voluptatis speciebus convenit, quare et boni; unde[3] et bonae[4] essent omnes. Bonae tamen[5] omnes esse non possunt, cum pleraeque dissimiles et[6] contrariae sint. Bonum vero bono neque contrarium est, neque dissimile; natura quidem boni est conservare et appeti, contrarii vero perimere atque fugare. Nullum bonum alterum bonum perdit et fugat, immo superius bonum bonum inferius servat et perficit, inferius autem superius expetit. Quatenus autem unum quod bonum dicitur aliud bonum perderet, eatenus malum esset, siquidem malum est privatio boni. Sin privatio boni est malum, malum est et id quod bonum destruit. Neque dissimilia [*348r*] bona sunt invicem, immo similia potius, cum similium proprium sit sese conservare, sese mutuo libenter adsciscere. Omnis autem conservatio a bono est bona et est ad bonum. Appetitio quoque omnis quae[7] a bono excitatur in bonum vergit. Cum igitur bona invicem contraria et dissimilia non sint, voluptates autem multae invicem dissimiles atque contrariae, non omnes voluptates bonae; immo malae complurimae quae bonis scilicet dissimiles sunt et contrariae. Non ergo voluptas ipsum est bonum.

Voluptates inter se dissimiles sunt, alioquin sequentur impossibilia. Item de differentia specierum sub genere.
Cap. XIV.[8]

Rationem Socratis, qua voluptas prosternitur, Protarchus nequaquam admittit, sed ait illam se divisionem reicere, qua asseritur voluptates partim bonas esse partim malas, ne cogatur fateri voluptatem bonum ipsum non esse. Ad quem Socrates: At non potes partitionem hanc spernere, si admiseris voluptates

---

[1]et voluptatis *XP*   [2]invenitur *P*   [3]unum *W*   [4]bene *W*   [5]tandem *Y*
[6]et *om. W*   [7]quae *om. WXP*   [8]*no ch. heading, but paragraph break WXP*

admit pleasures are mutually unlike and opposite.'' Protarchus
says, ''In fact, I don't admit it; for, in so far as they are pleasures, they aren't unlike and opposite.'' But Socrates refutes
this, ''If, in order to avoid the dissimilarity and opposition of
pleasures, we were to say they aren't dissimilar in so far as
they're pleasures, we'll also say they don't differ in so far as
they're pleasures. But things that don't differ are entirely one.
So there will not be lots of pleasures. So pleasure will not be a
genus. Nor could many persons be affected by pleasure
together, especially from different things; but only one pleasure
will emerge. But all this is absurd.

''Certainly, pleasures don't differ as pleasure; but then they
aren't the species (or pleasures), but pleasure, that is, the genus
itself. But we're looking for the species not the genus. But since
pleasures exist, they exist as species, and as such they also differ;
for they presuppose a genus that has been divided already
through the differences and included in them under one or other
reason. So within the genus the species differ, since they don't
accept the genus until it's been divided. A genus differs within
the several species, since it belongs to them under one or other
of its reasons. The species differ among themselves through the
differences which establish them in actuality. So whoever denies
the species differ on the grounds they have the same genus in
them is denying the genus has been divided into them through
the differences. So he's doing away with the species and leaving
behind the genus alone. So every possible thing will be one.

''So what you have to say is that the species in the genus both
agree and differ. They agree in so far as some one common
nature of the genus imparts itself to them. But they differ in so
far as the genus, before imparting itself to them, has already
been divided through the differences (which are in it in potentiality and issue into act). Under one or other of its characteristics
the genus is imprinted in some or other of the species. For the
differences are not sought for entirely externally. They are
drawn out of the guts, as it were, of the genus itself.

''But the examples offered above will not persuade you. Yet
you've conceded them to be true. What's going to happen to us

inter se dissimiles et contrarias esse. Tum ille: Hanc equidem non admitto. Neque enim dissimiles[1] et contrariae sunt, qua voluptates sunt. At hoc refutat Socrates: Quia si, ut vitemus dissimilitudinem contrarietatemque voluptatum, dixerimus non ex eo esse dissimiles quod voluptates sunt, dicemus etiam non differre quantum[2] sunt[3] voluptates. Quae vero non differunt unum sunt omnino. Non multae igitur voluptates erunt, neque voluptas igitur genus erit, neque poterunt[4] multi simul affici voluptate, praesertim diversis ex rebus, sed una dumtaxat voluptas proveniet. Haec vero absurda sunt omnia.

Profecto voluptates non differunt ut voluptas sic autem non sunt species neque voluptates, sed voluptas[5] scilicet[6] ipsum genus. Nos autem de speciebus [*348v*] quaerimus non de genere. Ut autem voluptates sunt, sic species sunt et sic etiam differunt. Praesupponunt enim genus iam per differentias esse divisum et sub alia[7] et alia ratione illis inclusum. Differunt ergo in genere species, quoniam[8] non ante accipiunt genus quam divisum fuerit. Differt genus in speciebus, quoniam[9] sub alia[10] et alia sui ratione illis competit. Differunt inter se per differentias quae[11] species actu constituunt. Qui igitur differre species negat ex eo quod idem in se genus habent, negat genus illud in eis per differentias esse divisum. Tollit igitur species, genus relinquit solum; unum igitur erit quodcumque.

Quid ergo dicendum quod species in genere[12] et conveniunt simul et differunt: conveniunt quidem[13] quantum[14] una quaedam communis natura generis sese illis communicat; differunt vero[15] quantum,[16] antequam illis sese[17] communicet,[18] per differentias quae in eo potentia sunt exeuntes in actum iam distinctum est. Et sub alio sui[19] charactere aliis et aliis imprimitur speciebus. Neque enim omnino[20] extrinsecus quaeruntur differentiae, sed ex generis ipsius quasi[21] visceribus educuntur.

---

[1]sunt *add. P*   [2]inquantum *WXP*   [3]sunt *om. WXP*   [4]poterint *WY*
[5]voluptates *Y*   [6]scilicet *om. W*   [7,10](*for* sub alia) substantialia *W*
[8,9]inquantum *WXP*   [11]in *W*   [12]in genere *om. Y*   [13]quidem *om. WXP*
[14,16]inquantum *WXP*   [15]vero *om. WXP*   [17]se *XP*   [18]communicit *W*   [19]suo *W*
[20]omnino *om. WXP*   [21]quasi *om. WXP*

is what usually happens to cowardly people and people unused to debating; for they fall from one mistake into many and they aren't consistent and they don't pursue the truth but charge after their opponent. If I wanted to copy you (Socrates says), what you're doing to pleasure I could do to all the remaining genera. In the case of substance, I can say that none of its species differ among themselves in so far as they are substances, similarly in the cases of quantity, quality, relation, activity, passivity, and the rest. And in this way the highest member of each genus wouldn't differ in any way from the lowest member, nor would quality differ from quality (although many of them are opposite and in turn repel each other). I can even say that one genus doesn't differ from another in so far as both are genera, and that in the universal order the highest member doesn't differ from the lowest in so far as each is said to be a member of the same order. And thus all will be one and every dissimilar thing will be the same as and most like whatever it is most unlike. And if two things are said to be among themselves in some way the most dissimilar of all, I shall show by your reasoning they are also utterly similar to each other. Just as one thing is most unlike another thing, so the other thing is most unlike the one thing. So they don't differ in the fact that they are most unlike, for they are equally most unlike. Things which don't differ at all are alike. So the things that are most unlike are in turn things that are alike.

"So (says Socrates), if I shall dare to maintain dissimilar things are similar things, that is, if I want to wander around all the genera of things by means of these useless quibbles, I'll be doing the same thing that you've done with pleasure. It will follow from such arguing that the most dissimilar thing is most similar to the thing it is most dissimilar to. In fact, the puerile and pointless inquiry will make us ridiculous and do away with the discussion in hand; for, if we're going to linger over it too scrupulously, the problem under debate will not be resolved."

After this he turns towards the types of knowledge, saying they ought to direct themselves again to the separation of the genera under discussion and recall the previous argument. But

Exempla vero[1] in superioribus posita nihil persuadebunt, quae tamen vera esse concessa sunt. Idque nobis eveniet, quod evenire solet hominibus ignavissimis et ad disserendum minime consuetis. Solent enim ex uno errore in multos incidere, neque sibi constare, neque veritatem sequi, sed insequi disputantem. Ego enim te, inquit Socrates, si imitari voluero, quod et tu in voluptate facis, potero et in ceteris omnibus[2] generibus facere. In substantia enim qua substantiae sunt nullas eius species inter se differre dicam. In quantitate similiter, qualitate,[3] relatione, actione, et passione ac reliquis, atque ita supremum [*349r*] cuiusque[4] generis nihilo ab infimo differret, neque qualitas a qualitate, quamquam multae contrariae sunt seque invicem fugant. Neque etiam genus unum ab alio quantum[5] utraque sunt [genera] differre dicam. Neque in rerum ordine supremum ab infimo quantum[6] utrumque aliquid eiusdem ordinis esse dicitur. Atque ita omnia unum erunt et dissimillimum quodque dissimillimo cuique idem erit atque simillimum. Et siqua duo inter se dissimillima omnium esse dicantur, illa quoque simillima invicem[7] tua illa ratione esse monstrabo. Nempe sicut unum alteri dissimillimum est, ita et alterum uni est dissimillimum. In eo igitur quod dissimillima sunt non differunt, aeque enim sunt dissimillima. Quae nihilo differunt similia[8] sunt. Quare dissimillima quaeque invicem sunt similia.[9]

Ego igitur, inquit Socrates, si asserere hoc audebo quod dissimilia[10] similia[11] sint, id est, si voluero per inutiles cavillationes istas vagari in omnibus rerum generibus, idem quod et tu in voluptate efficiam. Ex quo discursu sequetur dissimillimum quodque dissimillimo cuique esse simillimum. Quae quidem puerilis et inutilis inquisitio nos ridiculos reddet sermonemque propositum e medio tollet. Nam si in hoc superstitiosius immorabimur, quaestio proposita minime absolvetur.

Post haec ad scientias se convertit, dicens rursus propositorum generum partitionem esse tentandam et superiorem

---

[1]autem *WXP*   [2]omnibus *om. P*   [3]qualitate *om. P*   [4]cuius *Y*
[5],[6]inquantum *WXP*   [7]invicem *om. WXP*   [8]dissimillima *W;* simillima *XP*
[9]simillima *WXP*   [10]dissimillima *WXP*   [11]simillima *WXP*

if there's a chance for him to return to the original point and so resume the line of approach which Protarchus pursued above, perhaps (he says) they could come to a mutual understanding very conveniently. He says, "Protarchus, say I'm asked by you as follows: 'Socrates, wisdom, knowledge, intelligence and the other things you called good above (when you were asked what the good itself was), won't they come under the same conditions as pleasure, since the types of knowledge will seem to be many and some mutually dissimilar?' But if I were thus asked and perhaps suspected some types of knowledge did appear to be contrary, and if (in order to avoid the question) I immediately denied one type of knowledge was dissimilar to another, surely I wouldn't be worthy of the present argument? Certainly, if you do this with pleasure and I do the same with knowledge, you won't let the genus of pleasure be divided into species through the particular differences, and I won't let the genus of knowledge. So neither of them will be understood by a perfect and definite knowledge. So neither of them can be compared to each other or to another; nor can the good be understood in case it's one of them or both or another or whichever of them is the better. Accordingly, we will be playing at debating and this theme of ours will vanish away, since nobody is listening to true reason because of stubbornness. As the proverb says: The legend will be lost when it's told to a corpse.⁷³ But we will escape safely through a lack of argument; because, since it can't be understood which is the better of the two, neither of us will be defeated. But it will be the result of a lack of argument. For either it will be we don't know how to reason because of inexperience, or we don't listen to reasons because of pigheadedness. Still, we mustn't tolerate this just so we can escape unharmed and safe and entire. We must think, so we can safely preserve our own reason at the same time as the argument under discussion.

"So, having cleared such trifles out of the way, it must be equally agreed and established in your argument and in mine that pleasures are dissimilar and many. There are also many and different types of knowledge. But there are no opposite types of

orationem revocandam esse, quod si vicissitudine quadam fiat et[1] in easdem ansas redeatur, ita ut ipse rursus eandem vicem subeat quam supra[2] Protarchus, commodius forte sibi invicem concessuros ait. Pone enim, inquit, interrogatum me ita abs te, Protarche: Nonne sapientia, [*349v*] scientia, mens, O Socrates, et alia quae supra dixisti esse bona interrogatus quid ipsum esset bonum, idem patientur quod et voluptas, multae siquidem scientiae[3] videbuntur esse et aliquae inter se dissimiles. Ego autem si ita rogatus suspicarer, ne forte et aliquae scientiae contrariae apparerent utque id declinarem, negarem protinus scientiam aliquam alicui dissimilem esse, an praesenti disputatione[4] dignus essem[5]? Nempe si tu ita circa voluptatem egeris, atque ego itidem circa scientiam, neque tu in species dividi per[6] proprias differentias voluptatis genus permittes, neque ego scientiae. Neutrum itaque perfecta et certa scientia comprehendetur. Quare nec invicem vel ad aliud comparari poterunt, neque intelligi bonum, ne sit corum alterum vel utrumque vel aliud vel quid eorum sit melius. Quapropter ludemus[7] operam et nostra haec oratio evanescet, cum propter pertinaciam vera ratio minime audiatur, et ut proverbio fertur: Fabula disperdetur cum verba fiant mortuo. Nos autem sospites evademus quodam rationis defectu, quia, cum non possit intelligi quid ex illis melius sit, neuter erit convictus. Id autem defectu rationis eveniet. Nam ex eo quod nec ratiocinari scimus ob imperitiam neque rationes ob pertinaciam auscultamus. Neque tamen id tolerandum est, ut sospites quidem nos et integri et incolumes evadamus. Ita est cogitandum ut et ratio simul nobiscum et disputatio proposita integra conservetur.

Nugis itaque huiusmodi[8] praetermissis, par istud in tua ac mea oratione ponendum ratumque habendum ut multae sint et dissimiles voluptates. Multae quoque differentesque scientiae;

---

[1]et *om.* W   [2]super W   [3]et *add.* XP   [4]disputationi P   [5]esse W
[6]per *om.* W   [7]laudemus W   [8]huiuscemodi WXP

knowledge. For if there were any, the types of knowledge of
opposite things would be completely opposite; which is not true,
for they are in the same soul at the same time. On the contrary,
it is the same knowledge generally which knows opposites. So
don't let us conceal the differences between your good and
mine, Protarchus, but let's draw together for the common
good, so we can learn by careful refutation whether pleasure is
the good itself or wisdom or some third thing. For we ought not
to defend our own views obstinately, or hold them doggedly,
but we ought to search for the truth." For the worst deception,
as Plato writes in the *Cratylus,* is self-deception, for the
deceiver never forsakes the deceived.[74] But the person who
persuades himself in a thoughtless way that false things are true
deceives himself. This obstinacy in arguing and the deception
too is bitterly deprecated in the *Gorgias* and the *Phaedo.*[75] And
in the *Republic* Book 10, in condemning his friend Homer,
Plato says: A man must not be put before the truth.[76] Also
mentioning it in the *Letters* he says: I will not be afraid or
ashamed to tell the truth.[77] For the truth, as he says in the *Laws,*
is a solid good.[78] And elsewhere he says: nothing is sweeter to
the ears of a sensible man than the truth.[79] But in the *Phaedrus*
he says: neither among the gods nor among men has there ever
been or will there ever be anything more venerable than the
truth.[80]

*Chapter 15. Concerning the intelligence and truth and the
immortality of the intelligence. Again, concerning the
source of the power to divide and unite.*

However, after this, three things have to be considered
especially: first, what is intelligence, wisdom, knowledge? Now
the intelligence is the countenance looking back towards the
truth and it has two eyes—a right and a left. The right eye gazes
at the truth of those things that are inside the divine intelligence,
the left eye at those things that derive from it. The former
glance is wisdom, the latter knowledge. But the names can often

contrariae tamen [*350r*] scientiae nullae sunt. Siquae enim tales essent, maxime contrariorum scientiae contrariae forent, quod quidem falsum est. In eodem enim animo sunt eodem in tempore. Immo oppositorum eadem ferme est disciplina. Ergo ne differentias tui meique boni abscondamus, Protarche, sed in medium adducamus, ut ex recta redargutione comperiatur utrum voluptas ipsum bonum sit vel sapientia vel tertium aliquid. Non enim opiniones nostras pertinaciter defendere mordicusque tenere debemus, sed veritatem investigare. Pessima namque deceptio est, ut in Cratylo scribit Plato, qua quis se ipsum decipit, nam deceptor numquam deceptum deserit. Decipit autem se qui falsa sibi pro veris temere persuadet. Quam pertinaciam disputandi deceptionemque in Gorgia atque Phaedone acerrime detestatur. Et in decimo[1] de Republica cum amicum suum Homerum damnaret ait[2]: Virum non esse veritati anteponendum. Quod et in Epistolis observans ait: Verum dicere nec formidabo nec erubescam. Veritas enim, ut in Legibus ait, solidum est bonum. Et alias inquit nihil esse sanis auribus dulcius veritate. Immo vero in Phaedro inquit: Neque apud deos neque apud homines veritate venerabilius quicquam aut fuit umquam aut erit.

De mente et veritate et mentis immortalitate. Item unde sit virtus ad dividendum atque uniendum. Cap. XV.[3]

*Post haec autem tria praecipue consideranda sunt.[4] Primo quid mens, sapientia, scientia sit. Est autem mens vultus ad veritatem conversus, huius duo sunt oculi dexter et sinister. Ille veritatem eorum quae in divina mente sunt inspicit; hic eorum quae ab illa. Ille intuitus sapientia, hic scientia. Saepe autem vocabula haec confundantur,[5] quia quisquis quae in mente**

[1]sexto *Y*   [2]ait *om. X*   [3]*no ch. heading or break W; a break and the subscript* Finite hoc capite *only XP*   [4]*in X and P this sentence merely reads* Tria sunt consideranda
[5]confunduntur *XP*   *-**om. W (cont.)*

be confounded, because whoever perceives the things which are in the intelligence sees in them the things which derive from the intelligence, and whoever perceives the things which derive from the intelligence infers the things which are in the intelligence from them.

The second thing to be considered is this. If there are any opposite types of knowledge, would the greatest such be the knowledge of the biggest thing compared to the knowledge of the smallest? But they aren't opposites, because they supplement each other. For whoever recognizes the biggest thing sees in it the cause of the smallest; and whoever recognizes the smallest thing ascends by these steps to the biggest things. Again, things associated with opposites would be totally opposite, but these types of knowledge are identical.

But now, since the intelligence is adapted equally to the biggest things and to the smallest, and is able (when given anything) to recognize a bigger thing while seeking the cause of each, and since it doesn't stop in anything while it can be investigating its cause, it rests only in that which is causeless and infinite. Therefore it is an infinite capacity which is adapted equally to the smallest things and to the biggest and which is filled by the infinite alone. The sense isn't like this, for the biggest object defeats the sense's power and the smallest object isn't perceived and the biggest blocks the smallest. What can be defeated or is confined to a mean point is finite. Therefore the intelligence is immortal, but a bodily organ is mortal. And since corruption arises from opposites, the soul isn't corrupted because it doesn't have opposites. Rather, it is so far removed from contrariety that what are opposites in themselves fully cohere in the soul. The good and the bad, the true and the false, light and darkness, hot and cold cohere in the notions of the soul.

The third point to be considered is that truth is the correspondence of the thing and the intelligence, and the truth of the intelligence is the intelligence's correspondence to things, and the truth of things is the things' correspondence to the intelligence. There are two intelligences: the divine and the human.

*sunt intuetur in eis videt quae a mente, et qui quae post mentem ex his quae in mente sunt conicit.

Secundo considerandum quod siquae scientiae contrariae sunt maximae tales essent ea quae de maximo ad eam quae de minimo quodam. Hae vero non sunt contrariae[1] quia sese[2] iuvant. Qui enim[3] maximum novit in eo causam videt minimi, et qui minimum his gradibus conscendit ad maxima. Item quae de contrariis sunt maxime essent contrariae, hae vero eaedem sunt.

Iam vero[4] quia mens ad maxima et minima aeque se habet et quocumque dato maius potest nosse dum causam quaerit cuiusque, neque sistit se in aliquo dum causam eius indagare potest, in solo eo quod sine causa est et infinitum quiescit. Infinita ergo capacitas est quae aeque se habet ad maxima et minima et solo infinito repletur. Non ita sensus, maximum enim obiectum vim eius superat, minimum non percipitur et maximum impedit minimum. Finitum est quod superatur et quod ad medium quoddam determinatur. Immortalis igitur mens, mortale autem[5] corporis organum. Et cum corruptio a contrariis sit, anima non corrumpitur, quia non habet contraria. Immo adeo a contrarietate remota est, ut quae in se ipsis contraria sunt in ea admodum cohaerescant. Bonum, malum, verum, falsum, lux, tenebrae, calidum, frigidum in notionibus animae cohaerescunt.

Tertio notandum quod veritas est adaequatio rei ac mentis; et veritas mentis est eius ad res adaequatio; veritas rerum est rerum adaequatio menti. Duae sunt mentes: divina, humana. Duae res: opera divinae mentis, opera mentis humanae. Unde**

---

[1] *XP merely read* Hae non   [2] se *P*   [3] enim *om. XP*   [4] *for* Iam vero *XP read* et
[5] autem *om. XP*   *(cont.)* *-** *om. W (cont.)*

There are two sorts of things: the products of the divine intelligence and the products of the human intelligence. So in the *Statesman* Plato says there are two arts; there are two products of art, the divine and the human.[81] The truth of a human product is its correspondence to the human intelligence, that is, for the product to be such that it can correspond to the artificer's idea. The truth of a natural product, which is the product of the divine intelligence, is its correspondence to the divine intelligence, [that is,] for the product to exist in that purity and completeness where it strives to become its idea in the intelligence. The truth of the human intelligence is its correspondence to things, not to its own products, but to the products of the divine intelligence. Consequently it perceives things as they are in themselves through knowledge, but as they are in the divine intelligence through wisdom. However, the truth of the divine intelligence is not its correspondence to the things which are below it, but to those which are inside it. That is, its correspondence is to those seeds of things existing within its essence, for it is to them that the intelligence always coheres.

But there is a light from the good penetrating through all intelligences and species and things, which is the cause of all correspondence and consequently of all truth, for it is the light of truth. So in the *Republic* Book 6 Plato shows the good is the fountain of light, and the light emanating from the good is the cause of truth.[82] That good light is grace. So firstly there's the good, secondly grace, thirdly truth, fourthly life, that is, joy in the truth. "Above us is imprinted the light of your countenance."[83]

Plato takes great pains with the one and the many. The one itself is the creator. The one and the many is the rational creature. The many and the one is something lower. Certainly, a creature is what proceeds from the simplicity of the divine substance by means of duality. In so far as the creator is on one side, on the other side has now been made a creature. Within itself the creature proceeds from the one into two, that is, the one thing is divided into substance and accident. Again, the one substance is divided into two, essence and existence. Finally, the

*in Politico dicitur duae artes sunt, duo sunt artis opera, divina[1] et humana. Veritas humani operis est adaequatio eius ad hominis mentem, id est, ut tale sit ut ideae artificis correspondeat. Veritas operis naturalis quod est divinae mentis opus adaequatio ad divinam mentem, ut in ea puritate et integritate sit, qua ipsum fore idea sui in mente conatur. Veritas mentis humanae adaequatio rebus, non operibus suis, sed divinae mentis operibus; ut ita de his sentiat ut sunt in se ipsis per scientiam, et ut sunt in mente divina per sapientiam. Mentis autem divinae veritas adaequatio rebus non his quae infra[2] se sunt, sed his quae intra, id est, seminibus rerum in sua essentia existentium, illis enim semper mens cohaeret.

Est autem lumen a bono per mentes et species omnes et res penetrans quod omnis adaequationis causa est, et ideo veritatis omnis, quod est veritatis lumen. Ideo in Republica sexto significatur quod bonum est fons luminis, et lumen inde manans est causa veritatis. Illud bonum lumen gratia. Primo ergo bonum est, secundo gratia, tertio veritas, quarto vita, id est, gaudium in veritate. Signatum est super nos lumen vultus tui.

[3]Plato assidue circa unum et multa laborat. Unum ipsum est creator; unum et multa est creatura rationalis; multa et unum inferior. Profecto creatura procedens a substantiae divinae simplicitate per dualitatem. Quantum[4] inde est creator, hinc creatura iam facta. Merito intra se ab uno procedit in duo, videlicet una res in substantiam accidensque dividitur. Item substantia una in duo, †essentiam atque esse. Denique accidens unum in duo,†† virtutem et actionem. Hinc fit ut intellectus noster a**

---

[1]scilicet *add. XP*   [2]*in Y*   [3]*ch. break in X and P; heading reads* Caput octavum. Quomodo unum derivetur in multa, atque multa colligantur in unum. Item de dialectica divisione, compositione, definitione *(cf. ch.* XVI, p. 171*)*   [4]Inquantum *XP*   *(cont.)* *-**om. W (cont.)* †-††*om. Y*

one accident is divided into two, power and action. As a result, our intellect, having been made by God in the order of creatures, wanders around the one and the many. But since it is composed more of the one than of the many, it is, accordingly, moved in the first place towards the one—when it initially sees something as one with a sort of confused glance. But next, by looking more carefully at the thing and by dividing it into parts, it proceeds from the one into the many. Thirdly, by gathering the parts together, it inclines towards the one away from multiplicity. Fourthly, by composing the parts that have already been gathered together, it defines. In this process of defining, it is now brought back into the one. In the restoration, the circle from the many into the one and back again has been completed, just as in definition, the definition [is completed] when it is returned to what has been defined. Fifthly, it demonstrates why such a thing proceeds from another and why another proceeds from it. In the demonstration there's a movement: now from the one to the many, that is, from the one effect to the many causes, now from the many causes to the one effect.

Chapter 16. How the one is drawn into the many and the many gathered back into the one. Again, on dialectical division, compounding and definition, and on the Ideas.

Because he's mentioned the many species of pleasure and knowledge above and because he's put that many into one genus of pleasure and one of knowledge, the uncertainty arises whether the many can be one or the one can be many. To approach this uncertainty, Plato says we must try to reach a decision ratified by common assent. He admonishes us to discuss it the more intently as such an ambiguity fatigues the minds of all men—willing and unwilling (that is, those who inquire into such problems and everybody else). It tires certain people at certain times. That is, it tires those in the main, who, though they've condemned the senses, rely too little on the reason. And it tires them chiefly at that time when they have

14C-E

*Deo[1] in creaturarum ordine factus circa unum et multa vagetur. Quoniam vero unius magis quam multitudinis compos est, ideo primum ad unum movetur quando rem primo percipit confuso quodam intuitu tamquam unam. Sed deinde distinctius percipiendo distribuendoque in partes ab uno procedit in multa. Tertio partes invicem conferendo a multitudine vergit in unum. Quarto partes collatas iam componendo definit. In qua definitione iam restitutio facta est in unum. In qua restitutione fit circuitus a multis in unum atque vicissim, prout in definitione definitio ipsa cum definito convertitur. Quinto demonstrat qua ratione res talis procedat ab alio et qua aliud procedit[2] ab ipsa. In qua demonstratione fit motus, tum ab uno in multa, id est, ab uno effectu in multas causas, tum a multis causis in effectum unum.[3]**

Quomodo unum derivetur in multa atque multa colligantur in unum. Item de dialectica divisione, compositione, definitione et de ideis. Cap. XVI.[4]

Quia de speciebus multis voluptatis et scientiae mentionem fecit supra, et eam multitudinem in uno voluptatis genere et uno genere scientiae posuit, suboritur dubitatio, numquid multa unum esse possint et unum multa. Circa [*350v*] quam dubitationem conandum dicit Plato ratam aliquam communi assertione ferre sententiam, quod eo propensius discutiendum monet, quod huiusmodi ambiguitas omnium mentes fatigat et volentium et nolentium, id est, tam eorum qui[5] talia perscrutantur quam ceterorum omnium, et quorundam et aliquando, id est, eorum maxime qui, cum sensus damnaverint, rationi tamen parum confidunt, tunc praesertim cum primum aggressi

---

[1]adeo *Y*   [2]procedat *P*   [3]His premissis propius iam accedamus ad textum *add. XP*
[4]*no ch. heading or break W; no heading but a break XP; in XP the heading is transposed (cf. p. 169)*
[5]quam *W*   *(cont.)* *-**om. W*

acquired for the first time the subtlety of arguing, but not reached yet the full mastery of the art of disputation. However, this conflict occurs in our souls, because the senses drag them towards the consideration of the scattered multitude of bodily objects, but the intelligence towards the simplicity of incorporeal things. But for the most part we mingle together the perceptions of the senses with the intelligence's power to discern. So we are turned back towards the power of the unity and the divine nature less confidently than we ought to be. But Plato will explain at once what kind of doubts these are about the one and the many.

But you can think about the one being many in three ways: either one something has opposing aspects; or a whole something is made from its own many parts; or one simple something is shared by many things and diffused through many separated things. The last idea is fantastic and it can be doubted whether it is possible: whether you say one simple thing is borne through separated things or many separated things contain some one simple thing in common, you can be opposed as will shortly appear.

There's no need to wrangle about the first and second ideas. 15A Whoever says Protarchus is one thing and many things—big, little, light, heavy (that is, if he's compared to various things)— isn't introducing anything extraordinary about the one and the many. For everybody knows this isn't marvellous and there's no need to deny Protarchus is one because he has opposing aspects. Such quibbles are considered puerile and facile and unworthy of consideration, since they'll hinder the pursuit of truth if they're admitted, as you can go on wandering like this through innumerable paradoxes. However, if it means the one is opposite things in an absolute sense, it must be rejected at once as an impossibility needing no discussion. Even were it admitted, we couldn't discuss it properly, since we would have already granted that opposites are one and everything is mixed with everything. Hence nothing could be refuted. But if it means the one has opposing aspects when compared to diverse things, that's easily admitted and it would be childish to wonder about

disserendi subtilitatem nondum ad absolutum disputationis artificium pervenerunt. Accidit autem haec in nostris animis colluctatio, quia sensus ad corporum dispersam multitudinem cogitandam trahunt, mens vero ad incorporalium rerum simplicitatem. Ut plurimum vero sensuum visa cum mentis iudicio commiscemus. Unde ad unitatis ipsius divinaeque naturae potentiam diffidentius quam decet convertimur. Quales vero dubitationes istae sint circa unum et multa statim aperiet.

Unum vero esse multa tribus modis considerari potest: vel aliquid unum opposita circa se habens; vel totum aliquid ex pluribus suis partibus constitutum; vel unum aliquid simplex commune pluribus esse et per multa dispersaque diffundi. Postremum hoc quidem mirabile dictu et an fieri possit ambiguum, et quodcumque istorum dicatur, sive quod unum simplex per dispersa feratur, seu quod multa et dispersa commune quiddam unum et simplex[1] capiant, repugnari potest, ut paulo post patebit.

De primo autem atque secundo ambigere nullus debet. Neque mirum quicquam inducet circa unum et multa, qui Protarchum unum esse et oppositos dicet [*351r*] — magnum, parvum, levem, gravem — hoc est, si ad diversos aliquos comparetur. Vulgo enim notum est non esse istud mirabile, neque esse negandum Protarchum unum esse ex eo quod circa illum opposita sint. Cavillationes huiusmodi pueriles facilesque censentur, neque studio dignae, quippe, si admittantur,# veritatis inquisitioni impedimento erunt, cum per innumerabiles similiter ambages vagari liceat. Immo si intelligatur quod unum contraria sit absolute, id tamquam impossibile statim reicitur neque inquisitione indiget. Quin etiam[2] si admittatur, non poterimus recte disserere, cum liceat contraria[3] unum facere et miscere omnibus omnia unde nihil redargui poterit.[4] Sin intelligatur quod unum contraria sit, si ad diversa comparetur, istud admittitur facile et puerile esset de hoc ambigere. Sed neque de

---

[1] et simplex *om.* Y ends   [2] etiam *om.* WX   [3] et *add.* Y   [4] potitur *W*   #*P frag. II (48v)*

it. Nor do people disagree at all about the second idea: that the one is many and the many one in so far as some whole, composed from many parts, is many parts and again the many parts are one whole. In the same way certainly our body is one thing made out of many members and parts.

So Socrates says there aren't going to be extraordinary facts about the one and the many emerging, if someone first of all divides the body into members and the members into smaller parts and keeps on cutting to infinity and then infers it is a marvellous and monstrous thing that the one is infinite things (and so strives to do away with the one).

Certainly, with any one thing that has been created and diffused through matter it's no wonder if it degenerates from perfect unity and endures opposites and multiplicity. But if someone introduces one simple, uncreated thing, it will seem wonderful: first, if such a thing can exist; then, if it can be diffused through multiplicity too, since each form is divided by body. Plato touches here on a one under the Ideas when he posits one Protarchus; again, on a one in the Ideas when he posits one man or one ox in a species; again, on a one coming from the Ideas when he posits one beauty (for it is the ornament of all the Ideas); again, on a one above the Ideas when he posits the good itself (that is, the first God), by whom the one goodness of nature, that is, creativity, is given to the intelligence (through which the Ideas are brought forth). And when he talks about the Idea of the good in the *Republic,*[84] he means both the good itself by way of cause and the goodness of the intelligence by way of form; for the good is the Idea as cause, goodness the Idea as form. The one is the leader of the Ideas, the other is their principle. Plato often talks about the good, the beautiful, the just. The first is the divine creativity, the second the order in its understanding, the third the order in its will, the distributor of the first order.

Indeed, nobody doubts there is some one thing in created things—bodies are obviously single—; and who doubts this one is many things? But if someone introduces the one eternal and incorporeal man, the one ox, the one beauty, the one good, he

secundo ulla inter homines discrepatio est, quin unum ita sit
multa et multa unum, ut totum quoddam ex partibus multis
compositum multae sit[1] partes, rursusque partes multae unum
illud sint. Ut corpus nostrum unum profecto est multis ex
membris partibusque compositum.

Quapropter dicit Socrates neque mirabilia ista fore circa
unum ac multa, siquis corpus dividat in membra primum,
membraque in particulas,[2] iterum in infinitum secans, inferat-
que deinde mirum istud monstrumque esse ut unum infinita sit
atque ita contendat unum e medio tollere.

Profecto in eo uno quod genitum est et circa materiam est
diffusum nihil mirum est, si a perfecta unitate degeneret oppo-
sitaque patiatur et multitudinem. At vero siquis unum simplex
ingenitumque induxerit, mirabile videbitur: primum [*351v*]
quidem, siquid tale sit, deinde, si et illud in multitudine sit dispersum, cum divisio cuiusque formae[3] a corpore fiat. Tangit hic
Plato unum quod sub ideis est, cum ponit[4] Protarchum unum.
Item unum quod in ideis, scilicet[5] hominem vel bovem unum in
specie. Item unum quod ex ideis, cum dicit pulchrum unum, est
enim omnium idearum decor.[6] Item unum quod super ideas,
cum dicit ipsum bonum, scilicet Deum primum, a quo bonitas
una naturae scilicet foecunditas menti datur per quam ideae
parturiuntur. Et cum ideam boni in Republica dicit, utrumque
intelligit, bonum ipsum per modum causae, bonitatem mentis
per formae modum; bonum enim idea ut causa, bonitas idea ut
forma. Istud idearum caput, illud[7] idearum principium. Plato
dicit saepe bonum, pulchrum, iustum. Primum est divina foecunditas, secundum ordo in eius intelligentia, tertium ordo in
eius voluntate primi ordinis distributor.

Quod vero sit unum aliquod in rebus genitis, ut de singulis
corporibus patet, nemo ambigit, quodve unum illud sit multa
quis dubitat? Siquis vero unum hominem aeternum et
incorporeum, unum bovem, pulchrum unum, unum bonum

---

[1]sint *W*   [2]particulis *W*   [3]formae *om. Y*   [4]posuit *W*   [5]scilicet *om. WX*
[6]*X has both* decor *and* decus *as alternatives*   [7]istud *Y*

appears to be dreaming at first, as Aristophanes derisively says of Socrates, and the comedians, Timon, Alexis and Cratinus, say of Plato.[85] Diogenes the Cynic said he couldn't see Plato's Ideas. Plato replied he obviously didn't have an intelligence with which to see them.[86]

So it is that unless somebody reduces the orders of individual things to one common species, it's obvious he won't be able to understand anything, or know anything for certain. But if he brings in just one separate species for every order, everybody will think he's dreaming. Aristotle was not afraid to slander the divine Plato on this issue.

Nevertheless, in the *Phaedo* Plato proves the Ideas must exist. And in the *Timaeus* he says, since there are separate sensual and intellectual powers, they must have separate objects, and the universal objects of the intelligence must be more true and exist more absolutely than sensible objects to the extent that the intellect is superior to the sense.[87] The objects of the intellect are the rules with which you can distinguish between the truth and falsity of sensible objects and recognize the defects of existence. Therefore they are and they exist more truly and absolutely. Among the wise men of Greece arose the saying that Plato had three eyes: one with which he looked at human things, another at natural things, another at divine things (which was in his forehead, while the others were under his forehead).

However, given such species, whoever carefully and diligently tries to find out how they exist with regard to individuals will immediately come upon a problem concerning the division. For if each species isn't divided into many things, it won't appear to be capable of agreeing with many things. But, if it is divided, it will no longer appear to be one separate thing, nor remain incorruptible and eternal.

Chapter 17. Three doubts about the Ideas and their verification.

15B   Concerning these unities three major problems present themselves.[88] One, are the species true or just conceptions of our

induxerit, primum somniare videbitur, ut Aristophanes de Socrate obloquitur, et de Platone Timon, Alexis et Cratinus comici. Huiusque ideas videre se negavit Diogenes Cynicus, cui respondit Plato, carere eum videlicet mente qua ideae cernuntur.

Ita enim se res habet, ut, nisi quis singulorum ordines ad speciem unam[1] communem redigat, intelligere nihil posse videatur, neque certum aliquid [*352r*] scire; sin autem cuiusque ordinis speciem unam separatam induxerit, somniare vulgo videbitur. In quo et Aristoteles haud veritus est divum Platonem calumniari.

Oportet tamen eas esse quod in Phaedone probat. Atque in Timaeo dicit, cum sint distinctae vires sensualis et intellectualis, habere obiecta distincta et obiecta mentis universalia tanto veriora esse debere et magis existentia quam sensibilia quanto intellectus est sensu superior. Obiecta intellectus sunt regulae per quas inter veritatem falsitatemque sensibilium discernitur defectusque existendi recognoscitur. Ergo verius magisque sunt et existunt. Inter prudentissimos Graecorum natum est proverbium Platonem habuisse tres oculos: unum quo humana, alium quo naturalia, alium quo divina suspiceret qui in fronte esset cum alii sub fronte.

Positis autem huiuscemodi speciebus, siquis diligenter studioseque perquirat[2] quomodo se ad singula habeant, statim circa divisionem ambiguitas orietur. Nam si non dividatur species quaeque in multa, multis convenire non posse videbitur; sin autem dividatur, neque unum esse separatum amplius, neque incorruptum aeternumque manere.

Tria circa ideas dubia et confirmatio idearum. Cap. XVII.[3]

Tres potissimae contra has unitates dubitationes insurgunt. Una, utrum verae sint hae species an potius nostrae mentis

---

[1]unum *W*   [2]inquirat *WX*   [3]*no ch. heading or break WX*

intelligence? Two, if they really do exist, is each species one alone although it's in agreement with the many, and immutable although it's the cause of mutable things? Three, if each is one and immutable, how can it impart itself to many things and things which are mutable in such a way that it isn't made mutable in them, nor they made immutable by the fact that it's there? Also, can it be divided through the individual things, or can the whole of it be in them? It's obviously absurd that the species, if it is an eternal thing, should be divided by means of corruptible things. It's obviously incredible that one and the same whole should be at the same time in many things which are mutually separated, for the whole would also be separated from itself. Plato voices these doubts also in the *Parmenides.* But how they can be resolved can in large part be deduced from that dialogue and from the *Timaeus,* the *Republic* and the *Phaedo,* as we shall subsequently show.[89]

But Plato says such doubts are not those above, which are principally concerned with the one and the many. For to ask about the unities and species is to ask about the origin and substance of each thing. The person who gets this wrong is wrong over everything and handicapped; the person who gets it right can decide correctly and easily about everything. For in the *Phaedo* he says nothing is more sure and certain than the Ideas, and in them is revealed the total divinity of the soul.[90]

But because Plato calls the species of things "unities," you have to remember that whenever Plato says one something he's introducing individual things. But when he says "the one itself" he wants you to understand the first principle of all things; whenever "monads," the principle of number; whenever "unities," the eternal reasons of all things which are in the divine intelligence, the maker of the whole world. And since one reason is enough to make many things—a simple reason to make compounds; an eternal reason to make temporal things—therefore the species are called simple and eternal unities. The species for creating things are in God's intelligence exactly as the models for products are in an artificer's mind, or the reasons for all the members and parts are in the seed of an animal or tree. But the

conceptiones. Secunda, si revera sint, utrum quaeque sit una dumtaxat cum multis conveniat, et immutabilis cum sit mutabilium ratio. Tertia,[1] si sit una et immobilis,[2] quomodo multis[3] et mutabilibus se communicet, ita ut neque ipsa in eis fiat mutabilis neque illa per eius praesentiam immobilia, et numquid per singula dividatur an tota [*352v*] sit in singulis. Absurdum quidem[4] videtur quod dividatur per corruptibilia, si res aeterna est. Mirum videtur quod unum et idem totum sit simul in multis invicem separatis. Nam illud quoque a se ipso erit seiunctum. Dubia haec etiam in Parmenide movet, quae vero haec solvant[5] multa inde et ex Timaeo, Republica, Phaedone colligi possunt, ut in sequentibus ostendemus.

Dicit autem Plato haec[6] dubia non illa superiora esse, quae circa unum et multa plurimum important. Quaerere enim de his unitatibus et speciebus est quaerere de origine substantiaque cuiusque, in qua qui aberrat in omnibus errat et claudicat, quam qui bene ponit vere et facile cuncta diiudicat. Dicit enim[7] in Phaedone nihil habere se[8] certius et firmius quam[9] ideas et in his totam monstrari animi divinitatem.

Quia vero[10] species rerum unitates vocat[11] Plato, ideo meminisse oportet quod quotiens Plato unum aliquid dicit, singula profert; cum autem ipsum unum[12] dicit, primum omnium principium intelligi vult; quotiens[13] monadas, principium numeri; quando vero unitates, rationes aeternas omnium quae fiunt in mente divina mundi totius opifice. Et quia ad multa efficienda una, ad composita simplex, ad temporalia aeterna ratio sufficit, ideo species istae unitates simplices aeternae dicuntur. Neque minus sunt in Dei mente procreandorum species quam in artificis animo suorum operum exemplaria, et in semine animalis et arboris membrorum omnium et partium rationes. Quae vero in materia distincta sunt in

---

[1]tria *W*   [2]immutabilis *WX*   [3]sit *W*   [4]quidem *om. WX*   [5]solum autem *W*
[6]hae *WY*   [7]enim *om. WX*   [8]se *om. WX*   [9]in *add. WY*   [10]vero *om. WX*
[11]vocavit *WX*   [12]unum *om. W*   [13]monas vel *add. Y*

things which are distinct in matter are joined together in the
efficient cause, where there is distinction without separation,
union without confusion. This is demonstrated by the unity of
parts and the variety of qualities in a material product.

In any element or compound body the forms are present. It is
by their power that similar forms are generated in matter. In
trees and animals there are seeds; in the seeds there are reasons
that can be kindled. In the arts there are notions. In the contemplative's soul there are the lights and principles of all the conclusions he produces. So it's undeniable that the species of all
God's works, the seeds, the powers, the reasons, the models,
the notions are present in His intelligence, which is the creator
of all things. Plato wants them both to be Ideas, namely the reason by which God conceives of individual men and creates man
himself, and the Idea of such men; and similarly with all the
Ideas. But as the ancient theologians said—those whom Plato
followed, Zoroaster, Hermes Trismegistus, Orpheus, Aglaophemus, Pythagoras—the vain belief in many gods arose
universally from the many names of the Ideas. But the Christian
theologians, Dionysius the Areopagite and St. Augustine, also
maintain that the Ideas must be thus accepted as true and that
they were so accepted by Plato. Arguments selected from
Plato's books, which I'll bring in later, will prove it. So it is in
vain that the Aristotelians howl against Plato's majesty.

Chapter 18. Concerning the Ideas and the true and untrue forms.

We'll demonstrate from Platonic arguments that the Ideas
exist, if we show first that the Platonists introduced the Ideas to
oppose neither Christian theology nor counter the view of the
Aristotelians. Listen to St. Augustine in the *Book of the 83
Questions* saying as follows: "Whoever acknowledges all
existing things (that is, whatever is contained in its own genus
by an appropriate nature), [must also acknowledge] that in
order to exist they have been created by God the originator and

efficiente causa sunt unita, ubi sine separatione distinctio, sine confusione est unio. Quod quidem[1] in opere materiae unitas partium et qualitatum varietas ostendit.

In quolibet elemento [*353r*] corporeque composito formae insunt quarum vi formae similes in materia generantur: in arboribus et animalibus semina, in seminibus rationes et fomites, in artibus notiones, in contemplantis animo lumina et principia conclusionum omnium quae proferuntur. Quis ergo negabit in Dei mente omnium effectrice[2] operum suorum inesse omnium species, semina, vires, rationes, exemplaria, notiones? Has esse ideas Plato vult, rationem qua Deus homines singulos concipit procreatque ipsum hominem, et hominum istorum ideam similiterque de ceteris. Quod, cum ab antiquis theologis Zoroastre, Mercurio, Orpheo, Aglaophemo, Pythagora quos secutus Plato est diceretur,[3] ex plurimis idearum nominibus deorum plurium[4] vulgo vana est exorta suspicio. Ideas autem ita revera accipi debcre, et ita a Platone acceptas fuisse, theologi quoque Christiani Dionysius Areopagita, et Aurelius Augustinus perhibent; atque[5] rationes ex Platonis libris excerptae, quas adducam postea, demonstrabunt. Itaque[6] frustra contra Platonis maiestatem Peripatetici latrant.

De ideis et de formis veris atque non veris. Cap. XVIII.[7]

[8]Ideas esse Platonicis argumentationibus demonstrabimus, si prius ostenderimus neque contra Christianorum theologiam neque praeter Peripateticorum opinionem a Platonicis ideas inductas fuisse.[9] Aurelium Augustinum in libro octuaginta trium quaestionum audi ita dicentem: Quisquis[10] fatetur omnia quae sunt, id est, quaecumque in suo genere propria quadam

---

[1]quidem *om. WX*   [2]affectrice *W*   [3]doceretur *W*   [4]plurimum *Y*   [5]et *W; om. X*
[6]Ex quo *WX*   [7]*no ch. heading or break W; ch. numbered* VIIII *by X; no ch. heading in P but a penstroke before* Ideas *and* XVIII *in the margin faintly*   [8]*see appendix I for a passage added here by X, and in the middle of which P frag. III (52r) begins*   [9]Quippe *add. WXP*
[10]Quisque *XP*

that individual things are ruled by His providence. Once this has been conceded, who will dare say God established everything irrationally. The conclusion must be that all has been established by a rational principle. A man hasn't the same rational principle as a horse, for that's an absurd notion. Therefore individual things have been created by their own rational principles. But where else can the rational principles be thought to exist except in the intelligence itself of the Creator? For God didn't look to something placed outside Himself in order to establish what He was establishing according to it. But if the rational principles for creating all things (or for creatures) are contained in the divine intelligence, and if nothing can be in the divine intelligence unless it's eternal and unchangeable, and if Plato is calling these principal reasons for things "Ideas," not only are there Ideas, but they are true, because they remain eternal and always the same and unchangeable. It is through their participation that anything may be in whatever way it is.

"But among the things created by God the rational soul surpasses all; and it is closest to God when it is pure. To the extent that it clings to Him in love, it discerns (being in a way perfused and illuminated by that intelligible light) the rational principles. It does not discern them through corporeal eyes, but through the principal part of itself which excels, that is, through its understanding. By this vision the soul may be made utterly happy."[91] Therefore Augustine is the most reliable witness among Christians.

But among the Aristotelians Averroes says the same in commenting on books 11 and 12 of the *Metaphysics:* he says Aristotle, while denying Plato's Ideas, is also positing them as long as he puts the forms of things in the first mover of the heavens. Albert the Great maintains the same in his commentary on Dionysius, when he says Aristotle meant the first cause of things to be a cause in three ways: that is, to be the efficient cause, and (to use his own words) the final cause and the formal cause. The patterns for things he refers to the formal cause. Nor do we lack the testimonies of Simplicius and Themistius and Eustratius.[92] So let's go back to the Platonists.

natura continentur, ut sint, auctore Deo esse procreata, singulaque eius [*353v*] providentia regi. Quo concesso, quis audeat dicere Deum irrationabiliter omnia condidisse? Restat ut omnia ratione sint condita. Nec eadem ratione homo qua equus, hoc enim absurdum est existimare. Singula igitur propriis sunt creata rationibus. Has autem rationes ubi esse arbitrandum est nisi in ipsa mente creatoris? Non enim extra se quicquam positum intuebatur ut secundum id constitueretur quod constituebat. Quod si hae rerum omnium creandarum creatarumve rationes divina mente continentur neque in divina mente quicquam nisi aeternum et incommutabile potest esse, atque has rationes rerum principales appellat ideas Plato, non solum sunt ideae, sed ipsae verae sunt, quia aeternae et semper eiusdem modi atque incommutabiles manent, quarum participatione fit ut sit quicquid quoquomodo est.

Sed anima rationalis inter eas res quae sunt a Deo conditae omnia superat; et Deo proxima est, quando pura est eique in quantum caritate cohaeserit in tantum ab eo lumine intelligibili perfusa quodammodo et illustrata cernit non per corporeos oculos sed per ipsius sui principale quod excellit, id est, per intelligentiam suam[1] istas rationes, qua visione fiat beatissima. Inter Christianos igitur Augustinus testis est locupletissimus.

Inter Peripateticos autem testatur idem Averroes in Metaphysicis undecimo et[2] duodecimo libro, ubi dicit quod Aristoteles dum Platonis ideas negat ipse interim ponit ideas, dum in primo coeli motore rerum formas ponit. Idem quoque in Dionysii commentariis Albertus Magnus asserit Aristotelem dicens primam rerum causam tribus [*354r*] modis esse causam voluisse: efficientem scilicet et, ut verbis ipsius utar, finalem et formalem. Ad formalem vero causam rerum exemplaria refert. Neque nobis Simplicii desunt et Themistii et Eustratii testimonia. Quare ad Platonicos redeamus.

---

[1] *em. adopted from Augustine's text*, suas *WXYP*   [2] undecimo et *expressly excluded in the corrigenda list of Y*

We want to know especially whether this universal world which can be seen with the eyes comes from itself or rather from a higher cause. Obviously, it doesn't come from itself, because everything that does come from itself is necessarily indivisible. For everything that makes and creates from itself is incorporeal; for no action is appropriate to a body in so far as it is a body. A body, in fact, is composed of two things, that is, matter and quantity. It only possesses from matter the ability to receive from somewhere else, and from quantity the fact that it can be divided. But these are passivities—in fact, quantity not only does not help action, it hinders it; for action is most effective when the agent's power is completely united and the agent is as close as possible to what is being acted on. But quantity results in the power being dispersed through different parts; and it prevents things joining together, since by means of extension it forces them to be separated in space. So if no action is appropriate to a body in so far as it is a body, whatever bodies do they do through some incorporeal quality. But a quality is incorporeal, because there are many qualities in the same body, but many bodies can't be at the same time in the same place. But a quality, since it's in another, comes from another, but not from the body, as the body can do nothing on its own account. So it comes from something incorporeal, which isn't a body (because it can act) and isn't in a body (lest we go on to infinity).

Therefore there's a certain incorporeal species existing through itself above bodily things, whose job it is only to act, not to be passive. Just as the function of the body is to be passive only not active, so the function of quality which is in the body is both to be passive, since it is in the body (for it is divided and perishes with it), and to be active, since it is incorporeal in itself. Therefore it is appropriate for an incorporeal species or power to be active, and for this reason corporeal things act through incorporeal powers—fire through heat, but snow through coldness.

So two things follow: one, there is a certain incorporeal essence above the body of the world and its nature, and this essence is the first to act. Whatever the world does, it does

De hoc universo qui cernitur oculis mundo imprimis quaerimus, utrum ex se ipso sit an superiori ex causa. Quod ex se ipso
non sit ex hoc patet, quia omne quod tale est necessario est
impartibile. Omne enim quod proprie facit et gignit incorporeum est. Nulla enim actio corpori convenit quantum[1] corpus.
Corpus siquidem ex duobus constat materia scilicet et quantitate. Ex materia solum habet ut aliunde recipiat; ex quantitate
ut dividatur. Haec vero passiones sunt. Immo vero quantitas
non modo ad agendum non iuvat sed impedit actionem, actio
enim tunc maxime provenit cum et agentis virtus unita est
maxime et agens patienti proximum. Quantitas autem efficit ut
diversas per partes dispersa virtus sit, et unionem rerum invicem
impedit cum cogat propter extensionem distantiam in rebus esse
locorum. Quare si in quantum corpus est[2] nulla corpori competit actio, siquid agunt corpora incorporea quadam efficiunt
qualitate. Est autem qualitas incorporea, quia multae eodem in
corpore sunt qualitates, multa vero corpora simul et[3] eodem in
loco esse non possunt. Qualitas vero cum in alio sit ab alio est;
non autem a corpore, cum nihil corpus ex se ipso agat, ab
incorporeo igitur aliquo, quod neque est corpus ut agat, neque
in corpore est ne in infinitum progrediamur.

Est ergo quaedam species incorporea per se existens supra
corpora, cuius officium [*354v*] est ut agat tantum non
patiatur. Sicut corporis opus est ut patiatur tantum, non agat,
qualitatis autem quae in corpore ut patiatur, quia in corpore est
nam cum eo dividitur atque interit, et ut agat, quia ex se est
incorporea. Incorporalis itaque speciei atque virtutis proprium
est ut agant. Unde et corpora incorporalibus agunt virtutibus,
ignis caliditate, nix autem frigiditate.

Unde duo sequuntur: unum, ut supra mundi corpus eiusque
naturam essentia quaedam sit incorporea quae ipsa prima[4] agat.

---

[1]inquantum *WXP*   [2]est *om. WXP*   [3]et *om. Y*   [4]primo *WXP*

because of the power of this essence. From the nature which is impressed in the world all the forms of things arise in matter. The forms are made by the power of the nature. So the seeds of the forms are present in the nature. And because the nature acts through the power of the higher essence, the reasons for all the seeds which are in it are also in the essence. We call them the Ideas. Therefore from the creativeness of the divine substance the nature is also made creative; and from the nature various offspring are drawn into matter.

So this is the reason for our first argument for demonstrating the existence of the Ideas. Our second argument for again demonstrating the existence of the Ideas follows from the fact the world can't exist by itself. For what is from itself acts on itself. When something acts on itself, the actor and the thing acted on are the same; but what acts is indivisible, and therefore the thing acted on is indivisible. So the world, since it is divisible, can't be of itself. So it needs a higher cause.

Again, all that subsists through itself also operates of itself; for what produces itself is able before all else to operate in itself. But the world can't move itself, since it is corporeal; for, universally, no body can at the same time move itself and be moved by itself. For no totality can at the same time heat itself and be heated by itself, because what is being heated isn't hot yet, but what is doing the heating already has heat. And so the same thing will be, and will not be, hot. And if the whole heats a part, or a part heats the whole, or a part heats a part, the same thing is not heating itself. But if the same thing is heating itself, the whole is heating the whole. So the same thing will be hot and will not be hot. But just as it's impossible for some body to move itself in the sense of altering itself, so it's impossible for it to move itself in the sense of any sort of motion, since generation and corruption, and similarly getting bigger and getting smaller and rarefaction and condensation, all presuppose alteration. So what can't move itself by altering itself also can't move itself by any other interior movement. What isn't capable of producing from itself its own interior movement in itself is even less capable of producing from itself an exterior movement

Et mundus quicquid agit eius agat virtute. A natura autem mundo impressa omnes rerum proveniunt in materiam formae, quae formae vi naturae illius fiunt. Ergo in natura ipsa formarum insunt semina. Et quia natura agit vi superioris essentiae, omnium seminum quae in natura sunt sunt et in ea essentia rationes, quas ideas vocamus. Foecunditate igitur divinae substantiae fit et natura foecunda, ex qua in ma#teriam partus varii educuntur.

Ex hac itaque ratione hoc primum sequitur ex quo ideas esse monstramus. Sequitur et alterum per quod ideas esse iterum ostendemus, scilicet ut mundus ex se esse non possit. Nam quod ex se est se ipsum agit; ubi aliquid se ipsum agit, idem est agens et factum. Quod autem[1] agit impartibile est, ergo ibi quod agitur impartibile. Mundus itaque, cum partibilis sit, ex se ipso esse non potest, quare superiorem exigit causam.

Item omne quod per se subsistit ex se etiam operatur. Multo enim prius quod se ipsum gignit in se ipsum operari potest.[2] Mundus autem nequaquam est per se mobilis cum sit corporeus, nullum enim [*355r*] corpus universaliter simul per se movere et moveri potest. Neque enim simul totum se ipsum calefacere et[3] a se ipso calefieri, quia quod calefit nondum calidum est, quod autem calefacit iam habet caliditatem, atque ita idem erit et non erit calidum. Et[4] si totum[5] partem vel pars totum vel pars[6] partem calefacit, non idem se ipsum. Quod[7] si idem se ipsum, totum calefacit totum. Quare[8] idem calidum erit et non calidum. Quemadmodum vero secundum alterationem aliquod corpus movere se ipsum impossibile est, ita et secundum quemlibet motum, quia generatio et corruptio alterationem praesupponunt et diminutio augmentatioque similiter rarefactioque et condensatio. Quare quod motu alterationis movere se ipsum non potest, nullo quoque alio[9] interiori motu. Quod vero ad interiorem motum suum non sufficit ex se in se producendum,

---

[1]autem *om. WX*   [2]quia hoc ipsum facere et generari operari *est add. WX*   [3]et *om. W*
[4]et *om. X*   [5]totam *W*   [6]pars *om. Y*   [7]quod *om. X*   [8]igitur *X*   [9]actio *W*
#P frag. III (53v) ends

around a place or to another place, especially since what changes itself alters its own position, situation, disposition, shape and state of being affected.

But, universally, each corporeal movement seems to be more like being passive than being active, since passivity is appropriate to bodies. But the power to move oneself is activity. So it's the function of some indivisible thing to be moved of itself. Therefore, because it's a body, the world doesn't move itself. So it doesn't exist through itself either. So it depends on another more pre-eminent cause.

But, in order to work, the pre-eminent cause either needs choice and judgement, or it can operate through being alone. If it's the latter, it doesn't need to choose; but if it's the former, if it needs choice to act, absolutely nothing will be found which can do something without choice. For if the divine being itself isn't great enough to be able to act through itself, surely nothing at all will be able to act through itself. But we see each thing that now acts through choice also does something through being, for choice requires the soul. But if the soul presupposes another choice in order to be, and that in turn presupposes another, and that in turn another to infinity, no action will ever begin, since the result presupposes infinite decisions and innumerable choices. But you can never pass through an infinite series. So there is some operation and choice which proceeds from being alone, with no other interjected operation or choice. In fact, a man's soul, though it does many things through choice, nevertheless without choice gives life to the body through being: as soon as matter has been prepared, without choice the soul enlivens it straight away with its own life. For if this life resulted from our choice, either it would never leave the body in the men always obsessed with the body, or it would frequently and easily do so in the men who separate the soul for the sake of contemplation, or in others who renounce the union of the soul with the body because of bodily disease. Moreover, the soul would know all that it does in the body, for choice presupposes judgement.

But not everything that operates through being alone has choice or can operate through it even: for example, the elements

multo minus ad exteriorem motum ex se circa locum vel[1] ad
locum alium deducendum, cum praesertim quod se mutat locis,
situ, habitu, figura, affectione permutet.

Universaliter autem omnis corporalis motus passioni magis
quam actioni similis esse videtur, cum corporum sit[2] propria
passio. Vis autem sese movendi actio est. Ergo impartibilis
cuiusdam sese moveri officium est. Mundus itaque ex eo quod
corpus est sese non movet. Quare neque per se existit; ex alia
itaque causa pendet praestantiori.

Haec autem causa aut electione indiget consilioque ad opus,
aut ipso esse solo efficere potest. Si ipso esse *potest, electione
non indiget. Quod si non** potest indigetque ad agendum electione, nulla reperientur omnino quae sine electione quicquam
agant. Nam si ipsum esse divinum non tanti est, ut per se
[*355v*] possit agere, nullius certe rei esse per se operari poterit.[3]
Nunc autem videmus[4] omne quod per electionem agit aliquid
etiam ipso esse facere. Nam et eligere opus animi est. Quod si
aliam electionem a qua sit praesupponit, et illa aliam rursus, et[5]
rursus illa aliam in infinitum, numquam incipiet actio, cum
opus infinita praesupponat consilia et electiones innumeras.
Infinita vero numquam pertranseantur.[6] Quare est aliqua
operatio et electio quae a solo esse, nulla alia operatione et electione interiecta, procedit. Etenim hominis anima licet multa per
electionem agat corpori tamen sine electione ipso esse dat
vitam. Et cum primum apta materia fit, illam mox sine electione
sui ipsius vita vivificat. Nam si vita haec a nostra electione
fieret,[7] vel[8] numquam discederet a corpore vita in hominibus
semper cum corpore conversantibus, vel facile et frequenter in
hominibus qui ob contemplationem animam separant,[9] vel aliis
qui ob morbum corporis communionem renuunt. Quin etiam
cognosceret anima quaecumque in corpore facit. Nam electio
iudicium praesupponit.

Non omne autem quod ipso esse operatur electionem habet
per quam etiam operetur: ut elementa solo esse agunt, electione

---

[1]vel *om.* Y   [2]sint X   [3]potitur W   [4]vides Y   [5]et *om.* Y   [6]pertranseuntur Y
[7]manaret WX   [8]vel *om.* Y   [9]superant W   *-**potest, electione non indiget. Quod si
non *om.* Y

act through being not through choice—fire through heat, water through wetness. Therefore, if an operation which is completed through being has greater scope than an operation completed through choice, it's obvious it derives from another more noble cause, especially since any action proceeding from being always precedes an action made by choice—an example would be the action by which choice is produced or another action.

An action brought about through being alone is not unjustly attributed to divine things; for the action of those who act through being alone is effortless. But an effortless and happy operation must be attributed to divine things. Indeed, we live more easily and with less trouble when we lead a divine life according to virtue. So the cause of the world does everything through its own being, and so by its own substance. What acts by its own substance, however, is in first place; in second place is whatever is being effected. And what is in first place gives [something] to what is in second place, just as fire gives heat to another thing and is itself hot, and the soul gives life to the body and itself has life. Therefore the cause of the world, since it acts upon the world through being alone, is in first place. What is in second place is the world. So, if the world is the combination of all forms of the species, as Plato says in the *Timaeus* and Hermes Trismegistus too,[93] all the species will be present primarily in the world's author. For the same cause produces the sun, the moon, the horse, the man, and the rest of the forms in the world. So they are all primarily in the world's creator: another more outstanding sun than the one which is seen, another and more noble man, and so with all the rest.

Chapter 19. Confirmation of the above; and above the untrue forms are the true forms, that is, the Ideas.

This is also proved by what Plato argues in the *Phaedo,* the *Republic,* the *Timaeus* and the *Letters.*[94] The diversity of powers indicates a diversity of objects. But the sense is one thing, the intellect another. So the sensible object is one thing, the

nihil, calore ignis, aqua humore. Si ergo operatio quae per esse expletur[1] ad plura se extendit quam quae per electionem, patet quod ab alia venit causa digniore, praesertim cum actionem quae fit[2] per electionem semper actio secundum esse aliqua antecedat: puta illa qua electio producitur, vel alia quaedam.

Nec immerito divinis actio quae fit per esse tribuitur. Nam illaboriosa est actio eorum quae ipso esse agunt. Oportet autem divinis illaboriosam felicemque operationem tribuere. Nempe et nos facilius vivimus [*356r*] minorique cum labore, quando divinam secundum virtutem agimus vitam. Causa igitur mundi ipso sui esse omnia facit, ergo et a sui substantia. Quod vero sua agit substantia illud primo est; quicquid secundo est id quod efficitur. Et quod primo est dat ei quod est secundo, ut ignis et alteri caliditatem dat et ipse est calidus, anima vitam dat corpori et habet ipsa vitam. Causa itaque mundi, cum ipso esse agat mundum, primo est quicquid secundo est mundus. Si ergo mundus est omniformium specierum complexio, ut et[3] Plato in Timaeo et Mercurius inquit, omnes hae primo in mundi inerunt auctore. Eadem enim causa solem procreat, lunam, equum, hominem et ceteras in mundo formas. Haec ergo omnia primo sunt in opifice mundi, alius sol et praestantior quam qui videtur, homo alius et nobilior et reliqua omnia.

Confirmatio superiorum, et quod super formas non veras sunt verae formae, id est, ideae. Cap. XVIIII.[4]

Testatur et hoc Platonis ratio quae ex Phaedone, Republica, Timaeo, Epistolisque colligitur. Diversitas potentiarum diversitatem indicat[5] obiectorum. Sed aliud sensus est, aliud

---

[1]completur *W*
[5]arguit *WX*   [2]quae fit *om. WX*   [3]et *om. Y*   [4]*no ch. heading or break WX*

intelligible object another. And just as the intellect excels the
sense, so the intelligible object excels the sensible. But the
sensible object is something through itself, therefore the intelligible object is something through itself too. But the latter is a
universal rational principle that one understands. So the intelligible and universal species of things, which we call the Ideas,
exist.

Moreover, in matter we see the forms of things mixed in a
way with opposites: a circle with a square, equality with inequal-
ity, likeness with difference, beauty with ugliness, the good with
the imperfection of a potentiality, and one thing in another, just
as the forms seem to be confused in the elements. So none of
these things truly is what it is said to be, and each form loses its
perfection in matter, for, being impressed into a passive potentiality, it doesn't entirely retain the power to act. Moreover, all
bodies are in time and space and consist of matter and form.
Because they're in time they are measured by time, so each
body's condition corresponds to the condition of time. But time
is perpetually flowing in such a way that one moment always
succeeds another without a break. Therefore in the body one
quality follows another in individual moments, and so in the
individual moments each quality simultaneously begins and
ends. What begins isn't yet. What ends isn't any longer. So the
bodies' qualities are never true.

And if someone maintains some quality lasts for a particular
time, we'll ask him at once whether the quality has the same
power at the time's end as at its beginning. If he says it will stay
exactly the same, I'll ask the same question about a subsequent
period. If it's going to retain an identical power, it will always
stay exactly the same. But it's not true that bodies always stay
the same. So when the person is asked the question, he will be
forced to answer the power is not the same in the quality at the
time's end. It will be obvious it didn't stay the same because it
lost part of its power. Therefore bodily qualities don't even last
the shortest time. So, as Heraclitus and Timaeus maintain, as
often as you say "this is" when demonstrating something,
you're lying, for it's being changed while you speak.[95]

intellectus; aliud ergo sensibile, intelligibile aliud. Et sicuti praestat intellectus sensui, ita sensibili intelligibile praestat. Est autem sensibile per se aliquid, quare et per se aliquid est[1] intelligibile. Illud vero est universalis aliqua species, semper enim universalis ratio intelligitur. Extant ergo intelligibiles communesque rerum species, quas ideas vocamus.

Adde quod formas rerum videmus in materia contrariis quodammodo mixtas: circulum recto, aequalitatem inaequalitati, similitudinem dissimilitudini, pulchritudinem turpitudini,[2] bonum imperfectioni[3] potentiae, et alias [*356v*] in aliis, ut in elementis apparet formas esse confusas. Nullum ergo istorum vere est quod dicitur, et quaeque forma in materia perfectionem suam amittit. Nam cum passivae potentiae sit impressa, vim actus omnino non retinet. Corpora quin etiam sub tempore sunt et in loco omnia et ex materia constant ac forma. Quia sub tempore sunt, tempore mensurantur. Quare conditioni temporis corporis cuiusque conditio correspondet. Tempus autem ita fluit iugiter, ut[4] aliud semper sine mora momentum alteri momento succedat. Semper ergo in corpore alia qualitas aliam[5] momentis singulis subsequitur,[6] quare in singulis quaeque qualitas incipit simul et desinit. Quod incipit nondum est; quod desinit non est amplius. Numquam ergo verae sunt istorum corporum qualitates.

Ac siquis aliquam stare aliquod[7] tempus dixerit, eum statim interrogabimus, numquid par in ea vis est in temporis illius fine atque[8] in principio; si par stabit tantundem, de sequenti tempore quaeram quoque similiter. Et semper tantundem stabit, si vim retinebit aequalem. Stare autem semper corpora falsum est. Quare interrogatus ille respondere cogetur, non parem esse in ea qualitate[9] vim in temporis illius fine. Unde patebit non stetisse eam cum partem virtutis amiserit. Ergo ne minimum quidem tempus affectiones corporum permanent. Quotiens ergo aliquo demonstrato, ut Heraclitus et Timaeus inquit, hoc est, dicis,[10] mentiris utique, nam te loquente mutatur.

---

[1]erit *WX*   [2]pulchritudini *W*   [3]imperfectiori *Y*   [4]per *add. X*   [5]alteram *WX*
[6]subsequetur *WX*   [7]per *add. WX*   [8]atque *om. W;* ac *X*   [9]qualitatis *Y*
[10]dicit *Y*

Moreover, since bodies exist in space, they are extended in many parts. No one body exists as any one of its parts. But you can think of the parts in anything as infinite. And you can say about every part that it isn't the whole itself: this part isn't the whole man, nor this and so on with the individual parts. Therefore a man is not a man in infinite ways, but only in one way. So a man is nothing else but man.

Again, every body is made from matter and form. A body isn't called "man" or "fire" on account of matter, since matter is sempiternal and they aren't, and since matter itself is equally open to all forms. And so on account of matter some body is no more called "fire" than "air" or "man." Therefore a body is called such and such only on account of the form. But the form is a part. So [a body is called such and such only] on account of a part. But what is partly a man isn't a man, but man-like; what's partly a fire isn't a fire, but fire-like. So not one of these bodies truly is what it is said to be.

Moreover, truth itself is eternal and changeless. For if you were ever to deny truth exists, either you would say it falsely or truly. If falsely, then truth exists. If truly, it is true truth doesn't exist. If what you say is true, it's true because of truth. Therefore truth exists.[96] Therefore truth is eternal and changeless. So it can't be sustained in a changing thing, for what is situated in a changing thing is also changed with it. But all bodies undergo change, so the truth exists in none of them. Therefore they aren't true, nor do they truly exist.

If, therefore, corporeal forms are imperfect, they are not the first forms. For what is the first of its type is completely such, for the rational principle of each nature is established in its totality in the first member. So above the imperfect forms there are some perfect, primary and complete forms which aren't sustained in a subject (for they wouldn't be complete). We call these the reasons and the Ideas of the imperfect forms.

But if bodies' forms are not true, where, in fact, are the true forms? Nowhere? But the false would be more powerful than the true if it existed and the true didn't. But this is impossible, for what is stronger is stronger because of the truth; for, unless

Praeterea quia in loco corpora sunt, in partes plurimas extenduntur. Neque corpus aliquod aliqua partium suarum existit. Partes autem [*357r*] in quolibet infinitae considerari possunt. De quacumque vero dicere potes, haec totum ipsum non est: ut haec non est homo, neque haec, et ita de singulis. Infinite igitur non est homo, uno tantummodo homo est. Unde magis homo non est quam homo.

Item corpus quodlibet ex materia constat et forma, et secundum materiam nec homo dicitur nec ignis, quia[1] materia sempiterna, ista nequaquam, et materia ipsa ad omnes aeque se habet formas. Atque idcirco non magis per eam corpus aliquod ignis quam aer vel homo cognominatur. Secundum formam igitur tantum tale vel tale dicitur. Forma vero pars est. Igitur secundum partem. Quod vero per partem homo non homo, sed humanum; quod per partem ignis non ignis, sed igneum. Nullum ergo istorum vere est quod dicitur.

Praeterea veritas ipsa aeterna est et immobilis. Nam siquando dixeris eam non esse, aut falso hoc dices aut[2] vere. Si falso, est utique veritas. Si vere, verum est non esse veritatem[3]. Si verum est, veritate verum est. Est itaque veritas. Sempiterna ergo veritas est et immobilis. Quare nulla in re mobili sustinetur, quod enim in re mutabili iacet cum ea quoque mutatur. Omnia vero corporalia permutantur. Itaque in nullis est veritas; non ergo sunt vera, neque vere existunt.

Si ergo *formae corporum imperfectae sunt, primae formae non sunt; quod enim primum tale est integrum tale, tota enim ratio naturae cuiusque in primo fundatur. Sunt itaque** formae aliquae super istas perfectae primae et integrae, quae non in subiecto sunt, neque enim integrae essent. Illas istarum rationes ideasque vocamus.

Ac si formae corporum verae non sunt, ubinam verae sunt? Nusquamne? At potentius esset falsum quam verum, si illud quidem esset, hoc nequaquam; impossibile vero istud; quod enim potentius veritate potentius est, nisi enim verum sit esse

---

[1]quam *W*   [2]an *W*   [3]unitatem *W*   *-**om. *W*

it's true that it's stronger, it won't be what it's said to be. Or rather, what are called false forms can't exist without the truth's presence, for they won't exist, unless it's true they exist. So somewhere the true species exist.

But surely our soul has the species which are more true than the ones which are perceived? With the former the soul judges the latter, approves and condemns and corrects them and gets to know the extent to which they've fallen away from the true species or the extent to which they agree. However, the person who doesn't see the true species can't compare other things to them. The soul, in fact, corrects the visible circle when it doesn't touch the plane at a particular point, for otherwise it would never rest content. And it approves or condemns every structure made by art and the measures of music, and decides about the goodness and badness of natural things, the utility, the bad effects, the beauty, the ugliness. The soul possesses the truer forms and with them it judges concerning corporeal things. For the judge is more perfect than what is being judged.

But the forms in the soul aren't the first forms, for they're changeable and although they don't exist in space, still, they do traverse the intervals of time. Nor do they always exist in act either, for the soul doesn't always act through them. Nor do they exist in the whole of the intelligence, but in a part of it. For just as the whole soul is not the intelligence (since it adds the nature of both moving and perceiving), so the intelligence in the soul isn't the total or first intelligence. For the intelligence is in the soul. But what is in another also comes from another, for what can't sustain itself can't produce itself (for that's the more difficult job). Nevertheless, this intelligence doesn't come from the soul, since the rational principle for producing the intelligence would be in the soul. So the whole soul would be the intelligence and be the whole and perfect intelligence; and every soul would possess the intelligence, since the rational principle of the soul is present in every soul.

Therefore, above the soul and above the intelligence, which is part of the soul, is a certain prime intelligence which is completely itself and entirely absolute. In it will be the first and

potentius, non [*357v*] erit quod dicitur. Quin immo sine veritatis praesentia esse illae non possunt quae falsae formae dicuntur, nisi enim verum sit illas esse, non erunt. Alicubi ergo verae sunt species.

Nonne animus noster veriores habet species quam quae cernuntur. Quibus iudicat eas et probat damnatque et corrigit et quo a veris discedant intelligit quove[1] congruant. Qui autem vera non videt ad ea comparare alia minime potest. Visibilem quidem circulum animus corrigit cum in puncto planum non tangat, neque enim quiesceret umquam; et omnem artificiorum structuram musicaeque modulos vel probat vel damnat, et naturalium rerum bonitatem vel pravitatem, utilitatem et nocumenta, pulchritudinem, turpitudinem iudicat. Veriores igitur habet formas animus, quibus de corporalibus iudicet. Perfectior enim iudex est quam quod iudicatur.

Sed neque hae quae sunt in animo primae sunt formae, mobiles enim et quamquam in loco non sunt, per temporis tamen intervalla discurrunt. Neque actu semper existunt, non enim semper per eas animus agit. Neque tota in mente sunt, sed mentis parte. Nam, sicut anima tota mens non est quoniam addit et movendi et sentiendi naturam, ita mens quae in anima non est mens tota nec prima. Est enim mens in anima; quod vero in alio est, et ab alio est, quod enim se sustinere nequit neque potest producere, maius enim id opus. Neque tamen haec mens ab anima, quia in anima mentis producendae[2] ratio esset. Unde et tota anima esset mens et mens quidem tota atque perfecta; et omnis anima mentem haberet, quia in omni anima ratio inest animae.

Quamobrem super animam et mentem quae pars animae est, mens est [*358r*] quaedam prima in se ipsa integra ac penitus absoluta. In qua primae ac verissimae erunt rerum omnium

---

truest species of all things, because they exist now above space and time and change. If they are the prime species—for one must arrive at the prime ones—they're not in another subject. So you haven't on the one hand the essence of the intelligence, and on the other the species in the intelligence. For there the rational principles of everything are the essence and the life. Whatever has been made by this intelligence, the world's creator, exists in life itself. Therefore Plato says in the *Timaeus* that the creator of the world, the intellect, contemplates the Ideas in the living substance and constructs the machine of the world according to his own likeness.[97]

Chapter 20. Confirmation of the above; and on the natural truth of the universal forms.

The special powers and forms of things are not only in an imaginary way in our intelligence, but also in a natural [i.e. real] way in God, in the angels, in the celestial souls and our souls, and in the heavens and the vegetable nature and in prime matter. In all these the universal powers exist, although we may know nothing about them. The powers are in the creativeness itself of the divine essence and so in a way they are in the angelic creativeness, although [the angels] are not thought to understand [the powers as such], since for understanding they too [like us] turn towards internal objects [i.e. the Ideas]. But such forms are also in the vegetable nature, although it does not need to understand. For who is going to deny there are powers in the vegetable nature which produce teeth and hair; or, if there are, that they are not different or that one teeth-producing or one hair-producing power is not enough to produce all the teeth and hairs?[98]

But we know also the universal powers are natural [i.e. real] from the beginning, middle and end of the universe: firstly, because the world's order is established by the intellect acting through the forms. The forms, since they are the first reasons and the universal causes of things are the most natural [i.e. real].

species, quia supra locum iam et tempus motumque existunt. Quae si primae sunt, ad primas enim deveniendum est, in alio subiecto non sunt. Non ergo aliud ibi mentis essentia, aliud in mente species. Essentia enim ibi sunt et vita omnium rationes, et quicquid ab hac mente mundi opifice factum est in ipsa vita est. Quapropter Plato in Timaeo mundi opificem intellectum contemplari ideas dicit in vivente substantia et ad sui similitudinem mundi machinam fabricare.

Confirmatio superiorum; et de naturali veritate formarum universalium. Cap. XX [1]

*Speciales rerum vires et formae non solum imaginario modo sunt in mente nostra, sed etiam naturali modo in Deo,[2] angelis, animabus[3] coelestibus, nostrisque animis, et in[4] coelis et[5] natura vegetali et in[6] materia prima. In his omnibus universales sunt vires, etsi[7] nos nihil intelligamus. Atqui et in ipsa divinae essentiae foecunditate et inde[8] in angelica foecunditate quodammodo, etsi[9] fingantur non intelligere, quandoquidem et illi intelligendo ad[10] intima[11] se convertunt obiecta. Iam vero[12] in natura vegetali sunt tales formae, etiamsi cognitione non egeat.[13] Quis enim dixerit in vegetali[14] vel non esse vim dentificam et pilificam, vel, si sunt, non esse differentes, vel non sufficere dentificam unam unamve pilificam ad omnes dentes atque pilos?

Universalia vero etiam[15] naturalia esse cognoscimus ex principio, medio, fine universi. Primum quidem,[16] quia ordo mundi fit ab intellectu agente per formas, quae, quia primae rerum rationes causaeque sunt communes, maxime sunt naturales. Deinde, non dicimus de essentia universi principaliter**

---

[1]*no ch. heading or break WX*   [2]*X merely reads* sed naturali in Deo   [3]animalibus *Y*
[4]animis, et in *om. X*   [5]et *om. X*   [6]et in *om. X*   [7]etiamsi *X*   [8]inde *om. Y*
[9]etiamsi *X*   [10]in *X*   [11]intrinseca *X*   [12]Iam vero *om.; et add. X*   [13]egeant *Y*
[14]vegetativa *X*   [15]vero etiam *om. X*   [16]quidem *om. X*   *-**om. W (cont.)*

Secondly, we don't say the essence of the universe is the genera principally, since, like the powers, the genera are referred to the species; nor is it principally the individual things, since they're infinite, orderless and changeable, and the universe is perfect without any numbering off of the single things one by one. Therefore the universe's essence is constituted from the species. So it is they especially which are the real (as it were), that is, the natural things. Thirdly, the purpose of the nutritive nature is to have real nourishment. But, primarily, it's for nourishment as a species, for hunger's stimulus drives us towards food even when we've no mental picture of it; then, when we have, it drives us to food in general before driving us towards this or that particular food. The purpose of the reproductive nature is also the species; it has been implanted for the sake of propagating the species. But it wants the real species not an imaginary one. Finally, all the inclinations and movements in the world through their own particular goods contribute towards the general good of the whole, according to the primary purpose of nature. But what moves everything and is the perfection of everything is natural [i.e. real].

Consequently, notice that all men, in that they share the accidental appearances peculiar to man and differ from the beasts, have among themselves one common origin for the accidental factors, that is, the nature which they share and which distinguishes them from the beasts. This common nature is the real cause of real effects and it is true and one, even when mental activity has ceased.

Don't let it disturb you that subsequent accidents seem to have divided this nature; for what is subsequent and unnecessary and changeable doesn't detract from that prior, one community of the nature. For when you divide one flame into two little flames, just as there was one fieryness, so one fieryness remains; for division, which is the enduring of dimension, doesn't affect fieryness. But fieryness, as Avicenna maintains, precedes dimension, although its immediate accidents may come after dimension (or at any rate fieryness properly adheres not to dimension but to matter).

*esse genera, quia tamquam potentiae referuntur ad species; neque individua praecipue, quia infinita, inordinata, mutabilia, et singula singulatim dinumerando sine quolibet perfectum est universum. Ergo essentia universi constat ex speciebus. Praecipue ergo reales (ut ita dixerim) sunt, id est,[1] naturales. Tertio, intentio naturae nutritivae est ad alimentum reale.[2] Est autem primo ad speciem alimenti. Stimulus enim famis nos etiam non imaginantes ad[3] cibum urget; et deinde prius imaginantes cibum communem quam hunc vel illum. Intentio quoque genitivae est[4] ad speciem cuius propagandae gratia est inserta. Non autem est ad imaginem, sed ad rem eius intentio. Denique omnes in mundo inclinationes motusque per propria bona ad commune totius bonum conferunt praecipua intentione naturae. Est autem naturale quod movet omnia et omnium est perfectio.

Proinde attende cunctos homines, sicut in apparentibus accidentibus homini propriis conveniunt inter se differuntque a brutis, sic[5] habere in se unam communemque accidentium eorundem originem, naturam scilicet illis communem a brutis differentem. Communis haec natura realis[6] est realium[7] effectuum causa et vera unaque, cessante etiam mentis discursione.

Neque te turbet quod divisa videtur posterioribus accidentibus. Quod enim posterius et superfluum et mutabile est non aufert priorem illam[8] unamque[9] naturae communitatem. Nam cum flammam unam in duas diviseris flammulas, igneitas sicut erat una, ita restat una. Non enim ipsam attigit divisio quae dimensionis passio est. Igneitas vero, ut Avicenna putat, antecedit dimensionem, licet praesentia eius accidentia dimensionem sequantur; vel saltem igneitas non dimensioni proprie haeret sed materiae.**

---

[1] reales (ut ita dixerim) sunt, id est, *om. X*　　　[2] naturale *X*　　　[3] ad *om. X*　　　[4] est *om. X*
[5] sic *om. X*　　　[6] naturalis *X*　　　[7] naturalium *X*　　　[8] illam *om. X*　　　[9] -que *om. X*
(cont.) *-**om. W (cont.)*

Moreover, subsequent to division, the Idea which is in nature, like a nursery garden in matter, makes fieryness continue on here and there.

I omit that the species are predicated of individuals with a real predication; also, that natural knowledge is not about individual things but about the species.

Besides, all things try to propagate their own power; so, as far as they can, they exhaust it in generation. Firstly, they generate themselves in themselves. Then they generate themselves outside themselves. The elements produce appropriate qualities in themselves from the power of the appropriate species: from heat in potency comes the actual heat in the fire; from potential cold the actual cold in water. You can see this if you put water that's been heated by fire into coolish air; the water will restore itself to its usual coldness. The air won't do it, for coldness will be more intense in the water than it is in the air. But, when it has stopped being impeded by its opposite, the potential cold in the water gives rise in itself to its usual offspring, that is, actual cold. Each mature plant also generates itself in itself from the integral creativeness of its nature, that is, it generates the seed. In the seed is the plant's total power, its total reason. Similarly in animals the seed is the whole animal being produced in itself.

Moreover, the soul, when it has been instructed in the sciences of other things, recovers natural power and generates itself in itself. For it can fashion its total nature in itself by knowing itself. And the intelligence does it even better, because in the intelligence is the first knowledge; in it is the most perfect knowledge, therefore the knowledge closest to the thing that's known. So what's knowing, the thing known, and knowing are identical. Therefore essential generation will be in the intelligence. For all things are by way of essence in the very first essence.

But in individual things external generation follows internal generation. For after the fire's power has made the fire hot, it also makes the wood hot. The plant too, when the seed has been fashioned in itself, brings it forth and creates a plant, and an animal does the same. The soul, when it knows itself and

*Adde quod post divisionem tam idea quae in natura est quam seminarium quod est in[1] materia igneitatem hic et ibi continuat.

Mitto quod species de individuis praedicantur praedicatione reali.[2] Item[3] quod naturalis scientia est de rebus non individuis sed speciebus.**

Praeterea omnia suam vim propagare nituntur. Ideo quoad possunt eam exhauriunt generando; generantque se ipsa in se ipsis primum, extra se deinde se ipsa. Elementa ex virtute propriae speciei proprias in se qualitates gignunt: ex calore in[4] virtute, actu calor in igni; ex frigiditate in virtute, actu frigus in aqua.[5] Quod apparet siquis aquam igne calefactam in aere temperato posuerit; aqua ad solitam se ipsa redibit frigiditatem. Nec aer eam dabit, nam intensior erit in aqua quam in aere illo frigus;[6] sed in aquae potentia frigus remoto contrarii sui impedimento solitam suam in se ipso gignit prolem, scilicet[7] frigus in actu. Et planta quaeque adulta ex integra naturae foecunditate se ipsam generat in se ipsa, id est, semen, in quo tota vis est[8] tota ratio plantae. In animalibusque similiter semen animal totum in se ipso producitur.

Anima insuper cum in aliarum rerum disciplinis instructa est, naturalem vim recuperans, se ipsam generat in se ipsa. Nam se cognoscendo totam sui naturam in se ipsa figurat, idque mens efficit[9] multo melius, quia enim in ea prima cognitio[10] est,[11] in ea est [*358v*] perfectissima, proxima igitur cognito.[12] Idem ergo cognoscens et[13] cognitum et cognitio. Essentialis igitur erit in mente generatio. In prima enim essentia sunt per modum essentiae omnia.

Generationem vero interiorem in singulis exterior sequitur generatio. Postquam enim[14] virtus ignis ignem fecit calidum, calidum facit et lignum. Et planta semine in se concreto extra promit et plantam concreat, animalque similiter. Anima, cum

---

[1]est in *transposed Y*   [2]naturali *X*   [3]Ita *X*   [4]in *om. WX*   [5]aquam *X*
[6]frigiditas *X*   [7]scilicet *om. WX*   [8]*for* vis est *X reads* vis cuius est, *Y reads* vis eius
[9]faciet *WX*   [10]cogitatio *W*   [11]est *om. WX*   [12]cognitio *WX*   [13]et *om. WX*
[14]enim *om. WX*   (cont.) *-**om. W*

understands the true reasons of things which are inside itself, produces outside itself in its own likeness laws, artifacts, books, words, morals (producing them according to the rule of its rational principles). Therefore all things first generate themselves in themselves, then generate themselves outside themselves too. So the world's intelligence, which is the first essence, the first creativeness, and from which proceeds all creativeness and external generation (as we've seen), creates the world. So the world, which is the intelligence's particular child, is in a way the intelligence. For every single thing produces itself. And since nothing produces itself outside itself till it has first produced itself in itself, so the intelligence first generates the world in itself when (unfolding itself in itself) it conceives its creativeness. Now joy accompanies the internal generation, just as pleasure accompanies the external.

Chapter 21. Confirmation of the above and concerning the first intelligence.

Again, if there's no cause to the universe, but everything occurs by chance, how is it the degrees of things have been mutually ordered, the powers distinguished, the places separated? How is it all things always function in the same steady way and individual things proceed from individual things according to the nature of each? Such order consists in the union of opposite things, and since opposites shun each other, they are joined into one from elsewhere. But there must be one something that bestows union on the multitude of different things. Therefore outside the individual parts of the world there is the one coordinator of all things. But this order is more marvellous and more beautiful than every order that can be caused by any other reason. Now every order has been generated by order, and every reason has been generated by reason. It follows therefore that in the world's coordinator there is a more beautiful order than the world's order, a more outstanding reason than all our reason, a more venerable intelligence than every intelligence.

se noverit et rationes veras rerum quae in se sunt comprehenderit,[1] ad sui similitudinem extra se porrigit leges, artificia, libros, verba, mores, ad rationum suarum normam educit. Omnia ergo se in se ipsis generant primo, deinde etiam se generant extra se ipsa. Mens igitur mundi quae prima essentia[2] est, prima foecunditas a qua et foecunditas omnis et generatio extra se, ut vidimus,[3] gignit mundum. Mundus igitur propria mentis proles mens est quodammodo. Nam unumquodque se ipsum gignit. Et quia nihil se extra se gignit, nisi ante in se genuerit, ideo in se primo mens generat[4] mundum, dum se ipsam in se suam explicans foecunditatem concipit.[5] Generationem vero interiorem gaudium comitatur, sicut voluptas exteriorem.

Confirmatio superiorum et de prima mente. Cap. XXI.[6]

Item si nulla est causa universi, sed casu currunt omnia, quomodo invicem ordinati sunt rerum gradus, distinctae vires, loca discreta? Quomodo eundem semper agunt universa tenorem et secundum naturam cuiusque a singulis singula proficiscuntur? Ordo huiusmodi in oppositorum unione consistit, et quia opposita se invicem fugiunt, aliunde copulantur in unum. Unum vero esse debet quod diversorum multitudini exhibet unionem. Unus itaque est extra singulas [*359r*] mundi partes omnium ordinator. Ordo autem iste omni ordine qui ab aliqua alia ratione fiat mirabilior est et pulchrior. Et omnis ordo genitus est ab ordine, et genita ratio a ratione. Ex quo sequitur ut in mundi ordinatore ordo sit mundi ordine pulchrior, ratio omni nostra ratione praestantior, mens omni mente venerabilior.

---

[1]comprehendit *Y*   [2]essentiae *Y*   [3]videmus *WX*   [4]genuit *X*   [5]conciperet *WX*
[6]*no ch. heading or break* WX

At all events, this intelligence understands itself much more than our reason understands itself. But it is the cause of the total order. So it understands it is the order's cause, the creator of all things, the beginning of all and the end of all too. But it couldn't know that it's the order's cause, the creator, the beginning and the end of all, unless it knew the order and knew all things. Therefore the notions of all things, which we call the Ideas, subsist in that intelligence. If it is the prime intelligence, undoubtedly its understanding is completely perfect. But the most perfect is the most certain. But the most certain understanding is closest to the thing which is understood and in it what understands and what is understood are identical. So it is the same intelligence's essence which understands and is understood. And so to an even greater extent the intelligence's understanding is the same as its essence, since understanding is the intermediary whereby the knower knows what is being known. So in the intelligence to be and to understand are the same, therefore to be and to live also. For to live is the mean between to be and to understand. In the same way movement is the mean between rest and conversion. Therefore essence, life, intelligence, being, living, understanding are identical: it is essence when it is at rest, life when it acts and is moved, intelligence when it goes back into itself. Returning into itself it sees all things in itself; they are in that essence as in their principle.

But the intelligence doesn't look outside in order to understand all things, for it understands them before they can be externalized: they presuppose its understanding just as they do its being. But understanding can't exist without something being understood. So before everything can exist, the intelligence understands everything.

But it doesn't understand everything in order to make everything, for it would be referring the internal operation to the external one which is less perfect. Or rather, if it contemplated everything in order to make everything, contemplation would presuppose intending everything. But whoever intends everything already knows about everything beforehand.

Haec utique mens multo magis se ipsam intelligit quam ratio nostra se ipsam. Ipsa vero est totius ordinis causa. Quare se ordinis causam esse cognoscit, omnium effectricem, omnium principium, omnium quoque finem. Neque vero se esse causam[1] ordinis, effectricem,[2] principium, finemque omnium nosse potest, nisi ordinem illum et omnia noverit. Omnium itaque notiones ea in mente consistunt quas ideas vocamus. Haec si prima mens est, est utique perfectissima eius intelligentia. Haec vero quae certissima. Certissima vero quae rei cognitae proxima et in qua quod intelligit et quod intelligitur idem. Eadem ergo mentis essentia est quae intelligit et quae intelligitur eadem. Quare et intelligentia eius multo magis cum essentia eadem, cum ea medium sit quo intelligens aliquid intelligit quod intelligitur. Idem itaque in ea et esse et intelligere est, ergo et esse et vivere. Vivere enim inter esse et intelligere medium, sicut motus inter statum et conversionem medium est. Eadem ergo essentia, vita, mens, esse, vivere, intelligere: essentia ut stat, vita ut agit moveturque, mens ut in se ipsam redit. In se rediens in se videt omnia quae tamquam in principio suo in ea essentia sunt.

Neque vero extrinsecus respicit ut intelligat omnia, prius enim intelligit quam externa sint, quae sicut eius esse sic eius intelligentiam [*359v*] praesupponunt. Intelligentia vero sine re intellecta esse non potest. Quare antequam sint omnia, omnia mens haec intelligit.

Neque vero[3] intelligit omnia[4] ut faciat omnia. Nam internam operationem ad externam quae minus[5] perfecta est referret.[6] Immo si, ut faciat omnia, contemplatur omnia, contemplatio haec intentionem omnium praesupponeret. Qui vero intendit omnia cogitationem[7] omnium iam praesupponit. Quare vel

---

[1]casum *Y* (*in corrigenda list only;* causum *in printed text as such*)   [2]efficientem *WX*
[3]vere *Y*   [4]Neque vero intelligit omnia *repeated W*   [5]minus *om. W*   [6]referre *W*
[7]cognitionem *WX*

So either you will advance to infinity, or the contemplation of everything precedes the intending and effecting of everything.

Chapter 22. Confirmation of the above and how the Ideas are related to God and to lower things.

So all things are conceived in God's intelligence before they are drawn out into matter. The conceptions are one and many. They are one in essence, otherwise there'd be a compounding of essences in the first essence which has to be the simplest of all (since whatever is the first in any genus of things is also the simplest). But the conceptions are many in their role as cause, otherwise everything they bring about would be entirely one. But they are called "unities" by Plato mainly because, just as individual men can be reduced to one common nature in themselves and individual horses to theirs, so can these common factors in individuals be referred to common factors outside individuals. Now the one factor in a multiplicity, as it's in another, must come from another. But it can't come from any one thing in the multiplicity, because it would be peculiar to that and not belong to the rest. Nor can it come from the many things in so far as they are many, because it too would be many things. Therefore it's from one something and the rational principle of the one something that surpasses the many. So above the nature common to individual men and the nature common to individual horses there has to be the one rational principle of a man and the one of a horse. And just as all the natures exist in one matter, so all the rational principles exist in one essence.

The former change in time, the latter stay still in eternity. The former have been divided by quantity, the latter are undivided. Therefore the rational principles of all the former exist prior to them all in the one intelligence, and are absolutely one and absolutely unchangeable.

Each death either accords with the form being abandoned by its subject, or in the case of a compound with the dissolution of the parts. But the rational principles aren't in a subject, nor are they compounded from corporeal parts.

procedetur in infinitum, vel contemplatio omnium omnium intentionem effectionemque praecedet.

Confirmatio superiorum et quomodo ideae se habent ad Deum atque ad inferiora. Cap. XXII.[1]

Concepta ergo sunt omnia Dei mente antequam in materiam educantur. Conceptiones istae et unum sunt et multa. Unum essentia, ne in prima essentia essentiarum compositio sit quae debet esse omnium simplicissima, quia quicquid primum in quolibet rerum genere id et simplicissimum. Multa vero sunt ratione, ne unum penitus sint quaecumque inde efficiuntur. Unitates vero ex eo maxime appellantur a Platone, quia, quemadmodum singuli homines ad unam communem in ipsis naturam et singuli equi ad suam reducuntur, sic istae communes in singulis ad communes extra singula referuntur. Nam quod est[2] in multitudine unum, cum sit in alio, ab alio debet esse; non tamen ab uno multorum quia proprium illi esset et reliquis non competeret; non a multis illis qua[3] multa sunt quia et multa esset et illud. Ergo ab uno aliquo et ratione unius alicuius quod multitudinem supereminet. Quare supra naturam communem singulis hominibus et communem naturam equis singulis ratio una hominis, una equi debet esse; et sicut istae omnes in una materia [*360r*] sunt, sic illae in una essentia omnes.

Sub tempore istae fluunt, illae in aeternitate consistunt. Istae in quantitate divisae, illae simplices. Ergo rationes istorum omnium ante haec omnia sunt mente in una et unae maxime et incommutabiles maxime.

Omnis[4] enim interitus vel formae convenit a subiecto desertae vel composito ex partium[5] dissolutione. Illae vero neque in subiecto sunt, neque ex partibus corporalibus sunt compositae.

---

[1] *no ch. heading or break* WX   [2] est *om.* WX   [3] quia X   [4] Omnes Y   [5] partim W

But if someone argues corruption also comes from an opposite, he must understand that nothing can be a corrupting opposite for the forms which aren't in matter. For one thing doesn't destroy another, except to impart its own form to the other's matter; for nature doesn't aim at the bad. So where there's no shared matter, the reciprocal corruption of opposites can't exist. And if the intelligence is above bodies, it exists above bodily conditions which are division, time, place. Therefore the intelligence surpasses all time, place and division. So it includes and encompasses them as well. Because bodies derive from the intelligence, the intelligence is present everywhere in all things, preserving by its power the things that it makes. Because the intelligence exists above the conditions of bodies, it is present in all time but is eternal; it is present in all division but remains undivided; it is present in every place but isn't circumscribed. Therefore it is in all things but not included in them; it is above all things but not excluded from them.

If all this is true, and each Idea is present in its entirety everywhere and imparts itself to single things, it is not mixing itself with anything. It is manifesting its power not its substance, its similitude not its essence. To sum up in a word, the countenance of the divine intelligence when it gazes into the mirror of matter manifests none of its parts, but copies of the individual parts. People who stare at matter don't see true things, but some things having the appearance of truth and certain empty adumbrations of true things. Consequently, a person, who doesn't see the true things also while looking at the copies, is said by Plato to be dreaming, since he's being deceived by false images and like a dreamer he's supposing those things true which are just images. The doubts which Plato here introduced now seem to be sufficiently resolved by all this. So what's been said about such problems is enough.

Therefore, just as the image of one face is at the same time in its entirety reflected back from a number of mirrors and just as the one image is multiplied in a fractured mirror, so the total image of each Idea is in its individual things and is multiplied on account of the extent and distribution of matter.

Sed et siquis dixerit a contrario etiam venire corruptionem, sciat formis quae in materia[1] non sunt nihil esse contrarium corruptivum. Neque enim unum destruit aliud, nisi ut in eius materia[2] suam inducat[3] formam. Nam intentio naturae non est ad malum; ubi ergo non est communis materia, mutua[4] contrariorum corruptio esse non potest. Ac[5] si mens illa supra corpora[6] est, super corporum conditiones existit: hae vero sunt partitio, tempus, locus. Ergo mens omne supereminet tempus, omnem locum, omnem partitionem; ergo et ea complectitur ambitque. Quia a mente corpora sunt, ideo omnibus ubique praesens adest mens sua virtute conservans quae facit. Quia super eorum conditiones existit, ideo toti adest tempori sed aeterna, toti partitioni sed simplex, omni loco non circumscripta. Est ergo in omnibus non inclusa; super omnia non exclusa.

Si ita est, et idea quaeque ubique adest tota, et se communicat singulis, nulli se miscet; virtutem suam exhibet non substantiam, similitudinem non essentiam. Et, ut verbo uno complectar, divinae[7] mentis vultus in materiae speculum intuens nullas suas exhibet partes, sed singularum partium simulacra. [*360v*] Neque veras res vident, qui in materiam vertunt oculos, sed verisimilia quaedam et verarum rerum inanes quasdam adumbrationes. Quo fit, ut quisquis dum haec inspicit illa quoque non suspicit somniare a Platone dicatur, quia falsis decipitur imaginibus, et somniantis instar, quae imagines sunt res esse veras existimat. Ex his omnibus dubitationes quae introductae hic sunt a Platone iam satis solutae videntur. Quare de his haec dicta sufficiant.

*Proinde,[8] sicut vultus unius imago in multis tota simul est speculis[9] et quolibet fracto fit ex una multiplex, ita tota imago cuiusque ideae est in suis individuis et ob materiae dimensionem divisionemque[10] fit multiplex. Ac etiam sui ipsius unitatem**

---

[1]natura *W*   [2]materiam *X*   [3]inducit *W*   [4]mutuo *W*   [5]Et *WX*
[6]corpora *om. W*   [7]divae *WX*   [8]proinde *om. X*   [9]specialis *Y*   [10]-que *om. X*
*-**om. W (cont.)*

And still it preserves its own unity, just as the sun's light still remains one, although it is sustained in various colours in various ways.

Notice that matter, the vilest of all things, nevertheless retains its unity beneath all things. Notice that the primary extension too, which is made to be divided, similarly preserves its unity in every division. But since corporeity is nothing but matter in extension, it too retains its common unity in everything. Therefore animality and humanity can retain a common unity much more easily in their fewer derivatives than the meaner [universals] can in their many derivatives. If these corporeal [universals] can do it, subjected as they are to division and motion, the divine Ideas will be able to do it even more.

But even if you don't understand the way in which they can do it, still don't deny what reason is telling you for certain. In the *Phaedo* Plato tells us to stick close to reason, even if the lower faculties are unreliable.[99] Galen applied this to reason in the art [of medicine]; he tells us to stay with reason even if the result is not successful.[100] For who's going to alter a foundation that's been laid correctly just because the wall on top of it hasn't been properly erected? In the *Gorgias* the same is applied to morals: we are told to stand firm in what reason approves.[101] To the extent the soul excels the body, so the soul's health is better than the body's and its disease worse than bodily disease; and the health of the soul must never be neglected, even at the cost of everything—of the body and this life. In the *Republic* and the *Laws* the same is applied to piety.[102] For when, according to the *Timaeus,* you've deduced from the world's imperfection that the world depends on another and depends on the order, just proportion and power of that other by the highest power, goodness and providence, and that one result comes from one cause, you ought to stick fast to this conclusion even if you don't see how it is brought about.[103] Otherwise, human error would appear to be disparaging providence. For nobody in his right mind denies a clock is made by a clockmaker or juggling tricks are done by a juggler simply because he doesn't know exactly how they're done. Similarly,

*servat, sicut lumen solis quamvis in variis coloribus vario suscipiatur modo unum tamen extat.

Attende materiam omnium vilissimam tamen servare se sub omnibus unam. Dimensionem quoque primam cuius passio est divisio similiter unam in omni se divisione servare. Cum vero corporeitas nihil aliud sit quam extensa materia, ipsa quoque una communisque restat in cunctis. Ergo[1] animalitas et humanitas multo facilius in paucioribus suis retinere possunt communem unitatem quam viliora illa in pluribus. Si corporea haec divisioni motuique subiecta id possunt, multo magis ideae divinae id poterunt.

Tu vero, etsi modum quo id valeant non cognoscis, tamen negare noli quod certa tibi dictat ratio, cui firmiter inhaerendum in Phaedone iubet, etiamsi posteriora vacillent. Quod Galenus ad artis transtulit rationem cui monet manendum etiamsi exitus non succedat. Nam quis fundamentum rite iactum mutet, ex eo quod paries non examussim fuerit superstructus? Idem in Gorgia transfertur ad mores, ubi iubemur rationi huic stare probanti. Quanto animus praestat corpori, tanto sanitatem animi, quam corporis meliorem esse, morbumque peiorem; ipsamque animi sanitatem numquam esse negligendam, etiamsi ob eius studium iactura rerum omnium et corporis et huius vitae fuerit subeunda. Idem transfertur in Republica et Legibus ad pietatem. Postquam enim ex defectu mundi secundum Timaeum iudicaveris ipsum pendere ex alio atque ex eius ordine, commoditate, virtute pendere a summa potentia, bonitate, providentia, et opus unum ab uno, debes in hac sententia permanere, etiamsi non videas quo id modo fiat, ne[2] error humanus derogare providentiae videatur. Nemo enim sanae mentis negat orologium factum esse a fabro, vel a praestigiatore praestigias propterea[3] quod modum quo fiant non**

---

[1] et *add.* X　　[2] vel X　　[3] ex eo X　　*(cont.)* *-**om. W (cont.)*

nobody will deny it is the father's foresight that governs a home, whatever some small child has to babble about it.

Chapter 23. *Why we ought to approach dialectic with caution; and how we ought to divide the one into the many or resolve the many into the one.*

It's said in the *Cratylus* that in a long debate great diligence must be applied in establishing the first principles.[104] After that you can think about what follows. But if this must be done when you're establishing the principles of any particular art, it must be done even more with life's end which is the principle of all arts and actions. Hence, when the subject is felicity, the dialectical faculty is quite rightly introduced into the discussion as the way to examine truth; otherwise we'd perhaps make a wrong or unfortunate judgement about the most important thing of all. Elsewhere the penalty for erring is ignorance, here the penalty is misery as well. But why so much caution just at the beginning? It's because everything is contained in the beginning and comes from it. Consequently knowledge as well as ignorance about it is propagated through all that follows, and with the multiplication of the consequences there's a multiplication of mistakes.

Pleasure and wisdom are the subjects of the debate, but both are common to a number of species and innumerable individual things. So, in order to know about them best, you have to have the skill that can draw the one common thing out into many things and lead the many things back into the one (the former so that you don't stay in the genus, the latter so that you don't wander on through an infinite sequence of single things). As we said above, the person who's going to have definite and perfect knowledge of a thing has to think about this. However, the skill isn't easy at all, but difficult: it doesn't confine itself to dividing and uniting corporeal things, but aspires to the level of uniting or multiplying the incorporeal species. Therefore many problems confront us on all sides, as we've said, so we ought to

*teneat. Item nullus negabit domum patris providentia gubernari ob id quod puellus aliquis ibi[1] balbutiat.

Qua cautione dialecticen aggredi debeamus et qua ratione dividere unum in multa vel solvere[2] multa in unum. Cap. XXIII.[3]

In Cratylo dicitur in principiis constituendis summa diligentia cum longa disputatione est adhibenda. Post haec quae consequuntur considerandum. Quod si in principiis cuiuslibet artis id est faciendum, maxime circa finem vitae, qui est actionum omnium artiumque principium; ideo ubi de felicitate agitur, merito dialectica facultas[4] in medium adducitur tamquam veritatis examen, ne forte in re omnium gravissima male infeliciterque iudicemus. Alibi enim erroris poena est ignorantia, hic insuper poena miseria. Sed cur tanta in principio cautio? Quia in eo et ab eo cuncta, quo fit ut tam scientia quam inscitia circa ipsum per reliqua propagetur multiplicatisque his quae inde sequuntur multiplicentur errores.**

Positum est de voluptate et sapientia esse tractandum, utrumque vero commune est ad species multas et singula plurima. Igitur ut optime cognoscantur habenda est ea peritia quae unum commune in multa producere possit et multa in unum reducere: illud quidem ne insistat in genere; hoc vero ne per singula infinita[5] vagetur. Quae (ut supra diximus) observanda sunt illi qui certam perfectamque rei scientiam sit habiturus. Peritia autem haec[6] haudquaquam levis est, sed ardua; neque in rebus corporeis moratur dividendis et uniendis, sed usque ad incorporeas species uniendas et multiplicandas sese evehit. Unde et multae, ut dictum est, se illi undique dubitationes opponunt, quare diligenti cautione ad hanc nos conferre

---

[1]aliquis ibi *om. X*   [2]resolvere *X*   [3]*in X this ch. is numbered ten*   [4]facultas *om. X*
[5]infinite *W*   [6]ista *WX*   *(cont.)* *-**om. W*

approach dialectic with great care. This is what has been learnt so far from Socrates' conversation. Protarchus assents to the arguments and says he has to try mainly to achieve the following: that is, to acquire such a skill and with it divide the subject of the controversy into many things and in turn gather the many things into the one and do both correctly. However, in order to urge Socrates on in the present argument, he says,

15C   "Socrates, I personally and the people with me can easily agree with you over such things, and if you're afraid of the stubbornness of this argumentative fellow Philebus, dismiss him and don't have anything to say to him. For, as the saying goes, 'Let a sleeping dog lie.' Pythagoras' symbol is similar, 'Don't stab the fire with a sword'; and Heraclitus', 'It's a hard thing, to fight against anger. When it rushes out at full tilt you pay with your life.' The first proverb originated in Rhodes.[105] For after a huge colossus, that is, a statue, had fallen down and in so doing had brought about the ruin of many homes, the Rhodians didn't want it re-erected. And they countered the king who was thinking about putting it up again with the saying, 'A bad thing that's lying quietly mustn't be disturbed.'"

But Philebus' previous stubbornness immediately appeared, for he was tired of arguing before he was convinced by Socrates, and in a little while he added, "Pleasure seems to me to excel wisdom and it will always seem to." He showed here he wasn't ready to be taught anything, since he was going to stop his ears against future arguments, preferring to err in his own opinion rather than judge correctly by using other people's arguments even though they were true.

Plato inveighs against such men in the *Phaedo* and elsewhere.[106] He says they are annoying companions to other people and they are their own silent and familiar enemies as they indiscriminately deceive themselves. He tells us not to argue with them over important matters, since (passing over Philebus in a way) he admits Protarchus [alone] to the debate about the good which follows.

So, complying with Protarchus' request, Socrates advances
15D   to dialectic. He says three things must be recognized. First,

debemus. Haec hactenus ex verbis Socratis colliguntur. His
assentitur Protarchus et conandum imprimis ait ista perficere,
id est, peritiam huiuscemodi consequi ac per eam id quod in
controversiam deductum est in multa ut decet partiri et multa
rursus in unum colligere. Ut autem Socratem ad praesentem[1]
disputationem [*361r*] exhortetur,[2] addicit: Ego, o Socrates,
atque isti mecum tibi talia facile assentimur. Ac si contentiosi
huius Philebi pertinaciam vereris, mitte illum neque cum eo
verbum habeas ullum, nam ut habet proverbium: Malum quod
bene iacet non est movendum; cui simile Pythagorae symbo-
lum: Ignem gladio ne fodias; atque illud Heracliti: Durum est
adversus iram pugnare, nam cum in impetu est, vita emitur.
Rhodi ortum hoc est proverbium. Nam cum vastus quidam
colossus, id est, statua, cecidisset, quo ex casu domorum plurium ruina secuta est, noluerunt Rhodii in altum rursus attolli
colossum, regique de elevando colosso deliberanti opposuerunt:
Malum quod bene iacet movendum non esse.

Philebi vero[3] pertinacia in superioribus statim apparuit. Nam
prius defessus est disserendo[4] quam a Socrate persuasus, et
paulo post addidit:[5] Voluptas #mihi sapientiae praestare videtur
semperque videbitur. Ubi indocilem se esse testatus est, utpote
qui futuris rationibus obstrueret aures, ac potius propria cum
opinione errare vellet quam cum alienis rationibus etiamsi verae
sint recte sentire.

Hos homines detestatur in Phaedone et ubique Plato et aliis
molestos esse dicit socios, sibi vero tacitos et familiares hostes,
cum se ipsi passim decipiant. Cum his non esse de rebus
maximis disputandum monet, cum Philebo quodammodo prae-
termisso Protarchum ad sequentem de bono disputationem
adsciscat.

Socrates igitur Protarcho obtemperans eam aggreditur disciplinam, ac tria in ea observanda esse monet. Primum ne

---

[1]sequentem *WX*   [2]exhortatur *W*   [3]vero *om. WX*   [4]differendo *Y*   [5]reddidit *W*
#*P frag. IV (65r) begins*

adolescents aren't admitted to it. Next, those who attempt it must guard against the illusions of the senses and the phantasy and proceed towards it by the divine light of the intelligence. Third, they mustn't dash from one extreme to another without going through the intermediary stages. To understand these admonitions, you must notice that Plato divides the art of debate into two branches: one is called logic, the other dialectic. The first is the ability that concerns itself with the properties of nouns and verbs, with what's compounded from them, namely the sentence, with the various species of sentences and their combinations, with the resulting proofs, and finally with the various classes of proofs. Logic is pre-occupied with language; it is not properly knowledge, but the instrument of all knowledge. But dialectic is a divine craft which is no longer concerned with words, but with things. By the pure probing of the intelligence above the senses it inquires into each thing's substance, and from all things it ascends to their one principle without the need for any other principle. In the *Sophist* and the *Statesman* Plato calls dialectic the true philosophy.[107] In the *Republic* he calls it the outstanding task of the philosopher.[108] In the *Parmenides* he says nobody will ever be able to get to the truth without it.[109]

So dialectic either compares the principle of all things to all things or all things to the principle, or it considers single things individually, or refers them to each other. Whichever of these it does, it is always uniting and dividing and considering the one and the many. If it compares God to all things, it is bringing in the one and the many, for it's considering the power of the one God propagated through many things. If it compares all things to God, it's considering the perfection of the many as bordering on one end. If it compares things in themselves, it's looking at some one whole constituted from many parts. For whatever is subsequent to the principle, because it is degenerating from the first one, falls away into multiplicity; and the further it descends the less unity it retains while sustaining greater multiplicity. The spiritual intelligences consist of substance and species. Souls have in addition to the species distinct powers and

adolescentes ad hanc[1] admittantur; secundum ut qui eam tractant sensus et phantasiae illusiones caveant [*361v*] et divino mentis lumine ad hanc incedant; tertium ne ab extremo ad extremum sine mediis properent. Ad istorum intelligentiam advertendum est apud Platonem duo in membra artem disserendi distribui: et aliud logicam, aliud dialecticam dici. Illa quidem est facultas quae de proprietatibus agit nominum et verborum, de horum compositione quae oratio est, de orationis variis speciebus, de orationum cum orationibus compositione ex qua argumentationes conficiuntur, ac postremo de variis argumentationum generibus. Haec circa sermonem versatur, neque proprie scientia est, sed scientiarum omnium[2] instrumentum. Dialectica vero artificium divinum est quod non de verbis amplius, sed de rebus agit, et supra sensus pura mentis indagine substantiam cuiusque rei perquirit et a rebus omnibus nullo alio supposito principio ad unum rerum omnium ascendit principium. Hanc in Sophiste atque Politico veram philosophiam vocat. In Republica praecipuum philosophantis officium. In Parmenide dicit sine hac neminem umquam veritatem rerum consecuturum.

Quare aut principium omnium ad omnia comparat, aut omnia ad principium, aut singula in se ipsis considerat, aut invicem refert singula. Quicquid istorum agat, unit semper ac dividit et unum multaque considerat. Si Deum ad omnia comparat, unum profert et multa, nam unius Dei vim per multa considerat propagatam. Si ad Deum omnia, multorum perfectionem in finem unum conterminantem. Si res in se ipsis, totum quoddam unum cernit ex pluribus constitutum. Quicquid enim post principium est, quia a primo uno [*362r*] degenerat, abit in multitudinem, et quo discedit longius eo minus unitatem retinet dum maiorem suscipit multitudinem. Numinum quidem mentes ex substantia et speciebus constant; animae supra species vires adhibent operationesque distinctas; corpora insuper partes in

---

[1] eam *P*   [2] omnium *om. XP*

operations. Bodies have parts extended in space and quantity besides. Therefore the intelligence of the dialectician discovers the unity and multiplicity in individual things. And since it has to comprehend the nature of single things, it must ascertain how each thing's unity proceeds into the many and how the many are led into the one.

Moreover, if it compares the individual things together which are under the principle, it sees how they are distinguished and how they agree. According as they agree, they are one; according as they differ, they are many again.

In His works God everywhere joins the parts of each thing to the parts for the sake of the whole itself, and joins the whole to something compatible. And He separates parts from incompatible parts, just as He separates a whole from an incompatible whole. Similarly, nature separates incompatible things from a subject and joins compatible things to it. It unites a created thing to something compatible and divides it from its opposite. Similarly, and last of all, art is concerned with uniting and dividing. Accordingly, divine and natural things and human skills, as they are made in their issuing forth, so they are preserved in their turning back by uniting and dividing; and the same goes for the management of life. So, since the manner of knowing ought to follow on the manner of the things it knows, it is quite appropriate that the mistress of the sciences, dialectic, always regards the one and the many equally, and alternates them in turn in the proper way now by dividing, now by uniting.

But note that dividing upwards aims at the simple thing, for it distinguishes the nature [of something] from the contingencies. When these have been put aside, it reduces the many to the power of the one simple form. But dividing downwards ends in a compound, for it divides the general nature through its properties (which aren't abandoned but joined now to the nature itself in act), so that it ends up quite correctly in a compound. Whichever way it is done it is called division, but the division which ends up with the more simple nature is properly called resolution. Like fire, resolution, when it divides, leaves behind the additional and as it were terrestrial accidents on the ground.

loco quantitate porrectas. In singulis itaque dialectici mens unitatem et multitudinem reperit. Et quia singulorum debet naturam comprehendere tenere debet quo pacto unitas cuiusque in multa progrediatur et multa in unum ducantur.

Quin etiam si singula quae sub principio sunt invicem refert, quo distinguantur videt et quo conveniant. Ut conveniunt unum sunt; multa rursus ut distinguuntur.

*Deus in operibus suis ubique et unit partes rei cuiusque partibus ad ipsum totum, totumque unit convenienti rei, et tam partes ab alienis partibus, quam totum ab alieno dividit toto. Similiter natura dividit a subiecto aliena unitque propria; rem[1] genitam unit convenienti, dividit ab opposito. Demum ars similiter in uniendo et dividendo versatur. Ergo divina, naturalia, artificia tam in processu fiunt, quam in conversione servantur uniendo atque dividendo; similiter[2] et gubernatio vitae. Cum ergo scientiae modus rerum sequi debeat modum, haud ab re dialectica, magistra scientiarum, unum semper et multa pariter contuetur, eaque[3] vicissim tum dividendo tum uniendo decenter alternat.

Sed nota divisionem in ascensu tendere ad rem simplicem, dividit enim naturam a contingentibus, quibus posthabitis, redigit multa in unius simplicis formae virtutem. Divisionem vero in descensu desinere in rem compositam, dividit enim generalem naturam per eiusdem proprietates, quas non relinquit sed actu iam ipsi naturae continuat, unde merito in rem compositam desinit. Quocumque id modo fiat, divisio nominatur, sed divisio in naturam desinens simpliciorem proprie dicitur resolutio, quae ignis instar, dividendo supposita relinquit humi[4] accidentia quasi terrestria, atque interim ab his specialem**

---

[1] -que *add. XP*   [2] -que *add. XP*   [3] eoque *XP*   [4] humi *om. XP*   *-**om. W (cont.)*

Meanwhile evaporating the special nature from the accidents, it resolves it as if it were air into the sky.

The dialectician does three things in the process of comparing things together by dividing and uniting through the one and the many. First, he resolves; second, he defines; finally, he demonstrates. First, this is how he sets about resolving. He determines there are many men, as he can see the dissimilar qualities of individuals. So by dividing from the fact of dissimilarity he proceeds into multiplicity. But because he sees individuals do similar things—that is, they reproduce, reason, laugh—accordingly, he finds the one nature in the individuals which produces the one result; and he calls the nature, "humanity." And this is how by uniting from the fact of similarity he ascends from the many to the one. One by one he does the same for all the individual species of animals and plants as well. Next, just as he's reduced the many individuals in any class to one species, so he reduces the many species to one genus. Because thinking, barking and neighing are dissimilar, he determines there are a number of species: of man, dog, horse. But he determines, because they have walking and feeling in common, that they belong to one genus of many [species]; and he calls the genus, "animal." He divides this one genus through the differences into the many species, and brings the many species back through the similar nature to the one genus. Moreover, he perceives animals differ from plants, because animals can feel and walk, plants can't. But, since animals and plants have nutrition in common, the dialectician can accordingly reduce the many species to one genus and call it the genus of "animate bodies." And so he goes on till he comes to body and substance and essence. We always see the dialectician considering here the many and the one.

After he's thus resolved the many individual things into one species and the many species into one genus and the many genera into the supreme genus, he divides the supreme genus up again through the opposing differences and establishes the many species. For example, he divides substance into the divisible and the indivisible and establishes from them body and

*exhalans naturam quasi aerem in sublime resolvit.**
¹Tria dialecticus agit dum dividendo et uniendo per unum ac multa res invicem comparat. Resolvit primo, secundo definit, postremo demonstrat. In resolutione primum ita procedit. Quia dissimiles singulorum hominum inspicit qualitates, multos esse homines iudicat. Unde a dissimilitudine dividendo processit in multitudinem. Quia vero similes effectus singulorum videt hominum, hoc est, hominem gignere, ratiocinari atque ridere, ideo unam in singulis naturam a qua sit unus eventus esse reperit atque eam vocat humanitatem. Et hac ratione a similitudine uniendo ex multitudine ascendit in unum. Idem quoque in singulis speciebus animalium et plantarum efficit sigillatim. Deinde, sicut in quolibet ordine singula multa ad unam retulit speciem, sic et species multas ad genus unum. Nam ex dissimilitudine ratiocinandi, latrandi et hinniendi, multas esse species [*362v*] hominis, canis et equi iudicat. Ex similitudine vero et gradiendi et sentiendi, unum multorum esse genus, idque vocat animal. Quod unum genus in has multas species per differentias dividit; et species multas per naturam similem in unum redigit genus. Praeterea haec animalia differre a plantis intelligit, quia ista sentiant gradianturque, illae nequaquam. Quia vero tam animalibus quam plantis nutritio communis est, ideo genus in unum multa haec redigit, illudque corpus animatum vocat. Atque ita efficit quousque ad corpus et substantiam et essentiam veniat, ubi semper cernimus dialecticum multa et unum considerare.

Postquam ita resolvit singula multa in speciem unam, et species multas in genus unum, et genera multa in genus supremum, itcrum² gcnus illud per oppositas differentias dividit, multasque constituit species: ut substantiam per partibilem³ et⁴ impartibilem, unde corpus efficit incorporeamque substantiam;

---

¹In quo certe *add. W*   ²interim *W*   ³partibilia *W*   ⁴et *om. W*
(cont.) *-**om. W*

incorporeal substance. Body he divides into the animate and the inanimate and establishes animals and trees from the one, and all the rest of corporeal things from the other. Animal he divides into rational, barking, etc. From the one he makes a man, from the other a dog. So the dialectician, when he is going upwards, resolves by dividing and uniting; and again, when he is going downwards, defines by dividing and compounding. And after he has defined, he demonstrates by dividing and compounding. For, given the definition of something in which the thing's substance is comprehended, through it the dialectician can arrive at some conclusion by an ordered process of reasoning. Through the conclusion he can either, by being positive, compound certain things with the substance of the thing itself, for example those things which accompany it; or, by being negative, he can divide extraneous things from the substance. And, universally, whoever says anything is either being positive or negative. Whoever's being positive joins the many to the one. Whoever's being negative separates something else from the one and proceeds from the one into the many.

Chapter 24. The relationship between definition and demonstration. Again, on resolution, division and compounding.

The next problem is whether definition precedes the syllogism or the reverse. Definition apparently precedes it, since no condition can be assigned to anything through a syllogism unless the thing and the condition have both been understood first through a definition. But you could say perhaps there must be at least two syllogisms before a definition can emerge. For, since definition consists of the genus and the difference, the division of the genus through the differences precedes definition. Again, the comparing of each difference, then the rejection of one difference and finally the acceptance of another [all] precede a definition. When you divide a genus, you argue thus: Each animal is either rational or irrational. Man is an animal. Therefore

corpus per animatum et inanimatum, inde animalia arboresque
constituit, hinc reliqua corpora. Animal per rationale, latrabile,
etc.: hinc hominem inde canem conficit. Unde dialecticus dum
ascendit dividendo et uniendo resolvit; ac etiam dum descendit
dividendo et componendo definit. Et postquam definivit, dividendo et componendo demonstrat. Nam posita rei definitione
in qua substantia rei comprehenditur, per eam ratiocinatione
composita conclusionem aliquam infert. Per quam vel affirmando componit aliquid cum rei ipsius substantia, ut puta quae
illam sequuntur, vel negando ab ea extranea dividit. Et universaliter quisquis loquitur vel affirmat vel negat. Quisquis
affirmat multa ligat in unum. [*363r*] Qui negat ab uno separat
aliud et in multa procedit ex uno.

Quomodo se habeat definitio ad demonstrationem. Item de resolutione, divisione, compositione. Cap. XXIIII.[1]

[2]Quaeritur utrum definitio praecedat syllogismum an contra.[3]
Videtur illa hunc praecedere, cum nequeat rei conditio assignari
per syllogismum, nisi per definitionem prius et res et conditio
cognita fuerit. Forte vero licet dicere antequam definitio oriatur
duobus saltem syllogismis opus esse. Cum enim definitio constet ex genere atque differentia, definitionem praecedit divisio
generis per differentias; item comparatio differentiae utriusque,
deinde reiectio alterius, denique alterius assumptio. Sic argu-
mentando dum dividis genus: Omne animal vel rationale est vel
irrationale. Homo est animal. Ergo homo est rationale vel

---

[1]*no ch. heading or break WXP*   [2]*the last paragraph of this chapter, beginning* Universa haec industria . . . Plato conqueritur *(my p. 229), transposed here W*   [3]*e converso WXP*

man is either rational or irrational. Again, man is either a
rational or an irrational animal. But he isn't an irrational one.
Therefore, he's a rational animal. This conclusion is the definition of man, and it is the consequence of two syllogisms. Given
the definition, the next problem is to consider the accompanying
condition. As I find docility accompanies it, I conclude man is
docile by this sort of syllogism: Man is a rational animal. But a
rational animal is docile. Therefore man is docile. Again, a docile animal is not a wild one. Man is a docile animal. Therefore
he is not a wild animal. We saw that two syllogisms already preceded the definition and two succeeded it and that in both cases
the positive one was put before the negative.

However, if someone says an animal is already defined in
itself before it is divided, we'll accept this. But we'll add that
before the animal can be defined, body has been divided; and
that before body can be defined, substance has been divided;
and that before substance can be defined, entity has been divided. But entity can't be defined at all, since the general notion
of entity is entirely undefinable and it can't be constituted from
a genus and a difference. So you have to say first there's a confused description; then a division where the syllogisms originate
which lead to a definition; third, a distinct definition; fourth, a
distinct division (since more demonstrative syllogisms than the
first ones follow the definition).

By means of resolution the sight seizes the one simple image
of colour. The image has been cut off from colour itself which
is multiple and compound. In the process the image is both
divided from the colour and joined to the sight. Similarly, by
way of resolution the imagination conceives of the pure image
[i.e. the phantasm] from the visual image. And by resolution
the intellect conceives of the species which has been freed from
the particular phantasm. So the intellect knows the universal
before knowing the particular. It knows the particular by turning back towards the phantasm. In the same way the imagination when it's awake knows something as a pure image. Afterwards it is turned back towards the sight and dreams about the
something as a visual image. Thus resolution is everywhere first

irrationale. Item homo est animal rationale vel irrationale. Non est autem irrationale. Ergo est animal rationale. Haec conclusio est hominis definitio duos sequens [*363v*] syllogismos. Qua assignata, consideratur quae eam conditio comitetur, cumque inveniam eam comitari docilitatem, concludo hominem esse docilem tali quodam syllogismo: Homo est animal rationale. Sed animal rationale est docile. Ergo homo est docilis. Item animal docile non est ferum. Homo est animal docile. Ergo non est[1] ferum. Vidimus iam duos syllogismos definitionem antecessisse et duos successisse atque utrobique affirmativum negativo praeponi.

Siquis autem dicat animal prius in se definiri quam dividi, fatebimur, sed addemus, antequam definiatur animal, corpus esse divisum; et ante corporis definitionem divisam esse substantiam; et ante huius definitionem ens fuisse divisum, definitum vero nequaquam, cum et indefinita omnino sit communis entis notio, et[2] ex genere differentiaque constitui nequeat. Ergo dicendum est primo esse confusam descriptionem, secundo divisionem in qua syllogismi oriuntur ad definitionem conducentes, tertio definitionem distinctam, quarto distinctam divisionem, postquam definitionem sequuntur syllogismi magis demonstrativi quam primi.

Visus per modum resolutionis capit imaginem coloris simplicem unamque a colore multiplici et composito segregatam, ubi illa et a colore dividitur et unitur visui. Similiter imaginatio resolutionis modo concipit puriorem imaginem ex imagine visus. Et intellectus resolutione ex particulari phantasmate solutam[3] concipit speciem; unde prius universale cognoscit quam particulare, scilicet per conversionem ad phantasma,[4] sicut imaginatio prius imaginibile vigilans quam visibile somnians in visum conversa. Sic primum ubique est resolutio ascendens ad

---

[1]est *om. WXP*   [2]et *om. W*   [3]absolutam *XP*   [4]phantasmata *XP*

ascending towards the simple, dividing in the meantime impurer things from the purer thing and joining the purer thing to the soul. This is proper to fire. By the sudden impulse of the rational nature it proceeds thus far by resolving from the individuals to the species, from the species to the genus. But by dividing from the genus through the differences and compounding species from the differences, and so by defining and after defining by demonstrating, the whole process is brought to completion—to some extent by a natural movement but to a greater extent by an artificial one. When it demonstrates, it makes a compound resolution, since the first resolution was simple. So in demonstrating it resolves now upwards from the cause, now downwards from the effect, now laterally from those things accompanying it. In this it's like fire. It's called "resolution" as if it were a "solution," [a setting free,] that's repeated. For the forms of things are first free in the Ideas, then they are bound in matter, third, they are made free again by the power of Apollo and of Saturn. Saturn is apart from matter, Apollo is the bearer of light and heat. Therefore, in the *Cratylus* Plato refers to Apollo as "the Apolyon," that is, "the resolver."[110]

The entire activity (which in dividing and compounding leads the one out into the many and the many back into the one), when it joins nouns and verbs and makes sentences and then joins sentences together to make the structure of an argument and either denies or affirms something, and when it resolves, defines, and demonstrates, is called in part logic and in part dialectic. Although it must be understood completely, still, it must be approached with this caution at first. As Plato tells us in the *Republic* Book 7, we should impart it to adults not to adolescents.[111] For boys who depend on the subtlety of such questioning go around contradicting various things indiscriminately and use it to destroy the legitimate civic institutions of the life of mankind. But they haven't yet discovered better institutions themselves. So either they are too puffed up with pride or they surrender themselves to pleasures or judge ill of religion. Plato complains about this bitterly in the *Laws*.[112]

simplex, interimque dividens impuriora a puriori, et uniens cum anima purius, [*364r*] quod ignis est proprium. Et hactenus subito rationalis naturae fit instinctu resolvendo ab individuis ad speciem, ab hac ad genus. Hinc vero dividendo per differentias et ex his species componendo sicque definiendo et post definitionem demonstrando, tota progressio fit discursu quodammodo naturali, magis vero artificioso. Atque dum demonstrat resolutionem facit compositam, cum prima fuerit simplex. Resolvit ergo demonstrando tum sursum a causa tum[1] deorsum ab effectu[2] tum in latus a comitantibus, quod ignis est proprium. Dicitur resolutio quasi repetita solutio. Nam formae rerum prius in ideis sunt solutae, deinde in materia ligatae, tertio resolvuntur virtute Apollinis et Saturni. Hic enim a materia separatus; ille lucens et calens. Hinc Apollon quasi Apolyon,[3] id est, resolvens dicitur[4] in Cratylo.

[*363r*] [5]Universa haec industria, quae dividendo et componendo unum in multa producit et multa reducit in unum, dum verba nominaque iungit et orationes constituit iungitque invicem ad ratiocinationis structuram, negatque aliquid vel affirmat, resolvit, definit, demonstrat, partim logica partim dialectica nuncupatur. Quae cum percipienda sit omnino, tamen hac primum cautione tractanda, ut non adolescentulis eam sed adultis communicemus, ut in septimo de Republica iubet Plato. Nam pueri hac freti perscrutandi subtilitate redarguunt absque delectu singula, tolluntque per eam[6] legitima et civilia vitae hominum instituta, ipsi vero nondum reperiunt meliora. Unde vel fastu nimio tument, vel se voluptatibus dedunt, vel male de religione sentiunt, quod in libro[7] de Legibus Plato conqueritur.

---

[1]cum *W*   [2]*for* ab effectu *P reads* affectu   [3]Apologlyon *W;* Apoglyon *XP*
[4]dicitur *om. WXP*   [5]*in W this paragraph is transposed (see my p. 225)*   [6]singula *add. X*
[7]quinto *XP*

Chapter 25. On the art of dividing and uniting and why we ought to use it cautiously.

About to attack something difficult as it were, Socrates first of all examines how he should approach the problem, the gravest of those confronting us. That is, he thinks about how he can describe rationally and talk diligently about the ability which concerns itself with dividing and uniting the one and the many. Many doubts spring up in succession in dealing with them, that is, the one and the many—either the sort of doubts we've already mentioned or others you can think of. But Socrates demonstrates immediately that such an ability is absolutely necessary in order to know not only about wisdom and pleasure, but about anything at all. For we are all always forced to divide and unite in everything we think about or talk about, and to go from the one into the many and the reverse, from the many into the one. This has been shown above in greater detail. But if we use dialectic properly (which traverses everything), we will feel and talk about everything correctly; but if we abuse it, incorrectly. You can conclude therefore that the art which deals with dividing and uniting the one and the many is absolutely vital to knowledge.

15D-
16A

Plato also tells us why we ought to treat dialectic cautiously. First, he shows it must not be given to adolescents because they are led by it into three vices: pride, lewdness, impiety. For when they first taste the ingenious subtlety of arguing, it's as if they have come upon a tyrannous power for rebutting and refuting the rest of us. They are inflated with inane opinion and puffed up with arrogance. They deceive themselves with opinion and stubbornness, they molest others with their insolence and impudence. Plato exclaims against this pride in all the dialogues opposing the sophists and their disciples. He calls them not philosophers, but "philodoxers," that is, men covetous of opinion and glory.[113] Add to this what Plato writes in the *Phaedrus* and the *Republic* Book 7. He says two leaders preside over man from the earliest years: the innate desire for pleasures, and the opinion acquired from civil and moral codes which leads us

[*364r*] **De arte divisionis et unionis et qua observatione trac-**
tanda. Cap. XXV.[1]

Socrates tamquam ad rem arduam accessurus consultat
primum unde hanc pugnam, quae plurima est circa ea de quibus
dubitamus, aggrediatur. Hoc est qua ratione declaret et qua
diligentia tradat facultatem illam, quae dividendo et uniendo
circa unum ac multa versatur. In quibus tractandis, scilicet uno
et multitudine, multae suboriuntur dubitationes, sive quales
praediximus, sive quaevis aliae. Statim vero ostendit facultatem
eiusmodi non modo ad voluptatis et sapientiae sed ad cuiuscumque rei cognitionem esse admodum necessariam. Omnes enim[2]
ac semper et in omnibus quaecumque vel cogitamus vel dicimus
dividere et unire cogimur,[3] ex unoque in multa et contra ex
multis in unum deducere, quod sane latius in superioribus est
ostensum. Eo [*364v*] vero quod per omnia currit, si recte utimur, de omnibus vere sentimus et loquimur; sin abutimur,
falso. Ex quo concluditur ut ars illa quae circa unum et multa
dividendo et uniendo versatur summopere sit cognitu necessaria.

His addit qua sit cautione tractanda, primumque ostendit
adolescentulis non esse tradendam, quia ex hac[4] tria in vitia[5]
adolescentes incidunt: superbiam, lasciviam, impietatem. Nam
cum primum artificiosam hanc disserendi subtilitatem gusta-
runt, quasi tyrannicam quandam ad ceteros refellendos et con-
vincendos vim nacti; inani inflantur opinione, fastu tumescunt.
Se ipsi opinione pertinaciaque decipiunt; aliis sunt insolentia et
procacitate sua molestiores. Quam quidem superbiam omnibus
in dialogis Plato adversus Sophistas eorumque discipulos exec-
ratur, eosque non philosophos, sed philodoxos, id est, opinionis
et[6] gloriae cupidos nominat. Accedit ad haec quod ut in
Phaedro et septimo de Republica scribitur a Platone: duo a
primis annis hominibus duces praesunt, innata voluptatum
cupiditas, et acquisita opinio ex civilibus et moralibus institutis

---

[1]*a break, but no ch. heading W; in X and P the ch. is numbered eleven* [2]*WXP read* Quippe
omnes [3]coguntur *W* [4]hoc *Y* [5]vita *Y* [6]et *om. W*

towards the things adjudged by men to be honest and just.[114] Nine companions are present in every human soul. There's one god and two demons: that is, the soul's companion star and an airy and watery demon. Again, inside the soul there is one charioteer and two horses, a white and a black: that is, there's reason, the rational appetite and the appetite that obeys the sense. Again, there's one impulse and two leaders: that is, the impulse to the good, the desire that draws the soul towards the enjoyable good, and the opinion that leads the soul towards the honourable good.

But adolescents who are given to the study of arguing often confute men's beliefs about just and honest things. It's as if human institutions weren't good in actual fact but just seemed good, and weren't established by nature herself but were simply the result of a particular convention or usage. So the youths no longer venerate them. But they can't replace them with anything better because of their inexperience. Consequently, now the legitimate opinion has been discarded, they have another leader to follow, that is, the desire for pleasure, "and having talked about virtue, they go whoring."[115] Thus arose the lasciviousness that took possession of the Cyrenaics, whom Plato calls "philosomaters" not philosophers, that is, lovers of the body.[116]

These youths, moreover, when they've started on an argument, will assert that nothing exists except the thing for which they can apparently give a reason. But they don't yet grasp the reasons for divine things. Plato maintains in the *Parmenides* that adolescents aren't ready for them.[117] For, in order to understand divine things, you must have long practical experience and be sustained by all the sciences, and you have to turn your intelligence away completely from the things the eyes are accustomed to seeing. And since adolescents are deficient in all three, they can't yet grasp the reasons for divine things. However, they don't believe in the authority and the laws of the rest of us, inasmuch as they demand a reason for everything. So they judge ill of religion out of impiety, since either like Diagoras they deny that God exists, or like Protagoras they wonder whether there is a God or not, or like Democritus and Epicurus

quae ad ea nos ducit quae honesta et iusta ab hominibus esse censentur. Cuique animae humanae novem comites adsunt. Deus unus, daemones duo; stella scilicet sua compar et daemon aereus et humecteus. Item intra animam, auriga unus, equi duo albus et niger; ratio scilicet et appetitus rationalis et appetitus[1] sensui parens. Item impetus unus et duces duo; impetus quidem ad bonum, cupido trahens ad bonum iucundum, opinio ad bonum honestum.

Saepe vero adolescentes ratiocinandi studio dediti opiniones hominum de honestis ac iustis confutant, quasi humana haec officia haud [*365r*] revera bona sint, sed videantur, neque natura ipsa, sed positione et usu constent. Quapropter ea non amplius venerantur, meliora vero ipsi propter imperitiam reperire non possunt. Quo fit ut opinione illa legitima iam abiecta alium sui ducem sequantur voluptatum scilicet cupiditatem; et de virtute locuti clunem[2] agitant. Unde lascivia illa exorta est[3] quae Cyrenaicos, philosomatos non philosophos ut Plato inquit, id est, corporis amatores invasit.

Quin etiam cum argumentationum viam ingressi sint, nihil asserunt esse, nisi id cuius rationem posse reddere videantur. Divinarum vero rerum rationes nondum capiunt, ad quas ineptiores adolescentes esse in Parmenide testatur Plato. Oportet enim ad divinorum intelligentiam et longo rerum usu callere et scientiis omnibus esse fulctum, et mentem ab oculorum consuetudine prorsus abducere. Cumque his omnibus adolescentes carcant, rationes divinorum nondum assequuntur. Ceterorum vero auctoritati legibusque non credunt, utpote qui omnium exigant rationem. Quare impietatis causa[4] de religione male sentiunt, quoniam vel, ut Diagoras, Deum negant; vel, ut Protagoras, sitne an non Deus dubitant; vel, ut Democritus et Epicurus, Dei providentiam negant. Atque de hac impietate in

---

[1] rationalis et appetitus *om. W*   [2] clunem *om. W, but a space provided*   [3] est *om. W*
[4] rei *WXP*

they deny God's providence.[118] In the *Laws* Plato complains bitterly about this impiety[119] and in the *Apology* he attests to the infamy that befell legitimate philosophers, particularly Socrates, from it.[120] The adolescent quibbler falls into three vices. As soon as he stumbles on verbal paradox, he congratulates himself as if he'd come upon a treasure-house of wisdom and exults and throws his arms around with delight and promptly assays every paradoxical argument, now twisting the many round and round into the one, now unfolding and untwisting the one into the many. This gives rise at once to pride and impudence. Moreover, he injects the doubts caused by questions both into himself and into others, doubts about civil customs as well as religious institutions; and this gives rise to both lewdness and impiety. And his conversation is universally disagreeable to everybody. While he is engaged in refutation he spares no one: no one younger (here clemency and humanity perish) nor a peer (here friendliness dies) and no one older (here charity and reverence is wanting). To give even more vehement scope to his insance impudence, he'd start to quarrel with beasts and barbarians, Socrates says, if they could understand his paradoxical statements.

Since Socrates had said these derogatory things about adolescence in the middle of a circle of adolescents, Protarchus, to urge him to instruct the young men more openly, says jokingly to him: "Socrates, aren't you scared that all of us, being young ourselves, will attack you along with this impudent fellow, Philebus, if you provoke and irritate us with such threats and disparage adolescence so much and don't, moreover, instruct us in the proper discipline? But continue, Socrates, please, for we understand what you're talking about." Protarchus still thought there was another and better way to the truth over and above the art of dividing and uniting through the one and the many, and that here Socrates was condemning the latter art. So he meant to imply, "We realise you've condemned this art. So go on. If there's some way to clear up the muddle and confusion in arguing and you can find a better road to reason, look around, please, and we'll follow it as best we can. For this isn't

16A

Legibus Plato conqueritur, atque infamiam[1] adversus legitimos
philosophos Socratem praesertim hinc exortam in Apologia
testatur. Tria haec incurrit vitia adolescentulus cavillator. Qui
ut primum captiunculas attigit admodum congratulatur, tamquam thesaurum sapientiae nactus, laetitiaque exultat ac gestit
et argumentatiunculas omnes prompte pertentat, tum gyro
multa retorquens in unum, tum unum in multitudinem explicans et evolvens, ubi superbia et [*365v*] procacitas statim exoritur. Inicit sibi praeterea et aliis dubitationum scrupulos, tam
contra civiles mores, quam contra religionis institutiones, ubi et
lascivia et impietas emergit. Et universaliter molesta ad omnes
eius redditur conversatio; dum refellit quemque parcit nemini,
neque iuniori, ubi clementia et humanitas perit, neque aequali,
ubi amicitia moritur, neque maiori, ubi caritas et reverentia
deficit. Utque eius insanam procacitatem exprimeret vehementius etiam cum barbaris et bestiis litigaturus est, inquit, si ab eis
percipi eius argumentatiunculae possint.

Cum haec Socrates in adolescentum illorum corona contra
adolescentiam ipsam dixisset, Protarchus, ut eum ad planiorem
instructionem iuvenum incitaret, in Socratem ita iocatus[2]
inquit: An non metuis, Socrates, ne omnes cum iuvenes simus[3]
una cum protervo hoc Philebo in te irruamus, si hisce nos
lacessitos conviciis irritaveris tantum vituperaverisque adolescentiam, nec nos praeterea decenti instruxeris disciplina? Sed
age amabo Socrates. Intelligimus enim quod ais. Credebat enim
Protarchus potiorem esse aliquam ad veritatem viam, praeter
artem illam dividendi et uniendi per unum[4] ac multa, et hanc
artem hic[5] damnasse Socratem. Ideo inferre voluit: Intelligimus
quod artem hanc damnas. Age ergo, siquis modus est ad hanc
disputandi turbationem confusionemque auferendam,[6] et
semitam ad rationem rectiorem[7] reperire licet, tu quaeso, circumspice, pro viribus ipsi sequemur. Neque enim exiguus hic est

---

[1]infamia *Y*   [2]est *add. W*   [3]sumus *W*   [4]et uniendi per unum *repeated XP*
[5]hinc *W*   [6]auferandam *P*   [7]rectorem *W*

a trivial discussion, and the present argument isn't about something frivolous; it's important rather, that is, it's about the highest good and the way that leads to the truth.'' He added this because he'd said, ''We'll follow as best we can,'' and also to provoke Socrates to continue. However, Socrates agreed they aren't

16B   dealing with a trivial problem. He called them **boys** (when he'd previously called them youths), because he was continually blaming them for their ignorance for not noticing he'd been censuring the abuse of dialectic not dialectic itself. But Socrates said they were accustomed to being called **boys** by Philebus, in order to sting Philebus' pride (because Philebus calls young men **boys**). What's more, Socrates denied there was another better way or that there could be another; and he said he himself had always loved dialectic. It was as if he had had to be by nature a philosopher, but the way had often deserted him when he was younger—which is to say, a person shouldn't start on it in adolescence. Here he confirms that the fault underlying the confusion mentioned above lies in the abuse of dialectic rather than in dialectic itself. Therefore, for us to proceed successfully with dialectic, he will come momentarily to a second caution which must be observed in the art. But first he easily shows—to stop them losing confidence in his words—how the dialectical way is made more pleasant because of the subsequent cautions. Yet, to prevent them trusting too much in their own strength, he says the employment of dialectic will be difficult to begin with. To

16C   make them more attentive, however, he says all the inventions of art have shone forth because of it, for every art consists in the discovery of truth. But, as we demonstrated above, the ability to do dialectic is the best way to the truth.

In the *Phaedrus* Plato says you need for any major ability loftiness of mind and the skill to make things work.[121] The first is given by the power to resolve, the second by the power to divide. The two together are dialectic. In the *Parmenides* he says nobody will be wise without dialectic.[122] In the *Phaedrus* Socrates says that if he could find a man who knew how to proceed by uniting and dividing through the one and the many he would worship him as if he were divine.[123]

sermo. Hoc est non levi quadam de re, sed magna oratio praesens habetur, id est, de summo bono et de via ad veritatem
ducente. Hoc adiecit, quia [*366r*] dixerat, sequemur pro
viribus, atque etiam ut Socratem ad sequentia provocaret.
Consensit[1] autem Socrates non esse rem levem qua de agitur,
atque eos vocavit **pueros** cum antea iuvenes appellasset, *quia
continue magis eorum arguebat ruditatem, cum nequaquam
advertissent** quod abusum increpaverat non artem. Dixit
autem eos a Philebo pueros appellari solitos, ut eius morderet
fastum, quia[2] adolescentes[3] vocat pueros. Negavitque aliam esse
meliorem viam, aut esse posse et eam se semper amasse, quasi
natura philosophum esse oporteat, sed eam deseruisse eum
saepe iuniorem, quasi non sit in adolescentia adeunda. Ubi
confirmat vitium[4] perturbationis[5] illius in abusu esse potius
quam in arte. Et ideo ut per eam proficiamus, paulo post[6] ad
secundam cautionem quae observanda est ea in arte descendet;
ante vero, ne illi diffiderent verbis, facile ostendit[7] quo pacto
via illa reddatur commodior per cautiones, scilicet sub-
sequentes. Ne tamen opibus[8] nimis confiderent, usum eius prae-
dicit fore difficilem. Ut autem attentiores redderet, omnia
artium inventa per eam eluxisse dicit, nam quaelibet ars in veritatis inventione consistit. Ea vero facultas potissima est ad
veritatem via, ut supra monstravimus.

†In Phaedro dicit in qualibet facultate magna opus esse et
sublimitate mentis et efficacia ad operandum. Primum dari per
vim resolutivam; secundum per divisivam. Totum est dialectica.
In Parmenide dicitur nullum sine dialectica fore sapientem.
Socrates in Phaedro dicit, si reperiat hominem scientem per
unum et multa uniendo et dividendo procedere, se illum quasi
divinum adoraturum.††

---

[1]Assensit *WXP*   [2]qui *WXP*   [3]adaltisfrontes *W*   [4]vitam *W*   [5]turbationis *WXP*
[6]se *add. W*   [7]ostendi posse *WXP*   [8]operibus *WXP*   *-**om. W*   †-††*om. W*

*Chapter 26. How God illuminates our intelligences and how
Prometheus brought us the divine light from heaven, which
consists in the art of dividing, uniting and demonstrating.*

In the *Republic* Book 6 Plato argues that as in the corporeal
world the most outstanding thing, that is, the sun, produces colours in matter and sight in the eyes with the same light
(and when this is taken away the colours won't be seen and
the sight won't see anything), so in the higher world the first
thing, that is, the good itself and the one principle of things,
creates with its light all the species of things and all intelligences
and illuminates the intelligences and the species with the same
radiance.[124] The splendour, in fact, gives grace to all things
and displays truth and knowledge to the intelligences when it
joins the enlightened intelligences with the illuminated things.
Therefore, it is also agreed among Platonists that the light,
which the intelligences have in order to understand everything,
is the same thing as God Himself by whom all things were
made. Dionysius the Areopagite agrees. In the book *On the
Celestial Hierarchy* he writes: Just as the ray of the sun descends
through the heavens, through the sphere of fire and the sphere
of air into the eyes, so God's light passes through the highest
and intermediate and lowest ranks of the angelic army into the
soul.[125]

For just as the sun illuminates any star directly and also one
through another indirectly, so God illuminates any intelligence
directly and also one through another indirectly.

Certainly you can learn from Plato's *Timaeus* that the divine
intelligence itself, which the Hebrews call the Seraphim, has
some three offices. For first, it lifts its head towards the good
from which it emanates. (In the *Phaedrus* the charioteer of the
soul is described by Plato as doing the same.[126]) Next, it keeps
its breast to itself in the process of contemplating the beauty of
itself. In the *Timaeus* Plato refers to this as "remaining in its
own seat and sight." Finally, in providing and creating it
extends its thigh towards the lower things. On this account
Plato calls it "father" and "creator."[127]

Quomodo Deus mentes illuminet et quomodo Prometheus divinum lumen coelitus in nos traiecit, in quo consistit ars dividendi, uniendi, demonstrandi. Cap. XXVI.[1]

Plato in sexto de Republica disputat, quemadmodum quod in mundo corporeo praestantissimum est, id est, sol, colores eodem lumine producit in materia et in oculis visum, quo subtracto nec videbuntur colores, nec visus videbit quicquam, ita quod in mundo superno primum, hoc est, ipsum bonum et unum rerum principium species rerum mentesque omnes suo procreat lumine, eodemque fulgore et mentes illustrat et species. Qui sane splendor gratiam rebus omnibus praestat, et veritatem mentibus exhibet et[2] scientiam, [*366v*] dum illustratas[3] mentes cum rebus illuminatis coniungit. Unde et hoc apud Platonicos ratum est lumen esse mentium ad intelligenda omnia *eundem ipsum Deum, a quo facta sunt omnia.** Quod secutus Dionysius Areopagita in libro de Angelica Hierarchia scribit: Quemadmodum solis radius per coelos, ignem et aerem descendit in oculos, ita Dei lux per supremum, medium et postremum angelorum exercitum in animam penetrat.

†Sicut enim[4] sol illuminat quamlibet stellam sine medio et rursus aliam per aliam, sic Deus quamlibet mentem tum absque medio[5] tum aliam per aliam.††

Profecto ex Timaeo Platonis colligitur mentem ipsam divinam, quam Seraphin Hebraei nuncupant, tria quaedam habere officia; nam et ad[6] ipsum bonum a quo manat caput attollit, quod de auriga animi in Phaedro scribitur a Platone; et pectus secum ipsa retinet, dum sui ipsius pulchritudinem contemplatur, quod in circumspectu suo ac sede manere in Timaeo nuncupat; et ad inferiora femur providendo porrigit et creando, ex quo patrem nominat et opificem.

---

[1]*a break, but no ch. heading W; in X and P the ch. is numbered twelve*   [2]et *om. WXP*
[3]illustratas *om. WXP*   [4]enim *om. XP*   [5]*for* absque medio *X and P read* immediate
[6]ad *om. W; in XP*   *-***om. P*   †-††*om. W*

Therefore Dionysius in his book, *On the Divine Names,* says an angel has three movements: circular, straight, spiral.[128] Now it is moved in a circle because, starting out from God, its operation turns (together with its being) back to God through understanding. It is moved in a straight line because it offers its power to subsequent things. But it is moved spirally in so far as it pays attention to itself. This act comes back to where it started from, so it is said to participate in the circle; yet it isn't a perfect circle because it isn't brought back to its very first point of departure, namely God. You find the same in the soul.

So the ray of the good itself, although one in itself, becomes triple as well in the triple intelligence. When it strives towards the good, which some call the Sky, it is Saturn. When it turns back into itself, it is Jupiter. When it turns towards lower things, it is Prometheus, that is, providence. And when it descends, the same ray produces in matter every species of forms. It pours into the soul a similar number of rational principles. These are for judging the things which are produced and for fabricating the products of human skill.

The soul in turn, since it is midway between the spirits and bodies, is accordingly endowed with a triple power. One power is that by which it is joined to higher things. Another is that by which it is extended to lower things. The middle power is that by which it retains its middle position and its proper energy. In the soul's highest part the ray received from the divine intelligence is called the light of the human intelligence, and it raises the soul upwards to the contemplation of higher things. The ray situated in the middle of the soul is the ability of the reason to make judgements; it teaches the civic disciplines. The ray residing in the soul's lowest part is the force of the phantasy; it supplies the skills necessary for human livelihood and for adorning matter with the [various] crafts.

In the *Protagoras* Plato embodies all this in a more extended Prometheus parable.[129] He says Epimetheus, by whom he signifies nature, had armed the animals' bodies, but wasn't able to give men the skill to create things. The latter was bestowed by Prometheus, that is, by the ingenious providence of the divine

¹Ideo Dionysius in libro de divinis nominibus dicit tres esse in angelo motus, circularem, rectum, obliquum. Moveri autem circulo, quia una cum eius esse et operatio eius a Deo² incipiens in eum redit intelligendo. Moveri recte, quia vim suam porrigit ad sequentia. Oblique autem prout se ipsum³ animadvertit. Redit enim hic actus illuc unde venit, ideo circuli dicitur particeps; non tamen perfectus est circulus, quia ad primum sui exordium, Deum scilicet, non reflectitur. Idem in anima reperitur.

Ergo ipsius boni radius quamquam in se unus hac tamen in mente triplice resultat et triplex: dum ad bonum quod coelium⁴ aliqui⁵ dicunt nititur, Saturnus; dum in se reflectitur, Jupiter; dum vertit⁶ ad inferiora, Prometheus, hoc est,⁷ providentia. Idemque radius quot descendens in materia gignit formarum species, totidem et in animam fundit rationes ad ea quae producuntur diiudicanda atque ad artium opera fabricanda.

Anima rursus quia media est inter numina corporaque, ideo triplicem est sortita potentiam: unam qua supernis coniungitur, unam qua ad inferiora porrigitur, mediam qua mediam suique vim propriam retinet. In suprema animi parte radius divinae mentis acceptus mentis humanae lumen dicitur, [*367r*] et animam ad supernorum contemplationem erigit; in media fixus rationis iudicium est ad civilem instruens disciplinam; in postrema⁸ residens phantasiae industria est ad artes victui suppeditantes humano et materiam artificiis⁹ exornandam.

Haec omnia in Protagora prolixiori quadam¹⁰ Promethei parabola Plato significat, dum¹¹ Epimetheum, quo natura significatur, dicit animalium armavisse¹² corpora, industriam vero artium dare hominibus minime potuisse, sed eam a Prometheo fuisse traditam, hoc est, ab artificiosa mentis divinae

---

¹*this paragraph in margin W*   ²adeo *WY*   ³*em.,* ipsam *WXYP*   ⁴coelum *WXP*
⁵aliqui *om. WXP*   ⁶vergit *WXP*   ⁷est *om. W*   ⁸postremam *W*
⁹artificii *W;* artificis *X*   ¹⁰modi *add. W*   ¹¹de *W*   ¹²armasse *XP*

intelligence, the artificer of the world. He adds that Prometheus had taken the skill from the workshop of Minerva and Vulcan. The lowest part of the intelligence, which is called Prometheus, takes light and power from the middle part. The middle part looks three ways: towards its higher part from which it depends, towards itself as it is in itself, towards the production of the lower part. The first two are called Jupiter: Jupiter the greatest and best, and Jupiter the amicable and hospitable [one] and the preserver. The third is called Pallas and Vulcan. It is Pallas in so far as it gives the knowledge to create things to the lower part; it is Vulcan in so far as it gives the desire to create. So Pallas is born from Jove's head, because she gives to the lower part from the prime power. But Vulcan is called "lame," because there is something wrong in what is the product of desire.

Nevertheless, he says, the civic disciplines have not come down to men from Prometheus, but from Jove via Mercury. For the institution of the civil law has been shown to us to be derived from nowhere else but the disposition of the divine law, which the divine intelligence can see in itself when it reflects on itself. Now at that time it is called Jupiter. But it sent men the institution of the law via Mercury, that is, via the intermediate ray which Plato calls Mercury, since Mercury explains the mysteries of the divine law to human reason so that the civil law can be modelled on it.

But in the *Statesman* Plato writes that the contemplation of divine things is bestowed by Saturn,[130] since the ray of his intelligence, as it is raised to God, so in descending to us raises our intelligence too towards the divine countenance. In the *Laws* Book 4 Plato says Saturn is the true master of those who have intelligence.[131]

Moreover, in the same book Plato divides the capability of the human intelligence into three parts; for, either it inclines to contemplation alone, or to action alone, or to something in between. In the first case there is wisdom, in the middle case sovereignty, in the third what ministers to sovereignty, things like geometry, architecture, the artificer's skill. All these

providentia, mundi huius artifice. Ubi addit Prometheum eam accepisse[1] ex officina Minervae et Vulcani.

Accipit[2] enim haec postrema mentis pars quae Prometheus dicitur lumen et vim a media quae tres[3] habet respectus: unum ad superiorem sui partem unde est; alium ad se ipsam ut in se est; alium[4] ad producendam partem inferiorem. Illi duo Jupiter[5] dicuntur: Jupiter[6] maximus optimus, et Jupiter[7] amicabilis et hospitalis[8] et servator. Tertius dicitur Pallas et Vulcanus. Pallas quantum[9] inducit in[10] partem inferiorem cognitionem procreandorum; Vulcanus prout inducit illi affectum ad procreandum. Ideo Pallas nascitur ex capite Jovis, quia ex prima vi ad inferiorem partem. Vulcanus autem[11] dicitur claudicare, quia[12] in effectu qui ex affectu est, defectus existit.[13]

Disciplinam tamen civilem non a Prometheo, sed ab Jove per Mercurium ad homines descendisse. Nam legum civilium institutio nobis non aliunde monstrata est quam a dispositione divinarum legum, quam in se ipsa mens intueatur[14] divina dum in se ipsa reflectitur. Tunc vero Jupiter nominatur. Misit autem eam ad homines per Mercurium, per radium scilicet medium, quem appellat Mercurium, [*367v*] quoniam mysteria divinarum legum rationi interpretatur humanae ad civilium legum descriptionem.

Divinorum vero contemplationem a Saturno datam in Politico scribit Plato, quia eius mentis prout in Deum erigitur radius in nos descendens mentem quoque nostram in divinum attollit intuitum. Et[15] quarto Legum dicit Saturnum esse verum dominum[16] eorum qui mentem habent.

Porro in eodem libro Plato mentis humanae solertiam in tria dividit membra, quia vel ad contemplationem vergit tantum, vel ad actionem dumtaxat, vel ad medium. In primo sapientia est; medio[17] imperium; in tertio ministerium, veluti geometria, architectura, fabrilis opera. Omnis haec industria nobis a divina mente est tradita: prima ab eius capite, scilicet Saturno; secunda

---

[1] *WXP read* Ubi addit quod Prometheus eam accepit   [2]accepit *XP*   [3]tertius *W*
[4]tertium *WXP*   [5,6,7]supra *Y*   [8]hospitabilis *XP*   [9]inquantum *WXP*   [10]ad *Y*
[11]autem *om. WXP*   [12]qua *W*   [13]*WXP read* affectu est, est defectus   [14]intuetur *WXP*
[15]in *add. W*   [16]divinum *W*   [17]in secundo *WXP*

abilities are handed down to us by the divine intelligence. The
first comes from the head, that is, from Saturn. The second
comes from the breast, that is, from Jove. The third comes
from the thigh, that is, from Prometheus. So the one ray of the
highest good (which has become triple in the triple divine
intelligence and been triplicated in the triple soul similarly) is
said to have revealed three abilities to us: philosophy to the
intelligence, the prudence which can govern things to the
reason, the skill to employ the rest of the arts to the phantasy.
As Plato says in the *Timaeus* and in detail in the *Statesman* and
here too, all the things that men know are therefore God's
inventions and God's gifts.[132]

However, here Plato said each such gift has been obtained
from the gods through Prometheus. For these secrets are
derived for us from the Sky out of the higher powers of the
divine intelligence, that is, out of Saturn and Jove, through the
lower part closest to us, that is, Prometheus. As the distributor
himself, Prometheus gives us an ingenious quickness of mind.
But as the intermediary and the preparer, he turns our intelligence and reason towards wisdom, and towards civic skills too,
especially since the intelligence and the reason are stimulated
and prepared in us for more important things by the agency of
the primary human skills. Because of this, Plato mentions
Prometheus most, though the gifts of all the sciences derive
from every single divine spirit.

We can also refer to Epimetheus as the moon cherishing the
body, that is, ensuring the safety of the species through Venus,
and the individual through Jove. But we can refer to Prometheus as the sun cherishing the rational spirit especially: that is,
ensuring through himself its power to perceive, through Mars
its power to divide, through Saturn its power to resolve,
through Mercury its power to define, through himself again its
power to demonstrate. And since the powers to perceive and to
divide are the first parts of the gift, and since perception comes
through light and division through heat, Prometheus is said to
give these two with the brightest fire, that is, under the prime
influence of the Sun and Mars.

a pectore, id est,[1] Jove; tertia a femore, id est, Prometheo. Unus itaque summi boni radius in mente divina triplice triplex effectus,[2] et in anima itidem triplice triplicatus, tres nobis explicavisse dicitur facultates[3]: menti quidem philosophiam; rationi gubernandi prudentiam; phantasiae artium ceterarum industriam. Quare omnes hominum disciplinae Dei inventa sunt Deique munera, ut in Timaeo et Politico latius et hic asseritur.

Dixit autem hic Plato omne donum huiusmodi ex diis esse per Prometheum delibatum. Nam a coelio ex superioribus divinae mentis potentiis, Saturno scilicet ac Jove, per inferiorem nobis proximam, id est, Prometheum, a nobis arcana haec hauriuntur. Prometheus autem iste, ut ipse est largitor, artificiosam praebet solertiam, ut autem medius est et praeparator, mentem nostram et rationem ad sapientiam convertit civilemque peritiam, praesertim cum ab artium primarum industria mens [368r] et ratio ad maiora excitetur in nobis atque paretur. Quapropter licet dona scientiarum omnium ab unoquoque divino numine sint, Promethei potissimum Plato mentionem facit.

*Possumus etiam Epimetheum dicere lunam faventem corpori, videlicet per Venerem ad salutem speciei, per Jovem ad salutem individui. Prometheum vero solem faventem spiritui praesertim rationali, per se quidem ad percipiendum, per Martem[4] vero ad dividendum, per Saturnum ad resolvendum, per Mercurium ad definiendum, per se rursus ad demonstrandum, et quia percipiendi et dividendi vires partes sunt muneris huius primae, et perceptio fit per lumen, divisio per calorem, dicitur dare haec cum lucidissimo igne sub prima scilicet virtute solis et Martis.**

---

[1]id est om. WXP   [2]affectus W   [3]WXP read tres nobis explicuit facultates
[4]mortem Y   *-**om. W (cont.)

In the first use of the names, the Sky means God, Saturn means the intelligence, Jupiter means the soul. But in the second use, the Sky means God's creativeness, Saturn means God's understanding, Jupiter means God's will. In the third use, in any spirit, the Sky means looking upwards to higher things (so in the *Cratylus* it is referred to as "Uranos," the upward-looking), Saturn means pure self-regarding (so in the same dialogue he is called "Cronos," the pure and inviolable intelligence), Jupiter means the glances downwards providing for inferior things (so in the *Cratylus* he is called "Zeus," that is, the vital, and "Dia," that is, he through whom others live[133]). In any spirit, Prometheus and Epimetheus mean Jove's providence: it is Prometheus in so far as it pertains to rational things, Epimetheus to irrational things. Again, in the case of the demons, those who promote the functions of the reason are under Prometheus; those who promote natural functions are under Epimetheus. The firmament shows the image of the invisible heaven: the first planet is Saturn's, the second planet Jove's. Again, in the sun there is beauty, light, heat. Read all about this in the introduction to the *Cratylus*.[134]

16C   Plato adds that these gifts **were handed down with the brightest fire,** for individual things have been revealed by the ray of the divine truth. The ray of a fire has two powers: one burns, the other illuminates. So it is with the sun's ray too, so too with God's ray: it purges intelligences and souls with heat, separating them from lower things; it illuminates them with light. With the fervour of heat it inflames and excites the appetite of everything towards itself. With the splendour of light it reveals to all those who desire it the clarity of truth. Therefore the ancient theologians, Zoroaster, Hermes Trismegistus, Orpheus, Aglaophemus, Pythagoras, since they brought themselves as near as possible to God's ray by releasing their souls, and since they examined by the light of that ray all things by uniting and dividing through the one and the many, they too were made to participate in the truth. In fact, everyone must heed this caution who wants to reach the truth, that is, they must prepare themselves especially by purity of soul for the flowing in of the divine

*Prima nominum positione coelius[1] significat Deum, Saturnus mentem, Jupiter animam; secunda vero coelius[2] Dei foecunditatem, Saturnus Dei intelligentiam, Jupiter Dei voluntatem; tertia coelius[3] in quolibet numine aspectum ad superiora, unde Uranos in Cratylo suspiciens dicitur, Saturnus respectum ad se purum, unde Cronos ibidem pura inviolabilisque mens dicitur, Jupiter prospectus ad inferiora providendo, ideo ibidem dicitur Zeus, id est, vitalis et Dia, id est, per quem alia vivunt. Prometheus Epimetheusque in quolibet numine significant providentiam Jovialem. Sed Prometheus quatenus ad rationalia, Epimetheus quatenus ad irrationalia pertinet. Item in daemonibus Promethei sunt qui rationali favent officio, Epimethei qui naturali. Imaginem invisibilis coeli refert firmamentum; Saturni planeta primus; Jovis planeta secundus. Item in sole forma, lux, calor. De his lege in argumento Cratyli.**

Addit[4] Plato[5] **dona haec simul cum lucidissimo igni[6] fuisse tradita.** Nam divinae veritatis radio sunt singula revelata. Ignis radius duas habet vires: una urit, illuminat altera. Ita et solis radius. Ita quoque et Dei radius: calore purgat mentes et animas, ab inferioribusque secernit; luce illustrat. Caloris fervore in se omnium inflammat et incitat appetitum; lucis fulgore appetentibus omnibus veritatis exhibet claritatem. Unde et prisci theologi, Zoroaster, Mercurius, Orpheus, Aglaophemus, Pythagoras, quia se solutione animae ad Dei radium quam proximos reddiderunt, et eo lumine per unum et multa uniendo et dividendo omnia perscrutati sunt,[7] veritatis compotes effecti[8] sunt. Quae quidem cautio adhibenda est omnibus qui veritatem assequi cupiunt, ut imprimis puritate animi sese comparent[9] ad

---

[1],[2],[3]coelus *XP*　　　[4]-que *add. W*　　　[5]Plato *om. W*　　　[6]igne *XP*　　　[7]sunt *om. P*
[8]affecti *W*　　　[9]comparem [?] *Y*　　　*(cont.) *-**om. W*

splendour. When it is this that is leading them along the correct path and by sure traces, they will discover the truth of things, and distinguish things' individual hiding places—when, that is, they proceed by dividing and uniting through the one and the many, not with the opinions of the senses but with the scrutiny of the intelligence and the reason. For the senses will never reduce the many single things to the universal one, since the universal species are unknown to them; and they will never understand the one is present in the many without being dispersed. For the senses always see bodies, and no whole body can be present in many separate things at the same time, but it has to be divided. Now all this has made the second caution much more obvious, which, Plato says, must be observed in the employment of dialectic. But he hurries to the third caution straight away.

Chapter 27. Except for the first one everything is composed from the one and the many. Also, the species are finite.

16C-D   Plato refers here to three arguments that were handed down by the ancient theologians. First, **everything** that the one universal principle itself has made **is composed from the one and the many.** Second, in the universal order **the species are finite, the individual things infinite.** Third, **you mustn't pass from one extreme to another without mediation.** The first has been more than sufficiently demonstrated above, but it can be put briefly in this way. The universal principle has total power devoid of weakness. Power consists in unity, weakness in diffusion. So the one is simple, devoid of all multiplicity. What follows the one would be equally powerful if it were equally one. Therefore, it could make itself and the things dependent on it; consequently, it could make just as many things as the first one can. But it can't do this. So it isn't equally as powerful. So it isn't equally one. But what is less one is less one because it is made impure by the admixture of multiplicity, just as something is less hot because of the admixture of coldness. So in all

divini splendoris influxum. Quo ducente recto calle certisque
vestigiis veritatem rerum investigabunt singularesque[1] latebras
rerum discutient, dum videlicet non sensuum opinionibus, sed
rationis ac mentis examine per unum ac multa dividendo et
uniendo procedent. Sensus enim[2] singula multa in universale
unum reducent numquam, cum universales illis species sint
incognitae, et unum multis inesse numquam sine sui dispersione
comprehendent, semper enim corpora intuiti sunt, quorum
nullum simul in multis divisis totum inesse potest, sed dividatur
oportet. In quo iam secunda cautio patefacta est, quam obser-
vandam in hac dialectica facultate [*368v*] Plato iubet. Statim
vero ad tertiam properat.

*Omnia praeter primum ex uno et multitudine componun-
tur. Item species sunt finitae. Cap. XXVII.*[3]

Tria hic Plato refert ab antiquis theologis tradita: primum
quod **ex uno et multis constant omnia,** quae ab ipso uno rerum
principio sunt producta; secundum quod in rerum ordine
species finitae sunt, singula infinita; tertium quod **ab extremo
ad extremum sine medio non est eundum.** Primum illud supra
satis superque est ostensum, sic autem breviter patet.
Principium omnium omnem habet vim debilitatis expertem. In
unitate vis consistit, in dispersione debilitas. Quare unum simplex[4] est, multitudinis omnis expers. Quod ipsum sequitur, si
aeque unum esset, aeque[5] esset potens; posset ergo se ipsum
facere et sequentia, ut totidem possit quot et primum. Id autem
nequit. Non est igitur aeque potens, non igitur aeque unum.
Quod autem minus unum per admixtionem[6] multitudinis inqui-
natum minus est unum, sicut minus calidum per[7] frigoris
mixtionem. In omnibus ergo sequentibus cum unitate desuper

---

[1]singulasque *WXP* [2]quippe *WXP* [3]*a break, but no ch. heading W; in X and P the ch. is*
numbered thirteen [4]simpliciter *WXP* [5]aeque *om. W* [6]adnexionem *W*
[7]propter *XP*

subsequent things the multiplicity of external degeneration con-
tends with the unity infused from above.

16D   We can demonstrate the second argument thus. Because of
the dissimilar and disparate outcomes and effects of things, we
can conjecture there are dissimilar and disparate species, and
the universal series is distinguished by higher and lower degrees.
It is obvious in the case of the numbers descending from one.
But the progression of the species can't ascend infinitely nor
descend infinitely. If the species went on infinitely upwards,
there'd be no first in the series, so there'd be no middle one
either, since the first in a series is the cause of the middle. But
when you've removed the principle, you've removed its effects.
Again, within the species themselves, some are more one, true,
good; others are less so. But whatever is more or less such and
such is so called because of its smaller or greater distance or propinquity to that which is primarily and totally such and such.
For instance, things are more or less white or hot or bright
because of the first thing that is bright or hot. Therefore, either
these species are equally distant from what is primarily and
totally one, true, good, or they aren't equally distant. If they
were equally distant, they'd be on a par in goodness, etc. But
they aren't on a par. Therefore it must be that some of them are
nearer to it, but others are further away. So what is primarily
and totally one, true, good isn't separated from them by an infinite distance, because no one species would be closer to it than
another. But what is first and is totally one and good and true is
the first principle of things, as we've shown elsewhere. Or
rather, if there were no first good, there'd be nothing that was
totally good. If nothing were totally good, nothing else could be
called more or less good. But things are more or less good, so
there is a first good. Therefore the species of things don't
ascend to infinity; nor do they endlessly descend, since the end
has to correspond to the beginning, the descent to the ascent,
the decrease to the increase, the least to the greatest.

Moreover, with these intermediate degrees, the higher is the
cause of the lower. But the effect falls short of the cause, because it doesn't have the same power, since the cause produces

infusa externae degenerationis multitudo congreditur.

Secundum vero sic ostendimus: propter dissimiles et inaequales rerum eventus atque effectus, dissimiles et inaequales
esse species coniectamus[1] seriemque rerum superioribus et
inferioribus gradibus esse distinctam, quod in numeris ab uno
descendentibus est perspicuum. Haec vero progressio specierum
neque ascendere in infinitum potest, neque in infinitum descendere. Si sursum abeant infinitae nulla erit prima, nulla ergo erit
et media, quia primum est causa medii. Principio vero sublato
sublata sunt opera. Item in speciebus alia est magis una,[2] vera,
bona, alia minus. Quaecumque vero magis et minus talia sunt,
propter minorem vel maiorem[3] distantiam [*369r*] et propinqui-
tatem ad id quod primo et maxime tale est[4] dicuntur: ut alba,
calida, lucida magis et minus propter primum lucidum atque
calidum. Aut ergo species istae aeque distant a primo et maxime
uno, vero, bono, aut non aeque. Si aeque, pares essent in bonitate et cetera. Sunt tamen impares. Fit itaque ut alia illi sit propinquior, alia vero remotior. Non ergo ab eis infinito intervallo
distat quod primo et maxime unum, verum, bonum, quia nulla
ipsi esset propinquior alia.[5] Primum vero et maxime unum et
bonum et verum primum rerum principium est, ut ostendimus
alias. Immo vero si non esset primum bonum, non esset aliquid
maxime[6] bonum. Si non maxime bonum, nulla dicerentur magis
minusve bona. Sunt tamen ista, ergo et primum bonum. Non
itaque in infinitum species rerum ascendunt, sed neque sine fine
descendunt, siquidem finis principio, descensus ascensui, decrementum incremento, minimum maximo respondere debent.

Quin etiam in his intermediis gradibus superior inferioris
causa est. Effectus autem a causa deficit, quia non par in eo vis,

---

[1]arguimus *WXP*   [2]una *repeated Y*   [3]vel maiorem *om. XP*   [4]esse *Y*
[5]alia *om. XP*   [6]maximum *XP*

both it and those things under it but the effect doesn't produce itself. So the effect's power won't extend to the same number of things as the cause's power, because it hasn't the same amount of power. But if there were infinities under it, it would extend to the same number of things. Again, movement decreases in the direction of the imperfect. Imperfection becomes defect. Defect eventually results in death. So the power which decreases is defective. But the cause's power decreases by degrees in its effects. Therefore you can deduce that the species of things are defined by a certain number.

But the individual things under the species are said to be infinite, because of the fact that the species are eternal, as we proved in the case of the Ideas. Therefore the species are always active, lest they become idle. But each species communicates itself to many things and when these perish new things succeed them endlessly, as the Platonists maintain. So the production and diversity of single things goes on to infinity. Therefore, Orpheus, when he was talking about nature, said, ἀτελής τε τελευτή ,[135] "the endless end": "endless," I think, because of the single things; "end," however, because of the definite number of the species. Also, he said about Saturn: "You who destroy all things and revive them again, you who are master of the unbreakable chains through the infinite world, oh Saturn, creator of a universal eternity, oh Saturn, you who are possessed of the manifold plan."[136] In these lines Orpheus is saying first that the divine intelligence itself, Saturn, creates all things, and in destroying them transforms them into new things (here he proclaims the infinity of the generation of single things). In order to introduce some limit, he said: "You who possess the unbreakable chains of eternity through the infinite world." For [Saturn] arrests the infinite generation by means of the eternal species and contains them in a certain limit. And the things which have been destroyed he remakes from the same species, with the result that, although individual things in the world are changed, nevertheless, by recreating through similar species and similar things, nothing will ever seem to be wanting. In the *Universal Hymn,* therefore, Orpheus calls God, Ἀρχήν τ᾽ ἠδὲ

cum causa producat et ipsum et quae sub ipso, ipse vero se non producat. Non ergo vis effectus istius ad paria se extendet cum vi causae, quia est vis impar. Sin autem infinita sub eo essent, ad paria se extenderet. Item decrementum motus est ad imperfectum; imperfectio ad defectum; defectus denique ad interitum. Deficit ergo vis quae minuitur. Minuitur autem vis causae in effectibus paulatim. Ex his colligitur rerum species certo esse numero definitas.

Singula vero sub speciebus infinita dicuntur, propterea[1] quod species, ut de ideis probavimus, aeternae sunt. Semper ergo agunt, ne sint otiosae. [*369v*] Quaeque vero plurimis se communicat, quibus intereuntibus, nova, ut Platonici volunt, sine fine succedunt. Quare in infinitum generatio et varietas singulorum progreditur. Idcirco Orpheus, cum de natura loqueretur, ait, ἀτελής τε τελευτή,[2] infinitus finis: illud quidem[3] arbitror propter singula; hoc autem[4] propter species definitas. Item de Saturno dixit: *Qui destruis omnia iterumque resuscitas, insolubilia vincula possidens per infinitum mundum Saturne aeternitatis universae genitor, Saturne multiplici consilio praedite.** In his primo dicit quod ipsa divina mens, Saturnus, gignit omnia, et perimendo in nova permutat; ubi infinitatem generationis singulorum indicat. Et ut terminum induceret, ait: Qui habes insolubilia aeternitatis vincula per infinitum mundum. Nam per[5] aeternas species generationem infinitam certo sistit continetque in termino. Et quae destructa sunt ex eisdem reficit speciebus, ut, licet in mundo mutentur singula, recreando tamen per similes species, et similia nulla[6] umquam deficere videantur. Ideo in universali hymno Deum vocavit Ἀρχήν τ᾽ ἠδὲ Πέρας,[7] id est,[8] principium et finem. Nam idem terminat certis

---

[1]ex eo *WXP*   [2]*Greek om. W*   [3]quidem *om. WXP*   [4]autem *om. WXP*
[5]propter *W*   [6]ulla *W*   [7]*Greek om. W*   [8]id est *om. WXP*   *--**om. WXP;*
ὃς δαπανᾷς μὲν ἅπαντα καὶ, αὔξεις ἔμπαλιν αὐτός δεσμὼς ἀρρήκτως ὃς
ἔχεις κατ᾽ ἀπείρονα κόσμον αἰῶνος κρόνε παγγενέτωρ, κρόνε
ποικιλόμυθε *add. XP*

Πέρας ;[137] that is, the beginning and the end. For He, who lays the foundations of all things, terminates all things in fixed degrees.

16D   There remains the third argument: that we mustn't turn from one extreme to another without going through the intermediate steps. For the right way to approach things is to follow the way things themselves proceed. The obvious order in the case of things is this. Any cause out of its own nature makes things. So the process of making follows the nature. But what's made follows the process of making. So the nearest effect to any cause is the one most like it. But as it's deficient it has something dissimilar. But if this effect also makes something, it makes something similar to itself, and that in its turn is deficient. Thus gradually you arrive at something dissimilar. Therefore, between extremes there is a mean point. Or rather, extremes would never exist unless there were an interval and an assumed distance. In the *Timaeus,* therefore, Plato puts at least two intermediaries between the extremes.[138] One is more like the one extreme, the other is more like the other. The result is the first extreme has something like it next to it, and the last extreme is understood by the something similar next to it. Now a mean point is made from extremes. Extremes are opposite each other. If, therefore, there were only one mean point, there would be opposites in one and the same thing; and they would be equally powerful and mutually incompatible. So there are two means. Consequently in one mean the one opposite prevails, in the other the other opposite. And in this way one opposing subject is subordinate to the other and there is concord in the whole.

Perhaps you could posit a mean which contained both opposites equally, that is, each in a diminished degree. Because of the modification each would be reduced to a third form which each would obey. But the mean has to be divided so that the extremes don't touch. Therefore there must be a beginning, a middle and an end. I repeat there must be a middle so that the beginning doesn't touch the end.

So the one itself, since it only uses one power to do everything, straightway produces an effect which is wholly similar to

in gradibus omnia qui inchoat omnia.

Restat tertium illud, ne ab extremo ad extremum sine mediis adventemus. Verus enim ille est investigationis modus qui rerum progressus sequitur. In rebus autem hic ordo conspicitur. Quaelibet causa ex natura sua facit. Sequitur ergo naturam factio.[1] Effectionem vero factum sequitur. Quare cuilibet causae proximus est effectus persimilis. Dissimile vero quid habet ut[2] deficit. Siquid vero et iste facit, simile sibi facit, deficitque rursus et illud. Ex quo gradatim ad dissimile pervenitur. Itaque inter extrema medium est. Immo vero nisi intervallum sit, sublata distantia, extrema non essent. [*370r*] Itaque in Timaeo duo saltem media inter extrema ponit, quorum unum uni similius sit, alteri alterum. Ut et primum sibi simile habeat proximum, et postremum a simili proximo comprehendatur. Medium quippe ex extremis constat; illa opposita sunt. Si ergo unum esset medium, in uno eodemque essent opposita, aeque vehementia,[3] neque sese compaterentur. Duo itaque sunt, ut in uno unum praevaleat oppositum, in altero alterum. Atque ita unum oppositum alteri subiectum pareat, fitque[4] in toto concordia.

Posset forte poni medium aeque utrumque[5] continens, scilicet sub gradu utrumque remisso, ob quam temperiem ad tertiam redigatur formam, cui utrumque pareat. Oportet vero[6] medium esse dividuum, ne extrema se contingant. Ergo oportet habere principium, medium, finem. Medium, inquam, ne principium tangat finem.

Unum ipsum igitur, cum sit ex una[7] virtute admodum efficax, mox effectum sibi simillimum unitissimumque producit. Illud,

---

[1]effectio *XP*   [2]quid *P*   [3]aeque vehementia *om. XP*   [4]sitque *WXP*
[5]utrumque *W*   [6]vero *om. WXP*   [7]unita *WXP*

itself and utterly one. The effect, because it is from the one, is one; because it is outside the one, it degenerates from oneness. Then the opposite of unity enters, that is, multiplicity itself, for it regards both its cause and itself. But this too, since it is wholly united, is endowed with immense power, and therefore with creative oneness. It too produces a one which is wholly similar. This immediately degenerates and regards itself: it regards both its immediate cause and its remote cause. Therefore, after the one, two things appeared. After the two a trinity emerged. The same thing happens with all the rest of the steps [in the hierarchy], until in the process of decreasing you come down to the unlike thing and finally to the lowest thing. From the one you come to a united and finite many which is very similar to the one. From this many you come to another, and finally from the finite many you come to the infinite many which is unlike the one.

16E

Now things themselves also proceed out of the one into the intelligence, out of the intelligence into the soul, out of the soul into the nature, out of this into quality, out of quality into matter extended in quantity. At this point, therefore, the many is called infinite, since the division of quantity proceeds to infinity. Nature's progress stops at this, the sixth link of the golden chain introduced by Homer. So Orpheus tells us to stop ornamenting the song at the sixth generation: Ἕκτῃ δ᾽ ἐν γενεᾷ ... καταπαύσατε κόσμον ἀοιδῆς.[139]

Consequently, the universal genera go thus. One genus is distinguished into a finite number of species. The species descend into infinite individual things. Here the one has again fallen down through the finite many in the middle to an infinite extreme. So the conclusion is you have to pass from one extreme to another through intermediate points. Unless you observe this, you won't understand the extreme which is above, as you won't know how much of its power it needs to produce the intermediate stages. Nor will you understand the extreme which is below, as you won't have the nearest cause, because it is an intermediate stage.

Having described all this, Plato tells us how the ability to do dialectic was handed down. He described the tradition in full in

quia ab uno, unum; quia extra unum,[1] ab unione degenerat. Ubi unitatis subintrat oppositum, ipsa videlicet multitudo, nam et causam respicit et se ipsum. Sed et hoc, cum admodum unitum sit, ingenti est potentia praeditum; foecunda igitur unione. Et unum gignit admodum simile. Continuo[2] degenerat illud seque ipsum respicit, respicit causam proximam, respicit et remotam. Ergo post unum duo eluxerunt, post duo emersit et trinitas. Idem contingit in gradibus ceteris, quousque decrescendo ad dissimile ac tandem ad infimum descendatur. Et ex uno in multitudinem unitam finitamque tamquam similiorem uni, ex hac in aliam, ac tandem ex finita multitudine in infinitam uni dissimilem veniatur.[3]

Nam et res ipsae ab uno [*370v*] in mentem procedunt, a mente in animam, ab anima in naturam, ab hac in qualitatem, a qualitate in materiam quantitate extensam. Ubi multitudo ideo dicitur infinita, quia in infinitum procedit quantitatis partitio. Atque in hoc sexto anulo catenae aureae ab Homero inductae cessat naturae progressus. Ideo iubet Orpheus[4] ut in sexta generatione ornatum cantilenae finiamus: Ἕκτῃ δ᾽ ἐν γενεᾷ ... καταπαύσατε κόσμον ἀοιδῆς.[5]

Proinde[6] rerum genera sic se habent, ut genus unum in species finitas distinguatur; species in singula infinita descendant. Ubi rursus unum per finitam multitudinem mediam ad extremam infinitam est prolapsum. Quare concluditur ab extremo ad extremum esse per media transeundum. Quod nisi quis servaverit, neque extremum quod supra est[7] intelliget, cum quanta vis eius sit ad media producenda ignoret; neque extremum quod est infra cognoscet, cum causam eius proximam quod medium est non teneat.

His propositis, exsequitur Plato dialecticae facultatis traditionem, quam in Sophiste atque Politico abunde descripsit. Hic

---

[1]*for* extra unum *W reads* extremum [2]continue *W* [3]venatur *W* [4]Orpheus *om. W*
[5]*Greek om. W* [6]Et *WXP* [7]est *om. Y*

the *Sophist* and the *Statesman*.[140] Here, however, he says that since you find in the universal order the one and the many and some end and infinity, and since knowledge is about the universal rational principles of everything (because single things can't be known) so accept that, whenever you're trying to understand something, there is the one universal rational principle for a number of things. It is present in things in a way, and it is present more perfectly in the reason, and it is present most outstandingly in the intelligence. So you will find out about it. When you've accepted it, don't stay in the principle itself. For each thing's power can be more accurately assessed when it has been articulated in its effects. So you will go to the things which follow it most closely; and you will go to the genus. For all the universal rational principles must be accepted first, so you can descend from the most simple things to compounds. I repeat, you may divide the genus (if you're able to) through two differences; for the most convenient division is that done through opposites. But division occurs between two things and the first division consists in dividing something into two. For instance, essence becomes one thing in itself, another thing in something else; in the first case it is substance, in the second, accident. Substance becomes corporeal or incorporeal. Or you can divide into three. For instance, the genus of speech divides into judicial, deliberative and demonstrative. Or you can divide into four. For instance, an element can be either fire, or air, or water, or earth. And divide every single member again. For instance, body becomes animate or inanimate. But bodiless substance is either separated from the body or joined to it. Or again animate body becomes either a tree or an animal. Thus you can keep dividing them until you've uncovered the individual species included in any genus. When you've enumerated them, you can talk about the infinite multitude of individual things contained under them. You can't subject the multitude to one genus until you've found out how many intermediate species there are. In the case of the genus, knowledge is confused; in the case of the single things, it is uncertain; in the case of the species, it is certain and distinct. So you mustn't

autem dicit, quia in rerum ordine unum reperitur et multa et
finis aliquis et infinitas, et cognitio de universalibus rerum
rationibus est, quia singula sunt incerta, quotiens scientiam
investigas,[1] unam ipsam universalem plurium accipe rationem.
Inest enim quoquomodo in rebus, inest et in ratione perfectius,
inest et in mente praestantius. Itaque eam reperies. Cum eam
acceperis, ne in ea steteris, nam vis cuiusque in sequentibus
explicata apertius iudicatur. Ibis ergo ad proxima quae sequuntur et genus illud. Nam communissimae quaeque rationes
accipiendae prius, ut a[2] simplicissimis ad composita descendatur. Genus illud, inquam, [*371r*] in species dividas, si potes,
duas per differentias. Haec enim commodissima partitio est
quae fit per opposita. Ea vero inter duo est, et prima divisio in
dualitate consistit, ut[3] essentia per se alia, alia per aliud; illud
substantia, hoc accidens. Et substantia alia corporea, alia
incorporea. Vel saltem in tria partiaris, ut dicendi genus, aliud
iudiciale, aliud deliberativum, aliud demonstrativum. Vel in
quattuor, ut elementum aut ignis, aut aer,[4] aut aqua, aut terra.
Et unumquodque membrum divide rursus, ut corpus aliud animatum, inanime aliud. Incorporea vero substantia aut a corpore semota, aut coniuncta corpori. Rursusque animatum corpus, aliud arbor, aliud animal. Atque ita[5] utrinque dispertias,
quousque singulas species in quolibet inclusas genere patefacias.
Quibus adnumeratis,[6] infinitam singulorum sub illis multitudinem arguas contineri, quam uni generi non prius subicias quam
quot mediae species sint comprehenderis. In genere quidem
cognitio confusa; in singulis autem[7] est incerta; in speciebus
certa habetur atque distincta. Quare neque morandum in

---

[1]investigans *Y*   [2]ad *W*   [3]ut *om. W*   [4]aut aer *om. P*   [5]ita *om. XP*
[6]dinumeratis *WXP*   [7]autem *om. WXP*

linger in the genus, nor yet wander on through single things, nor pass over from one extreme to another without going through the intermediate stages.

Chapter 28. *Concerning divinity and the right use of the art of dividing and uniting.*

Now he's established the art of debating and dealt with the three cautions which must be observed in approaching it (and in order not to have passed on the precepts in vain), Socrates immediately exhorts his listeners to employ the art of dialectic with great circumspection; and he warns them in a way against the rival discipline [opposed to dialectic]. Then through examples he makes them tractable and ready to perceive and understand. But most of all he encourages them when he introduces the divine authority. He says the gods bestowed on us the ability **to contemplate** everything in this way [i.e. with dialectic], when, relying on our own ingenuity, we try to discover something. And they bestowed on us the ability **to be taught,** that is, the ability to learn things from others through instruction and also the ability **to teach** others, that is, to teach them what we've found out ourselves and learnt from others.

But we explained above that the gods gave us this [ability]: first, since they produced all things so they were one and many and between the one and the infinite many there was an intermediate finite many; and second, since they poured a ray from the same light with which they had thus distinguished things into our intelligence and reason. The ray can have the power to distinguish in the same way as the light. But Socrates warns them straight away against the rival discipline when he points out its accompanying vice. The rival discipline is the one which introduces the one and the many more quickly or more slowly than it ought to. For Socrates says **among the wise men** who are their contemporaries (that is, among those wandering around without the higher light who are guided by the senses and by human opinion) and **however it occurs,** that is, wherever

16E

genere, neque est[1] tamen per singula pervagandum, neque ab illo extremo ad hoc sine mediis transeundum.

De divinitate et recto usu artis dividendi et uniendi. Cap. XXVIII.[2]

Socrates, posita iam disserendi arte et tribus cautionibus declaratis quibus tractanda sit, statim, ne frustra haec praecepta tradita sint, ad hanc artem tali observatione capessendam auditores hortatur, dehortaturque ab aliena quodammodo disciplina. Deinde vero per exempla dociles reddit ad percipiendum et ad exsequendum faciles. Hortatur autem eos magnopere cum divinam inducit auctoritatem, dicens deos tribuisse nobis, ut hunc in modum **consideraremus** quaeque, dum proprio freti ingenio invenire quicquam nitimur. Atque etiam [*371v*] ut **disceremus,**[3] id est, ab aliis per disciplinam perciperemus, rursusque ut **doceremus** alios, scilicet, quae per nos invenimus et quae ab aliis quibusdam didicimus.

Quod autem dii nobis hoc dederint in superioribus est expositum, cum ea conditione res[4] omnes produxerint, ut unum essent et multa, et inter unum multitudinemque infinitam media esset multitudo finita; cumque ipsi ex eadem luce, qua res ita discreverant, radium nostrae menti rationique infuderint,[5] qui discretionis eiusdem vim habeat. Statim vero dehortatur eos ab aliena disciplina, dum monstrat quid eam sequatur vitii. Ea vero est quae unum et multa celerius vel tardius quam deceat infert. Dicit enim quod eorum temporum **sapientes inter homines,** id est, qui sensibus opinioneque humana sine lumine superiori vagantur **utcumque contingit,** id est, quo sors eos trahit, nam

[1]est *om. P*   [2]*a break, but no ch. heading W; in X and P the ch. is numbered fourteen*
[3]diceremus *Y*   [4]rationes *W*   [5]infuderunt *Y*

fate drags them (for the senses and opinion are moved by external force), there are some who introduce the one and the many **more quickly** than it is proper for them to do. For example, there are the followers of Democritus, who posited infinite intervals and numberless atoms straight after the one void. There is also Anaxagoras, who posited infinities straight after the one intelligence; for after it nothing was one, but anything was infinite (for indeed everything was mixed with everything). But others are **too slow** in searching out the one. For instance Protagoras, Pyrrho and Herillus consider nothing is more one thing in itself than another, but there are innumerable aspects to things according to each man's judgement. So they never come upon the one, but claim eventually that the one exists simply as a term we use in everyday conversation. Around the time of Socrates there were certainly many adherents to both parties. Though some of them introduced the one too quickly, others too slowly, nevertheless, as a result of an error they all had in common, they brought in infinities right after the one—the one either as a thing or just as a term. They didn't enumerate the definite intermediate stages between the one and infinities. It is through these intermediate stages you can show who is arguing dialectically, and who is arguing out of sheer obstinacy. For the person who comprehends the species midway between the genera and single things can give a firm and definite reason for everything. He can give a distinct reason for the genus in the species. He can give a firm reason for the single things in the species. He can give an appropriate reason in turn for [one] species in [other] species. But the person who doesn't have any intermediate stages, or just a few, can't assign an appropriate or true reason, since he doesn't know the one genus distinctly nor the single things in any firm way. And so he retreats into verbal quibbles and overcomes his opponents with tricks, and deceives them with verbal ambiguity, and beats them by threatening and brawling rather than convincing them by reason. But this is the vice which accompanies the rival discipline.

But next, after encouraging and warning his listeners, Socrates makes them eager and ready to learn. So he opens up the

sensus et opinio externo[1] iactu moventur, partim **celerius** quam
decet unum multaque ponunt: ceu Democritii, qui post unum
vacuum mox infinita intervalla et innumerabiles atomos posue-
runt; et Anaxagoras, post mentem unam infinita statim, nihil
enim esse unum post illam sed quodlibet infinitum, omnia namque omnibus esse commixta. Partim vero **tardius** unum quaerunt: ut Protagoras, Pyrrho atque Herillus, qui nihil magis in se
tale esse quam tale sed innumeras esse rerum facies pro
cuiusque iudicio volunt. Unum ergo isti numquam inveniunt,
sed tandem unum nomen propter communem loquendi usum
esse dicunt. Multi certe et illorum et istorum sectatores circa
Socratis erant tempora. Qui, quamvis[2] partim celerius, partim
tardius unum ponerent, tamen[3] communi errore post unum,
sive rem unam sive nomen unum, infinita protinus inferebant;
neque certa media inter unum et infinita dinumerabant. [*372r*]
Quibus mediis demonstratur qui dialectice et qui contentiose
loquantur. Nam qui medias comprehendit species inter genera
atque singula firmam ac certam potest de omnibus reddere
rationem: de genere distinctam in specie; de singulis firmam in
specie; de specie propriam rursus in speciebus. Qui vero vel
species nullas habet medias, vel paucas, cum neque genus unum
clare cognoscat neque stabiliter singula, propriam ac veram
assignare rationem non valet. Ideoque ad verborum captiunculas confugit, versutiis disputantes subducit, fallit ambiguitate
verborum, conviciis iurgiisque superat potius quam ratione con-
vincat. Atque hoc est vitium quod alienam illam sequitur disciplinam.

Sequitur autem,[4] ut post exhortationem dehortationemque
faciles auditores docilesque reddat. Quare exemplis rem omnem

---

[1]extrinseco *WXP*   [2]licet *WXP*   [3]tantum *WXP*   [4]autem *om. WXP*

whole problem by using examples. All of men's urge to do
things either stops in the cunning of the intelligence, or it
is articulated out of the intelligence into speech, or it needs
singing or playing as well, or more than this it acts on its own
body, or it effects something in external matter. The first is
contemplative knowledge, like dialectic, geometry and the
rest like them. The second is grammar. The third is vocal or
instrumental music. The fourth is dancing and gymnastics.
The fifth is craftsmanship in any of the arts. Of all these the
three middle ones have the best known effect, because they
offer themselves in a way to the senses and operate with
regard to their own body. And, since we ought to take our
examples from better known things, as Plato insists in the
Republic and the *Sophist*,[141] Plato bases his examples on
17A-B these three mainly, and on letters first (for each person
understands best of all the things which he learned first). Now
for us the voice is one, that is, it's a sound coming out of our
mouth. On the other hand the voice is infinite, for everyday each and every person produces various voices and the
variety and repetition of voices goes on to infinity. If someone recognizes a man's voice is one (that is, one particular
sound issuing from a man's mouth), he isn't a grammarian yet;
for everybody knows this, but everybody is not a grammarian.
Again, someone who recognizes you can hear a countless
diversity of voices isn't a grammarian yet, for who questions
this fact? But a grammarian is someone who knows into how
many and into what sort of species a voice can be divided
when it's being articulated clearly into the words conceived
17B in the intelligence. Furthermore, the person who knows the
voice is one, or the person who knows it is endlessly varied
17C isn't a musician; even the person who knows that one voice
is high-pitched, another low, another of medium pitch, isn't
a musician yet. The person who doesn't know them is com-
17D pletely non-musical. But the musical person is the one who
knows how many intervals of voices there are in the upper and
lower registers and what sort they are, and considers their limits
and the number of combinations that can be made from them.

aperit. Omnis industria hominum vel in mentis cessat acumine, vel in vocem ex mente producitur, vel etiam cantum requirit aut[1] etiam sonum,[2] vel praeter haec in corpus agit proprium, vel in[3] externam materiam quicquam efficit. Prima scientia contemplativa est, ut dialectica, geometria, et reliquae similes; secunda grammatica; tertia musica vocum vel sonorum; quarta saltatio ludusque gymnasticus; quinta artis cuiusque fabrilis opera. Ex his omnibus tres mediae, quia et sensibus se quodammodo offerunt et circa corpus proprium operantur, notissimum habent eventum. Cum vero ex notioribus, ut in Republica et Sophiste docet Plato, exempla trahere debeamus, in his tribus exempla potissimum Plato conficit, atque in litteris primum, patent enim cuique maxime quae primo quisque percepit. Vox quidem una est nobis, id est, sonus ex ore nostro emanans. Est iterum infinita, nam et omnes et singuli quotidie voces proferunt [*372v*] varias, atque in infinitum varietas replicatioque vocum progreditur.[4] Siquis cognoscit hominis vocem esse unam, id est, unum quendam sonum ex ore hominis erumpentem, nondum grammaticus est. Id enim sciunt omnes, non tamen[5] grammatici omnes. Item qui percipit diversita#tem vocum innumerabilem audiri posse, nondum grammaticus. Nam cui hoc dubium? Sed ille grammaticus est qui tenet quot[6] in species vox distingui possit et quales, dum ore articulatim in verba mente concepta distinguitur. Quin etiam neque musicus qui vocem unam esse intelligit, vel qui sine[7] termino variam. Neque etiam qui vocem esse aliam acutam, aliam gravem, communis toni aliam noscit tantum, qui haec scit nondum musicus; qui ignorat a musica est admodum alienus. Ille vero in ea sapiens est qui intelligit quot intervalla vocum sunt in acumine et gravitate, et qualia, et terminos intervallorum considerat, et quot compositiones ex istis efficiantur.

---

[1]vel *XP*   [2]somnum *W*   [3]in *om. Y*   [4]egreditur *WXP*   [5]tam *Y*   [6]quod *W*
[7]sive *Y*   #*P frag. IV (81v) ends*

A musical interval signifies the difference in pitch of one voice from another. The difference is brought about in several ways. For either one voice is higher than another in pitch and tension by an eighth making a whole tone, or by less than an eighth making a semi-tone, as is described in the *Timaeus*.[142] Plato calls the first interval "epogdoum;" but the second interval he calls "limma." Or the voice is a third higher and this interval is called "epitritos" and it produces the harmony of a fourth. Or it can be higher by a half octave and this interval is called "hemiolios" and it produces the harmony of a fifth. Or [hemiolios] can double itself and this duplicated, that is, doubled interval produces the harmony of an octave. But two and two-thirds [hemiolios] produces the octave and a fourth. [Hemiolios] tripled produces the octave and a fifth. [Hemiolios] quadrupled produces the harmony of a double octave. The first ratio is 9:8, the second is 243:256, the third is 4:3, the fourth is 3:2, the fifth is 2:1, the sixth is 8:3, the seventh is 9:3 and 9:27, the eighth is 4:1. In the first ratio we put the tone, in the second the semi-tone. In the third ratio we put the interval of the fourth, in the fourth of the fifth, in the fifth of the octave, in the sixth of the eleventh, in the seventh of the twelfth, in the eighth of the fifteenth. Yet all the species of the intervals are included in the octave. So the differences are the intervals.

But the intervals' limits are the consonances brought about by the differences (whose species we've enumerated). But the combinations of the intervals are tetrachords, pentachords, or octachords and similar orders of chords, which differ from each other through the intervals we've mentioned. But Orpheus introduced the tetrachord: for in the *Hymn to Phoebus* he gives Phoebus a lyre with four strings and he says summer comes when Phoebus touches the top string, winter when he touches the bottom one, autumn and spring when he touches the two middle ones.[143]

But since Plato says a would-be musician must not only know how many intervals there are, but also what sort they are, you have to understand that in these differences of voice from voice

Musicum intervallum significat consonum excessum vocis unius[1] ad alteram. Qui sane excessus pluribus fit modis, nam aut superat una vox in acumine et intentione[2] aliam octava sui parte tonumque efficit, aut minori parte quam octava et efficit semitonum, ut scribitur in Timaeo. Primam Plato proportionem epogdoum[3] vocat; limma vero secundam. Aut superat tertia sui parte, quae proportio epitritus dicitur efficitque diatessaron harmoniam. *Aut dimidia parte excedit quae proportio hemiolios,[4] harmoniam procreat diapente. Aut totam se tota bis aequat, quae proportio diplasia,[5] id est, dupla diapason harmoniam** gignit. Proportio vero dupla duarumque tertiarum, diapason et diatessaron; tripla, diapason et diapente; quadrupla, bis diapason. Primus excessus est novem ad octo; secundus ducentum quadraginta tres ad ducentum quinquagesimum sextum; tertius quattuor ad tres;[6] quartus trium ad duo; quintus duorum [*373r*] ad unum; sextus[7] ipsius octo ad tria; septimus novem ad tria[8] et novem ad viginti septem;[9] octavus quattuor ad unum. In primo tonum ponimus,[10] in secundo semitonum; in tertio quartam vocem; in quarto quintam; in quinto octavam; in sexto undecimam; in septimo duodecimam; in octavo quintam decimam. Verumtamen omnes intervallorum species intra octavam clauduntur. Excessus itaque intervalla sunt.

Termini vero intervallorum consonantiae quae his excessibus conficiuntur, quarum species numeravimus. Compositiones vero intervallorum sunt tetrachorda, vel pentachorda, vel octachorda[11] et similes chordarum ordines sese invicem per intervalla quae diximus excedentium. Induxit autem tetrachordum Orpheus. Nam in hymno[12] Phoebi lyram Phoebo dat quattuor cum fidibus, dicitque aestatem produci cum acutam tangit, hiemem cum gravem, cum medias duas autumnum[13] atque ver.[14]

---

[1]unus *W*   [2]tensione *WX*   [3]epogdonum *Y*   [4]*em.*, emiolus *XY*
[5]*em.*, diplasion *XY*   [6]tria *X*   [7]sextum *W*   [8]tres *W*   [9]novem *WX*
[10]primum *W*   [11]vel octachorda *om. W*   [12]hymnis *X*   [13]aestatem *X*
[14]aestatem *W*   *-***om. W*

you can proceed mainly in three ways. For if you cross from semi-tone to tone[s], you have the diatonic scale, serious and steady. If you go through several semi-tones, you have the soft chromatic scale. But if you go in a way through lesser [tones], you have the difficult harmonic scale.[144] And this is what Plato tells us to notice about music. Our ancestors, whom we follow, knew it too, that is, the Pythagoreans and the Orphics. They called harmony the measured arrangement which results in one voice being adjusted to another when all is observed.[145] But they called rhythm—to come to the third

17D   example—the dexterity and quickness which is pleasing to those who watch, and which can be seen everywhere in the dancers' and players' limbs when they observe the "arithmoi," that is, the numbers and measures similar to those in music. Plato also talked about it in the *Laws* Book 2 and the *Republic* Book 3; you have to observe the same thing in dancing as you do in grammar and music, and so with all the rest.[146] For

17E   whenever you consider them in this way, you'll end up knowing about them; and when you consider the rest similarly, similarly you'll end up knowing about the rest. But the infinite multitude of single things and within single things—of single things meaning of individual things numerically distinct, and within single things meaning within the parts of each body—this multitude will make you ignorant and totally devoid of wisdom. It won't make you rational, harmonious or orderly, since you'll never be looking at a number in anything.

Plato touches on three concepts here: wisdom, reason and number. Wisdom is the definite comprehension of something. Therefore the something has first to be distinguished by reason in order to be perceived with certainty, then defined by number in order to be understood. Therefore reason distinguishes the thing into parts and assigns a finite number to them; then it understands. But single things are all of them infinite in number and qualities, and any one is infinite in its particles and the variety of its flux and contingencies. So there's no definite number of single things; so there's no certain comprehension of them.

Quia vero dicit Plato quod futurus musicus nosse debet non solum quot sint intervalla, sed qualia, intelligendum est in his excessibus vocis ad vocem tribus modis potissimum posse procedi. Nam si semitonio in tonum ac tonum sit transitus, diatonos oritur melodia gravis et constans; si per[1] semitonos plures eatur, chromatica mollis; sin autem per minora quodammodo, harmonica difficilis. Atque haec sunt quae iubet Plato circa musicam animadverti, quae cognoscentes maiores nostri, quos sequimur, id est, Pythagorici atque Orphici, harmoniam vocaverunt eam concinnitatem, quae in vocum modulis ex eiusmodi observatione resultat; rhythmum vero vocaverunt, ut ad exemplum tertium veniamus, eam dexteritatem[2] gratamque aspectantibus promptitudinem, quae in saltantium ludentiumque [*373v*] membris ex arithmis, id est, numeris et mensuris musicae consimilibus passim apparet. Quod in Legibus quoque libro secundo et Republica libro tertio declaravit, in qua idem est quod in grammatica et musica observandum, idem quoque in ceteris omnibus. Quotiens enim haec ita tractas circa haec sapiens evadis et cum similiter cetera similiter et in ceteris sapiens. Infinita autem multitudo singulorum et in singulis, singulorum scilicet individuorum numero distinctorum, et in singulis scilicet partibus corporis cuiuscumque, imperitum te et expertem sapientiae passim reddet, neque rationalem, neque numerosum atque compositum, utpote in nullum in aliquo numerum[3] quandoque respicientem.

Tria hic tangit Plato: sapientiam, rationem, et numerum. Sapientia enim certa rei comprehensio est. Quare[4] prius ratione distincta sit res oportet ut certe percipiatur. Deinde numero definita ut comprehendatur. Ratio ergo distinguit in partes, finitumque illis assignat numerum. Mox vero comprehendit. Singula vero et omnia numero et qualitatibus infinita, et quodlibet particulis et varietate fluxus et contingentium infinitum. Ergo nullus eorum definitus est numerus; nulla igitur illorum certa comprehensio.

---

[1]per *om.* W   [2]ad exteritatem W   [3]numero W   [4]distincta *add.* X

Chapter 29. You must proceed from the one to the infinite many and back again from the infinite many to the one by means of the finite many.

Socrates' listeners have been sufficiently persuaded by the argument above to pursue the art of debating with due care. So Protarchus turned to Philebus and approved of what Socrates said. While Philebus didn't deny Socrates was right, he did ask what it all had to do with the present debate over pleasure and wisdom; and Socrates replied that this was a good question. Protarchus, therefore, begged him to unravel the problem now in hand through the suggested arguments. Socrates promises to do so, only first of all he will finish with the examples. Since it's been agreed from the foregoing examples that you mustn't rush from the one to infinities without going through the intermediate stages, it remains for them to demonstrate that you mustn't return from the infinities to the one without going through the proper intermediate stages. Socrates demonstrates it by taking the example of letters.

Now men start to think about everything either by using the intelligence's reason, or by using the senses. If they use the reason, they have to divide from the one into its many by way of the intermediate stages. But if they use the senses, they are brought back from infinities to the one by way of the intermediate stages. The first was established above; the second is shown here in the case of letters.

The use of letters has been continual, as Pliny shows in Book 7 and Plato indicates in the beginning of the *Timaeus* and in the *Laws* Book 3.[147] But certain fixed systems of letters have been invented by different people. In order for his priests to have their own secret literature apart from the vulgar, Zoroaster established letters in the characters of the celestial signs and constellations. Hermes Trismegistus, who was moved by Zoroaster's example, gave letters to his priests in the shapes of animals and plants, so that the vulgar should not partake of theology. But there flourished in Egypt's Naucratis (as Plato describes in the *Phaedrus*[148]), among those worshipped by the

18A-B

18B

Ab uno in multitudinem infinitam[1] at vicissim ab hac ad unum per multitudinem finitam est procedendum. Cap. XXIX.[2]

Satis ex superioribus persuasi sunt Socratis auditores ad eam disserendi artem debita[3] diligentia prosequendam.[4] Idcirco Protarchus ad Philebum conversus Socratis dicta probavit. Quod ille quidem non renuit, sed quid ista ad praesentem de voluptate et sapientia quaestionem conferrent, interrogavit. Quod recte quaesitum respondit Socrates. Oravit [*374r*] ergo Protarchus ut his propositis per haec iam[5] quaestionem propositam enodaret.[6] Quod se facturum Socrates pollicetur, modo prius, quod in exemplis restat, peragat. Siquidem ex superioribus exemplis constitit[7] non esse ab uno ad infinita sine mediis festinandum, reliquum est exemplis ostendere non esse ab infinitis ad unum absque debitis mediis redeundum, idque in litteris aperit.

Porro autem[8] homines aut[9] a mentis ratione considerare quaeque incipiunt aut a sensibus. Si a ratione, ab uno in multa sua per media partiantur oportet. Sin a sensibus, ab infinitis per media revertantur in unum. Primum supra constitit, alterum hic in litteris declaratur.

Usus litterarum sempiternus fuit, ut in septimo libro ostendit Plinius et in Timaei principio Plato significat et tertio Legum. Sed certi quidam litterarum modi a variis inventi sunt. Zoroaster, ut sacerdotes sui propriam seorsum a vulgo haberent[10] litteraturam, in signorum siderumque[11] coelestium characteribus litteras instituit. Mercurius eius exemplo commonitus[12] suis sacerdotibus in animalium et plantarum figuris dedit litteras, ne vulgus theologiae esset conscium. Floruit autem in Aegypti Naucrate,[13] ut Plato scribit in Phaedro, quidam ex his quos

---

[1]*em.,* finitam *XY*   [2]*a break, but no ch. heading W; in X the ch. is numbered fifteen*
[3]delata *W*   [4]persequendam *X*   [5]iam *om. Y*   [6]enodare *W*   [7]consistit *Y*
[8]aut *WX*   [9]aut *om. W*   [10]habent *Y*   [11]sideraque *Y*   [12]commotus *X*
[13]*em.,* Naucratia *WXY*

Egyptians as gods, one whose name among them is Theuth; among the Greeks it is Hermes Trismegistus and the Latins call him Mercury. In Hermes' time the king of Egypt was Tamus of Thebes (where Jupiter is worshipped as Hammon). Hermes was a friend of this Tamus. Inspired by the god Hammon, Hermes discovered arithmetic, geometry, astronomy and moreover introduced the use of letters as an aid to wisdom and a prop to the memory. Tamus, however, considered the use of letters would make men forgetful, because they would confide in writings and neglect to think; and it would make them careless about finding things out, inasmuch as they'd rely on the mental skill of their superiors and not on their own. The use of letters generally harms the memory; for the things we've laid aside in writing, we stop guarding as it were, and in that very security we abandon them. All this is in the *Phaedrus*.

But here Plato says that when [Hermes] was considering the voice's infinity, he was either **some god, or some divine man: god,** because by God's light he was next to God; **divine** because no man must be called God, as Plato says in the *Sophist*.[149] But the philosopher ought to be called divine. In the *Phaedrus* Plato also calls the philosopher "a demon," that is, wise.[150] Since, as I said, that divine and wise philosopher, Hermes Trismegistus, was considering the voice's infinity and wanted to ascend to the one voice, he investigated certain intermediate species of voices.

18C   In the first species he put vowels and divided them into seven: αεηιουω. Into the species which remained he put those which aren't in themselves voiced, but which bring a certain stress and tension when added to other letters. These we call consonants and the letters are seventeen in number: βγδζθκλμνξπροτφχψ. He divided the consonants into two species: into semi-vowels, which Plato calls here the intermediaries, and into mutes. The semi-vowels are eight: ζξψλμνρσ, the mutes are nine: βγδκπτθφχ. Again, he divided the vowels into three species: some are long: ηω, some are short: εο, some are both: αυ. But the eight semi-vowels he divided into three species: into doubles, and immutables, and sigma, there being three doubles: ζξψ, and four

Aegyptii ut deos venerati sunt, cuius nomen est apud Aegyptios Theuth; apud Graecos Hermes Trismegistus; Latini hunc Mercurium vocant. Eius tempore Tamus Thebarum Aegypti rex erat, ubi Jupiter celebratur¹ Hammon. Huius Tami familiaris fuit Mercurius. Hammonis autem Dei afflatu, arithmeticam, geometriam, astronomiam invenit et usum praeterea litterarum induxit tamquam sapientiae adminiculum memoriaeque subsidium. Quamquam Tamus propter scriptorum confidentiam cogitationisque [374v] negligentiam obliviosos homines litterarum usum putaverit² effecturum et ad inventionem negligentiores, utpote non suo, sed superiorum ingenio fretos. Obest plerumque memoriae litterarum usus, nam ea quae in scriptis reposuimus veluti custodire desinimus, et ipsa securitate dimittimus. Haec in Phaedro.

At vero Plato hic ait, cum vocis infinitatem consideraret, **sive quis deus, sive divinus vir aliquis: deus,** quia Dei lumine Deo proximus; **divinus,** quia, ut in Sophiste dicit, nullus³ hominum Deus dicendus est.⁴ Divinus vero est appellandus philosophus, quem et daemonem in Phaedro vocat, hoc est, sapientem. Cum inquam divinus ille et sapiens philosophus Mercurius Trismegistus vocis infinitatem animadverteret, velletque ad unam vocem ascendere, medias quasdam species vocum investigavit.

In prima specie⁵ vocales posuit, distinxitque in septem: αεηιουω; reliqua in specie eas posuit quae vocem quidem per se non habent, sed casum aliquem et tensionem inferunt litteris aliis additae, quas consonantes vocamus septem ac decem numero litteras: βγδ𝛇θκλμνξπρστφχψ. Has consonantes duas in species partitus est: in semivocales, quas hic medias vocat Plato, et in mutas. Semivocales octo: 𝛇ξψλμνρσ; mutas novem: βγδκπτθφχ. Rursusque vocales in tres; alias longas: ηω, alias breves: εο, alias duorum temporum: αυ. Semivocales autem octo in tres: in duplas⁶ et immutabiles et in sigma.⁷ Duplas tres: 𝛇ξψ,

¹colebatur WX   ²putaverunt W   ³nullum W   ⁴est om. Y   ⁵species Y
⁶scilicet add. WX   ⁷em., sima WXY

immutables: λμνρ. The mutes he divided into three species: thin, thick, and in between. There are three thin ones: κπτ, three thick ones: θφχ, and three in between: βγδ. Priscian divides them into vowels and consonants. The vowels are: a e i o u. All the rest he calls consonants: some among them are semi-vowels, some are mutes, some are liquids. The semivowels are: l m n r s, the mutes are: b c d f g h p q t, the liquids are: m n l r. Cadmus brought letters into Greece from Egypt and Phoenicia; the Pelasgi from Greece into Latium, as Pliny says in Book 7.[151]

But let's go back to Hermes. He divided letters so that he could arrive at individual letters; and each separate letter he called an "element," that is, an element of a syllable. He also called letters as a whole an element, that is, an element of diction and of speech. But as he reflected nobody would know any one letter without knowing them all (that is, nobody could know the power of any one letter without linking it with the others, or could distinguish clearly the nature of the one common voice without the individual voices), accordingly, he divided the one voice into many letters. And he intertwined any letter with others in such a way that he introduced the one discipline of dividing and joining. This discipline, which was concerned with the one common nature of the letters and their mutual relationships, he called grammar.

When Socrates finished, Philebus says the last example has made him understand the nature of letters more clearly than the nature of music or gymnastics, which Socrates had glanced at earlier. Or rather, now, he says, he understands at last the nature of letters more clearly than when they were previously mentioned. But he still wanted to know the same thing as before.

Socrates replied, "Aren't you asking what it all has to do with the problem in hand?" Philebus replied that it is just what he and Protarchus had been inquiring about for some time. And Socrates says, "Though, in actual fact, you know the answer already, you keep asking. For this long investigation means, since we have to decide between pleasure and wisdom (which of them ought to be chosen preferably as the better one),

18C-D

18D

18E

immutabiles quattuor: λμνρ. Mutas in tres: tenues, densas, medias. Tenues tres: κπτ, densas tres: θφχ, medias tres: βγδ. *Priscianus ita dividit in vocales et consonantes. Vocales: a e i o u; consonantes alias omnes vocat. Ex his alias semivocales, alias mutas, alias liquidas. Semivocales: l m n r s; mutas: b c d f g h p q t; liquidas: m n l r. Ex Aegypto et Phoenicia litteras in Graeciam transtulit Cadmus; e Graecia in Latium Pelasgi, ut in septimo libro inquit Plinius.

Sed ad Mercurium redeamus. Hic litteras**[1] ita distinxit, ut ad[2] singulas litteras perveniret, et unamquamque [*375r*] vocavit elementum, syllabae scilicet elementum; et cunctas etiam elementum vocavit,[3] dictionis scilicet orationisque[4] elementum. Cum vero cogitaret ille quod nemo unum quiddam illorum sine cunctis cognosceret, id est, quod unius cuiusdam litterae vim sine aliarum commercio non posset† aliquis scire, et communis unius vocis naturam distincte non posset†† dignoscere sine singulis, ideo et unam distinxit vocem multas[5] in litteras et quamlibet litteram cum aliis ita contexuit ut unam istius discretionis connexionisque disciplinam induceret, quae de una litterarum communi natura mutuaque inter se habitudine cogitaret, quam grammaticam nominavit.

His dictis, infert Philebus se in hoc postremo exemplo hanc litterarum conditionem planius percepissc quam conditionem musicae vel gymnasticae quam supra perstrinxit. Immo etiam clarius nunc tandem litterarum conditionem intelligere quam supra, cum de eisdem litteris facta mentio fuit. Sed adhuc idem quod et supra requirere.

Ad haec Socrates: Numquid postulas quid haec ad[6] quaestionem propositam conferant? Id ipsum esse respondit Philebus quod dudum ipse et Protarchus requirerent. Atqui Socrates ait: Cum iam id proprie[7] assecuti sitis, quaeritis tamen. Nam id sibi vult diuturna haec investigatio ut cum de voluptate et sapientia disceptandum sit, utrum eorum potius sit ut melius

---

[1]Atque *add. WX*   [2]in *W*   [3]in *add. W*   [4]ornationisque *W*   [5]mutas *Y*
[6]ad *om. W*   [7]prope *XY*   *-**om. WX*   †-†† *om. W*

we must understand them both first by knowledge. But since each is a genus divided into many species (and the species are again divided into an infinite number of single things), the higher discipline requires we consider how both must be divided into definite species and in what order, before we descend to the infinite number of single things."

So Protarchus says, "Philebus, the question isn't a frivolous one. I say again, Socrates has led us round **in a circle**." He said **in a circle** because Socrates, starting out from pleasure and wisdom, after a very long digression, came back again to pleasure and wisdom. He also said it because Socrates had ascended into the intelligence through the senses (from the many towards the one), and descended into the senses through the intelligence (from the one into the many). [Protarchus continues,] "Let's see, therefore, who of us will reply to these points. Perhaps it's absurd, [Philebus,] that I, your successor in replying, cannot act on your behalf and am asking you to do the replying. Yet it would be more absurd if neither of us could reply and we were to remain for ever in the state of ignorance. (Here he is saying people ought

to put up with anything rather than ignorance.) So let's see what we can do.

"It seems to me Socrates is asking about pleasure and wisdom, whether they have many species under them and how many they are and of what kind." Socrates confirms this, saying, "Protarchus, son of Callias, what you're saying is true, for unless we can observe the points mentioned above both in everything which is said to be one, similar and identical, and in the things which are opposite, that is, in the many, dissimilar and different things, none of us will be of any use at any time." With these words Socrates challenges them to the utmost to take up the dialectical discipline. At the same time he shows them what a terrible drawback it is not to have it. You must note, since he talked about **the one, the similar, the identical,** that the one pertains to every sharing in common. If the sharing is in the case of a quality, it produces the similar; if of a substance, the identical; if of a quantity, the equal.

eligendum, utrumque prius scientia comprehendatur. Cum vero utrumque unum sit genus multas in species distributum, et in singula iterum infinita, considerandum iubet superior disciplina, quomodo utrumque et quo ordine in species definitas sit partiendum, prius quam ad infinita singula descendatur.

Ait ergo Protarchus: O Philebe, haud levis ista quaestio est; inquam **circulo quodam** Socrates nos deduxit. Dixit **circulo,** quia a voluptate [*375v*] et sapientia incipiens, longiori quodam ambitu in voluptatem rursus et sapientiam rediit; ac etiam, quia per sensum a multitudine ad unum processit in mentem et[1] per mentem ab uno in multitudinem descendit in sensus. Vide igitur uter nostrum ad haec sit responsurus. Forte vero absurdum est, ut ego tibi in respondendo successor gerere vicem tuam non possim, tibique respondendum praecipiam. Absurdius[2] tamen esset, si neuter nostrum respondere posset, atque ita diutius in hac inscitia commoraremur. In quo docet quodvis aliud esse ferendum potius quam inscitiam. Vide igitur quid agamus.

Videtur mihi Socrates quaerere de voluptate et sapientia, utrum plures sub se species habeant, quotve sint et quales. Confirmat haec Socrates dicens: Vera narras, O Protarche, Calliae fili. Nam nisi possimus[3] quae supra dicta sunt observare in omni eo quod unum, simile, idem dicitur, et in contrariis, scilicet multis, dissimilibus, diversis, nullus nostrum quandoque ad aliquod[4] alicuius erit pretii. His verbis eos Socrates ad eam disciplinam vehementissime provocat, dum quam grave sit in eius privatione detrimentum ostendit. Quia dixit **unum, simile, idem,** advertendum est quod unum ad omnem pertinet communionem, quae, si in qualitate est, simile efficit, si in substantia, idem, si in quantitate, aequale.

---

[1]a mente *add.* W   [2]absurdus W   [3]possumus W   [4]aliquid WX

However, any one thing ought to be drawn into the many. What appears to be similar in itself [ought to be drawn] into dissimilar things if they are hidden under it at all: for instance, one hot thing into dissimilar hot things (in so far as they differ among themselves by degrees), taste into dissimilar species of taste. Or what appears the same in the common nature [ought to be drawn] into diverse things if they are under it at all: for instance, an animal into beasts and men. On the other hand, the many ought to be drawn back again into the one, dissimilar things into something similar, diverse things into something the same. For all things, however many or dissimilar or different they are, at least agree in some one condition, either of being, or living, or acting, or being acted on, or being good, or proceeding from the one, or returning to the one.

Since Socrates had thus put his listeners under too great an obligation, Protarchus shrank from the important task and referred it back to Socrates. Protarchus says, "It's obviously a beautiful thing for a wise man to know everything; but if he can't, the next best thing, that is, the safe way for him to sail, is obviously to recognize his own ignorance. Otherwise he'll be ignorant of the thing itself and of his own ignorance and he'll go wrong when he launches on what he doesn't know, and he'll be unteachable or too proud." Plato tells us so in the *Alcibiades*.[152] It's as if Protarchus were saying, "We acknowledge, in fact, that everything must be examined diligently and the best line of approach is the one you've told us about. But, being adolescents, we are inexperienced in such things, that is, we don't have the ability to do dialectic and we aren't yet ready for philosophizing. But you, you are better suited in age and experience and, besides, it concerns you to discuss all this. For at the time Philebus was saying pleasure is the highest good, you denied it on the spot and objected that wisdom is the more excellent. So you are the cause of the contention; for when an objection occurs, then the debate begins. So it concerns you to unravel what you yourself have tangled. Moreover, when the points were raised in the discussion, we warned you we were not going to let you go until

19C

19C-D

19D-E

Oportet autem quodlibet unum in multa deducere: sive simile quoddam in se videatur in dissimilia, siqua sub eo latent, ut calidum in dissimilia calida in quantum[1] ea inter se gradibus differunt, saporem in dissimiles saporis species; sive idem communi in natura appareat in diversa, siqua subter sunt, ut animal in bruta et homines. Ac rursus multa in unum: dissimilia in simile aliquod; diversa in aliquod idem. [*376r*] Omnia enim quantumcumque[2] multa vel dissimilia vel diversa in una quadam[3] saltem conditione conveniunt, vel essendi, vel vivendi, vel agendi, vel patiendi, vel boni, vel procedendi ab uno, vel redeundi ad unum.

Cum per haec Socrates auditores nimium astrinxisset, refugit grande hoc onus Protarchus, reiecitque in Socratem. Temperato inquit viro pulchrum videtur omnia nosse quod si fieri non possit, secunda quaedam, id est, tuta navigatio illi videtur suam ignorantiam recognoscere, ne et rem ipsam ignoret et ignorantiam, neque, dum quod ignorat temptat, aberret, neque sit indocilis, neque superbior; quod in Alcibiade Plato docet. Quasi dicat: Probamus quidem omnia esse diligenter examinanda, et eam esse optimam discussionem quam narrasti, sed ipsi ad haec ineptiores sumus adolescentuli, scilicet dialecticae expertes, neque dum ad philosophandum idonei. Tu vero peritia et aetate aptior ac praeterea tua interest ista discutere. Nam Philebo dicente voluptatem summum esse bonum, tu protinus negavisti, obiecistique sapientiam esse praestantiorem. Tu ergo contentionis causa. Unde enim obiectio oritur, inde et disceptatio. Tua ergo interest explicare quod ipse implicuisti.[4] Quin etiam his[5] in disceptationem positis, praediximus tibi te nos minime dimissuros prius quam absolveris. Ipse vero

---

[1]quantis *Y* [2]quaecumque *W* [3]*X reads* in uno quodam [4]explicuisti *W*
[5]him *om. W*

you resolved them. Now you yourself promised to and you put yourself at our disposal as an arbitrator. But what has once been given ought not by right to be retracted."

20A   Having given three reasons why it should be Socrates who should proceed with the argument, Protarchus now outlines the way he wants it explained. "Therefore, stop talking like this, Socrates; it's both vague and perplexing. And don't inject scruples either. And don't keep asking us for something we cannot tell you. You brought up the uncertainty. We can't resolve it ourselves and people should not remain in a state of uncertainty. For uncertainty isn't the goal of a discussion but discovery. So it concerns you to do the inquiring, especially since you promised to. So accept the job now of demonstrating the highest good. Discuss pleasure and wisdom yourself, either by dividing them into their species, or by some other method—if by some other convenient method you can and wish to explain the things we are uncertain about."

Plato called this **a second voyage.** He says the same in the *Phaedo*.[153] The second voyage means a safe journey, for people who go wrong on the first voyage sail more safely on the second. Accordingly, the Roman mime, Publius [i.e., Publilius Syrus], says, "The person who gets himself shipwrecked a second time is wrong to accuse Neptune."[154] Moreover, Protarchus said, "Socrates, you were the cause of this gathering, and you yourself promised us you would set about inquiring what is the best thing in life." Protarchus has demonstrated that the subject of the book is to debate not about pleasure, but about the highest good, not in the absolute, but for man.

But when he referred to the "intelligence," "knowledge," "understanding," "art," by the "intelligence" he meant the highest power of the soul, by "knowledge" the soul's disposition, by "understanding" the experience in action coming from it, finally by "art" the rational skill that produces things. But when he said the goal of a discussion is discovery, not uncertainty, he is making it obvious that Plato proposes to pass on doctrine, not ambiguities. When the Sceptics and Arcesilas and Carneades pursued ambiguities, they fell away from Plato.[155]

promisisti, dedistique te nobis disceptatorem, quod vero semel iure est datum, non est auferendum.

Postquam tribus rationibus ostendit haec a Socrate esse[1] tractanda, hic iam modum declarat quo explanari ista desiderat. Mitte igitur modum istum loquendi, Socrates, et[2] vagum et[3] turbulentum, neque scrupulos inicias, neque a nobis exquiras quae declarare non possumus. [*376v*] Dubitationem tu movisti; solvere ipsi non valemus; in ea resistendum minime est, neque enim inquisitionis finis est dubitatio, sed inventio. Tua[4] ergo[5] interest quaerere, praesertim cum promiseris. Quare ad summum bonum demonstrandum iam accede. De voluptate tu et sapientia dissere[6], sive eas in suas species dividendo, sive quomodocumque aliter, si aliter commode potes ac vis ea de[7] quibus dubitamus exponere.

Quod dixit **secundam navigationem**; idem in Phaedone inquit.[8] Tutum significat iter, nam qui prima navigatione erraverunt in secunda tutius navigant. Unde Romanus ille Publius mimus: Improbe ait Neptunum accusat qui iterum naufragium facit. Quod praeterea dixit: O Socrates, tu huius coetus causam nobis dedisti, teque ipsum nobis praebuisti investigaturum quid in humanis rebus sit optimum. Ostendit huius libri propositum esse non de voluptate, sed de summo bono non absoluto sed humano disserere.

Quando[9] autem dixit mentem, scientiam, intelligentiam, artem, per mentem accepit animi vim supremam, scientiam eius habitum, intelligentiam vero[10] prudentiam agendorum inde manantem, artem denique[11] rationem faciendorum operum. Quod vero dixit finem disputationis inventionem esse, non dubium, docet Platonis propositum esse doctrinam tradere non ambiguitates; quas Sceptici et Arcesilas et Carneades secuti, a Platone degeneraverunt.

---

[1]haec *W;* esse *om. X*   [2]et *om. X*   [3]et *om. W*   [4]tu *W*   [5]erga *W*
[6]disserere *WX*   [7]de *om. Y*   [8]et *add. WX*   [9]Quod *X*   [10]vero *om. WX*
[11]denique *om. WX*

Chapter 30. That the good is superior to being and to the intelligence. Or that the condition of the good itself is that it is perfect, sufficient and desirable.

After this, Socrates comes to the fourth part of the dialogue where he describes in detail the attributes of the good itself, in order that the good itself should be understood and what from among the various goods is closer to it. For the person who's going to compare the two, pleasure and wisdom, to the third thing [the good itself] has to know about the third thing. Now there are two ways of comparing them to it. One way is the negative way, where you show that neither of them is the third thing. The other way is the positive way, where you try to find out which of the two is nearer to it. You don't need the art of dividing and defining, which we've described above, for the first way. So Plato postpones using that art to the time when he will compare them to each other and to the third thing by being positive.

However, in order to know that neither of them is the good itself, there's no need to divide each one into its species or to define it too exactly; for some general understanding of both and a proper notion of the third thing, which is the object of the comparison, is quite sufficient. So, since Protarchus had told him he could gladly prepare for the comparison either by dividing or by not dividing, whichever way he wanted, Socrates began the discussion with this liberty. He joked initially thus, 20B "There's no longer any need for me to be afraid of something bad happening now you're giving me permission to speak my mind." He directed this at the adolescents who'd previously fallen into the habit of both threatening and encouraging him. Since they were now tractable and scared by the general difficulty, they bent their necks under the yoke of Socratic reason. But indeed nothing bad happens in a debate to the person who's been given permission to approach or abandon the discussion according to his own free choice, and to select the plan for the discussion intelligently. Young people ought to concede this right to their seniors.

#*Quod bonum sit ente atque mente superius. Quodve ipsius boni conditio est ut sit perfectum, sufficiens, expetendum. Cap. XXX.*[1]

Post haec quartam dialogi partem aggreditur Socrates, in qua, ut et ipsum bonum cognoscatur et quae ex aliis bonis illi sint propinquiora, conditiones boni ipsius enarrat. Tertium enim hoc cognoscat oportet [*377r*] qui ad ipsum duo illa voluptatem et sapientiam sit comparaturus. Comparatio vero istorum duplex est ad tertium. Una negativa, qua neutrum illud esse monstratur; altera adfirmativa, qua quaeritur utrum duorum tertio sit propinquius. Ad primam[2] non est opus ea dividendi et definiendi arte quam supra descripsimus. Ideo eius artis usum ad id tempus differet[3] quando adfirmando illa[4] invicem et ad tertium comparabit.

Ut autem cognoscatur quod neutrum ipsum bonum sit, non est opus utrumque in species suas dividere et exactissime definire, sufficit enim utrorumque communis quaedam intelligentia, et propria quaedam illius tertii ad quod comparatio dirigitur notio. Ideo, cum Protarchus dixisset Socrati, ut ad hanc comparationem seu dividendo sive non dividendo quomodocumque vellet sese accingeret[5] libenter, hac libertate disputationem inivit Socrates. Imprimis ita iocatus: Nihil grave mihi[6] amplius metuendum, postquam arbitratu meo loqui me sinitis. Hoc obiecit adolescentibus illis qui supra et comminari illi eumque urgere soliti erant, qui, quoniam dociles erant difficultate rerum perterriti, iugo Socraticae rationis iam cervicem[7] subiciebant. Immo vero nec grave illi quicquam in disserendo, qui pro voluntatis arbitrio et aggredi et dimittere disputationem permittitur, et disputationis rationem ex mente deligere,[8] quam auctoritatem iuniores senioribus concedere debent.

---

[1] *a break, but no ch. heading W; in X and P the ch. is numbered sixteen*   [2] primum *W*
[3] differt *Y*   [4] illam *W*   [5] accingere *W*   [6] mihi *om. Y*   [7] colla *WXP*
[8] diligere *X; P gives both as alternatives*   #*P frag. V (88r) begins*

Relying on this right, Socrates approaches the negative comparison, namely, that neither pleasure nor wisdom is the good
itself. You can't know the comparison until you know the good.
The good (as we've shown elsewhere) is above the intelligence,
because the power of the intelligence only extends as far as the
forms, since it is a species itself and acts through species. Each
intelligence acts by understanding. Therefore the intelligence
conceives in itself the form for producing an effect, and it puts
the form into effect according to the model it possesses. Again,
each craftsman's intelligence puts only the form into effect, not
matter at all, for nature produces the matter. Just as the potter
produces the dish's form, nature produces the clay. But just as
part is to part in the same genus, so whole is to whole. Accordingly, just as a particular intelligence is to a particular matter,
so the universal intelligence is to universal matter. But a
particular intelligence doesn't create a particular matter but
gives it form. Therefore the universal intelligence does the same
to the universal matter. Therefore the power of no one intelligence extends as far as matter. So the good exists above the
intelligence.

The good is also above being, because the power of being
only extends as far as the things which have been formed; the
being of these things is through form. But the power of the
good is extended even as far as privation and matter, because
they aim at good in actuality because of some power implanted
in them by the good.

So, since the good is above the intelligence and being, it is
above the power of the intelligence and its object, which is the
first being. For the first object of the intelligence is its own
being, for the first thing it understands is itself. The being of the
intelligence is the first being, because the intelligence is the first
species. Being comes after the form. Therefore the first being is
where the first species is. Here you have the species' subject and
the species itself. The subject of the species doesn't lead itself
into act, because it would already be an act not a potentiality.
But already its species, because it is in another, is therefore
from another; and it is from an act. Therefore above every

Qua sane auctoritate fretus Socrates comparationem negativam adit,[1] scilicet quod neutrum ipsum bonum est,[2] *quod nosse non potest, nisi bonum ipsum norit. Bonum ipsum, ut alias demonstravimus, supra mentem est,** quia vis mentis usque ad formas protenditur, cum [*377v*] ipsa species sit et speciebus agat. Omnis enim mens agit intelligendo; ergo faciendi operis formam concipit in se ipsa, ad eiusque exemplar agit formam.[3] Item cuiusque artificis mens formam agit tantum,[4] materiam minime, eam enim natura gignit. Ut figulus vasis formam, natura lutum. Sicut autem se habet pars ad partem in genere eodem, ita totum ad totum. Quare sicut mens particularis ad particularem materiam, ita universalis mens ad materiam universalem. Sed particularis# mens particularem materiam non gignit, sed format. Ergo et mens universalis universalem similiter[5] materiam. Nullius ergo mentis potentia[6] ad materiam usque porrigitur. Bonum igitur supra mentem est.

Est et super esse, quia vis ipsius esse usque ad formata tantum, quorum esse per formam est, extenditur. Vis autem boni etiam ad privationem atque materiam, quia haec in actum bonum tendunt propter vim aliquam ipsis a bono insitam.

Cum ergo bonum supra mentem et esse sit, est super potentiam mentis eiusque obiectum, quod ipsum[7] primum esse est; primum enim mentis obiectum suum[8] esse est, nam primo se ipsam intelligit.[9] Mentis esse primum est esse, quia prima species est. Esse vero formam sequitur. Ideo primum esse ubi prima species. Ubi haec, ibi subiectum speciei et species. Subiectum se ipsum in actum non educit, quia esset actus iam non potentia. Iam vero[10] species eius, quia in alio, ideo ab alio, et ab actu. Ideo super omnem speciem actus est, non subiecti actus,

---

[1]addit *Y*   [2]sit *P*   [3]forma *W*   [4]tamen *W*   [5]similiter *om. WX*   [6]portio *Y*
[7]ipsum *om. Y*   [8]suam *W*   [9]interfugit *W*   [10]Iam vero *om. WX*   *-**om. Y*
#*P frag. V (88v) ends*

species there is an act; not the act of a subject, but the utterly
absolute act. Every species, which is the act of a subject, comes
from it. Being presupposes an act which is imprinted in a
subject (that is, in an essence). So the good exists above being
and the intelligence. Therefore it exists above the object and the
power of the intelligence.

So Socrates ascends towards the perception of the good not
by his own strength, but by the favour of this very same good.
20B   For we don't see the sun, unless it's by the light of the sun.
Accordingly, he says **some god** has now made him recall the
things he had learnt through God's light, while listening long
ago to Diotima the prophetess who'd been inspired by God to
talk about the nature of the good. When Diotima talked,
Socrates at that time understood it all **as if in a dream,** being
young and addicted to the senses and mere opinion. That is,
instead of believing in the good itself, he believed in its replica.
For example, Diotima had said the good was perfect, sufficient,
desirable. In the first stage of their lives young men attribute
such qualities to the life of pleasure; in the second stage to the
political and social life. Socrates had acted perhaps in this way
himself. But at length, having woken up, that is, having used
the intelligence to contemplate the truth, he gazed in reality at
the good itself, not at its replica. This was because he had come
to recognize by means of a long examination by the intelligence
that sufficiency and perfection were present in neither life. Now
with the god inspiring him again, he is reminded of what he
heard and thought about long ago. He will conclude shortly
through such recollections that neither wisdom nor pleasure is
the good itself, but the third more excellent thing is. But if it is
so agreed, Philebus' pleasure will no longer surpass all good
20C   things, since it and the good itself are not the same. Nor will
there be any need to divide pleasure or wisdom into their species
to understand which of them is the highest good. For we can
demonstrate through a general knowledge of them both and an
appropriate notion of the third thing that neither of them is.
You have to remember Socrates learnt music from Connus and
the art of speaking from Aspasia, as Plato writes in the

sed actus penitus absolutus a quo omnis species est quae subiecti est actus, quem actum esse praesupponit in subiecto illo hoc est essentia impressum. Bonum igitur super esse et mentem existit. Igitur supra obiectum vimque mentis ipsius extat.[1]

Quare ad eius perceptionem non [*378r*] propria vi, sed ipsius eiusdem boni favore ascendit Socrates. Solem enim non, nisi solis lumine, cernimus. Ideo dicit quod **deus aliquis** in mentem sibi reduxit iam quae quondam Dei etiam lumine noverat audiens[2] a Diotima vate, Deo rapta de boni natura loquente. Quae, cum diceret[3] Diotima, Socrates utpote iunior ac sensibus et opinioni deditus, **quasi somnians,** tunc primum accepit, id est, pro ipso bono boni est suspicatus imaginem. Bonum namque dixerat esse Diotima quod perfectum, sufficiens, expetendum. Quod quidem prima aetate iuvenes voluptuosae vitae tribuunt; secunda aetate vitae civili. Ita forte egerat Socrates. Demum vero excitus, id est, mente usus ad veritatis contemplationem, ipsum revera bonum non imaginem intuitus est, cum recognosceret longo mentis examine in neutra vita sufficientiam et perfectionem inesse. Nunc quoque adspirante deo eorum recordatur quae audivit olim et quae examinavit, per quae hic paulo post concludet quod neque sapientia neque voluptas ipsum bonum est, sed tertium quiddam praestantius. Quod si constiterit, voluptas ipsa Philebi non amplius bona omnia superabit, cum non idem sit ac bonum ipsum. Neque opus erit voluptatem vel sapientiam in species suas dividere ad cognoscendum utrum istorum summum sit bonum, nam quod neutrum illorum sit per communem utriusque cognitionem et propriam tertii notionem concludere possumus. Meminisse oportet Socratem musicam didicisse a Conno, ab Aspasia dicendi artem, ut in Menexeno scribit Plato; atque ut in Symposio

---

[1]extat *om. WX*   [2]audiens *om. WX*   [3]dicent *Y*

Menexenus.[156] And, as Plato mentions in the *Symposium,* Socrates received the art of love from the prophetess, Diotima.[157] Through her he learnt to love, since he had come to understand through her what ought to be loved in reality, since she taught him what the truly beautiful itself is and what the good itself is. So he will introduce into the discussion (concerned as it is with the good and with the desirable) what Diotima said.

But who was that god, who inspired Diotima when she was telling Socrates about the beautiful and the good, and who enraptured Socrates when he was listening to her and then here, after the lapse of a long time, brought Socrates back to the same state of contemplation? It was surely the god, love. Dionysius the Areopagite put love third among the divinities; since in the first place he put power, in the second beauty, in the third he put love.[158] Power which has been unfolded becomes beauty; power which has been turned towards beauty becomes love. Plato also put the good first, the beautiful second, love third. He bestowed the good on the one principle, the beautiful on the divine intelligence, love on the soul which has been turned back towards the beauty of the divine intelligence. So love strives towards beauty. Love first flourishes among the celestial souls who are gazing at that beauty from near at hand. From there love flows down into our souls. Like a sunbeam descending from on high, it turns our souls back towards the splendour from which it came, namely, towards the beauty of the divine intelligence. From there it leads them into the light which is the source for the splendour of beauty shining in the divine intelligence. But that is the good itself. Therefore love guides our souls by means of the representations of the beautiful into the beautiful itself, by means of the beautiful into the good.

For the good itself is the principle of all. With the beauty of the species, of the reasons, of the forms, it forms the intelligence and the soul and matter. It converts matter into the soul. It lifts the soul into the intelligence. At length it enraptures all things to itself. So matter longs for the adornment of the soul. The soul loves the beauty of the intelligence. All these thirst for the good itself, the fountain of beauty. They have been enticed

refert, amatoriam artem a vate Diotima accepisse, per quam amare didicit, cum ex ea intellexisset quid[1] revera amandum sit, ea siquidem docuit quid ipsum vere pulchrum [*378v*] sit, quid ipsum[2] bonum. Ideo Diotimae dicta ad propositam de bono et appetendo quaestionem adducet.

Quis autem deus ille fuit qui et Diotimam afflavit, cum pulchrum et bonum Socrati revelavit, et rapuit Socratem audientem et reduxit demum post longa tempora in eandem hic Socratem contemplationem? Profecto ille fuit amor, quem Dionysius Areopagita tertium in divinis posuit; in primo siquidem potestatem posuit, pulchritudinem in secundo, in tertio locavit amorem. Potestas explicata pulchritudo fit; in pulchritudinem revoluta fit amor. Plato insuper primo bonum posuit, secundo pulchrum, amorem tertio. Bonum uni principio, pulchrum menti divinae, amorem[3] animae in divinae mentis decorem conversae dedit. Amor itaque in pulchritudinem nixus est. Hic primum viget[4] in coelestibus animis qui proxime decorem illum intuentur, inde et in nostros permanat; et quasi radius quidam superne descendens, in splendorem unde descendit nostros convertit animos, in divinae scilicet mentis ornatum. Inde in lucem illam perducit unde pulchritudinis splendor in divina emicat mente. Id autem ipsum est[5] bonum. Unde amor per pulchri imagines in ipsum pulchrum, per pulchrum perducit in bonum.

Ipsum enim bonum omnium principium; et mentem et animam et materiam specierum rationum et formarum pulchritudine format. Materiam convertit in animam; animam attollit in mentem. Ipsum[6] denique ad se rapit omnia. Materia itaque animae ornatum appetit. Anima mentis amat decorem. Haec omnia ipsum bonum decoris fontem sitiunt, decore ipso quasi

---

[1]quod *Y*   [2]pulchrum *W*   [3]amore *W*   [4]viget *om. WX*   [5]est *om. Y*
[6]haec *WX*

by beauty itself, as if by a certain foretaste of the good. So love
is a circle emanating from the good, proceeding through the
beautiful, running into the images of the beautiful, and through
the images turned back towards the beautiful and at last
returned through the beautiful into the good. In the *Phaedrus*
and the *Symposium* love was the god who goaded on the
enraptured Socrates.[159] It is the same god who advised him here
as he carried on the argument. And therefore Socrates will show
immediately that the good itself has three conditions: it is
sufficient, desirable and **perfect.**

20D

That the good is the principle of all things, because the good
and the one are the same and the one is the first principle, we've
shown elsewhere. Some part of the demonstration seems worth
repeating straight away. Since all things come from the one
principle, that principle is either the good itself, or it is better
than the good. If it is better than the good, either something
proceeds from it into the nature of things, or nothing does. If
nothing does, it doesn't make sense, for it wouldn't be the principle of things unless something were given by it to things. But if
something is given to things by the principle, just as something
is given to things by the good, which is of course goodness,
something will be given to things by the first cause which is
better than goodness. For, if it is above the good and better
than it, it certainly gives better gifts to things than the good
itself. But what's better than goodness, since something is said
to be better because it has a greater share of goodness? Besides,
since all things only desire the good, if there's something above
the good, will they or will they not desire it? If they don't desire
it, it doesn't make sense that the first cause by which everything
is created and preserved isn't also desired by everything. But if
they do desire it, they don't desire the good most of all, nor will
they examine everything because of the good. But since the
good is that towards which all things are converted when they
desire something, the good will be what creates all things. For
all things are converted to the point from which they set out.

So the good is the first principle of things. Because it is the
principle, it is said to be sufficient, desirable and perfect. I say it

quadam boni ipsius praelibatione pellecta. Ideo amor circulus quidam est a bono manans, per pulchrum progrediens, in pulchri [*379r*] imagines currens, perque illas ad pulchrum conversus, et in bonum per pulchrum denique revolutus. Hic deus in Phaedro et Symposio concitavit Socratem debacchantem; idem hic disputantem admonuit. Atque ideo statim tres esse boni ipsius conditiones significabit, ut **sufficiens** sit, ut **expetendum,** ut **perfectum.**

Quod bonum rerum omnium sit principium, quia[1] bonum et unum idem sit, unum vero primum sit principium, alias demonstravimus. *Cuius demonstrationis pars aliqua mox sequens repetenda videtur.** Cum omnia ab uno principio sint, principium illud vel ipsum bonum est, vel bono melius. Si bono melius, aut aliquid ab ipso in naturam rerum procedit, aut nihil. Si nihil, absurdum id quidem, non enim esset rerum principium, nisi aliquid ab ipso rebus tribueretur. Sin autem aliquid a principio isto rebus datur, quemadmodum[2] a bono rebus istis datum est aliquid, quod quidem bonitas est, erit aliquid[3] in rebus melius bonitate a causa prima tributum. Nam si super bonum sit ipsoque melius, meliora certe rebus munera elargitur quam ipsum bonum. At vero quid bonitate melius, quippe cum melius aliquid ex eo[4] dicatur quod bonitatis magis est particeps? Quin etiam cum omnia bonum dumtaxat cupiant, si supra bonum est aliquid, utrum et illud appetant necne? Si non appetunt,[5] absurdum est causam primam a qua quaeque fiunt atque servantur non appeti et ab omnibus. Sin appetunt, non bonum maxime appetunt,[6] neque sub ratione boni cuncta perquirent. Cum vero bonum sit ad quod omnia appetendo convertuntur, bonum erit a quo omnia procreantur, quo enim omnium est conversio illinc et omnium est processio.

Bonum itaque [*379v*] primum rerum est principium. Quia principium est, ideo sufficiens dicitur, expetendum, perfectum. **Sufficiens** inquam,[7] quia[8] in se ipso permanens ex foecunditate

---

[1]et *add. W*   [2]et *add. X*   [3]aliquod *WY*   [4]esse *add. X*   [5]appetunt *om. WX*
[6]appetent *X*   [7]inquantum *WX*   [8]quia *om. WX*   *-**Ad quam demonstrationem haec ad praesens est adhibenda *WX*

is **sufficient**, because it produces the essences of everything out of its overflowing creativity while remaining in itself. It is **desirable**, because it immediately converts the essences which have been produced towards itself. It is **perfect**, because it perfects and completes the converted essences. On the first count, it is called the principle, the truth, and the one; on the second, the middle and the way; on the third, the end and the life. Therefore Plato says in the *Laws* Book 4: God, as the ancient saying testifies, contains the beginning, end and intermediate points of all things, and in accordance with nature passes through and encircles them with righteousness.[160] But the ancient saying is Orphic, for it refers to Jupiter the principle, Jupiter the middle—all things are born from Jove—, Jupiter the foundation of the earth and the starry sky.[161] On account of all this He is called the good.

That the good is **sufficient** can be shown from the fact that it creates without moving or changing. For if it created through movement, the movement would be either internal or external. If internal, it would change from the one and the good and so in a way recede from the one and the good and so be weakened. But something appears to be most powerful when it produces another. But the good would appear to be weak at that very point when its greatest power was most in evidence. But if the movement is external, then is the movement it produces produced through movement or without movement? If the former, you will go on to infinity. If the latter, it's agreed the good creates without changing or moving. Or rather, since every movement is an impulse towards something that's needed, the first good needs something if it is moved. Either it is moved towards something better, or worse, or of equal value. It isn't moved towards something better, for nothing is better than the good. Nor is it moved towards something worse, for it isn't ignorant or coerced, since nothing is above it. But if it is moved towards a condition equal to its former condition, why is it moved, for it has the condition already? So, why is it looking? Therefore, since the good produces without any internal change, it creates while resting in itself. So it does not set out to

exuberante producit essentias omnium.[1] **Expetendum,** quia essentias statim productas in se convertit. **Perfectum,** quia conversas perficit atque complet. Propter[2] primum quidem[3] principium et veritas et unum dicitur; propter[4] secundum vero[5] medium et via; propter[6] tertium finis et vita. Ideo quarto Legum dicit Plato: Deus, ut antiquus sermo testatur, principium, finem et media rerum omnium continens, rectitudine secundum naturam peragit omnia atque circuit. Antiquus autem ille sermo est Orphicus, inquit enim[7] Jupiter principium, Jupiter medium—ex Jove nata sunt omnia—, Jupiter fundamentum terrae coelique stelliferi. Propter[8] omnia bonum dicitur.[9]

Primum sic ostenditur, quod scilicet immobile permanens creat. Nam si per motum, aut motus ille in eo est, aut extra. Si in eo, ipsum mutatum[10] esset ab uno et bono, ergo quodammodo ab uno et bono discederet, debilitaretur igitur. Maxime vero potens apparet aliquid, cum aliud efficit. Hoc autem tunc debilius appareret, cum maxime vis eius maxime[11] eluceret.[12] Sin extra sit, ergo motus ab eo productus utrum per motum an sine motu? Si primum, in infinitum ibitur. Si secundum, constat quod manens immobilis generat. Immo vero cum omnis motus impetus sit ad aliquid quod deest, deest aliquid primo si movetur. Item vel ad aliquid melius movetur, vel deterius, vel aequum. Ad melius quidem[13] non, nihil enim[14] bono melius. Ad deterius quoque[15] non, non enim ignorans est aut cogitur, cum nihil supra sit. Ad aequum vero statum priori cur movetur, habet enim iam? Cur quaerit ergo? Quare cum nulla sui transmutatione producat, [*380r*] stans in se ipso creat. Non ergo[16] defectu proprio extrinsecus aliquid quaerens ad agendum exit,

---

[1]rerum *WX*   [2,4,6,8]secundum *WX*   [3]quidem *om. WX*   [5]vero *om. WX*
[7]inquit enim *om. WX*   [9]bonum dicitur *om. W;* dicitur *om. X*   [10]motum *WX*
[11]maxime *om. WX*   [12]elucet *WX*   [13]quidem *om. WX*   [14]enim *om. W*
[15]quoque *om. WX*   [16]enim *W*

look for something to do externally from any internal defect. Rather it propagates itself out of overflowing creativity. As Dionysius says, "The infinite goodness of God did not let Him remain in Himself without a seed."[162] In the *Timaeus* Plato agrees when he says God's goodness, devoid of malice, supplied the cause for producing things.[163] And in the *Republic* Book 2 Plato wants this principle to remain motionless.[164] So the good itself is said to be sufficient because of its motionless creativity. That is, it is sufficient both to itself and to others; while not emptying itself, it gives water to other things.

That the good is **desirable** is obvious first from the testimony of Dionysius the Areopagite, who says all things seek God's likeness, each in its own way: those things which exist only in accordance with being, those which live in accordance with life, those which feel in accordance with the sense, those which understand in accordance with the understanding.[165] It is desirable also because it immediately converts the appetites of young creatures to itself. For every single thing desires well-being. A thing has well-being from where it has being. Therefore it is turned back towards its cause. In fact, everything wants to be preserved in its being. That preserves being which gives being. For the preservation of being is also the continuation of being, which is like a perpetual and never-ending production as an image from an object in pools or mirrors, or as light from the sun. So it is the job of the same thing to preserve whose job it is to produce. So the effect desires its preserving cause. Therefore the good itself, since it is the cause of all, ought to be desired by all. Again, *the order in the case of ends follows on the agents' order.*[166] *For just as the supreme agent moves all the secondary agents, so the ends of the secondary agents ought to be arranged in accordance with the end of the supreme agent. For whatever the first agent does, it does for its own end. But the first agent performs all the actions of all the secondary agents by moving them towards its own action and consequently towards its own ends too. Hence it follows that all the ends of subsequent agents are directed by the first agent towards its own end. But God is the first agent of all things. But there is no other end for His will*

sed exuberante foecunditate se propagat. Atque ut Dionysius ait, infinita Dei bonitas non permisit eum sine germine[1] in se ipso manere. Quod in Timaeo innuit Plato dicens bonitatem Dei livore carentem generandis rebus dedisse causam; atqui immobile manere principium in secundo de Republica Plato vult. Ex immobili igitur foecunditate sufficiens ipsum bonum dicitur, id est, quod et sibi una et aliis sufficit; dum se non exhauriens, irrigat alia.

Quod **expetendum** patet primo Dionysii Areopagitae auctoritate dicentis omnia modo suo Dei similitudinem petere: quae sunt tantum[2] secundum esse; quae vivunt secundum vitam; quae sentiunt secundum sensum; quae intelligunt[3] secundum intelligentiam. Deinde ratione sic, quia convertit in se statim nascentium appetitus. Unumquodque enim bene esse desiderat. Bene esse habet unde et[4] esse. Ad causam ergo convertitur. Etenim suo in esse servari quodcumque appetit. Conservat esse quod esse dat. Nam et[5] conservatio essendi essendi continuatio est, quae quidem est tamquam iugis perennisque productio, ut imago in aquis et speculis ab obiecto et a sole lumen. Eiusdem igitur conservare est, cuius et generare. Effectus igitur causam appetit conservantem.[6] Ipsum ergo bonum, cum sit omnium causa, est omnibus expetendum. *Item ad agentium ordinem ordo in finibus sequitur, nam, quemadmodum agens supremum omnia agentia secunda movet, ita ad agentis supremi finem oportet fines secundorum agentium ordinari. Quicquid enim agit primum ipsum agens propter finem suum agit. Agit autem primum secundorum omnium agentium actiones* [380v] *omnes ad actionem suam movendo, atque ita et ad suos fines. Unde sequitur omnes posteriorum agentium fines[7] a primo agente ad finem suum proprium dirigi. Agens autem primum omnium Deus est. Voluntatis autem ipsius nihil aliud finis*

---

[1]germino *Y*   [2]tactum *W*   [3]intelligant *W*   [4]et *om. Y*   [5]et *om. WX*
[6]servatricem *W*   [7]fines *om. W*

*than His goodness. Therefore all things are turned back
towards God. Besides, the ultimate end for any producer, in so
far as he is a producer, is himself. For the things we've
produced we use for ourselves. If someone at any time does
something for someone else, eventually it has a bearing on his
own good, being either enjoyable or useful or honourable. God
is the author of all things: of some things directly, of others indirectly. So He is the end of all things. Moreover, the end
holds principal place among the other causes, and thanks to it
all the remaining causes can actually exist as causes. For the
efficient cause does not act except for the sake of the end. But it
is by the efficient [cause] that matter is drawn into a form's act.
So matter is actually made the matter of this thing, form too is
made the form of this thing on account of the action of the efficient [cause]; and therefore on account of the end. Moreover
the ultimate end is the first cause. By means of the first cause an
end preceding [the ultimate end] is understood as an end, for
nobody is moved towards a proximate end unless urged to do so
by the ultimate end. Therefore the ultimate end is the first cause
of all. It and the good itself are the same.* Therefore the good
itself ought to be desired by everything.

The good is also called **perfect**, because it brings all things'
natures to completion and satisfies their appetites. The person
who makes something is the one responsible for perfecting it.
The person who begins something is the one responsible for
bringing it to completion. What is superabundant, as it's above
all things and is all things, is responsible for fulfilling them. But
the first cause of all things makes, begins and converts them all.
Or rather, since to satisfy is to arrest the appetite, and since
what moved something towards itself is responsible for
arresting it in itself, the good, which moves every appetite
towards itself, also arrests each appetite in itself and satisfies it.
In the good itself the appetite discovers whatever can be desired.
Because the good exceeds the capacity of the thing desiring it, in
comprehending that capacity it brings it to rest and fulfils it.
Therefore, the good itself, which is God, is said to be sufficient,
desirable and perfect.

est quam sua bonitas. In Deum igitur omnia reflectuntur. Prae-
terea finis ultimus facientis cuiuslibet, in quantum faciens est,
est ipsemet; rebus enim a nobis factis propter nos utimur. Et
siquis quandoque aliquid propter alium efficit in suum denique
bonum refert, vel iucundum, vel utile, vel honestum. Deus est
omnium auctor, quorundam proxime, aliorum per media. Est
itaque finis omnium. Accedit quod finis inter alias causas prin-
cipatum tenet, atque ab ipso ceterae omnes causae habent quod
actu causae sint. Agens enim causa non nisi propter finem agit.
Ab agente vero[1] *materia in actum formae deducitur, unde*
materia actu fit huius rei materia, forma quoque huius rei
forma fit propter agentis ipsius effectionem, atque idcirco prop-
ter finem ipsum. Finis quin etiam ultimus prior causa est, per
quam praecedens finis intendatur ut finis. Nemo enim in proxi-
mum movetur finem, nisi fine ultimo provocatus. Finis igitur
ultimus prima est[2] *omnium causa. Illa et ipsum bonum idem.*
Bonum igitur ipsum omnibus expetendum.

Perfectum quoque dicitur, quia complet naturas omnium, et
implet omnium appetitus. Perficere illius est, cuius est et facere;
complere cuius inchoare; implere illius quod exuberans est, quia
super omnia est, et omnia. Facit autem, inchoat, convertit
omnia causa prima omnium. Immo cum implere sit appetitum
sistere, et illius sit in se ipso sistere, quod ad se movit, ipsum
bonum, quod ad se movet [*381r*] appetitionem omnem,
omnem quoque in se ipso sistit et implet; in quo quicquid appeti
potest appetitio reperit, quod, quia appetentis supereminet
capacitatem, comprehendens eam sistit ac firmat. Ipsum igitur
bonum qui Deus est sufficiens, expetendum, perfectumque
dicitur.

---

[1] ex *add.* Y   [2] est *add.* W

Chapter 31. In what way the good itself is to be admired, loved, enjoyed; and what the principal good is in every single thing.

In the *Cratylus* Plato refers to the *agathon* as if it meant *agaston* from the verb *agamai,* which means three things: to admire, to love, to be delighted.[167] For the good is to be admired when we come to it, loved when we cling to it, delighted in when we are satisfied by it. Firstly, it turns us back from other things towards itself by making us recognize its beauty. Secondly, it draws us towards itself by making us love this same beauty. Thirdly, it transforms and diffuses us into itself through pleasure and surrounds us with itself and satisfies us through goodness. Perhaps somebody is going to ask therefore: "You say the good itself is the principle of things, and is sufficient, desirable and perfect. But you say it is the good in itself, and isn't the good of another or in another. Therefore, what is the good in other things?" I say it is the image of the good according to each thing's capacity to receive it. All secondary lights are images of the primary light, and they depend on the primary light. Therefore the habitual disposition of each thing is to be sufficient, desirable and perfect in so far as its nature allows. This is its highest good. It depends on the absolute good, just as colour depends on light, a hot thing on heat. Then what is the one thing which enables us to call the principle good, and other things good? It is act. What do all things flee from as bad? It is privation. Therefore all things follow act, the opposite of privation, as the good. Now matter, which is perpetually receding from formlessness itself, desires to receive form. It offers itself obediently to what is forming it. In the case of animal bodies pain comes when the form of the soul separates from them, pleasure when it adheres to them. But form is an act, since it is the principle of acting. Again, form bursts forth into action and motion and never stops operating. The movements and generations of the sky and elements testify to this. Souls are also always borne into act through the power of nourishing and producing, of feeling and understanding.

Quomodo ipsum bonum sit admirandum, amandum, iucundum; et quid potissimum in unoquoque sit uniuscuiusque bonum. Cap. XXXI.[1]

*Plato in Cratylo dicit ἀγαθόν dici[2] quasi ἀγαστόν ἀπὸ τοῦ ἄγαμαι. Quod tria significat: **admirari, amare, delectari.** Bonum enim admirandum est[3] cum ad illud accedimus, amandum cum haeremus, iucundum cum eo implemur. In primo ab aliis convertit ad se per cognitionem pulchritudinis suae. In secundo trahit ad se per amorem eiusdem. In tertio transfert in se diffunditque per voluptatem, circumfunditque se ipsi et implet per bonitatem.** Interrogabit igitur[4] forte aliquis: Bonum ipsum principium rerum esse dicis, idque esse sufficiens, expetendum atque perfectum; id vero ipsum in se bonum est, neque est alicuius, nec in aliquo; quid ergo in rebus[5] aliis bonum? Huius, inquam, pro captu cuiusque imago. Omnia sequentia lumina primi luminis imagines sunt, a primo lumine dependentes. Habitus ergo cuiusque rei, quoad eius natura patitur, sufficiens, expetendus, perfectus; supremum eius est bonum. Hic a bono absoluto dependet, ut color a lumine, calidum a calore. Quid unum istud est tandem, quo et principium bonum dicimus, et alia bona? Actus. Quid ut malum fugiunt omnia? Privationem. Ergo ut bonum sequuntur omnia actum privationis oppositum. Materia quidem ab ipsa informitate discedens perpetuo ad formam suscipiendam inhiat, seque formanti exponit obedientem; animaliumque corporibus dolor innascitur cum ab illis animae forma disiungitur, voluptas cum adhaeret. Forma vero actus quidam est, quoniam est agendi principium. Forma item in motum actionemque prorumpit, nec ab operatione cessat umquam; quod et coeli et elementorum motus generationesque demonstrant. Et animae per vim nutriendi gignendique, sentiendi, intelligendi semper in actum feruntur. Ergo sicut materia et

---

[1] *no ch. heading or break W; numbered seventeen X*   [2] *dici om. Y*   [3] *amandum, iucundum: admirandum add. X*   [4] *igitur om. W*   [5] *in rebus om. X*   *-***om. W*

Therefore, just as matter and bodies always look for the first act, so forms and souls always look for the second act. The first act is form. The second act is operation. Intelligences also look for the same thing, since the part of the intelligence which is present in us delights completely in operation as the good. And every soul which desires the types of knowledge and the virtues desires the species and act of the soul. Whatever soul desires the comforts of fortune or the body desires them in order to do something by using or enjoying them. Or rather, people desire both being and living in order to make use of both. But they use them by acting according to their capacities. Therefore act is what must be desired by all things. Act is also sufficient. For the first act, when it comes down, indicates the subject has now been sufficiently prepared and the compound is sufficient for acting. The second act indicates a thing is fully formed and has sufficient energy. For that which either moves another or produces another is now a complete, fully grown thing. Act is also perfect. The first act satisfies the longing of matter, puts a limit to its infinity, adorns its deformity. The second act brings the drive of the forms to completion and perfects the external result. Hence you can gather that these three are the conditions appropriate to the good itself and appropriate to act itself. Therefore the good and act are the same. Each act has the three conditions in one respect or another. Therefore in one respect or another each act is good. The purer act has the conditions more abundantly. So it is more good. The purest act has the conditions totally. And so it is the highest good. It does not have them externally, since it has them for no other reason than the reason which makes it an act. For it happens that one act has the conditions less than another because of the admixture of a subject, an impediment, privation. Therefore nothing has to be added to act to make it better; rather, the blemish it receives from having anything added to it has to be removed. Straight away it blazes out as pure act. When this, its natural purity, blazes out, the three conditions increase at once to accord with its purity. Then goodness is revealed. Moreover the good, as we said above, consists in unity. Unity consists in act. Therefore

corpora primum semper expetunt actum, ita formae animaeque
[*381v*] secundum. Primus actus forma est. Secundus est[1]
operatio. Idem et mentes quaerunt, siquidem pars mentis, quae
nobis inest, in operatione tamquam bono admodum delectatur.
Et quisquis animus scientias et virtutes appetit, speciem animi
actumque appetit. Quisquis fortunae aut corporis commoda, ut
per illa et circa illa utendo vel fruendo quicquam agat. Immo
vero et esse et vivere appetunt, ut utroque utantur. Utuntur
autem secundum eorum vires agendo. Actus igitur est quod
omnibus expetendum. Est etiam sufficiens. Actus enim primus
cum advenit[2] subiectum significat sufficienter iam praepara-
tum, et compositum ipsum ad agendum est sufficiens. Actus
secundus rem sufficienti vigore adultam declarat. Quod enim
vel movet vel gignit aliud integrum ipsum iam et adultum est.
Est et perfectus. Primus actus implet materiae desiderium, eius
terminat infinitatem, ornat deformitatem. Secundus actus formarum nixum complet et externum perficit opus. Sic est igitur
colligendum tres[3] illae boni ipsius conditiones sunt propriae,
sunt et actus ipsius[4] propriae. Ergo bonum et actus idem. Quisquis actus illa tria habet quodammodo; quisquis ergo quodammodo bonum est. Actus purior habet ea magis; ergo et magis
bonum. Actus purissimus habet omnino; ergo et summum
bonum. Neque habet haec actus extrinsecus, quia non alia
ratione quam ea ipsa qua actus est. Nam quod ea minus habeat
unus actus quam alius, subiecti et[5] impedimenti et[6] privationis
admixtione contingit. Nihil ergo actui est addendum ut magis
bonum sit, sed additamenti inquinatio removenda. Statim
purus emicat. Statim, cum sua haec naturalis puritas emicat, ad
puritatem suam tria crescunt illa, et bonitas demonstratur.
[*382r*] Quin etiam in unitate bonum consistit (ut supra dictum
est). Unitas in actu. Ergo in actu bonum. Materia enim tota una

---

[1]est *om.* X   [2]cum advenit *repeated* W   [3]tertius W   [4]ipsius *om.* X   [5],[6]et *om.* W

the good consists in act. For matter is said to be completely one, because it comes from the first act, and because it lies under the one form of the world. Every matter is one from one particular form. For every matter is indifferent as regards the number of effects. When it has been given a form, matter has been made into one particular thing. And all the parts of a compound thing are naturally or artificially made one from the certain form of the whole; for instance, the parts of a house. But the form establishes itself best in the second act, that is, in operation, when it is preserving, renewing and increasing its unity most. This one act shows there is one energy in the form, and it determines one result. The agent aims most at one [result] when it acts; and it acts most, when with one intention it joins all its little parts into the result.

Therefore the first thing, since it is the good and the one, is act. And, since it is the highest good, it is purest act. For it is act which is a law to itself. It isn't bound in by the limits of any subject. Since it isn't properly the act of any one thing, it is the act of all things; and, since it isn't contained by any one thing, it is present to all things. Therefore the good of all things is above all things and in all things, just as the sun's light, since it is peculiar to no one eye, is the light of all eyes and in all eyes. A ray of light, however, which is peculiar to a particular eye, is the ray of that eye alone, and is in it alone. So in the *Republic* Book 6 Plato represented the good itself by means of the image of the sun. He says the sun produces both visible bodies and eyes that see.[168] The sun pours a lucid spirit into the eyes so that they can see, and paints bodies with colours so that they can be seen. Yet the ray peculiar to the eyes and the colours peculiar to the bodies wouldn't be enough to produce vision, if it weren't for the one light itself. This light is above the many lights. From it the many and appropriate lights have been distributed to eyes and bodies; and it comes down, illuminates, awakens and strengthens. In the same way the first act itself, in the process of producing, has given a species and act to individual things. Of course, when this act is received in a passive subject, it is weak and powerless to execute an effect. But the everlasting and

dicitur, quia a primo actu, et quia sub una iacet forma mundi. Quaelibet materia una, ex una quadam forma, indifferens enim materia[1] quaevis ad multa opera. Data forma, unum quiddam est facta; et omnes partes compositae rei per naturam vel per artem, ut domus partes, unum ex certa totius forma fiunt. Forma vero cum maxime suam servat, restituit, augetque unitatem, tunc in[2] secundum actum, operationem scilicet, optime sese comparat. Qui unus actus unum in forma testatur esse vigorem et unum opus determinat. Et tunc maxime in unum dirigitur agens, cum agit; et agit maxime, cum una intentione in opus suas omnes unit particulas.

Primum[3] ergo, cum bonum sit et unum, actus est; et quia summum bonum, actus est purissimus. Est enim actus sui iuris; nullius subiecti limitibus coarctatus. Cumque nullius proprie actus sit, actus est omnium; cumque in nullo sit inclusus, omnibus adest. Est ergo bonum omnium super omnia et in omnibus, quemadmodum solis lumen, cum nullius oculi proprium lumen sit, omnium est lumen et in omnibus. Radius autem, qui alicuius est oculi proprius, illius solius est et in solo. Ideo Plato in sexto de Republica bonum ipsum per solis imaginem figuravit, dicens quod sol et corpora visibilia et oculos videntes procreat. Oculis, ut videant, lucidum infundit spiritum; corpora, ut videantur, coloribus pingit. Neque tamen proprius oculis radius, propriive corporibus colores ad visionem perficiendam sufficiunt, nisi lumen ipsum unum supra multa, [*382v*] a quo multa et propria lumina oculis et corporibus distributa sunt, adveniat, illustret, excitet atque roboret. Eodem modo primus ipse actus speciem actumque rebus singulis producendo largitus est. Qui sane actus, cum in subiecto patiente susceptus fuerit, debilis est et ad operis executionem impotens. Sed divini solis perpetua et invisibilis lux una semper omnibus adstat, fovet, vivificat, excitat,

---

[1]materia *add. W*   [2]et *W*   [3]principium *W*

invisible light of the divine sun is always close at hand to assist all things; to cherish, vivify, awaken, fulfil and strengthen them. Concerning the sun, Orpheus says divinely that "it cherishes all and bears itself above all things."[169] Also Hermes Trismegistus says that God is the potentiality of all acts and the act of all potentialities.[170] As all the first acts are created by Him, God is said to be the effective potentiality of all acts. As all the second acts are aroused and strengthened by Him, He is said to be the act of all potentialities; that is, the one who leads all potentialities into act. Each act bestowed by God, the first as well as the second, is called the good of each thing. It is called the highest good of each thing when it exercises its full power for action without any hindrance, and according to its nature, and when it operates without the least difficulty. But this it can do by the favour of the first act, when it is turned back towards the first act, which is called the good not of some one thing but of all things equally.

Therefore the first act completes and sets free the act of each thing. When it completes and strengthens, it is called the good itself. When it sets free and renders something pleasing and active, it is called the beautiful itself. But the act of something is at its best when it has been strengthened; is delightful and beautiful when it has been set free. But this total act, strengthened in itself and freed from any impediment, is the highest good of each thing since it is the highest act of each thing. That it can be an act in the first place comes from the first act. Then, that it can be strengthened and freed comes also from the first act and turning back towards the first act. So God bestows the good on things in putting them forth; but in turning them back He gives them the highest good. God's magnificence alone is enough for the first gift. For the second the future recipient of the gift must itself turn back.

The one itself produces all things, that is, the intelligence, the soul, matter. But, since the character of each cause is preserved in its effect, in the individual effects there is one particular unity, imprinted in them by the first one. An act of something

complet, et roborat. De quo divine Orpheus: Cuncta fovens atque ipse ferens super omnia sese. Mercurius quoque ait: Deum esse omnium actuum[1] potentiam et omnium potentiarum actum. Quia[2] omnes primi actus ab eo creantur, potentia efficax omnium actuum Deus dicitur. Quia omnes actus secundi ab eo excitantur et roborantur, potentiarum omnium dicitur actus, id est, omnes potentias in actum reducens. Actus quisque tam primus quam secundus a Deo datus cuiusque bonum dicitur. Et dicitur cuiusque summum bonum, quando sine ullo impedimento integram agendi[3] secundum sui naturam vim exercet et expeditissime operatur. Hoc autem favore primi actus assequitur, quando ad ipsum convertitur, quod non alicuius sed aeque omnium bonum dicitur.

Primus igitur actus complet cuiusque actum et expedit. Ut complet et roborat ipsum bonum, ut expedit gratumque reddit et agilem ipsum pulchrum dicitur. Actus autem rei ipsius ut roboratus optimus, ut expeditus iucundus et pulcher. Totus[4] autem hic[5] actus, roboratus in se, et quoad impedimenta alia expeditus, summum cuiusque est bonum, quia summus cuiusque est actus. Quod primo actus sit, a primo actu habuit. Quod deinde robustus sit, et expeditus, a primo quoque actu, et a sua in eum [*383r*] conversione. Dat ergo bonum Deus rebus in procedendo; dat bonum summum in convertendo. Ad primum munus sola Dei magnificentia sufficit, ad secundum conversio rei ipsius suscepturae requiritur.

Producit quidem ipsum unum[6] omnia, mentem scilicet, animam, materiam. Cum vero cuiusque causae character in opere suo servetur, in horum singulis una quaedam sua unitas est, a primo impressa uno. Actus quidam rei productae ab

---

[1]actum *Y*   [2]Qui *W*   [3]augendi *X*   [4]*em.*, totum *WXY*   [5]*em.*, hoc *WXY*
[6]unum *om. W*

produced comes from the absolute act of the producer. For each object possesses its principal something in itself: its one power or one subsistence or one condition. The one something is like the object's centre for which and from which all the rest of the things in it exist, just as every line [comes] to the centre of a circle and [goes] from the centre to the circumference. But through this one act and centre all things are turned towards the first act and the first one. But they can't attain the one, except through one something. For if the one were to be touched by plurality, it would be divisible and wouldn't be one. So all things gather themselves together into their one act, so that through this, their one centre, they may adhere to the centre of all things. The good itself is the centre of all things, because all things [come and go] from it and to it. Just as all the lines emanating from the central point have the point in themselves and returning to the centre touch the circle's point with their point, so all the things depending on God, on the one act, retain one act. With this one act they return to the first one and attain it.

Therefore the intelligence which has been produced by the one (because it is outside the one and has spread out into nothingness) falls away from the one act. Beyond the one act it has unformed hypostasis. The good's beginning is the first act and the one in the hypostasis. Through this one act the essence of the intelligence is turned back towards the one supreme act. This turning back is the second act; it's the good's augmentation. Having been turned back, the intelligence is embellished with the species for creating all things. This is the third act; it's the good's perfection and splendour. So the highest good of the intelligence is the perfected act of its nature: that is, when it has been turned back through one act towards the one act, for it to become all acts and all things in act. Again, the soul, when it's been gathered into its unity, that is, into its principal power and highest point, and when it has reached the one by rejecting the senses, clings to the one good. And the one good illuminates the soul through the intelligence and fills it with the reasons and the species of all things. Therefore the highest good of the soul is

absoluto productoris actu. Nam quaeque res principale aliquid sui in se habet, vel vim unam, vel subsistentiam unam, vel conditionem unam; quod unum quasi eius centrum est ad quod et a quo cetera quae in eo sunt existunt, ut ad centrum et a centro omnes ad circumferentiam lineae. Omnia vero per hunc actum[1] unum centrumque ad primum actum unumque vertuntur. Neque vero attingere unum nisi uno quodam possunt. Nam si illud pluribus tangeretur, divisibile esset atque non unum. Omnia igitur in suum unum actum se colligunt, ut uno hoc centro sui centro omnium haereant. Ipsum bonum centrum est omnium, quia ab illo omnia et ad illud. Et sicut lineae omnes, a centro puncto manantes, punctum in se habent, et in centrum terminantes puncto suo punctum circuli tangunt, sic omnia a Deo[2] uno actu pendentia unum actum retinent, quo uno redeunt in unum primum illudque attingunt.

Mens igitur ab uno producta, quia extra unum et circa nihil manavit, ab uno degenerat actu, et ultra actum unum hypostasim habet informem. In qua hypostasi[3] primus ille actus et unum; boni inchoatio est. Per quem actum unum essentia mentis in unum supremum actum convertitur. Conversio haec actus secundus est et [*383v*] boni incrementum. Conversa formatur producendorum omnium speciebus. Qui tertius[4] actus boni est complementum[5] ac splendor. Quare summum mentis bonum est actus eius naturae completus, id est, ut per unum actum conversa ad actum unum omnes fiat actus, omniaque actu fiat. Item anima in suam unitatem, id est, principalem vim apicemque ipsius collecta, et sensibus reiectis unum effecta, uni bono haeret; ab eoque per mentem illuminatur, rerumque omnium rationibus speciebusque completur. Summum igitur animae bonum eius unius actus[6] completio est, id est, ut per

---

[1]atque *W* [2]adeo *X* [3]hypostas *W* [4]tres *W* [5]complentum *W*
[6]*em.*, actusque *WXY*

the completion of the soul's one act: that is, when it has been turned back through its one act towards the one act of the intelligence and the one act of all things, for it to become all acts, that is, the plenitude of all the species. Matter also, when it has been turned back towards the one soul through one hypostasis and towards the acts of the soul, and when it has been turned back towards the intelligence through the soul, and towards the good itself through the intelligence, is adorned with all the forms. Therefore the highest good of matter is the fulfillment of its natural conversion, which is a certain act: that is, when it has been turned back towards the one act through one act, for it to become all acts and be arrayed with all the forms.

Therefore the absolute good itself is the one above all things, the one act. The highest good of the intelligence, of the soul, of matter, is the one which is all things and all acts. For the things which come after the first one cannot be the one in its simplicity. Therefore they must be one and many. But it is better to be one and all than one and some, so long as all things are possessed in the one. For the highest good of the intelligence isn't really that multiplicity of the species, but the one comprehension of the highest one in all the species. It is the one act in all the acts which exists for the pure act. Therefore the highest good of the soul too isn't the various and manifold probings through the reasons, but the one glimpse of the one God in all the reasons. Moreover, matter's good isn't the division itself of quantities and qualities, but the one loveliness that comes from them all, the one life that comes from the union with one soul. Therefore one thing is enough for individual things, that is, one enjoyment of the one, one glimpse of the one light, one act for the sake of the one act. So this one thing is the good, both in itself and in others.

But the multitude of all acts everywhere follows the supremely creative presence of the one itself. This multitude is beauty. So the splendour of the good is beauty. In the intelligence the beautiful series of all the Ideas accompanies the glimpse of the one itself. In the soul the loveliness of all the reasons accompanies the consideration of the one. In matter the

unum suum actum ad unum mentis omniumque unum conversa actum omnes actus efficiatur, id est, specierum omnium plenitudo. Materia quoque per hypostasim unam ad unam conversa animam actusque animae, perque animam ad mentem, perque mentem ad bonum ipsum formis omnibus exornatur. Bonum ergo summum materiae naturalis eius conversionis quae conversio actus quidam est expletio, id est, ut per actum unum ad unum actum reflexa omnes actus fiat, formis omnibus insignita.

Ipsum igitur absolutum bonum unum est super omnia, actus unus. Bonum summum mentis, animae, materiae unum omnia, actus omnes. Unum enim simpliciter quae post primum sunt esse non possunt. Unum ergo multa sint oportet. Melius autem est esse unum omnia, quam unum aliqua, dummodo in uno omnia possideantur. Summum enim mentis bonum non illa multiplicitas specierum est proprie, sed una unius summi in speciebus omnibus intellectio, in omnibus actibus actus unus ad purum actum. Ita quoque animae bonum summum non varii per rationes multiplicesque discursus, sed unus in rationibus omnibus Dei [*384r*] unius intuitus. Materiae insuper bonum non ipsa quantitatum¹ qualitatumque discretio est, sed unus ex omnibus decor, ex unius animae unione vita una. Unum ergo sufficit singulis, una scilicet unius fruitio, unus luminis unius intuitus,² unus actus ad actum unum. Unum ergo hoc et in se et in aliis bonum est.

Sed ad³ foecundissimam ipsius unius praesentiam omnium actuum passim sequitur multitudo, quae quidem pulchritudo est. Quare boni splendor est pulchritudo. In mente ipsius unius intuitum idearum omnium pulchra series comitatur. In anima unius inspectum rationum decor omnium. In materia unius animae fruitionem formarum sequitur ornamentum. Comes ergo boni pulchrum est. Comes itaque fruitionis eius⁴ est

---

¹quantitate *X*   ²unus luminis unius intuitus *om. X*   ³ad *om. W*   ⁴eius *om. X*

adornment of the forms follows the enjoyment of the one soul. Therefore the beautiful accompanies the good. Therefore joy accompanies its enjoyment. But what is the good? That which is sufficient, desirable and perfect; or rather, desirable and perfect sufficiency; or rather, the sufficient act, the desirable life, the perfect one; or rather, the sufficient life, the perfect unity, the total act; or rather, the one act of the one life in the one. In that it is absolutely such, it is the highest good absolutely. In that it is such proportionate to the natural capacity of each thing, it is the highest good for that thing. So Plato says here in the text the condition of the good itself is that it is the most perfect thing of all, that is, because it perfects all things; also, that it surpasses all existing things in sufficiency, since it exists above being and does whatever being does through unity and act.

It's also necessary to maintain the good is desirable. For the natural instincts are necessary, because they have been put there by the higher mover and they precede choice and decision. But the good is desired by the natural instinct, because both those things that lack knowledge seek the good, and men immediately they are born desire the good. But those things that have knowledge (and after they have it) desire the beautiful. So the desire for the good is older than the desire for the beautiful. So the good is older than the beautiful. Or rather, it's enough for the majority to seem to have beauty, but to seem to have the good is not enough. So the desire for the good is more important than the desire for beauty. Just as the intellect necessarily understands the principles of contemplating by a higher light, so the will necessarily wills what is a good principle of action by a higher instinct. For the universal principle draws all things towards itself. But the universal principle is the good. Therefore all things necessarily desire the good. As a result of this instinct, as Plato says in the *Republic,* things guess something is the good, but they don't know what it is.[171] Yet they divine it's something sufficient and perfect. So they choose as the good whatever seems to possess the species of sufficiency and perfection. So men proceed by various routes; nevertheless, they strive towards one end, that is, to attain life's sufficiency. Some think

gaudium. Quid tandem bonum? Quod sufficiens, expetendum, perfectum; immo sufficientia expetibilis atque perfecta; immo vero sufficiens actus, expetibilis vita, perfectum unum; immo vita sufficiens, perfecta unitas, actus integer; immo unius vitae actus unus in uno. Quod tale absolute, absolute¹ est summum bonum; quod tale pro cuiusque capacitate naturae, summum cuique bonum. Ideo hic in textu dicit conditionem ipsius boni esse ut sit omnium perfectissimum, quia scilicet perficit omnia; item quod omnibus quae sunt praestet sufficientia, quippe cum super esse existat et quicquid esse agit per unitatem et actum agat.

Necessarium quoque est asserere quod expetibile est. Naturales enim instinctus necessarii sunt, quia a superiori movente insunt et electionem iudiciumque praecedunt. Bonum vero naturali instinctu appetitur, quia et quae cognitione carent bonum quaerunt, [*384v*] et homines statim nati bonum appetunt. Pulchrum² vero appetunt, quae cognoscunt et postquam cognoverunt. Ideo appetitus boni antiquior est quam pulchri. Unde et bonum pulchro antiquius. Immo quod pulchritudinem videantur habere sufficit multis; quod bonum videantur non sufficit. Ideo appetitus boni principalior est quam pulchri. Et sicut intellectus necessario intelligit principia contemplandi superiori lumine, sic voluntas necessario vult bonum agendi principium instinctu superiori. Trahit enim ad se omnia principium³ rerum; id autem bonum est. Necessario igitur omnia bonum appetunt. Quo instinctu vaticinantur, ut in Republica inquit Plato, aliquid esse bonum. Quid⁴ vero illud sit ignorant. Esse tamen sufficiens quiddam et perfectum divinant. Ideo quicquid sufficientiae et perfectionis speciem habere videtur⁵ ut bonum eligunt. Diverso igitur homines calle procedunt, nituntur tamen ad unum finem, id est, vitae sufficientiam pervenire. Alii in voluptuosa vita, in militari alii, in civili alii, alii in

sufficiency belongs to the life of pleasure; others to the military life; others to the civic life; others to the life of contemplation. So the four dispositions of men by means of the four sorts of life seek one and the same thing, that is, sufficiency. But only the contemplatives reach it, for the contemplative life is closer to the good itself, which is God. For it seeks nothing externally; it is content with inner things; it is least in need. By fleeing the body, it avoids the bad things which afflict the body.

20D
Since all things desire the good, why did Socrates say here that each thing that has knowledge **hunts after and desires the good**? It's not because the things that don't have knowledge don't desire the good, but because they don't hunt it or choose it. For all bodily things always proceed by one and the same path towards the good, that is, towards the perfect act. Or rather, they are borne towards it, as an arrow is borne to the target by the archer's impetus alone. But those things having knowledge over and above a mover's impetus also exhibit a proper sagacity and skill for tracking down the good; and they devise stratagems for catching it, and often deliberate in order to choose one thing or another out of the many things that appear to be good.

Here Socrates is positing three things: desiring, wanting, hunting after. The first is common to everything; the second and third are peculiar to men employing knowledge. Men want the end, that is, the good itself. They hunt after it, that is, by deliberating they try to find out what it really is, where it is hidden, how it can be taken. They search for it in order to comprehend it truly, not merely to seem to have it. They want to comprehend it in order to possess it firmly and securely. Nor do they search for anything other than the good. And whatever they choose, they choose because they think it will lead to the good. For all things are desired because of the first desirable good. They are said to be perfected in the company of good things because they participate in perfection to the extent that they contribute to the good. Socrates also talks about **possession with regard to the good,** since whatever we long to possess, we long to possess to the extent that it pertains to the

contemplativa inesse sufficientiam arbitrantur. Quattuor igitur affectiones[1] hominum per quattuor vitae genera unum et idem, id est, sufficientiam expetunt. Soli autem contemplantes adipiscuntur. Nam vita haec ipsi bono qui Deus est propinquior. Nihil quaerit extrinsecus, interioribus contenta est, minimis indiget. Per corporis fugam mala vitat quae corpus affligunt.

Cum omnia bonum appetant, cur[2] dixit hic Socrates omne quod cognoscit **venatur bonum et appetit?** Non quia quae non cognoscunt non appetant, sed quia non venantur, nec eligunt. Omnia enim corpora in bonum, id est, actum perfectum, uno semper eodemque calle procedunt. Immo feruntur, ut sagitta [*385r*] ad signum solo iaculatoris impetu. Quae vero cognoscunt ultra moventis impetum ipsa quoque sagacitatem propriam et solertiam ad vestigia boni invenienda[3] adhibent, et machinamenta ad consequendum moliuntur,[4] et ex pluribus quae bona videntur ut eligant alterum saepe consultant.

Tria hic ponit: **appetit, vult, venatur.** Primum commune omnibus; secundum et tertium hominibus cognitione utentibus proprium.[5] Volunt finem bonum scilicet ipsum. Venantur, id est, consultando perquirunt quid proprie[6] id sit, in quo lateat, quomodo capiatur. Quaerunt ut vere comprehendant, non ut videantur habere. Comprehendere volunt ut illud firme stabiliterque possideant; nec aliud quaerunt quam bonum, et quicquid eligunt, quia ad bonum conducere putant, eligunt. Nam sub ratione boni appetibilis primi omnia appetuntur, quae dicuntur una cum bonis perfici, quia eatenus perfectione participant quatenus ad bonum conferunt. Dicit etiam **circa bonum possidere,** quia quaecumque possidere cupimus, quantum[7] ad bonum attinent cupimus possidere. Quin etiam ipsum bonum

[1]effectiones *Y*　　[2]cum *W*　　[3]reperienda *WX*　　[4]noluuntur *W*　　[5]propriam *W*
[6]prope *W*　　[7]inquantum *WX*

good. Moreover, we want to possess the good itself, that is, to enjoy it securely and perpetually. So what leads to satiety isn't the good.

Chapter 32. Neither pleasure nor wisdom is the good itself.

Having stipulated the conditions of the good itself, Socrates now shows that neither wisdom nor pleasure is the good itself. He says, "Now let's **consider** and **decide**; that is, let's **consider** what sort of life is appropriate to each. Then let's **decide** whether it's the good itself. Certainly, the good itself is sufficient, so it's wanting in nothing. So what has the good itself doesn't require anything else. Let's take the life of pleasure, devoid of all wisdom, and let's see whether it alone is sufficient for us. If it isn't, it's not the good itself, as the good itself is sufficient for the person who has it. And similarly, let's divide wisdom from pleasure. Whichever of the two is the good itself will be sufficient for us without the other. But if neither one is going to be sufficient in itself, neither in itself is the good." Given this standard with which to judge, Socrates reverts to his examples and proceeds to judge according to Protarchus' own choice. For it's from will and choice that one judges the nature of the good. Accordingly, Socrates arranges the argument in this way. "You call pleasure the good itself. So it is sufficient in itself. So a life always flooded with pleasure, denuded of any particle of wisdom, will be enough for you. If you have pleasure, you won't need wisdom, or anything else further. So there'll be no need **to know** anything, or **to understand**, or **to deliberate** about useful things, or to do anything else of that sort, or even **to see** anything." He said **to see**, because sight has the incorporeal intellect's image, since it is the result of a moment and tends towards an incorporeal light. Protarchus agreed he'd have every good if he had pleasure. Socrates infers from this, "Granted the event, perpetual pleasure will be present in your life. All wisdom will be absent. Therefore the **intelligence**, that is, the faculty for understanding, the

20E

21A

21B

possidere volumus, id est, firmiter et perpetuo frui. Ideo quod fert[1] satietatem non est bonum.

Neque voluptas, neque sapientia est ipsum bonum. Cap. XXXII.[2]

Positis ipsius boni conditionibus, iam ostendit neque sapientiam, neque voluptatem ipsum esse bonum, dicitque: **Consideremus** iam et **iudicemus, consideremus** scilicet propriam utriusque vitam qualis sit.[3] **Iudicemus**[4] deinde utrum sit ipsum bonum. Certe ipsum bonum sufficiens est, nullo igitur indiget. Quod ergo bonum ipsum habet nihil ultra requirit. Ponamus voluptatis vitam, sapientiae [*385v*] totius expertem, videamusque utrum ipsa nobis sola sufficiat. Si non sufficit, non est ipsum bonum, quod ipsum per se sufficit possidenti. Atque similiter a voluptate sapientiam secernamus. Utrumvis illorum bonum ipsum sit absque altero nobis[5] sufficiet. Sin neutrum per se sufficiet, neutrum per se bonum. Hac norma iudicii data ad exempla recurrit, et iudicium secundum Protarchi ipsius electionem peragit. Ex voluntate enim et electione boni iudicatur natura. Argumentatur itaque Socrates hunc in modum: Voluptatem ipsum bonum vocas, ergo per se sufficiens. Vita[6] igitur semper voluptate perfusa,[7] omni sapientiae parte nudata tibi sufficiet, quam si possederis, nec sapientiam nec aliud quicquam ultra requires. Non igitur opus erit **sapere** quicquam, vel **intelligere,** vel de opportunis **ratiocinari,** nec alia id genus habere, neque etiam **videre** quicquam. Dixit **videre,** quia visus, cum momento fiat et ad incorpoream lucem tendat quandam, intellectus incorporalis habet imaginem. Consensit[8] Protarchus, quia, si voluptatem habeat, omnia habeat bona. Hic infert Socrates: Ex casu posito, perpetua inerit tuae vitae voluptas, sapientia aberit omnis. **Mens** igitur, id est, intelligendi facultas,

---

[1]gignit *WX*   [2]*a break, but no ch. heading W; in X the ch. is numbered eighteen*
[3]sit *om. W*   [4]-que *add. WX*   [5]vobis *W*   [6]Una *X*   [7]etiam *add. W*
[8]Assensit *WX*

recognition of principles, and **knowledge**, that is, the sure perception of the conclusions from the principles, they will be absent. And **reasoning** too, that is, the elaborate process of arguing from principles to conclusions, from causes to effects, it will be absent. **Opinion** also will be wanting, that is, the conjectural estimating of when things will occur; and **memory** too, that is, the steadfast preservation of the things which have happened. But **to know** is the common term for all these [terms]. Since you won't have the intelligence or knowledge, you won't know whether you're happy or not. Since you won't have the memory, you won't record you were happy at some

21C   point nor preserve even for a moment the perception of present pleasure. Since you won't have true opinion, you won't ascertain you're happy when you are happy. Since you won't have the ability to reason, you'll never predict you'll be happy in the future. You'll be leading the life not of a man, but of some insensate jelly fish, or a stupid animal—a life like that of the marine oyster. These animals only have touch, a little taste, and none of the other senses. The jelly fish is a maritime animal. It's very white and seems compacted from the foam. It has the shape and motion of a lung, for it's always opening and closing. It has little hairs inside. The whole of it is very soft and most delicate like snow, and it can be punctured on all sides by a finger. Often it is cast up by the waves of the sea onto the shore. It can't move forward and it has no differentiation of organs.

This at least is the life of pleasure without wisdom. Nobody

21D   would ever choose it as sufficient: firstly, because it's considered the lowest form of life, the one closest to death, the one having the least of life to it; next, because pleasure would be present to the soul in such a way that the soul would enjoy pleasure to the minimum, for it wouldn't come from the past or the future, or last any interval of time—or rather, it would be exactly as if it were not there, since it wouldn't be known to be there and the soul wouldn't form the opinion it was there.

You ought to notice that the soul by its nature, being the mean between the intelligences and bodies, as it regards the body, does the work of nutrition, growth and reproduction in

principiorumque cognitio, et **scientia,** id est, ex principiis conclusionum certa perceptio aberit.[1] Aberit et **ratiocinatio,** id est, a principiis ad conclusiones, a causis ad effectus artificiosa discursio. **Opinio** quoque deerit, id est, incidentium rerum per coniecturam existimatio; **memoria** insuper, id est, eorum quae contigerunt stabilis conservatio. **Sapere** autem commune vocabulum est ad haec omnia. Quia deerit mens et scientia, utrum laeteris necne ignorabis; quia memoria, quod laetatus quandoque fueris non recordaberis et voluptatis praesentis perceptionem ne [*386r*] momentum quidem[2] servabis; quia opinio vera, dum laetaberis, laetari te nequaquam existimabis; quia ratiocinatio,[3] quod in futurum laetaturus sis, numquam praesagies. Agesque vitam non hominis, sed pleumonis cuiusdam insensati et stupidi animalis, et ostreae marinae persimilem, quae animalia tactum habent solum, gustus parum, sensus alios minime. Pleumon animal est maritimum, albissimum, quod videtur ex spuma compactum. Habet pulmonis formam et motum, semper enim et aperitur et clauditur. Intus habet villos. Totum est nivis instar tenerrimum et mollissimum, et undique digito perforatur. Defertur maris[4] undis saepe ad litus. Progressum habet nullum, aut organi distinctionem.

Haec utique voluptatis sine sapientia vita est, quam nemo umquam ut sufficientem eligeret. Primo, quia vilissima existimatur[5] et morti proxima, minimum quiddam habens vitae. Deinde, quia ita adesset animae voluptas, ut minima ex parte anima voluptate frueretur, neque enim ex praeterito, neque ex futuro, neque per aliquam temporis moram. Immo perinde esset, ac si non adesset, cum adesse ignoraretur, et cum animus non adesse opinaretur.

Advertendum est, quod anima natura sua, cum media sit inter mentes et corpora, ut corpus respicit, in eo nutritionis, augmenti, generationis opus exercet et per illud sentit. Nutrit

---

[1]aberit *om. W*   [2]quidem *om. W*   [3]ratiocinatione *Y*   [4]naris *W*   [5]estimatur *WX*

the body and perceives things through it. So the soul in the body
nourishes the body and perceives bodily things through the
body. But as it regards the intelligence separated from the body
and depends on it, so now it acts in such a way that it acts neither in the body nor through the body. So, to the extent that the
soul has been granted the power of the higher intelligence apart
from the instruments of the senses, it knows things by itself.
Either through opinion it knows the images and natures of
single things. Or through the intellect and the reason it knows
their universal and eternal reasons. Or through the process of
reasoning it proceeds by itself from image to image, or from
reason to reason. But it preserves them all through the memory.
All these functions it does without the body—therefore in so far
as it depends on the intelligence which operates without the
body entirely. But any operation which follows the nature of
the intelligence is called by the general name wisdom. So, if the
soul is utterly deprived of wisdom, it won't retain any of the
intelligence's power. So it will be said to be without memory,
opinion, reasoning, knowledge, intellect. So, if pleasure is
present to the external and corporeal senses, it will be present to
the body alone; it will not pass over into the undiluted soul. For
the soul enjoys pleasure through inner comprehension, which is
called opinion, and through memory and reason and intellect.
But the soul separated from the intelligence doesn't have these.
So the soul will not enjoy pleasures, since it cannot grasp hold
of them by any internal power or transfer them into itself. Perhaps there'll be some agreeable feeling in the instruments of the
body, but there'll either be no delight, or very little, in the soul,
since the agreeable feeling will pertain to the body not the soul.
This is because the soul won't comprehend it from nearby but
from afar. The soul will suppose it is in another (because
whether the pleasure is perceived or not will be hidden from it).
The senses, in fact, perceive the body's external changes, but
they don't perceive or retain their own perceptions, for that's
the job of internal thinking. Thinking directs itself not only to
corporeal images but also to incorporeal concepts. So, if there's
an exterior sense without an interior one, some pleasurable

ergo corpus in corpore; sentit per corpus corpora. Ut autem mentem respicit a corpore absolutam atque inde pendet, ita agit iam, ut nec in corpore agat, neque per corpus. Ideo quantum[1] supernae mentis vim sortita est sine sensuum instrumentis secum ipsa res cogitat. Vel per opinionem singulorum imagines atque naturas; vel per intellectum et rationem [*386v*] communes aeternasque rationes; ac per ratiocinationem secum ipsa de imagine in imaginem vel de ratione discurrit in rationem. Per memoriam vero haec omnia servat. Omnia haec sine corpore transigit. Ergo ut a mente dependet, quae omnino sine corpore operatur. Quaelibet vero operatio mentis naturam sequens communi nomine sapientia nuncupatur. Quare si sapientia omnino privata sit anima, nullam mentis vim retinebit. Ergo sine memoria, opinione, ratiocinatione, scientia, intellectu esse dicetur. Adsit ergo sensibus eius exterioribus corporeisque voluptas, soli erit corpori praesens, in meram animam non transibit. Anima enim ipsa in se per interiorem cogitationem, quae opinio dicitur, et memoriam et rationem et intellectum fruitur. Haec autem animae mentis experti deficiunt. Non ergo fruetur[2] voluptatibus, cum non interiori vi capiat et in se transfundat. Eritque forte conveniens aliqua in corporis instrumentis affectio, in anima vero vel nulla vel minima inerit delectatio, quia non ad eam sed ad corpus illa affectio pertinebit, quia non apprehendet cominus, sed eminus et in alio suspicabitur, quia latebit eam, percipiaturne[3] voluptas, necne. Sensus enim exteriores corporis mutationes percipiunt, suas vero perceptiones non percipiunt neque reservant; id enim interioris est cogitationis officium, quae non solum ad imagines corporum, sed et[4] ad incorporales[5] conceptus se confert. Quare, si exterior sensus sine interiori sit, levi quadam gustatione et subita affectio aliqua

---

[1]inquantum *WX*   [2]frueretur *W*   [3]participaturne *W*   [4]et *om. WX*
[5]corporales *X*

feeling in the body can be felt a little as a slight and sudden foretaste, but the soul won't know whether it's feeling or not. Just
as it often happens when we are looking at or listening to
various things with our external senses, yet we don't perceive
whether we see or hear. It's because we don't notice the external
changes when our internal thinking is attending to something
else. And so the soul feels no pleasure arising from shapes and
sounds. There is a change only in the organs. No pleasure exists
in a soul which isn't thinking. Moreover, since there is no
existing communion with the intelligence, the opinion won't
make any correct decision. So we won't be able to form the
opinion that something agreeable to the body is present when it
is offered. So from the soul's point of view it would be exactly
as if it were not there. This life, therefore, would resemble the
life of the animals we call sponges, purple-fish, mussels, and
oysters, which have no internal sense, only two external ones.

If someone wants to know why nature produces animals thus
deprived, he must understand the universal series are distinguished by gradations so that what is the lowest member of a
higher order is next to the principal member in the order subsequent to it. If it weren't, things wouldn't be bound together; the
work of the one God wouldn't be one. The highest angel is
closest to God, the lowest is next to the demon of fire. The
lowest demon, that is, the demon of water, is related to the most
outstanding man. The stupid man is just like the clever brute.
The inactive brute is next to the most beautiful tree. The most
lowly plant, like the truffle, is almost the same as an inanimate
body. Therefore, since the lowest member in the animal genus
ought to be next to the tree, but since the tree nourishes itself
without senses, it is appropriate we find animals which are virtually senseless, that is, which [only] have the senses which are
absolutely necessary and are diffused through the whole body,
namely, touch and taste. For the latter are necessary and sufficient for self-preservation and the production of offspring.
Through the taste the proper nourishment is taken in and the
improper rejected. Through the touch heat and cold and the
other things which can maintain or destroy life are perceived.

corporis voluptaria sentiri paululum poterit. Latebit tamen animam sentiatur necne. Quemadmodum saepe in nobis accidit videntibus [*387r*] et audientibus aliqua externis sensibus, quae tamen utrum videamus et audiamus non percipimus, quia interiori cogitatione ad aliud intendente externas mutationes illas nequaquam advertimus. Ideoque nulla animo ex figuris illis vocibusque iucunditas provenit. Sola est in organis[1] transmutatio; in animo non cogitante nulla iucunditas. Quin etiam, cum mentis nulla insit communio, verum deerit opinionis iudicium. Ideo, dum conveniens corpori res offeretur,[2] adesse non aestimabitur.[3] Erit ergo animo perinde ac si non adsit. Vita itaque ista persimilis erit animalium illorum quae spongiae, purpurae, conchae, ostreae appellantur quae sensum interiorem habent nullum, exteriores duos dumtaxat.

Siquis quaerat cur animalia haec usque adeo manca natura producit, intelligat his gradibus rerum series esse distinctas, ut[4] quod in superiori ordine infimum[5] est ei, quod in sequenti ordine est primum, sit proximum; alioquin res invicem minime necterentur, nec unum esset Dei unius opus. Supremus angelus Deo[6] propinquus; infimus daemoni igneo proximus. Daemon infimus, id est, aqueus, homini praestantissimo est cognatus. Homo stupidus sagaci bruto persimilis. Brutum iners arbori pulcherrimae proximum. Planta vilissima, ut[7] tuber, inanimato corpori ferme est idem. Ideo infimum in animalium genere cum proximum arbori esse debeat, arbor autem nutritionem habeat sine sensibus, conveniens est nonnulla animalia reperiri quae ferme nullum habeant sensum, habeant scilicet eos qui maxime necessarii et qui per omne corpus funduntur, tactum scilicet atque gustum. Hi enim ad sui conservationem et alterius generationem necessarii sunt, hi sufficiunt. Per gustum conveniens adsciscitur [*387v*] nutrimentum, quod conveniens non est

---

[1]in organis *om. W* [2]offertur *W* [3]*em.,* extimabitur *WXY* [4]et *W* [5]infinitum *W*
[6]Dei *Y* [7]et *W*

But these senses are sufficient for the animals we were referring to, since (fixed as they are to stones and soil like trees) they don't seek food at a distance, but suck nourishment from nearby. They can't avoid things by running away, nor seize hold of them by running up to them. In so far as they can, they turn aside and seize food by their drawing back and reaching out. But nobody would choose the life of such animals.

So for these reasons it is obvious the life of pleasure isn't the good itself, since it isn't in itself sufficient; nor would anybody choose it when it is apart from wisdom. Furthermore, it is obvious the life of wisdom isn't the good itself either, because it isn't sufficient in itself. For let it be entirely separated **from all pleasure and pain: from pleasure**, so that we can see whether it is sufficient in itself; **from pain**, so that what might be desired perhaps for its own sake isn't avoided because it's in a bad mixture (so that, in avoiding it, we may reject the bad thing mixed with it). We certainly don't seek the understanding itself as the sufficient good when it's devoid of all pleasure. For we desire to understand, just as we desire to feel. Now just as the sense is related to feeling, so the intellect is related to understanding. But, since we don't want to feel indiscriminately, but to feel with pleasure—in fact, pleasure's what we look for with all the senses—, so we don't want **to understand, to know, to remember, to form an opinion** indiscriminately either, but to do it with joy. To understand is to act and to operate. But we avoid acting with pain as a bad thing. However, we are not drawn towards acting without pain or pleasure as that action's indifferent; or, if we've started on it, we soon leave off, having had enough. So what we want to do most is to act with pleasure. Therefore the act of understanding without pleasure is not what we choose most. So it's not sufficient in itself. So it's not the good itself.

We demonstrated above that the good itself is act itself, and the utterly good act is the one that is utterly an act. But that action is utterly an action that is not mixed with passivity or an impediment and that is drawn towards the best object, that is, to what can be utterly in act. Something moves the sense.[172] The

reicitur. Per tactum calor, frigus et reliqua quae vel servare possunt vel perimere sentiuntur. Sufficiunt autem hi in his, quae narravimus, animalibus, quoniam instar arborum affixa lapidibus aut terrae procul alimenta non quaerunt, sed cominus alimoniam sugunt. Et quae fugiendo vel accurrendo vitare et capessere nequeunt; retractione[1] sui et protractione declinant quoad possunt et capiunt. Horum autem *vitam nemo eligeret.

Ex his igitur rationibus patet voluptatis** vitam ipsum bonum non esse, quia ipsa per se non est sufficiens, nec eam quisquam a sapientia separatam eligeret. Quin etiam quod neque sapientiae vita ipsum bonum sit ex eo patet, quia non est per se sufficiens. Separetur enim ab omni penitus **voluptate** ac **dolore: voluptate,** ut videamus numquid per se sufficiat; **dolore,** ne quod per se forte appeteretur mali admixtione vitetur, ut eo vitato malum quod admixtum est declinetur. Certe intelligentiam ipsam omnis voluptatis expertem ut sufficiens bonum non expetimus. Ita enim appetimus intelligere, ut et sentire. Nam sicut se habet sensus ad sentiendum, sic intellectus ad intelligendum. Cum vero non quomodocumque sentire concupiscamus, sed cum suavitate sentire, id enim per omnes sensus quaerimus, neque etiam **intelligere** et **sapere** et **meminisse** et **opinari** quomodocumque, sed cum gaudio cupimus. Nempe intelligere agere et operari est. At vero cum dolore agere tamquam malum fugimus. Agere autem cum neutro, nec dolore, nec voluptate ut indifferens non adsciscimus, et si coeperimus,[2] cito satietate affecti dimittimus. Quod ergo potissimum petimus est cum voluptate agere. Non ergo intelligentiae actus sine voluptate optabilissimum.[3] Non itaque per se sufficiens. Non [*388r*] igitur ipsum bonum.

In superioribus ipsum bonum actum ipsum esse monstravimus, et bonum esse maxime actum eum qui actus est maxime. Illa vero actio maxime actio est quae passioni et impedimento mixta non est, et quae ad obiectum optimum, id est, quod

---

[1] retractatione *Y*   [2] percepimus *W*   [3] expetendissimum *WX*   *-**om. W*

sense perceives it. If the thing is good, it then agrees with [our] nature. For something has to strike the sense as something before it can agree [with our nature]. Immediately the sense perceives the agreement. The feeling then accords first with the sense's perception, then with the agreement. The agreement is as it were the blind pleasure; so too is the feeling's accord. But the seeing pleasure is in the sense, when here it perceives the natural agreement of [its own] movement with [our] nature, and there the feeling's accord first with itself (that is, with [its] perception of the agreement), then with the agreement. The good is threefold. That is, there's the good of [our] nature when there's the agreement of [the sense's] movement with [our] nature. There's the good of the feeling, namely, the said accord. And there's the good of the sense, namely, the perception of both. Note that the feeling's accord is not only a quietness deprived of stimulus but an extending and striving towards the good of [our] nature and sense. It's like the principle of levity which both moves and stops itself and vehemently directs whatever it has moved and stopped. Read about these things in Olympiodorus. There you'll find pleasure is in the cognitive part also, and so is pain, although for the opposite reason.[173]

Therefore, let the sense be a potentiality free from passivity, and best prepared to perceive something. Let all external impediments be removed. Let the sense cling to some excellent object with which it's in accord and which is also perfect and totally an act, for instance to a shape or harmony that's perfect, or to some sweetest flavour. Immediately, the sense's act, being a pure, unhampered act, will act freely and completely. The sense will start to act eagerly, it will proceed gladly and it will cling [to the object] indissolubly. The completeness itself of the pure and unhampered act is the same thing as the perfect act and total act. Because it proceeds gladly to stop in itself the potentiality which was acting eagerly, it is called pleasure. Therefore completeness of the act and pleasure are the same. But completeness of the act is nothing other than total act. Therefore the same movement is both action and pleasure, although they differ in concept. For action is when the potentiality does something

maxime actu sit, fertur. *Aliquid movet sensum; sensus illud sentit. Mox illud, si bonum, convenit naturae. Prius enim occurrit ut aliquid sensui quam ut conveniens. Statim persentit convenientiam. Mox affectus consentit tum persensioni tum convenientiae. Convenientia est quasi caeca voluptas; similiter affectus ipsius consensio. Voluptas vero videns est in ipso sensu, dum hinc persentit naturalem motionis convenientiam cum natura, inde vero consensionem affectus, tum secum, id est, cum ipsa persensione convenientiae, tum cum ipsa convenientia. Hic triplex est bonum: scilicet bonum naturae ut motionis convenientia cum natura; item bonum affectus, scilicet dicta consensio; et bonum sensus, scilicet persensio utraque. Nota consensionem affectus esse quietem non privativam solum stimuli, sed diffusionem et nixum in bonum naturae sensusque, sicut levitas et movet et sistit applicatque vehementer quod movit atque firmavit. De his in Olympiodoro, scilicet quod voluptas sit etiam in parte cognitiva, similiter dolor, licet opposita ratione.**

Sit ergo sensus potentia passionis expers optime ad sentiendum affecta; remota sint impedimenta externa;[1] haereat obiecto cuidam optimo et consentaneo, quod et perfectum et actus maxime sit, ut figurae vel harmoniae perfectae, vel sapori alicui[2] suavissimo. Statim ipsius sensus actus tamquam merus et expeditus actus libere et integerrime aget. Avide agere incipiet sensus, libenter perseverabit, indissolubiliter adhaerebit. Haec ipsa meri et expediti actus integritas idem est quod actus ipse completus et maxime actus. Et quia potentiam avide operantem libenti perseverantia in se sistit, voluptas dicitur. Idem igitur integritas actus atque voluptas. Integritas autem actus nihil aliud quam[3] maxime actus est. Quare motus idem et actio est et voluptas, quamquam differunt ratione. Actio enim est ut per

---

[1]extrinseca *WX*   [2]alicui *om. Y*   [3]quam *om. W*   *-**om. W*

through movement. Pleasure is when the potentiality, which is
thus acting gladly with regard to the object, stops in the movement. What we said about the sense, apply to the intellect as
well. Completeness in the sense's action is both total act and
pleasure. Each sense aims at the completeness as its highest
good. Completeness in the intellect's action is both total act
and pleasure, and the intelligence seeks this completeness as
its good. Therefore wisdom's operation is not its own good
no matter how it works. On the contrary, if it can be with pleasure, it is with pleasure. If it can be complete, it is such.
When it is unimpeded, unmixed and joined to the best object,
which is the highest act, then it is total act. When the act is
total, then there's pleasure. So this, which is in actuality one
(but for different reasons) and is mixed in a way from two
things, wisdom and pleasure, is the highest good of the intelligence. So it is man's highest good as well, for man uses the
intelligence and the crown of the intelligence as his highest part.
Plato in the *Phaedrus*, the *Phaedo* and the *Theaetetus*
maintains this, and Aristotle in the *Ethics* Book 10 accepts it
willingly.[174]

Now pleasure is said to be dual. One pleasure is in the act itself of knowing: this pleasure is knowing completely, and it's in
the knowing power. The other pleasure accompanies knowing:
this is in the power of the appetite. The former pleasure
is the same as the pure unimpeded act, the latter is the assent
of the appetite. The former is in the same genus as knowing,
since it belongs to the genus of the limit, as it's the limit of
unimpeded knowing. The latter is in the genus of the infinite,
since it's the inclining and reaching out of the appetite
towards the thing that knowing has decided is good. Plato
doesn't bring the first sort of pleasure into the argument to
compare it with the intelligence, for it's the same. Rather, he
introduces the second sort (which is in the power of the appetite and is different from knowing) to compare it to knowing.
We will show below that it isn't sufficient in itself, and it's
what both we and Plato are referring to here, when we say pleasure isn't sufficient. For the pleasure which is present in the

eum potentia aliquid agit; voluptas ut in eo motu circa tale obiectum libenter potentia sic operans conquiescit. Quod in sensu diximus in intellectu quoque intellige dictum. Integritas in actione sensus et actus maxime est et voluptas. Et hanc integritatem quisque[1] sensus ut summum sui bonum affectat. Integritas in intellectus actione et actus maxime est et voluptas; et hanc integritatem[2] ut suum[3] bonum mens expetit. Non ergo sapientiae operatio[4] quomodocumque se habeat suum[5] bonum est. Immo si cum voluptate sit, est cum voluptate. Si integra sit, talis est. Cum non impedita, non mixta, et cum obiecto [*388v*] optimo qui summus actus est coniungitur, tunc vero est actus maxime. Cum itaque maxime actus est, tunc est voluptas. Hoc igitur quod re ipsa unum est varia quadam[6] ratione ex duobus quodammodo sapientia et voluptate mixtum, summum mentis est bonum. Ergo et hominis qui mente et mentis capite suprema sui parte utitur. Quod et Plato in Phaedro et Phaedone et Theaeteto vult, et Aristoteles in decimo Ethicorum libenter accipit.

Verum voluptas duplex esse dicitur. Una in ipso cognitionis actu, quae cognitionis integritas est, et est in cognoscente potentia. Altera cognitionis comes, quae in appetitus potentia est. Illa idem est quod merus et expeditus actus; ista est appetitionis assensio. Illa eiusdem generis cuius cognitio, quia in genere termini ponitur, cum sit expeditae cognitionis terminus. Ista in genere infiniti, quia est inclinatio et diffusio appetitus in id quod cognitione iudicatum est bonum. Illam[7] Plato in disceptationem non trahit,[8] ut cum mente eam comparet, idem enim est. Immo secundam voluptatem, quae est in appetendi potentia et aliud quiddam est quam cognitio, ad cognitionem confert, quam non esse per se sufficientem[9] infra monstrabimus. Atque de hac et ipse hic intelligit et nos cum sufficientem esse negamus. Nam quae in cognitivae potentiae actu inest

---

[1]quisquis *W*   [2]quisque sensus *add. X*   [3]summum *WX*   [4]operatio *om. X*
[5]ipsum *WX*   [6]varia quadam *om. WX*   [7]illum *W*   [8]transibit *W*   [9]*W reads* per
sensus facientem *for* per se sufficientem

act of the cognitive power is sufficient, because, as soon as this, the integral pleasure occurs, wisdom has been joined to the second pleasure which is the assent of the appetite. Therefore, when the integral pleasure occurs, the wisdom of the intelligence and the pleasure of the appetite have been mixed together.

22A   Accordingly, Socrates says here the life mixed from pleasure and wisdom is desired more than either of them are singly because it's more sufficient. Also it's desirable to everybody, because contemplative men desire it for wisdom's sake, voluptuaries want it as they are drawn to it for pleasure's sake, the men in between also want it as they are drawn to it on both counts.

From the above he concludes animals wouldn't choose either life as sufficient, if they were given the choice. Men don't think wisdom is enough without pleasure. The beasts too, if they are aware at all and are given the choice, won't judge the external pleasure of the body is sufficient without the delight of the internal senses, a delight which pertains in a way to wisdom. It is said of the beasts chiefly, because even the men who only live as beasts, that is, are delivered over to the senses, don't consider the most external and silliest pleasure is enough without the unbroken delight of inner thinking.

22B   So Socrates concludes neither life is the good itself, because neither is sufficient or perfect. For if either were sufficient, it would have to be chosen before the rest and given precedence by all those who use their reason to deliberate and decide what they ought to choose. This goes even for the more perfect among the beasts, like dogs, horses, elephants. These animals receive things from the consideration of the inner phantasy over and beyond the external senses. For they seek something from both: to enjoy the delight of the sense and to be delighted by the inner phantasy and memory. This is obvious with monkeys and playful dogs, musical birds and honour-loving horses, the skilful bees and ants. It even appears with plants. Their nature—eager as it were for the pleasure of the external

sufficiens est, quia cum primum haec integritas est sapientia coniuncta est cum alia voluptate quae est appetitus assensio. Ubi ergo haec est ex sapientia mentis et appetitus voluptate facta est mixtio.

Quapropter dicit hic Socrates vitam ex voluptate et sapientia mixtam magis quam utrumlibet illorum expeti, quia sufficientior. Et cuique expetibilis est, quia contemplativi homines [*389r*] ratione sapientiae eam quaerunt, voluptuosi quoque voluptate pellecti eam cupiunt, medii quoque eandem utriusque studio tracti.

Ex superioribus colligit quod neutram vitam ut sufficientem animalia, si optio detur, eligerent. Homines quidem sapientiam sine voluptate ut sufficientem non putant. Bruta quoque, si id persentiant et optio detur, exteriorem corporis voluptatem sine sensuum interiorum iucunditate, quae ad sapientiam quodammodo pertinet, ut sufficientem minime iudicabunt. Hoc de brutis ob id maxime dicitur, quia etiam homines, qui ut bruta dumtaxat vivunt, id est, sensibus mancipati, voluptatem extimam et laevissimam illam sine cogitationis interioris continuata iucunditate sufficere non arbitrantur.

Per haec concludit quod neutra vita ipsum bonum est, quia neutra sufficiens et perfecta. Si enim sufficiens esset, prae ceteris eligenda et praeponenda esset ab omnibus[1] qui ratione de eligendis consultant atque diiudicant. Immo etiam a brutis perfectioribus, ut canibus, equis, elephantibus, quae praeter sensus exteriores interioris phantasiae examine res adsciscunt. Haec enim utriusque aliquid quaerunt, et sensus iucunditate perfrui et interiori phantasia et memoria delectari. Quod in simiis, et iocosis canibus, musicis avibus, et ambitiosis equis, *artificiosis apibus formicisque** apparet. Immo etiam plantis, quarum natura quasi exteriorum sensuum voluptatis avida, gustu quasi

---

[1]hominibus *WX*   *-**artificio sis opibus formatisque *W*

senses—sucks the healthgiving moisture up through the roots
and extends the roots out everywhere for the moisture as if by
some sense of taste. It turns the leaves towards the sun's heat
and embraces the nearest support with little twigs and twines
and in creating brings forth the buds as if by some sense of
touch. It paints and forms the body with artful shapes and with
the countless species and variety of colour as if by some conscious art of the inner phantasy.

So you see that in all things there is a certain innate feeling for
both wisdom and pleasure, or rather, that all men seek each one
mixed. This goes for the stupid men who are given to sloth or
the stomach who live an indolent life; and those who are given
to luxury and avarice; and those who are given to rage; and
those who are given to busy reason; and those who are given to
tranquil contemplation. We call the first sort vegetables, the
second pigs and asses, the third lions, the fourth men, and the
fifth gods. For they all desire both wisdom and pleasure as far
as they can; and they want to possess it through the whole of life
as long as they can.

But whoever **chooses** differently, that is, whoever chooses
death, or a troubled life, doesn't do so voluntarily. But either it's
through ignorance—for instance, the person who devotes himself to some study of life thinking it will be pleasant which at
length is troublesome. **Or** it's through the compulsion of **necessity and force**—for instance, the person who is commanded by a
tyrant either to die or to live as a hired man, who chooses the
hired life; or the person who is going to die and is told to choose
either a cross or an axe, who chooses an axe. Nevertheless,
whoever it is who chooses, he always chooses either what's
better or less bad. But to choose the less bad instead of what's
worse is to choose the good. Plato justifiably used the word
choice; for we want the end, and choose those things which contribute to the end. We always want the good. Often we choose
what is less bad, as Plato argues in the *Gorgias* and in the
Protagoras. He says the bad is chosen by unhappy necessity,
that is, the necessity which is contrary to felicity (which consists
in the highest good).[175]

quodam humorem salubrem radicibus sugit, atque ad illum radices passim protendit; et quasi quodam tactu ad solis calorem vertit folia, ramusculis et viminibus proximum amplectitur sustentaculum, germinaque gignendo producit; et quasi sapienti [*389v*] quadam phantasiae interioris arte artificiosis figuris, colorum varietate numerosa specie corpus suum pingit ac format.

Vides ergo in omnibus esse innatum aliquem utriusque affectum; immo vero homines omnes utrumque mixtum quaerunt: et qui somno et ventri dediti stupidi per inertiam vitam agunt; et qui luxuriae et avaritiae; et qui iracundiae; et qui rationi negotiosae; et qui tranquillae contemplationi. Primos plantas vocamus; secundos porcos et asinos; tertios leones; quartos homines; quintos denique deos. Omnes enim hi utrumque appetunt quoad possunt, et quamdiu possunt per omnem vitam cupiunt possidere.

Siquis vero aliud quam hoc, id est, vel mortem, vel vitam anxiam **elegerit,** non sponte istud, sed **vel per ignorantiam,** puta qui ad studium aliquod vitae se confert putans iucundum esse quod tandem est anxium; **vel necessitate et vi** coactus, ut qui tyranno iubetur vel mori vel mercenarium vivere eligit mercenariam vitam; vel qui moriturus iubetur vel crucem eligere vel securim securim eligit. Verumtamen quisquis eligit semper vel melius vel minus malum eligit. Minus vero malum ad maius, bonum est. Merito Plato **electionis** nomine usus est, volumus enim finem. Eligimus quae ad finem sunt. Volumus semper bonum. Eligimus saepe quod minus malum, ut in Gorgia et Protagora Plato disputat. Electionem mali a necessitate infelici esse dicit, id est, quae contra felicitatem est, quae in bono summo consistit.

Chapter 33. The good itself is superior to the intelligence. Neither wisdom nor pleasure is the highest good, but rather something they share. This something is totally superior; nevertheless, wisdom is more nearly related to it than pleasure.

22C   From the argument above Socrates concludes that Philebus' **particular goddess**, namely pleasure, is not the same as the good. He didn't say **goddess** in order to maintain pleasure is a goddess, for this would be to despise God, but rather to ridicule Philebus who had referred to pleasure as a goddess. Socrates denies here that pleasure is a goddess on the grounds that pleasure isn't happy. But since he wanted to infer in the same conclusion that the intelligence, that is, wisdom, also isn't in itself the good, [and] since the intelligence is a divine name he was not allowed to desecrate, Socrates wanted the assertion to be made by his adversary, Philebus. So Philebus replied, "Socrates, what you're defending, the intelligence, isn't the good itself either. For, as we showed above, it's open to the very same objections as pleasure: it's not sufficient, nor perfect, nor alone desirable before all else."

For some conclusion to be drawn from the foregoing, however, Socrates agreed his intelligence and wisdom are not the good. It's as if he were saying "his" to stress the wisdom which is human and imperfect. For he doesn't possess the complete understanding, nor that pleasure which is the highest repose and consent of the will. And therefore the intelligence isn't sufficient in itself. However, in order to show not only what the good is not, but also to indicate some ways for tracking down what the good is, he added that, while he agreed the imperfect intelligence wasn't the good itself, the perfect intelligence behaves otherwise. That is, it is different from the imperfect intelligence because it is happy.

Nevertheless, he didn't say it was the good itself, because all things desire the good, but not all things desire the intelligence. For not all things are capable of attaining the intelligence and wisdom (therefore many things would desire them in vain). And

Ipsum bonum est mente superius. Neque sapientia neque voluptas est summum bonum, sed potius commune quiddam. Potissimum vero superius aliquid, cui tamen sapientia est cognatior quam voluptas. Cap. XXXIII.[1]

Ex superiori disputatione concludit Socrates quod **dea illa** Philebi,[2] id est, voluptas non idem est ac bonum. Non dixit **deam,** ut affirmaret esse deam, [*390r*] nam Deum sperneret; immo ut illuderet Philebum potius, qui deam dixerat voluptatem, quae dea esse hic negatur a Socrate cum beata non sit. Cum autem vellet in eadem conclusione inferre quod neque etiam mens, id est, sapientia per se ipsum sit bonum, id a Philebo adversario pronuntiari voluit quia mens divinum est nomen quod non erat a Socrate temerandum. Intulit ergo Philebus: Neque tua illa mens, quam tutaris, o Socrates, ipsum est bonum. Nam easdem quas et voluptas, ut supra monstravimus, obiectiones patitur, quod neque sufficiens sit, neque perfecta, neque sola prae ceteris expetenda.

Ut autem superioribus aliqua adderetur conclusio, consensit[3] Socrates mentem et sapientiam suam, id est, sui quasi dicat humanam et imperfectam,[4] bonum non esse. Nam neque integram habet intelligentiam, neque voluptatem illam quae voluntatis suprema est requies et consensio. Ideoque ipsa per se sufficiens non est. Sed ut non modo quid non sit bonum concluderet, verum etiam vestigia nonnulla ad inveniendum quid bonum sit indicaret, dum negavit mentem imperfectam ipsum bonum esse, adiecit quod mens perfecta aliter se habet, scilicet, quam imperfecta, quia scilicet beata est.

Neque tamen dixit eam ipsum esse bonum, quia omnia bonum appetunt, mentem vero non omnia. Neque enim assequi mentem et sapientiam omnia possunt. Ideo multa eam frustra appeterent. Et ea quae mente carent non omnia mentem adipisci

---

[1]*a break, but no ch. heading W; in X the ch. is numbered nineteen* [2]Phebi *W*
[3]consentit *W*   [4]imperfectum *W*

not all things which lack the intelligence try to acquire it. However, those which have the intelligence don't stop; they keep searching for the good. For to understand is proper to the intelligence. To understand is a particular movement. After this movement, the intelligence finds itself either better or worse or just as before. It won't be worse, because action is perfection and nothing descends towards the worse except through ignorance or coercion. It won't be the same as before, for what accomplishes nothing is moved in vain, and nothing is moved towards something it already has. So it is moved in order to be better. So it isn't the good itself, for nothing is better than the good. Moreover, we seek wisdom and intelligence because of reason's impulse alone, but we seek the good before reason provides any incentive at all.

For the same reasons it's obvious the good is above the intelligence. Firstly, it's because, in the process of desiring, all things are turned back towards the good, but not all things are turned back towards the intelligence. But the point towards which things are turned back is the point they started out from. So all things start out from the good, but not all things start out from the intelligence. So not the intelligence, but the good is the first cause of all. Secondly, it's because the natural appetite of men is each and always for the good, but not each and always for the intelligence. So the natural appetite values the good more highly than it does the intelligence. Therefore the good is adjudged by natural instinct to be of more value and therefore of greater excellence than the intelligence. Thirdly, it's because the intelligence imbibes goodness in the process of understanding (since it finds itself better). But it imbibes from elsewhere. If it had goodness in itself, there'd be no need of the movement, no need to profit from action. What it imbibes goodness from is the good itself, which is above the intelligence (since it pours the liquor of its perfection into the intelligence).

So Socrates didn't call the intelligence, though perfect, the good itself, since something else prior to the intelligence is the good. But he did say the intelligence was blessed when he said it was better than his own intelligence.

student. Quae vero mentem habent nondum cessant, sed adhuc bonum quaerunt. Mentis enim proprium est intelligere. Intelligere motus quidam est. Aut post hunc motum melius se mens habet, aut deterius, aut aeque. Non deterius, quia actio perfectio est et ad deterius nihil, [*390v*] nisi aut vi aut inscitia, labitur. Non aeque, frustra enim movetur quod nihil proficit, et nihil ad id quod habet movetur. Ergo ut melius se habeat movetur. Non igitur ipsum bonum est, nihil enim bono melius. Quin etiam sapientiam mentemque ex solo[1] rationis impulsu petimus, bonum autem etiam ante omne rationis incitamentum.

Iisdem rationibus patet bonum esse supra mentem. Primo sic omnia appetendo convertuntur ad bonum, non ad mentem omnia. Quo vero conversio est, illinc et processio. Omnia ergo a bono procedunt, non a mente omnia.[2] Quare non mens, sed bonum est[3] causa[4] prima *omnium. Secundo sic appetitus hominum naturalis omnis et semper ad bonum, non omnis et semper ad mentem; pluris ergo facit bonum quam mentem.** Igitur naturali instinctu bonum mente pretiosius, et idcirco eminentius iudicatur. Tertio sic mens intelligendo haurit bonitatem, cum sese melius habeat. Aliunde autem haurit. Si enim in se haberet, non esset motu opus ut agendo proficeret. Illud unde haurit bonitatem ipsum bonum est, quod et supra eam est, cum in eam perfectionis suae liquorem infundat.

†Quare mentem licet perfectam ipsum bonum esse non dixit, cum et aliud quiddam sit bonum et ante mentem. Sed beatam esse eam innuit, dum dixit melius se habere quam suam.††

---

[1]solo *om.* WX   [2]omnia *om.* WX   [3]*W and X read* Quare bonum non mens est   [4]ea *W*
*-** *and* †-†† *(cont.) inserted in margin W; in both cases we have the scribe's normal hand*

In fact, the good creates the intelligence immediately next to itself. This intelligence, since it is the prime intelligence, is the total intelligence. Therefore it's the true intelligence, because it is pure and entire. It's also divine, because it has always been shaped by God. This intelligence creates our soul. The soul, since it is born from the intelligence, has part of the intelligence. But because it falls away from the intelligence and turns towards matter, it's not the entire, the pure intelligence, but the intelligence which is in the soul and is part of the soul (the soul possesses beyond the intelligence: opinion, sense and the productive nature). So the soul's intention is not always and entirely directed to the intelligence but more often to bodily objects. But since the intelligence's nature is closest to and appropriate to the good (as it was created next by the good) and since it's the receptacle of blessedness, the soul won't accept total blessedness till its other powers and functions have been abandoned and it has been turned back with its whole intent towards the intelligence, its chief part, and been made in a way into the total intelligence alone. Then the soul will be the true and divine intelligence, that is, the first intelligence born immediately from God; and it will drink down the fullness of the good and be blessed. In this true, divine intelligence, surely, the most abundant blessedness is present. Because it's wisdom's total act, pleasure is innate in it. And so such wisdom is the sufficient good. There's no need for another, external pleasure to accompany it, because whatever's there is the intelligence: there isn't one power for willing and another for understanding (otherwise, to attain sufficiency, the will would have to assent to the understanding, and thus the appetite's pleasure would have to be united to the understanding's pleasure). It's obvious the power for willing isn't different there, because the will which does differ from the intellect is what stimulates [us] to attain the good with the understanding. But full possession of the good resides there where the intelligence, which is the closest receptacle of the good, is total and alone.

Such is the blessedness of the prime intelligence and the blessedness of the soul, when with its whole intent it has been

†Ipsum quidem bonum mentem proxime creat. Haec mens, quia prima est mens, tota mens est. Ideo vera est mens, quia pura et integra. Est et divina, quia semper a Deo formata. Mens ista nostram gignit animam, quae prout a mente nascitur mentis habet partem, quia vero a mente degenerat et ad materiam vertitur, non tota et pura mens est, sed mens in anima atque pars animae habentis ultra mentem opinionem, sensum et gignendi naturam. Idcirco intentio animae non omnis semperque ad mentem, sed ad corpora plurimum.†† Cum vero mentis natura, quia proxime a bono creata, proximum sit et proprium boni, et beatitudinis receptaculum, beatitudinem integram anima non prius accipiet, quam reliquis potentiis et officiis praetermissis tota sui intentione in mentem sui caput conversa fuerit,[1] tota et sola quodammodo mens effecta. Tunc anima vera erit mens et divina, ut mens prima statim ex Deo nata, bonique hauriet copiam eritque beata. In hac utique vera et divina mente plenissima[2] beatitudo inest. Quia sapientiae actus integer cui est innata voluptas. Ideoque sapientia huiuscemodi sufficiens bonum est. Nec opus est voluptatem aliam exteriorem sibi comitem adhibere, quia quicquid [*391r*] ibi est[3] mens est. Nec est ibi alia volendi potentia, intelligendi alia, ut necesse sit ad sufficientiam consequendam voluntatem intelligentiae assentiri, atque ita voluptatem appetitus cum intelligentiae voluptate coniungi. Quod autem volendi potentia ibi diversa non sit patet, quia voluntas quae ab intellectu differt stimulus est ad bonum intelligentia consequendum; ibi autem boni est adimpleta possessio, ubi tota ac sola mens est quae boni est proximum receptaculum.

Talis quidem est beatitudo primae mentis et beatitudo animae, cum tota erit in mentem intentione transfusa. Quo loco

---

[1] sunt [?] *W*   [2] et *add. W*   [3] est *om. Y*   *(cont.)* †-††*inserted in margin in the scribe's normal hand W*

poured into the intelligence. The souls of the spheres, whose whole intent is directed towards the intelligence, are always in that condition. For they don't move the heavens by busy intention but by the supereminent power of the essence and the seeds. But the soul's blessedness, in so far as it's a human soul, is compounded both from the understanding (which is entire to the extent that it can belong to the soul which is busy ruling the body) and from the consent of the will and each appetite. This consent is external pleasure. It's necessary for human sufficiency, so that there should be no internal sedition, but all the parts should in one way or another come together into one to possess the one gift of blessedness. In this book [Plato] often mentions the soul's human felicity which is in the first degree of wisdom, that is, in the evening vision of the good, in the splendour cast by the good itself. But the intelligence's divine felicity is in the second degree of wisdom; it's the morning vision of the good, in the very light of the good.[176] The morning vision Plato sometimes secretly points to in this dialogue, but he argues at length, therefore publicly, about the evening vision. But now he's shown that neither the life of wisdom nor pleasure is the good itself, Socrates concludes the shared life is more excellent than either of them because it's more sufficient. He says he will not fight to take away the palm of victory from the shared life, or to set up wisdom alone in front of it. However, he didn't mention pleasure, because it's the duty of Philebus and Protarchus to make such a concession for pleasure; and also because it's been demonstrated very clearly above that pleasure isn't enough. But now

22D Socrates will prepare for the second comparison. Here the problem is to find out, since it's apparent neither of them is the supreme good, which one is nearer to it and occupies second position. But Socrates suggests questions, he promises, encourages, and prepares. Finally, he'll take up the comparison proposed in the fifth section of the book. He says in the comparison perhaps one of them will defend the intelligence. To show it's closer to the highest [good], this person will maintain that the intelligence is mainly the reason why the shared life is the good. But the person who defends pleasure will do the same for pleasure.

semper sphaerarum animae sunt, quarum tota in mentem est intentio. Neque enim intentione negotiosa coelos movent, sed supereminenti essentiae et seminum potestate. Beatitudo autem animae, quantum[1] anima est[2] humana, composita est ex intelligentia, eatenus integra quatenus animae regendo corpori occupatae competere potest, et voluntatis appetitusque omnis consensione, quae exterior est voluptas. Quae consensio ad humanam sufficientiam necessaria est, ut nulla interior sit seditio, sed omnes partes quoquomodo in unum concurrant ad munus unum beatitudinis possidendum. De hac humana animae felicitate ut plurimum hoc in libro loquitur, quae est in primo illo sapientiae gradu, in boni scilicet visione vespertina, in boni ipsius splendore. Divina vero illa mentis felicitas in secundo sapientiae gradu, matutina boni visio est in boni luce, quam nonnumquam hoc in dialogo clam significat. De alia vero latissime disputat, palam[3] igitur.[4] Iam vero, cum ostenderit neutrum ipsum esse bonum, concludit Socrates quod communis vita praestantior est quam istorum alterum, quia sufficientior, dicitque minime se pugnaturum quo palmam communi vitae [*391v*] auferat, eique solam[5] sapientiam anteponat. De voluptate vero subticuit, quia ad Philebum et Protarchum ea concessio pertinet, ac etiam quia liquidius demonstratum fuit in superioribus eam nequaquam sufficere. Mox vero ad secundam comparationem illam se praeparabit, in qua, cum pateat neutrum esse summum, utrum illorum sit summo propinquius secundamque obtineat sortem est inquirendum. Movet autem quaestiones, pollicetur, exhortatur, et praeparat. Exsequetur demum comparationem propositam in quinta libri particula. In ea inquit forsan comparatione, qui partem mentis tutabitur, ut eam summo propinquiorem ostendat, asseverabit mentem potissimum causam esse ut commune id bonum sit; qui vero voluptatis voluptatem.[6]

---

[1]inquantum *WX*   [2]est *om. WX*   [3]*em.*, palmam *XY; om. W*   [4]igitur *om. W*
[5]solum *X*   [6]Quare ex communi concessione neutrum ex his ipsum erit bonum; boni vero causa erit utrumvis horum pro vario iudicantium arbitratu *add. W*

But one mustn't persist in such partisan attitudes, for the perfection of one thing comes eventually from the one, and the
perfection of a compound thing from what is simple. And so
some one thing must be placed above the compound life, so that
there can be one something common to the parts given to this
life and both the parts can be good and the whole can be good.
Certainly, it is to this one thing that you have to compare wisdom and pleasure. Thus we'll see which is the better; for what is
more nearly related to the one cause will be the better. Such will
be the right way to make the comparison. Socrates says, "I'd
certainly fight against Philebus to affirm that the intelligence is
closer to and more like the one thing than pleasure—whatever
this thing is that makes the mixed life exist as **good** and
eligible." He said the mixed life is **good** relative to itself (as it's
almost perfect), **eligible** relative to the appetite (as it's almost
totally desirable). He said the intelligence is **closer to the good,**
that is, nearer to its genus, **and more like it,** that is, more in
agreement with its property. This will be demonstrated subsequently. However, if we agree, in first place we'll put what
endows the compound life with perfection, in second the compound life, in third the intelligence, in fourth the intelligence's
participation in the soul's processes of reasoning, in fifth,
finally, pleasure. This will be obvious at the end of the book.
22E   Socrates adds that, if any credence is to be given to **his** (that is, a
human) **intelligence, for the present** (that is, before he has
rationally demonstrated what the proposal is), this is the way
such things must be decided. It's as if he were saying, "Perhaps
you don't believe me at the moment, until I give you the reason.
I'll certainly give you the reason when I come to it. Meanwhile,
accept it is so, having put your trust in what [my] intelligence
anticipates (the very intelligence Philebus has scorned). The
intelligence certainly excels pleasure principally because of the
fact that, as you can see for yourself, we're now deliberating
about the intelligence and pleasure through the power and the
light of the intelligence itself. But we're not inquiring into either
pleasure or wisdom through the light of pleasure, which is blind
itself (for the appetite is blind too). So who will doubt the

Neque tamen in his partibus insistendum, unius enim perfectio ab uno tandem, et compositi a simplici manat. Atque ideo aliquod unum supra compositam hanc vitam est ponendum,[1] quo[2] vitae huic datum unum aliquid partibus commune sit, quo et bonae partes et totum sit bonum. Ad quod unum certe sapientiam et voluptatem comparare decet. Atque ita videbimus quid ex his melius sit, quod enim uni causae cognatius id melius. Atque hic erit rectus comparandi modus. Certe ego,[3] inquit Socrates, adversus Philebum pugnarem affirmaturus mentem esse **illi uni cognatiorem et similiorem** quam voluptatem, quicquid illud sit quo vita haec mixta **bona** et **eligenda** existit. **Bonam** dixit, quoad[4] se ipsam quasi perfectam; **eligendam,** [*392r*] quoad appetitum quasi maxime expetendam.[5] Mentem dixit **cognatiorem** bono, id est, eius generi propinquiorem, **et similiorem,** id est, eius proprietati magis convenientem; quod in sequentibus ostendetur. Quod si[6] constiterit, primo loco ponemus illud quod compositae vitae perfectionem tribuit; secundo compositam vitam; tertio mentem; quarto mentis participationem in discursibus animae; quinto denique voluptatem, ut in fine huius libri patebit. Addit Socrates ita esse de his iudicandum, siquid **suae,** id est, humanae, **menti** credendum est, **in praesentia,** id est, antequam ratione quod propositum est demonstret; quasi dicat, Forte mihi nunc non creditis[7] prius quam afferam rationem. Afferam certe loco suo. Interim ita esse ponite, vaticinio mentis confisi, mentis eius quam Philebus[8] spreverat, quae certe voluptati praestat ex eo maximo quod, ut nunc cernitis, mentis ipsius vi ac lumine et de mente et de voluptate consultamus. Lumine autem voluptatis, quae ipsa caeca est, nam et appetitio caeca, neque de voluptate neque de sapientia

---

[1]ponendam *W*   [2]qq° *W;* a quo *XY*   [3]ergo *Y*   [4]quod ad *Y*   [5]*W and X read* quasi
expetendissimam   [6]si si *W*   [7]credis *W*   [8]Philebi *W*

intelligence excels pleasure when it so judges pleasure that it isn't judged by pleasure at all?''

After this Protarchus accepted Socrates' first conclusion (derived from the first comparison), namely, that neither pleasure nor the intelligence is the good itself. He says pleasure has fallen, struck down by Socrates' **arrows**, that is, by reasons, and is now so prostrate it can no longer contend for the **first prize** among the goods; for pleasure surrenders and lies vanquished. But in the judgement of those who know, the intelligence won't lay claim to the first victory either, since, if it tried to, the same things can be objected to it as to pleasure, namely, it is insufficient in itself and imperfect. (I am referring to the human intelligence, which is part of the soul.) Granted this, Protarchus encourages Socrates to pursue the other comparison, that is, the one where Socrates shows which one is the better (especially since he is going to demonstrate pleasure is inferior). Protarchus says, "This will benefit men's life. For, since people value pleasure most highly, they're caught by it, like fishes by a hook,[177] and they sink into vices. 'For the snake lies hidden in the grass.'[178] If you can show she occupies the lowest place among good things, men will despise her, and live more temperately and justly. If she's deprived of the **second prize** as well, the men who now love her because they think her a wonderful thing will despise her because they'll see she is ignoble." But Socrates, before entering the argument, warns us we ought to strive for victory as modestly as possible, so that we should study to defeat the adversary rather than extinguish him. For it is proper to human beings to search for the highest good without destroying another. And so Socrates pretended he thought Protarchus had said those things in order to frighten him away from the contest, so that he wouldn't offend the many followers of pleasure. Socrates said, "Is it not better then to let pleasure go, and not **pain** her with an exacting scrutiny?" Protarchus said, "Nonsense!" Again, as he usually does, Socrates pretended not to understand. So he said, "Perhaps you're censuring me, because I talked about **paining pleasure**, which is an impossibility. For contraries don't admit each other,

23A

23B

quaerimus. Quis igitur dubitet quin mens voluptati excellat, quae ita eam iudicat ut ab ea minime iudicetur?

Acceptavit posthaec Protarchus conclusionem Socratis primam prima illa ex[1] comparatione inductam, scilicet quod neque voluptas ipsum bonum est, neque mens, dicens quod voluptas Socratis **iaculis**, id est, rationibus, percussa concidit et prostrata est usque adeo ut de **palma prima** bonorum non ultra contendat. Succumbit enim et iacet. Sed neque mens, eorum iudicio qui sapiunt, sibi primam victoriam vendicabit,[2] quia, si id temptet, eadem sibi obicientur quae voluptati, scilicet, quod insufficiens per se sit et imperfecta. Mentem [*392v*] humanam dico quae pars animae est. His acceptis Socratem ad comparationem alteram exhortatur, scilicet in qua ostendit[3] quid ex his melius sit, praesertim cum ostensurus sit voluptatem esse inferiorem. Proderit sane[4] hoc hominum vitae. Nam quia voluptatem plurimi faciunt, ab ea capiuntur tamquam pisces ab hamo, et in vitia delabuntur. Nam latet anguis in herba. Quam, si ostenderis in bonis locum infimum obtinere, contemnent temperatioresque et iustiores vivent. Ideo dixit, si etiam **secundis** privetur[5] **honoribus**, homines qui nunc eam amant, quia rem praeclaram existimant, contemnent, quia esse ignobilem recognoscent. Socrates vero, antequam hanc discussionem ingrediatur, admonet nos quam modesti in victoriae contentione esse debeamus, ut vincere studeamus adversarium potius quam extinguere. Humanitatis enim est bonum summum[6] sine alterius interitu quaerere. Ideoque dissimulavit quasi suspicaretur Protarchum ea dixisse ut eum a pugna absterreret, ne multos voluptatis sectatores offenderet. Praestatne, inquit, eam dimittere, neque exacta redargutione **affligere**? Id quidem Protarchus renuit. Dissimulavit rursus more suo Socrates, quasi non intelligeret. Ait ergo, Reprehendis me forte, quod **affligi voluptatem** dixi,

---

[1]ex *om. W*   [2]iudicabit *W*   [3]ostendat *WX*   [4]quippe *WX*   [5]priventur *W*
[6]suum *WX*

because, when one draws near, the other either immediately perishes or goes away. Therefore, where pain is, pleasure is absent. But I didn't mean pleasure is pained, but that her followers are." Why did Socrates pretend all this? It was in order to seem kinder to them; in order to seem to be entering on the final struggle unwillingly; in order to avoid their envy and capture their good will. (He advises us to make sure of doing the same.) So Protarchus recalled Socrates, who was in a way making off. Protarchus said, "It wasn't only because of your argument I said you were talking nonsense, but also because you seem to be ignoring the fact that we aren't going to let you go until you've proved all this rationally, not just left it with us on trust." Here Plato is instructing young men in the attitude with which they ought to inquire into, pray for and extract the learning of their seniors. So Socrates does not approach the contest willingly, but provoked in a way, as is proper; for he was beseeched to start with, then coerced. (He is not coerced when he teaches, but he is coerced when he gives offence.) Therefore at the beginning he wins their indulgence and makes them attentive, when he says the following discussion will be particularly full and must be pursued by a new approach (as it isn't easy to resolve using the present reasoning). They need other reasons and other weapons to win a favourable victory for the intelligence and wisdom. This is because, in order to make the comparison between wisdom and pleasure, first you have to have defined each one and each one's genus and discovered the difference, and also distributed each one into its parts. The more such knowledge is distinct from the knowledge you had first, the more diligent an examination it needs. Therefore Socrates says they need new stratagems, although among those we've already mentioned there are some which will do again: for instance, the idea that the intelligence is more like the third good thing, and what was said about the finite and the infinite. These are things he has touched on above and they will have to be discussed in what's to follow so that the genus of wisdom and the genus of pleasure can be tracked down. Therefore, having asked for indulgence because of the difficulty of

quod impossibile est; contraria enim se invicem non recipiunt, uno enim accedente, statim alterum vel interit vel discedit. Ubi ergo afflictio est, voluptas abest. Ego vero non affligi voluptatem, sed eius sectatores intelligebam. Cur haec dissimulat Socrates? Ut mitior his appareat, ut ad extremum certamen invitus descendere videatur, ut invidiam [*393r*] vitet, captet benevolentiam. Ita certe nos facere monet. Revocavit ergo Protarchus Socratem quodammodo fugientem, dicens, Non ob id tantum te nihil dicere asserebam, sed etiam quia ignorare videris nos te non antea dimissuros quam ista ratione non fide declares. Ubi iuvenes admonentur quanto oportet affectu doctrinam seniorum exquirant, exorent, extorqueant. Accedit ergo Socrates ad eam pugnam non sponte, sed ut decet, quodammodo lacessitus, exoratus enim primo deinde coactus. Non coactus docet, sed coactus offendit. Captat ergo veniam imprimis et attentos reddit, dum dicit confertissimam esse sequentem disputationem et nova quadam via peragendam, quia[1] non facile sit per praesentem rationem eam transigere, sed aliis opus sit rationibus et iaculis ad victoriam secundam menti et sapientiae vendicandam. Quia scilicet ad comparationem sapientiae et voluptatis inter se faciendam, opus est definisse[2] utrumque prius et genus utriusque et differentiam invenisse, in partes quin etiam distribuisse suas utrumque. Quae quidem cognitio quo distinctior est quam prima eo diligentiori examine indiget. Ideo dicit novis esse opus machinamentis, quamquam inter ea quae iam diximus nonnulla sunt quae ad futuru conducant: ut quod dictum[3] est mentem similiorem bono tertio, et finitum et infinitum. Quae in superioribus tetigit, quae et in sequentibus ad genus sapientiae et voluptatis investigandum discutienda sunt. Statim ergo petita venia ex rerum difficultate, capta

---

[1] qui *W*   [2] defuisse *W*   [3] *for* quod dictum *W reads* addictam

everything, having caught their attention because of the novelty and variety of the argument, and having made them willing to listen mainly because he had said some of the present and past ideas will do again, Socrates added, "So, there still has to be a
23C   fight, does there?" Protarchus says nothing can prevent it. Socrates warned them on the spot they would have to show great care in establishing the principles of each thing, since the way everything else follows is derived from them. What seem to be trifling deviations in the small and narrow beginning are multiplied in the course of the many, broad intermediary steps. For instance, at the crossroads you go wrong by just a small distance, then the more you proceed the greater the deviation. So Socrates says, "While we're laying the foundations of this argument, let's take great care to accept only the good things, to use the greatest caution in sorting out the things we introduce, and to distinguish everything very clearly."

Chapter 34. The ultimate end has to be some one simple thing. How it is put into a compound made from the understanding and pleasure. The conditions which make this compound blessed. Also, the reason why the understanding excels pleasure.

Before we come to the fifth part of the book, we must think about some of the things discussed above. Plato seems to be putting the ultimate end of life in wisdom and pleasure together. This is what he seems to argue from what precedes and to conclude from what follows. But the end has to be one thing, not many things. Were there two ends, either each would move the appetite equally, or unequally. If unequally, the one which moves more is the end, the other one contributes to the end. If equally, the appetite is similarly and equally drawn towards them both. This similar and equal response is the result of the similar and equal nature of the person desiring. But a similar and equal nature hurries towards what is similar and equal. So things are not equally desired in so far as they are

attentione ex novitate et varietate sermonis, et docilitate incepta per hoc maxime quod ait aliqua ex praesentibus et praeteritis ad futura conferre, adiecit, Nonne ergo iam pugnandum. Nihil prohibet ait ille. Monuit [*393v*] Socrates illico quanta sit cuiusque rei principiis diligentia adhibenda, cum ex eis omnium sequentium trahatur conditio, et quae minima in exiguo et angusto principio videntur esse delicta, in plurimis et latis mediis propagentur. Ut error in bivio parvo distat intervallo, eo deinde distat magis quo ultra proceditur. Ideo, inquit, dum sermonis huius fundamenta iaciemus, omni studio annitamur ut bene accipiamus et maxima cautione quod inducimus discernamus et plane admodum distinguamus.[1]

Finis ultimus unum aliquid et simplex esse debet, et quomodo ponatur in composito quodam ex intelligentia et voluptate, et quae conditiones compositum hoc beatum faciant. Item qua ratione intelligentia superet voluptatem. Cap. XXXIIII.[2]

Antequam ad quintam libri partem veniamus, quaedam ex superioribus discutienda censemus. Plato finem vitae ultimum sapientiam et voluptatem simul ponere videtur, ut ex superioribus significare et sequentibus videtur concludere. Finis autem unum quiddam esse debet non plura. Sint duo, aut aeque appetitum movet utrumque, aut non aeque. Si non aeque, illud unum quod magis movet finis est, aliud est ad finem. Si aeque, similiter pariterque ad utrumque afficitur appetitus. Affectus iste par et similis a pari et simili natura est appetentis ipsius. Par autem similisque natura ad par et simile rapit. Non igitur quantum[3] diversa sunt appetuntur aeque, sed quantum[4] una quaedam

---

[1] διευλαβεῖσθαι significat: bene cauteque accipere et distinguere componitur enim ex

εὖ διὰ λαμβάνω. *add X*   [2]*a break but no ch. heading W; in X ch. is numbered twenty*
[3],[4]inquantum *WX*

different, but in so far as there's some one nature they share in common through which they are similar and equal and demanded in a similar and equal way. So what's being demanded is one thing. So there's one end. Moreover, each one thing seeks as an end that which contains its entire good. Therefore, if each thing looks for two things, its entire good must be contained in them. So either of the two things has either the whole good, or just a part. If either of them has the whole good, one of them is enough; and since every first movement begins initially for the sake of the one, it looks for nothing further when it arrives at the one. If either of the two ends has a part of the good, there won't be two ends, but one end which is the result of them both. Again, the person desiring them either decides the two things are equally good, or he decides they are unequally good. If unequally, the one he decides is the better he'll desire more vehemently. But that one will be the end. If equally, he'll either decide they are equally good in so far as they differ, or in so far as they agree. It will not be in so far as they differ, for difference does away with equality. (It is agreement in a nature and power which produces equality.) Therefore he decides they are equally good in so far as they agree. If they agree, they agree over some one nature and power. Because of it, both are equally good. Therefore the appetite looks for one thing. For just as there is one outstanding part and one being to each thing, although it is made from many parts, so there is one outstanding power. Also there's one outstanding appetite, one outstanding result. Therefore there's one outstanding end towards which the one movement of [its] one being and nature is directed. Moreover, every single thing seeks as its end its own perfection. But of [its] one being there is a certain one perfection. Therefore it desires one end. For though it seeks many other things, it reduces them to this one perfection. So this is their one end.

As the end of each thing has to be one, just as the beginning has to be one too, man's end has to be one. Therefore, how can it be two, pleasure and wisdom? These two aren't the end if they're separate, because neither is sufficient. But when they are

natura communis est in[1] utrisque per quam paria et similia sunt et pariter similiterque petuntur. Unum ergo est quod quaeritur. Unus itaque finis. Praeterea unumquodque ut finem petit quod totum suum continet bonum. Si ergo duo petit, oportet in[2] eis[3] totum illius contineri bonum. Aut ergo quodvis illorum totum habet, aut quodvis partem. Si quodvis totum, unum sat est; et quia omnis primus [*394r*] motus ad unum primo incipit, cum ad unum pervenerit, nihil quaeret ulterius. Si quodvis partem, non duo fines erunt, sed unum quod ex utrisque resultat. Item aut aeque bona illa duo iudicat qui appetit, aut non aeque. Si non, quod melius iudicat vehementius appetit. Illud autem erit finis. Si aeque, aut quantum[4] differunt iudicat aeque bona, aut quantum[5] conveniunt.[6] Non quantum[7] differunt, differentia enim aequalitatem tollit; convenientia[8] in natura et potestate praestat aequalitatem. Ergo quantum[9] conveniunt aeque iudicat bona. Si conveniunt, in una quadam natura et potestate conveniunt, per quam utraque aeque sunt bona. Unum igitur quiddam appetitio quaerit. Nam sicut cuiusque rei, quamquam ex pluribus constitutae, una pars est praecipua et unum esse, ita vis una praecipua. Una quoque praecipua appetitio, unum opus praecipuum; unus ergo finis praecipuus quo unius[10] esse et naturae motus dirigitur unus. Praeterea unumquodque ut finem sui ipsius perfectionem expetit. Unius autem esse una quaedam perfectio est. Unum igitur appetit finem. Nam etsi multa quaerit alia, ad unam hanc reducit perfectionem. Haec itaque ceterorum unus est finis.

Cum igitur cuiusque rei finis unus esse debeat, sicut et principium unum, necesse est ut hominis unus sit finis. Quo pacto igitur duo? Voluptas et sapientia. Non duo haec finis sunt, si seiuncta sunt, quia neutrum sufficit, sed cum coniuncta unum

---

[1]in *om. W*   [2]in *om. X*   [3]eis *om. X;* eius *Y*   [4],[5],[7],[9]inquantum *WX*   [6]aeque iudicat bona *add. W*   [8]enim *add. X*   [10]unus *W*

joined they make one thing. One compound made from both of them is the end, because it is sufficient. But it's proper for one compound thing to be the end for the soul, because the soul too is one compound thing made from the power which knows and the power which desires. From the first it has its need for wisdom, from the second for pleasure. But one thing results from them, the one thing that comes from both powers. Or rather, just as the two powers are reduced to the soul's one essence which is common to them both, so wisdom and pleasure, when they've been joined together, have one thing in common. Because of it each is good and both are the good and the end for man. Accordingly, the one compound is the end because of the one which is in the compound. Or rather, there is one thing in the compound and because of it the compound is called "the end" and "the good." It is the sufficient and outstanding "end" and it is man's "good."

What is this one thing? It isn't wisdom, because if the whole compound were good because of wisdom, the whole power and rational principle of the good would dwell in wisdom. In that case wisdom would be sufficient by itself. For the same reason it isn't pleasure. It isn't both together, because each one would either contribute the whole good, or each would separately contribute part of the good. If each contributes the whole good, one of them is enough. If each one separately contributes part of the good and therefore contributes to the one good, either they contribute to that one good in so far as they differ, or in so far as they agree. In so far as they differ, they don't contribute to one thing, but to different things. Therefore, when they agree over one thing, they contribute to one thing. Therefore there is some one thing in them both and through its power they work for the one good of man. The one thing whose power brings this about is more outstanding than either of them and more outstanding than both together; and it is the one end of the one soul.

But above this one thing, which is in the compound and in something else, is the one which is the simplest of all things and above them all. The one thing in the compound derives from it. The one which is above all is called both the one itself and act

faciunt. Unum ex utrisque compositum finis est, quia
*sufficiens. Merito autem animae unum compositum finis est,
quia** et ipsa unum quiddam compositum est ex ea quae
cognoscit potentia, atque ea quae appetit. Ex illa sapientiam
postulat, ex alia voluptatem, sed ex his unum fit, ut ex utraque
potentia unum. [*394v*] Immo vero quemadmodum duae potentiae ad unam animae essentiam reducuntur utrisque communem, ita sapientia et voluptas invicem iuncta[1] unum quiddam
habent commune ratione cuius utrumque bonum est, et ambo
ipsum bonum hominis atque finis. Unum itaque compositum
finis gratia unius quod in composito est. Immo illud unum in
composito potius per quod compositum dicitur finis et bonum
et sufficiens finis praecipuus est et hominis bonum.

Quid unum hoc? Non sapientia, quia si ratione eius totum
hoc esset bonum, tota vis in ea boni ratioque consisteret. Ipsa
ergo sola sufficcret. Non etiam voluptas hac eadem ratione.
Non utrumque simul, quia vel quaeque totum praestant bonum,
vel singula boni partem. Si quaeque totum, unum sat est. Si
singula partem boni, atque ita ad unum conducunt bonum, aut
quantum differunt ad id unum conferunt, aut quantum[2] conveniunt. In quantum differunt non ad unum sed ad diversa con-
ducerent. Ad unum ergo conferunt, ut in uno conveniunt.
Unum igitur quiddam est in[3] utrisque cuius unius vi ad[4] unum
hominis bonum perducunt. Unum illud, cuius vi istud efficitur,
praestantius est utrisque, praestantius est ambobus, unusque est
animae unius finis.

Sed et super hoc unum quod in composito est et in alio est
unum quod simplicissimum et super omnia, a quo et unum hoc
quod est in composito manat. Unum quod super omnia et unum
ipsum et ipse actus dicitur, ut alias disputavimus. Unum igitur
actum huic composito praebet; a primo bono secundum bonum.

---

[1]cuncta *W*   [2]inquantum *WX*   [3]in *om. W*   [4]id *W*   *-**om. W*

itself, as we've argued elsewhere. So it gives one act to the compound. From the first good derives the second good. This one gift of God is our good. The habitation and the temple where we receive and preserve the gift is the mixture from wisdom and pleasure. The temple's foundations are the intellect and the will. For we can't seize hold of the highest good except with the highest part of ourselves.

The highest part is a certain unity, the crown of the soul, and this, the soul's head, is lifted by two wings and flies to the one good itself. For it explores and looks around with the intellect and searches out with the will; it seizes hold with the intellect and retains with the will. When the intellect seizes hold, it is wisdom, that is, understanding; when the will clings on, it is pleasure. The ultimate end always corresponds to the first mover, because what moves moves for its own sake. For victory corresponds to the general; the intermediary steps between the general and victory correspond to his subordinates. For the end for every single thing subsequent to the general is some limited objective; for the general the end is the ultimate end perfected through the limited objectives. However, the first thing is what moves the soul towards the one good. That unity is the soul's "head." For in the *Phaedrus* it is written:

"The souls which were about to be blessed raised their head to the heavens." Plato also refers to it as the "charioteer" when he says:

"The charioteer, when he's stopped the horses at the stable, throws them ambrosia and also potable nectar."[179] For the soul's crown, which at first spurred the intellect and the will towards the good, having attained it, arrests the intellect's pursuit and the will's ardour; that is, it no longer moves them. It stops them so they don't depart from it (for lightness drew fire upwards and detains it in the upper regions) and throws ambrosia to the intellect, that is, sight, and nectar to the will, that is, joy. It isn't because the soul's unity can initially see or rejoice, for it is above the understanding and the will, but because it was the first to move them and the mover is the one which secures and restrains the moved. What is the good of the soul's unity? It's to

Hoc unum Dei munus bonum nostrum est. Habitaculum et templum in quo id recipimus et servamus mixtum ex sapientia [*395r*] et voluptate.[1] Fundamenta huius templi intellectus et voluntas. Supremum enim bonum capere, nisi suprema nostri parte, non possumus.

Suprema pars est unitas[2] quaedam, apex animae, quod animae caput duabus alis ad unum ipsum bonum instigatur et advolat. Nam intellectu explorat atque circumspicit, voluntate petit; intellectu rapit, retinet voluntate. Raptus intellectus sapientia, id est, intelligentia est; adhaesio voluntatis est voluptas. Semper primo moventi ultimus respondet finis, quia quod movet sui gratia movet. Duci enim respondet victoria; aliis agentibus[3] media quae inter ducem et victoriam sunt. Unicuique enim sequentium certum opus finis est, principi[4] ultimum quod per opera illa perficitur. Primum autem quod ad bonum unum movet animam. Unitas illa eius caput est. Nam in Phaedro dicitur:

Animae quae beatae futurae sunt supra coelum extulerunt caput. Quem etiam[5] aurigam vocat cum dicit:

Auriga ad praesepe sistens equos obicit illis ambrosiam et super ipsam nectar potandum. Nam apex animae, qui primo ad bonum intellectum instigavit calcaribus et voluntatem, eo accepto, intellectus indaginem sistit et voluntatis ardorem, id est, non movet amplius, sed retinet, ne inde discedant. Levitas enim ignem sursum traxit, et ignem in superioribus detinet et obicit intellectui ambrosiam, id est, visionem, voluntati nectar, id est, gaudium. Non quia unitas illa primo videat aut gaudeat, est enim super intelligentiam et voluntatem, sed quia primo movit et quae movit firmat et cohibet. Quid huius unitatis bonum? Ut primo uno formetur, ut aer lumine, igne ferrum.

---

[1] et voluptate *om. W*   [2] unita *Y*   [3] inter *add. WX*   [4] principii *Y*   [5] et *WX*

be formed by the first one, like air by light, iron by fire. But the unity is formed by the one, when it has formed the intellect and the will, and converted them from their diversion towards lower things to higher things, and united them to itself. When this conversion has been completed in so far as it is humanly possible, the intellect is formed by vision and the will by pleasure. After they've been formed, at last the unity, since it's no longer impeded, will plunge itself into the first one absolutely. The unity's good will be to become the one itself. But the intellect's and the will's good will be to become the one act for the one's sake.

Three ends or happinesses become apparent here. The first is when through the impulse of the charioteer the soul enjoys wisdom and pleasure, having been converted through the intelligence and will towards higher things, in so far as it can attain them while it is still busy ruling the body. The second is when, having relinquished the body, the soul directs every intention towards the intelligence. Here the understanding is entire and its entirety is inner pleasure. The third follows it instantly. It is the fashioning of the unity itself by the one. The first sort of happiness is human and pertains to the soul as soul. The second sort is divine and pertains to the intelligence, and to the soul when it's been transformed into the intelligence. The third sort is [to be] a god, for where God's form is, there God dwells. Plato talks about the last two sorts of happiness in the *Phaedrus*.[180] In this dialogue he enlarges on the first sort, the human happiness, which, by virtue of the fact that it's human, consists in a compound made from understanding and pleasure in the intellect and the will. But this doesn't happen until the elements have been first joined together in the best possible way. For the good doesn't dwell in a mass of things badly put together.

Chapter 35. How three things are necessary for the happy mixture of wisdom and pleasure: truth, proportion, beauty.

However, for two things to be well mixed together there are three particularly necessary things. This is so they may desire

Formatur autem uno, cum ipsa intellectum [*395v*] voluntatemque formaverit, haecque ad inferiora diversa ad superna converterit et ea secum univerit. Qua quidem conversione, quoad homini possibile est, peracta, intellectus visione formatur, voluptate voluntas. Quibus formatis tandem unitas, utpote non amplius impedita, in unum primum se prorsus immerget; eritque huius unitatis bonum unum ipsum fieri. Intellectus autem et voluntatis bonum unus actus ad unum.

Hic tres fines beatitudinesque elucent. Primus est quando anima aurigae ipsius instinctu, mente et voluntate conversa ad supera, quatenus dum regendo corpori occupatur assequi potest, sapientia et voluptate fruitur. Secundus cum relicto corpore omnem intentionem in mentem direxerit, ubi intelligentia illa integra est, cuius integritas interior est voluptas. Tertius post hanc e vestigio sequitur: unitatis ipsius ab uno formatio. Prima humana est et animae quantum[1] anima est; secunda divina et mentis est et animae, cum mens erit effecta;[2] tertia deus quidam est, ubi enim Dei forma, ibi est Deus. Has duas in Phaedro exponit Plato. Hoc in libro primam illam atque humanam, quae, quoniam humana est, in composito quodam ex intelligentia et voluptate in intellectu et voluntate consistit. Neque in hoc est prius quam optime iuncta fuerint. Neque enim bonum est in congerie male disposita.

Quomodo ad felicem sapientiae voluptatisque mixturam tria necessaria sint: veritas, commensuratio, pulchritudo. Cap. XXXV.[3]

Ut autem duo aliqua bene invicem misceantur, tria maxime exiguntur, ut gratia quadam naturae mutuo sese appetant, ut

---

[1] inquantum *WX*   [2] affecta *X*   [3] *no ch. break or heading WX*

each other by a natural grace like heat and a dense liquid. For heat and cold avoid each other because they aren't mutually pleasing. And it isn't enough for them to gladly seek each other. They must be glad to the extent that they can mutually penetrate each other. For example, the heat in iron and the wetness in gold don't mix together; they have to be thin and pure so they can flow together into one. And this purity and natural grace isn't enough, unless they've been brought together in the right quantities and are mutually adjusted to each other. For, if you wanted to mix the hottest of heats with a small drop of a dense liquid, there would be no mixture; for the heat will immediately evaporate the liquid. If you try to do the reverse, the liquid will immediately extinguish the heat. So they have to be mutually adjusted in weight and power, so the things which have admitted each other through grace, and freely and easily come together through purity, can become absolutely equal to each other through moderation and remain together without the threat of being separated. Nature's grace is the inner beauty through which all things attract each other and by whose power Zoroaster wanted works of magic performed. Plato agreed. Each thing's purity is each thing's truth, for each thing's pure and entire nature is its truth. So Plato says in the *Laws* Book 5, Ἀλήθεια δὴ πάντων μὲν ἀγαθ ῶν θεοῖς ἡγεῖται πάντων δὲ ἀνθρώποις — Truth is the leader of all good things among gods and men.[181] So he says in the *Phaedrus,* οὔτ ἐν ἀνθρώποις. οὔτε θεοῖς τῆς ἀληθείας τιμιώτερον οὔτε ἔστω οὔτε ποτὲ ἔσται — Among men and gods nothing is more venerable than the truth.[182] Plato's wonderful love for the truth appears here, because he expresses it in poetry in both passages. But purity and entirety are the same thing. A pure quality, which isn't restrained by any impediment, surely exercises its full power. But mutual moderation among things is called proportion. At the end of this dialogue, therefore, Plato is right to require three things for the best mixture: **truth, proportion, beauty.** For things that are pure moderately and amicably and eagerly seek each other; they easily agree together; they firmly cling together. When such things have been joined, because the parts are true, the whole is true too.

calor et pinguis humor; nam[1] calor et frigus sese invicem fugiunt, quia grata sibi invicem non sunt. Neque [*396r*] sufficit ut se libenter petant, nisi adeo expedita sint, ut sese invicem valeant penetrare. Calor enim in ferro et humor in auro invicem non miscentur; tenuia sint[2] haec oportet et pura, ut in unum conflentur. Neque satis est puritas haec et gratia illa naturae, nisi quantitate moderata, sibique vicissim consona sint. Nam, si intentissimum caloris aestum exiguae pinguis humoris guttae miscere volueris, mixtio nulla fiet, subito namque aestus humorem resolvet; sin contra, protinus calorem humor extinguet. Sint ergo competenti vi et pondere moderata oportet, ut quae per gratiam sese adsciverunt[3] et per puritatem expedite et facile congressa sunt per moderationem sese penitus aequent atque una procul a dissolutione permaneant. Naturae gratia interior pulchritudo est, qua sese adliciunt omnia, cuius vi magicae opera exerceri Zoroaster voluit et Plato probavit. Puritas cuiusque cuiusque[4] est veritas, mera enim et integra sui natura cuiusque veritas est. Ideo in quinto Legum dicit Plato, Ἀλήθεια δὴ πάντων μὲν ἀγαθῶν θεοῖς ἡγεῖται πάντων δὲ ἀνθρώποις.[5] Veritas tum diis tum hominibus bonorum omnium dux est.[6] Itaque et[7] in Phaedro, οὔτ ἐν ἀνθρώποις οὔτε θεοῖς τῆς ἀληθείας τιμιώτερον οὔτε ἔστω οὔτε ποτὲ ἔσται.[8] Veritate nihil venerabilius est apud deos et apud homines. Ubi apparet mirus amor Platonis in veritatem quod utrobique cam expressit carmine. Idem autem merum est et integrum. Nempe mera qualitas, nullo impedimento detenta, totam vim suam exercet. Moderatio autem rerum inter se mutua commensuratio nuncupatur. Merito igitur in fine huius dialogi tria ad optimam mixtionem Plato requirit: **veritatem, commensurationem, pulchritudinem.** Purae[9] enim res moderate [*396v*] invicem et amice et se avide petunt; congrediuntur[10] facile; firmiterque cohaerent. Quibus iunctis, quia verae partes sunt, verum est et totum; quia moderatae, consonum et concinnum;[11]

---

[1]nec *WX*   [2]sunt *W*   [3]adsciverint *X*   [4]cuiusque *om. W*   [5,8]*Greek om. W*
[6]est *om. Y*   [7]et *om. X*   [9]verae *X*   [10]congredientur *W*   [11]consonum *and*
concinnum *are written as alternatives X*

And because they are moderated, the whole is harmonious and in proportion. Because it's harmonious, it's comely and beautiful. So our good will consist in the mixture made from wisdom, i.e., understanding, and from pleasure, at the time when they are mixed in the best possible way. They will be mixed together best at the time when they are true, in proportion and beautiful, and the mixture they make is true, in proportion and beautiful. Therefore because of truth, proportion and beauty the compound is the good. So truth, proportion and beauty are the good for man. For to join together true wisdom, that is, the wisdom that is certain, entire and universal, with true pleasure, that is, the pleasure that is pure and unmixed with contraries, it is necessary for them to be also in proportion. The result is only those pleasures can be accepted which can have some connection with wisdom. And the wisdom and the pleasure which should be bound together are those which are in turn eager for and agreeable to each other. Here the mixture will be true because of the truth, and congruent because of proportion, and comely because of beauty.

Plato calls this mixture not properly the good, but the good's **home**. Also, the three things in the mixture aren't the good, but the good's **vestibule**. Our good he calls in actual fact the one power, the one act, which is given by the highest good itself to the three. Because of the one act they are first of all true, in proportion and beautiful; secondly, they come together and in this coming together again you can see truth, proportion and beauty. Therefore there is one end, not many.

Chapter 36. The manner in which God is called the measure, the moderator, the suitable.

Plato signifies the highest good itself, the one principle of things, by three terms: **the measure, the moderator, the suitable.** As **the measure** it gives the truth to all things; as **the moderator** it gives proportion; as **the suitable** it gives beauty. The one itself is called **the measure**. It is also called this in the *Laws* Book 4,[183]

quia consonum, decorum et pulchrum. Tunc igitur in mixtione ex sapientia, id est, intelligentia et voluptate bonum nostrum consistet cum optime mixta erunt. Tunc erunt optime iuncta, cum[1] vera erunt, commensurata, pulchra, eorumque commixtio vera, commensurata, pulchraque existet. Ratione igitur veritatis, commensurationis, et pulchritudinis compositum illud bonum est. Veritas itaque, commensuratio, pulchritudo hominis est bonum. Iungenda enim sapientia vera, id est, certa, integra, universa, cum voluptate vera, id est, pura, contrariis non permixta, commensurata sint etiam necesse est. Ut illae dumtaxat voluptates accipiantur quae commercium habere cum sapientia possunt, et sapientia et voluptas[2] illae invicem vinciendae quae sui vicissim avidae sunt et gratae; ubi et per veritatem vera erit mixtio, et per commensurationem congrua, et decora per pulchritudinem.

Hoc mixtum non bonum proprie, sed boni **domum** Plato nuncupat. Tria illa quoque in mixto non bonum, sed boni **vestibulum.** Bonum vero nostrum vocat proprie vim unam, actum unum ab ipso summo bono his tributum, per quem primo vera sunt, commensurata, pulchra; deinde congrediuntur et in congressu rursus veritas, commensuratio, pulchritudoque elucet. Unus ergo finis est non plures.

Quomodo Deus appellatur mensura, moderans, opportunum. Cap. XXXVI.[3]

Ipsum quidem summum bonum et unum rerum principium tribus nominibus Plato significat: **mensura, moderans, opportunum.** Ut **mensura** rebus omnibus tribuit [*397r*] veritatem; ut **moderans** commensurationem; ut **opportunum** pulchritudinem. Dicitur **mensura** ipsum unum, ut in quarto Legum etiam dicitur,

---

[1]cum *om. W*   [2]et voluptas *om. X*   [3]*no ch. break or heading WX*

because God is for us the greatest measure of all things—
because, that is, He measures the ascent and the descent of all
things. For you can go up to Him, but you can't go higher; and
the gradations of nature go down as far as His power extends,
to diffused external things, but no lower. Again, He measures
the power and the worth of everything. For everything is worth
as much as that which imparts it. He is the measure making all
things equal according as His presence fills all things. As He
exceeds all things, He is the measure embracing all things.
Again, He measures the movement of single things. He
measures their going forth, because they proceed no further
than from Him, and their turning back, because they are turned
back no further than to Him. Again, He is also the measure of
comparison. For in the same way as we decide about secondary
hot or bright things by looking back to the first thing that is hot
or bright, so we measure all things by Him when we compare all
good things to the first good thing. Consequently, things are
said to be better the nearer they are to Him and worse the
further they are away from Him. He is also the measure of
repetition. For what is compound and divisible doesn't measure
what is simple and indivisible; for, if they are brought together,
the compound either equates the whole of the simple thing with
its whole self, or with a bit of itself. If with its whole self, the
thing we've called simple would also be compound. But if with
a bit [or point] of itself—for we equate one point with another
point—, what is being measured is indivisible, hence the measure is simple too. Therefore a compound can't be the measure
of a simple thing. But by repeating itself the simple thing can be
the measure of the compound. The point can be the measure of
corporeal magnitude, for it surrounds objects on the outside
and penetrates through them all. But the moment of time terminates the past, inaugurates the future, manifests the present and
brings about the whole of time by its repetition. Just as the
point becomes equal by its repetition to the total mass of a corporeal object, so eternity does to all the moments of time. For
the point of eternity, in remaining single, views all the hastening
moments of time from the viewpoint of the present, as the

quod Deus nobis rerum omnium maxime est mensura, quia
scilicet ascensum rerum omnium et descensum metitur. Usque
enim ad ipsum ascenditur, supra nequaquam; et quatenus se
porrigit vis eius ad exteriora diffusa eatenus graduum naturae
descensus, infra autem minime. Item vim cuiusque rei pretium-
que metitur, tanti enim est quodcumque quanti est quod ipsum
impertit. Est mensura adaequans omnia prout praesentia sua
implet omnia. Est mensura complectens omnia, ut[1,2] omnia
supereminet. Item motum singulorum ipsum metitur, processum quidem, quia non altius quam ab eo procedunt, conversionem autem, quia non ulterius quam ad ipsum convertuntur.
Est et comparationis mensura, ut enim ad primum calidum et
primum lucidum respicientes de secundis calidis lucidisque sententiam ferimus, sic ad primum bonum bona omnia comparan-
tes eo ita metimur omnia, ut quo propinquiora illi sunt eo
meliora dicantur, quo remotiora ab illo eo deteriora. Est et
replicationis mensura. Quod enim compositum est et partibile
id quod est simplex et impartibile non metitur. Nam invicem
admoveantur, aut compositum se toto adaequat simplex totum,
aut puncto sui. Si se toto, compositum esset et id quod simplex
dicimus. Sin puncto sui, puncto enim punctum adaequamus,
impartibile est quod metitur ergo et simplex est mensura. Ideo
compositum simplicis mensura esse non potest. Simplex autem
compositi [*397v*] potest replicatione sui esse mensura. Punctum quidem magnitudinis corporum, nam et exterius corpora
circumscribit et per omnia penetrat. Momentum autem
temporis praeteritum[3] quidem terminat, futurum inchoat, praesens ostendit et sui replicatione totum efficit tempus. Quemadmodum punctum replicatione sui totam corporis molem adaequat, aeternitas omnium temporalium momentorum. Nam unicum aeternitatis punctum permanens omnia temporis momenta

---

[1]prout *WX*   [2]praesentia sua implet *add. X*   [3]praesertim *W*

unchanging centre views the points of a moving line. Moreover, the monad does the same for all numbers. For a number is nothing else but the repetition of the monad. What's ten? The monad repeated ten times. So the monad reckons all numbers. Therefore, since the one is the most simple of all things and is unchanging and supreme, [the following happens]. Because it is supreme, it encompasses all things. Because it is unchanging, it begins and ends and decides on the movements of all things; for every movement is discerned when it has been compared to some unchanging thing. Because it is the one, it fulfils and contains all the multitude of different things. Because it is the most simple, it measures all other things and isn't measured by other things. And by its repetition it perfects the nature of compounds; for every single thing possesses as many parts and powers as it participates in the modes of the one God Himself. Therefore God is the measure of all things. He is measured by nothing. He isn't the measure peculiar to this thing or to that thing, so He is the measure which is equally appropriate to all things because He is above all things. As a measure He is neither big nor small: if He were small, He would not fill big things; if He were big, He would not agree with small things. God is also the measure of limitation. For He establishes for single things by a fixed law the limits of substance, power, action, value and life. These limits it is impossible to transgress. He arranges everything by distinct grades, in a fixed number and ordered series, and imparts to each according to its natural capacity or merited worth. He determines matter with form, nature with seeds, the soul with reasons, the intelligence with Ideas, and, finally, all things with Himself. Therefore we've said enough about the way in which God is the measure.

He is also **the moderator.** The job of measuring is more absolute, whereas the job of moderating consists in bringing things together. For He is the measure according as He gives to each thing a fixed, appropriate and determined nature and power. But natures could be present in single things so exclusively that there would be no communication between them. And so each thing would be one, but there would not be one overall result

currentia praesens aspicit, ut centrum stans lineae currentis puncta.[1] Monas insuper omnium numerorum, nihil enim aliud numerus quam monadis replicatio. Quid decem? Monas decies replicata. Omnes ergo monas computat numeros. Cum ergo ipsum unum sit omnium simplicissimum sitque permanens et supremum: quia supremum, omnia circumscribit; quia permanens, motus[2] omnium inchoat, sistit et iudicat, nam ad stabile aliquid comparatus omnis motus discernitur; quia unum, omnem diversarum rerum multitudinem implet et continet; quia simplicissimum metitur alia nec ab aliis mensuratur. Et replicatione sua naturam explet compositorum; tot enim partes totque vires possidet unumquodque quot modis Dei ipsius unius est particeps. Mensura igitur Deus est omnium a nihilo mensurata. Mensura nec huius nec illius propria ut omnium aeque mensura sit quod est super omnia. Mensura nec parva nec magna; si parva est, magna non implet; si magna parvis non congruit. Est et limitationis mensura Deus. Ipse enim singulis certa lege substantiae, potentiae, actionis, et dignitatis et [*398r*] vitae statuit limites, quos transgredi impossibile est. Omnia distinctis gradibus, certo in numero, ordinata serie digerit, et cuique pro naturae capacitate vel meriti dignitate impertit. Terminat materiam forma, naturam seminibus, animam rationibus, mentem ideis, se ipso denique omnia. Quomodo igitur Deus mensura sit satis est dictum.

[3]Est et **moderans.** Mensurae quidem opus absolutum magis, moderationis opus in collatione consistit. Prout enim cuique certam, propriam, determinatamque naturam et vim tribuit, mensura est. Possent autem ita proprie singulis inesse naturae, ut nulla esset inter illa communio, ideoque quodcumque unum

---

[1]puncta *om. Y*   [2]motum *X*   [3]*em., no paragraph break Y*

from the individual things. But the work of one God must be one. Accordingly, there has to be moderation whereby single things can be joined to single things. Because of measure the proper nature is present to the intelligence. It makes the intelligence differ from the soul. But because of moderation the power to perceive the truth is common to them both. Again, because of measure the proper nature is present to the soul. It makes the soul separate from the body's nature. But because of moderation they are joined together so that movement and life are common to them both. Moreover, with the elements you can see the power appropriate to each, and you can also see a mutual harmony whereby fire agrees with the air in heat, but differs from it in dryness. The air agrees with water in wetness, but the water differs from air in coldness. Water agrees with earth in coldness, but differs from it in wetness. Therefore to measure is to give individual determination to everything; but to moderate is to join things together in such a way that they also agree in some nature. It is to make sure one of them doesn't have so much power that it subsumes all the others. It is to make sure things mutually coexist and move and act, and in turn resist each other. But to make sure individual things agree among themselves is the job of the person who makes them, and makes them one and the one all things. Therefore God is both the measure and the moderator.

Moreover, He is **the suitable.** Suitability means a certain grace and fitness among things which makes them mutually pleasing to each other and makes them in turn admit each other. But they're mutually pleasing and eligible because they agree together in having a nature and a regulated quality in common. But He who brings this about is the one who balances all things together through moderation. For He immediately makes things mutually suited and pleasing. On this account He is called the suitable. Therefore, in so far as He is called the measure, He bestows truth on all things, which is the pure and determined nature appropriate to each thing. In so far as He is the moderator, He bestows proportion, which is the concinnity and mutual harmony of all things. In so far as He is the suitable, He

esset, ex singulis autem unum opus nequaquam efficeretur. Dei autem unius opus unum esse debet. Moderatione igitur opus est, qua singula cum singulis connectantur. Propria natura menti per mensuram inest, qua differt ab anima. Sed per moderationem vis ad veritatem percipiendam communis utrique. Item propria per mensuram animae inest natura,[1] qua a natura corporis est seiuncta. Per moderationem vero ita comparata sunt invicem ut motus et vita sit utrique communis. In elementis quin etiam vis propria cuiusque conspicitur, et mutua insuper consonantia, qua ignis in calore cum aere convenit, siccitate distinguitur. Aer cum aqua in humore consentit. Aqua ab illo frigiditate dissentit. Aqua terrae in frigore convenit, liquiditate discrepat. Metiri igitur est unumquodque in se ipso determinare. Moderari autem ita res invicem comparare ut et in aliqua natura conveniant, nec tanta vis insit in aliquo ut reliqua adsumat omnia, sed [*398v*] invicem simul sint, moveantur, agant, vicissimque resistant. Facere autem ut singula inter se conveniant, illius est qui singula facit et qui singula facit[2] unum et unum omnia. Deus ergo et mensura est et moderans.

Est insuper **opportunum.** Opportunitas gratiam quandam et commoditatem rerum significat, qua sibi invicem mutuo placent seque vicissim adsciscunt. Quod autem grata sibi sint et optanda ex eo est quod invicem ex communi natura et temperata qualitate congruunt. Id autem ille facit, qui per moderationem libravit invicem omnia. Statim enim opportuna et grata ea invicem reddidit, ex quo dicitur opportunum. Ut ergo mensura dicitur, veritatem rebus omnibus tribuit, quae est propria cuiusque mera et determinata natura. Ut moderans, commensurationem, quae est concinnitas et mutua omnium consonantia. Ut opportunum, pulchritudinem, quae est gratia et rebus singulis

---

[1]naturae *W*   [2]et qui singula facit *om. W*

bestows beauty, which is the grace which is both innate in single things individually and accompanies that comeliness which comes from the mutual congruity of all things.

Or rather, as He is the one, He is those three things, and He makes these three things. As the one above all things who produces all things, He circumscribes individuals within fixed limits. He purges away extraneous things from them. He establishes each in the purity of the proper nature. But individuals are one in themselves to the extent that they are circumscribed by one limit, cleansed from irrelevancies, and retained in [their] nature's one peculiarity. Therefore, as He is the one above all, He gives the one in the way we have described. But, as is evident, in this respect He is the measure and provides truth. However, as He is the one who keeps all things together in all things, He binds all things together in an indissoluble way so that they are one. But in this respect He is being the moderator bestowing proportion. As He is the one towards which everything moves and who rouses everything, He excites single things through the grace which he gives to them as individuals in themselves. And through the grace which results in them all [as a group] He seizes them all to Himself. Here He is both joining individuals to individuals and all things to the one. But in this respect He is the suitable and produces beauty. Therefore as the one He is both the measure and the moderator and the suitable. So individual things also, according as they share in some one thing, are true, proportionate, beautiful. For this reason what is mixed from wisdom and pleasure is the dwelling place of the human good; for the good is contained in it. The three attributes are the good's vestibule; for through them the good is received and admitted. But the unity given by the one, which causes the three attributes to be present in a compound and which itself blazes forth when it has been perfected by their presence, is man's good and depends on the good of the whole of nature. But that one and this unity are acts. The one is the act enacting all, by which all act, for which all act. The unity is the act which is impressed in things by the first act, enacting all for the sake of the first act. Therefore act and the one are the same.

ad singulas res innata et gratia decoris illius comes qui ex congruitate rerum omnium mutua nascitur.

Immo vero ut est unum est illa tria et haec tria facit. Ut unum super omnia, producens omnia, singula certis limitibus circumscribit. Ab extraneis purgat singula, sistitque in propriae[1] puritate naturae. Sic vero singula unum sunt in se ipsis ut uno limite circumscripta, ut ab extraneis defaecata, ut in una naturae proprietate retenta. Ut ergo unum est super omnia, unum dat eo modo quo diximus. Eo autem modo, ut apparet, mensura est et veritatem exhibet. Ut autem est unum in omnibus conservans[2] omnia, indissolubili modo[3] invicem vincit [*399r*] omnia, ex quo cuncta unum sunt. Eo autem modo moderans est commensurationemque largitur. Ut est unum ad quod omnia, citans omnia, singula per gratiam quam tribuit singulis in sese[4] invicem concitat, et per gratiam quae resultat in cunctis ad se ipsum rapit cuncta. Ubi et singula unit singulis et universa uni. Hoc autem modo opportunum est et pulchritudinem exhibet. Ergo ut est unum et mensura est et moderans et opportunum. Quare et singula ut uno quodam participant vera sunt, commensurata, pulchra. Quamobrem mixtum ex sapientia et voluptate humani boni est habitaculum, in hoc enim bonum capitur. Illa tria vestibulum boni sunt, per illa enim bonum excipitur et intromittitur. Unitas autem data ab uno, per quam et illa tria insunt composito et ipsa illis praesentibus[5] completa relucet, hominis bonum est a bono totius naturae dependens. Unum autem illud et unitas ista actus sunt. Unum actus agens omnia, quo agunt omnia, ad quem agunt omnia. Unitas actus a primo actu rebus impressus, agens ad primum actum omnia. Idem igitur actus et unum. Summum itaque bonum hominis est unius

---

[1]propria *Y*   [2]continens *W*   [3]nodo *W*   [4]se *Y*   [5]adsentibus *add. W*

Therefore man's highest good is the act of one life. It is one, it is for the one and it is in the one. Therefore the one end is the one act of the mixed life, the life that has been properly mixed and directed towards the one itself. For, in the process of understanding and rejoicing, it joins itself to the good itself absolutely. This joining is a most powerful act, merging itself into the good, transforming itself into the good. That is, in this life [it is in the process of transforming itself]; in another life, however, the transformation is complete. It is the one act of one entire soul, I say again, in so far as it is humanly possible. It occurs only at that point in time when both the act of the intellect through understanding, and the act of the will through pleasure have been directed towards the one good itself. But they are so directed when they join together in accordance with the three attributes. These are present through the power of the one. Therefore the one act of the one soul, which is from the one, for the one and in the one, is man's highest good. Therefore, since the one act of this, the mixed life, is the highest good, it is certainly more outstanding than either pleasure or wisdom.

Chapter 37. Happiness seems to belong more to wisdom than to pleasure, and to be received more by the intellect than by the will.

But if somebody were to ask which one of these was the better, wisdom or pleasure, you'd have to reply that wisdom is the better, because it is closer to the conditions of the perfect life.

Undoubtedly, intelligence (and wisdom) accords more with the truth than pleasure does, for it is capable of the truth and is perception; pleasure impedes the truth. Moreover, it accords more with proportion, for intelligence (and wisdom) is tranquil and at peace, while pleasure is in a state of complete frenzy. And it accords more with beauty. Men lead wisdom into the light as a beautiful and comely thing and show her off;

vitae actus. Unus ad unum atque in uno. Unus igitur finis est actus unus vitae mixtae, bene mixtae, et in unum ipsum directae. Nam et intelligendo et gaudendo ipsi bono penitus sese unit. Unitio haec actus quidam est vehementissimus, in bonum sese mergens, in bonum se transformans, in hac scilicet vita, in alia vero transformatus actus. Actus inquam unus totius unius animae, [*399v*] quoad homini licet, qui tunc demum adest cum et actus intellectus per intelligentiam et actus voluntatis per voluptatem in unum ipsum bonum directi fuerunt.[1] Directi vero sunt cum secundum tria illa congrediuntur. Tria illa unius vi adsunt. Unus ergo animae unius actus ex uno, ad unum atque in uno summum est hominis bonum. Cum ergo mixtae illius vitae actus unus summum sit bonum, et voluptate certe et sapientia praestantius est.

Felicitas pertinere videtur ad sapientiam potius quam ad voluptatem et intellectu magis accipi quam voluntate. Cap. XXXVII.[2]

Siquis vero quaesiverit utrum istorum melius sapientiane an voluptas,[3] respondendum meliorem esse sapientiam, quia[4] conditionibus vitae illius perfectae est propinquior.

Veritati procul dubio magis consonat mens et sapientia quam voluptas, illa enim veritatis capax et perceptio est, haec veritatis impedimentum. Commensurationi quin etiam tranquilla enim et pacata mens et sapientia est, voluptas admodum furiosa. Pulchritudini quoque. Sapientiam quippe ut rem pulchram atque decoram in lucem educunt homines atque ostentant; voluptatis usum tenebris dedicant tamquam obscenam rem

---

[1] fuerint *XY*   [2] *no ch. break or heading WX*   [3] voluptateas *W*   [4] qui *W*

pleasure's use they dedicate to the darkness as an obscene thing unworthy of the light. This proves those people are wrong who insisted the good itself is the tranquility of the will, which they call pleasure. For the highest good is contained in the higher rather than the lower power. But the intellect is more outstanding than the will: firstly, because it is the leader, the will the servant; for we know and decide before we want, and we only want something to the extent that the intellect decides we ought to want it. Secondly, it's because the intellect is never deceived, for where there's deception you have opinion not the intellect; the will is deceived by opinion and by the appearance of the good. Thirdly, the intellect is always of use in understanding the good or the bad and invariably becomes more and more acute in all things. The will becomes bad in the process of wanting bad things. Fourthly, the intellect draws things towards itself. The will is drawn away by things. For the intellect doesn't conceive of things as they are in themselves, rather it conceives of things in its own way, the many in terms of the one species, changing things in terms of stability, single things in terms of the universal and so on. With its own formulae it rectifies what is defective in things. But the will is drawn towards possessing things as they are in themselves. It is swept towards them by a notion which has been conceived of them. It doesn't alter them; but it itself is altered from a state of rest to one of motion. Again, since each motion is towards the good, the same nature which is moved towards the future good rests in the present good; [and] just as motion is related to the future good, so rest is related to the present good. But it isn't the good because the nature is moved towards it; because the object, [which is] end and mover, does not depend on the power which is being moved, but, on the contrary, the power depends on it. Therefore, because it's the good, there is movement towards it. Similarly, it's not the good just because there's repose in it. There's repose because it's the good. Therefore rest itself isn't the good itself, but something else is; towards it there was motion, in it there's rest. Because a higher place is the good for fire, accordingly fire is moved towards it and comes to rest in it. It isn't the good because fire is

lumineque indignam. Ubi certe eorum patefactus est error qui voluntatis quietem, quam voluptatem vocant, ipsum bonum adseruerunt. Etenim supremum[1] bonum in potentia capitur superiori potius quam inferiori. Intellectus autem praestantior est quam voluntas. Primo, quia dux est, illa ministra; cognoscimus enim et iudicamus[2] prius quam velimus, et tantum et eatenus et id volumus quod et[3] quatenus intellectu iudicamus esse volendum. Secundo, quia intellectus numquam decipitur, opinio enim est non intellectus ubi est deceptio; voluntas decipitur [*400r*] opinione et specie boni. Ter#tio, ille semper proficit[4] sive bonum seu malum intelligat,[5] fit semper in omnibus clarior; ista in volendis malis mala. Quarto, ille res ad se trahit; ista a rebus trahitur. Nam[6] ille non ut res in se ipsis sunt eas concipit, sed modo suo multa in una specie, mobilia stabiliter, singula universaliter, et cetera, et quae[7] claudicant in rebus formulis suis dirigit. Haec[8] autem inclinatur ad res ita possidendas ut in se ipsis sunt, rapiturque ad eas[9] notione concepta, nec mutat eas,[10] sed mutatur e statu in motum. Item cum omnis motus ad bonum sit et eadem natura quae ad bonum futurum movetur[11] in praesenti bono quiescat, sicut se habet motus ad futurum bonum ita ad praesens bonum requies. Non autem quia natura moveatur ad aliquid, illud bonum est, quia non obiectum[12] et finis et motor a potentia quae movetur, sed contra potentia[13] ab illo dependet. Igitur, quia bonum, ad illud est motus. Similiter, non quia in illo requies, bonum illud est, sed quia bonum, requies. Non igitur ipsa quies ipsum est bonum, sed aliud quiddam ad quod motus fuit, in quo est requies. Quia superior locus igni bonus est, ideo ad illum movetur ignis et quiescit in illo, non quia movetur et quiescit, bonum. Nam si

---

[1] *undecipherable W*   [2] iudicemus *W*   [3] et *om. W;* quantum *X*   [4] perficit *W*
[5] intelligant *W*   [6] et *add. W*   [7] quo *W*   [8] Ista *WXP*   [9,10] ea *WXP*
[11] moventur *W*   [12] obiecti *W*   [13] potentiam *Y*   *#P frag. VI (121r) begins*

moved and comes to rest. For, if by chance a stone were thrown upwards and it went up and stayed up, it still wouldn't be the good for the stone.

Again, happiness is the attainment of the ultimate end. But this attainment doesn't consist in the will's act, but rather in the act of the intellect. For the will is borne towards the absent end when it longs for it, and the present end when it comes to rest in it and is delighted. But it's agreed that longing for the end isn't attaining the end, but movement towards attaining it. But the will feels pleasure because the end is present. It isn't the reverse: the end isn't present because the will delights in it. Therefore there must be something other than the act of the will through which the end itself becomes present to the person willing it. You can see this with the ends of external things. For if the attainment of money were the result of the will's act, as soon as a person willed it, he would attain it. But in actual fact money isn't there first of all; then it is acquired through work. Once you have money, enjoyment begins, since pleasure consists in a certain quietness of the will. That the will comes to rest in something, however, is the exclusive result of the goodness of what it comes to rest in. So, if the will comes to rest in some operation, the will's repose proceeds from the goodness of the operation. The will doesn't seek the good in order to come to rest. If it did, the act of the will would be the end, which is untrue, as Plato will show. But, therefore, the will seeks to rest in the operation because that particular operation is the good for it. So you can gather that the operation of the intelligence in which the will rests is more excellent than the repose of the will.

The intellect comes to know the reason of a thing as a result of investigation. Then the intellect decides whether the thing is good, neutral or bad. The intellect can embrace these three concepts. The will is stimulated to want something only when it is decided it is good. So the intellect embraces more than the will. The intellect says, "This is good for me. I don't have it. So I must get it." Till now the will had been lying low; but, upon the pronouncement of such a decision, it is excited. Where does this act of the intellect originate? From its clarity. What is the source

forte lapis cogeretur et ascenderet illuc et maneret, non tamen illi id bonum.

Item felicitas est finis ultimi consecutio. Consecutio vero haec non in actu voluntatis, sed magis in intellectus actu consistit. Voluntas enim in finem fertur et absentem cum ipsum desiderat, et praesentem cum in ipso quiescens delectatur. Constat autem desiderium finis non esse finis consecutionem, sed motum [*400v*] ad consequendum. Voluptate[1] vero voluntas afficitur ex eo quod praesens finis est, non contra, quod praesens sit ex eo quod ipso voluntas gaudet. Oportet igitur aliquid esse aliud quam voluntatis actum per quod finis ipse praesens volenti fiat. Quod in finibus circa res externas intueri licet. Si enim pecuniae consecutio per voluntatis actum fieret, cum primum quis eam vult, consequeretur. Nunc autem abest primum, deinde operando paratur. Parata exoritur delectatio, voluptas siquidem[2] in quadam voluntatis quiete consistit. Quod autem in aliquo voluntas quiescat non aliunde est quam ex illius bonitate in quo quiescit. Quare si voluntas in aliqua operatione quiescat, ex operationis bonitate quies voluntatis procedit. Nec voluntas propter quietem bonum quaerit, sic enim voluntatis actus finis esset, quod falsum est, ut patebit. Sed ideo quaerit ut in operatione quiescat, quia sibi est illa operatio bonum. Unde colligitur praestantiorem esse mentis operationem in qua quiescit voluntas quam voluntatis ipsius quietem.

*Intellectus indagando rationem rei concipit, deinde iudicat vel bonam vel neutram vel malam; ad tria haec se extendit. Voluntas ex solo[3] boni iudicio ad volendum excitatur. Ideo latior est intellectus quam voluntas. Dicit intellectus, Hoc bonum meum est. Hoc careo. Hoc ergo est comparandum. Huc usque iacuerat voluntas, sed lata huiusmodi sententia excitatur. Unde trahit originem hic intellectus actus? Ex eius claritate. Unde voluntatis incitamentum? Ex indigentia. Perfectior ergo**

---

[1]voluptati *P* [2]quidem *W* [3]*XP punctuation alters the sense* Ad tria haec se extendit voluntas. Ex solo, etc. *-**om. W (cont.)*

of the will's excitement? Need. Therefore the origin of understanding is more perfect than the origin of wanting. Which was
the one to taste the good first? The intellect. It perceived the
rational principle of the good while the will was still sleeping.
But the person who was the first one to taste will be the first one
to find because he is the wiser. But the person who tasted first is
the one who drinks first. And in the hunt the person who's the
first to discover the tracks called upon his will to discover them.
In the same way the person who first finds and catches the
quarry will summon his will to catch it. And out of his own
abundance he will give to the friend who's been participating in
the hunt with him. Just as the friend was behindhand in following the quarry, he'll be behindhand in catching it. The initial
proposal is in the intellect and it's this: we must acquire the
good we lack. Given the proposal, the will springs up. The will
is nothing else but a certain stimulus of the soul which won't be
stilled until the good is acquired. The ultimate end is not the
allaying of the stimulus, but the attaining of the end. Once the
end has been acquired the stimulus itself is allayed. The ultimate
end corresponds to the initial proposal. The inciting of the
stimulus wasn't the initial thing proposed, but immediately followed it. So the allaying of the stimulus, which is pleasure,
won't be the ultimate end, but something accompanying the
ultimate end. Therefore the initial proposal is to acquire the
good. The ultimate end is the acquisition of the good. The
former was in the intellect, so the latter will be in the intellect
too. The inciting of the stimulus followed the former. The
allaying of the stimulus will follow the latter. But both the
inciting and the allaying are in the will.

Again, since man's happiness descends from above, it is
seized by the power which the soul shares with those above
rather than by the power which the soul shares with the beasts.
The intelligence is shared with those above, the appetite with
those below. Again,[184] *with all the powers which are moved by
their objects, the objects are naturally prior to the acts of the
powers (just as what moves naturally is prior to the movement
and the experience of being moved introduced into what is*

*origo est intelligendi quam volendi. Quis primo gustavit bonum? Intellectus, qui rationem concepit boni dormiente etiam voluntate. Qui autem primo gustavit, utpote sagacior, prior inveniet. Illius enim est potatio cuius et praelibatio; et qui in venatione prius investigans, ad investigandum convocavit voluntatem. Prius inveniens et consequens ad consecutionem similiter convocabit, reddetque ex propria plenitudine participem socium, qui sicut inferior fuit venando erit in consequendo inferior. Primum propositum est[1] in intellectu atque est eiusmodi[2]: bonum quo caremus comparandum. Hoc dato insurgit voluntas, quae nihil est aliud nisi quidam animi stimulus, qui non ante sedabitur quam comparetur bonum. Non est finis ultimus sedatio stimuli, sed consecutio eius, quo acquisito stimulus ipse sedatur. Finis ultimus primo proposito respondet. Stimuli incitamentum non fuit propositum primum sed illud secutum est e vestigio. Quare[3] sedatio stimuli quae est voluptas non ultimus erit finis sed finis ultimi comes. Primum ergo propositum bonum comparandum; ultimus finis boni comparatio. In intellectu illud,[4] ergo in intellectu et istud. Stimuli incitamentum secutum illud est; stimuli sedatio[5] istud. In voluntate autem est utrumque.**

Item cum felicitas hominis superne descendat, ea animi vi capitur potius, quae animae cum superis est communis, quam ea, quae illi cum brutis communis existit. Mens cum supernis communis[6] est, cum inferioribus appetitio. *Item in omnibus viribus, quae a suis obiectis moventur, obiecta secundum naturam priora sunt quam virium illarum actus. Quemadmodum id quod movet natura prius est quam motio passioque in id quod movetur illata. Eiuscemodi[7] vis voluntas est, res enim expetenda*

---

[1]est *om.* XP [2]hoc *XP* [3]et *add.* XP [4]*X and P have what is either a punctuation mark or the abbreviation for* id est [5]et *add.* X [6]communius *W* [7]eiusmodi *W* *(cont.)* *-***om.* W

moved). The will is such a power. For a desirable object seizes hold of the appetite. Accordingly, the object precedes the act of the will itself. Therefore the will's first object precedes its every act. So the will's act can't be the first thing the will wants. But this is the ultimate end. So the will's act can't be the ultimate end. Moreover, with all the powers that can be reflected onto their own acts, the power's act has to be directed first towards another object. Afterwards it can be reflected onto its own act. For, if the intellect is to understand it is understanding, it must first understand another thing. After the thing, it can understand it is understanding. Of course, the understanding which the intellect understands in itself is the understanding of some object. So, either you have to proceed to infinity; or, if you can arrive at the first thing which is understood, it won't be understanding itself, but some intelligible object. For the very same reason also, the first thing the will wants isn't willing itself, but some other good thing. But the first thing an intelligent nature wants is the intelligence's happiness.

Moreover, every single thing, in accordance with those things which constitute its substance, has its own natural truth. For a true man differs from a painted man because of the things which make up the substance of a man. But true happiness doesn't differ from false happiness because of the act of the will. For the will ends up loving and rejoicing equally in whatever it is that is presented to it as the good and as the highest good, whether this is truly or falsely such. But whether it is truly or falsely the highest good which is being presented is a distinction made by the intellect with the reason. Therefore the substance of happiness pertains more to the intellect than it does to the will.

Again, nature hasn't set up pleasure as the end, but has introduced it in order to bring operations to completion. For we see nature has given pleasure to those animal operations which are established for necessary ends. This is obvious in the case of food and sex. Animals would abstain from them utterly if pleasure didn't attract them. And so those who follow nature's lead won't set up pleasure as the end for themselves. Furthermore,

appetitum rapit. Obiectum igitur voluntatis *actum ipsius prae-
cedit. Primum igitur obiectum eius actum eius omnem praece-
dit. Non potest igitur voluntatis actus primum quod voluntate
petitur¹ [401r] esse. Id autem finis est ultimus. Actus igitur
voluntatis** ultimus esse finis non potest. Praeterea in viribus
omnibus quae suos in actus reflecti possunt, ante oportet poten-
tiae ipsius actum in obiectum aliud dirigi, postea suum in actum
reflecti. Si enim intellectus intelligere se intelligit, prius rem
aliam intelligat necesse est, post eam se intelligere recognoscat.
Nempe intelligere ipsum quod in se intellectus intelligit alicuius
obiecti intelligentia est. Quare oportet ut vel in infinitum eatur,
vel si ad primum quod intellectum est venire licet, hoc non
ipsum intelligere erit, sed res intelligibilis aliqua. Eadem quoque
ratione primum quod voluntas exigit non ipsum velle est, sed
aliud quoddam bonum. Primum autem quod vult natura mentis
particeps eius felicitas est.²

Quin etiam unumquodque secundum ea quae substantiam
eius constituunt habet³ naturae suae veritatem.⁴ Differt enim a
picto homine verus homo per ea quae hominis substantiam
complent. Vera autem beatitudo a falsa per actum voluntatis
non differt. Aeque enim⁵ voluntas in amando aut gaudendo sese
habet quicquid illud sit quod sibi ut bonum et ut summum
bonum proponitur, sive revera tale id sit, seu falso. Utrum
autem⁶ revera sit summum bonum quod tale proponitur aut
falso, ratione Intellectus hoc differt. Beatitudinis ergo substan-
tia ad intellectum magis pertinet quam voluntatem.

Item natura voluptatem ut finem non posuit, immo ad opera-
tiones explendas eam induxit. Cernimus enim quod natura eis⁷
animalium operationibus voluptatem dedit quae [401v] sunt
ad fines necessarios ordinatae, quod in usu cibi et veneris est
perspicuum, a quibus animalia penitus abstinerent, nisi volup-
tate adlicerentur. Ita et qui naturam ducem sequuntur volup-
tatem sibi finem non statuent. Adde quod voluptas nihil aliud

¹patitur *W*   ²est *om. XP*   ³habent *W*   ⁴*em. from Aquinas;* virtutem *WXYP*
⁵se *add. X*   ⁶aut *P*   ⁷eius *P*   *-***om. XP*

*pleasure is nothing else but the repose of the will in some appro-
priate good, just as desire is the inclining of the will towards an
appropriate good. But just as man is borne by the will towards
the end, so he rests in the end, just as natural things themselves
have certain natural inclinations too towards the end, which
stop when they arrive at the end. But it's ridiculous to say the
end of a heavy body's movement is not to be in its proper place,
but is its inclination's repose or cessation in the place aimed at.
For, if He had principally intended the inclination itself should
come to rest and cease, the Creator of corporeal things
wouldn't have given the inclination. But He gives the
inclination so a body may arrive at its proper place through it.
When the place has already been attained (as the end), the inclination's repose follows. And therefore this repose and cessation
is not the end, but rather it accompanies the end.*

*Again, if the end of something is some external thing, the
operation whereby it acquires the external thing in the first
place is also said to be the ultimate end. For instance, with the
people for whom the end is money, the end is said to be not to
love or long for money but also to possess it. But the end of a
rational substance is God. So the human operation whereby
man first attains to God is the one best suited for attaining
happiness. But this is understanding. For we are unable to want
something until we understand what we want.* Moreover, the
ultimate end corresponds to the first mover, just as victory does
to the general, the proper means for achieving it to his subordinates. But the intellect moves the will, which is in itself blind,
and it uses a particular notion to do this. So the ultimate end
concerns the intellect rather than the will. Now, if every single
thing operates for its own sake, the intellect moves the will for
its own good. The will, since it is servile and blind, is subordinate to the intellect. Therefore the will, as Plotinus says, isn't
sufficient, for it doesn't seek its own good.[185] And even were it
to seek pleasure, it wouldn't be seeking its own good. For
people are always delighted by something else, just as it is
something else that people desire. And yet the good itself (which
anyone covets for himself) must not be some passion or

est quam quies voluntatis in aliquo convenienti bono, sicut desiderium est eiusdem[1] *inclinatio in conveniens bonum. Sicut autem homo per voluntatem in finem fertur, sic in eo quiescit, sicut et naturales ipsae res quaeque naturales habent in finem inclinationes, quae cum pervenerunt ad finem cessant. Ridiculum autem dictu*[2] *est quod finis motus ipsius corporis ponderosi non sit proprio in loco esse, sed quies et cessatio inclinationis in hoc in quod*[3] *tendebat. Si enim hoc principaliter intenderet ut inclinatio ipsa quiesceret et cessaret, auctor corporum eam non daret. Dat autem eam ut per hanc proprium ad locum deveniat, quo quasi fine iam acquisito inclinationis sequitur requies. Atque ita requies haec et*[4] *cessatio non finis est*[5] *sed finem potius comitatur.*

Item si alicuius rei est aliqua res exterior finis, illa eius operatio etiam finis ultimus esse dicitur[6] *per quam primo rem illam assequitur. Ceu*[7] *in his quibus finis pecunia est, dicitur quoque possidere pecuniam finis esse, non amare neque cupere. Finis autem substantiae rationalis est Deus. Illa ergo hominis operatio ad felicitatem potior est per quam primo ad Deum attingit. Haec autem intelligentia est. Nam velle non possumus, nisi quod intelligimus.* Praeterea primo moventi ultimus respondet finis, ut duci victoria, subiectis [*402r*] propria ministeria. Intellectus autem sua notione voluntatem ex se caecam movet. Illi ergo potius quam isti ultimus respondet finis. Nam si unumquodque sui ipsius gratia operatur, ad sui bonum voluntatem intellectus movet, quae, quia servilis est et caeca, intellectui subest. Quapropter voluntas,[8] ut Plotinus ait, sufficiens non est, non enim quaerit idem. Neque etiamsi[9] voluptatem quaerat, idem quaeret. Semper enim aliud est in quo delectatur quis, sicut aliud quod appetit. Atqui oportet bonum ipsum quod esse sibi quis expetit non esse passionem et affectionem aliquam in

---

[1]eiusdem *om.* P [2]dictum P [3]quo P [4]et *om.* Y [5]est *om.* W
[6]dicetur *WXP* [7]cum *W* [8]voluptas *WXY (i.e., I have adopted the P reading)*
[9]enim si P

affection in the person who attains the good. Accordingly, the person, who has the state of being affected alone (which anyone can derive from the good) and thinks this state is the good, hasn't anything. So it's not enough for someone simply to think he has the state of being affected if he hasn't the thing actually causing the affection. For nobody chooses to be happy when his sons are absent as he would be if they were present. And nobody chooses to be happy when he's not eating as he would be if he were eating. Nor does he choose to be transported when he's not enjoying sex as he would be if he were enjoying it. Rather, a person chooses actually to have these things. Plotinus, in writing on felicity, proves that felicity isn't in pleasure on the grounds that just as the appetite exists for the sake of another good, so the appetite's repose takes place in another good.[186] Again, pleasure can be imaginary and it can be deceived. But the good doesn't consist at all in the passion of the person attaining the good. The passion can be the same because of a mistake even when the good is not attained. Nobody, however, would choose to be thus affected. The reasons above have put the act of the intellect in the happy man before the act of the will. In an epistle on felicity I have tried to deal with the reasons that make the opposite view the more probable. Ultimately, perhaps the safer approach is not to think of the will as [something] cut off from the intellect, but to think of it and pleasure as though they were in the intellect itself.[187]

From all that's preceded we can conclude man's end is one, that is, it is the one act of the life mixed from wisdom and pleasure which is for the one good and in the one. We can conclude too that wisdom is of more use in attaining the end than pleasure. This has certainly resolved your question, my dear Michael of San Miniato, most learned man and brother philosopher. For, in disputing with me (as your frequent custom has been from the earliest years), you have often demonstrated with a number of reasons that man's end has to be one and simple. And therefore you said you wondered why Plato set up man's end as mixed. So I've now replied to your reasons; and consequently I've gladly admitted and accepted them as being

eo qui consequitur. Unde et vacuus manet qui hoc bonum existimat habens passionem solam quam quis a bono haberet. Quapropter non satis sibi esse affectionem quis putat, dum re ipsa caret; neque enim eligit quisquam non praesentibus filiis ita laetari ac si adessent, aut non comedendo ita laetari ac si comederet, aut veneriis non potiundo ita gestire[1] ac si potiretur, sed habere exoptat. *Plotinus de felicitate quod non in voluptate sit ita probat, quia sicut appetitus est ad aliud bonum sic eius quies in bono alio. Item voluptas potest esse imaginaria et decepta. Omnino vero bonum non consistit in passione consequentis bonum, quae potest esse similis per fallaciam etiam in non consecuto. Nemo vero talem eligeret affectionem. Superiores quidem rationes intellectus actum actui voluntatis in beato praeposuerunt. Quibus vero rationibus oppositum probabiliter existimari possit in epistola quadam de felicitate tentavi. Denique, si consideretur non tam voluntas ab intellectu discreta quam quod in ipso intellectu est quasi voluntas et voluptas, erit forte tentatio tutior.**

Ex superioribus omnibus colligere possumus finem hominis esse unum, unum scilicet actum vitae ipsius ex sapientia et voluptate mixtae, ad unum bonum atque in uno, sapientiamque ad finem magis quam voluptatem conducere. In quo certe soluta est tua illa quaestio, vir doctissime[2] Miniatensis Michael conphilosophe noster plurimumque dilecte. Saepe enim mecum ut frequenter a primis annis consuevisti disputans unum et simplicem hominis esse debere finem rationibus multis confirma visti.[3] Ideoque mirari cur Plato mixtum finem [*402v*] posuerit dicebas. Illis ergo[4] rationibus tuis iam ita respondi, ut et[5] eas

---

[1]gestare *W*   [2]sapientissime *WXP*   [3]*for* multis confirmavisti *WXP read* illis quas supra retuli demonstrasti   [4]ego *WXP*   [5]et *om. Y*   *-**om. WXP*

completely valid, and at the same time I've defended our Plato's mixture. Elsewhere we'll respond to the rest of your extremely subtle questions about Plato.

THE END OF THE FIRST BOOK OF THE COMMEN-TARIES OF THE FLORENTINE, MARSILIO FICINO, ON PLATO'S PHILEBUS CONCERNING MAN'S HIGHEST GOOD.

libenter admiserim et tamquam verissimas approbaverim, et Platonis nostri defenderim mixtionem. Reliquis tuis circa Platonem subtilissimis quaestionibus alias respondebimus.

FINIS PRIMI LIBRI[1] COMMENTARIORUM MARSILII FICINI FLORENTINI IN PLATONIS PHILEBUM DE SUMMO HOMINIS BONO.[2]

---

[1] *W reads* Explicit liber primus   [2] sequitur eiusdem liber secundus *add. X;* sequitur eiusdem in eundem liber secundus *add. P (see p. 385 note 1)*

THE SECOND BOOK OF THE COMMENTARIES
OF THE FLORENTINE, MARSILIO FICINO,
ON THE PHILEBUS.

Chapter 1. On the one principle of things and how all things subsequent to it are constituted from an infinite and a limit. Also on the primary genera of things.

23C   **All the things that are now in the universe** ... [188] After Plato proposed in the first part of the book what ought to be the main topic of discussion, and in the second part told us of a particular way and approach to discuss it, in the third part he told us why it ought to be discussed carefully. In the fourth part he began to treat of the good; and, since he was about to compare pleasure and wisdom to it, he explained what it is so you could see whether either of them is the good itself. In the process of comparing each one to it, he showed that neither is the good itself.

All this so far. Now it remains to find out which contributes more to the good. You cannot find this out, unless each is defined and divided into its parts. But definition first needs the genus, then the difference. Therefore in the fifth part Plato inquires into the genus of each, and introduces a certain genus of **the infinite** and also the genus of **the limit**.[189] Pleasure he refers to the infinite; the intelligence and wisdom to the limit. And therefore, to the extent that the limit excels the infinite, he wants the intelligence and wisdom to excel pleasure.

Here you have to understand before all else that the infinite is talked of in two ways. The first sort excludes the limit; the

SECUNDUS LIBER COMMENTARIORUM
MARSILII FICINI FLORENTINI
IN PHILEBUM.[1]

De uno rerum principio et quomodo post ipsum omnia ex infinito quodam ac termino componuntur atque de primis rerum generibus. Cap. I.[2]

Omnia quae nunc in universo sunt ... Postquam in prima libri parte quod tractandum erat proposuit Plato, et in secunda tractandi modum[3] quendam et ingressum tradidit, in tertia qua cautione disserendum sit docuit. In quarta tractare coepit de bono, et quoniam collaturus ad ipsum erat voluptatem et sapientiam, ut inspiceretur numquid istorum alterum ipsum sit bonum,[4] quid bonum sit explicavit,[5] et ad ipsum utraque conferens neutrum esse ipsum bonum ostendit.

Haec hactenus. Deinceps investigandum restat utrum istorum magis ad bonum conferat. Quod inveniri non potest, nisi et definiatur et dividatur in partes utrumque. Definitio autem genus requirit primo, postmodum differentiam. Ideo quinta hac in parte genera utriusque perquirit et **infiniti** quoddam genus necnon **termini** genus inducit. Ad infinitum voluptatem, ad terminum [*403r*] mentem et sapientiam refert. Ideoque eo praestare vult mentem et sapientiam voluptati quo praestat terminus infinito.

Ubi ante omnia intelligendum est quod duplex esse dicitur infinitum. Unum quod excludit terminum, alterum quod

---

second sort is in need of the limit. For the infinite is what does not have the limit. But something can lack the limit in two ways. Either it's so simple by nature and supereminent and absolute it has neither an inner limit of parts (that is, a first part, middle part and last part) since it is indivisible, nor anything above it by whose limits it might be circumscribed; nor does it lie embedded in anything by whose capacity it might be restricted. Or it's formless and vague and wanders away from itself and is in need of the limit and is powerless by nature to provide itself with the limit it longs for. The infinite is talked about in both these ways; but the first infinite is excluding the limit, the second infinite is in need of the limit.

The first infinite, since it doesn't have the limit above or within or below itself and since it's above and outside all things, is itself the limit of all things. It encloses all, forms all, sustains all, circumscribes all. Therefore the infinite which excludes the limit and the unlimited limit of all things are identical. For the limit is not itself limited; for it would be limited by another, and that other by another, and so you'd go on to infinity. So the first limit excludes the limit. So it's infinite. So the infinite which excludes the limit and the limit of all things are mutually convertible. Such is God, namely the one itself whose infinity Plato praises in the *Parmenides*.[190] There he called Him the infinite, but in this book he first calls Him the limit of all things, then the measure of all things. Plato added that God was the universal measure, in order to show He is not the limit which is imprinted in things, but the limit which encloses all things from the outside and which separates all things into their proper natures by imprinting in them the inner limit.

The second infinite is in need of the limit in the sense that it is the limit of nothing but is limited by everything. Therefore the first infinite, which excludes the limit, is the infinite which limits another. The second infinite is limited by another. In the first instance infinity is better than the limit, because the limit of all things comes from it, since it is not itself limited. But in the second instance the limit is better than infinity, because the limit has been sought for by infinity. The *Parmenides* is concerned

termino caret. Infinitum enim est quod non habet terminum. Quod autem aliquid non habeat terminum duobus modis contingere potest. Aut quia tam simplex natura est et supereminens et absolutum, ut neque interiorem partium habeat terminum, scilicet primam partem, mediam atque ultimam, cum impartibile sit, neque supra se quicquam habeat cuius limitibus circumscribatur,[1] neque in aliquo iaceat cuius coarctetur capacitate. Aut quia informe vagumque et errans ex se est et termini indigum et suapte natura praestare sibi optatum terminum impotens. Infinitum utrumque dicitur; sed primum infinitum excludens terminum,[2] secundum infinitum termino carens.

Primum infinitum, cum ipsum nec terminum habeat[3] supra nec intra nec infra, sitque super omnia et extra omnia, omnium est terminus, omnia limitans, omnia formans, omnia sistens, omnia circumscribens. Idem igitur est infinitum excludens terminum et terminus omnium sine termino; neque enim terminus terminatur, nam ab alio terminaretur, illudque ab alio atque ita in infinitum procederetur. Primus ergo terminus terminum excludit. Est igitur infinitum. Infinitum igitur excludens terminum et terminus omnium invicem convertuntur. Talis Deus est, ipsum scilicet unum cuius infinitatem [*403v*] in Parmenide laudat Plato, et ibi infinitum pronuntiavit, hoc autem[4] in libro primo terminum omnium deinde omnium mensuram. Adiecit mensuram omnium, ut ostenderet Deum non esse terminum rebus impressum, sed extrinsecus omnia limitantem et interioris termini impressione omnia in natura propria distinguentem.

Secundum infinitum ita indiget termino ut nullius[5] sit terminus, sed ab omnibus terminetur. Igitur infinitum primum excludens terminum infinitum est aliud[6] terminans. Secundum infinitum est[7] ab alio terminatum. Ibi quidem melius infinitas quam terminus, quia ex eo est terminus omnium, quia ipsum non terminatur. Hic autem terminus infinitate melior, quia terminus

---

[1]circumscribitur *P* [2]et *add. X* [3]habeat *om. XP* [4]autem *om. WXP*
[5]nullus *W* [6]illud *W* [7]est *om. WXP*

with the one God himself, that is, God as the infinite.[191] Here, however, [in the *Philebus*] Plato is concerned with Him as the limit of all things and as the measure. For, as the infinite, God is the good for no one but Himself. But as the measure and the limit, He is the good for all things, because He is the substance, the salvation and the perfection of all. So, since Plato is concerned in this dialogue with the good for man, he calls God by the title which denotes Him as He communicates Himself to things and does them good, not as He flees from them.

Therefore, whenever Plato mentions in this dialogue the limit and measure of all, understand that it means God. Whenever he talks about the infinite which is in need of the limit either here or in the *Timaeus*,[192] understand that it means the completely universal matter which in the intelligence is formed and limited by the Ideas, in the soul by the reasons, and finally in bodies by the forms. As infinite material it comes from God as the infinite, so that from God's infinity comes the infinity of matter. From God as the limit and measure comes the limitation of matter. And although God as the infinite is more excellent in Himself than He is as the limit, nevertheless matter which is dependent on the former is not more excellent than the limitation which derives from the latter. For what does the pre-eminence of God's infinity do towards making things subsequent to it excellent? In a way that sublimity, which is free and impatient of circumscription, abandons everything else. Therefore universal matter, like some shadow, follows after God who is fleeing away. But the form in matter, as in a mirror, results from a certain beneficent glance of the divine countenance. Matter is forced by necessity to accompany the necessity of the divine pre-eminence, form to accompany the goodness of the [divine] glance. Therefore in the *Timaeus* Plato calls matter necessity, but the form he calls the intelligence.[193] As matter is first, it is the first thing above nothingness. So it is only a little distance from nothingness. Form, being second, is the first thing above something. So there there's potentiality; here there's act. There there's essence; here there's being. There there's inchoation; here there's perfection. There you have matter as the

ab infinitate quaesitus. De ipso uno Deo, scilicet ut infinitum in Parmenide. Ut autem terminus omnium et mensura hic agitur. Ut enim infinitum nulli bonum praeter quam sibi. Ut autem mensura et terminus omnibus bonum, quia omnium substantia, salus atque perfectio. Ideo cum hoc in libro de hominis agatur bono, Deum ea significat appellatione qua se rebus communicat atque prodest non qua omnia fugit.

Quotiens igitur terminum omnium dicit et mensuram hoc in libro, intellige[1] Deum. Quotiens termino carentem infinitum[2] vel hic vel in Timaeo significat, materiam intellige communissimam, quae in mente formatur terminaturque ideis, in anima rationibus, in corporibus denique formis. Haec ut infinita materies a Deo est ut infinitum, ut a Dei infinitate materiae sit infinitas. A Deo[3] ut terminus et mensura materiae profluit limitatio. [*404r*] Ac licet Deus ut infinitum in se ipso praestantius sit quam ut terminus, tamen non praestantior materia illinc pendens quam hinc emanans terminatio. Illa enim praestantia quid ad sequentium excellentiam? Deserit enim quodammodo reliqua exempta illa et impatiens circumscriptionis sublimitas. Ideo communis materies velut umbra quaedam fugientem[4] sequitur Deum. Forma vero in materia velut in speculo ex quodam benefico[5] divini vultus aspectu resultat. Necessitatem divinae praestantiae necessario materia comitatur; bonitatem aspectus forma. Ideo necessitatem in Timaeo materiam vocat, formam vero mentem. Materia ut primum, inde primum super nihilum, parvo igitur intervallo distat a nihilo.[6] Forma ut secundum, inde primum super aliquid. Ideo ibi potentia, hic actus; ibi essentia, hic esse; inchoatio ibi, hic est perfectio. Materia quidem ut a Deo processus, forma ut in Deum conversio.

---

[1]intelligit *P*   [2]infinitatem *WXP*   [3]Adeo *WX*   [4]fugiendem *W*   [5]beneficio *YP*
[6]idcirco in Timaeo dicitur materia inter esse et nihil esse media *add. WXP*

proceeding from God. Here you have form as the turning back towards God. Turning back towards God is better than proceeding from God. The one separates things from the good and compels them to degenerate; the other joins them to the good, repairs the harm, forms them into the good again. From God comes matter. From the pure act comes the pure potentiality. From the act enacting all comes the potentiality which sustains all.

Understand by matter the first thing God's super-eminence threw above the infinity of nothingness itself. Understand by form the second gift which God extended above the first. These two remain as constants through all the levels of God's creation. The infinite which is in need of the limit call matter. The limitation of matter call form. From the infinity which excludes the limit you can derive the infinity which needs the limit. For by the same token the former excludes the limit, the latter is born without the limit. From the limit which accompanies God's infinity you derive the limit which accompanies matter's infinity. Not that there are two things in God, infinity and the limit; for He is His own infinity, His glance is the limit of other things. But necessarily there are two things in things, just as things necessarily go forth and are turned back.

Set aside for the present the infinity of God Himself, for it is dealt with in the *Parmenides.*[194] Accept the fact that in this dialogue on the good Plato is dealing with the beneficent limit. Secondly, accept the infinity of all things which proceed from God. Thirdly, accept in the case of this infinity that limit has been given to it by the limit. Fourthly, accept that there's a mixture from both. You need only concern yourself here with these four points, because the higher limit itself has been and will be discussed elsewhere. You're now concerned with the second sort of limit and with infinity. But let's deal with infinity first, because matter is the first to emerge. Accept that it is, and accept what it is. God is always equally powerful. Therefore the power to make things is always equal in Him. Therefore the potentiality to be made is always equal outside Him. For He wouldn't always be capable of making everything, if everything

Melior conversio in Deum quam a Deo processio. Illa enim disiungit a bono degenerareque[1] compellit. Haec bono coniungit, detrimentum restaurat, reformat in bonum. A Deo[2] materia. Ab actu puro potentia pura. Ab actu agente omnia potentia suscipiens omnia.

Materiam intellige primum a Dei supereminentia iactum super ipsius nihil infinitatem. Formam intellige secundum Dei donum super primum inde porrectum. Haec duo per omnes rerum gradus a Deo[3] permanant. Infinitum termini indigum voca[4] materiam; terminum, materiae formam. Ab infinitate terminum excludente infinitatem[5] deducas [*404v*] termini indigam. Nam eo ipso signo quo illa excludit terminum ista nascitur sine termino. A termino infinitatis illius comite terminum infinitatis istius comitem. Nec duo in Deo sunt, infinitas et terminus, nam infinitas ipsa sua est, aliorum aspectus est terminus. In rebus autem duo quaedam necessario[6] sunt, sicut necessario et manant et reflectuntur.

Mitte ad praesens Dei ipsius infinitatem, nam de hac in Parmenide. Accipe in dialogo de bono beneficum terminum. Accipe secundo infinitatem rerum omnium a Deo manantium. Accipe tertio in hac infinitate terminum datum a termino. Quarto quod ex utroque est mixtum. De his quattuor hic est dumtaxat agendum, quia vero de superno ipso termino alias et dictum est et dicetur. Nunc de termino secundo et infinitate, sed de hac primum, quia prima procedit materia. Quod ista sit et quid sit accipe. Semper Deus aeque potens est, semper ergo in illo aequa faciendi potestas, semper igitur aequa exterius fiendi potentia. Neque enim facere semper omnia potest, nisi fieri semper omnia possint.[7] Aeterna igitur omnium factiva[8]

---

[1]degeneratque *W*   [2],[3]adeo *W*   [4]vocat *P*   [5]infinitem *P*   [6]necessaria *XP*
[7]possunt *W*   [8]factura *XP*

weren't always capable of being made. Therefore the potentiality capable of making everything is eternal; eternal too is the potentiality of everything to be made. This potentiality to be made something (as it were) is either nothing, or something, or everything. It isn't nothing; for nothingness is opposed to being and repels being. But the potentiality to be made something longs for being. It isn't something; for it would already be something, it wouldn't be the potentiality to become it. Or rather, if it were something, it would be one distinct thing; in which case it wouldn't have an equal regard to everything. Or rather, it would have already actually been made into something; it wouldn't be the potentiality to be made it. Therefore it is everything. It isn't everything in act, because there'd be no need for it to be made into anything. Therefore it is the state of being prepared for everything. Therefore it is indifferent as regards individual things. Therefore it is the undetermined potentiality for everything.

But if somebody said the potentiality [to be made] is always from God and therefore God is always able to make it and it can always be made, and if this somebody asked about the [possibility of] any other passive potentiality, you ought to reply that forms and compounds presuppose both the active and the passive potentiality, but matter, (as it is itself all passive potentiality) only requires the active potentiality, and the active potentiality alone follows the passive potentiality. The passive potentiality, which precedes everything and is placed midway between nothingness and being, either of itself determines to be, or not to be, or it is indifferent to both. If to be, it wouldn't need the action of the superior potentiality to possess form and being, since its own rational principle would include these and so it wouldn't be the possible being, but the necessary being. If not to be, its rational principle would be the same as nothingness; so it would be nothing. Or rather, since its rational principle demands non-being for itself, being would be contrary to its rational principle. So it would be impossible for it ever to be. Therefore it is indifferent. So God is the necessary being, matter is the possible being, nothingness is what cannot possibly be.

potentia, aeterna et omnium potentia susceptiva. Haec (ut ita dixerim) fiendi potentia aut nihil est aut aliquid aut omnia. Non nihil, nihil enim ipsum ipsi esse oppositum et esse fugat; potentia vero fiendi esse appetit. Non aliquid, esset enim iam, neque esset ad fieri potentia, immo etsi esset aliquid unum esset distinctum, ergo non omnia aeque respiceret. Immo vero iam factum actu aliquid esset, non fiendi potentia. Est igitur omnia. Non actu omnia quia non opus esset aliquid fieri. [*405r*] Est igitur omnium praeparatio, quare ad singula est indifferens. Est igitur ad quaelibet[1] indeterminata potentia.

Quod siquis dixerit hanc potentiam a Deo[2] esse semper, ergo semper Deum eam facere posse, et semper eam posse fieri, quaeratque de alia fiendi potentia, respondendum formas et composita activam et passivam potentiam praesupponere, materiam vero, quia ipsa est omnis passiva potentia, activam dumtaxat exigere, et solam faciendi potentiam fiendi potentiam sequi. Haec fiendi potentia omnia antecedens, quae inter nihil et esse media ponitur, aut esse sibi ipsa determinat aut non esse aut ad utrumque est indifferens. Si esse, superioris actione ad formam et esse non indigeret, cum ratione propria haec includeret, esset ergo non possibile, sed necessarium. Si non esse, ratio sua cum nihilo eadem, nihil igitur esset. Immo cum ratio sua non esse sibi exigat, contra rationem suam erit esse. Impossibile igitur erit, ut sit quandoque. Est ergo indifferens. Unde Deus necessarium, materia possibile, nihil impossibile.

---

[1]quaecumque *WXP*   [2]adeo *W*

And therefore Orpheus calls God "necessity" when he says, "Strong necessity contains all things."[195] Plato says the same in the *Republic* Book 10.[196] Accordingly, matter is the undetermined potentiality for being or non-being, and it's the indifferent inchoation for all the forms. Therefore it is in need of the limit. Therefore it is infinite.

As there is for all things one universal act—not one with reference to number, species or genus, but one, because from the one and for the one—, so there is for all things one universal matter. This is called one, because it follows after the supereminence of the one God, and because it has been made the subject of one act. Although this matter is appropriate to incorporeal things and is incorporeal in them, yet it does not disagree with corporeal forms; for when it's in them it is also incorporeal, as it precedes quantity (from the dimensions of which bodies are made). Or rather, this matter suffices on the one hand for the incorporeal qualities and powers, and on the other it will also suffice for the Ideas. In the latter instance, in a way it is sustaining something corporeal, namely the rational principles of corporeal objects. In the former instance, it is sustaining something incorporeal, namely the indivisible qualities.

That this matter subsists in all things after God, however, can be demonstrated again thus. Things which are made by God as the principle don't proceed from themselves; if they did, they wouldn't need the principle. So they receive being and act from God, for being means the act which is present in the nature of things. So things either contain in themselves something else over and beyond the act of being, or they don't. If they contain nothing else, the act of being is pure, free from all deprivation, free from all the circumscription of a subject; it is utterly one, an infinite overflowing energy which excludes all limit and subsists through itself. And because it is existing in itself, it comes, accordingly, from itself. But this is only appropriate to the first thing, God. Therefore the act in things has something else added, otherwise it would be the first thing and infinite and subsisting through itself. The act in things is in another as in a subject. Consequently it isn't like the first utterly abundant act

Quocirca et necessitatem Orpheus Deum vocat, cum ait, Fortis necessitas omnia continet. Et in decimo de Republica Plato. Est itaque materia ad esse et non esse indeterminata potentia et ad omnes formas indifferens inchoatio. Est igitur indiga termini. Est itaque infinita.

Atque ut est omnibus unus communis actus, non unus numero, specie aut genere, sed quia ab uno ad unum, ita omnibus una est communis materies, quae ideo dicitur una, quia unius Dei supereminentiam sequitur, et uni actui est subiecta. Neque ex eo quod incorporeis [*405v*] haec materia convenit in eisque incorporea, ideo a corporeis dissentit[1] formis, nam et in his quoque est incorporea; antecedit siquidem quantitatem, cuius dimensionibus corpora constant. Immo quae hic qualitatibus et viribus incorporeis sufficit, illic quoque ideis sufficiet. Illic quidem corporale aliquid quodammodo sustinet, corporum scilicet rationes. Hic nonnihil incorporale, impartibiles qualitates.

Quod autem omnibus post Deum rebus haec subsit materies, iterum sic ostenditur. Quae a principio illo fiunt se ipsis non sunt; neque enim principio indigerent. Inde igitur esse actumque accipiunt, esse enim praesentem actum in rerum natura significat. Aut ergo praeter hunc essendi actum aliud quicquam in se continent, aut nihil. Si nihil aliud, actus hic purus est sine omni privatione, liber ab omni circumscriptione subiecti, unum penitus, infinitus vigor atque exuberans, omnem excludens terminum, per se subsistens. Et quia in se ipso existens, ideo ab se ipso. Id autem soli primo Deo convenit. Ergo actus ille aliquid aliud habet annexum, ne sit primum, ne infinitum, ne se ipso subsistens, et in alio est ut subiecto,[2] ne sit ut primum vigore plenissimum. Est ergo in sequentibus omnibus et actus simul et

---

[1]descendit *P*   [2]subito *W*

in energy. So there are in all things subsequent [to God] both act
and potentiality at the same time, potentiality being the subject
of act. Furthermore, we understand by a thing's "essence" the
rational principle of each thing's substance; but by "being" the
act of the essence itself which is present in the nature of things.
You can learn this from the *Parmenides*.[197] Therefore essence is
one thing, being another. For whatever isn't included in the
rational principle and the understanding of the essence comes
from outside and produces a compound when added to the
essence. Since any essence can't be understood without the
things which constitute its parts, but each essence can be understood even if it doesn't exist—for we can understand what a
phoenix is or a man is and at the same time not know whether
they exist in the universe—, it's consequently obvious that being
is other than essence, unless perhaps there's something whose
essence is its being itself. But this can't happen except in the
case of what is one and first. For it's impossible for something
to be divided into many things except [for the following rea-
sons]. Either you get the addition of some difference; for
instance, the nature of the genus is multiplied into the species.
Or you get the form received in different materials; for
instance, the nature of the species is multiplied in the different
individual things. Or you get one thing that is absolute by itself,
but becomes something different when it's lying in another; for
instance, a colour can be one thing separated from a material,
another joined to it, the difference being caused by the separation. But if you can posit something which is only being, that is,
subsisting being itself, it won't receive the addition of a difference. For then you'd have one thing in the position of the genus
and the shared potentiality, and another in the position of the
difference and the act. So it wouldn't be the pure act. But being
subsisting through itself is the pure act, for Plato calls being
"act alone." So where you have being alone, you have act
alone. This being doesn't even sustain the addition of matter;
for, if it did, it wouldn't be subsisting through itself. So
something like this, which is its own being, can only be one
thing. In order to be pure existence, which is what we mean by

potentia actus ipsius subiectum. Praeterea essentiam rei rationem cuiusque substantiae intelligimus; esse vero actum
essentiae ipsius in rerum natura praesentem, ut ex Parmenide
discitur. Igitur aliud essentia est, aliud esse. Quicquid enim in
ratione intelligentiaque essentiae non includitur extrinsecus
advenit et illi additum compositionem efficit. Quoniam essentia
nulla sine his, [*406r*] quae partes eius[1] sunt, intelligi potest,
omnis autem essentia potest sine esse intelligi, intelligere enim
possumus quid phoenix, quid homo, ignorare simul quod in
natura rerum existant, ex quo patet quod esse aliud quam
essentia est, nisi forte res aliqua sit, cuius essentia ipsum suum
esse sit. Quae quidem res, nisi una et prima, esse non potest;
impossibile enim est aliquid in plura dividi, nisi vel per alicuius
differentiae additamentum, sicut generis natura multiplicatur in
species, vel propter id quod forma in materiis diversis recipitur,
sicuti natura speciei in diversis individuis multiplex redditur, vel
ex hoc quod unum absolutum est aliud autem in alio iacens,
sicut si esset color[2] aliquis a materia separatus, alius a
coniuncto, ex ipsa sua separatione differens. Si autem aliqua res
ponatur, quae sit esse tantum ita ut ipsum esse sit subsistens,
hoc esse additionem differentiae non recipiet. Esset enim ibi
aliquid loco generis communisque potentiae, aliud loco differentiae atque actus. Non ergo esset actus purus. Esse autem per
se subsistens purus est actus, esse enim actum dicit solum.
Quare ubi solum ponitur esse, solus ponitur actus. Neque etiam
esse illud additamentum materiae suscipit, neque enim per se
subsisteret. Quare res talis, quae suum esse est, una est tantum.
Certe primum tale est, ut pura existentia sit, quod per esse

---

[1]eius *om.* W   [2]calor W

being, such a thing is certainly the first thing. And therefore, in all the things subsequent to it, essence has to be one thing, being another. For all that agrees with something is either derived from the principles of that thing's nature, for example, the ability to laugh in man; or else it comes from an external principle, as light comes to the air from the sun. But it is impossible for the being in things, which is distinct from the essence, to be made from the essence and nature of a thing as if from the efficient cause. Should this happen, anything would be the cause of itself and would bring itself into being. So everything which is such that its essence is one thing, its being another, derives its being from another. And since everything which exists through another can be derived from what exists through itself, namely the first cause, and since it receives being from this, it finds itself with regard to the first cause in the position of the receiving potentiality. But corresponding to this potentiality is the act of being which is received. So all things after God are compounded from potentiality and act, that is, from essence and being.

You can see this firstly from what I shall call created nature's possibility, secondly from the fact that nature endures limitation, thirdly from the fact that it has composition. The first is obvious as follows. Because a thing has been produced by another, it is not from itself. It is from another, and placed apart from the other, it would not exist. So the thing can both be and not be; and it isn't its own being but the potentiality for being. For nothing is the potentiality for itself, and nothing sustains itself and nothing is created as a result of sustaining itself. For the agent, when it acts, always makes what is such and such potentially such and such actually. Therefore every production is not the result of potentiality being impressed into potentiality, because, if it were, the product would still be in the state of potentiality and wouldn't yet exist. Nor is it even the result of act being poured into act, or the same thing into itself, because, [if it were,] the thing produced would exist before it existed. Rather, act is being poured into potentiality. But since act and potentiality are in a way opposed and the one is not the

significamus. Ideoque oportet ut in omnibus id sequentibus aliud essentia sit, aliud esse. Omne autem quod alicui convenit vel ex naturae suae principiis est eductum, ut ridendi facultas homini, vel ab externo principio advenit, ut aeri [*406v*] a sole lumen. Fieri autem nequit ut ipsum esse in rebus quod ab essentia[1] est distinctum ab ipsa rei essentia et natura sit effectum, tamquam ab effectrice causa. Nam sic aliquid sui ipsius esset causa, seque ipsum in esse produceret. Omne itaque quod tale est ut aliud in eo essentia[2] sua[3] sit, aliud esse, esse habet ab alio. Et[4] quia omne quod per aliud est ad id quod per se est reducitur ut ad causam primam, et ab illo esse recipit, ad illud se ut potentia recipiens habet. Huic autem potentiae susceptus essendi actus respondet. Ex potentia igitur atque actu, essentia scilicet et esse, post Deum omnia componuntur.

Quod praeterea ostendendum est primo ex naturae creatae (ut ita dicam) possibilitate; secundo ex ipsius limitatione; tertio eiusdem compositione. Primum sic patet: nempe ex eo quod res producta ab alio, ex se non est. Est quidem ab alio et ab illo destituta non esset. Ideo et esse potest et non esse; et suum esse non est, sed ad esse ipsum potentia est. Nihil enim ad se ipsum potentia est; nihilque se ipsum suscipit et nihil suscipiendo se ipsum gignitur. Semper enim agens cum agit quod potentia tale est actu efficit tale. Fit ergo productio quaeque non quia potentiae potentia imprimatur, quia si ita fieret adhuc producta res in potentia esset, nequedum esset. Nec etiam actus infunditur actui, vel idem sibi ipsi, quia res producta esset antequam foret. Sed potentiae infunditur actus. Quoniam vero actus et potentia quodammodo opponuntur,[5] neque unum idem est

[1]*for* ab essentia *Y reads* absentia   [2]substantia *XP*   [3]sua *XP*   [4]Et *om. W*
[5]componuntur *W*

same as the other, in creation, accordingly, the being which is given to the essence possesses the rational principle of act, but the essence which receives [the being] possesses the rational principle of potentiality.

You can see it is so from [nature's] limitation. Since the essence of souls and intelligences isn't in matter, the essence certainly isn't contracted on account of matter's capacity. So from the point of view of what's below it, it is infinite and excludes the limit. Accordingly, if the essence doesn't receive being different from itself, but is its own being, then the being hasn't been received in another. Therefore it exists through itself. Everything that is such is pure and utterly infinite and excludes all limit. Its being isn't defined from above because it isn't in another; and its essence isn't defined from below because it isn't in another. Therefore on all counts it excludes all limit. But this is only true of what comes first, not of what comes second; for all that the first thing surpasses is constrained by its limits. Therefore with higher substances essence is one thing, being another. But, since every compound found in the higher substances must also be found in corporeal things, all corporeal things and incorporeal things have essence distinct from being.

You can see it is so from [nature's] composition. If created nature were to exist as its own being, it would be entirely simple, since being itself doesn't participate in anything in any way. For being is the substantial act; or rather, the total act of the total thing. But participation is brought about because of potentiality. Therefore whatever has been created to be just being can't participate in anything else. So it exists as an entirely simple thing, therefore by nature entirely unchangeable. But this is not at all true of a thing that's been created. Therefore with all things subsequent to God Himself you find potentiality and act and essence and being.

Matter I call the potentiality itself which is shared by all things and is in itself indifferent to being and non-being alike; it is midway between nothingness and being and is unformed and equally receptive to all the individual forms. Matter is the first

quod est[1] et aliud, ideo in creatione ipsum esse quod essentiae datur rationem actus habet, essentia vero quae suscipit[2] habet potentiae rationem.

Ex limitatione [*407r*] sic apparet. Profecto cum essentia animorum et mentium in materia non sit, non est pro materiae capacitate contracta. Ideo si ad inferiorem partem comparetur, infinita est excludens terminum. Quare si esse non suscipit a se differens, sed ipsum suum esse est, iam esse id in alio non est receptum. Itaque per se existit. Omne tale purum est et penitus infinitum, omnem excludens terminum. Neque sursum finitur esse, quia in alio non est; neque deorsum essentia, quia non in alio. Undique igitur omnem excludit terminum. Id soli primo competit, nulli vero secundo, nam omnia ab eo superata eius limitibus coercentur. Quapropter aliud in supernis substantiis essentia est, aliud esse. Quoniam vero quaecumque compositio in supernis substantiis invenitur in rebus quoque corporeis insit necesse est, tam corporea omnia quam incorporea[3] essentiam habent ab esse distinctam.

Ex compositione sic ostenditur. Si natura creata esse suum existeret, omnino simplex esset, quoniam ipsum esse nullo modo aliquo participat. Est enim substantialis actus; immo totus rei totius actus. Participatio vero ratione potentiae fit. Siquid ergo creatum solum esse est alio nullo participare potest. Omnino igitur simplex existit, ergo omnino immutabilis per naturam, quod creatae rei convenire nullo modo potest. Quare in omnibus Deum ipsum sequentibus potentia reperitur et actus essentiaque et esse.

Potentiam ipsam communem omnibus se ipsa ad esse et non esse indifferentem mediamque inter nihil et esse, informem et

---

[1]est *om. WXP*   [2]suspicit *Y*   [3]incorpora *Y*

infinity in need of the limit. Because it is indifferent to being and non-being, it is therefore indeterminate as regards both, and is said to be indefinite and limited by another. Since it is midway between nothing and something, it occupies, accordingly, infinite space; for there is no greater distance than the distance between nothingness and being. Since it is unformed, it lacks the limit of the forms. Since it is equally disposed towards all the forms, it is disposed towards them indefinitely. Through infinite time it offers itself as the receptacle for the innumerable forms, and it accommodates itself equally and in like manner to all the possible movements of the forms. Moreover, it accommodates itself equally to all the places to which the movements of the forms lead. Therefore it has nothing of its own, nothing certain. Therefore it has no limit. Therefore it is absolutely infinite. What is matter? The potentiality for all, the infinite interval between being and nothingness, the infinite capacity to recieve forms, the indeterminate inchoation of movements. Matter is the first infinity of all things and in all things. All things are made from it and from the limit according to the Pythagorean Philolaus. Hermes Trismegistus calls the infinite "malignity and darkness," the limit "benignity and the splendour of God."[198] Orpheus calls the infinite "chaos," the limit "ornament."[199] Zoroaster introduced two principles, that is, he introduced prime elements from which all things are constituted, the good and the bad. In the place of the limit he put the good, in the place of the infinite he put the bad.

Chapter 2. Confirmation of the above. The hierarchy among the principles and elements which make up an entity.

Plato accepted the two principles, [the infinite and the limit] and was right to introduce the two only after the one. The one is above all things; the two principles are what all things consist of. After the two, Plato numbered off three, that is, the infinite accompanying the limit, the limit in the infinite, and a third mixed from both. But when he mentioned the cause of the

aeque ad formas singulas praeparatam materiam voco, primam ipsam termini [*407v*] indigam infinitatem. Quia ad esse et non esse indifferens, ideo ad quodvis illorum indeterminata est, et indefinita dicitur, et ab alio terminatur. Quia inter nihil et aliquid media, ideo infinitum tenet spatium, nulla enim distantia maior quam quae inter nihil et esse. Quia informis termino formarum caret. Quia ad omnes aeque se habet, indefinita est ad formas; et innumeris formis per infinitum tempus susceptaculum se exponit, quibuscumque formarum motibus aeque se pariterque accommodat; locis quin etiam ad quae formarum motus ducunt aeque congruit omnibus. Nihil igitur habet proprium, nihil certum. Nullum itaque terminum; prorsus igitur infinita. Quid materia[1]? Potentia omnium, infinitum inter esse et nihilum[2] intervallum, infinita formarum capacitas, indeterminata motuum inchoatio. Haec prima est omnium et in omnibus infinitas, ex qua et termino constant omnia, ut Philolaus inquit Pythagoreus. Mercurius infinitum vocat malignitatem tenebrasque, terminum benignitatem Deique splendorem. Orpheus infinitum[3] vocat chaos, terminum ornatum. Zoroaster duo principia induxit, id est, elementa prima ex quibus constituuntur omnia, bonum et malum; loco termini bonum, loco infiniti malum.[4]

Firmatio superiorum. Gradus principiorum elementorumque entis. Cap. II.[5]

Plato haec duo accepit principia, et merito post unum solum duo induxit. Unum super omnia; duo ex quibus omnia. Post duo tria connumeravit, id est, infinitum cum termino, terminum in infinito, mixtum ex utrisque tertium. Statim vero

---

[1]nam *W*   [2]nihil *XP*   [3]infinitam *W*   [4]*em., WXYP read* loco mali infinitum
[5]*no ch. break or heading WXP, though P has a faint* Cap. II *in the margin*

23D   mixture, he immediately introduced four principles. But in the
Sophist Plato posited five elements in what is called "an entity."[200] Plato understands by this something compounded from
essence and being, although the term "entity" itself refers more
to the compound's being than to its essence. Therefore Plato
didn't say an entity consists of being, essence, rest, motion,
[identity, difference,] for that would be six. But he posited five
and left out being, because being plays the major part in the expression "an entity." So "entity" refers principally to the being
given by the limit, which is above infinity, to infinity. Plato
added five things to entity: essence (namely the infinity which
being presupposes), rest, motion, identity, difference. For in the
case of every single thing that exists, five elements are added to
being. First comes essence, that is, the formal cause of each
thing. Identity is next, as each essence is entirely similar to and
identical with itself and also always shares something with
others. Immediately difference arises, because being and essence
differ, and [every entity] is often made from many things and it
differs from other things which are outside itself. There is also
rest in so far as it stays for some time in its own nature and persists in its unity. Motion arises too, which is nothing else but the
movement away from essence; that is, motion is a certain operation (for all things do something). In the same way as the two
principles, the limit and the infinite, are in all things after God,
so the five [elements] are in them too. Because of the limit every
single thing has being, that is, because of the higher limit. The
fact that it has being doesn't increase the number [of the ele-
ments], since being is included in the meaning of the term
"entity." But because of the infinite this first thing, namely entity, possesses essence. Again, because of the limit every entity
has identity and rest; because of the infinite, difference and
motion.

    You can make the elements into six as long as you say every
entity consists of being, essence, identity, difference, rest and
motion. Plato indicated this can happen when he said the
adorning of the song is completed, according to Orpheus, in the
sixth generation.[201] But six is the most perfect number because

intulit quattuor, cum mixtionis causam nominavit. Quinque vero in Sophiste posuit elementa [*408r*] eius quod ens dicitur. Ens intelligit compositum ex essentia atque esse, quamquam nomen ens illius compositi magis exprimit esse quam essentiam. Ideo non dixit quod ens[1] constet ex esse, essentia, statu, motu, et cetera, essent enim sex. Posuit autem quinque et esse praetermisit, quia in expressione entis esse praevalet. Significat ergo ens[2] praecipue ipsum esse a termino, qui super infinitatem est, infinitati datum. Huic adiecit quinque, essentiam, scilicet infinitatem ipsam quam esse id praesupponit, statum,[3] motum, idem, alterum. In unoquoque enim quod est ipsi esse quinque[4] sunt annexa. Essentia primo, scilicet ratio cuiusque rei formalis. Idem, quia essentia omnis sibi ipsi penitus similis est et idem, et cum aliis etiam semper in aliquo convenit. Statim oritur alterum, quia et esse et essentia alterum et saepe ex pluribus constituitur et ab aliis quae extra se sunt differt. Est et status quantum[5] in sui natura aliquamdiu moratur, et sua in unitate persistit. Oritur et motus qui nihil est aliud quam exitus de essentia, id est, operatio quaedam. Omnia enim aliquid operantur. Sicut in omnibus post Deum sunt duo illa, terminus et[6] infinitum, ita et ista quinque in omnibus. Ratione termini esse habet unumquodque, termini scilicet superioris, quod quidem esse[7] non auget numerum, quia in ipsa entis denominatione exprimitur. Ratione vero infiniti illud primum scilicet ens habet essentiam.[8] Ratione rursus termini est illic[9] idem et status, infiniti alterum atque motus.

Potest et numerus senarius addi ita ut dicatur constare ens omne ex esse, essentia, eodem, altero, statu ac motu. Quod fieri posse significavit Plato cum dixit in sexta generatione [*408v*] secundum Orpheum ornatum cantilenae finiri.[10] Is autem numerus perfectissimus est, quia proprie ex partibus suis

---

[1] eos *W*   [2] eas *W*   [3] statim *XP*   [4] *X has what is either the letter S (abbr. for* scilicet*) or the number 5;* scilicet *P*   [5] inquantum *WXP*   [6] et *om. W*   [7] quidem esse *om. WXP*   [8] *for* scilicet ens habet essentiam *W reads* ex quaque est essentia scilicet, *and XP read* ex quinque est essentia scilicet   [9] est illic *om. WXP*   [10] fieri *P*

it is properly constituted from its parts: from one, from two, and from three. And though the elements are six, the first one, which is being, Plato didn't mention in the *Sophist* when he enumerated them, because in talking about entity he meant it to include being (for in entity being prevails over the other elements).[202] So, in talking about five elements, he meant five over and above the one which is being, which is what he had principally meant by the term "entity." So there are six universal genera. After one correctly comes two, since two is what follows closest to one. After two comes three—from which you get six. Firstly there's God. Secondly there's the limit and the infinite. Three of the elements come under the limit: being, identity, rest. Three of the elements come under the infinite: essence, difference, motion. So the one becomes two, the two three. Consequently after two, when three emerges, six also emerges simultaneously; for the three derivatives of each of the two make up six. You can't, as it so happens, go any further. For each of the two, in coming from the one, returns to the one through its three derivatives—when it is in the one and proceeding from it and returning to it.

Or rather, there are seven elements, for above the six is God. However, the number seven is the limit of nature.

Or rather, the total is nine: God, the infinite, the limit, being, essence, rest, motion, identity, difference. All things come to an end in this number. For the one, in resting, moving and returning to itself, effects three things which undergo the same process in themselves and effect nine. You can't go any further because the three sets of three, which are in the number nine, make up the total power of one entity. For it rests, is moved, returns, [that is,] is, lives, understands. You have three things here: [essence, life, intellect.] Again, in the essence there is life and intellect by way of essence; in life there is essence and intellect by way of life; in the intellect there is essence and life by way of intellect. So every going out and turning back is terminated in the number nine because, from the triple correspondence within any one thing through the sets of three, the maximum conversion into the one occurs in so far as it's possible.

constat: uno, duobus, tribus. Ac licet sex sint, illud primum
quod est esse in Sophiste tacuit Plato in numerando, quia cum
ens diceret significavit, in eo enim esse alia praevalet.
Ideo cum quinque dixit, intellexit quinque ultra unum, quod esse est,
quod per ens praecipue significaverat. Sex itaque sunt genera
rerum. Merito post unum duo, hoc enim proxime sequitur
unum. Post duo tria, ex quibus sex complentur. Est primo
Deus. Secundo terminus et infinitum. Sub termino tria: esse,
idem, status. Sub infinito tria:[1] essentia, alterum, motus. Ergo
unum in duo, duo in tria. Ex quo post duo, dum tria oriuntur,
sex quoque pariter oriuntur. Nam sub unoquoque duorum tria
pendentia sex conficiunt. Neque forte potest ultra procedi, nam
quodvis duorum per tria sua ut ab uno est ita redit in unum dum
et est in eo et procedit et redit.

Immo vero septem[2] sunt, nam Deus supra sex. Septenarius
autem naturae est terminus.

Immo et novem: Deus, infinitum, terminus, esse, essentia,
status, motus, idem et alterum. In hoc numero finiuntur omnia.
Unum quippe dum stat, movetur,[3] reditque in se ipsum tria efficit. Tria pariter in se redeuntia novem. Neque ultra proceditur
quia tres quae sunt[4] in novenario trinitates omnem unius entis
vim explent. Nam et stat, movetur,[5] redit, est,[6] vivit, intelligit.
Ubi tria sunt. Item in essentia est vita et intellectus per modum
essentiae; in vita essentia,[7] intellectus per modum vitae; in intellectu essentia, vita per intellectus modum. Quare in numero
[*409r*] novenario omnis progressio est, omnis reflexio terminatur, quia ex hac[8] trina adaequatione in quolibet uno per trinitates maxima quoad fieri potest fit in unum conversio.

---

[1] tertia *W*   [2] septimum *W*   [3] movet *Y*   [4] insunt *W*   [5] et *add. WXP*
[6] et *add. W*   [7] essentiae *P*   [8] hoc *W*

*Chapter 3. The conditions which all things share because of
the infinite and those they share because of the limit.*

But let's return to the point from which we digressed. Let's
see what all things generally have in common from the nature of
the limit and the infinite, then see what is particularly appropriate to individuals from the same. Because the limit, that is, act,
has been given to things by God, a certain unity is present which
copies the first one. Because infinity is present, that is, the potentiality which falls away from the one, multiplicity is present
which degenerates from the one. Again, from the former comes
being, from the latter, essence. From the former comes identity,
from the latter, difference. From the former comes rest, from
the latter, motion. For every single thing gladly persists in its act
and limit. But it is moved towards something out of the need
supplied by the passive potentiality. What isn't moved is the
same as itself, but what digresses is different. If the limit alone
were present, there would be only act, rest, identity. If infinity
alone were present, there would be only potentiality, motion and
diversity. But in things the latter have been mixed together;
therefore the former have been mixed together too. From the
limit comes the good; from the infinite, the bad, or the decrease
of good. This is because act comes from the former, privation
from the latter. Beauty comes from the former, from the latter
comes deformity or ugliness. From the former comes action,
from the latter, passivity; for everything acts through act, sustains through potentiality. They are what everything has in
common.

From the limit in the intelligence is eternal essence and
operation and the fixed series of the Ideas. From the infinite is
the multitude of the Ideas and because of them unceasing repetition. From the infinite the soul proceeds by operating through
the intervals of time, and in addition to the number of the
species it supplies the number of operations and temporal intervals. From the limit the essence stays still and repeats the same
operations at fixed intervals. From the limit the universal world
is continuous and connected in its parts and contains the finite

Quae conditiones competant omnibus ratione infiniti et quae ratione termini. Cap. III.[1]

Sed redeamus illuc unde digressi sumus. Videamus quid communiter omnibus rebus competat ex termini et infiniti natura; deinde quid proprie singulis ex eisdem conveniat. Quia in rebus terminus est, id est, actus a Deo datus, inest unitas quaedam unum imitans primum. Quia infinitas, id est, potentia ab uno discedens, inest multitudo ab uno degenerans. Item ex eo esse, ex hac essentia. Ex eo idem, ex hac alterum. Ex eo status, ex hac motus. Quia unumquodque in actu et termino suo libenter permanet. Movetur autem ad aliquid ex indigentia quam passiva praebet potentia. Et idem secum est quod non movetur, alterum vero quod digreditur. Si solus inesset terminus, solus actus, status, identitas. Si sola infinitas, sola potentia, motus atque diversitas. Haec autem in rebus mixta sunt; mixta igitur sunt et illa. Ex illo bonum, ex hac malum sive decrementum boni, quia ex illo actus, ex hac[2] privatio. Ex illo pulchritudo, ex hac deformitas sive informitas. Ex illo actio, ex hac passio, nam quaeque per actum agunt, per potentiam capiunt. Ista omnibus sunt communia.

Ex illo in mente aeterna essentia et operatio est et certa idearum series. Ex hac idearum multitudo perque eas incessabilis replicatio. Ex infinito anima per temporis intervalla operando progreditur et supra specierum numerum operationum et temporis adhibet numerum. Ex termino stat essentia et operationes easdem certis replicat intervallis. Mundus universus [*409v*] ex termino continuus[3] est partibusque[4] connexus[5] et finitas rerum

---

[1] *no ch. break or heading WXP*   [2] hoc *WY*   [3] continuum *WXP*   [4] -que *om. P*
[5] connexum *WXP*

species of things. From the infinite the world makes various progressions and produces numberless single things; but by measuring through the limit it also restores the progressions to fixed intervals. Again, from the limit the qualities and quantities of the lower bodies in a way possess the ability to check the capacity of matter and to limit the flux. From the infinite quantity possesses the ability always to be divided and increased. For it is appropriate to quantity which is in matter to be divided and extended. But each part of a quantity is a quantity. Therefore each part can be divided and extended, for quantity isn't made from non-quantities but from its parts; and unless it possesses a part it isn't quantity, so you can divide it to infinity. Each part of a quantity is a quantity. Each quantity has parts, therefore each can be divided. What can be divided to infinity can also be increased to infinity. For, by virtue of the fact that something descends to infinity, it leaves behind an infinite series above. Therefore, where there is an infinite descent, there is an infinite ascent behind it; for the descent isn't infinite unless there is an infinite series through which it can descend. As many steps in the series as are taken up in front, that number is left behind. In front they are taken up to infinity, therefore they are left behind to infinity. So an infinite thread is rolled up behind while an infinite thread is unrolled in front. But what can be extended to infinity doesn't disagree with itself. But it does disagree with a species, which requires a definite quantity just as it does an appropriate quality. But quantity can be extended to infinity because it's in matter. For, if it's above matter, it will certainly be the rational principle itself of quantity—which isn't large (in order to agree with small things), nor small (in order to agree with large things). Therefore because of matter's infinity quantity finds itself open to any amount of extension or division. Again, quality, when it partakes of the limit, forms matter and possesses the one property appropriate to its nature. But when it degenerates into matter's infinity, it can always be relaxed in its degrees to infinity or intensified to infinity. For to be intensified and relaxed is appropriate to the quality which is in matter. Each

continet species. Ex infinito progressus efficit varios et singula
generat infinita, sed et progressus per terminum metiendo[1]
certis restituit intervallis. Item qualitates et quantitates inferiorum corporum ex termino habent ut materiae quoquomodo sis-
tant capacitatem et fluxum terminent. Ex infinito quantitas
habet ut et dividi possit semper et augeri. Proprium enim quantitatis est quae est[2] in materia dividi et extendi. Quaecumque
vero quantitatis pars quantitas est. Igitur quaeque pars et[3] dividi
et extendi potest, neque enim quantitas ex non quantis constat,
ex partibus autem suis constat et nisi habeat partem[4] non est
quantitas. Quare in infinitum dividitur. Quaeque pars
quantitatis est quantitas. Omnis quantitas habet partes; ergo
omnis dividitur. Quod dividi potest in infinitum et in infinitum
augeri, eo enim ipso quod descendit in infinitum, supra relinquit gradus in infinitum. Ergo post tergum fit ascensus infinitus, ubi descensus fit infinitus; non enim descensus est infinitus, nisi infiniti sint gradus per quos descenditur. Quot gradus
ante capiuntur tot retro linquuntur; ante in infinitum capiuntur,
retro ergo linquuntur in infinitum. Ergo tela retro convolvitur
infinita, dum ante infinita revolvitur. Quod autem in infinitum
extendatur nequaquam sibi repugnat. Repugnat autem speciei
quae ita certam quantitatem postulat ut propriam exigit qualitatem. Id autem quantitati contingit, quia in materia est. Si enim
sit supra materiam erit utique ipsa ratio quantitatis, [*410r*]
quae nec magna est ut parvis congruat, nec parva ut congruat
magnis. Ab infinitate igitur materiae quantitas habet ut ad
quamlibet extensionem et divisionem sit indifferens. Item qualitas ut termini est particeps materiam format unamque[5] habet
suae naturae proprietatem. Ut autem in materiae infinitate
degenerat et remitti in infinitum potest et in infinitum[6] gradibus
semper intendi. Proprium enim qualitatis est quae inest materiae ut intendatur et remittatur. Quaeque pars qualitatis est

---

[1]metuendo *W*   [2]quae est *om. W*   [3]et *om. YP*   [4]partes *W*   [5]unaquaeque *XP*
[6]finitum *W*

part of a quality is a quality, so each part can always be intensified or relaxed.

But if quality exists outside matter, it is nothing else but the
rational principle itself of quality. It isn't in a state of intensity,
so that it can agree with a relaxed quality; nor is it in a state of
relaxation, so that it can agree with an intense quality too.
Again, the quality which is in matter is received according to the
capacity of matter itself. Matter's condition is worse than the
form. So the quality is not received in matter in its total
fullness. Therefore it can be diminished since it's disabled or increased since it's not entire. It's received by the subject more
and more or less and less according to the subject's various
states of preparedness. But the quality which has been freed
from the limits of a subject has the total completeness of its
energy; it has it in an instant since it surpasses time, and it has it
in one spot since it is above place. So it isn't stretched out in
degrees nor extended from part to part.

Moreover, because of matter there are infinite individuals in
the same species of each thing or quality. For as matter nowhere
possesses the total fullness of the form and is prepared to
receive it everywhere, it keeps on desiring what remains. It is
able to receive it and receive it in various parts. So matter
receives the form's same nature in various ways and at various
intervals of time and space. You can see this with the things
which we say are in the same species. The one common property
and one act indicates there is one form. Yet there's the
distinction which comes from certain conditions of matter
itself: from time, from situation, from shape. So when you've
subtracted them from the form one thing is left. But this
diversity of individuals in the same species is caused by
quantified matter in the case of bodies; but in the case of souls it
is caused by the distinction of reason which is in the souls' Idea.
Here each Idea receives some distinction in itself from the participation of infinity, as we've described.

Conclude that the infinite is manifested in the intelligence
only in the multitude of the reasons, in the soul in the multitude
of the reasons and instants, in bodies in the multitude of the

qualitas, semper igitur quaeque pars intendi potest atque remitti.

At si extra materiam sit qualitas, nihil aliud est quam ipsa ratio qualitatis. Ipsa vero nec intensa est ut remissae congruat, neque remissa ut competat et intensae. Item quae in materia est pro captu materiae ipsius suscipitur. Conditio materiae forma deterior est. Quare non tota sui plenitudine in materia suscipitur qualitas. Ideo minui potest, cum sit debilis, et augeri, cum tota non sit, et pro subiecti varia praeparatione magis magisque, vel etiam minus ac minus accipi a subiecto. Quae vero absoluta est a subiecti limitibus totam sui vigoris integritatem uno habet momento, cum tempus supergrediatur, et uno habet in puncto, cum sit supra locum. Non ergo de gradu in gradum protenditur, neque ex parte in partem extenditur.

Quin etiam ratione materiae in eadem specie rei cuiusque et qualitatis infinita sunt individua. Nam cum nusquam materia totam formae habeat plenitudinem et ubique ad recipiendum parata sit, adhuc quod superest appetit, potestque accipere et in diversis accipere[1] [*410v*] partibus. Igitur et temporum et locorum intervallis diversis, diversis modis suscipit eandem formae naturam. Quod ex eo patet quia in his quae in eadem specie esse dicimus communis una omnium proprietas et actus unus unam esse indicat[2] formam. Est distinctio tamen ex quibusdam materiae ipsius conditionibus tempore, situ, figura. His ergo subtractis a forma unum remanet. Hanc vero diversitatem individuorum in specie eadem in corporibus materia quanta facit, in animis rationis distinctio quae in animorum idea est. Ubi distinctionem idea quaeque in se suscipit aliquam ex infinitatis participatione quam diximus.

Collige infinitum in mente in rationum multitudine dumtaxat ostendi, in anima rationum et momentorum, in corporibus

---

[1]accipere *om. W*   [2]arguit *WXP*

reasons and instants and points in space. Therefore infinity increases in bodies, because the universal matter is the first to receive quantity as it's subjected to the forms of bodily things.

There is a certain condition of the limit inserted into everything by the one itself; because of it individuals are one in themselves and everything is one. There is also a certain condition of the limit coming down from the intelligence with the energy of the one above; and because of it there is one unchanging order for all the species, reasons and forms. In a fixed and continuous series the order is turned back eventually towards the first one. There is also a certain condition of the limit given to matter by the soul from the energy of the intelligence and the one. This limit is form itself, quantity and quality. Moreover, in quantity's dimensions there is a fixed and measured and mutual proportion. In quality's degrees there is some number's species and a mutual moderation of the qualities among themselves. Given all this, vague movement ceases.[203] All things are bound together. From the various proportions of the quantities and moderations of the qualities various corporeal substances and natures also arise. So, as the Platonist, Philo, says, individual things are made from the condition of the limit itself in weight, measure and number. "Weight" he calls the fixed substance and nature of a thing. "Measure" signifies the determined proportion of the quantity; "number," the finite and consonant degrees of the quality.[204]

Chapter 4. Again, the way in which the infinite is under God and the limit depending on it; and how these two are mixed together.

23C   **All things which are now in the universe** . . . [205] Therefore Socrates says, "All things which are now in the universal order of things and descend from the one leader of the entire order let's separate into two elements; that is, into the limit and the infinite, that is, into the universal matter and the universal form and the conditions which follow them." He says "now" in

rationum, momentorum atque punctorum. Crescit ergo in corporibus infinitas, quia materia illa communis ut subest corporalium rerum formis prius accipit quantitatem.

Est quaedam conditio termini ab ipso uno omnibus insita qua singula in se unum sunt et unum cuncta. Est et a mente quaedam superioris unius vigore descendens qua unus et stabilis omnium specierum, rationum et formarum ordo certa et continuata serie in unum denique primum reflectitur. Est et ab anima mentis et unius vigore quaedam materiae termini conditio data, ipsa videlicet forma, quantitas et qualitas. Quantitatis insuper dimensionibus certa et mensurata mutuaque proportio; qualitatis gradibus numeri alicuius species et qualitatum inter se mutua moderatio. Quibus [*411r*] datis vagus cessat motus. Simul omnia vinciuntur. Et aliis aliisque quantitatum proportionibus et qualitatum moderationibus aliae quoque et aliae corporum substantiae naturaeque consurgunt. Unde singula, ut Platonicus inquit Philon, ex termini ipsius conditione in pondere, mensura ac numero sunt constituta. Pondus certam dicit rei substantiam atque naturam. Mensura quantitatis proportionem determinatam, numerus finitos et consonantes qualitatis gradus significat.

Iterum quomodo sub Deo est[1] *infinitum atque terminus inde dependens et quomodo duo haec invicem misceantur. Cap. IV.*[2]

Omnia quae nunc in universo sunt ... Dicit igitur Socrates, Omnia quae sunt in universo ordine rerum ab uno totius ordinis principe descendentium in duo elementa partiamur, scilicet in terminum et infinitum, materiam videlicet illam communem et communem formam et conditiones quae illas sequuntur. Dicit nunc, ut ostendat terminum, scilicet formam, non ex materiae

---

[1]est *om.* Y   [2]*a ch. break, but no heading W; in X and P the ch. is numbered two*

order to show that the limit, that is, form, isn't born from the
bowels of matter by matter's energy, but is caused by God. It's
as if he were saying that form didn't always exist, and wasn't
the equivalent of matter's handmaid. Rather, before matter was
turned back towards God and the divine countenance blazed in
it as in a mirror, it was formless, it was chaos—a confused mass
(as Orpheus says),[206] an empty and vacant potentiality,
darkness above the face of the abyss, that is, of infinity (as
Hermes says).[207] But "now," that is, after God regarded
matter, and the spirit of God (as the same Hermes says) was
borne above the flowing matter of the world, the limit and every
beauty shone forth, as is described in the *Timaeus*.[208] But the
infinite didn't precede the limit in time, but in origin. St. Augustine also acknowledges this when he's expounding Moses, and
Origen before him didn't deny it.[209] To the two elements
23D   Socrates adds a third besides, that is, what is compounded from
them both; for a certain third nature results from the two when
they've been mixed together properly. He said, "Let's entertain
some points from the arguments above." For he had also said
above that God mixed the one and the many, the finite and the
infinite in all things—which we described in its [proper] place.
Socrates said too that God himself through Prometheus, that is,
through His providence and light, had **manifested** these things
to the ancient theologians and to us—"manifested," that is,
declared them to us. Moreover, by way of manifestation God
had created them. For there are three things: creating, effecting,
generating. "Creating" pertains indeed to God who operates
without the Idea and from a matter that did not exist before; for
He Himself produces both. "Effecting" pertains to the
intelligence which effects things in a stable way through the Idea
from a certain matter. "Generating" pertains to the soul which
(through the seeds and reasons and from corporeal matter) acts
with motion and in time. Accordingly, God "made manifest,"
that is, without any pre-existing matter He laid out the infinite,
the foundation of all; and without any pre-existing Idea He
applied the limit to the infinite. Socrates refers to all existing
things as part the infinite, part the limit. This is not because the

visceribus vigore materiae natam, sed a Deo exhibitam. Quasi dicat non semper forma fuit, non aequa materiae ipsius pedissequa. Immo vero antequam materia in Deum converteretur et divinus in eam vultus ut in speculum reluceret, erat informis, erat chaos, congeries indigesta, ut ait Orpheus, inanis erat vacuaque potentia, tenebraeque[1] super abyssi, id est, infinitatis faciem, ut Mercurius inquit. Nunc autem, id est, postquam in materiam aspexit Deus et Dei spiritus, ut idem ait Mercurius, super fluxam mundi materiam est delatus, terminus ornatusque omnis eluxit, ut dicitur in Timaeo. Neque vero infinitum hoc tempore, sed origine praecessit terminum. [*411v*] Quod et Aurelius Augustinus dum exponit Mosen confitetur, et Origenes antea non negavit. His insuper duobus adiungit tertium, quod scilicet ex utrisque compositum, ex duobus enim invicem bene mixtis tertia quaedam natura resultat. Dixit, Accipiamus aliquos ex superioribus sermones. Nam et supra quoque dixerat Deum in omnibus rebus unum et multitudinem, finitum et infinitum immiscuisse, quod loco suo exposuimus. Et dixit ea priscis theologis ac nobis Deum ipsum per Prometheum, id est, providentiam suam et lumen **ostendisse**; ostendisse, id est, nobis declaravisse. Quin etiam per ostensionis modum creasse. Est enim creatio, effectio, generatio. Creatio quidem[2] ad Deum attinet, qui et sine idea et ex nulla praecedente materia operatur, ipse enim ea producit. Effectio ad mentem, quae per ideam ex materia quadam stabiliter efficit. Generatio ad animam, quae per semina et rationes ex materia corporali cum motu agit ac tempore. Ostendit ergo Deus, id est, nulla praecedente materia infinitum iecit omnium fundamentum, et nulla praeexistente idea terminum applicuit infinito. Dicit eorum quae sunt alterum infinitum alterum terminum, non quia ibi quidem infinitum

---

[1] -que *om. Y*   [2] quidem *om. WXP*

infinite can appear here and the limit separately there, but because the infinite is one element of existing things and the limit is the other. So of the three species, that is, degrees of things, let's put first the two elements, the infinite and the limit; and what's constituted from them let's put third. The third thing is one something, because the two have been properly mixed together. For though the things that are mixed by the one itself are two separate things, still they are joined together through the one's power. Imitating the one author they are led to one being. For matter and form joined together are one being not two, just as the operation shines out as one. For matter exists by the being itself of the form. After this, as he wants to bring in a fourth element that isn't in the universe like the other three but above the universe, Socrates says, "**It seems** it's ridiculous of me, that is, I'm a figure of fun, if I assert I have sufficiently divided and enumerated everything." He says "it seems," because in fact he has sufficiently enumerated everything, because he only promised to enumerate the things existing in the universe and there are only three such things. And yet he would be ridiculous unless he introduced the cause which is above the universe. Or rather, Socrates did introduce it when he said that God made manifest. Yet it wasn't enough for him to say God manifested two separate and distinct things. For from the one there has to be one something. Therefore Socrates had to say also that the one God joined the two things into one being. So the one is not only given the job of producing them, but also of joining them into one. So first of all Socrates had made God the one who produces different things; now he also makes God the one who brings things together. Consequently it's obvious that as the world's parts don't come from themselves so they aren't made into one through themselves, but that whatever needed a producer also needs someone to join it together. For opposite things shun each other, therefore they come together through the power of the one above. So **look out** for the fourth element over and beyond the other three, that is, look out for the cause which mixes them together. For all things have been united through the one's strength. Socrates said,

appareat[1] illic seorsum terminus, sed quia eorum quae sunt elementum unum infinitum, alterum vero terminus. Harum itaque trium specierum, id est, graduum rerum, duas quasdam primo ponamus istas, infinitum et terminum, tertiam vero quod ex his constat, quod unum quiddam est, quia bene ista invicem mixta sunt. Quae enim ab uno ipso miscentur, quamquam duo sunt seorsum, tamen [*412r*] invicem iuncta unius ipsius vi. Unum ipsum imitantia auctorem in unum esse ducuntur. Nam et materiae et formae invicem coniunctarum non duo sunt esse sed unum, sicut operatio emicat una. Materia enim ipso formae esse existit. Post haec volens quartum inducere quod non in universo[2] est ut tria illa, sed super universum, ait, Ridiculus sum, id est, deridendus **ut videtur,** si asseverem me sufficienter omnia divisisse atque[3] numerasse. Inquit, ut videtur, quia sufficienter numeravit, quia sola quae in universo sunt se dinumeraturum est pollicitus, illa vero tria sunt tantum. Et tamen ridiculus est, nisi super universum causam induxerit. Immo eam induxit, cum dixit Deum ostendisse; neque tamen satisfecit dum diceret quod Deus duo diversa et seorsum ostendit. Ab uno enim unum esse debet. Ideo adiungendum erat quod Deus unus ea in unum esse coniunxit, ut non solum producendi sed uniendi uni detur officium. Primo igitur Deum productorem fecerat diversorum, nunc etiam conductorem facit, ut pateat sicut partes mundi ex se non sunt, ita neque per se una constare, sed et conducente indigere quicquid indiguit producente. Opposita enim sese fugiunt, unius ergo superioris vi coeunt. Ideo praeter haec tria **vide** et quartum, causam scilicet qua haec una miscentur. Nam unius vi unita sunt omnia. Dixit vide ut aperiret

---

[1]apparet *W*   [2]*for* in universo *Y reads* innumeroso   [3]atque *om. W*

"look out," to show that the cause is not fourth in the sequence, for it's first in the sequence, but that it's the fourth one to be discovered. For, since we see opposites come together into one, we conjecture there is one author of the union above them. On this topic first the Democriteans are certainly refuted, and then the Epicureans who thought that all opposites cling together because of a fortuitous dashing together.

Here you have to remember the first cause of the union is the first God Himself by whose power the intelligence and the soul bind all things into one. For the intelligence as intelligence only produces the forms. The soul in turn as soul produces the movement of the forms. But the two together give unity to something according as they participate in the first one's unity.

Protarchus asked whether there isn't a need for the fifth element, the highest cause, which can separate what's better from what's worse for the sake of the perfection of the better, just as the fourth element unites what's better to what's worse for the sake of the perfection of the worse. This Socrates didn't deny, but he did say there was no need in the present dispute to do it. For God both surpasses everything and communicates Himself to everything. The former is referred to as God's "sublimity," the latter as God's "countenance." The former produces the matter which is by itself, the latter joins form to it. When things after God copy the divine countenance, they always join themselves to lower things for the sake of the perfection of the lower things; and things which are equal meet and everything is brought to a single steady course. But when they desire God's sublimity, all the forms and essences, which can exist without lower things, free themselves from them for the sake of the completeness of each other and no longer communicate with what is worse. Therefore God is always the cause of unity. God's countenance is the cause of the unity which results in things joining together. God's sublimity is the cause of the unity which preserves the proper simplicity of each thing. But in the first case God joins separate things together by mixing them; in the second He unites every thing to Himself by separating them. So He is called on the one hand the cause of things

23E

causam istam non esse quartam gradu, est enim gradu prima, sed inventu quartam.[1] Quia enim videmus opposita in unum congredi, unum esse unionis super illa conicimus auctorem. Quo certe in loco Democritii primo[2] redarguuntur, [*412v*] et postmodum Epicurei, qui fortuito[3] concursu haec omnia putaverunt invicem cohaerere.

Ubi meminisse oportet quod prima unionis causa primus ipse est Deus, cuius vi mens et anima in unum omnia vinciunt. Mens enim ut mens est formas dumtaxat producit. Anima rursus ut anima formarum motum. Unionem vero dant ut primi unius unitate participant.

Interrogavit Protarchus num quinta[4] et suprema causa opus sit quae discernere possit a deterioribus meliora ad meliorum integritatem, sicut quarta unit meliora deterioribus ad deteriorum perfectionem. Non negavit Socrates, sed dixit in praesenti disputatione illa opus non esse, et enim Deus supereminet omnia et se communicat omnibus. Illa Dei sublimitas, hic Dei vultus dicitur. Illa solitariam producit materiam; hic illi unit formam. Atque ut sequentia vultum imitantur divinum, semper sese iungunt inferioribus ad illorum perfectionem, et paria congrediuntur, et omnia in tenorem unicum rediguntur. Ut Dei appetunt sublimitatem omnes formae et essentiae quae sine deterioribus esse possunt se eximunt ad sui ipsius integritatem, peiorumque[5] relinquunt commercium. Semper ergo Deus unitatis est causa. Dei vultus unitatis quae in coniunctione resultat. Dei sublimitas unitatis cuiusque propriam tutantis simplicitatem. Sed ibi quidem commiscendo discreta unit invicem; hic autem discernendo sibimet ipsi unit quodcumque. Ideo ibi[6]

---

[1]quarta *XP* [2]primo *om. P* [3]fortuitu *W* [4]quanta *W;* q̄ta [?] *X;* quarta *P*
[5]priorumque *XP* [6]ibi *om. Y*

mixing; on the other, the cause of things separating. So above the cause of the mixture there is also the cause of the separation. In this dialogue we're concerned with the mixed life, since we're concerned with the happiness of the human soul (which perfects the intellect and the will). Therefore the cause of the mixture is sufficient. There's no need to discuss the cause of the separation. For the imitation of this cause pertains to the happiness which is the intelligence's alone and is the soul's only when it has finally separated the intelligence from its other parts. Where there is no potentiality of the appetite and there's the complete act of understanding, there is happiness. It is just tasted in this life by the person who is seized by God, as Plato says in the *Phaedrus*.[210] But the soul actually enjoys it in another life, when it has come out of the body and is pure, as Plato says in the *Phaedo*.[211] The fifth life is so called since it imitates the fifth element, and since the first life is the concupiscible life, the second the irascible, the third the active, the fourth the contemplative (which is the life appropriate to the soul). The fifth life is the contemplative life appropriate to the intelligence. Given the opportunity, it's the life Socrates will follow gladly, whenever he recognizes it and is able to attain it. Protarchus willingly concedes him this point, although they are concerned here with protecting the mixed life. For we always ought to support the thing that is most true and not cling stubbornly to our opinions; we always ought to seize hold of what appears to be the better alternative.

But of this elsewhere. Now to deal with human happiness, for it's the way to the other life. Therefore, having dismissed the fifth element, Socrates proposes to treat of the other four which pertain to the subject of the argument. Before doing anything else he establishes the right approach: that is, since there are four elements, we'll consider the first three first, then the fourth one which is the cause of the mixture. For through the first three we can understand the cause. But with the three, we'll deal with the first two, that is, with the infinite and the limit, before dealing with the mixture. For from the first two comes the mixture. And with the first two, we'll deal with the infinite first,

23E

dicitur mixtionis, hic autem discretionis causa. Super igitur causam mixtionis est et discretionis causa. Hoc [*413r*] in libro de
mixta agitur vita, quia de humani animi beatitudine quae et
intellectum et voluntatem perficit. Ideo causa mixtionis sufficit.
De discretionis causa disserere nihil opus est, nam ad eius imitationem ea pertinet beatitudo quae solius mentis est, et animi
tunc demum cum mentem ab aliis partibus suis secrevit. Ubi
nulla est appetitus potentia, ubi integer intelligentiae actus felicitas est quam hac in vita gustat quisquis Deo rapitur, ut ait in
Phaedro. In alia vero fruitur animus qui mundus corpus
egreditur, ut in Phaedone. Haec vita quinta dicitur, quoniam ad
quinti illius imitationem et quoniam prima vita concupiscibilis[1]
est, secunda irascibilis, tertia activa, quarta contemplativa
animae propria, quinta contemplativa propria mentis, quam
vitam libenter sequetur Socrates, cum data opportunitate eam
et noverit et assequi poterit.[2] Quod libenter illi concedit[3] Protarchus, quamquam mixtam hic tutantur vitam. Semper enim ei
quod est verissimum favere debemus, nec opiniones nostras
mordicus tenere, sed quod melius semper apparet capessere.

Sed de hac[4] alias. Nunc de humana felicitate, haec enim ad
illam via. Quinto ergo dimisso quattuor tractanda[5] proponit
quae ad disputationis propositum pertinent. Modumque tractandi ante omnia statuit, quod[6] videlicet, cum quattuor sint,
primo tria consideremus, postea quartum, scilicet causam mixtionis. Nam per haec illam cognoscimus. Inter haec autem tria[7]
prius de duobus scilicet infinito et termino quam de mixto. Hoc
enim ex illis. Et inter haec duo prius de infinito, hoc enim terminum antecedit, et ad voluptatem praecipue confert de qua

---

[1]corruptibilis *W*   [2]potuerit *P*   [3]concedet *W* [?] *XP*   [4]hoc *XP*   [5]tractando *Y*
[6]quae *P*   [7]tertia *W*

for it precedes the limit and is the chief contribution to pleasure, which ought to be dealt with first. But Socrates taught us to proceed in the following way when dealing with the infinite and the limit. Since we see each is divided through the many and is scattered, we must try to gather each into the one common nature shared by individual things and so consider how each is one and many. This is Plato's usual precept and it's repeated in many dialogues; since all things after God are one and many, it's to make us investigate their unity and multiplicity and to do so with reference to individual things. But in every case, since the many individuals are outside knowledge, let's consider them in terms of the one species. In order to understand their principle, let's contemplate the many species in terms of the one genus.

24A   Protarchus asks for a plainer explanation. Socrates explains himself thus: "I repeat, first of all two things must be investigated, the infinite and the finite." Since he had talked about the limit above, he introduces something having the limit into the course of the argument. For something concrete is better known than something abstract. Socrates begins with the infinite. In it he first discovers the many, since the many is better known. He will then reduce [the many] to the one. So the topics to be dealt with are these and here is the way of dealing with them.

There follow, collected from the same lectures of Marsilio, some remains of annotations which have been separated.[212] *But Marsilio's commentaries have been summarily arranged according to the order in the text itself of the* **Philebus.**

Concerning understanding and pleasure and their mixture.

Porphyry says happiness can be called a simple good since the pleasure of understanding can be scarcely distinguished from it.[213] For when understanding is at the point of highest concentration, the height of its concentration is itself intimate pleasure. Plotinus also says this.[214] But then it is totally simple and one. But the understanding is delighted when it's been already

primo est agendum. [*413v*] Tam vero de infinito quam de termino hunc in modum tractandum praecepit.[1] Ut cum utrumque
videamus per multa divisum atque dispersum, conemur in unam
communem naturam singulis competentem utrumque[2] colligere, atque ita considerare quo pacto utrumque unum est et
multa. Haec solita illa Platonis praeceptio est et multis in dialogis repetita; ut cum omnia post Deum et unum et multa sint,
unitatem illorum et multitudinem investigemus, hocque facia-
mus in singulis. In cunctis autem individua multa cum praeter
scientiam sint, in una specie consideremus; species multas ut
earum intelligatur principium uno in genere contemplemur.
Petit Protarchus planiorem orationem. Socrates ita se aperit,
Duo primum investiganda, inquam, infinitum atque finitum. Et
cum supra dixisset terminum, hic in modo tractandi proponit
terminum habens. Concretum enim notius quam absolutum. Et
ab infinito incipit. Ubi multitudinem in eo utpote notiorem
prius reperit, deinde in unum rediget. Haec ergo tractanda sunt,
hic est[3] tractandi modus.[4]

[5]*Sequuntur divulsae quaedam annotationum reliquiae ex
eisdem Marsilii lectionibus collectae. Commentaria vero
Marsilii ordine disposita breviter sunt in ipso Philebi textu.*

De intelligentia et voluptate eorumque mixtura.

Porphyrius inquit felicitatem dici posse simplex bonum
quoniam voluptas intelligentiae vix ab ipsa distinguitur. Cum
enim intelligentia est in summo gradu penitus expedito, ipsa sua
expedita summitas est voluptas intima. Ut etiam Plotinus
inquit. Tunc vero maxime est simplex atque unum. Gaudet vero

---

[1]praecipit *WXP* [2]utcumque *WXP* [3]etiam *Y* [4]*in W the subscription reads* Commentaria haec ego Marsilius nondum absolvi, nec emendavi. Similiter neque Iamblici et Hermiae transla-
tionem. Finis; *in X* Finis. Exscripsit clara haec opera Sebastianus Salvinus Marsilii Ficini amitinus,
iij idus februarii 1490; *in P* Finis *(and then a few illegible words)* [5]*in WX (and P) ten excerpts
follow instead of these four odd chapters and the ch. divisions and summaries; see appendix II*

formed, as it were, by the higher light. And just as the utmost point of light in a concave mirror is already heat, so the utmost point of being is already life, and the utmost point of living is sensation, of sensation is the imagination, of the imagination is reason, of reason is understanding, of understanding is joy, and of joy is the good. But now we've arrived at the highest degree we don't reach division but union. And just as the elements seek and enjoy something agreeable with the same natural drive, so the pure intelligence with its same act turns towards the object as something true and enjoys it as something good. To be sure, in the understanding's knowing there is a certain pleasure, in so far as knowing participates in the nature of a person who desires. Now in the power itself of knowing there is inquiry and discovery. Similarly in the power of desiring there is wanting and getting. Inquiry is like wanting, discovery is like getting. Therefore, just as there is pleasurable getting, so also there is pleasurable discovery. Yet the power that desires is not precisely the same as the power that knows. This is especially true with us, for we come to know many things that we don't want and would have preferred not to have known, and vice versa. Again, we come to know for most certain what we least want; and in turn we very much want the things we do not come to know very well.

That neither understanding nor pleasure is the end, but pleasure least of all.

Neither understanding nor pleasure is the good itself, for we can desire neither the one nor the other; and now and then in one way or another we can reject or neglect either of them. But the good, in so far as it is the good, we cannot not desire; nor can we reject or neglect it. Pleasure isn't the end or the good itself, for it always accompanies either getting the good or moving towards it. But now, just as we desire the good as something other, so we rejoice in the good as in something other. But we don't desire desire, nor rejoice in joy. And just as pain is

se ipsa tamquam superiori lumine iam formata. Atque sicut summitas luminis in speculo concavo iam est calor, ita summitas essendi iam est vita, et vivendi sensus, sentiendi imaginatio, imaginandi ratio, rationis intelligentia, intelligentiae gaudium, gaudii bonum. Iam vero ad supremum gradum euntes non ad divisionem pervenimus sed unionem. Atque sicut elementa eodem naturae nixu petunt conveniens et fruuntur, ita mens pura eodem sui actu vergit in obiectum tamquam verum et fruitur obiecto tamquam bono. Profecto in cognitione sua quaedam est voluptas quatenus cognitio naturae appetentis est particeps. Nam in ipsa cognoscendi potentia inquisitio est et inventio. In potentia similiter appetendi est appetitio atque consecutio. Inquisitio quidem appetitioni similis est. Inventio vero consecutioni consimilis. Sicut igitur consecutio sic et inventio voluptaria. Neque tamen est idem penitus virtus appetens atque cognoscens. Apud nos praesertim, nam multa cognoscimus quae nolumus et quae cognovisse nollemus atque vicissim. Item certissime cognoscimus quae minime volumus et vicissim affectamus valde quae non valde cognoscimus.

Quod neque intelligentia neque voluptas est finis, minime vero voluptas.

Neque intelligentia neque voluptas est ipsum bonum, possumus enim neque hanc neque illam appetere et alterutrum interdum quoquomodo respuere vel negligere. Bonum vero qua ratione bonum neque possumus non appetere neque respuere vel negligere licet. Voluptas non est finis ipsumve bonum, semper enim comitatur vel adeptionem boni vel motum ad bonum. Iam vero sicut appetimus bonum tamquam aliud, ita gaudemus bono tamquam alio. Neque vero vel appetimus appetitum vel gaudemus gaudio. Atque sicut dolor aliud est quam malum, dolemus enim malo, nec omne malum dolor, ita

something other than evil (for we are pained by evil), and just as all evil is not pain, so pleasure is other than the good and vice versa. Understanding is also other than the good, for understanding is what looks towards the good and to ways towards the good; it isn't content with itself. To be sure, pleasure is a certain feeling and cheerfulness in the person who's rejoicing, and it is a sort of passive state. But the good itself cannot be like someone's feeling or passive state. Rather, it is in itself that which exists; but of other things it's the maker and perfecter and end. Besides, the good is shared by all those qualities which are mutually opposite. Therefore none of the opposite qualities is the good itself. Therefore, just as the good itself isn't pain, so it isn't pleasure either. Again, if all things participate in the good, but all things don't participate in pleasure, pleasure is certainly not the good itself.

Though the good itself is pleasurable, that is, sweet and delightful, still it isn't pleasure itself and it's perhaps cut off from formal pleasure. For what brings delight is separate perhaps from delight itself, just as what introduces movement is separate from movement. If the good were brought to completion by the pleasurable, then, just as the useful and convenient, so too the pleasurable would certainly be present to everything whatsoever because of the good. But many good things don't arrive accompanied by pleasure. If it is appropriate to the good to preserve, preservation at least is enough to insure the presence of the good. But something that isn't filled with pleasure at all is preserved too. If the pleasurable brings the good to completion, why doesn't the unpleasurable bring the bad to completion? But every so often the bad too is without pain [i.e., the unpleasurable]. If each action exists for the sake of the end, each passive state must do so even more. But pleasure is a passive state; it is the result of something that pleases. But if it exists for the sake of the end, it isn't the end. The arts use pleasure for attaining utility, just as medicine and learning do. Here the end for pleasure is utility. But art imitates nature.[215] It's as if nature instituted pleasure for an end. If pleasure's intention is to attain and to season properly an action which

voluptas aliud quam bonum atque vicissim. Intelligentia etiam aliud quam bonum, spectat enim bonum atque vias ad ipsum bonum; neque se ipsa contenta est. Profecto voluptas est affectio quaedam diffusioque gaudentis et velut passio quaedam. Ipsum vero bonum non potest esse velut alicuius passio vel affectio, sed est in se ipso potius id ipsum quod existit, aliorum vero effector et perfector et finis. Praeterea bonum omnibus oppositis inter se qualitatibus est commune. Neutra igitur oppositarum est ipsum bonum. Igitur ipsum bonum sicut non est dolor ita nec est voluptas. Item si bonum participant omnia, non tamen omnia voluptatem, merito non est voluptas ipsum bonum.

Etsi ipsum bonum est voluptarium, id est suave atque delectans, tamen non est ipsa voluptas, et forte segregatum a voluptate formali. Quod enim delectationem affert sic ab ea forsan est absolutum, sicut quod motum infert a motu. Si bonum a voluptario compleretur, certe quibuscumque per bonum adest utile atque conferens ita etiam voluptarium. At vero multa bonorum non simul cum voluptate proveniunt. Si proprium boni est servare, salus utique satis est ad boni praesentiam. Servatur autem etiam quod nulla voluptate perfunditur. Si voluptarium complet bonum, cur non et molestum complet malum? Passim vero malum est etiam sine dolore. Si omnis actio est ad finem, multo magis passio. Voluptas autem est passio quaedam ab ipso delectante procedens. Si vero est ad finem, non est finis. Artes sane voluptate utuntur ad utilitatem consequendam, sicut medicina atque disciplina, ubi utilitas finis est voluptatis. Iam vero naturam[1] ars imitatur. Quasi natura ad finem instituerit voluptatem. Si voluptatis intentio est attingere atque condire actionem proprie quae tendit ad bonum ut ad

---

[1] *em.,* natura *Y*

aims at the good as the end, it's agreed pleasure belongs to the genus of those things which exist for an end. But pleasure is either in the sense or in the reason, so it familiarly accompanies the [sense's] perception of the good and to some extent the [reason's] anticipation of the good. The result is it often confounds the judgement, and pleasure itself appears to be the good. Pleasure nevertheless can be distinguished from the good which is entirely present or anticipated as present, just as the appetite is distinguished from the good which is absent.

How an essence is compounded from the one, the many, the limit, the infinite. Also, on the genera of an entity.

16C

Plato compounds an essence from four elements as it were, that is, from the one and the many, and also from the limit and the infinite. It seems to me that, in order to compound an essence, the one precedes the limit, and the many, infinity. For the one exists in itself, before it can limit something else or be the limit of something else. Again, the many is thought of simply as the many, before it is thought of as infinite things. If you think of them from the viewpoint of the creator, the one and the limit precede their opposites. However, if you think of them from the viewpoint of the creature, perhaps the reverse happens and the many and the infinite give the appearance of preceding their opposites. Finally, if you think of creator and creature together, perhaps (to compound an essence) the one proceeds together with the many, and the limit with the infinite. Then in the essence, which is now compounded as it were, movement and difference arise because of the many and the infinite. But rest and identity arise because of the one and the limit. But, as I've said before, movement flows as it were out of the compounded essence before rest does. For the essence acts as soon as it is born, and there is a procession in it from one thing to another, however instantaneous. Again, with movement rest itself dawns. For the essence isn't moved correctly, unless at the same time the power itself remains the same.

finem, constat voluptatem esse in eorum genere quae sunt ad finem. Sed haec sive in sensu sive in ratione, ita familiariter comitatur perceptionem boni et quodammodo spem boni, ut confundat saepe iudicium, appareatque ipsa voluptas esse ipsum bonum, cum tamen ita distinguatur a bono omnino praesente vel sperato quasi praesente, sicut appetitio distinguitur ab absente.

Quomodo essentia componatur ex uno, multitudine, termino, infinito. Item de generibus entis.

Plato essentiam componit quasi ex quattuor elementis, scilicet ex uno et multitudine, item ex termino et infinito. Mihi quidem videtur ad essentiam componendam prius esse unum termino, et multitudo prius infinitate. Prius enim est unum in se quam terminet aliquid, vel sit terminus alicuius. Item multitudo prius consideratur ut simpliciter multitudo quam ut infinita. Si considerentur haec respectu creatoris, unum atque terminus praecedunt opposita. Si autem respectu creaturae, fit forte vicissim ut multitudo et infinitum opposita praecedere videantur. Si denique simul conspiciantur creator atque creatura, forte procedit unum quidem simul cum multitudine, terminus autem simul cum infinito ad essentiam componendam. Mox in essentia iam quasi composita nascitur motus et alteritas propter multitudinem atque infinitum. Status autem identitasque propter unum atque terminum. Profluit autem ab essentia ut modo supra dixi composita motus quasi ante statum. Agit enim statim nata, fitque in ipsa ab alio processus in aliud quamvis subitus. Item cum motu status ipse lucet. Non enim recte movetur, nisi et virtus ipsa consistat. At vero post motum

But, after the movement, which is the beginning of difference, follows difference itself. For because of the procession another openly appears and another differing from it. But along with difference identity is equally preserved.

How the function and craft of dialectic is God's gift and imitates the divinity.

The art of division refers to the procession of things, the art of resolution, to their conversion. The art of definition refers to independent existence, the art of demonstration, to dependent existence. But all the arts are reduced either to the art of joining or unjoining. For to divide and to resolve is to unjoin, but to define and to demonstrate is to join. Defining joins parts to the whole; demonstrating joins wholes to wholes.

Plato says the art of dividing and resolving was given by God. This is dialectic in its totality. For in dividing one understands the procession of things, but in resolving, their conversion. The art of definition includes the conversion of the parts to the whole, the art of demonstration, the procession of the effect from the cause.

Dialectic is said to be divinely given, since it is the power which resolves from matter into the divine form, and in dividing leads the images of the divine and universal form down into matter and separates unlike things from unlike things and compounds like things with like things. This entire function is divine, especially since in resolving it can refer to things' conversion, in dividing, to their procession, in defining, to their existence midway between procession and conversion. But in demonstrating it refers now to the procession from the cause, now to the conversion from the effect, now to the existence which is the result of them both being there. But dialectic is given with fire, that is, with the same sort of power that fire has. In rising fire resolves the subtle things, in sinking it divides off the gross things; in leading back to itself it defines, in lighting it demonstrates. Dialectic illuminates the intellect, heats the will, raises

qui alteritatis est principium alteritas ipsa sequitur. Nam per processum palam apparet alterum atque alterum inter se differens. Sed cum alteritate simul identitas aeque servatur.

Quomodo dialecticae officium artificiumque sit Dei munus divinitatemque imitetur.

Ars divisiva refert processum rerum, resolutiva conversionem; definitiva existentiam independentem, demonstrativa existentiam dependentem. Omnes vero ad coniunctivam vel disiunctivam rediguntur; nam dividere et resolvere est disiungere, definire vero et demonstrare est coniungere. Illud partes toti, hoc tota quaedam totis.

Plato dicit artem dividendi et resolvendi a Deo datam, id est, totam dialecticam. Nam in dividendo subintelligit processum rerum, in resolvendo vero conversionem. At definitiva conversionem includit partium ad totum; demonstrativa processionem effectus a causa.

Dialectica dicitur data divinitus, quoniam est virtus resolvens a materia in divinam formam, atque dividendo deducens divinae universalisque formae imagines in materiam, discernens aliena ab alienis, componens propria cum propriis. Totum hoc officium est divinum, praesertim cum resolvendo referat conversionem rerum, dividendo processum, definiendo existentiam inter processum conversionemque mediam. Demonstrando vero tum a causa processum refert, tum ab effectu conversionem, tum a comitantibus existentiam. Datur vero cum igni, id est, cum tali virtute qualis est ignis. Qui resolvit elevando subtilia; dividit demittendo crassa; definit in se reducendo; demonstrat lumine. Illuminat intellectum; calefacit voluntatem; elevat

both to divine things. In the *Timaeus* and the *Protagoras* and here Plato refers to this faculty (which can procure the divine truth) as the gift of God, for we are drawn by Him and to Him.[216] Plato calls it a gift, so that, when you realise you've received it from God not from yourself and received it free, you may be grateful to God and hand it on freely. In the *Statesman* and the *Protagoras* Plato writes that in the beginning itself of the world (either at the very first or after the floods) God's providence entrusted the race of men, which was entirely untutored and lacking in everything, to the care of the divine shepherds.[217] Through the shepherds certain men, who as a result of their birth were more fortunate than the others and were God's sons as it were, could be taught to discover the arts, in particular the divine arts. Origen's book *Against Celsus* proves it was necessary in that ruder age, and Avicenna maintains the same when he's talking about the prophets.[218] Therefore, just as a child while he is led and instructed by his parent (being too weak himself) does not slip nor err in his replies, but then, walking and replying by himself, often falls over and errs, so those first inventors of the arts (being guided by God) did not err. Therefore their successors who can err (being abandoned by God to themselves) ought to venerate the first men as if they were the adopted sons of God. And just as the animals, who wouldn't otherwise preserve themselves if they didn't fly away into the air or burrow into the earth, have some of them been given wings by God with which to lift themselves, others sharp claws with which to dig into the earth, so the soul, which has been created for the divine truth, has been given dialectic. Through dialectic the soul can both fly away towards higher things in resolving, and emulate the creative efficacy of those above in dividing.

But dialectic divides the genus into the species, just as God divides matter into the forms. For the genus doesn't make the species, since with regard to them it's like matter and open to opposite species indifferently. So it would through itself make none of the species or all of them everywhere. Or rather, if it were going to make the species, it would actually have to possess opposite species; and this is what a nature that's been

utrumque in divina. In Timaeo et Protagora et hic facultatem divinae veritatis comparatricem donum Dei nominat, ab ipso enim trahimur et ad ipsum. Donum inquit, ut agnoscens te non abs te, sed a Deo, gratisque accepisse, et Deo sis gratus et des gratis. In Politico et Protagora scribitur in ipso mundi principio, seu primo sive post illuviones, Dei providentia hominum genus rudissimum omnium egenum divinis pastoribus commendasse, per quos viri quidam inter alios genitura feliciores quasi Dei filii illustrarentur ad artium inventa, praesertim divinorum. Quod Origenes contra Celsum necessarium probat in saeculo rudiori fuisse. Idemque Avicenna disputans de prophetis. Itaque sicut puellus quamdiu propter infirmitatem ducitur a parente atque instruitur, neque pede labitur, neque errat in respondendo, deinde vero per se deambulans atque respondens, saepe cadit et errat, sic ipsi primi artium inventores a Deo recti non erraverunt. Eos ergo quasi adoptivos Dei filios posteriores, qui a Deo sibi ipsis relicti errare possunt, venerari debent. Et sicut Deus animalibus quae aliter servari non possunt quam vel ad sublime confugiendo vel penetrando terram largitus est partim alas quibus elevarentur partim aculeos quibus terram dividerent, sic animo ad veritatem divinam creato largitus est dialecticam, per quam tum resolvendo ad supera revolaret tum dividendo superiorum efficaciam producentem emularetur.

Dividit autem ita genus in species, sicut Deus materiam in formas. Neque enim genus efficit species, cum ad eas se habeat quasi materia indifferensque sit ad oppositas. Unde per se vel nullas vel ubique omnes efficeret. Immo si facturum sit, actu habere debet oppositas, quod creata determinataque natura

created and determined can neither possess nor make. So the divine intellect draws the general nature into the special natures within itself and produces them outside itself when it distinguishes matter into the forms—first into the elemental or shared forms, as it were, then into others which are, as it were, particular forms. And in the generation of animals, the body is made before the animal, and the animal before the man. Similarly, the artificer first makes the form of the work and proclaims it in general before proclaiming it in particular. But, since knowledge is brought about through the form, and its quality depends on the quality of the form, knowledge through the material form of the genus is confused, and knowledge through the actual form of the species is distinct.

Dialectic is concerned with uniting and dividing with regard to the one and the many. Division is twofold: either it divides the nature of the species from the individual things and in resolving joins it to the Idea; or it divides the nature of the genus into the species and the nature of the species into individual things and in compounding and defining joins the more common with the less common. Thus far, the compounding is the compounding of simple things with simple things. After this, you get the compounding of compound things with compound things. So dialectic makes a demonstration either by substituting the effect for the cause, or by putting the cause in front of the effect, or by juxtaposing things that are equal. In the first case you get the perfect demonstration: from cause to effect. In the second case you get the imperfect demonstration: from effect to cause. In the third case you get the demonstration that is least perfect: from parity, namely induction. Though the third demonstration is the clearer one for us, yet in itself it is less perfect, since it makes something known by using something almost identical. We begin with induction in the process of conceiving an opinion through the sense, or of building up experience through the frequency of both the sensation and the [resulting] opinion. From experience comes art too. So the conclusion which comes from induction presents us with the first step of the syllogism.

neque habere potest neque facere. Ergo generalem naturam in speciales intellectus divinus et intra se deducit et extra se producit, dum materiam distinguit in formas, elementales primum quasi communes deinde alias quasi proprias. Et in generatione animalium prius corpus fit quam animal, animalque quam homo. Similiter artifex prius formam operis facit pronuntiatque communiorem, deinde distinctiorem. Cum vero cognitio per formam fiat et per talem talis, cognitio per materialem generis formam est confusa, per actualem speciei formam est distincta.

Dialectica circa unum et multa uniendo dividendoque versatur. Divisio duplex est: vel dividit specialem naturam ab individuis, unitque ideae resolvendo; vel dividit generalem naturam in species, specialemque in individua, unitque communius cum minus communi componendo atque definiendo. Hactenus est simplicium cum simplicibus compositio; post haec componit composita cum compositis. Unde facit demonstrationem aut causae supponendo effectum, aut effectui causam praeponendo, aut paria paribus apponendo. In primo gradu est demonstratio a priori perfecta. In secundo a posteriori imperfecta. In tertio a pari imperfectissima, scilicet inductio, quae, quamvis nobis sit manifestior, in se tamen est imperfectior, cum idem declaret quasi per idem. Nos quidem ab hac incipimus per sensum concipiendo opinionem et per utriusque frequentiam congregando experientiam, per quam et artem. Unde conclusio inductionis principium nobis porrigit syllogismi.

This is the material that has so far been hastily collected from Marsilio's lectures on the first parts of the Philebus. *[In the future,] however, read the rest of the exposition in his commentaries on the whole* Philebus. *So what follows next are the chapter divisions in the* Philebus *and chapter summaries in lieu of the commentaries.*

Hactenus collecta cursim ex Marsilianis lectionibus in priores Philebi partes. Expositiones autem reliquas in commentariis eiusdem in totum Philebum legito. Sequuntur ergo deinceps distinctiones capitum in Philebo, capitumque summae pro commentariis.[1]

---

[1] *see appendix V*

APPENDICES

Appendix I: Additions and Omissions

A. *Fragments omitted in the* editio princeps *of Florence 1496 (Y).*

i. ut decet audendi atque metuendi; temperantia scientia circa bona et mala (p. 123).

ii. essentiam atque esse. Denique accidens unum in duo (p. 173).

iii. potest, electione non indiget. Quod si non (p. 189).

iv. quod nosse non potest, nisi bonum ipsum norit. Bonum ipsum, ut alias demonstravimus, supra mentem est (p. 285).

B. *Passages added in MSS. Laur. 21, 8 (X) and Oliver. 620 where extant (see Appendix IV).*

i. *(Inserted after* iam disputationis totius ordo est tradendus [*ch. IX end of para. 1*]; *see* p. 127*).*
De subiecto lege Olympiodorum. Nota qualitatem puta lumen multis modis esse; est enim lumen per causam in spiritibus super coelum, per formam in sole, per participationem veram in stellis, per imaginariam in diaphanis, per umbratilem circa solida, praesertim quo oblique pervenit. Ita mens per causam in Deo, per formam in angelis, per participationem veram in animabus rationalibus, per imaginariam in carentibus ratione, per umbratilem in corporum formis. Similiter voluptas, cuius umbra quaedam inest corporibus, quae ut inclinantur ad conveniens referunt appetitum, ut se applicant illi voluptatem. Hic Proclus una cum Iamblico et Siriano. Bonum ex mente voluptateque mixtum, ait, sub Deo usque ad formas corporeas procedere, in quibus formalis ordo mentem, applicatio voluptatem refert. Id autem cui mirum? cum Plato in Timaeo dicat omnia ex necessitate menteque componi. Sed ad disputationis ordinem redeamus.

ii. *(Inserted at the beginning of ch. XVIII before* Ideas esse Platonicis argumentationibus demonstrabimus; *see* p. 181*).*

Idea dicitur in quantum est formalis actus vel actualis forma; ratio in quantum per ipsam res intelligitur facien#da; exemplar in quantum res intellecta prout intellecta est iam voluntate et per ipsam fit et refertur ad ipsam. Idea praecipue in divinae potentiae fecunditate viget radicitus; ratio in sapientia pululat; exemplar floret in voluntate. [# *P frag. iii begins (see Appendix IV)*.]

iii. *(See* p. 253*) X and P supply a quotation in the original Greek.*

C. *Passages and/or fragments omitted in MSS. Vat. lat. 5953 (W) and/or Laur. Plut. 21, 8 (X) and Oliver. 620 where extant (see Appendix IV).*

i. *Iam vero in arte . . . causae assignari (p. 73) W & X.

ii. *Aristoteles tertio . . . infinitum. Praeterea (p. 85) W.

iii. *Finis ultimus . . . ultimus appetitus (p. 87) W.

iv. opponuntur. Nam . . . se invicem (p. 93) W.

v. *Id totum sic ab . . . ipsa principium motus existit (pp. 101-103) W.

vi. *Agit mens sed . . . ipsa principium motus existit (pp. 101-103) XP (see v.).

vii. Ut in obiectis . . . gratia, et pulchritudo (p. 111) W.

viii. scientia boni . . . Platonis colligitur (p. 123) W.

ix. scientia malorum . . . iustitia (p. 123) W.

x. Aliunde igitur eius perfectio pendet (p. 125) W.

xi. *Cum enim quaelibet . . . quod omnino conducat (p. 131) W.

xii. *Item voluptas et . . . comes est veneris (p. 139) W.

xiii. *Origines in libro . . . litteris exprimi. (pp. 141-145) W.

xiv. *Sicut locum superiorem . . . propriam esse putant (p. 151) W.

xv. *Post haec autem . . . in effectum unum (pp. 165-171) W.

xvi. formae corporum. . . . Sunt itaque (p. 195) W.

xvii. *Speciales rerum vires . . . individuis sed speciebus (pp. 199-203) W.

xviii. *Proinde, sicut vultus . . . multiplicentur errores (pp. 211-215) W.

xix. *Deus in operibus . . . in sublime resolvit (pp. 221-223) W.

xx. quia continue magis . . . advertissent (p. 237) W.

xxi. *In Phaedro dicit . . . divinum adoraturum (p. 237) W.

xxii. Sicut enim sol . . . aliam per aliam (p. 239) W.

xxiii. *Possumus etiam Epimetheum . . . in argumento Cratyli (pp. 245-247) W.

xxiv. Qui destruis omnia . . . consilio praedite (p. 253) WXP [in X and P the Greek original is added, however].

xxv. Aut dimidia parte . . . diapason harmoniam (p. 267) W.

xxvi. *Priscianus ita dividit . . . Hic litteras (p. 275) W & X.

xxvii. aliquis scire . . . non posset (p. 275) W.

xxviii. *Plato in Cratylo . . . implet per bonitatem (p. 299) W.

xxix. vitam nemo eligeret . . . patet voluptatis (p. 323) W.

xxx. *Aliquid movet sensum . . . licet opposita ratione (p. 325) W.

xxxi. sufficiens. Merito . . . est, quia (p. 351) W.

xxxii. *Intellectus indagando . . . autem est utrumque (pp. 373-375) W.

xxxiii. actum ipsius praecedit . . . igitur voluntatis (p. 377) XP — the only omission unique to X and P.

xxxiv. *Plotinus de felicitate . . . tentatio tutior (p. 381) W & XP.

The asterisked passages are the more significant omissions. Kristeller in his *Supplementum Ficinianum*, Vol. I, pp. 79-80, neglects to mention nos. i, vi, xi, xii, xiv, xix, xxiii, xxvi, xxx, xxxii, among those I have asterisked.

Appendix II: The Ten Excerpts

The ten excerpts are found in their entirety only in the two complete manuscripts of the *Philebus* commentary (the Pesaro MS. 620 [P] has excerpts I, II, III, V and, incompletely, VI). Although untitled in MS. *Vat. lat.* 5953 (W), the sequence is prefaced in MS. *Laur. Plut.* 21, 8 (X) and in MS. P by the words: "Item alia excerpta breviter ex lectionibus Marsilii Ficini [*om.* X] in Philebum." However, MS. W refers to excerpts VII, IX and X as "apologues" and MS. X refers to excerpts IV, VII, IX and X as "apologues on pleasure." This has confused some scholars. I have referred to the sequence as "the ten excerpts" and reserved the term "apologue" for the four pleasure apologues in MS. X.

In the edition of 1496 (and in all subsequent editions) the excerpts were replaced with the four unattached chapters which bore no relation to them (my pp. 425-437).

I have adopted the order in MS. W. In MS. X the four apologues were transferred to the end. Later Ficino moved them to the end of the tenth book of his letters and dedicated them to Martin Preninger, alias Martinus Uranius (*Op. Om.,* 921, 2). To judge from its omission of excerpt IV (i.e. apologue I), MS. P was following the same order as MS. X.

My text is based on MS. X, but it has been collated with MSS. W and P. Professor Kristeller's *Supplementum Ficinianum,* I, 80-86, has the six non-apologue excerpts in a text also based on MS. X, but without the MS. P readings and with a few readings which differ from mine.

Marsilio Ficino's account of the triple life and the triple end. [*I*]

Paris, the son of the eastern king, is pasturing wild animals in the wood; that is, the soul, created by God, is nourishing the senses in the disordered matter of the elements. Three goddesses

Alia Excerpta

SYNOPSIS. [*I*] Allegorical account of the judgement of Paris. The three lives, those of wisdom, pleasure and power, and why pleasure is closer to genuine tranquillity than power. Allegorical account of Ulisses' visit to the underworld in the *Aeneid* Book VI. The wood and the bough and their Christian meanings. [*II*] For lower things the end consists in inactivity, for middle things in moving activity, for higher things in motionless activity. [*III*] God gave us the ability to choose between wisdom, power and pleasure. Why we are mainly drawn to pleasure. Its ubiquity. The three pleasures pertaining to the body and the three to the soul. Men pursue even wisdom and power for pleasure's sake. Why the *Philebus* has Socrates choose between wisdom and pleasure without mentioning power. Power is "the least tranquil of things." [*IV*] The evil demon leads us towards the false by means of verisimilitude, towards the bad by means of pleasure. God uses both to lead us towards the true and the good. [*V*] Whether pleasure consists in the absence of pain or in motion or in rest. The various theories are considered with regard to the body and the intelligence. The nature of true pleasure in this life and the next. [*VI*] The many species of pleasure between the two extremes of the intelligence's joy and the pleasures of touch and taste. Pleasure can be a quality, a movement, a tranquillity. [*VII*] A fable. The envy that drove the Bad to produce bad things in imitation of the Good. How the Good kept Pleasure subordinate and how the Bad wanted to advance her and ridiculted the Good for not doing so. The self-destructiveness inherent in bad things. [*VIII*] Why bad things can be mutually opposed, but good things cannot: the latter partake of unity, the former do not. [*IX*] A fable. How the Pleasures managed to defend themselves against their worldly power-seeking critics by choosing Shamelessness as their patron. But how they were defeated by Pallas, the philosophers' patroness, when they elected Thoughtlessness as their spokesman: having tried to demonstrate Pleasure's origin and the extent of her power before the tribunal of Jove, Thoughtlessness and the pleasures were suddenly routed when Pallas mentioned Fear, the most abject of all things. [*X*] A fable. Jupiter's first attempt to conquer Pleasure, who lived on earth, was to send Mars and Vulcan to defeat her; but they were defeated in turn. His next attempt was to send Pallas; but Pleasure not only managed to evade Pallas continually, she also penetrated her shield. Pallas' bid to enlist the aid of Pain did not work either and she returned to heaven unsuccessful. Jupiter therefore summoned old Saturn on Rhea's advice and Saturn told them to try to bring Pleasure to heaven instead of killing her. The demons were given this task but to no avail. Then Pallas consulted with Saturn again and they eventually decided to send Mercury, Apollo, the Muses and the Graces to entice Pleasure into heaven instead of compelling her to come as the demons had tried to do. The plan succeeded and Pleasure was happy to be brought singing and dancing into heaven. However, in order to help men to get along without her on earth, Jupiter gave them Hope. Then Pleasure and Pallas became one and the same. Meanwhile, Pluto, the king of the earth, had to find a way to keep souls in the lower world; so he created a false Pleasure by using the clothes and ornaments that the true Pleasure had left behind when she went away to heaven. The task of being this false Pleasure was given to Waste who was one of the Furies.

Marsilii Ficini[1] *expositio de triplici vita et fine triplici.*

Paris regis orientalis filius in silva pascit bestias, id est, animus a Deo creatus in confusa elementorum materia fovet sensus. Huîc tris deae: Pallas, Juno, Venus se offerunt

---

[1]Ficini *om. X*

come to him: Pallas, Juno, Venus.[219] They are quarrelling over
who has the most beautiful form, and present themselves to him
as the judge. Paris inclined to Venus and so the wars of Mars
arose. Because of the three sorts of life, the contemplative, the
active, the pleasurable, three things present themselves to us as
ends: wisdom, power, pleasure. Most people pursue bodily
pleasure; a considerable number pursue power; a few pursue
wisdom. Those who pursue power and wisdom also do it for
pleasure's sake in a way. But the voluptuary locates pleasure in
the sense, the active man in the imagination, the contemplative
man in the intelligence. The active man, that is, the ambitious
man, the worshipper of Juno, is further from the end than the
others are. For the end consists in a certain tranquillity. But
nothing is further removed from tranquillity than power and
the follower of power. But the voluptuary is closer [to the end].
The contemplative man is closest [of all]. Moreover, the truest
pleasure is in the intelligence, the less true in the sense, the least
true in the imagination. So Aeneas is depicted as someone
who's afflicted with worry because of Juno, that is, because of
his desire to rule; and Ulisses is disturbed for the same reason.
But whenever each in a way inclines with moderation towards
the things of Venus, that is, towards things associated with love,
he is less miserable; and each is sometimes happy whenever he
seeks refuge in contemplation. But without celestial inspiration
neither was able to be perfectly content. So it's said that when
Ulisses had been given a certain flower by Mercury,[220] that is,
light from God through an angel, he escaped the poisoned cups
of Circe; that is, he escaped the allurements of corporeal love
which transforms the human soul out of a man into a beast,
that is, out of the reason into the sense. So at some point
through this flower Ulisses is said to have escaped both the
poisons of pleasure and the worries of ambition, and attained
the secret mysteries of things divine. For the same reason in the
Aeneid Book VI,[221] when Aeneas wandered through the
immense old wood (that is, through the world's matter) and
became exhausted and implored divine help from the oracle,
divine mercy allotted him the golden bough (that is, the light of

tamquam iudici de formae praestantia inter se certantes. Paris declinavit ad Venerem, unde orta sunt proelia Martis. [*414r*] Profecto pro triplici vitae genere scilicet contemplativae, activae, voluptuosae tria se nobis offerunt velut fines: sapientia, imperium, voluptas. Plurimi corporis voluptatem sectantur, plerique imperia, pauci sapientiam, et qui haec duo etiam quodammodo gratia voluptatis. Sed voluptuosus voluptatem in sensu ponit, activus in imaginatione, contemplativus in mente. Activus scilicet ambitiosus Junonis cultor magis quam reliqui aberrat a fine. Finis enim in quadam quiete consistit. Nihil autem a quiete remotius quam imperium eiusque sectator. Voluptuosus vero propinquior, contemplativus est proximus. Adde quod voluptas in mente verissima est, in sensu minus vera, in imaginatione minime. Propterea fingitur Aeneas ob Junonem perturbatione vexatus, id est, ob studium imperandi, eademque ratione agitatur Ulixes. Sed uterque minus miser, siquando ad Venerea, id est, amatoria quodammodo et moderate declinat, et uterque felix interdum, quatenus confugit ad contemplandum. Quod quidem neuter implere perfecte potuit absque inspiratione coelesti. Quapropter fertur Ulixes accepto quodam a Mercurio flore, id est, lumine a Deo per angelum devitasse venefica pocula Circes, id est, illecebras corporalis amoris, qui humanam animam ex homine in bestiam, id est, ex ratione transformat in sensum. Ergo Ulixes per huiusmodi[1] florem aliquando et voluptatis venena et ambitionis perturbationem dicitur declinasse et secreta divinorum attigisse mysteria. Eadem ratione Aeneas in sexto, dum per silvam immensam et antiquam, id est, mundi materiam pererraret iamque[2] defessus divinum ab oraculo auxilium imploraret, divina clementia impetravit [*414v*] ut ramum

---

[1]eiusmodi *W*   [2]-que *om. XP*

the intelligence poured in from above). With it he could penetrate into the obscure retreats of things with clarity and safety. This bough is imagined existing in the same wood: "For the light shines in the darkness."[222] Nobody is imagined capable of plucking it unless he's someone who's been accepted by God: "For the darkness didn't comprehend the light."[223] Nobody is imagined as being able to return from the wood below to the upper world unless he's born from God, that is, reborn by the divine grace. Hence the line: "They could do it who were sons of Gods";[224] also the line: "But they were born from God."[225] But when the line says, "If the fates call you,"[226] take it to mean, "If the providence of the divine mercy helps you." Hence the line: "None ascends to heaven unless drawn there by the heavenly father."[227] But because He is the father there is no need for us to spend a long time outwardly striving to be drawn by Him; it's enough for us to wish to be drawn by Him. So whoever stops being carried away by created things and wishes to be seized by the creator alone, and directly he has this wish, he seizes the golden bough in his hand, "and the bough will yield to him willingly and easily."[228] When he has the bough, however, "nothing else is missing."[229] For a spiritual gift is like light; it is neither diminished by being poured forth, nor is it ever wanting to those who desire it.

The end for lower things consists in inactivity, for middle things in moving activity, for higher things in motionless activity. [II]

Since we said the end has the character of rest, take note of the following. Terrestrial bodies descend into rest in order to be inactive. Water and air, however, proceed to their ends on condition that they can not only rest there but also act, although in a disorderly way—that is, they may be blown about in some way or other by the winds. Fire, however, retires to its end above not only for the sake of rest but also action, but action of a much more orderly kind. The sky, however, possesses its place

aureum sortiretur, mentis videlicet lumen infusum ab alto, quo perspicue tutoque posset per¹ obscuras rerum latebras penetrare. Fingitur eiusmodi ramum in eadem esse silva. Lux enim in tenebris lucet. Fingitur neminem posse decerpere, nisi qui Deo sit acceptus. Tenebrae enim lucem non comprehenderunt. Fingitur² neminem posse ab ima³ silva ad superna redire, nisi Deo genitum, id est, gratia divina regeneratum. Hinc illud: Dis⁴ geniti potuere. Item illud: Sed ex Deo nati sunt. Ubí vero dicit: Si te fata vocant, intellige, Si divinae clementiae te adiuvat providentia. Hinc et illud: Nemo ascendit in coelum, nisi coelestis pater traxerit illum. Sed quia pater est, idcirco ut trahamur haudquaquam longo externoque opus est conatu, sed sufficit velle trahi. Quisquis ergo cessat a creaturis rapi soloque creatore rapi vult, cum primum vult, aureum ramum carpit manu et ille volens facilisque sequetur.⁵ Sed hoc accepto non deficit alter. Spiritale namque donum luminis instar neque transfusione minuitur neque umquam volentibus⁶ deficit.⁷

Finis inferiorum in otio, mediorum in actione mobili, supernorum⁸ in actione immobili.

Quod diximus finem rationem quietis habere, nota terrena corpora ad quietem descendere ut otientur, aquam vero et aerem ad terminos suos ea conditione procedere ut ibi non quiescant tantum, sed agant, quamvis inordinate, id est, ventis utcumque accidit agitentur, ignem vero ad finem sui supernum se recipere non quietis tantum [*415r*] gratia, sed actionis atque huius quidem magis admodum ordinate. Coelum vero locum possidere suum non solum ut quiescat in ipso, sed etiam ut agat,

---

¹per *om. W* ²fingit *W* ³una *W* ⁴em. *from Virgil:* Dei *W;* Diis *XP*
⁵sequitur *P* ⁶violentius *W* ⁷*sentence barely legible P* ⁸superiorum *Sup. Fic.*

not only in order to rest in it, but also to act and, though in
motion, yet to act in the most orderly way possible. The soul
hurries towards its end in order to find rest in the act itself of
the reason. The angel clings to its end in order to find rest in the
motionless act of the intelligence. Finally God Himself is act
and rest and the end itself of all things.

Why we are mainly drawn towards pleasure before all things. [*III*]

The poets tell us Jove entrusted Paris with the task of judging
between the three goddesses; that is, God gave our soul the
freedom to choose and didn't subject us like beasts to a peculiar
end. For when He gave us the triple powers—the rational, the
irascible, the concupiscible—surely He also gave us the ability
to choose between wisdom, power and pleasure. Man is more
drawn to Venus, however, because the soul and the body alike
are produced by and incline towards and are nourished by a
certain pleasure: firstly, because God Himself is pleasure and
by pleasure He makes all things. This is because God uses His
will to make things and in Him the will is pleasure itself. He
certainly creates the soul with a pleasure that is infinitely greater
than that with which parents produce offspring. Next, it is with
an instinctively natural pleasure that the soul inclines towards
the body. Lastly the soul is immediately nourished by pleasure
when it gets into the body: first with the ditties one sings to
infants, then with stories, then very soon with little praises and
promises. In the same way, as everybody knows, the body is
conceived as a result of the parents' pleasure. Then it is with a
certain natural pleasure that it eagerly admits the soul, as sul-
phur admits fire. Then once it is born it is with pleasure that it is
nourished by milk. So far, therefore, we have enumerated six
pleasures: three pertaining to the body, three to the soul. So,
since the whole man advances in every direction by means of
pleasure, pleasure is certainly as it were the end or the seventh
step where he mainly rests, or at least hopes to rest. For should

et licet mobiliter, ordinatissime tamen. Animam ad finem pro-
perare ut quiescat in ipso rationis actu. Angelum haerere fini ut
quiescat in mentis actu stabili. Deum denique esse actum sta-
tumque ipsum omniumque finem.

Quare ad voluptatem maxime omnium[1] proclives simus.

*Tradunt poetae Jovem iudicium illud[2] inter tres deas ad
Paridem demandasse, id est, Deum animae nostrae iudicium eli-
gendi liberum tradidisse neque ut brutis fini proprio mancipa-
tum. Siquidem cum tres dedit vires ratiocinandi, irascendi, con-
cupiscendi, nimirum et facultatem dedit per quam possemus
sapientiam et potentiam voluptatemque eligere.** Quod autem
homo proclivior sit ad Venerem, inde provenit, quod tam animus quam corpus voluptate quadam nascuntur et inclinantur et
nutriuntur. Principio cum Deus ipse ipsa sit voluptas eaque
faciat omnia. Siquidem Deus voluntate facit voluntasque in eo
est ipsa voluptas. Certe voluptate procreat animam et infinite
maiori quam filios ipsi parentes. Deinde anima naturalis voluptatis instinctu vergit ad corpus. Quin etiam in ipso corpore
statim voluptate nutritur, dum infantibus cantilenae primum,
deinde fabellae,[3] mox laudatiunculae pollicitatiunculaeque
adhibentur. Corpus similiter nullus ignorat parentum concipi
voluptate, mox naturalis cuiusdam voluptatis aviditate sic animam adsciscere ut sulfur ignem, deinde natum lactea voluptate
nutriri. Sex ergo hactenus [*415v*] voluptates connumerantur:
tres ad corpus, totidem ad animam pertinentes. †Cum ergo
totus homo per voluptatis undique vias progrediatur, nimirum
in voluptate veluti fine septimoque gradu plurimum conquiescit
vel saltem quieturum esse se sperat. Nam cui mirum videri††

---

[1]omnium *om. W* [2]illum *W* [3]fabellas *P* *-**barely legible P* †-††*barely legible P (cont.)*

it surprise anybody that when pleasure presents itself to us we recognize it immediately and embrace it as father and also as mother, as male nurse and also as female nurse, as tutor and tutoress? So it is that most people propose pleasure to themselves as the end. Those who desire it never desire it for the sake of power or wisdom; but those who pursue power or wisdom very often want them for the sake of pleasure. Also, there is nothing that the soul's three powers have more in common than pleasure. The concupiscible power acquires the pleasure of the lower senses; the irascible power pursues the delights of the higher senses and the imagination; the rational power, lastly, strives in so far as it can for the joys of heaven. But now at last let's come to the *Philebus*. Just as Paris was given the task of judging between three goddesses, so Socrates was given the task of judging between two. To do it, however, Socrates called upon two arbiters, Philebus and Protarchus. But why did Plato introduce only two goddesses, that is, wisdom and pleasure, into the contest but not power? It's precisely because anyone in his right mind can see without a debate that you can't hope to find rest, which is proper to the end, in power, which is the least restful of all things. However, wisdom can hope to find true rest in eternal things; and, as with the beasts, the desire for pleasure dreams about a certain rest existing in the body.

A fable. The evil demon leads us to the false through verisimilitude, to the bad through pleasure. But through verisimilitude and pleasure God leads us to the true and the good. [IV]

God is truth and goodness and so He composed all things from truth and goodness. For anything is called true in so far as it remains in its integral purity and remains what it was made by God. But to the extent it is profitable to others, it is called the good for them. Again, to the extent one of its parts within itself is profitable to another, it is called the good for itself. But God imprinted the truth of things with a verisimilar mark as it were;

†debet, quando voluptas sese nobis offert, eam nos statim agnoscere amplectique[1] tamquam patrem simul atque matrem, nutritorem pariter et nutricem, tutorem quoque atque tutricem. Hinc fit ut plurimi voluptatem sibi proponant velut finem, et qui eam concupiscunt, numquam vel potentiae vel sapientiae gratia concupiscant,†† at vero qui sapientiam secuntur aut potentiam, ea saepissime voluptatis gratia cupiant. Fit etiam ut in tribus animae viribus nihil sit communius voluptate. Nempe concupiscibilis voluptatem sensuum adsciscit inferiorum; irascibilis superiorum imaginationisque oblectamenta sectatur; rationalis denique coelestium gaudia utcumque potest aucupatur. Sed ut tandem[2] ad Philebum perveniamus. Sicut trium iudicium delatum fuit ad Paridem, ita duorum ad Socratem. Ille vero duos convocavit arbitros, Philebum scilicet atque Protarchum. Sed cur Plato duo tantum, scilicet sapientiam et voluptatem in certamen produxit, potentiam vero nequaquam? Quoniam videlicet absque controversia quilibet sane mentis iudicat in potentia tamquam inquietissima quietem quae finis propria est sperari non posse. Sapientia vero veram in aeternis sperare quietem potest, et concupiscentia brutorum more quietem aliquam in corpore somniat.

Apologus.[3] *Malus daemon per verisimile ad falsum, per voluptatem [416r] trahit ad malum; Deus vero per haec ad verum et bonum.*[4]

Deus veritas est et bonitas, ideoque omnia ex veritate et bonitate composuit. Res enim quaelibet quantum[5] in integra sui puritate id quod a Deo facta est permanet vera denominatur. Quatenus vero aliis conducit ad aliquid, bona aliis nuncupatur. Item quatenus intra se aliud sui conducit ad aliud, bona sibi. Impressit autem Deus veritatem rerum verisimili quasi nota, bonitatem vero voluptate perfudit quasi esca ut occulta cuiusque

---

[1]complectique *Sup. Fic.*   [2]ut *add. W*   [3]Apologus *om. W*   [4]*whole apologue om. P*
[5]inquantum *W*   *(cont.)* †-††*barely legible P*

goodness, however, he bathed with pleasure as a bait. This is so the hidden truth of each thing may be discovered through the image resembling it, and God's truth may then be discovered through the truth of all things. On the other hand, it's also so single things may be drawn towards the good (which is hidden in itself) lured by the bait of pleasure, and then drawn through all good things to the good of God. But when the envious demon saw God drawing all things towards Himself, partly through the verisimilar mark and partly through the bait that resembled the good, he devised a scheme in emulation of the divinity whereby he could similarly draw all things principally towards himself. So he created a verisimilar mark and a bait that resembled the good. They were copies of the divine ones. He added the former to what was false and the latter to what was bad. Consequently he draws people's intelligences through the mark towards the false, and their affections through the bait towards the bad; and eventually he draws both towards himself. Since he is a rebel as it were and is utterly separated from the divine goodness and truth, there is a certain falsity and badness. Hence in the *Timaeus* Plato calls pleasure the bait that lures us towards bad things.[230]

Pleasure: [whether it consists] in the absence of pain or in motion or in rest. [*V*]

Jerome of Rhodes says desirable pleasure consists in the removal or absence of pain; he calls it painlessness. Aristippus and Eudoxus say it consists in movement; that is, in a return to the natural disposition. Democritus says it consists in the disposition itself, which he calls "euthymia" or cheerfulness. Epicurus in his youth agreed with Aristippus, in his age with Democritus. The first view is wrong because it doesn't take into account that privation [i.e. absence of something] is alien to the rational principle of the good; people don't particularly choose it nor can it satisfy. The second view is also wrong, for in the return [to the natural disposition] the pleasure is mixed with

veritas per imaginem verisimilem indagaretur, ac demum per omnium veritatem Dei veritas. Rursus ut per voluptariam escam singula ad bonum per se latens allicerentur, perque bona omnia ad Dei bonum. Cum vero daemon invidus Deum partim veri-simili nota partim boni simili esca ad se trahere cuncta contuere-tur, machinatus est tamquam divinitatis aemulus qua potis-simum ratione ipse similiter ad se omnia traheret. Itaque notam verisimilem et boni similem escam ad divinae illius expressit similitudinem; adhibuitque tum illam falso, tum hanc malo. Quo fit ut per illam mentes ad falsum, per hanc affectus trahat ad malum, ac denique ad se ipsum. Ipse enim, cum a divina veri-tate bonitateque quasi rebellis atque alienissimus sit, falsitas quaedam est atque malitia. Hinc Plato malorum escam in Timaeo nuncupat voluptatem.

Voluptas in privatione doloris vel motu vel statu.

Hieronymus Rhodius in privatione et vacatione doloris expe-tibilem voluptatem ponit quam nominat indolentiam; Aristip-pus Eudoxusque in motu, id est, in[1] quadam restitutione in habitum naturalem; [*416v*] Democritus in hoc ipso habitu quam vocat euthimiam. Epicurus in iuventute secutus est Aris-tippum, in senectute Democritum. Prima opinio ideo errat quia non considerat privationem a ratione boni alienam esse, neque vel eligi a quoquam praecipue vel posse sufficere. Errat et secunda. Voluptas enim in ipsa restitutione perseverante indi-gentiae molestia dolori miscetur tenditque[2] ad aliud sicut motus

---

[1] an *W*   [2] tendique *Sup. Fic.*

pain: it comes from the continual discomfort of being in need, and as the movement towards the disposition it aims at something else. But if somebody strays from the order of nature and assumes the return is the end, he is precipitated immediately from having a little, brief, impure pleasure into having pure, long-lasting and grievous pains. But since the second view thinks pain is the bad, it erroneously considers that pleasure to be the good which relapses of necessity into pain. The third view is the more likely one, for it's using the pleasure which is perceived in movement for that perceived in rest. Just as the end of the movement is the disposition and being at rest, so the end of pleasure's movement is the pleasure of being at rest. Indeed, if the return to the natural disposition is properly sweet because it's being directed towards the natural disposition, the disposition itself ought to be even sweeter. But why doesn't it seem so to us? It's because novelties arouse more wonder, and a quality impinges on the sense more in motion than in rest. It's because as long as we're in need the bait which will lead us to the end seems providently sweeter [than the end itself]. It's because daily we experience the state of returning [to the natural disposition]—now through heat, now through cold, through eating, through excreting, through motion and through rest—but we never experience the disposition in its integrity. And sometimes the portion of the disposition that we have acquired doesn't manifest its sweetness to us, because the soul for one reason or another has been continually intent on a complete return [to the disposition]. But the sequence that appears in the sense and in the intelligence is as follows. In the sense first there is painlessness when nothing in the body is being tortured or titillated. Then there's the pleasure of moving through the contrary states, as we've just described. Third, when some sort of return [to the disposition] has been achieved, the body is well disposed and able to do things energetically and quickly. As a result of a peaceful inner mildness and tranquillity and natural joyfulness it is either better prepared to accept some pleasures or more willing to produce them. In the intelligence too the first step in the sequence occurs when it neither rejoices nor grieves over the

ad habitum. Ac siquis ab ordine naturae aberrans eam sumat[1] pro fine,[2] mox ex voluptate impura levi brevi in dolores puros graves diuturnos praecipitatur. Cum vero opinio haec dolorem existimet ipsum malum, *falso iudicat eam voluptatem ipsum bonum, quae necessario relabitur in dolorem. Tertia opinio probabilior est, utitur enim voluptate illa quae est in motu illius gratia quae persentitur in statu. Et merito sicut status habitusque finis est motionis, ita voluptas haec illius est finis. Profecto si restitutio in habitum naturalem ob id suavis est proprie quia in naturalem dirigitur habitum, ipse habitus suavissimus esse debet. At cur nobis id minus apparet? Quia nova magis admirationi sunt; quia qualitas cum motu magis agit in sensum quam in statu;** quia durante indigentia esca suavior ad finem alliciens providenter est adhibita; quia quotidie in restitutione sumus modo per calorem modo per frigus, per impletionem evacuationem, per motum perque quietem, in habitu vero integro numquam sumus. Atque habitus ipsius portio quam aliquando nacti sumus suavitatem suam patefacit minus, animo [*417r*] continue hinc vel inde restitutioni prorsus intento. Apparet autem ordo hic in sensu atque mente. In sensu quidem indolentia quando nihil in corpore vel cruciatur vel fovetur, deinde voluptas in motu per contrarios modos quos modo narravimus, tertio quando restitutione qualicumque facta corpus bene se habet vivaciterque et ad officia prompte †cum intrinseca quadam et placida lenitate tranquillitate hilaritate naturae ad quaelibet oblectamenta sive accipienda paratius sive edenda propensius. In mente quoque gradus primus apparet quando ob nullius opinionis[3] vel praesentiam vel absentiam aut gaudet aut dolet, secundus quando per opiniones rationalesque discursiones in††

[1]summant *W* [2]prosit (?) *W* [3]-que *add. W* *-**barely legible P*
†-††*barely legible P (cont.)*

presence or absence of any one opinion. The second step occurs
when the intelligence is restored to its natural disposition either
by the recent acquisition, or by the recollection, of the truth via
opinions and discursive reasoning. The third step never occurs
in this life, since the light which is natural and proper to the
intelligence and in which its disposition consists cannot be
possessed among these shadows. For the closer we come to it
the more vehemently we rejoice in the return. But we don't
rejoice enough in the small portion of the disposition, since
we're too assiduously preoccupied with the return. Moreover,
in the body the sense is awake, but the intelligence is asleep.
Since the sense is what receives the body's sustenance but the
intelligence the image of its sustenance, the mental pleasures
seem very diluted in the body but the sensual pleasures seem
very concentrated. In the next life the reverse is true. For in the
next life the highest disposition will be found, constituted from
both the glorified body which obeys the soul absolutely and
from the glorified soul which has become one with its appropriate Idea. Hence the line: "The good for me is to cling to
God."[231] So the psalmist prays: "Strengthen me with your highest spirit."[232] Then at last, he says, he'll be in a state of exulta-
tion.

The species of pleasures are many. [VI]

The pleasure the intelligence is seen to take in immaterial
truth is similar in a way to the delight we receive from hearing
and seeing, for this delight is sufficiently spiritual and has a
bearing on the pursuit of truth. But it is dissimilar to the delight
we receive from smelling, for this delight already draws us
towards matter. It is totally dissimilar to the sweetness we
receive from touch and taste however moderated it might be,
since this sweetness is immersed in matter and penetrated by the
material object. But if this [lower] pleasure keeps no measure, it
is now assumed to be opposite to the intelligence's joy, since
both move from opposite ends to opposite ends. The [lower]

†naturalem mentis habitum restituitur vel nuper veritatem acquirendo vel reminiscendo, tertius in hac vita numquam quippe cum naturale mentique conveniens lumen in quo eius consistit habitus in his tenebris haberi non possit.†† At enim quo propinquius ad ipsum accedimus, eo restitutione vehementius delectamur, habitus vero partiuncula parvula parum, praesertim cum assidue restitutioni occupati simus. Adde quod sensus quidem in corpore vigilat, mens vero dormit; cumque ille alimoniam suam accipiat, haec alimoniae suae umbram, nimirum in hoc corpore remissae apparent voluptates mentis, sensus vero vehementissimae, sed in altera vita contra. Tunc enim et corpus glorificatum animae prorsus obtemperans et glorificatus animus ideae propriae congruens in habitu praecipuo constituetur. Hinc illud: Mihi vero adhaerere Deo bonum est. Unde petit: Spiritu principali confirma me; dicitque tunc demum se exultaturum. [*417v*]

Multae species voluptatum.[1]

Voluptas mentis circa immaterialem percepta[2] veritatem quodammodo similis est videndi audiendique delectationi satis quidem spiritali et ad veritatis indaginem conferenti, olfactus vero oblectamento dissimilis ad materiam iam trahenti, gustus tactusque suavitati etiam moderatae maxime est dissimilis, quandoquidem haec est immersa materiae et ab obiecto penetrata materiali. At si haec voluptas nullum servet modum, iam contraria mentis gaudio iudicatur, quia a contrariis terminis ad contrarios vergunt. Haec quidem ab immateriali ad materiale omnino detorquet, illud vero contra. Item contraria habent

---

[1]voluptas mentis *add. P*   [2]praecepta *W*   *(cont.)* †-††*barely legible P*

pleasure turns us away entirely from the immaterial towards the material, joy the reverse. They also have opposite functions: one divides the soul by scattering it into numerous moving things, the other unites it into the opposite. Again, the presence of one hinders or repulses or flees from the presence of the other and vice versa. Finally, within the genus itself of pleasure one is as far away from the other as possible. Now, since the movements are considered opposite which aim at opposite ends, the [various] reposes which exist in opposite [ends] must also be opposite. Therefore, whether pleasure exists in a movement or repose, the pleasures concerned with opposite things are entirely opposite. Nor can anybody object they are one in the genus of pleasure, for you could say that opposite motions and qualities are similarly one in the genus of motion or of quality. Again, nobody can object that the whiteness in some hot body is not opposite to the whiteness in a cold body; or, similarly, that in opposite things the pleasures are not opposite in turn. For the two bodies [the hot and the cold] aren't white because they're opposites, nor are they opposites because they're white. Contrariety doesn't entail whiteness nor the reverse. However, the pleasure you hope from and perceive in an immaterial thing is the reason why you move from a material thing towards its opposite. Similarly, the pleasure you perceive in a material thing is the reason why you move from an immaterial thing towards its opposite. Again, the intellect rejoices because it moves towards an immaterial thing; and the touch is pleased because it sinks towards a material thing. In sum, as the opposites in a light or heavy object are now lightness versus heaviness, now ascent versus descent, now one repose versus another—and particularly one repose versus another, since it's because of the repose which they have as their end that some things are judged to be opposite to others—so with pleasure (whether it's defined as a quality or as movement or as repose): when occupied with opposite things one pleasure becomes opposite to another (especially if the pleasures are judged to be the reposes so to speak in opposite things). This is confirmed by the fact that opposite moods are excited by opposite affections.

officia. Haec disgregat animam in res mobiles multiplicesque diffundens, illud congregat in oppositum. Item huius praesentia illius praesentiam impedit, fugat, fugit atque contra. Denique sub ipso voluptatis genere quam maxime distant.[1] Profecto cum motus illi oppositi iudicentur qui ad terminos tendunt oppositos, oportet et quietes in oppositis oppositas esse. Sive igitur in motu quodam sive in quiete voluptas sit, omnino voluptates circa opposita sunt oppositae. Neque obiciat quisquam eas in genere voluptatum esse unum. *Similiter enim dici posset contrarios motus et qualitates in genere motus qualitatisve unum esse. Neque rursus obiciat albedinem in corpore altero quidem calido altero vero frigido non esse contrariam; similiter neque voluptates in contrariis invicem esse contrarias. Non enim duo illa corpora vel quia contraria sint sunt alba, vel quia alba sint contraria sunt,** neque contrarietas ad albedinem conducit neque contra. Voluptas autem quae speratur percipiturque in re immateriali causa est quare a materiali [*418r*] in hanc illi oppositam fiat motus. Similiterque voluptas quae in re materiali percipitur causa motus est a re immateriali ad eius oppositam. Item et intellectus# quia ad immateriale se confert gaudet, et tactus quia ad materiale labitur oblectatur. Summatim sicut in corpore gravi et levi contraria sunt tum levitas gravitati tum ascensus descensui tum quies quieti, et multo magis quies quieti quam alia cum ob eam velut finem alia iudicentur opposita, sic voluptas sive definiatur ut qualitas sive ut motus sive ut quies quando circa opposita versatur altera alteri fit contraria, praesertim si tamquam quietes in contrariis iudicentur. Hoc inde confirmatur quod ex contrariis

---

[1]dictant *W*   *-**barely legible P*   #*P frag. VI (144v) ends*

The moods move towards opposite pleasures. The pleasures incite the opposite moods and are also the result of them. They are both the principles and the ends of opposite movements.

A fable about good and bad things. [*VII*]

Once upon a time there were only two things, the Good and the Bad. As long as the Good produced nothing, however, the Bad wasn't goaded to produce anything out of vanity since it thought it could resist the Good on its own. Eventually the Good began to produce good things. Then the Bad feared for itself because of the Good and the good things, and thought to oppose them by producing bad things. But since it couldn't produce anything because it was sterile, it went begging to Fortune and bewailed its fate. Fortune favoured it and the Bad began to produce bad things in a way contrary to the way the Good produced good things. The Bad saw that the good things resembled the Good and turned to it, possessed power and retained the good in which they existed, were united among themselves in their own health and kept Pleasure behindhand; so the Bad did the opposite: that is, it set up degeneration, obstacles, manifold commotion, impatience of what sustains the good, and the inability to accept the various good things together. Lastly the Bad put Pleasure in front of itself. At the same time it reproved the Good with Momus [i.e. ridicule], because the Good had concealed its bait, [i.e. Pleasure,] by keeping her behind the good things when it would have been perhaps more correct to put her in front. In order for its kingdom not to be destroyed by the Bad, the Good first decided bad things should suffer from two enemies, namely another bad thing and a good thing (since one good can't be opposed to another). Next it decided a bad thing should not only destroy another bad thing, but also itself; for a bad thing (whether it's constituted through defect or excess) eventually destroys the foundation on which it's sustained and apart from which it cannot exist. Consequently the Bad cannot possess infinite power but the Good

affectionibus contrarii excitantur affectus vergentes ad contrarias voluptates quae et incitant contrarios affectus atque sequuntur tamquam principia simul et fines motionum contrariarum.

Apologus de bonis atque malis.

Erant quondam duo quaedam sola, bonum scilicet atque malum. Quamdiu vero bonum generabat nihil, malum ad generandum haud irritabatur prae superbia, putans se solum posse bono resistere. Incoepit tandem bonum generare bona, tunc malum extimescens sibi a bono atque bonis concupivit contra haec generare mala. Cum vero ob sterilitatem non posset deflendo sortem suam invocavit fortunam, qua favente, coepit generare mala atque contrario modo quam bonum bona. Videns enim bona referre bonum ad ipsumque conferre, habere virtutem, servare id in quo sunt, salute sua concordare inter se, habere a tergo [*418v*] voluptatem, contra haec obiecit opposita, scilicet degenerationem, impedimentum, numerosam turbam, impatientiam eius scilicet quod sustinet bonum, item ineptitudinem ad varia simul bona; denique voluptatem posuit in fronte mali, reprehendens una cum Momo bonum ipsum, quod escam boni occuluisset, a tergo bonis eam subdens quam forte rectius praeposuisset. At vero bonum ipsum ne regnum suum a malo dissolveretur constituit primo quidem mala pati contraria duo, scilicet malum alterum atque bonum, cum bonum bono contrarium esse nequeat; deinde ut malum non modo alterum destruat malum sed etiam se ipsum. Sive enim per defectum fiat sive per excessum destruit tandem fundamentum quo sustinetur, a quo seorsum stare nequit. Hinc fit ut malum virtute infinitum esse non valeat, bonum vero valeat. Denique constituit ut

can. Lastly it decided that bad things, even though they preferred the brief bait of pleasure, nevertheless should fall into
lasting pain. Pythagoras meant this when he said: "Keep away
from the animal with a black tail, that is, from vices."[233]

The reason why bad things can be mutually opposite, but the good things cannot. [VIII]

Since the origin of good things is unity itself, good things are
certainly uniform among themselves and produce unity in
others; and so they can't be opposites (especially because
they're good to the extent that they look back to the good itself,
their own fountain, as the principle, and look forward to it as
the end). Therefore, since they're the same to a third thing,
they're also the same among themselves. The origin of bad
things, on the contrary, is division. Because outside the divine
unity something else arises which is already cut off from the
unity, a decrease of good occurs. Gradually by going through
subsequent division and multiplication the decrease draws
towards the bad. Therefore, since division is the origin and support of bad things, bad things are deservedly opposed to each
other. You can see this with the genus of morals: since the vices
arise through excess and defect, they become even more opposite to each other than they are to virtue. But the virtues, which
partake of the mean as a result of a certain temperance and con-
sonance, not only don't resist each other but contribute to each
other. But the vice in either of two extremes destroys its
counterpart and then itself. Take for instance the miser: in
always hoarding, he desiccates and destroys himself and greed
at the same time. The prodigal does the same when he
squanders everything. The same is true in the genus of nature.
For in the living body health consists in a certain tempering of
the humours, just as beauty consists in the tempering of shape.
Health and beauty are both good things and they help each
other. Disease, however, whether it's brought about through
too much dilution or too much concentration [of the

mala etsi voluptatis escam praeferunt brevem tamen in dolorem decidant diuturnum. Hoc significavit Pythagoras dicens: Ab animali caudam habente[1] nigram abstine, id est, a vitiis.

Quare mala esse invicem contraria possunt, bona nequaquam.

Cum origo bonorum ipsa sit unitas, nimirum bona uniformia inter se sunt et unifica ideoque contraria esse non possunt. Praesertim quia eatenus bona sunt, quatenus bonum ipsum ipsorum fontem referunt ut principium atque ad id conferunt velut finem. Itaque cum eadem sint uni tertio, inter se quoque sunt eadem. Contra vero malorum origo divisio est. Siquidem ex eo quod practer divinam unitatem fit et aliud iam ab ipsa divisum, accidit [*419r*] decrementum[2] boni quod gradatim per succedentem divisionem multitudinemque succedendo tendit in malum. Merito ergo cum malorum origo et alimonia sit divisio inter se repugnant. Id autem apparet in genere morum in quo vitia quia per excessum defectumque fiunt opposita sibimet magis etiam evadunt quam virtuti. Virtutes vero in quadam temperatione consonantiaque medii consistentes non modo invicem non repugnant sed conducunt. Vitium vero in alterutro extremorum alterum destruit et tandem se ipsum. Puta avarus omnino servans se exsiccat et perdit simulque avaritiam, prodigus quoque similiter omnia erogando. Idem apparet in ipso naturae genere. Nam in corpore vivo sanitas in quadam humorum temperatione consistit, sicut pulchritudo in temperatione figurae. Sanitas quidem et[3] pulchritudo utraque[4] bona sibique invicem conferentia. Morbus autem sive per remissionem *nimiam sive per nimiam**

---

[1]habentem *W*   [2]tum *add. W*   [3]et *om. W*   [4]citraque *W*   *-**om. W (cont.)*

humours]—and both are opposites and both are bad things—
destroys itself. The concentration destroys the dilution, and
both destroy the patient at the same time as they destroy
themselves. Similarly with shape you can either exceed or come
short through the gradations of colour and line. You proceed
through opposite modes and the excess destroys the defect and
vice versa and then each destroys the subject and itself at the
same time.

A fable about the pleasure which conquers the ambitious and is itself conquered by Pallas. [IX]

Once upon a time the Pleasures, when they heard they were
being blamed on every side by ambitious agitators, banded
together in their own defense and chose Shamelessness as
patroness of their cause. They said: "Shamelessness, look at
how ungrateful all these people are to us, seeing that all their
happiness depends upon us. Yet they dare to censure us
openly." Then Shamelessness said: "I wonder at your coward-
ice. Since you own the agitators and their homes, won't you be
brave enough at least to show your faces occasionally to the
people from the windows and doors? Thus all the people will
realize you are the agitators' favourites and that the agitators
are censuring you so nobody should steal you away." Then the
Pleasures, relying on the counsel of Shamelessness and on her
aid even more, showed their faces through the windows. They
did this so their ambitious censurers should lose all faith and
authority among the people and those who had censured Pleasure might be censured everywhere in turn on her account. But
when they had conquered these false and empty enemies, they
still had to defend themselves against their true and legitimate
enemies, the philosophers. However, since the philosophers put
Minerva before Pleasure, the judgement was transferred to
Jove, with Thoughtlessness as the new advocate. So when the
trial reached Jove, Thoughtlessness, the advocate for the Pleasures, said: "It's only right that Minerva should be brought to

*intensionem fiat quae duo et contraria et mala sunt se ipsum perdit; tum intensio remissionem** tum utraque subiectum simulque se ipsa.[1] Similiter in figura sive excedas sive deficias per gradus colorum atque linearum per oppositos procedis modos et excessus perdit defectum atque contra et uterque tandem subiectum simulque se ipsum.

Apologus. De voluptate quae vicit ambitiosos, victa est a Pallade.

Voluptates quondam cum audirent se ab ambitiosis concionatoribus passim vituperari in unum pro sua defensione conspirantes patronam causae impudentiam elegerunt his verbis: Vide impudentia quam ingrati hi omnes erga nos sint? quippe cum in nobis tota illorum sita sit felicitas, at tamen audeant palam nos improbare. [*419v*] Tunc impudentia: Ignaviam vestram,[2] inquit, admiror, nempe cum illos illorumque aedes possideatis, non audetis saltem e fenestris portisque vestros interdum vultus populo demonstrare, quo intelligant omnes in delitiis vos apud illos haberi, atque idcirco ab eis vituperari ne quis vos inde subripiat. Post haec voluptates impudentiae fretae consilio atque insuper ope vultus per fenestras aperuere suos. Hinc factum est ut ambitiosi illarum vituperatores omnem apud populum fidem auctoritatemque amitterent, et qui voluptatem vituperaverant ab ipsa vicissim ubique vituperarentur. Postquam vero vanos falsosque vicere hostes, reliquum erat ut adversus veros hostes legitimosque philosophos se defenderent. Quoniam vero voluptati Minervam anteponunt, iudicium, advocata nuper temeritate, in Jovem est translatum. Cum igitur perventum esset ad Jovem, temeritas in voluptatum causa declamatrix: Ius, ait, esse

---

[1]ipsam *Sup. Fic.*   [2]vestras *W*   *(cont.)* *-**om. W*

the trial. Her followers illegally put her before Pleasure as the mistress of all." When they had summoned Pallas, she appeared. Immediately Thoughtlessness made this charge: "Jupiter, according to the philosophers Pallas boasts she is your daughter and Pleasure is worth nothing. My reply is that Pleasure herself was born from you under the name of Venus. However Minerva is Pleasure's daughter under the name of Wisdom. All the philosophers follow Minerva for the sake of a certain pleasure. What more? Venus was born from you. But if Pallas boasts that she, Pallas, was born from your head, we declare she was also born with pleasure from your head." To which Pallas replied: "Pleasure, I say you arose from me. You arose from me in the presence of Jove who was rejoicing in the gift of wisdom. You arose from me among men too, for I was the person who invented their various delights. You arose among the philosophers on the other hand from my image, for they delight in and are enraptured by an image of my splendour." Then Thoughtlessness said: "Let's put aside these dialectical subtleties since Pleasure is too simple and innocent to protect herself with such prickly defenses. Jupiter, look around. How ample is the kingdom of Pleasure. Look at Venus. Look at Cupid assisting her. Look at the Graces following her. Look at the god of gardens, he is her servant too. Hers too is Ceres in the food-shop and Bacchus in the store. Hers is the ambrosia and the nectar which all the gods enjoy. Why do I need to remind you of Mars, the most ferocious of the gods; or yourself, Jupiter; or those others who are everywhere entangled in the delights of Venus? As for the rest they can scarcely seize and scarcely keep [anyone] eventually by using violence; [whereas] Pleasure by herself can happily satisfy with just one nod. She compels no one. She draws every one after her willingly. She retains them because they want to be retained. She rules not only those who live on earth but also those who live in heaven and rule in heaven. Pleasure takes to herself not only all the living but also the dead. Besides, so that Pallas or Diana or Vesta should not brag of their own barrenness and escape from Pleasure's power, Pleasure herself, Jupiter, orders Pallas to

Minervam in iudicium accersiri quam supra quam fas est sectatores eius voluptati omnium dominae anteponant. Pallas accer-
sita comparuit. Repente obiecit ita temeritas: Haec tua o Jupiter Pallas ex ore philosophorum voluptatem nihili pendens se
tuam esse filiam gloriatur. At ego respondeo voluptatem ipsam
sub Veneris nomine ex te natam, voluptatis vero filiam sub sapientiae nomine esse Minervam, quam voluptatis cuiusdam gratia
philosophi cuncti[1] sectantur. Quid plura? Ex te nata Venus est,
quod si ex tuo prodiisse capite se iactet Pallas, asseremus et
ipsam abs te cum voluptate progenitam. Ad haec Pallas: At ego
te o voluptas affirmo ex me ortam tum penes Jovem sapientiae
beneficio [*420r*] se ipso gaudentem, tum apud homines ex me
quoque variorum inventrice oblectamentorum. Immo vero ex
mea apud philosophantes imagine, hi enim imagine quadam
mei splendoris delectantur atque rapiuntur. Tunc temeritas:
Dialecticas, ait, mittamus argutias, voluptas utpote simplex et
innocens eiusmodi se non munit aculeis. Circumspice Jupiter
quam amplum sit voluptatis imperium. En Venus, en Cupido
huius astipulatores. Huius et pedissequae gratiae, huius et hor-
torum deus ipse minister. Huius in popina Ceres, atque Bacchus
in penu. Huius ambrosia nectareque coelestes cuncti vescuntur.
Quid memorem Martem deorum ferocissimum? Quid te ipsum
Jupiter? Quid ceteros venereis passim illecebris irretitos? Et
quidem ceteri[2] violentia tandem vix assequuntur vixque
retinent, una haec uno quodam nutu feliciter implet, nullum
trahens, omnes volentes ducens, retinensque libentes. Neque
solum quae in terris vivunt sed quae in coelo et quae coelum
ducunt ipsa ducit. Neque viventia solum sed etiam non viventia
rapit ad se[3] quaeque voluptas. Ceterum ne Pallas vel Diana vel
Vesta suam iactent sterilitatem imperiumque voluptatis
effugiant, voluptas, o Jupiter, ipsa et Palladem iubet arcibus,

---

[1]cunctis *W*   [2]ceteris *W*   [3]*em.,* sua *WX*

take pleasure in bows and Diana in hunting and Vesta in hearths.'' Pallas angrily replied: ''Jupiter, you will soon see how strong this Pleasure is, she who so insolently boasts of her power over everything. Bring Fear here—it's the most abject not only of the gods but of all things.'' Jupiter cried: ''Hey, bring Fear here.'' Directly he had summoned Fear by name, all the timid Pleasures together with Thoughtlessness took to their heels. Then all the gods laughed and condemned and ridiculed such abject flight. Finally, Pallas put a seal upon the sentence of the gods thus: ''What's more abject than Fear? For it's created out of what doesn't exist, when it's created from the image of some evil that isn't there. Again, it's killed by what doesn't exist, when it's destroyed by the image of a good that isn't there. But Pleasure is even more abject than such abject Fear. For she's put to flight not only by Fear but by the shadow of Fear. Not only when she's [actually] afraid, but when she thinks about being afraid she suddenly takes flight; or rather, to put it more accurately, she perishes. And in order to perish with greater ignominy she isn't changed into some amicable thing like herself, but into her enemy. And this happens suddenly: while still alive she's changed into Pain.''

A fable about Pleasure. You should not fight with her or hope for her on earth. [X]

When Jupiter learned that the souls didn't return to heaven because they were being retained on earth by Pleasure, he sent Mars and Vulcan, who were armed and very strong, to destroy Pleasure. But in the very first fight they laid down their arms; being young men they were seduced by the allurements of Pleasure. Next, Jupiter sent Pallas, who was armed and wise, [as] he thought the other two had succumbed through thoughtlessness. So Pleasure said to Pallas: ''Aren't you ashamed to fight with me? You're clothed and armed and a goddess and I'm naked and helpless and human.'' Pallas replied: ''I want to fight you in order to conquer you.'' Pleasure said: ''Since you won't

et[1] venatione[2] Dianam et Vestam laribus delectari. Ad haec indignata Pallas: O Jupiter, mox videbis quam fortis sit voluptas haec quae tam insolenter omnium gloriatur imperio. Accerse huc pavorem non deorum tantum sed omnium abiectissimum. Exclamavit Jupiter: Heus pavor, accede pavor. Confestim ad ipsum [*420v*] pavoris advocati nomen, voluptates omnes trepidae una cum temeritate fugam arripuerunt. Tunc omnes risere coelicolae fugamque tam vilem ridiculo damnavere iudicio. Denique Pallas deorum sententiam sic obsignavit. Quid nam pavore vilius? Hic enim ex eo quod non est creatur, quando ex absentis mali fit imagine. Hic rursus ex eo quod non est necatur, quando ex absentis boni imagine perditur. Pavore vero tam vili vilior est voluptas. Haec enim non ab ipso solum sed ab eius umbra fugatur, quando non solum pavens sed cogitans pavorem subito fugit, immo, ut verius loquar, interit. Atque ut maiori cum ignominia pereat non in simile quicquam amicumve transformatur sed in hostem et id quidem subito; dum in vita convertitur in dolorem.

Apologus. De voluptate, quod non sit cum ipsa congrediendum neque in terris speranda.

Cum cognosceret Jupiter animas ad coelum non redire quia voluptate in terris detinerentur, misit Martem atque Vulcanum ceu fortissimos et armatos ad voluptatem interimendam,[3] sed ii in primo congressu utpote iuvenes voluptatis illecebris deliniti arma deposuere. Misit iterum Palladem armatam et sapientem, putans illos ob temeritatem succubuisse. Ad hanc ergo voluptas ait: Nonne te pudet o Pallas deam vestitam, armatam certare mecum humana, inermi, nuda? Illa respondit: Sic placet te[4] certare quo te superem. Ad haec illa: Cum neque gloriae neque

---

[1]et *om. W*   [2]venationem *W*   [3]imperimendam *W*   [4]te *om. X*

acquire glory or gain in fighting me (for in conquering me you will achieve neither), it's obvious you are fighting only because you've been overcome by the pleasure of victory. You have no consideration of glory or gain." Then Pallas, who had been defeated by these words, lashed out and tried to strike her again and again. But Pleasure, who is by nature yielding and nimble and very quick, straightway avoided the strokes. Then Pallas put her broad shield over her head. But Pleasure penetrated the shield, for Pleasure's ability to penetrate is such that she can penetrate the body and the soul. Then Pallas called upon Pain in order to destroy Pleasure by her enemy opposite. However, since opposites do not mutually come together, Pain did not rush in to encounter Pleasure but kept drawing away to the side. Then Pallas, together with her associate Vulcan, who had brought his bellows, laboured to extenuate Pleasure and resolve her. But Pallas couldn't extenuate her, since she's as thin as she can be; and she couldn't resolve her into anything further, since she's an ultimate term. For if the question is: Why does somebody do this? The reply will be: Because of that. And again if the question is: Why that? The reply will be: Because it's pleasant. If there's the further question: Why is it pleasant? The reply cannot be anything else but: Because it's pleasant. Therefore (the story goes) Pallas returned to Jove pallid with pain because she hadn't conquered Pleasure. Then Rhea approached Jove very quickly (because of her natural fluidity) and said: "Son, now you can see you need the advice of old Saturn. Till now you've stolen the kingdom from him and kept him hidden in the bowels of the palace." That is, the active life has been distracting men completely from the contemplative. So, when the doors had been unlocked, Saturn was called for consultation. He said: "There are two principles of motion: pleasure for pursuing, pain for fleeing (painlessness does neither, however). So Pleasure mustn't be killed, otherwise souls won't want to come to heaven when Pleasure isn't even here. But Pleasure must be brought here and Pain left among men. In this way everybody will leave there for here." They were pleased with the old god's advice. The attendants of Mars and Vulcan, the

utilitatis in certando rationem habeas, neutrum enim victa me consequeris, constat te ipsa [*421r*] dumtaxat victoriae voluptate devictam certare, nulla gloriae vel utilitatis habita ratione. Tum Pallas verbis convicta prorupit in verbera telumque saepius in eam direxit. At illa cuius natura cedens est atque subintrans et fugacissima ictus protinus declinabat. Ergo Pallas latum clipeum *in caput eius protendit; at illa clipeum** penetravit, adeo enim ad penetrandum est potens ut corpus animamque penetret. Post haec advocavit Pallas dolorem, quo hoste contrario perderet voluptatem. At quoniam contraria se mutuo non accipiunt, dolor non voluptatis in faciem irruebat, sed iuxta tendebat in latus. Tum Pallas una cum socio Vulcano acceptis follibus extenuare et resolvere voluptatem molliebatur. Neque potuit extenuare eam cum tenuissima sit, neque resolvere in ulterius aliquid cum ipsa sit ultimum. Cum enim quaeritur: Quare quis facit hoc? Et respondetur: Propter illud. Rursusque: Quare illud? Ac respondetur: Quia placet. Si quaeratur iterum: Quare placet? Non aliter respondebitur quam: Quia placet. Palladem ergo pallidam prae dolore, quia voluptatem non superasset, ad Jovem rediisse ferunt. Tunc Rhea utpote a fluxu proprio properantior agressa Jovem ait: O fili, nunc agnosces tibi opus esse senis Saturni consilio, cui hactenus abstulisti regnum et in palatii penetralibus occlusisti. Activa videlicet vita homines a contemplativa plurimum distrahente. Reseratis ergo ianuis convocatur Saturnus ad consultandum. Tum ille: Duo sunt, ait, principia motus. Voluptas quidem prosequendi, dolor autem fugiendi, indolentia vero neutrum facit. Non ergo voluptas interimenda alioquin animae coelum non petent, [*421v*] voluptate etiam hic[1] extincta. Sed voluptas huc trahenda, dolor apud homines relinquendus ut inde huc cuncti confugiant. Placuit

---

[1]hinc *W*   *-**om. X

demons, were sent to seize Pleasure, for it was feared the gods
might fall for Pleasure's beauty and yield to her. The demons it
was agreed, however, would have no use for beauty. But the
demons could never get a firm hold on Pleasure. In a marvellous way she is softer and more slippery than eels, for the constant use of, and association with, soft and gentle things confirms the softness in her. Eventually Pleasure overcame the
gods and the demons. The result was nobody dared to encounter her (for she ought to be avoided rather than attacked).
But, so we shouldn't fail in our duties to the divine names for
too long, let's acknowledge that on earth Minerva and the other
gods, that is, human wisdom and power, are completely overcome by Pleasure; on the other hand Pleasure is overcome by
divine wisdom. For Saturn consulted again with Minerva to try
to seize Pleasure, not through violence which was her enemy but
through grace which was her friend. So they sent Mercury,
Apollo, the Muses and the Graces in order to allure Pleasure to
heaven. Mercury was the first to speak to her. He dissuaded her
from staying any longer on earth among her enemies—fear,
pain, wrath, hate, envy, toil, poverty and disease. Phoebus cap-
tivated her also with his lute, the Muses with songs and melo-
dies, and the Graces with leaps and choral dances. Having been
enticed by them, Pleasure joined the singing Muses, and with
outstretched hands she linked herself with the Graces who were
gently dancing. So in singing and dancing she accompanied the
gods (who were returning to heaven) and was brought into
heaven. Pleasure has deserted the earth, so men must go away
from earth to heaven; but go in such a way that you don't turn
back like Orpheus and lose the reward! When was it Pleasure
ran away into heaven? It was at the time when Astraea, that is,
original justice, ran away too (when Adam sinned).[235] But lest
mortals, having lost Pleasure, should fight among themselves
and kill each other among so many adversities, Jupiter pitied
our misery when he stole Pleasure away and multiplied hope for
us. But deceptive is the hope of attaining Pleasure here, that is,
of winning her from mortal things. When she was led away by
Mercury, Phoebus, the Graces and the Muses, she was

senis consilium. Mittuntur daemones Martis Vulcanique satellites ad voluptatem corripiendam. Timebatur enim ne dii illius pulchritudini indulgerent et cederent. Constabat autem daemones nullam rationem pulchritudinis habituros. At daemones numquam voluptatem tenere manibus potuerunt, mollitie lubrica anguillas mirabiliter superantem. Eius enim mollitiem confirmat assiduus mollium dulciumque usus et habitatio. Voluptas denique et deos et daemones superavit ut nemo audeat cum illa congredi; fugienda enim est potius quam invadenda. Verum ne diutius in divina nomina delinquamus, fateamur Minervam in terra et deos in terra alios, id est[1] humanam sapientiam et potentiam plurimum voluptate devinci, sed eam a sapientia divina superari. Nam Saturnus iterum una cum Minerva deliberaverunt ut tentandum esset voluptatem rapere non per violentiam illi oppositam, immo per gratiam eius amicam. Miserunt ergo Mercurium, Apollinem, Musas, Gratias ad voluptatem sursum alliciendam. Mercurius ad eam primus orationem habens dissuasit voluptati in terris moras trahere inter hostes suos, timorem, dolorem, iram, odium, invidiam, laborem et pauperiem atque morbum. Phoebus quoque eam[2] cithara delinivit; Musae cantilenis et modulis; Gratiae saltibus atque choris. His enim pellecta voluptas inseruit se canentibus Musis, manibusque porrectis implicuit se Gratiis blande ludentibus. Itaque numinibus his canendo atque [*422r*] ludendo coelum repetentibus comitata voluptas coelo invecta est. Terra a voluptate deserta est, hinc ergo illuc abeundum; ita tamen ut abeundo te retro ne vertas, ne Orphei more perdas praemium. Sed quonam tempore voluptas aufugit in coelum? Quo et Astraea originalis scilicet iustitia Adam peccante. Sed ne mortales orbati voluptate inter tot adversa se afflictarent et perderent, Jupiter miseriae nostrae misertus dum abstulit voluptatem spem nobis multiplicavit. Sed fallit spes voluptatis hic consequendae, id est, ex rebus mortalibus reportandae. Nam ad

---

[1] *for* id est *W reads* in   [2] tam *W*

transferred to Minerva. So we can only attain complete pleasure in the presence of divine wisdom (and there's a certain delight to be had from the liberal disciplines also). After this, Pluto, the king of the earth, perceiving the bait for keeping souls for himself in the lower world had been carried off, thought at least to model a bait with a face like Pleasure's. So, when he received the clothes and cosmetics which Pleasure had left behind and was accustomed to use on earth (for she went into heaven pure), he decided to equip and substitute another to take Pleasure's place. But he didn't adorn the demons for he needed them as attendants, nor the souls for they've been judged. He adorned one of the Furies. It wasn't Wrath or Envy or Hate or Fear or Pain, for Pleasure's clothes and shoes didn't fit them: they differed from her too much. But he adorned Waste, whom he had always known to be Pleasure's closest friend when she was on earth. So we ought to take warning and flee far away from pleasure. Otherwise we will immediately tumble into Waste who is hidden there in Pleasure's clothes.

THE END

Minervam translata est, Mercurio, Phoebo, Musis, Gratiis perducentibus. Quamobrem voluptatem plenam penes divinam sapientiam tantum assequi possumus, delectationem etiam quamdam ex liberalibus disciplinis. Post haec Pluto rex terrae, videns sublatam sibi escam detinendarum apud inferos animarum, cogitavit saltem escam fingere aspectu similem voluptati. Acceptis ergo vestibus fucisque a voluptate relictis quibus in terras solebat uti, in coelum enim abiit pura, subornare et substituere alium pro voluptate decrevit. Neque tamen subornavit daemones, ministri enim necessarii sunt; neque animas, adiudicatae enim sunt; sed aliquam furiarum. Non iram, non invidiam, odium, timorem, dolorem, non enim his, velut nimium diversis, congruebant vestes et calcei voluptatis, sed subornavit iacturam quam noverat semper terrenae voluptati familiarissimam. Hinc admonendi sumus ut voluptatem procul effugiamus, alioquin sub voluptatis praetextu in latentem iacturam protinus corruemus.

FINIS

Appendix III

Appendix III contains the following:

1. The preface to the second version of the *Philebus* commentary as found in MS. *Laur. Plut.* 21, 8. This preface was dedicated to Lorenzo and, like the first excerpt, refers to the judgement of Paris.

2. The *argumentum* which originally accompanied the translation of the *Philebus* in Ficino's first decade of Plato translations. Later it served as the preface to the *Philebus* commentary in the first and second Basle editions of the *Opera Omnia,* as well as continuing to serve as the preface to the *Philebus* translation in the various editions of the *Platonis Opera Omnia*; in these instances a third paragraph was added consisting of the passage found at the beginning of ch. 7 of the *Philebus* commentary (Cum multa de summo bono ... apparet accipe defendendam). The version presented here is that of the autograph MS. fragment in the Bibliothèque Nationale, *Lat. nouvelles acquisitions* 1633, which has been collated with the version in the Bodleian MS. *Canonicianus lat.* 163. Apart from the title and the final addition of *Finis argumenti,* however, the two versions are virtually identical.

3. The letter to Orlandini which Ficino appended to the Florence edition of his *Commentaria in Platonem* in 1496. In the Basle edition of the *Opera Omnia* it was used as a prefix to the commentary on the ninth book of the *Republic (Op. Om.,* 1425-26).

Marsilio Ficino's proem to Plato's Philebus [is] dedicated to Lorenzo de' Medici, the magnanimous, the saviour of his native land.

No living being endowed with reason doubts there are three lives: the contemplative, the active, the pleasurable. This is

Proemium

Proemium Marsilii Ficini in Philebum Platonis ad Magnanimum Laurentium Medicem Patriae Servatorem.[1]

Tres esse vitas nemo ratione vivens dubitat: contemplativam, activam, voluptuosam, quoniam videlicet tres ad felicitatem

[1] *this is the preface to X; see Op. Om., 919, 4*

because men elect three routes to happiness: wisdom, power, pleasure. However, we understand by the term "wisdom" any application to the liberal arts, also religious peace. In using the term "power" we think of having authority in civil government and likewise in the military, or having a lot of wealth or brilliant renown, or being actively engaged in doing things. Finally, and without a doubt, under the term "pleasure" are contained the delights of the five senses and the avoidance of labours and worries. Accordingly, the poets named the first Minerva, the second Juno, and the third Venus.

Once upon a time in the presence of Paris three goddesses contended for the golden apple, that is, for the palm and victory. Paris, having inwardly deliberated which he should choose as the best way to happiness, eventually chose pleasure out of the three. But since he'd rejected wisdom and power he deservedly fell into misery while hoping imprudently for happiness.[236]

It is said Hercules only encountered two goddesses, namely Venus and Juno.[237] Having neglected Venus, Hercules pursued the active virtue which was under Juno. Nevertheless because of this he was never happy among men, but vexed perpetually with the work of labours. But at last victory makes him equal to the sky; finally conquered Earth gives him the stars. Two goddesses also met a certain Philebus, pleasure and wisdom. Each strove for victory and with him as judge it seemed Venus had beaten Pallas. However, a little later when Socrates decided the issue more correctly Minerva gained the victory. Rejected Venus, however, together with Juno eventually sentenced Socrates to death, after he'd been harassed by false judges.

Finally, our Lorenzo, having been taught by the oracle of Apollo, has neglected none of the god[desse]s. For he has seen [all] three of them and he has, in addition, admired each one for her own merits. On this account he has won wisdom from Pallas and power from Juno and the graces and poetry and music from Venus.

15 February 1491

vias homines elegerunt: sapientiam, potentiam, voluptatem. Nos autem sub sapientiae nomine quodlibet liberalium artium studium religiosumque otium intelligimus. Sub appellatione potentiae auctoritatem in gubernatione civili pariter atque militari divitiarumque affluentiam et splendorem gloriae negotiosamque virtutem comprehendi putamus. Sub voluptatis denique cognomento quinque sensuum oblectamenta et laborum curarumque declinationem contineri non dubitamus. Primam igitur poetae Minervam, secundam vero Junonem, tertiam denique Venerem nominaverunt.

Tres olim apud Paridem de pomo aureo, id est, de palma et victoria certaverunt. Consultante videlicet Paride secum quam e tribus potissimam ad felicitatem viam eligeret, elegit denique voluptatem. Cum vero sapientiam spreverit et potentiam, merito imprudenter felicitatem sperans incidit in miseriam.

Duae tantum occurrisse traduntur Herculi, Venus scilicet atque Juno. Hercules neglecta Venere animosam sub Junone virtutem est secutus. Neque tamen inter mortales propterea felix, perpetuo certaminum labore vexatus. Sed hunc tandem exaequat victoria coelo; huic denique superata tellus sidera donat. Duae quoque Philebo cuidam obviae voluptas atque sapientia de victoria contenderunt, atque eo iudice Venus Palladem superavisse visa est. Sed paulo post Socrate rectius decernente Minerva victoriam reportavit. Spreta vero Venus simul atque Juno Socratem tandem sub falsis iudicibus agitatum morte damnarunt.

Laurentius denique noster Apollinis oraculo doctus nullum posthabuit superorum. Tres enim vidit, tres quoque pro meritis adoravit. Quamobrem et a Pallade sapientiam et ab Junone potentiam et a Venere gratias poesimque et musicam reportavit.

XV Februarii 1490

A summary for the Philebus, which is about the highest good, by Marsilio Ficino, the Florentine.

Plato wrote the dialogue, the *Philebus,* according to a wonderful order. It is so clear that it doesn't really need a summary, since Plato himself sets forth all his material and the order he's going to follow at the beginning of the debate, then midway he resumes it, then at the end he gathers it together. However, the book's object is to examine the highest good of the soul, which is called the highest good conditionally, since the principle itself of all things is called the highest good absolutely. So the conditional good is dealt with in this book, the absolute good in the *Parmenides.*[238] However, just as a particular light depends on the fountain itself of all light, so does the conditional good proceed from the absolute. Therefore in the *Phaedo*[239] and the *Theaetetus*[240] Plato says the soul's highest good is to be like God. But nothing can become like the sun except by some infusion of light itself. So the soul's good too will be the perfect attainment of the divine light. This light descends first into the intelligence, then into the will. Truth is in the intelligence, joy is in the will. Here and in the *Phaedrus* Plato refers to them as the ambrosia in the intelligence, the nectar in the will.[241] Hence he located man's highest good in the mixture of wisdom and pleasure.

However, before he did so, he denied happiness could consist in either wisdom's or pleasure's reason alone, because in neither do you find the highest good's three conditions: namely that it's utterly perfect and sufficient and desirable. It's perfect because it is wanting in nothing; sufficient because what possesses it is wanting in nothing; desirable because whatever can be desired is in it and from it. So because it's perfect it's sufficient, because sufficient desirable. Since it's sufficient for itself, it's sufficient for another. Since it's sufficient for another, it's desired by another. Neither pleasure alone nor wisdom are shown to satisfy these conditions, but some mixture from them both. In Plato's demonstration the genus, origin and nature of pleasure and wisdom are fully explored, along with the infinite and the limit, and compounding and the principle of compounding.

Argumentum Marsilii Ficini Florentini in Philebum de summo bono.[1]

Philebus dialogus miro quodam ordine a Platone conscriptus est. Atque adeo perspicuus ut ferme argumento non egeat, quippe cum omnem sui materiam atque ordinem in principio disputandi praeponat, resumat in medio, in fine denique colligat. Est autem huius libri propositum de summo animae bono disserere, quod quidem summum bonum cum conditione quadam dicitur, cum ipsum rerum omnium principium summum bonum absolute dicatur. De illo igitur quod cum conditione bonum hoc in libro; de eo quod absolutum in Parmenide disputatur. Ab absoluto autem aliud hoc manat quemadmodum lumen quoddam ab ipso luminis totius fonte dependet. Quamobrem in Phaedone in[2] Theaeteto dictum est a Platone summum animae bonum Dei similitudinem esse. Nihil vero soli sit simile, nisi quadam luminis ipsius infusione. Unde et animae bonum erit integra divini luminis consecutio. Id lumen in mentem primo, in voluntatem deinde descendit. In mente veritas, in voluntate gaudium; in mente ambrosia, in voluntate nectar a Platone et hic et in Phaedro cognominatur. Itaque summum hominis bonum[3] in sapientiae voluptatisque conmixtione locavit.

Sed ante in sola vel sapientiae vel voluptatis ratione beatitudinem consistere posse negavit, ex eo quod triplex boni summi conditio in neutro reperiatur. Ea est ut summopere perfectum sit et sufficiens et expetendum. Perfectum quia nihil sibi deest; sufficiens quia nihil deest illi quod ipsum capit; expetendum quia in illo et ex illo est quicquid appeti potest. Unde quia perfectum sufficiens; quia sufficiens expetendum. Nam quia sibi satest, alteri sufficit; quia sufficit alteri, desideratur ab altero. Haec neque soli sapientiae neque voluptati sed mixto cuidam ex utraque competere demonstrantur, ubi de voluptatis et sapientiae genere origine atque natura permulta dicuntur, de infinito

---

[1] *In MS. 163 the title reads* Argumentum Marsilii in Philebum   [2] *et MS. 163*   [3] bonum *om.*
MS. 163

Only then does he conclude that the highest and absolute good in nature is the measure of all things, that is, is the principle of all nature. But the highest good of the intelligence and soul is the enjoyment of that first good—an enjoyment which coincides with the mixing together of wisdom and pleasure through truth, proportion and beauty. So Plato puts the measure of all things in the first degree of goods; truth, proportion and beauty in the second; wisdom in the third; knowledge, skill and opinion in the fourth; and moderate pleasure in the fifth. A man is said to be happy when he's acquired wisdom concerning divine things and experience about human things (the knowledge that consists of skill and opinion). The whole man exults in the joy of contemplation, and indulges in the pleasure of the senses only to the extent that wisdom and knowledge and joy aren't hindered by it.

Marsilio Ficino, the Florentine, to Paolo Orlandini, monk at the church of the angels and brother philosopher, salutation.

Yesterday you argued with me over matters of divinity with your customary subtlety and you eventually asked me why I give precedence to the will in my letter on happiness, while in [my commentary on] the *Philebus* I've followed Plato in giving precedence to the intellect. Now I could reply that in the *Philebus* [commentary] I give you Plato's view, in the letter my own view. But I don't want Marsilio's view to differ from Plato's. So briefly I will reply that our intelligence proceeds in two ways: one natural, but the other supernatural, which might properly be referred to as the way of ecstasy. In the first case the intellect guides the will as a companion because of some naturally innate light. Eventually, when it has guided the will correctly, it satisfies it, and is therefore superior to it. In the second case, the case of ecstasy, however, a new light and power poured in by God doesn't fill the intellect with the divine splendour, until it has kindled the will with a wonderful love. When

et termino, de composito et compositionis principio. Ac demum concluditur summum in natura bonum et absolutum esse mensuram universorum, hoc est totius naturae principium. Summum vero bonum mentis et animae esse illius primi fruitionem, quae mixtioni ex sapientia et voluptate per veritatem commensurationem et pulchritudinem convenit. Quapropter in primo bonorum gradu rerum omnium mensura ponitur; in secundo veritas commensuratio pulchritudo; in tertio sapientia; in quarto scientia ars et opinio; in quinto temperata voluptas. Beatusque vir dicitur qui sapientiam habet divinorum, humanorum peritiam scientiam arte et opinione constantem; gaudio contemplationis totus exultat, voluptati sensuum eatenus se committit quatenus sapientia scientiaque et gaudium impedimentum inde nullum accipiunt.[1]

Marsilius Ficinus, Florentinus, Paulo Orlandino in angelorum aede monaco conphilosopho suo, salutem.

Postquam heri multa mecum de divinis ut soles subtiliter disputasti, quaesisti denique cur ego in Philebo tamquam ex Platonis sententia intellectum voluntati praefecerim, cur in epistola de felicitate praeferam voluntatem. Equidem respondere possem in Philebo quidem sententiam ferri Platonicam, in epistola vero meam. Sed nolim Marsilianam sententiam a Platonica dissentire. Itaque respondebo summatim duplicem esse mentis nostrae processum: alterum quidem naturalem, alterum vero supra naturam, quem proprie nominamus excessum. In illo quidem processu intellectus luce quadam naturaliter insita voluntatem ducit quasi comitem; ac denique recte ductam implet, ideoque praefertur. In hoc autem excessu nova lux

---

[1]Finis argumenti *add. MS. 163*

the will has been thus kindled through the transmitted power of heat and love, it draws the intelligence into God. There love itself, whose function in the universe is generation, regenerates the soul and makes it divine. We have discussed the intelligence's natural process in accordance with Plato in the *Philebus*; but we touch on the ecstasy which is higher than the natural motion in the letter, and we have treated it in accordance with Plato in the *Phaedrus* and *Symposium*. In the commentaries on Dionysius we've declared how the divine love, which has been kindled in the will, takes the intellect into the highest unity where we enjoy God absolutely. But this is enough for a letter. Proceed happily in your theological commentaries. Often commend me to your venerable father (or rather to the father of both of us), Guido Laurentinus, the restorer of the church of the angels.

Florence 13 November 1496.

virtusque infusa divinitus non prius intellectum divino splendore complet quam amore mirifico accenderit voluntatem. Quae quidem sic accensa per ipsam translatoriam caloris amorisque efficaciam mentem traducit in Deum, ubi amor ipse cuius est in universo generationis officium regenerat animum efficitque divinum. Naturalem quidem mentis incessum una cum Platone tractavimus in Philebo, excessum vero naturali motu superiorem attingimus in epistola atque una cum Platone in Phaedro Symposioque tetigimus, et qua ratione divinus amor qui in voluntate accenditur intellectum in unitatem summam transferat qua praecipue Deo fruimur in commentariis in Dionysium declaravimus. Sed haec pro epistolae modo satis. Tu vero in theologicis commentationibus tuis perge feliciter, et venerabili patri vestro, immo et nostro, Guidoni Laurentino angelicae aedis instauratori nos saepe commenda.

Florentiae xiii Novembris
MCCCCLXXXXVI.

Appendix IV: The Pesaro Fragments

The Biblioteca Oliveriana's MS. 620 is damaged in places, particularly towards the end, and consists of seven fragments first identified correctly by Professor Kristeller in 1967 as belonging in the main to some stage of the *Philebus* commentary (*Iter Italicum* II, p. 65). There are six fragments of the commentary, which I have called P frags. I, II, III, IV, V and VI (my pp. 87-109, 153-173, [444 and] 181-187, 217-265, 283-285, 371-425 and 447-455 and 457-463), and one fragment consisting of Ficino's *De Virtutibus Moralibus* together with some of his *De Quattuor Sectis Philosophorum*. The MS. has 68 folios and an older foliation (which I have used) going to 144v. It is written in a non-Italian, perhaps Spanish, hand and is largely unparagraphed. I would like to revise Kristeller's description of the contents thus:

f. 1(1)-5(5)v. (M)Arsilius Ficinus Antonio Canisiano S. D. Cum sepe mecum egisses ... ut deus efficiaris [i.e. the *De Virtutibus Moralibus* complete].

6(6)-8(8)v. De quattuor sectis philosophorum eiusdem. (M)Arsilius fficinus clementi ffortino s.d. Tria sunt mi Clemens ... mundos et refici. Animum no ... [i.e. the *De Quattuor Sectis Philosophorum* incomplete].

*

f. 9(17)-16(24)v. [Ficino's *Philebus* commentary: the last ⅔ of ch. 3, all of ch. 4 and the beginning of ch. 5].

f. 15(23)v. [at the bottom in an eighteenth century hand] Marsilii Ficini Comment. in prim. et secund. Tomum Perhihermen.

*

f. 17(41)-24(48)v. [the *Philebus* commentary: the end of ch. 13, all of chs. 14 and 15 and the beginning of ch. 16. Ch. 15 is not abridged: the heading to ch. 16 is simply transposed forwards, cf. MS. *Laur. Plu.* 21,8].

*

f. 25(52)-26(53)v. [*idem:* the beginning of ch. 18, including most of an opening passage otherwise found in MS. *Laur. Plu.* 21,8 only].

*

f. 27(65)-43(81)v. [*idem:* most of ch. 23, all of chs. 24-27, the beginning of ch. 28].

*

f. 44(88)-44(88)v. [*idem:* the beginning of ch. 30].

*

f. 45(121)-63(139)v. [*idem:* all but the opening few lines of ch. 37 and all of book two, i.e. chs. 1-4].

f. 49(125). Finis primi libri commentariorum Marsilii Ficini Florentini in Platonis Philebum de summo hominis bono. Sequitur eiusdem in eundem liber secundus.

f. 63(139)v. Item alia excerpta breviter ex lectionibus Marsilii Ficini in Philebum.

f. 64(140)-68(144)v. [excerpts I, II, III, V and two-thirds of VI (i.e. from the ten excerpts which conclude the commentary in the other MSS.)].

* * * *

But what stage of the commentary does Pesaro's MS. present? It must be the second stage (the stage presented in its entirety in MS. *Laur. Plu.* 21,8) for the following reasons:

a. the vast majority of P readings agree with X when X differs from W and/or Y (e.g. my pp. 229, 239, 249, 255, 391, 421);

b. P has additions otherwise unique to X (e.g. my pp. 235, 253, 405), as well as additions common to X and W *or* Y;

c. P has omissions otherwise unique to X (e.g. my pp. 251, 255, 377, 387), as well as omissions common to X and W *or* Y;

d. P shares X's spelling conventions when they differ from W and/ or Y (this is especially true of X and P's preference for *iis* over *his*);

e. P agrees with X in having fewer abbreviations than W and far fewer than Y;

f. P follows the word-order of X when this occasionally deviates from that of W and/or Y;

g. P follows the chapter numbering unique to X (my pp. 231, 239, 249, 261, 415).

Within these seven categories of agreement the exceptions are very infrequent and usually trivial: P has a few independent readings, even fewer agreements with W over and against X and Y, and only four agreements with Y over and against W and X. It has some unique omissions (e.g. my pp. 239, 247) but no unique additions. Very rarely, incidentally, have I opted for the XP reading, and only once for a unique P reading (my p. 379).

There seems to be no way of determining the relationship between X and P, but my feeling is that P was not a copy of X but of another MS. of the commentary's second stage.

Finally, since stage three had already appeared in 1496 and appeared, moreover, in an edition, it seems less likely the scribe was reproducing stage two in the 1500s than working at the time of stage two itself. Accordingly, we ought to extend Kristeller's (and Mazzatinti's) dating of P to include the 1490s.

Appendix V: The Chapter Summaries

Instead of the ten excerpts, Ficino added these chapter summaries to the third version of the *Philebus* commentary, i.e. the *editio princeps* in his *Commentaria in Platonem* of 1496; and they accompanied all subsequent editions of the commentary. My text incorporates the 1496 corrigenda list without comment.

Introductio ad dialogum.　　ca. i.
"Vide O Protarche quem nunc a Philebo, etc...." Proponitur tractandum quid sit hominis bonum, et utrum ad illud magis conferat voluptas an sapientia.

Dispositio dialogi.　　ca. ii.
"Age igitur praeter haec, etc...." Primo quidem invenienda ipsa summi boni conditio. Deinde perpendendum utra magis accedat ad illam voluptasne an sapientia.

Dispositio dialogi.　　ca. iii.
"At nunc expiationis gratia, etc...." Summopere verendum ne contra divina nomina delinquamus. Ut voluptas et sapientia cognoscantur iudicenturque, dividendum utriusque genus in species. Si voluptas ipsa esset ipsum bonum, omnis voluptas esset bona. Sunt tamen aliquae malae, quae videlicet sunt contrariae bonis. Bonum vero contrarium esse non potest.

Ambigitur quomodo unum multa.　　ca. iiii.
"Hoc item multo magis mutua confessione asseveremus, etc...." Vetus et difficilis dubitatio est quomodo unum multa sit atque vicissim. Facile quidem cognitu est quomodo unum hoc vel illud genitum et caducum, una cum unitate substantiae, habeat etiam multitudinem, et valde quidem diversam. Difficultas igitur non versatur circa eiusmodi unum sed circa unum sempiternum.

Ambigitur quomodo unum multa.   ca. v.

"Quando quispiam o puer, etc...." Siquis introduxerit unam cuiusque naturalium specierum ideam separatam, dubia multa nascentur. Primum, utrum existant unitates eiusmodi ideales? Secundum, quales sint? Tertium, quomodo insint mortalibus aut assint?

Artificium circa unum et multa et abusus logicae.   ca. vi.

"At unde potissimum exordiemur, etc...." Animae rationali naturaliter insita est quaedam disserendi facultas, quae communiter ab uno in multa vicissimque discurrit. Ingeniosissimi quique ad eiusmodi artificium propensiores existent. Si id adolescentulis concedatur absque delectu, insolentes evadunt; logicaque abutentes, non fiunt philosophi sed sophistae.

Divinitas ingenii circa unum et multa.   ca. vii.

"Donum profecto, etc...." Animus noster quatenus divinitatis est particeps eatenus ad dialecticam, id est, metaphysicam facultatem est propensus. Itaque philosophi divini praecipue Pythagorici dixerunt omnia entia ex uno multitudineque constare et in uno habere terminum, in multitudine infinitum. Atque in hoc mysterio fundaverunt nobis dialecticam facultatem, non in conceptibus cogitationis nostrae sed in ideis speciebusque naturalibus, ut in quolibet idearum spherarumque ordine genus unum inveniamus generalissimum, dividamusque ipsum per differentias suas in species gradatim usque ad species ultimas; neque praetermittamus medios differentiarum gradus, sub speciebus autem multis singula tamquam innumerabilia negligamus.

Quomodo considerandum unum et multitudo.   ca. viii.

"Quae modo dixisti, etc...." Vox humana unum genus est, multiplicari quoque singulatim possunt infinitae voces. Scientia vocum vel musica vel grammatica non habetur ex eo quod aliquis vel genus illud cogitet vel infinitas voces imaginetur, sed quod speciales gradatim vocum differentias distincte comprehendat. Similiter de litteris atque de omnibus est putandum.

Distinctio circa unum et multa ad scientiam necessaria.
ca. viiii.

"An non de sapientia, etc...." Neque sapientia neque voluptas neque res ulla perfecte iudicari potest, nisi genus ipsius in
suas species dividatur. Subiectum huius disputationis est summum hominis bonum, utrum sit sapientia an voluptas an
tertium.

Tres ipsius boni conditiones.　　ca. x.

"Nihil iam grave, etc...." Promittit se probaturum ipsum
bonum non esse sapientiam vel voluptatem vel utrumque simul,
sed tertium quiddam quod aliud est quam utrumque et melius
est ambobus. Tres ipsius boni conditiones ponit, scilicet esse
perfectum, sufficiens, omnibus expetendum.

Quomodo voluptas vel sapientia se habeat ad bonum.
ca. xi.

"Consideremus igitur, etc...." Si sapientia separatur a voluptate vel voluptas a sapientia et ab his quae sapientiae similia
sunt, scilicet opinione vera, praevisione, memoria, neutrum erit
ipsum bonum, quia neutrum ipsius boni conditiones habebit. Id
tamen sapientia praestantius habet quod delectationem secum
affert et hanc quidem mirificam atque intimam si intelligentia
fuerit expedita. Voluptas autem sapientiam non introducit
secum saepiusque excludit. Adde quod voluptas omnis plenitudinem habet a sapientia. Animadversio enim cum sit motio
circularis ubicumque fiat fit intelligentiae munere. Voluptas
autem animadversione perficitur. Nam ubi sensus corporeus
congruum voluptariumque attingit, nisi animadvertatur sentiendi motus, vel nulla vel stupida fit voluptas. Intelligentia
denique ad vitam mixtam atque sufficientem proprius accedit
quam voluptas, siquidem haec voluptatem propriam secum
affert, neque vicissim voluptas propriam affert sapientiam.

Quomodo bonum in mixto.　　ca. xii.

"Quid autem, etc...." Cum neque sapientia neque voluptas
sola sit ipsum bonum, quia non sufficit appetitui, reliquum est

ut summum nobis bonum consistat in quodam ex utrisque mixto. Bonum quidem humanae mentis in quodam mixto consistit, quoniam in hac aliud quidem est intellectus aliud vero voluntas. Purae vero divinaeque mentis bonum in simplici quodam, quoniam unum ibi magis est intellectus atque voluntas, gaudiumque ibi est ipsemet actus intelligentiae videlicet expeditus.

Quomodo bonum in mixto.   ca. xiii.

"Palmam igitur, etc...." Summum hominis bonum est unum quiddam occultum atque divinum quod desuper in ipsa sapientiae voluptatisque certa mixtione suscipitur. Huic autem divino similior est sapientia quam voluptas, ergo melior. Suscipitur autem illud in ipsa unitate quae est caput animae intellectu et voluntate superius, diciturque illud bonum capi a mixto, quoniam unitas est utriusque radix. Nec ipsa bono fruitur nisi vel prius vel interim satis utrique fiat, per visionem quidem intellectui per laetitiam vero voluntati. Illud vero bonum quasi per modum gustus tactusque efficitur atque est ineffabile.

De infinito et termino et mixto et horum causa.   ca. xiiii.

"Omnia quae nunc, etc...." Sub ipso uno rerum principio statim duo sunt amplissima entium omnium elementa, scilicet infinitudo atque terminus. Deus ex his duobus tertium quiddam, id est, universum ens commiscet. Utrumque vero genus est amplissimum multas species in se comprehendens. Ipsemet Deus ut communicabilis est causa mixtionis existit; ut autem supereminens causa discretionis apparet. Item per terminum unit, per infinitatem vero discernit. Ipsa quin etiam alteritas in mundo intelligibili causa discretionis existit.

Quae sint in genere infiniti.   ca. xv.

"Attende igitur, etc...." Qualitati materiali suapte natura non repugnat remitti intendive per gradus absque fine. Similiter neque id repugnat motui actionique ipsius. Similiter dimensioni non repugnat minui vel augeri absque fine. Certus autem modus his ab auctore specierum desuper adhibetur, ubi enim destinat

humanam speciem vel equinam, simul certum qualitatis et quantitatis motionisque modum terminumve decernit. Infinita igitur per se desuper finiuntur.

Conditiones generis infiniti.   ca. xvi.

"Benedicis, etc...." Progressio hinc inde per quoslibet gradus indifferens est proprium infinitae naturae. Haec autem fit aliter alibi, in materia quidem per formas, in dimensione vero per maius et minus, in numero per plus et paucius, in qualitate et actione per remissionem et intentionem, in motu per velocius atque tardius, in tempore per longius atque brevius. Praeterea in rebus incorporeis est aliquid suo quodam pacto infinitae naturae persimile. Sed intellectus auctor specierum in virtute ipsius unius atque per animam ut instrumentum speciebus omnibus addit terminos, tum unicuique, tum invicem imponens insuper aequalitatem proportionemque numeratam ad terminum pertinentem.

Mixta ex infinito et termino.   ca. xvii.

"Agedum, etc...." Mixta ex infinito et termino sunt formae rerum recta ratione compositae, ubi quae per se quodammodo infinita sunt vel etiam invicem opposita certum suscipiunt modum, et mutua proportione conciliantur in unum. In parte quin etiam animae sensuali affectus per se infiniti et oppositi modum terminumque accipiunt ab illa dea quae est causa mixtionis ac terminos amat, id est, ab ipsa mente.

Mixtum fit ab alio.   ca. xviii.

"Ceterum quid, etc...." Mixtum ex infinito et termino invicem oppositis neque per se coeuntibus factum est ab alio. Non enim efficitur a se ipso, alioquin qua ratione faceret iam esset. Qua vero ratione fieret nondum existeret. Causa vero a qua fit si dominatur operi non est pars operis aliqua. Partes enim non ipsae quidem causae sunt, sed ipsi causae serviunt. Vera causa supereminet atque est efficiens et exemplar et quodammodo finis.

De vita mixta, de voluptate et intellectu, de causa terminante.
ca. xviiii.

"Agedum deinceps, etc...." Vita quae ex voluptate et sapientia constat species quaedam est in genere mixtorum. Voluptas in genere infinitorum, est enim quasi motus quidam ad magis minusve indifferens atque multiplicabilis. Infinitudo haec voluptatem non efficit bonam, alioquin dolorem quoque faceret bonum. Mens scilicet intellectus aliquando deus dicitur, aliquando dea. Deus quidem si ad inferius, dea vero si ad superius ref[e]ratur. Est autem intellectus et sapientia in genere terminorum. Intellectus mundi rex alter quidem est in anima mundi, alter vero mundo superior. Mentem esse in genere termini confirmatur quia dum in se convertitur profecto terminat ordinatque se ipsam. Item speciem modumque et ordinem sequentibus adhibet, tum mens mundana mundanis, tum humana humanis praesertim affectibus per se infinitis. Affectus enim cum inferatur aliunde ducendi munus nullum habet. Mentis vero iudicium habet imperium. Hinc illud Platonicum atque Orphicum iudicium Jovis rex est universi. Quoniam vero intellectus manifestus est rerum definitor, ipsum vero bonum definitor occultus atque superior, ideo intellectus nominatur a Platone propheta quasi superioris interpres.

Corpus nostrum dependet ex universo.　　　ca. xx.

"Utrum o Protarche, etc...." Antiquiorum sententia est ex ipso mirabili mundanorum ordine confirmata, mundum non fortuna sed intelligentia regi. Elementa quae nobis insunt nec integra sunt nec pura. Dependent igitur ab integris purisque elementis quibus constat mundus. Ex toto igitur mundi corpore corpus nostrum conficitur et alitur atque regitur.

Mundus est animal intellectuale.　　　ca. xxi.

"Quid hoc, etc...." Mundanum corpus quanto perfectius est quam nostrum tanto magis est animatum, neque nostram susciperet intellectualem animam ab intellectu artifice mundi nisi mundus suam inde animam suscepisset. Vitam vero irrationalem habemus etiam a vita mundi, per quam praeparamur ad

intellectualem animam capiendam. Reliqua sic expone, si in nobis sunt terminus, infinitum, mixtum atque ex his ipsa causa hominem rationalem efficit, cur non et mundum ex isdem melioribus constitutum effecerit sapientem? Atque si nostrum hoc sapientia gubernatur et arte, cur non etiam universum? Causa ipsa his ordinem praebens est intellectus. Hic autem corpori non aliter quam per mediam animam inesse potest. Igitur in Jove, id est, in vivente mundo est mens et anima regia per virtutem causae, id est, et per modum causae mundanae et a virtute causae supermundanae. Mentis umbra est anima, animae umbra est vita corporis.

Mens, voluptas, vita mixta, bonum.   ca. xxii.
"Praecedentem, etc...." Mens illa vigens in mundi anima est causa mundanorum, et progenies supermundanae mentis quae est causa mundi totius. Mens supermundana progenies est ipsius boni quod est omnium causa. Nostra mens est progenies supermundanae mentis; est cognata quodammodo causis modo dictis, igitur in genere termini. Terminus enim proprietatem habet causae potius quam infinitum. Est ergo melior voluptate. Vita enim mixta ex sapientia et voluptate, ideo summopere est eligenda quoniam a divina causa eam constituente munus habet. Mens igitur et sapientia quia cognatior causae quam voluptas ideo melior.

Quomodo fiat in composito voluptas atque dolor.   ca. xxiii.
"Oportet itaque, etc...." Voluptas dolorque ad corporeum sensum praecipue pertinentes fiunt in composito quodam ex infinito et termino, ex materia atque forma: dolor quidem quotiens harmonia solvitur naturalis, voluptas autem quotiens restituitur.

Voluptates ad animum pertinentes vel ad corpus.   ca. xxiiii.
"Pone deinceps, etc...." Sunt aliae species voluptatis atque doloris ad solam animam pertinentes quando expectans bonum malumve futurum laetatur aut maeret. Tu vero si velis de voluptatis dolorisque conditione diiudicare, invicem omnino secernes

cognoscesque utrum omnis voluptas et semper sit eligenda aut dolor similiter respuendus, an potius aliquando et certa quadam conditione. Si enim voluptas non simpliciter eligenda, neque dolor simpliciter respuendus, certe neque voluptas idem erit atque ipsum bonum, neque dolor idem atque malum.

De indolentia et voluptate animi.   ca. xxv.
"Primum igitur, etc...." Si naturalis harmonia nec solvitur nec restituitur, non fit dolor in sensum vel voluptas. Item merus contemplationis status absquȩ motu laetitiae vel molestiae esse potest. Status eiusmodi forte maxime divinus est, siquidem talis habitus sit deorum. Denique sicut est in anima sola per expectationem futurorum dolor atque voluptas ita per memoriam praeteritorum.

De motu et sensu et passione.   ca. xxvi.
"Primum quidem, etc...." Levissimae corporis passiones latent animum, graviores innotescunt. Sensus est perceptio corporeae passionis in anima. Motus igitur factus in corpore per quem sensus excitatur corpori simul et animae quodammodo videtur esse communis, quamvis hic motus aliter sit in corpore quam in anima; in illo quidem passio, in hac vero iudicium atque actio.

De memoria et reminiscentia.   ca. xxvii.
"Sensus praeterea, etc...." Meminisse est simpliciter conservare vestigium vel imaginem quandam motionis quae sentiendo facta fuit in sensu. Meminisse proprie non includit in se praesentem horum animadversionem. Reminiscentia vero animadversionem praesentem habet et fit in anima sine corporis passione. Est autem duplex, una quidem in parte sensuali quando recolimus praeteritas sensuum passiones, altera in parte rationali quando post oblivionem quandam resumit quae senserat vel quae didicerat. Agere vero potest non solum sine passione corporis sed etiam sine communione cum corpore.

Quomodo voluptas quaedam animi propria. ca. xxviii.
"Multa considerare, etc. . . ." Cum primum ex obiecto quodam proportionali nobis fit restitutio in naturam, voluptas fit statim hoc praesente, servatur deinceps hoc in memoria. Post hac indigentia corporis ad idem vel simile nos incitante appetimus illud rursus adesse. Eiusmodi appetitus, non solum per indigentiam corporis sed etiam per ipsam animae memoriam incitatus ad consequendum id quod a nobis abest, non est in corpore sed in anima. Corpus enim agit vel patitur solummodo per contactum. In hoc autem gradu nihil adhuc attingitur. Praeterea in corpore quidem nunc indigéntia est; appetitus interim ad repletionem movet huic oppositam, quasi sit alibi quam in corpore. In corpore quidem passio est excitans appetitum. Appetitus autem in animo est, non tam passio quam motio quaedam similis actioni. Non autem hic de naturali vel quolibet appetitu loquimur sed sensuali.

Voluptas corporis impura est. ca. xxviiii.
"Hoc praeterea, etc. . . ." Vita voluptuosa servilis est, servit enim indigentiae corporali; est et anxia, mixtas enim voluptates cum doloribus habet, ut quando quis propter famem dolet sed interim propter spem mensae statim futurae laetatur.

Voluptas corporis falsa est. ca. xxx.
"Hac talium, etc. . . ." Sicut opinio, spes, formido, sic et voluptas partim quidem vera partim vero falsa esse potest. Opinio rursus quando circa iudicium boni malive fallitur voluptatem et molestiam reddit vanam.

Voluptas corporis falsa est. ca. xxxi.
"Distinguamus igitur, etc. . . ." Opinio alia quidem vera est, alia vero falsa, quamvis verum sit tunc hominem opinari etiamsi opinione fallatur. Similiter voluptas quaedam potest esse falsa, quamvis interea verum sit sic affectum hominem delectari. Item sicut ex opinione prava sequitur voluptas prava, sic ex falsa opinione falsa voluptas.

Voluptas corporis falsa est. Item de opinione et imaginatione.
   ca. xxxii.
"Nihil ne o amice, etc...." Hic quidem somniat se dulce
bibere. Hic vero vigilans dulce bibit utrobique voluptas est, sed
in vigilante sic vera voluptas sicut verum vinum, in somniante
sic falsa sicut falsum. Item tanto maior voluptas in vigilante
quanto vinum ipsam imaginem vini superat. Opinio ex sensu
memoriaque proficiscitur quando iterum sentimus aliquid
memoriterque iudicare de illo non nihil pergimus, scilicet quod
sit homo vel equus, amicus vel inimicus, bonus aut malus. Hac
ipsa quasi consultatione opinionem concipimus veram aut fal-
sam, quae quidem opinio sermoni vel scripturae similis esse
videtur. Praeterea est in nobis imaginatio quae actiones sensus
opinionesque imaginibus secum ipsa consignat profundiusque
imprimit et latius exprimit. Saepe vero ex opinione vera vel falsa
sequitur imaginatio vera similiter aut falsa. Potest utique imaginatio praeter id quod nunc existit quodve iam possidet alia
fingere multifariam et optare.

Voluptates quaedam animi propriae.   ca. xxxiii.
"Si modo recte, etc...." Opinio et imaginatio non solum ad
praesentiam sed etiam ad futura et praeterita pertinet, voluptates autem et molestiae de praeteritis futurisve susceptae ipsius
animae propriae sunt.

Bonus vir tamquam Deo similis veras habet imaginationes atque
voluptates, malus vero contra.   ca. xxxiiii.
"Age ad hoc, etc...." Bonus vir a Platone censetur qui in se
quidem temperatus, ad Deum autem pius est, ad homines vero
iustus. Animus eiusmodi propter similitudinem Deo prae ceteris
est amicus, malus autem propter dissimilitudinem inimicus.
Itaque cum Deus et moveat intrinsecus et ubique provideat
nimirum opiniones et imaginationes spesque bonorum virorum
verae frequenter evadunt, malorum vero falsae. Utrique gaudia
quaedam excogitant, optant, sperant. Haec bonis tamquam
divinis atque veridicis vera frequenter evadunt, malis vero falsa.
Mali enim tamquam sibimet mendaces, sicut frequenter quae

nec sunt nec fuerunt neque erunt fingunt atque optant, ita falsa saepius oblectamenta confingunt. Denique si pravis tamquam a Deo discordibus succedere spes non debent saepe tamen in externis succedere videntur, saltem sequitur ut intrinsecus non succedant. Semper igitur sollicitantur intrinsecus atque languent voluptatesque eorum similes sunt falsis voluptatibus aegrotantium, somniantium, insanorum.

Unde voluptas vera sit vel falsa, item bona vel mala.
       ca. xxxv.
"Num opiniones, etc...." Quaeritur an sicut opinio propter falsitatem prava est sic et voluptas quia falsa sit etiam sit et prava? An etiam propter aliam quoque causam iudicanda sit prava voluptas. Voluptas cognitionem appetitumque requirit, illinc igitur habet ut sit vera vel falsa, hinc autem ut bona vel mala.

Confirmatio superiorum et quomodo voluptas appareat maior quam sit.   ca. xxxvi.
"Aggrediamur iterum, etc...." Voluptates conferendae sunt ad obiectum quod delectat. Si hoc revera bonum voluptas bona, contra mala. Si hoc revera adest quodammodo vera voluptas, sin minus falsa. Dicuntur quoque verae voluptates tum propter obiectum vere bonum, tum propter veram obiecti praesentiam; falsae quin etiam tum propter malum, tum propter absentiam. Iam vero ubi voluptas apparet maior quam sit aut minor, est falsa voluptas, praesertim ea parte qua fallimur. Apparet autem maior voluptas praesens; praeterita vel futura sicut visibile comminus quidem maius, eminus vero minus esse videtur. Item voluptas apparet maior quae post molestiam sequitur vel quam appetitus acrior comitatur. Item maior saepe videtur quam sit quae post nullas vel minimas voluptates nova denique venit, modis quoque quam plurimis. Praeterea contingit ex comparatione fallacia.

Utrum voluptas omnis fiat ex indigentia.   ca. xxxvii.
"Post haec igitur, etc...." Dictum est quando solvitur

harmonia corpori naturalis dolorem fieri, quando restituitur voluptatem scilicet corporalem. Voluptates enim molestiaeque animo propriae alia quadam ratione contingunt. Voluptates insuper
quaedam levissimae fiunt in sensu corporeo etiamsi tunc non
fiat necessaria restitutio in naturam, ut dulce bibere sine siti.
Denique nisi fiat necessaria restitutio vel solutio noxia neque voluptas vehemens sequitur neque molestia. Quaeritur interea
utrum corpus aliquo tempore sine mutationibus sic oppositis
esse possit. Quaestio in Theaeteto Theologiaque solvitur, sed
quantum ad voluptatis corporeae naturam spectat; qualitas quidem eius in quadam congruentia rei ad sensum spiritumque consistit, quantitas autem in ipsa corporis et spiritus indigentia.

Quae voluptas in statu, quae in motu.　　　ca. xxxviii.
"Ista sane sic, etc...." Si non quilibet motus in corpore, sed
qui manifeste sensum movet voluptatem efficit vel dolorem,
sequitur ut in motibus sensum latentibus neutrum fiat. Affectio
eiusmodi neque voluptas est neque molestia vera, quamvis si
conferatur ad manifestum vehementemque dolorem voluptas
quaedam appareat, sin ad similem voluptatem molestia videatur. Siquis autem dixerit affectionem mediam esse optabilem
naturaeque gratam. Quoniam et ad vitam confert et actionem
possidet expeditam, hic iam se conferet ad laetitiam quandam
animo quidem propriam, nec satis ad sensum corporeum pertinentem. Voluptas quidem sensus in motu versatur potius quam
in statu. Mentis gaudium consistit in statu; quamvis status eiusmodi possit sua quadam ratione motus cognominari, quatenus
voluntas ad ipsum intelligentiae actum obiectumque quodammodo se diffundit. Siqua vero sit mens divinior in qua voluntas
ab intellectu non discrepet ibique aliquid nominetur gaudium,
vel etiamsi in quolibet intellectu iam absoluto gaudium appelle-
tur in ipsomet intelligentiae actu stabili, tunc eiusmodi voluptas
ad statum terminumque pertinere videbitur. Neque de hac ipsa
in hoc dialogo ulla fit disceptatio.

Quam inanis voluptas corporis.　　　ca. xxxix.
"Quomodo id, o Socrates, etc...." Democritii Epicureique

voluptatem ab eis electam in corpore quidem indolentiam, in animo vero tranquillitatem vocant. Pythagoras, Heraclitus, Empedocles, tamquam severi morum vitaeque censores, corporeas voluptates in contemptum trahere studuerunt, dicentes corpoream voluptatem non habere essentiam alicubi propriam, sed in ipsa doloris fuga illam aliquid apparere. Forte vero putant multa sensuum oblectamenta esse quaedam inferiorum daemonum veneficia, ut huiusmodi esca in rebus mortalibus nos illaqueent.

Voluptas corporis quam impura, falsa, procul ab ipso bono.
    ca. xxxx.
"Post haec autem, etc...." Tunc voluptas apparet in corpore vehementior quando indigentia maior molestiorque acriorem incitat appetitum. Eiusmodi est in corpore aegrotante vel similiter se habente potius quam in sano. Eiusmodi quin etiam in animo propter intemperantiam aegro potius quam in animo temperato. Igitur vehementia voluptatis cum habitu pravo et imperfecto concurrit. Nam in habitu meliore sive corporis sive animi voluptas purior stabiliorque existat. Aliud ergo est vehementia voluptatis, aliud vero eiusdem puritas atque veritas; et ubi voluptas apparet maior ibi minus vera quia sincera minus, siquidem cum stimulo indigentiae appetitusque molesto miscetur, quo cessante desinit simul et vehementia voluptatis. Quis ergo dixerit voluptatem habere rationem finis et boni atque perfecti, siquidem magnitudinem suam cum falsitate coniungat, et in habitu corporis adhuc imperfecto ad perfectumque tendente maior appareat quam in habitu iam perfecto, immo apparente perfectione dispareat?

Quomodo miscetur dolor cum voluptate.   ca. xxxxi.
"An non aliquas, etc...." Voluptas quae percipitur in perfricando pruritum vel calefaciendo frigidum corpus vel refrigerando calefactum saepe cum dolore miscetur. Eiusmodi mixtura fit in corpore propter mixtionem differentium qualitatum vel accidentium. Miscetur quoque in anima voluptas aliquando cum dolore propter mixtionem imaginationum

motuumque vel respectuum differentium. In ipsa vero voluptatis cum dolore confusione aliquando voluptas superat saepius dolor, nonnumquam simul aequantur. Saepe etiam non in anima vel in corpore seorsum sed in communi contingit voluptatis cum dolore concursus, quando corpore sitibundo delectatur animus interim spe vini iam proximi, vel quando dum sensus oblectatur potu animus cura maeret.

Quomodo miscetur dolor cum voluptate.　　　ca. xxxxii.

"Dic igitur, etc...." In scabie similique apostemate bilis vel sanguis fervidus vel etiam falsa pituita petit cutem. Pars quidem crassa residens citra cutem tumefactione dolorem creat. Pars autem media infusa cuti pruritum movet qui pertinet ad dolorem, sed pars subtilior per frictionem foras evolat atque propter evacuationem superflui quae naturae convenit voluptatem affert, sed dolorem iterum frictio durior cutis continuitatem rumpens. Si ad cutem sic infectam calentem pannum admoveamus, dolor iterum sequitur et voluptas: dolor quidem dum pungit cutem iam infectam, voluptas autem dum quod ibi superfluum est dissolvit. Sin abluamus mediocriter aqua rosacea, dolorem iterum voluptatemque reportabimus: voluptatem sane dum temperatur aestus, dolorem quoque dum humor includitur intus et tumefacit stimulatque inclusus. Hactenus dolor quidem plurimum intus est, voluptas vero foris, ac dolor superat voluptatem. Quandoque vero in hac vel simili quadam corporis affectione agitationeque nostra spiritus quidam qui hactenus torpuerant excitati per meatus nervorum usque quaque percurrunt lambentesque deliniunt, praesertim quia spiritibus diffusio motusque congruit, unde voluptas quaedam intima et occulta sequitur. Sed hanc interim comitatur exterior molestia quaedam, quatenus ad pulsus spirituum moventur vapores humorum mali, cutisque exteriores nervos tendunt aut gravant. Hic vero ambiguum est in utram partem declinatio fiat: ad internamne magis an ad externam; rursus ad condensationem vel rarefactionem atque diffusionem; item ad dolorem an voluptatem? Nonnumquam vero in hoc vel simili corporis habitu voluptas ita dolorem superat ut non tam molestia vel punctio

videatur quam titillatio quaedam, qualis revera fit quando spiritus genitalis exundans palpat tenditque nervos. Sed enim ibi voluptas vehementior oritur ubi et titillatio crescit, videlicet in effectu venereo, in quo voluptas quanto vehementior est tanto periculosior. Haec enim et occultum quendam timorem repentinae mortis incutit animo et discrimen interitus infert corpori tam nervorum concussione quam exhalatione spirituum proventuri. Itaque voluptas haec etsi videtur magna tamen cum dolore miscetur.

Mixtura doloris cum voluptate.   ca. xxxxiii.
"De voluptatibus o Protarche, etc...." Miscentur quoque voluptates in anima cum doloribus sicut in corpore, sed quandoque conditione contraria, quando videlicet in anima quidem voluptas quaedam est, in corpore vero dolor, aut contra. Item anima quando repletionem cupit tunc movetur in oppositum praesenti corporis passioni, id est, evacuationi, et interdum corporeo sensu dolente propter indigentiam simul animus aliqua spe laetatur. Multis practerea modis animus in affectibus a corpore discrepat. Sed iam dominandum est quomodo non in communi dumtaxat, sed in ipso etiam animo fiat quaedam voluptatis cum dolore permixtio. Iam vero in appetitu vindictae una cum iniuriae dolore inest laetitia quaedam in effectu vel spe vindictae victoriaeque fundata. Saepe etiam in timore, desiderio, quaerimonia, amore, spes quaedam inest, vel expurgatio quaedam atribilis pertinens ad laetitiam, in aemulatione cum solicitudine miscetur spes victoriae, in lamentationibus et tragediis re quidem ipsa dolemus, sed harmonia et ordine delectamur, in comicis similibusque spectaculis apparatus et artificium nos delectat. Mollior autem vox vel habitus aut gestus liquefacit spiritum et enervat. Lacrimae quin etiam sicut in maesta contractione spirituum exprimuntur, sic in dilatatione ob laetitiam nimiam videlicet humore roscido foras sparso funduntur.

Confirmantur superiora.   ca. xxxxiiii.
"Invidiae nomen, etc...." In invidia praecipue dolor cum voluptate proculdubio commiscetur. Praeterea sicut optimum

est se ipsum cognoscere, ita pessimum ignorare se ipsum. Multi quidem arroganter ignorant quomodo ad bona externa se habeant plures, item qua conditione ad corporis sui dotes quam plurimi, qua ad animi bona, quae quidem est ignorantia pessima, se videlicet aestimare scientem aut bonum cum non sit talis.

Ignorantia et confidentia.   ca. xxxxv.
"Hoc iterum, etc. . . ." Ignorantia et confidentia sui nacta quidem potentia terribilis est, si vero sit impotens fit ridicula.

Mixtura quaedam doloris cum voluptate.   ca. xxxxvi.
"Tristitia quaedam, etc. . . ." Quando videmus homines quosdam nobis amicos vel saltem non inimicos se ipsos adeo ignorare ut se pulchriores sapientioresve quam sint existiment, sintque etiam invalidi, solemus eiusmodi habitum irridere. Igitur et laetamur, laetamur autem illorum malo, id est ignorantia simul et arrogantia; livore igitur affecti sumus unde tristamur. Tristitiam itaque clam cum laetitia commiscemus. Haec utique mixtionis et invidiae species aliis forsan occulta deprehenditur a Platone.

Quae voluptates indigentiae minus, puritatis plus habeant.
          ca. xxxxvii.
"Secundum naturam, etc. . . ." Resolutiva ratio nos docet mixtum resolvere in simplicia formasque tandem ab oppositis segregare. Itaque post oblectamenta mixta maeroribus ad pura gaudia progredi. Dictat praeterea ratio inter opposita, quod praestantius est habere potius habitus rationem, quod vero deterius conditionem potius privationis habere, sicut calor atque frigus, album atque nigrum. Hac igitur ratione considerationeque simplici dolor ad voluptatem comparatus privatio quaedam esse videtur, potius quam vicissim. Quapropter etsi quoquomodo tamen non omnino credendum est dicentibus voluptatem privationem quandam vel sedationem doloris existere, praesertim quia voluptates purae haud palam sunt eiusmodi. Proinde voluptatem gustus et tactus praecedit, vel etiam comitatur indigentia ad essentiam necessaria, scilicet ad naturam singularem

vel specialem. Ideoque vehemens haec indigentia est et sensui manifesta. Hinc stimulat et affligit. Voluptates autem circa illa quae spectantur vel audiuntur vel odorantur non eiusmodi indigentiam stimulumve habent. Hi namque sensus quando bene naturaliterque se habent attinguntque suum aliquod obiectum congruitate delectans impleri videntur qualitate quadam (ut ita dixerim) peregrina quamvis grata iam et amica, sed ad aliud quiddam praeter essentiam attinente. Quapropter absque molestia esse possunt hae voluptates atque purae. Appellat autem visum auditumque sensus divinos, non solum quoniam ad sapientiam praecipue nos perducunt, sed etiam quia coelestibus insunt. Hinc Orpheus et Homerus solem dicunt spectare omnia et audire. Appellat iterum haec pulchra, scilicet figuras, colores, voces non ob aliquem corporeum usum qui speretur ex illis, nec tamquam ad aliud comparata, sed propter quandam ipsis propriam qualitatem atque proportionem quae puram secum delectationem sensibus quasi speculantibus affert. Quae quidem voluptas a voluptatibus discrepat quae in motibus passionibusque circa gustum tactumque versantur. Denique voluptates omnes eiusmodi quae non necessario cum dolore miscentur ad unum genus redigit oppositum impurarum generi voluptatum.

Voluptates disciplinarum purae.　　　ca. xxxxviii.
"Istis item, etc. ..." Voluptas disciplinarum pura censetur, quia non necessario dolorem habet ad mixtum. Stimulus autem discendi vel reminiscendi non in natura sed in opinione consistit. Tanta est animae excellentia ut re prorsus nulla indigeat ad essentiam.

Quae voluptates minus vehementes sed puriores.
　　　ca. xxxxviiii.
"Postquam voluptates, etc. ..." Voluptates plurimum corporales, scilicet gustus et praecipue [t]actus sunt vehementes, id est, acres, acutae, concitatae, et quasi violentae. Neque propter aliquam perfectionem suam tales sunt, sed propter necessariam corporis indigentiam. Voluptates aliae non sunt vehementes

quia nulla necessitate compulsae. Illae quidem nullum per se modum habent. Hae vero modum habere videntur. Illae igitur infiniti plurimum habent, hae autem infiniti minus; sed utraeque quoniam magis minusve suscipiunt et ad corpus animamve pertinent, ubi infinitum per magis minusve apparet, in genere infiniti procul dubio continentur. Laetitia vero intelligentiae purae, siquidem non habeat conditiones eiusmodi praesertim manifestas, omnino vel maxima ex parte est in genere termini.

Non quae acrior sed quae purior voluptas, ea est verior atque praestantior. ca. l.

"Socrates post haec, etc. . . ." Non dimensio vel numerus vel impetus aut passio vehemens efficit, ut substantia vel qualitas aliqua sit vera censenda, sed puritas et sinceritas per quam ipsa qualitas vel substantia revera sit hoc ipsum quod esse debet in specie sua, sitque ab alienis qualitatibus vel passionibus segregata. Voluptas igitur quanto purior tanto verior. Hinc efficitur ut corporeae voluptates tamquam mixtae molestiis voluptates verae iudicandae non sint, sed illae dumtaxat verae quae a molestiis segregatae, eiusmodi quidem sunt delectationes animi propriae, necnon visus auditusque, videlicet quasi contemplativae. Est autem imprimis eiusmodi purae intelligentiae gaudium.

Praeterea qualitatis puritas atque veritas indicat eam esse in suo genere summam. Quoniam et quae summa est sola videtur in naturali puritate sua et veritate consistere. Aliud igitur est in voluptatibus vehementia, aliud vero summitas. Siquidem vehementia in voluptatibus non veris, id est, mixtis atque corporeis potius quam in ipsis puris animi mentisque gaudiis esse solet. Itaque si summitas cum puritate veritateque concurrit, vehementia vero contra cum impuritate confluit atque falsitate, hic necessario concluditur vehementiam voluptatum a veritate summitateque longe distare, voluptatemque puriorem etiam suaviorem existere atque magis optabilem. Tametsi vehementia ex indigentia stimulante contingens, saepe iudicium fallit, ut suspicari vel somniare quis possit vehementiorem voluptatem esse potius eligendam, utpote qui stimulo quodam interim

urgeatur et vehementiam, immo violentiam impetumque pro
veritate suavitateque accipere compellatur.

Voluptas corporea propter motum remotior est a ratione boni,
intellectualis contra.   ca. li.
"Socrates, quid vero ad hoc, etc...." Quando voluptatem
appellat generationem de voluptatibus corporeis et mixtis similibusque praecipue loquitur. Generationem vero nominat quasi
motionem tendentem ad instaurandum habitum naturalem.
Voluptas enim corporea praesertim motionem eiusmodi comitatur, est igitur semper alterius gratia, scilicet habitus naturalis
qui dicitur essentia quaedam. Ratio quidem boni atque finis est
eadem. Bonum igitur est non proprie quidem quod alicuius
gratia fit, sed ipsum potius cuius gratia fiunt alia. Voluptas
igitur corporea aliena videtur a ratione boni et siqua in animo
huic assentitur, vel est quodammodo similis, siquidem talis sit
delectatio quae in discendo vel reminiscendo percipitur, in motu
videlicet quodam ad habitum acquirendum. Gaudium vero
quod in habitu statuque percipitur similius essentiae quam gene-
rationi videtur, sed habet interim non nihil simile motioni,
quatenus versatur in voluntate se ipsam in obiectum actumque
cognitionis suaviter diffundente. In mente quidem divina voluptas statui simillima iudicatur, siquidem ibi sit idem intellectus
atque voluntas, ibique voluptas sit ipsemet subitus intelligentiae
actus expeditus et gratus, firmus simulque totus. In ratione vero
intelligentiaque humana voluptas omnis imitatur motum,
quippe cum sit quasi actio quaedam temporaliter se expediens et
a minore proficiens in maiorem; idque quasi stabiliter et tran-
quille. Hanc imitantur nonnullae in videndo audiendoque
voluptates, et illa insuper quando quis sine impedimento vivit et
agit percipitque se bene naturaliterque habere.

Voluptas corporea remotior est a ratione boni.   ca. lii.
"Quin etiam, etc...." Voluptas praesertim corporea non est
ipsum nobis bonum, quia cogit deterioribus nos servire, scilicet
corporis evacuationi repletionique et alterationi inter oppositas
qualitates; item quia non in corporibus sed in anima bonum est

aestimatione dignum, id est divinum. Voluptas quidem animam deflectit ad corpus, virtutes autem cum divinitate coniungunt. Virtus igitur bonum nobis est potius quam voluptas. Praeterea per ipsum quod nobis bonum est appellamur boni, si vero desit, mali; per voluptatis vero praesentiam solam bonus nemo dicitur, neque per absentiam voluptatis malus. Rursus cum alia multa praeter voluptatem bona in nobis nostra et circa nos existant, non est voluptas ipsum nobis bonum, nec igitur ipsum universalem bonum, praesertim quia non est in omnibus. Sicui vero voluptati sit indulgendum, certe contemplationis voluptati potius incumbendum; voluptas enim corporis a maiori movetur frequenter in minus deficitque in habitu, delectatio vero mentis a minori procedit in maius et in habitu proficit.

Quam necessaria sit artibus mathematica. ca. liii.
"Ne tamen, etc...." Inter voluptates scientiasque eligenda est utrobique purissima, ut hae ad iudicium faciendum tam invicem quam ad ipsum bonum rectius comparentur. Scientiae quae utuntur manibus dicuntur artes. Hae perspicaciam perfectionemque suam habent imprimis a mathematica facultate, scilicet numerandi, metiendi, librandi quae maxime omnium Mercurialis et rationalis existit. Absque huius munere artes omnes titubant fallaci videlicet sensu vel imaginatione, experientia coniecturaque confisae. Architectura igitur omnisque consimilis quia maxime omnium artium ingenio utitur mathematico perspicacissima est. Musica consimilisque diligentia secundum tenet in artificio et perspicacia gradum quia gradu secundo mathematica nititur. Reliquae artes ob similem rationem tertium, quartumque deinceps gradum sortitae videntur. Memento vero hic de facultatibus rationalibus agi, quae mediae sunt et quodammodo mixtae; non autem de supremis in praesentia, scilicet de intellectualibus qualis est dialectica, id est metaphysica, neque de infimis, id est sensualibus atque servilibus.

Usus mathematicae varius in artibus. ca. liiii.
"Prorsus sed num o, etc...." Aliter mathematica industria utitur contemplator, aliter vero practicus. Ille quidem unitates

et numeros considerat per se formaliter existentes. Itaque apud illud unum non differt ab uno, binarius non discrepat a binario. Hic autem numeros in rebus resque considerat numeratas. Quapropter apud hunc hoc unum ab illo uno diversum, scilicet lignum magnum a parvo, vel lignum a ferro; similiter duo exercitus, bovesque duo. Ille rursus quae sit proportionum virtus et proprietas contemplatur, quae virtus in proportione aequali vel dupla vel sesquialtera. Hic autem utrum aedificii longitudo dupla ad latitudinem esse debeat. Alio quoque tendit contemplatoris, alio practici computatio.

Quae scientia sit purior aliis.   ca. lv.
"Probe sed num, etc...." Quaeritur in praesentia partitio quaedam scientiarum, partitioni voluptatum aequa proportione respondens. Est igitur alia scientia vel ars purior alia, quemadmodum voluptas voluptate purior; et quae facultas magis speculativa est adest facultati magis practicae tamquam obscuriori clarior. Iam vero mathematica disciplina etiam quae practicis inest artes omnes eiusmodi superat, quae vero mathematica lucet apud philosophum reliquam mathematicam splendore praecellit.

Excellentia mathematicae atque metaphysicae.   ca. lvi.
"Sunto igitur, etc...." Sicut mathematica speculativa practicam atque haec rursum practicas omnes excedit, ita dialectica, id est metaphysica, non solum istas sed etiam speculativas omnes excellit. Ipsa quidem scient[i]arum artiumque omnium iudex circa ipsum simpliciter ens versatur. Atque ad ipsum ens verissimum et aeternum praecipuo se studio confert, ideoque facultates omnes sinceritate, veritate, perspicacia, lumine supereminet.

Res et disciplinae humanae naturalesque et mathematicae et divinae.   ca. lvii.
"Numquid tale, etc...." Cognitio quidem humanorum naturaliumque opinio nominatur. Incerta sane et instabilis sicut et illa incerta et instabilia sunt. Cognitio vero mathematicorum

atque divinorum scientia nuncupatur certa stabilisque, sicut et illa certa stabiliaque semper existunt. Sed divinorum quidem scientia intellectualis dici solet, mathematicorum vero scientia rationalis potius appellatur, intelligentia denique sapientiaque praestantissima proprie pertinet ad divina. Inter haec nota mundum esse factum quomodocumque sit factus; item mundum coelumque semper fieri nec umquam idem prorsus existere; denique humana ad naturalia, haec ad mathematica, haec ad divina tamquam ad superiora referri debere.

Indagandum quomodo sapientia misceatur rite cum voluptate.
        ca. lviii.
"Ceterum siquis, etc...." Proponit indagandum quomodo voluptas cum sapientia misceatur ad beatitudinem consequendam. Repetuntur a principio dicta ipsius boni proprietatem esse ut sit perfectum et sufficiens ac omnibus expetendum. Cum vero neque sapientia seorsum a voluptate neque voluptas ab illa seorsum hanc boni proprietatem habeat, sequitur ut neutrum sit ipsum bonum; sapientia vero magis ipsius boni participem esse constat.

Quomodo bonum adsit mixto; item de Dionyso atque Vulcano.
        ca. lviiii.
"Aut igitur, etc...." Ipsum nobis bonum habitat in vita quadam ex sapientia et voluptate bene commixta. Haec igitur neque sapientia est neque voluptas neque vita mixta. Siquidem mixta vita boni habitaculum est, non ipsum bonum. Mixtum quidem hic accipitur non simplex hoc et illud, sed aliquid ambobus additum utrisque cognatum. Huic autem cognato divinitus adest ineffabile bonum; illius vero cognati praeparatio ad bonum non potest unico nomine designari. Explicabitur ergo deinceps per veritatem et commensurationem atque pulchritudinem.

Voluptas quidem melli similis, quia sicut dulcedine blanditur, ita nocet facileque in bilem desinit amarissimam. Sapientia vero non vino similis propter ebrietatem adversam intelligentiae, sed aquae potius similis appellatur; neque tamen cuilibet aquae sed

saluberrimae. Sed cur nam austerae? Ut ostendatur contemplationis fructum ex austero dulcem denique fieri, sicut voluptatis exitus ex dulci contingit amarus.

Dionysus atque Vulcanus mixturae passim harmonicae praesunt. Haec quatenus in mentibus et animis inest ad Dionysum praecipue pertinet, quatenus autem in naturis atque corporibus potius ad Vulcanum. Duo vero haec numina in diis super coelum atque coelestibus sunt eiusmodi proprietates duae, sed infra deos duo quaedam genera daemonum ad haec officia maxime conferentium.

Quomodo misceatur bene voluptas cum sapientia.   ca. lx.
"Dic age primum, etc...." Ut per mixtura scientiae cum voluptate beati simus, non quomodolibet sunt miscenda sed bene. Ut autem misceantur bene imprimis necessarium est eligere purissimam verissimamque scientiam scilicet theologicam similemque voluptatem. Haec autem est imprimis quae ex ipsa contemplatione percipitur. Non enim video quomodo voluptates quae a contemplatione distrahunt conflari cum contemplatione possint. Conceditur in praesentia si hic beati futuri simus necessariam nobis fore sapientiam divinorum, scientiam quoque sequentium et prudentiam humanorum et cognitionem cum speculativa practicam.

Qualis mixtio conducat ad felicitatem.   ca. lxi.
"Rursus ad voluptatum, etc...." Si hinc quidem voluptati, illinc autem intelligentiae detur optio, voluptas omnem cognitionem et hanc quidem exactissimam eliget. Cognitio enim circa rem congruam perspicacior exactiorem exhibet voluptatem; intelligentia vero non omnem voluptatem prorsus admittet, respuet enim corpoream atque furiosam ut inimicam, delectationem vero ex contemplatione perceptam volet [*em., Y reads* nolet] ut necessariam ac sibi penitus naturalem. Oblectamenta visus auditusque harmonica eliget tamquam consona; necessarias denique corporis voluptates siquae mentem nullo modo perturbant recipiet ut non dissonas. Ex intelligentia quidem ipsiusque gaudio mixtio perfecta conflatur. Ex his duobus atque

insuper ex delectationibus auditus et visus quae etiam purae dicuntur fit compositio quaedam congrua etsi mixtio non perfecta. Necessariae vero corporis voluptates etiam temperatae in compositionem cum intelligentia non conveniunt etsi non dissonant. Si omnem cognitionem artemque cum omni voluptate non perversa coniunxeris civilem efficies vitam Vulcaniamque mixturam. Sin autem contemplationem cum familiaribus gaudiis copulaveris contemplativam reportabis vitam mixturamque ad Dionysum potius pertinentem. Proinde ubi admixtionem perveneris in qua veritas et commensuratio pulchritudoque vigeat te iam ad splendorem boni pervenisse putato. Eiusmodi quidem splendor boni in universo est mundus intelligibilis ex ipso bono tamquam patre natus. Huiusmodi quoque splendor nostri iam advenientis boni erit in mente nostra mixtio intelligentiae cum gaudio per veritatem, commensurationem, pulchritudinem absoluta.

Quomodo veritas, commensuratio, pulchritudo ad felicem mixturam pertineant.   ca. lxii.
"Atqui ad hoc, etc...." Sicut in qualibet mixtione perfecta sic in eiusmodi mixtura voluptatis cum sapientia. Primo quidem est necessaria puritas atque veritas per quam utrumque sit in se ipso sincerum atque ex ambobus veris compositum fiat verum. Deinde necessaria commensuratio est, in qua comprehenditur tum utriusque certa in se ipso mensura modusque virtutis actionisque definitus, tum etiam alterius ad alterum sociabilis et amica proportio; ex his continuo nascitur pulchritudo, id est consummatio et absolutio formae. Quae quidem formarum forma est diciturque formositas. Quando igitur coniunctio voluptatis cum sapientia tria haec possidet et consequitur statim per haec suum assequitur bonum.

Sed unde nam? Ab ipso videlicet quod est omnium in universo bonum, a quo sane, cum prius acceperit veritatem et commensurationem atque pulchritudinem per quae perfecta fit mixtio, statim suum accipit bonum. Quod quidem et universi boni simulacrum est atque munus et in mixtione per tria quae diximus absoluta tamquam in aede dicitur habitare. Inter haec

memento commensurationem quidem ad mixturam conferre quam maxime, pulchritudinem vero ita repraesentare bonum ut facile appareat ipsum bonum, sicut splendor lucem perspicue refert. Neque tamen est ipsum bonum; quippe cum nec semper nec ab omnibus appetatur. Sed quoniam in compositione ultimum exactissimumque provenit, ideo artificem expressissime refert. Est etiam pulchritudo quaedam quamvis non perfecta in qualibet mixti parte. Denique bonum ipsum mixti causa per unum in se continet idque excellentius quod per tria in mixto suscipitur atque distribuitur; similiterque a nobis exprimitur, non potentibus exprimere manifeste per unum, nisi forte sub nube dicamus unum aut bonum aut causam. Illud vero si nominamus veritatem intelligimus ab omnibus segregatum; si commensurationem cogitamus amicum et propitium atque congruum; si pulchritudinem consideramus Deum ad se omnia provocantem. Eiusmodi trinitas videtur quasi quidam ornatus incorporeus, id est intelligibi[li]s atque divinus. Sed cuiusnam est hic ornatus? Corporis videlicet animati, id est illius mixti, in quo voluptas quidem est quasi corpus, intelligentia vero velut anima.

Sapientia est melior quam voluptas. ca. lxiii.
"Quisque iam, etc...." Cum trinitas illa, scilicet veritas, commensuratio, pulchritudo electo mixto data divinitus, sit causa per quam mixtum fiat bonum atque beatum, profecto sapientia quae huic trinitati est cognatior quam voluptas est mel[i]or voluptate. Est enim sapientia veritati, mensurae, pulchritudini longe propinquior quam voluptas. Immo vero voluptas quo vehementior eo remotior. Veritas est boni lumen in mente ita cognatum menti sicut solis lumen stellis, luna superioribus, animae vero rationali ita congruum sicut lumen solis lunae.

Multi bonorum gradus. ca. lxiiii.
"Cun[c]tis igitur, etc...." In primo bonorum gradu numeratur ipsum universi principium, qua videlicet ratione effector omnium est et perfector et finis. Hac ratione Pythagorici mensuram modumque et opportunitatem et persimilia nominant. In

secundo gradu ponitur mixtum illud ex intelligentia et voluptate, iam harmonicum veritatis, commensurationis, pulchritudinis beneficio, videlicet tributo divinitus. In tertio intelligentia quaelibet, sed imprimis segregatae mentis propria; consequenter autem intelligentiae munus inde communicatum animae. In quarto discursiones animae propriae, scientiae, artes, opiniones. In quinto numerantur voluptates purae quas non antecedit vel comitatur indigentia, ita naturae necessaria ut dolorem cum voluptate confundat. Quae quidem etsi quandoque accipiant occasiones a sensibus sunt tamen simplices perceptiones animi. Si praeterea introducantur necessariae aut vehementes corporis voluptates, gradus erit sextus, sed hae dimittuntur, quia vel non consonant in unam cum intelligentia compositionem vel ab illa dissonant.

Epilogus. Jupiter conservator gradus sextus.   ca. lxv.
"Tertio iam orationem, etc...." Epilogum totius dialogi facit eandemque summam iam tertio repetens inquit eam sacrificare se Jovi conservatori. Huic sacerdotes antiqui ter libare pateram cons[u]everant, declarantes egere nos conservatore deo, non solum in rerum nostrarum vitaeque principio, sed medio etiam atque fine. Tu vero singularem huius dialogi proprietatem considera, neque enim certum habet principium neque finem; imitatur sane bonum ipsum de quo quodammodo disputat. Hoc enim cum principium sit et finis omnium, merito neque principium habet neque finem. Atque hoc quidem ratione qua immensum in se est et penitus absolutum. Praetermisit ipsum in superioribus nec in illa distributione graduum numeravit. Est enim prorsus incognitum, nisi forte quis suspicetur significatum fuisse per generationem sextam, in qua Orpheus hymnos finiri iubet, quasi sit ineffabile. Ubi senarium celebrari ab Orpheo tamquam finem sicut a Mose videmus, quoniam sit perfectus intra decem, quippe cum suis partibus, uno scilicet et duobus atque tribus, deinceps dispositis componatur.

Impressum Florentiae per Laurentium Franci[s]ci de Venetiis
Anno ab incarnatione domini nostri Jhesu Christi
Mcccclxxxxvi, die ii. Decembris.

Footnotes to Introduction

[1]For a list of the humanist versions of Plato see Paul O. Kristeller, *Supplementum Ficinianum* (Florence, 1937), I, clv-clvi—hereafter cited as *Sup. Fic.;* also Eugenio Garin, "Ricerche sulle traduzioni di Platone nella prima metà del sec. XV," in *Medioevo e Rinascimento: Studi in onore di Bruno Nardi* (Florence, 1955), I, 339-74.

Prior to the humanist versions, the only Plato available to the West consisted of the *Timaeus* in Chalcidius' partial translation, the *Meno* and the *Phaedo,* and passages from the *Parmenides* embedded in Proclus' commentary. See R. Klibansky, *The Continuity of the Platonic Tradition During the Middle Ages* (London, 1939).

[2]Paul O. Kristeller, *Renaissance Thought I* (New York, 1961), ch. 3, passim; and Paul O. Kristeller, "Renaissance Platonism," in *Facets of the Renaissance,* ed. W.E. Werkmeister (New York, 1963), 105-107.

[3]"Renaissance Platonism," 109.

[4]See Sears R. Jayne, *Marsilio Ficino's Commentary on Plato's Symposium,* University of Missouri Studies, 19 (1944). See also, however, Josephine L. Burroughs' translation of the *Quaestiones de Mente* in Cassirer, Kristeller and Randall, *The Renaissance Philosophy of Man* (Chicago, 1948), 193-212; the many quotations translated in Paul O. Kristeller's invaluable work, *The Philosophy of Marsilio Ficino* (New York, 1943) — hereafter cited as *Philosophy;* and Josephine L. Burroughs' translation of the *Platonic Theology* III 2, XIII 3, XIV 3 & 4 in her article, "Ficino and Pomponazzi on Man," *Journal of the History of Ideas,* 5 (1944). 227-39.

[5]*Op. Om.,* 1965: "[Cosmus] divi Platonis libros decem, et unum Mercurii e graeca lingua in Latinam a nobis transferri iussit, quibus omnia vitae praecepta, omnia naturae principia, omnia divinarum rerum mysteria sancta panduntur." See Raymond Marcel, *Marsile Ficin* (Paris, 1958), 258 — hereafter cited as *Marsile.*

For the *Pimander* translation and the reason for its title see Kristeller, *Sup. Fic.,* I, cxxxi, and his article, "Marsilio Ficino e Lodovico Lazzarelli," *Annali della R. Scuola Normale Superiore di Pisa; Lettere, Storia e Filosofia,* 2nd Series, 7 (1938), 238-39.

[6]*Marsile,* 273.

[7]*Op. Om.,* 608, 1: "Contuli heri me in agrum Charegium, non agri, sed animi colendi gratia, veni ad nos Marsili quamprimum. Fer tecum Platonis nostri librum de Summo bono quem te isthic arbitror iam e Graeca lingua in Latinam, ut promiseras, transtulisse. Nihil enim ardentius cupio, quam quae via commodius ad felicitatem ducat cognoscere. Vale et veni non absque Orphica lyra."

[8]Paul O. Kristeller, "Marsilio Ficino as a beginning student of Plato," *Scriptorium,* 20 (1966), 41-54. Kristeller recently discovered two autograph manuscript fragments: one in the Bibliothèque Nationale (*Nouvelles acquisitions latines* 1633, f. 5-7), the other in the Biblioteca Palatina in Parma. The Paris fragment includes the introduction to the *Philebus* translation and the two fragments together constitute the original draft for the preface and the ten introductions of Ficino's first decade. Since this Parma-Paris manuscript exhibits the preface and the introductions without the actual translations, Professor Kristeller's wife, Dr. Edith Kristeller, suggests Ficino composed these pieces at the same time, after he had completed the translations. On the basis of Professor Kristeller's discovery I have presented the *Philebus* introduction as it appears in the Paris fragment (see Appendix III).

[9]Kristeller, *Sup. Fic.,* II, 103-105: "Cumque in Dei visione beatitudo nostra consistat, iure Philebus de summo bono hominis post Parmenidem de summo totius nature bono locatus esse videtur" (105). See Raymond Klibansky, "Plato's Parmenides in the Middle Ages and the Renaissance," *Medieval and Renaissance Studies,* 1 (London, 1943), 313: "With Proclus and Olympiodorus he [Ficino] holds that the Parmenides enshrines the essence of Plato's theology and that it is the innermost sanctuary of Platonic thought." Note the religious language.

[10]Kristeller, "Marsilio Ficino as a Beginning Student," 44-46.

[11]*Philebus* commentary (this edition), 325—hereafter cited as *Phil.* com.; also see Appendix I for another passage found only in MS. *Laur.* 21, 8, but containing a reference to Olympiodorus/Damascius.

L.G. Westerink, "Ficino's Marginal Notes on Olympiodorus in Riccardi Greek MS. 37," *Traditio,* 24 (1968), 351-78. Westerink notes that "Ficino's published work . . . [the commentary on and summary of the *Philebus*] shows hardly any evidence of his having referred to his notes [on the commentary on the *Philebus* which was traditionally attributed to Olympiodorus but which Westerink attributes to Damascius (see note 12)], though there are some points of contact with the Greek text of Damascius" (354). Westerink then gives three minor references: *Op. Om.,* 1223. 13-16 (the opening of ch. 17, my pp. 177-79) he compares to Damascius, paragraph 45; *Op. Om.,* 1229. 27-62 (the second half of ch. 23, my pp. 221-25, beginning, "Cum ergo scientiae . . .") he compares to Damascius, paragraphs 54-56; *Op. Om.,* 1269. 49-51 (part of the summary of ch. LXV, my p. 518) he compares to Damascius, paragraphs 11 and 259.

[12]L.G. Westerink, *Damascius: Lectures on the Philebus* (Amsterdam, 1959), 2, notes 1-6. The *Parmenides* incidentally was usually the culmination of a second teaching cycle.

It is in the introduction to this edition that Westerink argues the case for Damascius' authorship of the commentary on the *Philebus,* usually attributed to Olympiodorus.

Footnotes to Introduction   521

[13]Ibid. Cf. *Phil.* com., 127, where Ficino defines the *skopos.*
[14]Henry Sidgwick, *Outlines of the History of Ethics* (Boston, 1960),2.
[15]A.E. Taylor, *Plato: The Man and his Work,* 7th ed. (London, 1960), 410.

But see R. Hackforth, *Plato's Examination of Pleasure* (Cambridge, 1945), 12: "There is nothing to suggest that Socrates has referred to any metaphysical or supersensible Good, or discussed the Form of the Good. Both parties have however been concerned with something wider than the good for Man; but it is this that Plato is to make the subject of his dialogue..."

[16]Cf. *Phil.* com., 107, where Ficino juxtaposes the *Republic* Bk. 6 and the *Parmenides* in order to prove that the good and the one are identical.

[17]Marcel, *Marsile,* 273: "avec quelle ingéniosité Ficin s'était appliqué à faire un tout de ces éléments quelque peu disparates en les enchaînant dans une progression continue qui, partant du désir des biens terrestres, s'épanouissait dans la plénitude du Souverain Bien."

[18]Ibid., 273.

[19]Vespasiano da Bisticci, *Vite* (Florence, 1938), 292 and 372. Cosimo "volle per passare tempo, innanzi circa uno anno che morisse, farsi leggere l'*Etica* d'Aristotile a messer Bartolomeo da Colle, cancelliere in palazzo; e pregò Donato Acciaiuoli, che arrecasse in ordine gli scritti che aveva ricolti sotto messer Giovanni [Argyropoulos] sopra l'*Etica*; e secondo che Donato emendava, egli mandava i quinterni a Cosimo, e messer Bartolomeo leggeva; e lessela tutta; e questo comento che c'è oggi dell'*Etica*, di Donato, fu quello che s'emendò, mentre che Cosimo se la faceva leggere" (292). See Eugenio Garin, *La cultura filosofica del Rinascimento italiano* (Florence, 1961), 26-27 on Scala; 68, 69, 104-108 on Acciaiuoli's notes which later became a commentary; and 102-108 on the importance of Argyropoulos' lectures on Aristotle. Garin's book is hereafter cited as *La cultura.* On Cosimo's last years see Curt S. Gutkind, *Cosimo de'Medici* (Oxford, 1938), 242-46.

[20]*Op. Om.,* 649: "Itaque postquam Platonis librum de uno rerum principio, ac de summo bono legimus, sicut tu nosti, qui aderas, paulo post decessit, tanquam eo ipso bono, quod disputatione gustaverat re ipsa abunde iam potiturus." See Klibansky, "Plato's *Parmenides* ...," 315: "...the masterpiece of Platonic dialectic was chosen, with the *Philebus,* to be read to the dying Cosimo as the fitting preamble 'for his return to the highest principle and the fruition of the highest good'." Cosimo died on August 1st, 1464.

[21]See Ficino's preface to Xenocrates' *De Morte, Op. Om.,* 1965, Cf. Marcel, *Marsile,* 275-78; and André Rochon, *La Jeunesse de Laurent de Médicis* (Paris, 1963), 39—hereafter cited as *La Jeunesse.* The discussion must have occurred on July 20th.

[22]André Chastel, *Marsile Ficin et l'Art* (Geneva and Lille, 1954), 189-92, and Marcel, *Marsile,* 274.

[23]Marcel, *Marsile*, 321, suggests that Piero was disinterested while Arnaldo Della Torre, *Storia dell'Accademia Platonica di Firenze* (Florence, 1902), 565-66,—hereafter cited as *Storia*—and Rochon, *La Jeunesse*, 295-96, both argue for Piero's continuing support.

[24]Arnaldo Della Torre, *Storia*, 497. See Garin, *La cultura*, 63 note 1 on Tignosi; also A. Rotondò, "Nicolò Tignosi da Foligno," *Rinascimento*, 9 (1958), 217-55.

[25]Corsi's life of Ficino (which was dedicated to Bindaccio Ricasoli in 1506 but not published until 1771) is presented by Marcel in the first appendix to his book, *Marsile Ficin*; references to Corsi will therefore include the page reference in Marcel. For Corsi himself see Paul O. Kristeller, "Un uomo di stato e umanista fiorentino: Giovanni Corsi," *La Bibliofilia*, 38 (1936), 242-57.

Corsi, VII (*Marsile*, 683): "Publice itaque eo tempore Marsilius magna auditorum frequentia Platonis *Philebum* interpretatus est ..."

[26]*Marsile*, 322: "...étant donné que ce dialogue avait été traduit du vivant de Cosme, on peut supposer que, fidèle à sa méthode, il en discuta avec ses amis dès 1464, et que c'est l'enthousiasme suscité par l'exposé de la pensée platonicienne sur le Souverain Bien, qui amena ses amis et bienfaiteurs à souhaiter qu'il puisse faire profiter un plus large auditoire de son enseignement."

[27]Corsi, VII (*Marsile*, 683): "...in quem adhuc etiam illius temporis nonnulla eius exstant collectanea et cum iis quoque *declarationum Platonicorum* quatuor volumina."

See *Sup. Fic.*, I, 79-80, for further details on the manuscripts and their history.

[28]"Cum optimis civibus nostris placuerit, ut celebri hoc in loco sacram Divi Platonis philosophiam interpretemur, opere pretium fore censui, ut quid philosophia sit primum paucis perstringamus ..." (MS. *Vat. lat.* 5953. f. 321v).

[29]"Vobis autem viri praestantissimi qui meam hanc orationem vestra presentia honestare dignati estis, ingentes gratias habeo, immortalis Deus immortales referam [sic]" (MS. *Vat. lat.* 5953. f. 326v).

[30]Paul O. Kristeller, *Studies in Renaissance Thought and Letters* (Rome, 1956), 116—hereafter cited as *Studies*.

See Arnaldo Della Torre, *Storia*, 568 ff.

[31]Kristeller, *Studies*, 111. This could be the old church of S. Maria degli Angeli (Angioli) which has long been absorbed into what is now the office of the disabled veterans' administration. For details see Walter and Elizabeth Paatz, *Die Kirchen von Florenz* (Frankfurt am Main, 1943-54), vol. III (M), 107-47.

I would like to propose another intriguing possibility. Adjacent to the old church Brunelleschi began a new polygonal church for the Camaldolese in 1434 which is still standing and known as the Castellaccio or Rotunda. The Calimala provided money from the estate of Filippo Scolari (Pippo Spano)

for its erection, but this was apparently diverted to help pay for the war with Lucca and construction stopped altogether in 1437. From what remains of the original work, from Giuliano da Sangallo's floor-plan (Vatican cod. *Barberiniano lat*. 4424. f. 15v), and from other sketches, we can get some idea of its shape and dimensions. By 1437 the outer sixteen-sided wall and inner octagon of columns had reached some 27 feet and more in places, the floor's mean diameter was 45 feet, and there were already fluted pilasters without their capitals and also molding in the eight side-chapels and on the sixteen exterior faces. The precise details of the future entablature, drum, dome, oculi, window and main altar locations, ornamentation and much else are open to speculation, as are the models for the central planning: the temple of the Minerva Medica and the Pantheon in Rome, S. Vitale in Ravenna, and Brunelleschi's own work on the Cathedral tribunes and lantern in Florence (see Patricia Waddy, "Brunelleschi's Design for S. Maria degli Angeli in Florence," *Marsyas*, 15 [New York, 1972], 36-46, for a surview of the problems and further references).

Surely in its unfinished state the Rotunda (which probably resembled a Roman ruin by 1466-68) would have been ideal for Ficino's *Philebus* lectures, given its shape, size, otherwise uselessness and the Platonic enthusiasms of the convent priors? It would have been especially attractive to the Florentine Platonists on aesthetic grounds—and G.C. Argan has described it as " 'tutto al modo antico di dentro e di fuori' [quoted from Manetti's *Vita*] ... un esplicito tentativo di ricostruzione degli edifici rotondi classici o di un'opera d'indubbio carattere umanistico" (*Brunelleschi* [Milan, 1955], 131)—, but even more so on philosophical ones. Since it resembled the one ancient temple in Rome dedicated to *all* the gods and was itself to be dedicated ecumenically to the Virgin and *all* twelve apostles, it would have harmonized perfectly with Ficino's syncretism and his ideas on the historical relationship between Christianity and pagan theology. Second, if it was still open to the sky, as was most likely, Ficino's many references to the sun would be particularly pointed (and his audience knew too that the ancients habitually philosophized in the open air). Finally, as it was to be the first centrally planned, wholly concentric building of the Renaissance, it would have appealed immediately to Ficino's Neoplatonic love of both circle and number symbolism.

After five centuries of misuse and neglect, the Rotunda was disastrously completed by Mussolini in 1940; and in 1959, ironically, it did become a lecture hall. Today it is once more "in restauro."

I am indebted to Mrs. Geraldine Bass of UCLA for drawing my attention to Waddy's article and for sharing her own ideas on Brunelleschi's intentions with me.

[32]*Marsile*, 309, 476.

[33]*Op. Om.*, 886, 2: "Nos igitur antiquorum sapientum vestigia pro viribus observantes, religiosam Platonis nostri Philosophiam in hac media

prosequemur Ecclesia. In his sedibus angelorum divinam contemplabimur veritatem.'' The words *vestigia* and *media* would be especially appropriate if it is the Rotunda (see my note 31).

[34]Marcel, *Marsile,* 310: "Pour la première fois un latin, texte en mains, explique un dialogue de Platon à la demande de nobles citoyens et devant un auditoire aussi attentif que nombreux. A la vérité le choix du *Philèbe* était fort judicieux, car la thèse du Souverain Bien qui s'y trouve exposée ne pouvait que séduire cette élite qui avait grandi en cherchant la solution de ce problème en écoutant ses maîtres commenter l'*Éthique* d'Aristote.''

[35]*Phil.* com., chs. 1-6. See pp. 81-83, 87-89.

[36]Cristoforo Landino, *Disputationes Camaldulenses* II, 20r. "Dicunt enim deum summum esse bonum quod et ante Christum et hominem natum Platonem sensisse constat. Cuius quidem opinionem facile cum voles vel iis commentariis quos Marsilius non modo gravissime verum etiam in primis perspicue et enucleate in Platonis Philebum conscripsit cognoscere poteris . . .''

[37]*Marsile,* 321: ". . . les références à Ficin dans ces deux premiers livres sont suffisamment nettes et élogieuses pour que nous puissions juger de son influence à cette époque.''

[38]Ficino never did finish any of his Plato commentaries except for the one on the *Symposium.* More than any of the other dialogues which Ficino was particularly interested in commenting on, the *Symposium* has a clearly defined dramatic progression in which none of the speakers pre-empts material that is going to be used by the others. The structure of the *Philebus,* conversely, seems to invite digression and repetition.

[39]*Marsile,* 323: "Alors que Ficin avait annoncé à ses auditeurs que le *Philèbe* se divise en douze parties, sans aucun avertissement, il interrompt son exposé après la cinquième et bien qu'il ait par la suite, et par deux fois, manifesté son regret de n'avoir pu compléter cet exposé, nous le voyons se contenter de l'illustrer par des apologues, qui sont pour ce traité une étrange conclusion.''

[40]*Storia,* 567 ff.: ". . . per il Ficino nel decennio che va dal 1459 al 1469 cade un periodo di depressione morale, dovuto ad un combattimento interno fra le convinzioni filosofiche e il sentimento religioso.''

[41]Corsi, VIII (*Marsile,* 683): ". . . etiam Orphei hymnos ac sacrificia invulgare, sed divino prorsus miraculo, id quo minus efficeret, in dies magis impediebatur, quadam, ut aiebat, spiritus amaritudine distractus; id quod et divo Hieronymo in Cicerone accidisse memoriae proditum est.'' For the reference to Proclus compare *Op. Om.,* 1928 and *Sup. Fic.,* I, cxxxiv-v. Marcel (*Marsile,* 347), however, suggests that it is to Porphyry that we must turn in order to find a treatise on sacrifices; he translates Corsi's ambiguous phrase as "the hymns and sacrifices of Orpheus'' (the reference would be to Porphyry's *De Abstinentia* II, cf. *Op. Om.,* 1934).

[42]*Marsile,* 353.

⁴³*Studies,* 52, 191-213 and especially 204-205: "'. . . cioè non c'era bisogno di una crisi intima per condurlo dal paganesimo al cristianesimo . . . [perchè] non il passaggio dal paganesimo al cristianesimo è ciò che determina lo sviluppo del pensiero ficiniano; l'unico fatto che si può ammettere fino ad un certo punto è una crescente accentuazione dell'interesse teologico e dogmatico . . . egli fu cristiano durante tutta la sua vita."

⁴⁴It is important that Plato himself finishes the dialogue on an inconclusive note: when Socrates asks to go, Protarchus says, "There is a little which yet remains, and I will remind you of it, for I am sure you will not be the first to go away from an argument." This is reinforced at the thematic level too: problems have been raised but hardly solved.

⁴⁵See Kristeller, *Philosophy,* 114-15, 399. Apropos the theory of the soul developed in the *Platonic Theology* Kristeller writes: "Soul, in its connecting power and in its effect in the world, has taken the place of love and is characterized in almost the same words that characterized love . . . the Soul has absorbed the attributes of the all-comprehensive love as its own new and independent qualities" (115). See p. 34 of this introduction.

⁴⁶See Raymond Marcel, *Marsile Ficin: Commentaire sur le Banquet de Platon* (Paris, 1956), 41. Marcel gives July 1469 as the date of completion of the *Symposium* commentary. Hence in his *Marsile,* 393-94, he says, "'. . . c'est de l'échec de son commentaire du *Philèbe* qu'est née la Théologie [sic] et accessoirement son *Commentaire du Banquet.*" This is wrong, as we shall see.

⁴⁷Michele Schiavone, *Problemi filosofici in Marsilio Ficino* (Milan, 1957), 141 and 143—hereafter cited as *Problemi.*

⁴⁸*Op. Om.,* 914, 3: "Rediit enim mox in mentem absolvenda mihi superesse commentaria in Platonis Philebum de summo bono quondam ad dimidium usque producta."

⁴⁹Kristeller, *Sup. Fic.,* I, cxxiii; Kristeller was the first to note the difference between the February dating of the proem and the subscription. For Salvini see Paul O. Kristeller, "Sebastiano Salvini, A Florentine Humanist and Theologian, and a Member of Marsilio Ficino's Platonic Academy," in *Didascaliae,* ed. Sesto Prete (New York, 1961), 205-43.

⁵⁰See MS. *Vat. lat.,* 413v-422; *Op. Om.,* I, 921-24; *Sup. Fic.,* I, xli and 80-86. Raymond Marcel's note (*Marsile,* 323, footnote 2, is in error. The MS. *Laur.* 21, 8 contains all ten excerpts not just the four pleasure apologues.

⁵¹The sequence of the five commentaries in this collection is as follows: *Parmenides, Sophist, Timaeus, Phaedrus, Philebus.* This accords, Ficino says, with the universal order since the *Parmenides* treats of the one principle of all, the *Sophist* of the general character of being, the *Timaeus* of the physical world, the *Phaedrus* of worldly and human matters, and the *Philebus* likewise. However, Ficino makes a point here of praising the *Phaedrus* at the expense of the *Philebus*— "'. . . ob longiorem videlicet divinorum disputationem praecipuumque divini furoris munus Philebo divinior."

[52]Corsi, XIV (*Marsile*, 685).

Marsile, 456: "...et nous verrons Ficin jusqu' à la fin de sa vie tenter de compléter ceux du *Timée*, du *Philèbe*, et du *Phèdre*, qui, à juste titre, représentaient pour lui les assises du système platonicien." Why does Marcel omit the other three, however?

[53]*Sup. Fic.*, II, 81-82, 88-89; also Kristeller, *Studies*, 44-45.

[54]The episode is recorded in Baronius, *Annales ad annum* 411 (Cologne, 1624), 371. See *Sup. Fic.*, II, 216-17.

[55]Giuseppe Saitta, *Marsilio Ficino e la filosofia dell'Umanesimo*, 3rd ed. (Bologna, 1954), 210-11: "...nel suo bellissimo commento al *Filebo*, la superiorità del bene sul bello è vigorosamente affermata. Ogni bello è bene, ma non ogni bene è bello: è questo il concetto platonico che il Ficino a modo suo cerca di mettere sempre in luce. Pure un fondamento comune tra il bene e il bello esiste, ed esso è costituito dall'appetito ..." and 219: "Già nel suo magnifico commento al *Filebo* egli aveva esplicitamente identificato l'attività universale con il Bene."

[56]Ibid., 5, footnote 5.

[57]Cf. Paul Shorey, *Platonism Ancient and Modern* (Berkeley, 1938), 152-57 and 121. Shorey talks of Ficino's "meaty introductions" to the Plato dialogues and of his enormous influence. Interestingly, the *Philebus* is being increasingly recognized as an important source for Sir Thomas More: see Ernst Cassirer, *The Platonic Renaissance in England*, trans. P. Pettegrove (Austin, Texas, 1953), 110; and the recent article by Judith P. Jones, "The *Philebus* and the Philosophy of Pleasure in Thomas More's *Utopia*," *Moreana*, vol. 31-32, ed. Germain Marc'hadour (Angers, France: Amici Thomae Mori, 1971), 61-70. I suggest the *Philebus* commentary and Ficino's championship in general also played their part in directing More's attention to the *Philebus*. Another debtor to the *Philebus* and possibly to Ficino's commentary is, I suspect, Sir Francis Bacon.

[58]Paul O. Kristeller, *Renaissance Thought II* (New York, 1965), 15—hereafter cited as *Thought II*.

[59]Saitta, 51: "L'interesse etico predomina nel Ficino sull' interesse speculativo ..."

[60]*Thought II*, 34-35. Cf. Charles Trinkaus, *In Our Image and Likeness*, 2 vols. (London, 1970), 773—hereafter cited as *Image*.

[61]*Philosophy*, 289.

[62]Eugenio Garin, *Italian Humanism*, trans. by P. Munz (Oxford, 1965), 82 ff. See *La cultura*, 64, footnote 3, for the controversy surrounding Bruni's translation.

[63]Kristeller, *Thought II*, 34. Garin, *La cultura*, 60-71, and especially 62-63, examines Bruni's importance as a champion of the "ethical" as opposed to the "metaphysical" Aristotle extolled by the Scholastics.

[64]Della Torre, 497; Marcel, *Marsile*, 180-81. Ficino frequently lauds

Aristotle, e.g.: *Op. Om.*, 869: "Nam in eodem veritatis virtutisque cultu sumus unum. In quo Plato et Aristoteles non esse unum non potuerunt." *Op. Om.*, 1438: [Plato] . . . vel de naturalibus agit divine, quemadmodum Aristoteles, vel de divinis naturaliter agit."

[65]MS. *Riccardian.* 135, 1r-138r, and Garin, *La cultura,* 106-108. Cf. Marcel, *Marsile,* 215.

[66]See Rochon, *La Jeunesse,* 37: "[Argyropoulos] conserva cette charge jusqu'en août 1471. Pendant ces quinze années, il exerça sur la vie intellectuelle de la cité une influence décisive et forma d'illustres disciples, groupés autour de lui dans le *Chorus Achademiae Florentinae.* Bien loin d'être cantonné dans la philosophie péripatéticienne, son enseignement englobait toute l'histoire de la pensée et de la civilisation helléniques, et ce n'est pas un de ses moindres mérites que d'avoir fait connaître aux Florentins les textes de Platon." Rochon attributes Argyropoulos' election specifically to Donato Acciaiuoli and Alamanno Rinuccini. Cf. Marcel, *Marsile,* 189-97.

[67]Marcel, *Marsile,* 176 ff. See Garin, *La cultura,* 106-108, on the importance of Argyropoulos as a reconciler of Plato and Aristotle.

[68]Marcel, *Marsile,* 177. In 1478 Acciaiuoli published his own moderating contribution to the debate: *Expositio supra libros Ethicorum Aristotelis.*

[69]A.E. Taylor, *Plato: Philebus and Epinomis,* ed. by R. Klibansky (London, 1956), 49.

[70]See for instance R.G. Bury, *The Philebus of Plato* (Cambridge, 1897), section VI of the introduction; and Auguste Dies, *Philèbe* (Paris, 1949—the Budé edition), xcii ff.

[71]See E. Zeller - R. Mondolfo, *La filosofia dei Greci nel suo sviluppo storico* (Florence, 1961), part III, vol. VI, 106, 126, 229; and Westerink, *Damascius,* passim.

[72]Benjamin Jowett, *The Dialogues of Plato,* rev. 4th ed., 4 vols., (Oxford, 1968), III, 531 and 534.

[73]Bury, ix.

[74]J. Gould, *The Development of Plato's Ethics* (Cambridge, 1955), 219-24.

[75]Hackforth, 10.

[76]Dies, ix-x: ". . .une singularité de construction . . . Le caractère scolaire de la discussion. . ."

[77]Dies, ix: ". . .[une] masse à l'intérieur du dialogue et que l'analyse du plaisir fait bloc à l'intérieur de cette masse."

[78]Dies, xvi-xvii: ". . .La parfaite continuité logique du développement. . ."

[79]See Saitta, 52: ". . .ciò che gli manca è la coscienza critica della posizione vera di Platone nella storia del pensiero."

[80]Jowett, 533 and 545.

[81]Kristeller, *Philosophy,* 15. The genealogy was strictly defined. See

D.P. Walker: "The *Prisca Theologia* in France," *Journal of the Warburg and Courtauld Institutes,* 17 (1954), 204-59; "Orpheus the Theologian and Renaissance Platonists," ibid., 16 (1953), 100-20; and his new book, *The Ancient Theology* (London, 1972), especially the introduction on pp. 1-21. See also Trinkaus, *Image,* 502 ff., and 714; and Charles B. Schmitt, "Perennial Philosophy: From Agostino Steuco to Leibniz," *Journal of the History of Ideas,* 27 (1966), 507-11. I have adopted Ficino's spelling of Aglaophamus.

[82]This selection is in general accord with the selection adopted by the Neoplatonists. See Paul Henry's introduction to Stephen MacKenna's translation of the *Enneads,* 3rd ed. revised by B.S. Page (London, 1962), xxxix-xl, footnote 2; also the index to E. Bréhier's ed. of the *Enneads* (Paris, 1924-28).

[83]*Phil.* com., 281.

[84]Roberto Weiss, "Scholarship from Petrarch to Erasmus," *The Age of the Renaissance,* ed. Denys Hay (London, 1967), 139-40.

[85]*Studies,* 42.

[86]Ibid., 55. But Trinkaus rightly insists that "in making use of Thomas Aquinas, [Ficino] does so in a decidedly Augustinian way" (*Image,* 474).

[87]See Maurice De Wulf, *Introduction à la philosophie néoscolastique* (Louvain & Paris, 1904), 108-109; Saitta, 59.

[88]Trinkaus, *Image,* 504. See also Kristeller, *Thought II,* 38: "In a period in which the emphasis is on authority and tradition, originality will assert itself in the adaptation and interpretation of the tradition."

[89]Raymond Marcel, *Marsile Ficin: Théologie Platonicienne,* 3 vols. (Paris, 1964, 1970), 29—hereafter cited as *Théologie*: "...comme s'il voulait s'approprier leur pensée ou contraindre ses lecteurs à admettre des principes ou des arguments qu'ils auraient refusé a priori d'examiner s'ils en avaient connu la source." Cf. Ficino's preface to his Plotinus translation (*Op. Om.,* 1537) where he talks of a "philosophical lure" for those "acute minds" who rely on reason and must be led to religion gradually.

[90]*Théologie,* 29.

[91]Typical of the manifold problems are questions such as these: Did Ficino have any detailed knowledge of Henry of Ghent, of Bonaventura, Scotus or Ockham; of the works of Aquinas apart from the *Summa Contra Gentiles*? If so, when exactly did he acquire this knowledge? Why did he not make greater use of Olympiodorus' (Damascius') commentary on the *Philebus*? When did he read Proclus? Obviously, each one of these questions is of vital importance when we come to consider Marcel's "resonances," and Kristeller may be wrong about Ficino's ignorance of the scholastics. See my note 112.

[92]*Phil.* com., 109-111 ff. and 303-305.

[93]Trinkaus, *Image,* 468.

[94]See Frances A. Yates, *Giordano Bruno and the Hermetic Tradition*

(London, 1964)—hereafter cited as *Giordano,* and D.P. Walker, *Spiritual and Demonic Magic from Ficino to Campanella* (London, 1958) for full length examinations of Ficino's initiation of the hermetic revival.

⁹⁵*Op. Om.,* 1: "Nam cum animus ... duabus tantum alis, id est, intellectu, et voluntate possit ad coelestem patrem, et patriam revolare, ac philosophus intellectu maxime, sacerdos voluntate nitatur, et intellectus voluntatem illuminet, voluntas intellectum accendat, consentaneum est....

"O viri coelestis patriae cives, incolaeque terrae, liberemus obsecro quandoque philosophiam, sacrum Dei munus, ab impietate, si possumus, possumus autem, si volumus, religionem sanctam pro viribus ab execrabili inscita [sic] redimamus. Hortor igitur omnes, atque precor, philosophos quidem, ut religionem vel capessant penitus, vel attingant: sacerdotes autem, ut legitimae sapientiae studiis diligenter incumbant."

⁹⁶*Op. Om.,* 930: "Per quam sane quasi mediam quamdam viam, Christianam pietatem denique consequantur."

See Raymond Marcel, "L'apologétique de Marsile Ficin," *Pensée humaniste et Tradition chrétienne au XVᵉ et au XVIᵉs.* (Paris, 1950), 159-68.

⁹⁷See the Orlandini letter (Appendix III).

⁹⁸*Studies,* 99 and 121. Cf. the religious role played by Iamblichus in ancient Neoplatonism.

⁹⁹On the Augustinian, ascetic strains in Ficino see Charles Trinkaus, "The Problem of Free Will in the Renaissance and the Reformation," in *Renaissance Essays,* edited by Kristeller and Wiener (New York, 1968), 192; also his earlier book, *Adversity's Noblemen: The Italian Humanists on Happiness* (New York, 1940), 37-38. In his most recent book, however, Trinkaus stresses the more optimistic, anthropocentric aspects of Ficino (*Image,* ch. IX passim, and especially pp. 482 and 484-89).

¹⁰⁰See Kristeller, *Philosophy,* 296-97; also *Sup. Fic.,* II, 81 ff.

¹⁰¹For Diogenes, see R.R. Bolgar, *The Classical Heritage* (New York, 1964), 278 and 472.

For the impact of the newly discovered Lucretius on Ficino himself see Eugenio Garin, "Ricerche sull'epicureismo del quattrocento," in *La cultura,* 72-86.

See also Miss Yates' comments in *Giordano,* 224-25: "...in some Renaissance writers the Epicurean teaching on pleasure as a good becomes merged with the cosmic significance of *amor* as the intrinsic vital force in universal nature." This is extremely pertinent when we consider the propinquity of the *Philebus* and *Symposium* commentaries (cf. Garin, *La cultura,* 84).

¹⁰²*Plato, Philebus and Epinomis,* 15, 16 ff.

¹⁰³Hackforth, 5; Taylor, *Plato: Philebus and Epinomis,* 92.

¹⁰⁴*Op. Om.,* 108: "...voluptas, quae est dilatatio voluntatis in bonum, et quies voluntatis in bono." Cf. *Phil.* com., 353-55, 379-81.

¹⁰⁵*Philosophy,* 262.

[106]See *Phil.* com., 197, 325-29, 335-39.

[107]Taylor, *Plato: Philebus and Epinomis,* 15-25, and *Plato: The Man and his Work,* 409-10.

[108]Saitta, 81: "Il concetto d'una religione universale o naturale . . . presenta nel Ficino, tutti i caratteri, che saranno oggetto di più ampi e penetranti sviluppi." See also Kristeller, *Philosophy,* 318 ff., for further information.

[109]Saitta, 84; Trinkaus, *Image,* ch. XVI, pp. 722 ff.

[110]Kristeller, *Le Thomisme et la pensée italienne de la Renaissance* (Montreal, 1967), 97—hereafter cited as *Le Thomisme:* "Chaque chose est dirigée par son créateur vers un but naturel, et son essence s'accompagne toujours d'un désir, ou amour, ou appétit de ce but, et cet appétit ne peut être vain puisqu'il constitue un élément nécessaire de l'ordre même de l'univers."

[111]Kristeller, *Philosophy,* 328. See 328, footnote 16, for further references.

[112]Marian Heitzman, "L'agostinismo avicenizzante e il punto di partenza della filosofia di Marsilio Ficino," *Giornale critico della filosofia italiana,* 16 (1935), 295-322; 460-80; 17 (1936), 1-11. Page 299: "Tutti questi termini significano l'universale esistente nell'intelletto divino. . . ."

Heitzman deals at length with the problems of Ficino's epistemology and with the history of the controversies surrounding them with particular reference to Ficino's probable debt to Avicenna and his illuminationism.

See *Phil.* com., 199 ff.

[113]For example, *Phil.* com., 177-79.

[114]Charles Huit, "Le Platonisme pendant la renaissance," *Annales de philosophie chrétienne,* N.S., 33 (1895-96), 362 ff.; Kristeller, *Philosophy,* 240; Saitta, 50.

[115]*The Cambridge History of Later Greek and Early Medieval Philosophy,* ed. A.H. Armstrong (Cambridge, 1967), 55.

[116]*Philosophy,* 246.

[117]*Phil.* com., 251. See Kristeller, *Philosophy,* 126-31.

[118]*Republic* VII, 534E.

[119]*Phil.* com., 219.

[120]Heitzman, 460: "La relazione fra la ragione e la mente non è chiara nel Ficino."

[121]Ibid., 320: ". . . l'intelligenza non è la vera facoltà dell'anima ragionevole."

[122]Ibid., see 461. Previously Heitzman had explained why the intelligence is above the order of destiny to which the sensitive soul is subject, but is itself subject to the order of providence; the reason on the other hand is completely free: ". . . per la nostra ragione [*ratio*] discorsiva invece siamo completamente liberi e scegliamo una direzione ad arbitrio" (320).

See, however, Kristeller, *Studies,* 35-99. While agreeing that "Augustinianism is one of the important antecedents of Ficino's Platonism" (42, footnote 40), Kristeller doubts the extent of Ficino's "Augustinisme avicennizant"

and disagrees in particular with Heitzman's differentiation between the intelligence and the reason and consequently with his views on their respective freedoms.

[123]Heitzman, 464 ff.: "Se si tratta dunque dell'atto di comprensione, questo si compie nella mente, ma il vero fattore agente è Dio come agente primo, e le formule come agente secondo, e la mente da se non fa che la parte della materia."

[124]*Philosophy,* 253 ff. See Trinkaus, *Image,* 476, 488, 498, on man's "striving to be a god in all of his thoughts and actions" (498).

[125]Kristeller, *Philosophy,* 254.

[126]*Phil.* com., 249, 261, etc.

[127]Ibid., ch. 26 (i.e., pp. 241-47).

[128]Heitzman, 467: "... Le idee divine sono le più alte misure della verità; ma noi, nel nostro pensare, non usiamo queste idee, bensì le loro copie che sono nella nostra mente e che Ficino chiama *formulae idearum.*"

[129]Ibid.: "La mente ha dunque bisogno, in un certo senso, d'immagini sensibili per la sua funzione, benché non dipenda da essi, come asserivano i peripatetici."

[130]Ibid., 474: "... l'esistenza nella nostra anima di idee innate non è ancora equivalente colla loro conoscenza e comprensione."

[131]*Republic* VII, 534 B.

[132]See *Phil.* com., ch. 12 (i.e., pp. 143-45). This is an enormous topic, but the following two articles are of especial interest: D.P. Walker, "The *Prisca Theologia* in France," 231 ff.; and E.H. Gombrich, "*Icones Symbolicae:* The Visual Image in Neoplatonic Thought," *Journal of the Warburg and Courtauld Institutes,* 11 (1948), 163-92.

[133]*Phil.,* com., 143.

[134]Heitzman, 303 ff.; Kristeller, *Philosophy,* 49-54; Schiavone, 259-324.

[135]Frances A. Yates, *The Art of Memory* (Chicago, 1966), 240.

[136]See Marcel, *Marsile,* 663; "La vérité, pour Platon, n'était pas seulement le terme d'une induction ou d'une déduction, elle était avant tout le fruit d'une contemplation ..."

[137]See William J. Bouwsma, "Postel and Renaissance Cabalism," in *Renaissance Essays,* edited by Kristeller and Wiener (New York, 1968), 257-58. Bouwsma extends this idea further to embrace not only dialectic but language itself: "... for the cabalist, language is far more than an arbitrary instrument of communication between men. It is a general unifying principle, capable of comprehending all particular things. It originated in the words taught by God to Adam and hence possesses an absolute relation to what it designates: it represents the self-expression of God and reflects his creativity." We can derive from this that there is one, universal, magical language (for the cabalists themselves, this was usually thought of as being Hebrew), that can unify man's experience and give him absolute control over the universe.

[138]See also Frances Yates, *Giordano,* 111: "...the gnostic heresy that man was once, and can become again through his intellect, the reflection of the divine *mens,* a divine being."

[139]*Phil.* com., ch. 30 (i.e., pp. 289-91); also ch. 11 on the two Venuses.

[140]*Phaedrus* 265C-266D; *Symposium* 210A-211C; *Enneads* I, iii.

[141]Taylor, *Plato: The Man and his Work,* 417. Taylor says that Plato makes no attempt to unite these two concepts with the theory of the Ideas and that one cannot deduce a coherent ontology from them all.

[142]See Marcel, *Marsile,* 670-71.

[143]Sears Jayne, *John Colet and Marsilio Ficino* (Oxford, 1963), 57—hereafter cited as *Colet.* In Kristeller's *Philosophy* see the entire ch. XIII on will and love; see too his important article, "A Thomist Critique of Marsilio Ficino's Theory of Will and Intellect," *Harry Austryn Wolfson Jubilee Volume,* English section, vol. III (Jerusalem, 1965), 463-94—hereafter cited as "A Thomist Critique." Kristeller's article introduces some significant modifications to the account presented in his earlier chapter. Cf. too Edgar Wind, *Pagan Mysteries in the Renaissance* (rev. ed., New York, 1968), chs. III and IV.

[144]Jayne, *Colet,* 57. Cf. Kristeller, *Philosophy,* 269 ff; "A Thomist Critique," 483-85.

[145]*Colet,* 59-60.

[146]References are to the English translation by the Dominican Fathers (London, 1928). *Summa Contra Gentiles* III, ch. 26, p. 33.

[147]Ibid., 60.

[148]Ibid., 65. Cf. *In III Sent.,* dist. 27, q.1, a.4; *Summa Theologica* I, q.82, a.3; I-II, q.3, a.4.

[149]Ibid., 78.

[150]See James B. Wadsworth, "Landino's *Disputationes Camaldulenses,* Ficino's *De Felicitate,* and *L'Altercazione* of Lorenzo De'Medici," *Modern Philology,* 50 (1952), 29: and Rochon's refutation of Wadsworth in *La Jeunesse,* 475-543 and especially 480-81 and 495-503.

See too A. Buck, *Der Platonismus in den Dichtungen Lorenzo de'Medicis* (Berlin, 1936), 70-94 and Kristeller's review of Buck reprinted in *Studies,* 214-16.

[151]Saitta, 50: "Nei commentari al *Filebo* che, come si sa, è uno dei più significativi dialoghi di Platone, ciò che si riferisce alla natura volontaristica del bene è trattato con ampiezza e profondità, ma la ragione ne è chiara: il Ficino, pur discorrendo dei vari problemi toccati in quel dialogo da Platone, non poteva non obbedire al demone che l'agitava e che consisteva nella posizione d'un idealismo etico nettamente volontaristico, a spese, s'intende, della razionalità."

[152]*Philosophy,* 272. See the entire section 271-76; and also "A Thomist Critique," 474.

[153]*Philosophy,* 269. Cf. "A Thomist Critique," 471.

[154]*Philosophy*, 272. Cf. Kristeller, "A Thomist Critique," 475.

[155]*Philosophy*, 257.

[156]*Op. Om.*, 313: "...sicut appetitus irrationalis sequitur sensum, sic voluntas, quae est rationalis aviditas, sequitur intellectum."

[157]*Op. Om.*, 236: "...voluntas eousque affectat bonum, quousque intellectus offert ..." Cf. Kristeller, *Philosophy*, 259.

[158]*Philosophy*, 256.

[159]*Op. Om.*, 219.

[160]*Op. Om.*, 187, 307, 313.

[161]*Op. Om.*, 677: "...sub ratione veri intelligit, sub ratione boni appetit omnia." Cf. Kristeller, *Philosophy*, 260.

[162]*Philosophy*, 271 (cf. his p. 270). Cf. "A Thomist Critique," 474, 477.

[163]*Philosophy*, 256.

[164]Ibid., 290.

[165]Ibid., 292.

[166]Ibid., 304.

[167]*Op. Om.*, 78 [the proem to the *Platonic Theology*]: "Quicunque Philosophiae studium impie nimium a sancta religione seiungunt."

[168]*Op. Om.*, 1425-26. See my Appendix III for the Latin (pp. 487-89). Cf. "A Thomist Critique," 476.

[169]Saitta, 53: "Queste ultime parole sono una protesta, di cui non sappiamo che fare..."

[170]*Philosophy*, 276. But cf. "A Thomist Critique," 476.

[171]*Summa Contra Gentiles* III, ch. 26; *Quaestiones Disputatae: De Veritate*, q. 22, a. 11; *Summa Theologica* I, q. 12, a. 12; q. 26, a. 2; q. 82, a. 3.

[172]*Opus Oxoniense* IV, 49, q.4; *Reportata Parisiensia* IV, 49, q. 2-4.

[173]Paul O. Kristeller, *Le Thomisme*, 109-10: "Le problème préoccupa Marsile Ficin à plusieurs reprises à diverses époques de sa vie. De fait, c'est l'un des points au sujet desquels on peut observer des oscillations et des changements dans sa pensée." Cf. too "A Thomist Critique," 474-75. From the viewpoint of interpreting the *Philebus* commentary in the context of the intellect/will controversy, Kristeller's positions in "A Thomist Critique" (1965) and *Le Thomisme* (1967) are identical: they both give fuller recognition to the oscillations in Ficino's thinking, and the article even suggests there are three successive stages in his attitudes towards voluntarism. Further research might establish this to be true for other problems as well. If so, we would have a key to Ficino's overall development.

[174]*Le Thomisme*, 110: "Vers la fin de sa carrière, cependant, il se montre de nouveau indécis. En préparant son commentaire du *Philèbe* pour la publication, il y admet, à l'endroit propice, avoir résolu la question ailleurs en un sens opposé et il cherche à proposer un compromis, distinguant entre la volonté au sens de faculté distincte et comme partie de l'intellect." Cf. "A Thomist Critique," 475-76.

[175]*Le Thomisme,* 110-11: "Cette solution n'est ni très claire ni convaincante, mais elle nous fait voir que le problème continuait à le préoccuper et qu'il n'avait pas du tout réussi à se faire une opinion ferme ou catégorique sur ce point particulier." Cf. "A Thomist Critique," 476.

[176]*Le Thomisme,* 117-18. For Bandello, see Kristeller, "A Thomist Critique," passim.

[177]*Le Thomisme,* 119-20: "De son côté, Ficin, héritier de la tradition néoplatonicienne, n'admet pas que la différence soit aussi radicale entre la vie présente et la vie future. Il est convaincu que l'expérience suprême de la contemplation à laquelle le philosophe platonicien peut atteindre en cette vie est une anticipation authentique de la vie future ... il insiste sur le fait que les expériences des vies présente et future sont profondément semblables." Cf. "A Thomist Critique," 473.

[178]*Le Thomisme,* 108. "...il est intéressant de trouver des échos de la discussion dans les écrits des humanistes qui, par ailleurs, manifestèrent si peu d'intérêt pour les questions de théologie et de philosophie scolastiques." Cf. "A Thomist Critique," 478, 482.

[179]See Jayne, *Colet,* 82-83: "Intelligentia prior est, amor posterior. Intelligentia parit amorem: amor funditur in intelligentia. Intelligentia magis intus stat. Amor magis foris extat. Intelligentia denique simplicior, serenior, et verior est. Amor quodammodo compositior, crassior et concretior est ... intelligas voluntatem scilicet crassum esse intellectum. Intellectum autem serenam et liquidam voluntatem."

Kristeller took account of this oversight in a later article, "The European Significance of Florentine Platonism," *Medieval & Renaissance Studies,* ed. John M. Headley (Chapel Hill, 1968), 228, footnote 69. In alluding to the Colet letter Kristeller writes, "Here Ficino seems to treat the intellect as superior, but the entire treatment is different from Ficino's earlier discussions of the subject."

[180]Schiavone, *Problemi,* 191. See particularly Schiavone's explanation of Ficino's monism pp. 52, 57, and ch. I, passim; also, Kristeller's opposing views in his *Philosophy,* 229, 249-51, and in his review of Schiavone's book, *The Journal of Philosophy,* 58 (1961), 51-53.

[181]*Problemi,* 18-19: "...sotto una classificazione ed una terminologia classiche, si celino nuovi significati e nuove prospettive."

[182]Ibid., 142: "...risente troppo di un voluto ... e forzato concordismo ad oltranza verso Platone."

[183]Ibid., 143: "...nel commento al *Filebo* il motivo che assegna il primato all'intelletto è indicato dalla preminenza dell'attività senza divenire e della concretezza dinamica ... in questa fase giovanile, il dinamismo è inteso come azione statica sull'*altro* e non come autodeterminarsi mediante la determinazione dell'alterità: manca quindi quella circolarità e quel dialettismo che mostrammo *magna pars* nel Ficino della maturità."

[184]*Phil.* com., 307.
[185]Ibid., 307.
[186]Ibid., 309.
[187]Ibid., 307-309.
[188]Ibid., 389, cf. 421.
[189]Ibid., 421.
[190]Ibid., 305.
[191]Ibid., 307-309.

[192]Della Torre, 568: "Poco dopo aver finito il commento del *Simposio,* il Ficino si mise a quello del *Filebo*; ma a questo punto Piero lo invitò ad esporre pubblicamente la sua interpretazione."

[193]Ibid., 573, 591.

[194]*Marsile,* 322: "En tout cas ce qui est certain c'est qu'à l'époque où Landino a écrit ses deux premiers livres, Ficin avait 'composé' son Commentaire sur le *Philèbe,* car non seulement Landino le dit, mais s'en inspire textuellement. C'est donc bien entre 1464 et 1468 que fut commenté le *Philèbe...*"—surely a non-sequitur?

[195]Ibid., 314-22: "Donc le livre a été écrit avant la mort de Pierre et l'aggravation de son état nous permet de conclure que c'est au cours de l'été 1468 qu'eut lieu la rencontre aux Camaldules que Landino nous *rapporte ou imagine* [my italics] ..." (314). Marcel's own words, "rapporte ou imagine," are the operative ones and undermine his own hypothesis. Another counterproof to the 1468 dating is the mention in the dedication to Landino's first book of the defeat of the two Orsinis which took place in 1469; see Rochon, *La Jeunesse,* 40.

[196]*Marsile,* 313, 393. Marcel is in slight error here. It was on *August 21,* 1474, that Federico was named Duke of Urbino by Sixtus IV. Landino still uses the title "Count" and so the book must have been dedicated to Federico before August 21, 1474.

The most recent work on the dating of the *Camaldulensian Disputations* is by Peter Lohe. In his article, "Die Datierung der *Disputationes Camaldulenses* des Cristoforo Landino," *Rinascimento: Rivista dell'Istituto Nazionale di Studi sul Rinascimento,* 2nd series, 9 (Florence, 1969), 291-99, Lohe pushes the completion date of Landino's composition of the four books of the *Disputations* back to 1472: "...dann können wir jetzt zusammemfassend festsellen: Landino hat die *Disputationes Camaldulenses* zwischen dem April und Dezember 1472 verfasst" (297). He proffers no information, however, on the possibility of dating the composition of Landino's second book, the book upon which Marcel's line of argument devolves. Lohe's article was kindly brought to my attention by Professor Roger L. Deakins.

[197]*Marsile,* 322. See Kristeller, *Sup. Fic.,* II, 88-89.

[198]Marcel, *Marsile,* 322 and footnote 2: "Par exemple, la citation du *Cratyle* au commencement du ch. XXIII et celles des ch. XXIV et XXXI

manquent dans le manuscrit *Vat. lat.* 5953.''

[199]Kristeller argues on the basis of the Bodleian MS. *Canon class. lat.* 163 that Ficino composed the *argumentum* for each dialogue at the same time as he translated it (*Sup. Fic.*, I, xxxvii; *Studies*, 161.13). Since the chronological sequence in which he translated the dialogues seems to be the same as the sequence in which they appear in the Plato edition (*Sup. Fic.*, I, cxlvii ff.), and since we know that on April 1, 1466 he had translated 23 dialogues, the *Cratylus* being no. 22 (*Sup. Fic.*, I, cli, and II, 88), the translation of the *Cratylus* ⅂ the composition of its *argumentum* were probably both made early in 1466. Consideration of the *argumentum* therefore cannot be separated from consideration of the dating of the *Cratylus* as a whole.

[200]Marcel, *Marsile*, 603.

[201]Ibid., 610.

[202]Marcel, *Commentaire sur le Banquet de Platon*, 150, 221 (Zoroaster); 138 (Hermes).

[203]*Philosophy*, 17.

[204]Marcel, *Commentaire sur le Banquet de Platon*, 41.

[205]MS. *Vat.* 5953 is not an autograph. In the margins throughout the entire codex, however, there are a few intermittent jottings in a hand other than the scribe's formal hand. These marginalia consist of proper names and headings which are single words or phrases or sentences taken either directly from the text itself or modified so that they can stand independently. There are no corrections or additions. MS. *Laur.* 21, 8 has marginalia with the same general features, except that they are written in Salvini's "Roman" hand and are even briefer; they do not correspond to the marginalia in MS. 5953. The question which presents itself is this: Are the marginalia of MS. 5953 in Ficino's own hand?

Currently, there is some debate over Ficino's handwriting. One view is that Ficino had two distinct hands: a rough-copy hand which made liberal use of abbreviations, and a neat calligraphic script, i.e. a book hand, where the abbreviations are less frequent. For this view see Martin Sicherl's article, "Neuentdeckte Handschriften von Marsilio Ficino," *Scriptorium,* 16 (1962), 50-61. Page 169 of H.D. Saffrey's article, "Notes Platoniciennes de Marsile Ficin dans un manuscrit de Proclus," *Bibliothèque D'Humanisme et Renaissance,* 21 (1959), 161-84, contains a full page specimen of Ficino's rough-copy hand; this is the hand in which the Parma/Paris MS. containing the argument to the *Philebus* is also written (see Appendix III and my note 8). Samples of Ficino's book hand can be seen in Raymond Marcel's edition, *Marsile Ficin, Commentaire sur le Banquet de Platon,* in the plates facing pp. 32, 33, 38, 39, 134.

Paul Kristeller has questioned this easy distinction between the two hands in an article, "Some Original Letters and Autograph Manuscripts of Marsilio Ficino," *Studi di Bibliografia e di Storia in onore di Tammaro de Marinis, 3*

(Verona, 1964), 5-33. He notes that Ficino's Greek, Italian and Latin hands all differ and that his Roman may differ also from his Italic. But, he continues, "whether Ficino . . . also wrote a book hand remains to be seen" (10; cf. 21), for the book hands of the fifteenth century humanists as a group "resemble each other so closely that one may very well despair of establishing the work of individual copyists" (8-9).

Kristeller enumerates the characteristics of Ficino's rough-copy hand: "the long s, the round d, the h whose tail is drawn below the level of the middle line, the final m (which is turned around and looks like a z, according to a common medieval practice), the final i, which is often prolonged and without a dot, the initial f, which often has a double loop, and the g. . ." (10). See the illustrations in plates III, 3; III, 4; and III, 9. These characteristics, he says, "appear in all Ficino autographs from about 1469 on."

Judging from the available plates and the descriptions of Kristeller and Sicherl, I am firmly convinced that the marginalia of MS. 5953 are not by Ficino. They are possibly in the scribe's own less formal hand.

[206]Marcel, *Théologie,* vol. I, 29.

[207]*Summa Contra Gentiles,* trans. by the Dominican Fathers (London, 1923-28); and again under the title *On The Truth Of The Catholic Faith* by Dr. Pegis et al. (New York, 1956).

[208]Roy J. Deferrari, *A Latin-English Dictionary of St. Thomas Aquinas* (Boston, Mass., 1960).

[209]See, for instance, *Phil.* com., 369-75.

References in The Commentary and Appendices II and III

(a bracketed question-mark following the reference means the ascription is a guess)

¹*Alcibiades* II, 144D, 146D-147B; *Euthydemus* 280D-281D; *Republic* VII, 534BC; *Laws* I, 631B-D.

Cf. Aristotle, *Nicomachean Ethics* I, 1094a; Aquinas, *Summa Contra Gentiles* III, ii; and Lactantius, *Divine Institutes* I, ii-v.

The opening section of this commentary (my pp. 72-110) is directly concerned not with the *Philebus* but with the absolute good or one. Ficino says that this defense of the Idea of the good is in order to "explode the objections of the Aristotelians" (my p. 113, cf. pp. 177 and 181).

²*De Rerum Natura* I, 159-163 (a direct quotation).

³The following passage is borrowed in a somewhat abbreviated and emended form from the *Summa Contra Gentiles* III, ii, paragraphs 3, 4, 5.

⁴Cf. Aristotle, *Metaphysics* II, 994a, 1-10.

⁵*Metaphysics* II, 994b, 10-15 (cf. *Phil.* com. 85-87 and ref. 7).

⁶*Statesman* 269C-270A.

⁷*Metaphysics* III, 996b [?]. Cf. *Metaphysics* II, 994b and *Nicomachean Ethics* I, 1097a.

⁸The following chapter is borrowed in a somewhat abbreviated and emended form from the *Summa Contra Gentiles* III, iii, paragraphs 2, 3, 4, 5, 6 and 8.

⁹Cf. *Summa Contra Gentiles* I, xlii, paragraph 23.

¹⁰Cf. Cicero, *De Natura Deorum* I, 35; *Academica* II, 121.

¹¹Cf. Augustine, *City of God* VIII, 1; VII, 6.

¹²Plato, *Phaedo* 97C; Augustine, *City of God* VIII, 2; Cicero, *De Natura Deorum* I, 26.

¹³Cf. Cicero, *De Natura Deorum* I, 36; II, 22.

¹⁴Cf. Aquinas, *II Sent.*, 17, 1, 1 and Albertus Magnus, *Summa Theologiae*, IIa, t. 12, q. 72, membr. 4, a. 2, n. 4.

¹⁵Ficino's immediate source for these Alfarabi and Avicebron refs. may be Aquinas, *De Ente et Essentia* 4 and *Quodlibet* 11, 5, 5.

¹⁶*Parmenides* 151E-152A.

¹⁷*Parmenides* 137C-142B; 159B-160B.

¹⁸*Laws* X, 892A; 896A-898B, etc.

¹⁹Cf. Aristotle, *De Anima* I, 2, 404b.

²⁰*Parmenides* 160B-166B & passim; *Republic* VI, 508A-509B [?].

²¹*Republic* VI, 509B; *On The Divine Names* V, 1 (*PG*, 3, 816B).

[22]*On The Trinity* VIII, 3, 4: Tolle hoc [bonum] et illud, et vide ipsum bonum si potes: ita Deum videbis, non alio bono sed bonum omnis boni." Cf. Augustine, *Enarrationes in Psalmos* 134 (*PL*, 36, 1430-74).

[23]*On Mystical Theology* I, ii (*PG*, 3, 1000A ff.).

[24]*Republic* VI, 509B ff.

[25]See Ficino's *Opera Omnia*, 934, line 12 of the first hymn (cf. my page 305 and ref. 169). This "Orphei versus de deo" is, as D.P. Walker has shown, an extremely free rendering of the Orphic fragment known as the *Palinode* or *Testament* (Kern, frag. 24, i.e. the Aristobulus version). Ficino was working from George of Trebizond's incompetent translation of Eusebius' *Praeparatio Evangelica* XIII, 12. Though this was not published until 1470, Ficino had access to a MS. version in the Laurenziana in 1462 (D.P. Walker, "Orpheus the Theologian and Renaissance Platonists," *Journal of the Warburg and Courtauld Institutes,* 16 [1953], 110-111).

[26]The intelligence, reason and will [?].

[27]*Laws* I, 628CD. Plato talks of "peace" rather than "quietness."

[28]*Republic* II, 357B-358A.

[29]*Gorgias* 467C-468C.

[30]*Nicomachean Ethics* VII, 1152b-1154b and X, 1172a-1176a; *De Finibus* I, 29-57 and passim.

[31]Cf. the proem in X to Lorenzo (Appendix III).

[32]*Euthydemus* 306A-C.

[33]*Euthydemus* 280B-D.

[34]*Cleitophon* 408E-end; *Meno* 78C ff., 88D; *Alcibiades* II, 144D ff., 146E-147A; *Laws* I, 631B ff.; II, 661A ff.; III, 697B ff., etc.

[35]*Euthydemus* 281B-282A.

[36]*Protagoras* 352CD, 357C.

[37]*Republic* VI, 505A-509B.

[38]Cf. Augustine, *City of God* XI, 29 (cf. my p. 339 and ref. 176).

[39]*Republic* VI, 505A-509B.

[40]Diogenes Laertius (*Lives Of The Philosophers* III, 58) says it was Thrasylus who maintained the *Philebus* was "on pleasure." Thrasylus also maintained the *Parmenides* was "on Ideas," the *Symposium* "on the good," and the *Phaedrus* "on love"; and consequently that the four of them constituted "a tetralogy."

[41]Ficino's twelve parts presumably correspond to the following in the Stephanus pagination:

Part I: 11A-11D
Part II: 11D-15C
Part III: 15C-20A
Part IV: 20B-23B
Part V: 23C-27C
Part VI: 27C-30A

Part VII: 30A-31B
Part VIII: 31B-55C
Part IX: 55C-59C
Part X: 59C-61C
Part XI: 61D-66A
Part XII: 66A-67B

In my edition Part I begins on page 115, Part II on page 131, Part III on page 215, Part IV on page 283 and Part V on page 347.

In the opening sentence of the *argumentum* Ficino talks of "the wonderful order" Plato employed in composing the *Philebus*. All but the most recent editors of the *Philebus* have had greater reservations.

[42] *Euthydemus* 273E (cf. *Euthyphro* 13B ff.) [?].

[43] Cf. Hesiod's *Theogony,* 198-200.

[44] *De Rerum Natura* I, 1-5 (a direct quotation).

[45] *Hymn to Uranus* (4), 1-2.

[46] *Timaeus* 28B-29A.

[47] *Epistle* II, 312E.

[48] *Republic* VI, 508A, 509B.

[49] This Porphyry ref. may derive from Augustine's *City of God* X, 23: "[Porphyrius] dicit enim Deum Patrem et Deum Filium, quem Graece appellat intellectum vel paternam mentem." The source of the Neoplatonic Kronos/Nous identification is Plotinus' *Enneads* V, 1, 4; it derives in turn from Plato's *Cratylus* 396BC.

[50] *Timaeus* 48A.

[51] *Statesman* 269A.

[52] *Laws* IV, 715E-716A.

[53] *Protagoras* 322C-D.

[54] *Epistle* VI, 323D.

[55] *Timaeus* 30B; *Republic* X, 616C; *Statesman* 272E; *Laws* X, 897C; *Epistle* VI, 323D; *Phaedrus* 246E.

[56] *Symposium* 180D ff.

[57] *Theogony,* 178-206.

[58] *Cratylus* 390D-E, etc.

[59] *Cratylus* 400D ff.

[60] *Phaedrus* 234D — the reference is to the word "Δαιμονίως." Ficino is alluding to Socrates' demon, his attendent "spirit" or genius, a subject upon which the ancient Neoplatonists and their successors had speculated at some length. Cf. *Apology* 40A; *Theaetetus* 151A; *Euthyphro* 3B; *Cratylus* 398BC; Augustine, *City of God* VIII, 14; and my p. 273.

[61] *Laws* XI, 917B [?]. The more likely ref. is to *Laws* X, 907E.

[62] *Parmenides* 147D, 142B-157B.

[63] *On the Divine Names* passim.

[64] *Against Celsus* V, 613.

[65] *Epistle to the Philippians* 2: 9.

[66] *Aeneid* I, 327.

[67] Quoted in the *Cratylus* 391D.

[68] *Epistle to the Hebrews* 4: 12.

[69] *St. John's Gospel* 19: 26. There are five words in the Greek — Γύναι, ἰδοὺ ὁ υἰός σου.

[70] *Matthew* 1: 20-21; *Luke* 1: 31; *Acts* 4:7 — "...In qua virtute, aut in quo nomine fecistis hoc vos?"

[71] Here Ficino is referring to a pre-Areopagitian enumeration of the spirits. Dionysius' nine heavenly orders would be inappropriate here.

[72] *Sophist* 253D; *Statesman* 262A ff.

[73] Ficino has ingeniously tried to make sense of an allusion in the text of the *Philebus* which he did not understand. The Greek means literally: "our argument would *disappear and perish* like a fairy tale." Raymond Klibansky in his edition of A.E. Taylor's *Plato: Philebus and Epinomis* (London, 1956), p. 256, n. 5, says that Plato is alluding to a *formula* used at the end of fairy tales.

[74] *Cratylus* 428D.

[75] *Gorgias* 457C-458B [?]; *Phaedo* 90B-91B.

[76] *Republic* X, 595C.

[77] *Epistle* II, 310D.

[78] *Laws* II, 663E.

[79] Diogenes Laertius, *Lives Of The Philosophers* III, 39-40: "truth is the pleasantest of sounds" [?].

[80] *Phaedrus* 241C (a garbled reference — cf. my p. 357 and ref. 182).

[81] *Statesman* 258E. In fact, Plato's division is between the practical and purely intellectual sciences.

[82] *Republic* VI, 509B.

[83] *Psalm* 4: 6.

[84] *Republic* VI, 505 ff.

[85] Aristophanes, *Clouds,* 225 ff. (cf. Plato's *Apology* 19C). For the comedians' opinion of Plato see Diogenes Laertius, *Lives Of The Philosophers* III, 26-28.

[86] See Diogenes Laertius, *Lives Of The Philosophers* VI, 53.

[87] *Phaedo* 77A, 100B-E; *Timaeus* 47A ff.

[88] Successive scholars have differed as to whether Plato was asking two or three questions here. Ficino's solution, interestingly, is the one adopted by Raymond Klibansky in his edition of A.E. Taylor's *Plato: Philebus and Epinomis* (London, 1956), pp. 257-59, n. 9. The controversial second question, Klibansky says, is: Since each of the units is a particular being, how can they be said to be eternal and self-identical?

[89] *Parmenides* 128E-136C & passim; *Timaeus* 28A-29C, etc.; *Republic* V, 476A-480; X, 596A ff., etc.; *Phaedo* 77A, 100B-E.

[90]*Phaedo* 77A, 100B-E.

[91]*De Diversis Quaestionibus* LXXXIII, *Quaestio* XLVI: *De Ideis.* These two paragraphs — "Whoever acknowledges that all existing things ... the soul may be made utterly happy" — are copied almost verbatim from the concluding section of Augustine's *quaestio.* Typically, though, Ficino has left out one or two clauses and there are some minor variations.

[92]The passage in question is *Metaphysics* XII, 1072b-1074a. Eustratius is the least well known of these commentators. During the twelfth century he was metropolitan of Nicaea and composed, among other works, commentaries on the *Posterior Analytics* and the *Nicomachean Ethics,* commentaries which were often cited during the Middle Ages and even translated into Latin by Robert of Lincoln.

[93]*Timaeus* 30D. For the Hermes ref. see Ficino's own translation of the *Pimander,* chs. I and III (*Op. Om.,* 1837, 1841).

[94]*Phaedo* 100B-E; *Republic* V, 476C ff.; *Timaeus* 28A ff.; *Epistle* II, 312E-313A.

[95]Cf. Plato's *Cratylus* 401D.

[96]Cf. Augustine, *De Vera Religione* 39, 73.

[97]*Timaeus* 28A-31A, 39E.

[98]This is a confusing passage, partly because of the difficulty in determining the subject of the verb *fingantur* — angels? men? powers? creativenesses?

Ficino is stressing the distinction between the universal powers or forms as they exist naturally, or in reality, and as they exist as concepts in the angelic or human understanding, i.e. as they exist "in an imaginary way." Kristeller writes: "All forms are found on all levels of reality, from God down to matter. The *natura vegetalis* corresponds to the lower soul, the vegetative power, which obviously lacks knowledge. Yet it does have forms (the seeds or seminal reasons) which are the direct causes of corporeal forms." He continues, "The phrase *ad intima se convertunt obiecta* refers to the angels and means that their thought, at least in one of its aspects, is directed towards the forms or Ideas inherent in themselves, that is, towards an internal object. I take this to be a generalized application of the Plotinian view that the soul is active in three directions: upwards (towards the intellect), internally, and downwards (towards the body)" (private letter, Sept. 1972).

[99]*Phaedo* 90D-E.

[100]Galen, *On The Natural Faculties* III, x, 179-180 [?].

[101]*Gorgias* 480A-D.

[102]*Republic* IX, 591CD; *Laws* IV, 716A-E.

[103]*Timaeus* 28A ff.

[104]*Cratylus* 436D.

[105]For the Rhodes ref. see Strabo's *Geography* XIV, 2, 5 (but Strabo does not cite the proverb itself). For the Pythagoras ref. see Ficino's own translation

of the *Symbola* in his *Op. Om.*, 1979. For the Heraclitus ref. see fragment 105 (Bywater); it is quoted in the *Nicomachean Ethics* II, 1105a and in Plutarch's *Life of Coriolanus*, ch. 22.

[106]*Phaedo* 89D-91A.

[107]*Sophist* 253DE, etc.; *Statesman* passim.

[108]*Republic* VII, 534B-E.

[109]*Parmenides* 135D-136C.

[110]*Cratylus* 405BC ff.

[111]*Republic* VII, 537D-539D.

[112]*Laws* X, 908C ff.

[113]The ref. to philodoxers (or perhaps doxophilists) is in the *Republic* V, 480A.

[114]*Phaedrus* 237D, 246 ff.; *Republic* VII, 538CD.

[115]Juvenal, *Satire* II, 21.

[116]*Phaedo* 68C.

[117]*Parmenides* 135A ff. [?].

[118]Cf. Cicero, *De Natura Deorum* I, 2, 63, 117 and III, 89 (for Diagoras); I, 2, 29, 63, 117 (for Protagoras); I, 29, 120 (for Democritus); I, 18 ff. and 57 ff. (for Epicurus). Also Lactantius, *Divine Institutes* I, ii.

[119]*Laws* X, 908C ff.

[120]*Apology* 23CD and passim.

[121]*Phaedrus* 269E-270A.

[122]*Parmenides* 136C.

[123]*Phaedrus* 266B.

[124]*Republic* VI, 508B ff.

[125]*The Celestial Hierarchy* III, 1 (*PG*, 3, 164D) and passim.

[126]*Phaedrus* 248A.

[127]*Timaeus* 28C, 29A-E.

[128]*On the Divine Names* IV, 8 (*PG*, 3, 704D) ff.

[129]*Protagoras* 320D-322A.

[130]This is presumably a reference to *Statesman* 271D ff., or 274C, that is, to the Promethean fire (see my p. 245).

[131]*Laws* IV, 713A ff.

[132]*Timaeus* 47C; *Statesman* 274CD.

[133]*Dia* is the Greek accusative of Zeus! Ficino is also referring to Plato's derivation of the name via δίαιτα (a way of living) and διά (through) — see *Cratylus* 396A-C.

[134]The *argumentum* to the *Cratylus* is the introduction Ficino himself wrote to accompany his translation of the dialogue (cf. my third appendix for his *argumentum* to the *Philebus*).

[135]*Hymn to Nature* (10), 8.

[136]*Hymn to Saturn* (13), 3-5.

[137]*Universal Hymn* (i.e. the introductory hymn), 42.

[138]*Timaeus* 32AB. Cf. Aquinas, *Summa Contra Gentiles* II, lxviii, paragraphs 6 and 7.

[139]The "golden chain" of Homer is described in the *Iliad* VIII, 18-27 and referred to in the *Theaetetus* 153CD. The quotation from Orpheus is taken from the *Philebus* itself at 66C (see my pp. 403 and 405 and refs. 199 and 201). Cf. Plutarch, *The EI at Delphi* 391D; Proclus, *In Rempublicam* II, 100, 23; and Kern, *Orphica,* frag. 14.

[140]*Sophist* 253C ff. [?] *Statesman* passim.

[141]*Republic* II, 368D-369A; *Sophist* 218D.

[142]*Timaeus* 35B-36B.

[143]*Hymn to Apollo* (34), 21-23.

[144]Ficino is describing the three tetrachords of Greek musical theory. A tetrachord was a descending series of four tones that spanned the interval of a perfect fourth. Ficino has named and loosely described the diatonic and chromatic tetrachords, and described, but not named, the enharmonic tetrachord. See Gustave Reese, *Music in the Middle Ages* (New York, 1950), 23-24. For this and the following note I am indebted to Professors Charles W. Forker and Theodore Diaconoff.

[145]Whereas the musical theory and practice of Ficino's time included "harmony" in the modern sense of tones sounded simultaneously, Greek music did not. For the Greeks "harmony" apparently meant the proper adjustment of singly-sounded notes to one another. Plato is often careless or casual with musical terms and he uses this word loosely. Ficino follows him in this respect.

[146]*Laws* II, 654AC; *Republic* III, 412AB.

[147]Pliny, *Natural History* VII, lvi, 192-193 — "ex quo apparet aeternus litterarum usus" —; *Timaeus* 29B; *Laws* III, 677A ff. [?] (But in 680A Plato says that letters did not exist in the early period succeeding the flood.)

[148]*Phaedrus* 274C-275B. Cf. Cicero, *De Natura Deorum* III, 56; Lactantius, *Div. Inst.* I, vi; and Ficino's own preface to his *Pimander* translation (*Op. Om.,* 1836).

[149]*Sophist* 216B.

[150]See ref. 60; and also *Phaedrus* 249CD.

[151]See ref. 147. To us Hermes' classification is a strange one: his "semi-vowels" consist of double consonants, liquids, nasals and a sibilant. The liquids and nasals can become "vowel-like" when they are protracted, but normally, of course, we reserve the term "semi-vowel" for *w* and *y*.

Priscian is the famous and voluminous grammarian who lived in Constantinople in the sixth century.

[152]*Alcibiades* II, 146E ff.

[153]*Phaedo* 99D. The reference here is to the Δεύτερος Πλοῦς.

[154]*Sententiae,* line 331 (Loeb). Ficino is using the incorrect form "Publius." The correct form "Publilius" was established by Woelfflin in

Philol. xxii (1865), 439.

[155]Cf. Cicero, *Academica* II, 94-98 and *De Natura Deorum* I, 11; Lactantius, *Div. Inst.* III, lv-vi; Augustine, *Contra Academicos* III, xvii, 38-39.

[156]*Menexenus* 235E. For the ref. to Connus see *Euthydemus* 272C.

[157]*Symposium* 201D ff.

[158]*On The Divine Names* IV, 12 (*PG,* 3, 709B) and passim.

[159]*Phaedrus* 257A (see ref. 60); *Symposium* 202E.

[160]*Laws* IV, 715E-716A. (See ref. 161 and Kern, frag. 21).

[161]This is from the Orphic fragment known as the *Hymn of Jove* (Kern, frag. 21a, lines 2 and 3; and 168, lines 2 and 4). The fragment is quoted in the Pseudo-Aristotle, *De Mundo* 7, in Eusebius, *Praeparatio Evangelica* III, 9, and in Proclus, *In Plat. Tim.* 28C. Ficino's source is probably the Pseudo-Aristotelian version (which is shorter than, and differs from, the version in Eusebius and Proclus) since he had already translated it in a letter to Peregrino Alio (*Op. Om.,* 614, i.e. the *De Divino Furore*) dated December 1, 1457.

[162]*On The Divine Names* IV, x (*PG,* 3, 708B).

[163]*Timaeus* 29E.

[164]*Republic* II, 380D-381C.

[165]*On The Divine Names* IV, xx (*PG,* 3, 720A) and passim [?].

[166]The following passage is borrowed in a somewhat abbreviated and emended form from the *Summa Contra Gentiles* III, xvii, paragraphs 7, 8 and 9.

[167]*Cratylus* 412C.

[168]*Republic* VI, 508A ff.

[169]See Ficino's *Op. Om.,* 934, 1, line 12. This hymn is a version of the so-called *Palinode* of Orpheus (Kern, frag. 247; see my p. 111 and ref. 25).

[170]See ch. 13 of Ficino's own translation of the *Pimander* in his *Op. Om.,* 1856 (cf. ch. 12, *Op. Om.,* 1854).

[171]*Republic* VI, 505E.

[172]This is a difficult passage. *Natura* again refers to a part of the "irrational" soul, to a quality inherent in the body which is also called the "vital complexion." Ficino himself defines it: "In each living body there is a certain effective and vital disposition or complexion, which the animating power of its soul gives to the body. The Platonists say that this is the *nature* of bodies; it is like a trace or shadow of the soul in the body" (*Op. Om.,* 289). To emphasize this fact I have translated *natura* here as "*our* nature."

The *sense* is part of the "rational" soul and it alone is capable of pleasure "which has sight" (*videns*) as opposed to the blind pleasure (*quasi caeca voluptas*) which the feeling and the natural complexion experience.

[173]Olympiodorus (Damascius), *Lectures on the Philebus* 155, etc.

[174]*Phaedrus* 249B-D [?]; *Phaedo* 65C, 65E-66A & passim; *Theaetetus* 173E ff. [?] or 185C-E [?]; *Nicomachean Ethics* X, 1177a-1179a.

[175]*Gorgias* 468A-C, 509E; *Protagoras* 355A, 358CD, etc.
[176]Cf. Augustine, *City of God* XI, 29 (cf. ref. 38).
[177]Cf. Cicero, *De Senectute* xiii, 44.
[178]Virgil, *Eclogue* III, 93.
[179]*Phaedrus* 247E & 248A.
[180]*Phaedrus* 247C-248A, 249B-D.
[181]*Laws* V, 730C.
[182]*Phaedrus* 241C. This is a garbled version. (Cf. my p. 165 and ref. 80.)
[183]*Laws* IV, 716C.
[184]The following passage is borrowed in a somewhat abbreviated and emended form from the *Summa Contra Gentiles* III, xxvi, paragraphs 9, 10, 11, 14, 15, 16.
[185]*Enneads* I, iv, 2, 3, 6, 14.
[186]*Enneads* I, iv, 6.
[187]Cf. the letter to Orlandini (Appendix III) and my Introduction. Notice that this passage is omitted in the manuscripts: it suggests a solution which still subordinates the will. But see Kristeller, *Philosophy,* 275.
[188]Ficino is quoting from his own Latin translation of Socrates' proposal in the *Philebus* 23C to divide all existing things into two or three classes. Ficino's Latin runs: "Omnia quae nunc in universo sunt, bifariam distinguamus, immo, si vis, trifariam."
[189]The fullest Neoplatonic elaborations of the importance of the limit and the infinite as cosmogonic principles are Syrianus, *In Metaphysica Commentaria* 112, 14 ff. and Proclus, *Platonic Theology* III, vii-ix (and also Proclus' commentaries on the *Timaeus* I, 176 and *Parmenides* 1119 ff.). We do not know, however, if Ficino had direct access to any of these by 1469.

There is also the possibility Ficino is recalling the argumentation in Henry of Ghent's *Summa Theologica* 21, 2, 14.

The *terminus* (limit) and the *infinitum* (the infinite) are Ficino's choices for the Greek *peras* and *apeiron*. Although they seem to function with antinomic force in Plato there are many inherent ambiguities. Jowett, for instance, lists the bundle of associations surrounding the term *apeiron*: it "is the negative of measure or limit; the unthinkable, the unknowable; of which nothing can be affirmed; the mixture of chaos which preceded distinct kinds in the creation of the world; the first vague impression of sense; the more or less which refuses to be reduced to rule, having certain affinities with evil, with pleasure, with ignorance, and which in the scale of being is farthest removed from the beautiful and good" (*The Dialogues of Plato,* rev. 4th ed. [Oxford, 1953], vol. III, p. 537).
[190]*Parmenides* 137C-142B.
[191]*Parmenides* 137C-142B.
[192]*Timaeus* 51AB.
[193]*Timaeus* 47E ff.

¹⁹⁴*Parmenides* 137C-142B.

¹⁹⁵*Hymn to the Night* (3) 11: δεινὴ γὰρ ἀνάγκη πάντα κρατύνει.

¹⁹⁶*Republic* X, 616C-617D.

¹⁹⁷*Parmenides* 142B-157B.

¹⁹⁸See Ficino's own translation of the *Pimander* (*Op. Om.*, 1841) and my p. 417 and ref. 206.

¹⁹⁹*Philebus* 66C (scc my pp. 257, 405 and refs. 139 and 201) and *Op. Om.*, 1847. Cf. *Genesis* 2:1, "Igitur perfecti sunt coeli et terra, et omnis ornatus eorum"; and Plato's *Gorgias* 507E-508A and *Timaeus* 29D-30A. *Ornatus* is the adorning of chaos in the sense that it is the cancellation of the void, the result being the cosmos (i.e. order). In the *Symposium* commentary I, iii Ficino writes: "To designate this gathering together of all the forms and all the Ideas we use the word *mundus* in Latin and the word *kosmos* in Greek, that is to say, *adornment*" (Formarum omnium idearumque complexionem, mundum latine, grece kosmon, id est, ornamentum vocamus).

For "chaos" see Orpheus, *Argonautica*, 12 and Kern, frag. 66b [?].

²⁰⁰*Sophist* 254D ff.

²⁰¹See *Philebus* 66C (cf. my pp. 257, 403 and refs. 139 and 199).

²⁰²*Sophist* 254D-256E. Ficino translates τό τ᾽ ὂν αὐτὸ as *ens ipsum* (254D), though in English this is often rendered as "being."

²⁰³*Timaeus* 30A.

²⁰⁴This could be Philo of Larissa but is more probably Philo Judaeus. Cf. Eusebius, *Historia Ecclesia* II, 18 and *Praeparatio Evangelica* VII, 13. See too *The Wisdom of Solomon* 11:21, "Sed omnia in mensura, et numero, et pondere disposuisti" (this was an oft-quoted text); and Augustine, *De Libero Arbitrio* II, 16, 41ff.

²⁰⁵Ficino is again quoting from Socrates' proposal at 23C (see ref. 188).

²⁰⁶Orpheus, *Argonautica,* 12 and Kern, frag. 66b [?].

²⁰⁷See Ficino's own translation of the *Pimander,* ch. iii (*Op. Om.*, 1841).

²⁰⁸*Timaeus* 48A — a ref. to the cosmos (cf. ref. 199).

²⁰⁹Augustine, *De Genesi Ad Litteram* I, 15, 29 (cf. too his *De Genesi Contra Manichaeos* I, 17, 11), Oilgen, *De Principiis* II, 1, 4 [?].

²¹⁰*Phaedrus* 249B-D.

²¹¹*Phaedo* 66D-68B.

²¹²L.G. Westerink in his article, "Ficino's Marginal Notes on Olympiodorus in Riccardi Greek MS. 37," *Traditio,* 24 (1968), p. 354, identifies three of these four odd chapters as being Ficino's "reading notes" on Damascius' commentary on the *Philebus*. *De intelligentia et voluptate eorumque mixtura* (#1) are notes on paragraphs 10-13 in "a rewritten version"; *Quod neque intelligentia neque voluptas est finis, minime vero voluptas* (#2) are notes on paragraphs 121-126; *Quomodo dialecticae officium artificiumque sit Dei munus divinitatemque imitetur* (#4) are notes on paragraphs 54-56. But *Quomodo essentia componatur ex uno, multitudine, termino, infinito. Item de generibus*

entis (#3) Westerink says are "reflections" on the *Philebus* itself (i.e. on 16C9-10) and apparently have "no connection with Damascius."

Westerink has one surprising observation, however: he argues that the word *lectiones* must refer to Ficino's "private reading" of Damascius, not to his lectures, on the grounds that "otherwise the agreement could not be so complete." This is open to several objections. The word *iisdem* emphasizes the fact that the four odd chapters belong to the *same* (sic) category as the rest of the commentary and Westerink nowhere suggests that the whole commentary is simply a collection of reading notes. To the contrary, he is at pains to show how *little* evidence there is to suggest that Ficino ever referred to his reading of Damascius, apart from the three odd chapters and three other very minor references (see note 11 of my Introduction). Next, at the end of the four odd chapters there is a postscript containing the word *lectio* (p. 439); here it refers specifically to *lectures* on the *first parts* of the *Philebus,* and *reading* would not make sense. Finally, the word *lectio* also appears in the alternative title to the whole commentary and must again refer to *lectures* (see my note on the titles).

In short, the evidence indicates that the editor of the *Commentaria in Platonem,* or perhaps the "literary executor" who Westerink posits as finding "some separate sheets" in Ficino's manuscript volume, did not realize three of these four odd chapters were reading notes on Damascius: after all, he inserted a fourth chapter that had no connection with Damascius. He must have assumed automatically that the four chapters were stray lecture notes which Ficino himself had composed on the *Philebus* but not yet incorporated into the body of his commentary: hence the wording of the two postscripts (my pp. 425 and 439).

[213]See Porphyry's *De Abstinentia Animalium* as excerpted by Ficino, paragraph 2, entitled, "beatitudo non est divinorum cognitio sed vita divina" (*Op. Om.,* 1932).

[214]*Enneads* I, lv, 12.

[215]Aristotle, *Physics* II, 2, 194a, 21. Cf. too Seneca, *Moral Epistle* 65, 3.

[216]*Timaeus* 47BC; *Protagoras* 321E [?].

[217]*Statesman* 271DE [?]; *Protagoras* 320D-322A [?].

[218]Origen, *Against Celsus* IV, 560 ff. For Avicenna see M.E. Marmura, "Avicenna's Theory of Prophecy ...," in *The Seed of Wisdom,* ed. by W.S. McCullough (Toronto, 1964), 159-178.

[219]Fulgentius, *Mythologiae* II, i. Cf. Plutarch, *De Liberis Educandis* 10 (*Moralia* 8A); Plato, *Republic* IV, 439D ff. and IX, 580D ff; and Ficino's proem to Lorenzo (Appendix III).

[220]*Odyssey* X, 287-306.

[221]*Aeneid* VI, 136 ff. Servius, the first great Virgil commentator, explicated the word *silva* in terms of the Greek word *hyle,* meaning both "forest" and the "elemental chaos" (*In Vergilii Aeneidem* VI, f.256r). His explication

became the standard one for the Middle Ages and then entered into the Renaissance dictionaries and the variorum editions of Virgil.

[222]*St. John's Gospel* 1:5.

[223]Ibid.

[224]*Aeneid* VI, 131.

[225]*St. John's Gospel* 1:13.

[226]*Aeneid* VI, 147.

[227]*St. John's Gospel* 6:44.

[228]*Aeneid* VI, 146.

[229]*Aeneid* VI, 143.

[230]*Timaeus* 69D.

[231]*Psalm* 72:28 (Vulgate).

[232]*Psalm* 50:14 ff. (Vulgate).

[233]See Ficino's own translation of the *Symbola* (*Op. Om.*, 1979); see also *Sup. Fic.*, II, 98 where Ficino, in annotating Iamblichus and this particular apothegm, says: "The pleasures of the body have a black tail, though they present a beautiful face."

[234]Cf. Porphyry's *Life of Pythagoras*, 39.

[235]Cf. Aratus, *Phaenomena*, 96-136; Ovid, *Metamorphoses* I, 150; Virgil, *Eclogue* IV, 6; and Lactantius, *Div. Inst.* V, v.

[236]Fulgentius, *Mythologiae* II, i (see the first of the ten excerpts and ref. 219 above).

[237]Xenophon, *Memorabilia* II, i, 21-34; cf. Cicero, *De Officiis* I, xxxii and III, v.

[238]*Parmenides* passim.

[239]*Phaedo* 80AB.

[240]*Theaetetus* 176BC.

[241]*Phaedrus* 247E.

Select Bibliography

Aquinas, St. Thomas. *Summa Contra Gentiles*. Trans. the Dominican Fathers. London, 1928. Also trans. Dr. Pegis et al. under the title *On the Truth of the Catholic Faith*. New York, 1956.

Argan, Giuseppe C. *Brunelleschi*. Milan, 1955.

Armstrong, A.H., ed. *The Cambridge History of Later Greek and Early Medieval Philosophy*. Cambridge, 1967.

Bisticci, Vespasiano da. *Vite di uomini illustri del secolo XV*. Florence, 1938.

Bolgar, R.R. *The Classical Heritage*. New York, 1964.

Bouwsma, William J. "Postel and the Significance of Renaissance Cabalism." *Renaissance Essays*. Ed. P.O. Kristeller and P.P. Wiener. New York, 1968. Pp. 252-66.

Buck, A. *Der Platonismus in den Dichtungen Lorenzo de'Medicis*. Berlin, 1936.

Burroughs, Josephine L. "Ficino and Pomponazzi on Man." *Journal of the History of Ideas*, V (1944), 227-39.

Bury, R.G. *The Philebus of Plato*. Cambridge, 1897.

Cassirer, Ernst. *The Platonic Renaissance in England*. Trans. P. Pettegrove. Austin, Texas, 1953.

Cassirer, Ernst, et al. *The Renaissance Philosophy of Man*. Chicago, 1948.

Chastel, André. *Arte e umanesimo a Firenze al tempo di Lorenzo il Magnifico*. Trans. Renzo Federici. Turin, 1964.

——————. *Marsile Ficin et l'Art*. Geneva and Lille, 1954.

Deferrari, Roy J. *A Latin-English Dictionary of St. Thomas Aquinas*. Boston, 1960.

Della Torre, Arnaldo. *Storia dell'Accademia Platonica di Firenze*. Florence, 1902.

Dies, Auguste. *Philèbe*. Paris, 1949.

Ficino, Marsilio. *Commentaria In Platonem*. Florence, 1496.

In Convivium Platonis, sive de amore. Ed. and trans. Raymond Marcel. *Marsile Ficin, Commentaire sur le Banquet de Platon*. Paris, 1956.

——————. *Opera Omnia*. Basle, 1576.

——————. *Platonic Theology: III, 2; XIII, 3; XIV, 3 & 4*. Trans. Josephine L. Burroughs in "Ficino and Pomponazzi on Man," *Journal of the History of Ideas*, V (1944), 227-39.

——————. *Quaestiones de Mente*. Trans. Josephine L. Burroughs in *The Renaissance Philosophy of Man*. Ed. E. Cassirer, et al. Chicago, 1948. Pp. 193-212.

——————. *Supplementum Ficinianum*. 2 vols. Ed. P. O. Kristeller. Florence, 1937.

_____. *Theologia Platonica de immortalitate animorum*. Ed. and trans. Raymond Marcel. *Marsile Ficin, Théologie Platonicienne de l'immortalité des âmes*. Vols. I and II: Paris, 1964. Vol. III: Paris, 1970.

Garin, Eugenio. *La cultura filosofica del Rinascimento italiano, Ricerche e Documenti*. Florence, 1961.

_____. *Italian Humanism*. Trans. P. Munz. Oxford, 1965.

_____. "Ricerche sulle traduzioni di Platone nella prima metà del sec. XV." *Medioevo e Rinascimento: Studi in onore di Bruno Nardi*, I (Florence, 1955). Pp. 339-74.

Gombrich, E.H. "*Icones Symbolicae:* The Visual Image in Neoplatonic Thought." *Journal of the Warburg and Courtauld Institutes*, XI (1948), 163-92.

Gould, J. *The Development of Plato's Ethics*. Cambridge, 1955.

Gutkind, Curt S. *Cosimo de'Medici*. Oxford, 1938.

Hackforth, R. *Plato's Examination of Pleasure*. Cambridge, 1945.

Hay, Denys, ed. *The Age of the Renaissance*. London, 1967.

Headley, John M., ed. *Medieval and Renaissance Studies*. Chapel Hill, North Carolina, 1968.

Heitzman, Marian. "L'agostinismo avicenizzante e il punto di partenza della filosofia di Marsilio Ficino." *Giornale critico della filosofia italiana*, XVI (1935), 295-322 and 460-80; XVII (1936), 1-11.

Huit, Charles. "Le Platonisme pendant la renaissance." *Annales de philosophie chrétienne*, N.S., XXXIII (1895-96), 362 ff.

Jayne, Sears. *John Colet and Marsilio Ficino*. Oxford, 1963.

_____. *Marsilio Ficino's Commentary on Plato's Symposium*. University of Missouri Studies, XIX (1944).

Jones, Judith P. "The *Philebus* and the Philosophy of Pleasure in Thomas More's *Utopia*." *Moreana*, XXXI-XXXII (Angers, France, 1971), 61-70.

Jowett, Benjamin. *The Dialogues of Plato*. Rev 4th ed. 4 vols. Oxford, 1968.

Klibansky, Raymond. *The Continuity of the Platonic Tradition during the Middle Ages*. London, 1939.

_____. "Plato's Parmenides in the Middle Ages and the Renaissance." *Medieval and Renaissance Studies*, I (1943), 281-330.

_____, ed., *Plato: Philebus and Epinomis*. London, 1956. (See A.E. Taylor.)

Kristeller, Paul O. "The European Significance of Florentine Platonism." *Medieval and Renaissance Studies*. Ed. John M. Headley. Chapel Hill, 1968. Pp. 206-29.

_____. *Iter Italicum*. 2 vols. London, 1963 and 1967.

_____. "Marsilio Ficino as a Beginning Student of Plato." *Scriptorium*, XX (1966), 41-54.

552   Bibliography

—————————. "Marsilio Ficino e Lodovico Lazzarelli: Contributo alla dif-
fusione delle idee ermetiche nel Rinascimento." *Annali della R.* Scuola
Normale Superiore di Pisa; lettere, storia e filosofia, 2nd Series, VII
(1938), 237-62.
—————————. *The Philosophy of Marsilio Ficino.* New York, 1943.
—————————, and Philip P. Wiener, eds., *Renaissance Essays.* New York,
1968.
—————————. "Renaissance Platonism." *Facets of the Renaissance.* Ed.
W.E. Werkmeister. New York, 1963. Pp. 103-23.
—————————. *Renaissance Thought I.* New York, 1961.
—————————. *Renaissance Thought II.* New York, 1965.
—————————. Review of *Problemi filosofici in Marsilio Ficino* by Michele
Schiavone. *Journal of Philosophy,* LVIII (1961), 51-53.
—————————. "Sebastiano Salvini, A Florentine Humanist and Theolo-
gian, and a Member of Marsilio Ficino's Platonic Academy." *Didasca-
liae.* Ed. Sesto Prete. New York, 1961. Pp. 205-43.
—————————. "Some Original Letters and Autograph Manuscripts of
Marsilio Ficino." *Studi di Bibliografia e di Storia in onore di Tammaro
de Marinis,* III (Verona, 1964). Pp. 5-33.
—————————. *Studies in Renaissance Thought and Letters.* Rome, 1956.
—————————ed. *Supplementum Ficinianum.* 2 vols. Florence, 1937.
—————————. *Le Thomisme et la pensée italienne de la Renaissance.*
Montreal, 1967.
—————————. "A Thomist Critique of Marsilio Ficino's Theory of Will
and Intellect." *Harry Austryn Wolfson Jubilee Volume,* II (Jerusalem,
1965). Pp. 463-94.
—————————. "Un uomo di stato e umanista fiorentino: Giovanni Corsi."
La Bibliofilia, XXXVIII (1936), 242-57.
Lohe, Peter. "Die Datierung der *Disputationes Camaldulenses* des Cristoforo
Landino." *Rinascimento: Rivista dell'Istituto Nazionale di Studi sul
Rinascimento,* 2nd Series, IX (Florence, 1969), 291-99.
Marcel, Raymond. *Marsile Ficin.* Paris, 1958. (See also under Ficino.)
—————————. "L'apologétique de Marsile Ficin." *Pensée humaniste et
Tradition chrétienne au XVe et au XVIes.* Paris, 1950. Pp. 159-68.
Paatz, W. and E. *Die Kirchen von Florenz, ein Kunstgeschichliches Hand-
buch,* III. Frankfurt-am-Main, 1943-54.
Plato. *The Dialogues of Plato.* Ed. and trans. Benjamin Jowett. Rev. 4th ed.
4 vols. Oxford, 1964.
Plotinus. *Enneads.* Ed. with French trans. E. Bréhier. Paris, 1924-28. English
trans. Stephen MacKenna, rev. B.S. Page. 3rd ed. London, 1962.
Reese, Gustave. *Music in the Middle Ages.* New York, 1950.
Rochon, André. *La Jeunesse de Laurent de Médicis (1449-1478).* Paris, 1963.
Rotondò, A. "Nicolò Tignosi da Foligno." *Rinascimento,* IX (1958), 217-55.

Saffrey, H.D. "Notes Platoniciennes de Marsile Ficin dans un manuscrit de Proclus." *Bibliothèque D'Humanisme et Renaissance,* XXI (1959), 161-84.

Saitta, Giuseppe. *Marsilio Ficino e la filosofia dell'Umanesimo.* Rev. 3rd ed. Bologna, 1954.

Schiavone, Michele. *Problemi filosofici in Marsilio Ficino.* Milan, 1957.

Schmitt, Charles B. "Perennial Philosophy From Agostino Steuco to Leibniz." *Journal of the History of Ideas,* XXVII (1966), 505-32.

Shorey, Paul. *Platonism Ancient and Modern.* Berkeley, 1938.

Sicherl, Martin. "Neuentdeckte Handschriften von Marsilio Ficino." *Scriptorium,* XVI (1962), 50-61.

Sidgwick, Henry. *Outlines of the History of Ethics.* 6th ed. Repr. Boston, 1960.

Taylor, A.E. *Plato: The Man and His Work.* 7th ed. London, 1960.

——————. *Plato: Philebus and Epinomis.* Ed. R. Klibansky. London, 1956.

Trinkaus, Charles. *Adversity's Noblemen: The Italian Humanists on Happiness.* New York, 1940.

——————. *In Our Image and Likeness.* 2 vols. London, 1970.

——————. "The Problem of Free Will in the Renaissance and the Reformation." *Renaissance Essays.* Ed. P.O. Kristeller and P.P. Wiener. New York, 1968. Pp. 187-98.

Waddy, Patricia. "Brunelleschi's Design for S. Maria degli Angeli in Florence." *Marsyas,* XV (1972), 36-46.

Wadsworth, James B. "Landino's *Disputationes Camaldulenses,* Ficino's *De Felicitate,* and *L'Altercazione* of Lorenzo De'Medici." *Modern Philology,* L (1952), 23-31.

Walker, D.P. *The Ancient Theology.* London, 1972.

——————. "Orpheus the Theologian and Renaissance Platonists." *Journal of the Warburg and Courtauld Institutes,* XVI (1953), 100-20.

——————. "The *Prisca Theologia* in France." *Journal of the Warburg and Courtauld Institutes,* XVII (1954), 204-59.

——————. *Spiritual and Demonic Magic from Ficino to Campanella.* London, 1958.

Weiss, Roberto. "Scholarship from Petrarch to Erasmus." *The Age of the Renaissance.* Ed. Denys Hay. London, 1967. Pp. 133-44.

Westerink, L.G. *Damascius: Lectures on the Philebus.* Amsterdam, 1959.

——————. "Ficino's Marginal Notes on Olympiodorus in Riccardi Greek MS. 37." *Traditio,* XXIV (1968), 351-78.

Wind, Edgar. *Pagan Mysteries in the Renaissance.* Rev. ed. New York, 1968.

Wulf, Maurice De. *Introduction à la philosophie néoscolastique.* Louvain and Paris, 1904.

Yates, Frances A. *The Art of Memory.* Chicago, 1966.

_____. *Giordano Bruno and the Hermetic Tradition.* London, 1964.

Zeller, E., and R. Mondolfo. *La filosofia dei Greci nel suo sviluppo storico,* VI. Florence, 1961.

Index of Names in the Texts